Property and Political Order in Africa

In sub-Saharan Africa, property relationships around land and access to natural resources vary across localities, districts, and farming regions. These differences produce patterned variations in relationships between individuals, communities, and the state. This book captures these patterns in an analysis of structure and variation in rural land tenure regimes. In most farming areas, state authority is deeply embedded in land regimes, drawing farmers, ethnic insiders and outsiders, lineages, villages, and communities into direct and indirect relationships with political authorities at different levels of the state apparatus. The analysis shows how property institutions – institutions that define political authority and hierarchy around land – shape dynamics of great interest to scholars of politics, including the dynamics of land-related competition and conflict, territorial conflict, patron-client relations, electoral cleavage and mobilization, ethnic politics, rural rebellion, and the localization and "nationalization" of political competition.

Catherine Boone is Professor of Government and International Development at the London School of Economics and Political Science, where she teaches courses on political economy and African politics. She is former Professor of Government and Long Chair Fellow at the University of Texas at Austin. Boone has been a member of the board of directors of the African Studies Association, the executive council of the American Political Science Association (APSA), and the executive committee of the Comparative Politics Section of APSA. She was Treasurer and then President of the West Africa Research Association (2005–2008). She is author of *Merchant Capital and the Roots of State Power in Senegal, 1930–1985* (Cambridge, 1992) and *Political Topographies of the African State: Rural Authority and Institutional Choice* (Cambridge, 2003), which won the Society for Comparative Research Mattei Dogan Award in 2005.

D1224178

Cambridge Studies in Comparative Politics

General Editor

Margaret Levi   *University of Washington, Seattle*

Assistant General Editors

Kathleen Thelen   *Massachusetts Institute of Technology*
Erik Wibbels   *Duke University*

Associate Editors

Robert H. Bates   *Harvard University*
Gary Cox   *Stanford University*
Stephen Hanson   *The College of William & Mary*
Torben Iversen   *Harvard University*
Stathis Kalyvas   *Yale University*
Peter Lange   *Duke University*
Helen Milner   *Princeton University*
Frances Rosenbluth   *Yale University*
Susan Stokes   *Yale University*
Sidney Tarrow   *Cornell University*

Books in the Series

Continued after the Index

Property and Political Order in Africa

Land Rights and the Structure of Politics

CATHERINE BOONE

London School of Economics and Political Science

CAMBRIDGE
UNIVERSITY PRESS

CAMBRIDGE
UNIVERSITY PRESS

32 Avenue of the Americas, New York NY 10013-2473, USA

Cambridge University Press is part of the University of Cambridge.

It furthers the University's mission by disseminating knowledge in the pursuit of education, learning and research at the highest international levels of excellence.

www.cambridge.org
Information on this title: www.cambridge.org/9781107649934

First published 2014

A catalogue record for this publication is available from the British Library

Library of Congress Cataloguing in Publication data
Boone, Catherine.
Property and political order in Africa : land rights and the structure of politics / Catherine Boone.
  p.   cm. – (Cambridge studies in comparative politics)
Includes bibliographical references and index.
ISBN 978-1-107-04069-4 (hardback) – ISBN 978-1-107-64993-4 (pbk.)
1. Land tenure – Political aspects – Africa.   2. Land use, Rural – Political aspects – Africa.
3. Land use – Government policy – Africa. 4. Central–local government relations – Africa.
5. Ethnicity – Political aspects – Africa.   6. Ethnic conflict – Africa.   I. Title.   II. Series:
Cambridge studies in comparative politics.
HD963.B66   2014
323.46096–dc23   2013009770

ISBN 978-1-107-04069-4 Hardback
ISBN 978-1-107-64993-4 Paperback

To my family

Of course the land question in sub-Saharan Africa has dominated the political arena for over two centuries. Land and land resources were central to the imperial conquest, the colonial settlement and the extractive economy, administered in terms of imported legal frameworks which claimed to extinguish rights held under local customary law. Whether the purpose was agriculture, mining, administrative control or simply trade, land and property rights became the subject of fierce competition and conflict and, in most cases, were at the root of the freedom struggle.... For up to four decades after independence, issues of land and property rights have remained at the centre of contemporary politics in the region. Yet, with the exception of a few states, we have been reluctant to confront the land issue.

– Permanent Secretary, Kenya's Ministry of Lands and Housing,
Eng. E. K. Mwongera[1]

---

[1] Keynote Address: ACTS Seminar on Land Tenure and Conflict in Africa, Nairobi 2004, 4–5.

Contents

List of Figures, Tables and Maps

MAPS

Preface and Acknowledgments

Although analysts of African politics have focused mostly on the cities, civil conflict has played out mostly in the countryside. This pattern has become much starker in the past two decades. The 1990s and 2000s also drew observers' attention to the role and weight of rural populations as voters in national elections. These shifts underscore the pressing need for tools to understand political dynamics in rural Africa, home to 60–70 percent of the continent's population but still largely indecipherable to most political analysts.

Drawing on literatures in the new institutional economics, property rights, and the political science institutionalisms, this book proposes a model of *political and economic structure* in rural Africa, how it varies at the subnational level, and how it shapes subnational- and national-level outcomes. In the countryside, local political arenas are defined largely by land tenure regimes, which we define as property institutions (or rules) governing landholding and land access. The shape and political effects of these property regimes are visible in the *political expression* of land-related conflict. These same property regimes go far in structuring local patterns of social stratification and hierarchy, ethnic conflict, electoral mobilization, and representation in the national political arena.

Land-related conflicts are the empirical grist for this study. They are important substantively: they are often the stakes or the stimulus in larger conflicts that are shaping the course of African nations. A group of Nairobi-based observers stated that "land issues are almost always part of the conflict," and they are correct.[1] In agrarian society, land tenure relations go far in defining relationships among individuals, groups, markets, and the state. Land-related conflict is important in this study for purely analytical reasons as well. It is a phenomenon that manifests in a wide variety of observable instances of rural

---

[1] Huggins, Kumugi et al. ACTS, 32.

political expression. This allows us to probe the possibilities and limits of our argument, which attributes differences in the political expression of land-related conflict to variation in local property regimes and in how these connect to political institutions and processes at the national level.

Approximately thirty land-related conflicts, all played out in subnational (district level, mostly) political arenas, form a broad empirical base for this study. About a dozen cases (from eight countries) are presented as case studies in the book's main chapters. These are based on secondary literature, gray literature, field research including farm-level interviews, newspaper analysis, and research in national archives.

Many institutions, groups, and individuals have helped me with this project. A yearlong research grant from the American Council of Learned Societies to study land conflict in Africa got me started. I thank the ACLS and the proposal reviewers for their confidence in this study. Financial support for this project also came from the West Africa Research Association and the Long Chair in Democratic Studies at the University of Texas at Austin. The project was conducted while I was Professor of Government at UT, and I am grateful to this institution and especially to the staff of the university's Perry-Casteñeda Library for their support.

For help with launching and conducting field research and archival work in Kenya, I am very happy to thank John Harbeson, Tom Wolf, James Wilson, Susanne Mueller, Mutu wa Gethoi, Sandra Joireman, Ben Nyanchoga, and Mike Norton-Griffiths. For helping me plan and undertake field research and archival work in Tanzania, thanks to Goran Hyden, Greg Maddox, Howard Stein, Lydia Nyeme, Faustin Maganga, and Kelly Askew. For helping me put together a field project and the logistics to carry it out in Ghana, thanks to James Essegby, Beatrice Allah-Mensah, Helena Saele, Jon Kraus, and Cyril Daddieh. For help with archival and fieldwork in Côte d'Ivoire and Senegal, I thank Atta, Alfred Babo, Beth Rabinowitz, Alioune Badara Diop, and the archivists at *La Voie* in Abidjan in October 2010.

For research affiliations and assistance in Africa, I thank the University Cheikh Anta Diop in Dakar, Senegal; Université Gaston Berger, Saint-Louis du Sénégal; University of Nairobi, University of Legon, in Accra, Ghana; the Institute of National Resource Management at the University of Dar es Salaam, in Tanzania; and especially research assistants of exceptional commitment, goodwill, and resourcefulness: Lydia Nyeme, Dennis Duku, Desmond Koduah, and those in Côte d'Ivoire and Kenya to whom I remain indebted. In East and West Africa, many citizens, public officials, researchers, chiefs, drivers, and farmers took a keen interest in this project and spent hours – sometimes days – providing information, analysis, and assessments of the opportunities and challenges facing farmers and their families. I am very grateful for their openness and goodwill, and I hope that I have done justice to the subjects that we discussed. My sons, Joshua and Alexander Trubowitz, assisted me with this fieldwork in Senegal, western Ghana, and Tanzania. My brother, Jim Boone, accompanied me on one round of field research in northern Tanzania.

Several University of Texas at Austin graduate students read drafts of this work, including Giorleny Altamirano Rayo, Calla Hummel, Huseyin Alptekin, Christian Sorace, and members of the Politics-History-Society seminar in the Sociology Department. UT undergraduates also lent a hand, including Yasmin Frazelinia (collecting data on election violence in Kenya), Sharanya Rajan, Dhawal Doshi, and Emma Tran. Special thanks go to Amanda Pinkston, who read the *Ashanti Pioneer* on microfilm, helped with background research on Ghana, and wrote an undergraduate senior thesis on land conflict in Kenya and Ghana, all of which fed into this project.

I was very fortunate to have many knowledgeable readers of all or part of the manuscript. They offered excellent ideas and saved me from many errors: Robert H. Bates, Crawford Young, David Laitin, John Harbeson, Christian Lund, Steven Orvis, Catharine Newbury, Milton Krieger, Jesse Ribot, Amy Poteete, Robert Parks, Beth Rabinowitz, Norma Kriger, Sandra Joireman, Atul Kohli, Ambreena Manji, Carl LeVan, Pauline Peters, Anne Pitcher, Reo Matsuzaki, Luca Puddu, Paul Bjerk, Sara Berry (who read the original proposal), Jason Brownlee, and Olivier Tchouaffe. Although I have been unable to take full account all of their suggestions and critiques, I am eager to do so in future work. I look forward to continuing the discussion.

Talks I have given over the past six years helped me develop material that is presented here, including presentations at University of Michigan, Ann Arbor (twice); Northwestern University (twice); University of Florida, Gainesville; Princeton University; Brown University; Yale University (twice); University of Virginia; Indiana University Workshop on Political Theory and Policy Analysis and WOW IV meeting; Columbia University; Pomona College; University of Pennsylvania; University of Chicago (twice); the "Tanzania and the World Conference" hosted by Texas Southern University and Rice University; the International Food Policy Research Institute (IFPRI); SAIS/Johns Hopkins University; the Uppsala University Department of Peace and Conflict Studies; and the Africa Talks seminar series at the London School of Economics, which provided the occasion for a very educational discussion with Elliott Green, Sam Moyo, and Thandika Mkandawire. I thank those who invited me to present this work at these seminars and workshops.

Professor John Cotter of Saint Edward's University drew all the original maps in this book, and I thank him for his patience with a project that ended up stretching over several years. Wim van Binsbergen gave me permission to use his photo of the Tribal Territories Map of Zambia, which Kaila Wyllys redrew and enhanced for reproduction in this book. I thank Praeger Press for permission to reproduce the map of Zimbabwe that appears in Chapter 10, and Charles Ntampaka, editor of the Kigali journal *Dialogue*, for permission to use the colonial map of Kivu that appears in Chapter 2 (redrawn by Kaila

Wyllys). Laurie Sellars's help with the maps and reference list toward the end of the project was much appreciated and will be remembered fondly.

I thank Norma Kriger for her support and for allowing me to use some of our jointly published material on Zimbabwe in Chapter 10.

Professor Margaret Levi, editor of the Cambridge Studies in Comparative Politics series, hosted a book workshop in at University of Washington in January 2013 that was devoted to analysis and critique of this manuscript. I benefited greatly from this opportunity. Discussions were led by David Laitin, Joel Migdal, and Mary Kay Gugerty, and I thank them for their careful readings and critiques. Graduate students in the UW Department of Political Science offered comments on the manuscript that were very helpful. I also owe great thanks to Lewis Bateman of Cambridge University Press, who provided great encouragement and assistance in bringing this book to fruition.

All the translations from French-language sources are my own.

Josh Trubowitz, Sander Trubowitz, and Kit Boone helped with preparing the final manuscript. I thank my family for their patience and support. Most of all, I thank my husband, Peter Trubowitz, for his many great contributions to this endeavor, and for his confidence in the project from the outset.

CHAPTER I

Introduction

Property Regimes and Land Conflict: Seeing Institutions and Their Effects

> Arable land has long been under considerable social pressures. Control over land has served as an important component of control over people.
> (Fisiy 1992, 18)

> Democracy's prospects may lie not in the city but in the countryside.
> Munro 2001, 311

Policy analysts, academics, and journalists point to the increasing incidence and importance of land-related conflict in sub-Saharan Africa.[1] After four or five post-independence decades of relative political calm in most of rural Africa, rural districts and provinces in many countries now roil with land-related tension, sometimes expressed in politically charged ways. Tension arises from land scarcities and growing competition over land access, the assertion of citizenship and ethnic claims linked to land entitlements, and, in some cases, enclosure and the growing exclusiveness of land rights.

In some countries, land-related conflict has exploded onto the national political stage. In Kenya, more than 300,000 people were displaced and some 1,500 killed in the violent conflict over land rights in the 1990s. Almost as many were affected by land-related violence in 2007 and 2008. Land-related conflict fueled a political conflagration in Côte d'Ivoire that tore the country in two in 2003, and it paralyzed attempts to reconstitute order through the electoral process. Land conflict also fueled the Mano River Basin civil wars in Liberia and Sierra Leone, war and widespread violence in the villages of the eastern Democratic Republic of Congo, and the war in Darfur, Sudan.[2] In Zimbabwe,

---

[1] By contrast, a 1970s view was that political conflict and mobilization are phenomena of the *urban* areas. See Wiseman 1986.

[2] See Autesserre 2010; Peters forthcoming; Reno 2007, 2010; Vircoulon and Liégeois 2010; Kahl 2006.

land expropriation and reallocation has been at center of the Mugabe regime's desperate struggle to remain in power since 2000.

Land-related conflicts also find expression in ways that fail to capture international headlines. They often play out in more local and more systemic ways. In Cameroon, local political authorities expel "non-indigenous" farmers from localities so that ethnic insiders can take their land and prevent them from voting. Across the Sahel, the incidence of farmer-herder conflict has increased steadily over the past two decades. In parts of Ghana, chiefs who sell off communities' land can stoke protest against the abuse of political authority for private gain.

Africa's rising tide of land-related conflict is a phenomenon that is very poorly understood. It defies modernization theory and theories of economic development, which predicted that land politics would decrease in salience over time. Levels and patterns of land conflict do not bear any systematic correlation to rates of demographic increase, the prevalence of land scarcity, national regime type, or legal traditions imported from the colonial metropoles. Political science has just begun to notice this phenomenon, and is yet to confront the paradoxes and puzzles that it presents for existing theory and expectations. Framing some of the most striking of these puzzles helps identify questions that motivate this study.

Consider theories of state consolidation and power projection. Much discussion of land conflict conveys the impression that natural-resource disputes in Africa stem from the weakness (or absence) of state intervention in rural property relations. Jeffrey Herbst's *States and Power in Africa* (2000), for example, argues that central state authority barely penetrates rural Africa. From this vantage point, land conflict seems to lie outside the sphere of formal politics and beyond the reach of the state. Yet in many cases, this is clearly not so. Some of the most extensive episodes of violent conflict over property rights have happened in the commercial farming areas of states such as Côte d'Ivoire, Kenya, and Zimbabwe, all of which have long histories of deep state involvement in the ordering and reordering of rural property relations. Highly politicized land conflict has been central in recent political histories of some of the richest and most intensively governed regions of Africa's strongest states. What explains this apparent paradox?

Rising tides of land-related conflict also defy some basic expectations about transitions to democracy. The return to multipartism was supposed to mitigate social conflict by opening channels for peaceful dispute resolution. Yet in some countries, this very shift opened the door to the highly political and partisan expression of land grievances, culminating in extensive rural violence, as in Côte d'Ivoire, Zimbabwe, and Kenya. Why does the prospect of regime turnover sometimes heighten land-related tensions? Why does intensified electoral competition sometimes inflame land-related conflict?

In rural Africa, property itself is a paradox: its political character and evolutionary dynamics seem to defy theoretical expectations. Land conflict of the scale and scope that we observe today confounds basic expectations about Africa's "transition to the market." Since the mid-1980s, expert opinion has predicted that rising demographic pressure and land values would propel the gradual, bottom-up transformation of Africa's customary land rights into something more akin to private property in land. Although this expectation has held up in some cases, in others it has proved to be dead wrong. Demographic increase is sometimes a factor that contributes to violent and highly politicized conflict over land rights. More often, however, it feeds low-level tensions among and within communities, stoking struggles over authority, entitlement, and the legitimacy of the market. Why is the development of private property in land turning out to be such a deeply politicized and contested process?

These questions underscore the need for broader, more comparative, and more political theories of land tenure regimes and rural conflict. Africa's land regimes turn out to be far more varied and politicized than existing analysis has recognized. So far, however, there is no conceptual or empirical mapping of the character and contours of land-related conflict, and scholars have lacked the analytic tools needed to extract its broader implications for our understandings of African politics.

Deep and systemic connections between land politics and wider questions of interest to political scientists have gone largely unnoticed in comparative work on Africa. This is because the architecture and political character of *rural property regimes* has remained mostly invisible and untheorized in existing work.

This book aims to remedy this deficiency by advancing two core arguments. The first is that governments in Africa have created and upheld rural property institutions that create relationships of political dependency and authority, define lines of social cooperation and cleavage, and segment territory into political jurisdictions. In most places for much of the twentieth century, these arrangements have made rural Africa governable. It is in this sense that rural property regimes have been central in constituting the "political order" that is invoked in the book's title. The second core argument is that these rural land institutions vary across space (and time), and thus *account for* patterned variations in the structure and political character of land-related competition and conflict. In particular, I argue that variation in land institutions can explain where, why, and how ethnicity is salient in land conflict; whether land conflict is "bottled up" at the local level or "scales up" to national-level politics; and where and how land-related conflict finds expression in multiparty elections.

These features of land politics are the political outcomes that are the immediate focus of the analysis, but as I argue in the chapters and the Conclusion of this book, they are often mirrored in the larger or more diffuse dynamics of patronage and clientelism, civil society, ethnic mobilization, electoral mobilization, and rural rebellion and civil war. Part I of the book develops an analytic model and hypotheses that link land tenure institutions to political outcomes in the land domain. The hypotheses are laid out in Tables 3.2–3.6. In

Parts II, III, and IV of the book, these arguments are expanded, probed, and tested via comparative case study analysis.

The analysis offers solutions to the puzzles about the projection of state power, democracy and conflict, and the evolution of property rights that I have just outlined. Scholars of state-building will see how land-related conflict develops within institutions that have been molded by the state. Patterns of conflict are as much a *result* of state-building as a reflection of the absence or failure thereof. For analysts of democracy, I show where land tenure regimes create direct institutional linkages between landholding and partisan politics (and where they do not). This generates a theory that helps account for when and where land conflict connects local constituencies to larger social coalitions, and to national-level electoral processes. The property rights analysis underscores the politically contingent character of property holding in rural Africa. This is the key to unlocking the puzzle of politicized responses to the growing commodification of land.

AN INSTITUTIONAL ANALYSIS OF LAND TENURE REGIMES AND THEIR POLITICAL EFFECTS

This book argues that African land tenure regimes can be understood as institutions, or complexes of institutions, that structure local political arenas and link rural populations to the state. Following much of the work in the New Institutional Economics, I count both formal and informal institutions as "institutions." This makes it possible to transcend the dichotomy between formal-legal and customary arrangements that underlies studies of legal dualism in African land regimes.[3] Making visible this part of the architecture underlying state-society relations in these mostly agrarian societies undercuts the notion that modern African states are disconnected from their rural hinterlands, that rural social structure is uniform continent-wide (or unique in each locality), or that impersonal markets govern access to land.

Land tenure regimes are property regimes that define the manner and terms under which rights in land are granted, held, enforced, contested, and transferred. In all political economies, property rights lie at the confluence of the political-legal order and the economic order.[4] As rights, they do not exist

---

[3] Greif (2006) sees institutions as formal and informal legal/social frameworks in which activity takes place. See also North 1981, 1990; Ostrom 1990; Knight 1992; Ensminger 1997.

[4] As Perry Anderson pointed out (1974, 404–405, cited by Hann 1998, 46–47). A property regime, then, is the larger *system of rules* in which property rights per se are embedded: rules about classes of individuals or groups who have access to property rights; who can assign, transfer, enforce, or adjudicate rights; and the principles and procedures by which they can do so. In analyzing varieties of capitalism, Hall and Soskice (2001, 46) employ a notion of regimes as interlocking systems of complementary institutions – social, economic, political – that can structure interactions at macro, regional, and perhaps sectoral levels (or domains). Use of the term "regime" is consistent with the notion of institutional order proposed by Ostrom (1990, 50–51).

without third-party enforcement – like property rights everywhere, they establish a *political relationship* between the claimers of rights and the enforcer of rights, which, in unitary polities, is the state.[5] As economic institutions, property rights are the cornerstone of relations of production: they govern the use of productive assets and the distribution of the wealth so generated. Sociological traditions find the essential nature of property in this relational aspect: property rights are *social relations* concerning the access and use of things, including the land and land-based resources that sustain livelihoods and society for most of Africa's population.[6] In agrarian society, where socioeconomic life is organized around the use of land, land tenure regimes constitute an institutional template for sociopolitical organization.

In the land tenure regimes that are the focus of this analysis, political and economic rules overlap and are embedded in each other. This contrasts with the formal separation of political and economic rules that appears in settings where impersonal markets govern access to productive assets, and where the liberal conception of the economy and the polity as autonomous spheres prevails. Because of this, we can conceive of land tenure regimes in these largely agrarian societies and local political arenas as *roughly isomorphic*, with the degree of correspondence between the two varying with the degree to which local populations actually depend on land access for their livelihoods.

Seeing African land tenure regimes as configurations of rules and structured relationships that are amenable to comparative institutional analysis is a major departure from theoretical precedent, and – as this analysis hopes to show – a powerful tool for reinterpreting structure and variation in African politics. Although social science is rich in studies of the sociopolitical dynamics of African land tenure regimes in particular places, we have lacked an explicit conceptual framework for describing how these land systems vary across space (and time) and how they fit into the larger institutional superstructure of national government. A general pass at the question could yield an answer that points to the "customary" nature of land regimes across most of sub-Saharan Africa – and to the important role of nontraditional authorities such as chiefs, elders, and land chiefs – in the allocation of land rights and the adjudication of disputes. Much work on this topic explores the lack of fit between customary land tenure in rural localities and statutory land law and the ways that complex situations of legal dualism encourage actors to game the system to maximize their own situational advantage. Fine-grained studies of local practice often underscore, either implicitly or explicitly, the intricacy, variety, and even bewildering

---

[5] Joireman's (2011) recent contribution to the analysis of rural property rights in Africa emphasizes this aspect of property.

[6] By the 2008 World Development Indicators, rural population as a share of the national population dips below half in only eight of forty-five African countries (not counting the island states). These are Gabon, Republic of Congo, South Africa, Botswana, Liberia, Cameroon, Angola, and The Gambia.

diversity of local land regimes.[7] At the limit, analysts may find the very notion
of land tenure rules (or land "regime") to be oxymoronic in situations where
land tenure practices are "shrouded in a dense field of competing claims and
counterclaims around land rights, and embedded in complex local and 'hidden'
histories."[8]

The present analysis departs from received analysis by proposing a schematic
conceptualization of African land tenure regimes. It identifies these as political-
economic institutions (or institutional configurations), specifies their politically
salient features, and describes how they vary. Land regimes are defined as institutional orders that encode four critical aspects of local sociopolitical structure:
(1) property relations or rights, (2) authority rules, (3) citizenship rules, and (4)
territorial jurisdiction. Together, these elements define the political-institutional
character of different land tenure regimes and make it possible to compare and
contrast land regimes across space and time.

The overarching argument is that these land tenure institutions go far in
defining structure and variation in the character of local politics, government
control over rural populations, and the integration of the rural areas into
national political life. Evidence of these *political effects* is observable in *the
forms of conflict* that arise from mounting competition over land. As land
regimes vary, so too do forms of land-related conflict.[9]

This argument is important because land conflicts vary in ways that are of
great interest to political science. Land conflicts vary

- by whether and how ethnicity and ethnic hierarchy are implicated as axes
  of social conflict;
- by whether and how the central state is implicated in these local resource
  struggles;
- according to the political scope and scale at which land-related distributive
  conflicts play out; and
- in how land conflicts are connected to (or disconnected from) electoral
  dynamics.

By explaining these variations, this book generates new ways of understanding
ethnicity, the state, national political dynamics, and elections in Africa.

Chapters focus on cases of subnational-level land conflict that emerge as
farmland grows scarce and rises in value in provinces, districts, or localities in
Ghana, Côte d'Ivoire, Kenya, Burkina Faso, Cameroon, Rwanda, Democratic

[7] For example, Toulmin and Quan (2000a, 164) state that "numerous conflicting or competing rule-orders exist, characterized more often than not by 'ambiguities, inconsistencies, gaps,
   conflicts, and the like.'"
[8] Klopp 2001, 474.
[9] Berry (1989, 1993), Ribot and Peluso (2003), and others have argued for more processual
   conceptualizations of African land regimes and of property. Here I am opting for a theoretical model that identifies similarity and variation in the structured attributes of local
   settings.

Republic of Congo, Zimbabwe, and Tanzania. The array of cases spans the continent's regional divides, differences in colonial inheritance, and national variations in economic and political trajectories. This makes it possible to situate this institutional argument with respect to alternatives and rivals. The larger goal is to identify and track the effects of the state institutions that go far in organizing political space, political territoriality, and social hierarchy across the farming districts of sub-Saharan Africa.

RESEARCH DESIGN AND CONCEPTUAL INNOVATIONS

Seeing Institutional Effects

To use empirical evidence to see the political effects of variation in land regimes (and test arguments about institutional cause and political effect), this study employs a research design that is the workhorse of comparative political analysis. I first develop a model for describing spatial variation in the structure and character of land tenure regimes, using subnational territories as the unit of analysis. I then test the argument that common exogenous pressures, refracted through the distinctive institutional configurations of these local land regimes, produce political effects that vary across the subnational units. The common pressure is rising competition for land.[10] Institutional variations, I argue, produce patterns of distributive conflict in which central states are implicated directly (or not), that play out at different jurisdictional scales (local versus national), and that cleave local society along ethnic, gender and generational, class-like, or partisan lines.

The analytic strategy of tracing comparative responses to broad socioeconomic shocks or broad changes in the macroenvironment is well established in the field of comparative politics. In the study of agrarian society, work so configured includes Barrington Moore's *Social Origins of Dictatorship and Democracy* (1966), Charles Tilly's *The Vendée* (1964), Jeffrey Paige's *Agrarian Revolution* (1975), and Robert Brenner's *Past and Present* (1982) essays on the rise of agrarian capitalism in Europe. In these studies, distinctive subnational or regional political movements – the products of distinctive regional social structures and agrarian land tenure systems – are shown to affect the course of nations. Comparing across the industrialized democracies, Peter Gourevitch (1986) famously tracked "national responses to international economic crises," showing that the different responses to the Great Depression of the 1930s were shaped by sectoral-level institutions that structured relations between labor,

---

[10] I use the term "exogenous" to describe how these common pressures are treated in the analytic model, not to argue that, as an empirical matter, rising pressure on the land is a uniform, generic phenomenon that is unrelated to land tenure regimes. This study separates these two analytically, in order to make and test arguments about the political effects of different land tenure regimes.

industry, and agriculture. More recent "varieties of capitalism" literatures explain variations in capitalist states' responses to the pressures of globalization by highlighting differences in the national-level institutions that structure relations between labor, business, and the state.[11]

Common to these works is a logic of inquiry that follows the effects of "shocks," broad changes or stimuli, or rising pressures as they shake up and destabilize an established political order at the national or subnational level.[12] Under such pressures, existing lines of cleavage or tension can become axes of political mobilization or competition. Previously settled debates or disputes are reopened, and differently positioned actors move into action to protect past gains, or to take advantage of new openings.

This study follows this logic by modeling rising competition for land as a shock that strains established property relationships and relations among land users at the grassroots level.[13] Critics of Malthusian theories of social conflict have argued that rising land scarcity does not explain differences in the *political expression* of land-related conflict.[14] I agree. Rising land scarcity does not explain why land-related tensions among farming households would be bottled up at the local level in one region, while similar tensions in another region could explode onto the national stage (e.g., in the form of land-related violence at election time). Rising scarcity does not explain why land tensions would ever find expression in ethnic conflict or in different forms of ethnic conflict, or in grievances against chiefs in one locality and against the state itself in another, or in the national electoral arena in some countries but not in others.

This study argues that these political variations occur because tensions fueled by rising competition for land are refracted through the different local institutional configurations that make up land tenure regimes. Institutional structure shapes politics, producing effects that vary across space in predictable ways. In agrarian society, land tenure institutions play a strong role in defining lines of sociopolitical tension and cleavage (and alliance), economic and political hierarchy, rules of access to the local political arena, and the stakes of politics. The argument is that these political effects are visible in *variation in the forms*

---

[11] See, for example, Hall and Soskice 2001 and Jackson and Deeg 2006, 6, 32.

[12] Tilly (1964) modeled "urbanization" as a kind of exogenous shock to rural political institutions. B. Moore (1966) examined the varied effects of the rise of the "commercial impulse" in agriculture. Many studies that lie at the intersection of international relations and comparative politics model the effects of "international shocks" on national equilibriums. North (1981) conceptualized technological and demographic changes as "exogenous shocks" to prevailing institutional setups.

[13] The claim that there is a net rise, continent-wide, in the level of land-related conflict is not necessary to my argument. This argument and research design require only that local actors perceive that competition for land is rising in a given place at a given time. Land conflict and land scarcity per se are not new phenomena in Africa, and they do not affect all regions or locales. Both can either increase or decrease over time. See Hussein, Sumberg, and Seddon 1999.

[14] Homer-Dixon and Blitt 1998, Peluso and Watts 2001, Kahl 2006.

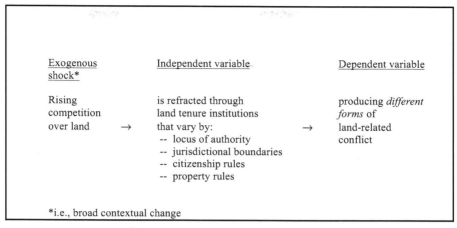

Exogenous
shock*

Independent variable

Dependent variable

Rising
competition
over land   →

is refracted through
land tenure institutions
that vary by: →
-- locus of authority
-- jurisdictional boundaries
-- citizenship rules
-- property rules

producing *different
forms* of
land-related
conflict

*i.e., broad contextual change

FIGURE 1.1. Structure of the Argument.

of land-related conflict. As a heuristic device, Figure 1.1 arrow-diagrams this logic in its most generic form. (The more focused, testable hypotheses explored in the case-study chapters are presented in Chapter 3.)

Land-Related Conflict as a Dependent Variable

This study innovates by considering land-related conflict a "class of phenomena" that is isomorphic to strikes and urban protests, civil wars, outbreaks of ethnic conflict, or military coups. Like a workers' strike, land-related conflict has causes and effects that are both systematic (patterned or common across cases) and unsystematic (random, contingent). Without denying the existence of particular and contingent causes of land conflict, this study follows a very large body of social science and policy research that identifies *systematic factors* – including demographic increase, rising land values due to commercialization, and environmental changes – that contribute to increases in the intensity, scope, and frequency of overt forms of land-related conflict.

The dependent variable is the form of land-related conflict.[15] We are interested in the *political expression* of tensions that arise around growing competition for land. Land-related conflict can be highly localized or wide in geographic scope; targeted at ethnic insiders, ethnic outsiders, or neither; shaped or fueled by government backing of either customary rights holders or "strangers" (or neither); manipulated directly by politicians or ostensibly beyond their effective reach; and played out within the local political arena of a chieftaincy, the national political arena, or at the molecular level of the family. Some land conflict finds expression in election-time political violence, but this is rare.

[15] Chapter 3 discusses coding and measurement.

Land-related conflict is usually nonviolent or else violent in small, private ways. Often it is evident in the "silent violence" of dispossessions that can lead to extreme social and economic vulnerability. This book argues that patterned variations in these land-conflict characteristics are largely explained by differences in land tenure institutions.

Cases, Case Construction, and Use of Cases

To develop this argument, we need to conceptualize units of analysis (cases), scales of analysis, and temporal framings in ways that make it possible to observe causes and effects that operate at the subnational level. The analysis must be scaled in a way that captures subnational variation in rural property regimes. The scale must also be defined to capture some of the major environmental, demographic, economic, and agronomic forces that shape land access and use.[16] The appropriate units for this study are thus rural territories defined roughly at the *provincial or district level*.[17]

Approximately thirty-two provincial- or district-level case studies constitute the empirical base of the study. The comparative case-study method conforms to the structure of the data: cases were developed from existing analyses of land rights processes in diverse rural localities, drawn from geography, anthropology, economic history, colonial and postcolonial rural-development literatures, land-rights and natural-resource-management think tanks, agrarian studies, and political science literatures on rural politics in Africa.[18] Case selection was driven by (a) the availability of longitudinal information about land regimes and land-related conflict in particular contexts and (b) the goal of maximizing variation in the study variables – that is, the hypothesized independent variable (features of land tenure regimes, especially variation in the locus of authority over land allocation), its rivals (ethnic heterogeneity, state weakness, levels of modernization, land scarcity, and national-level variables such as political regime type), and the dependent variable (forms of land-related conflict). Constructing longitudinal analyses was essential, given that the research

---

[16] For example, a drought or a spike or crash in the world price of one of Africa's export crops will not affect all farmers in a given country equally: farmers in the export-producing zone or in the drought-affected region will be affected much more directly than others.

[17] *Temporal framing* is also an issue, since this is an artifact of study design that is largely constructed on a case-by-case basis in order to (a) capture time periods in which we can plausibly make the case that land competition is rising and (b) assign a value to the dependent variable.

[18] What would the "total universe" of cases be? One way to imagine this is the following: most African countries have ten to twenty first-level administrative subdivisions (provincial-level subdivisions). (Nigeria and Uganda are outliers, with 36 and 111, respectively.) If all cases of subnational politics were defined at the provincial level, then the total number of cases in 45 countries of sub-Saharan Africa would be about 600. In the present study, many of the cases in are framed at the district (second-level administrative subdivision) or subdistrict level.

design is constructed to track social and political responses to *rising* competition for land. Rising competition for land is an observable aspect of agrarian social relations in all the case studies of land-related conflict featured in this study.[19]

Coding these cases on what we are conceptualizing as independent and dependent variables makes it possible to establish the plausibility of the general argument about institutional causes and political effects, as well as its analytic superiority over rival explanations of land-related conflict in its various forms. This analysis suggests that the argument can go far in capturing correlations between local institutional structure (encoded in land regimes) and forms of land-related conflict. As the land tenure regime varies, so, too, do forms of redistributive conflict over land.

The book's more focused arguments have to do with how land tenure regimes produce effects that are visible in patterns of ethnic conflict, in the political scale of redistributive politics, and in election-time conflict. To test these, we employ comparative case-study analysis, homing in on a subset of about twelve cases drawn from the larger pool.[20] In half of these, the research was grounded in, or supplemented by, fieldwork, including field observation, on-site archival research, and farm visits and interviews with farmers, land officers, local authorities, and land activists.

Not all the evidence fits into this descriptive mold or conforms to the causal hypotheses, but as Barrington Moore (1966, 469) said, "It is easier to perceive the meaning of these departures if we first grasp the general model." Discordant findings are tracked in an effort to reveal some of the limits and weaknesses of both the analytical model and the main argument. Often, discordant cases are those where the distinctions presented as categorical in the model are blurred. The success of the overall endeavor can be measured by how well the cases featured here (and other cases from sub-Saharan Africa) can be usefully described in terms of the model, and the extent to which they manifest

---

[19] This study focuses mostly on land conflict among smallholders (roughly defined, for the purposes of this introduction, as farmers working holdings of about 2 to 20 acres). It does not deal head-on with cases of land conflict that involve attempts by large-scale promoters of agribusiness ventures, such as foreign governments or multinational corporations, to acquire vast tracts of land for agriculture.

[20] The chapters feature nine subnational regions and two national units as case studies. Five of these are divided explicitly into two time periods to observe the effects of the introduction of multipartism on land politics. The national-unit case studies also feature analyses of key subnational regions, framed as cases-within-the-case. Part II follows the logic of a "most similar" case research design (Chapters 4 and 5). Part III is four illustrative case studies. Two of these also serve as in-country contrasts to cases featured elsewhere in the book, and one is a premultipartism study that pairs with a multiparty politics case that appears later. Part IV features a "most different" case research design (Chapter 9) and a least-likely/most-likely case selection logic (Chapters 9 and 10). Consideration of each unit involves within-case analysis, including identification of causal mechanisms, process tracing, and consideration of counterfactuals and empirical anomalies. On the cases, see Chapter 3 and the Appendix.

cause-effect patterns that conform to the hypotheses. Its success can also be judged by the coherence and straightforwardness of the theory in generating new hypotheses and insights about state structure and political dynamics in contemporary Africa.

STRUCTURE AND OVERVIEW OF THE ARGUMENTS

Part I, "Property Rights and the Structure of Politics" (Chapters 2 and 3), develops the analytic framework and hypotheses. Chapter 2 defines African land tenure regimes as property regimes that have been defined and redefined as part of state-building and power consolidation projects. The chapter is about institutional origins (or institutional choice). I argue that colonial and postcolonial rulers have *purposefully designed or redesigned* rural land regimes because these institutions help them to govern, and to create political order in the countryside. (In the rest of the book, I advance and test the theory that variations in land regimes *explain* outcomes of interest to political science.) The preliminary work is important. Although rural property regimes have been a systematic focus of comparative-politics literatures on agrarian societies, for many readers, land tenure regimes in general – and Africa's in particular – are completely unfamiliar. Political science has tended to see rural property regimes in Africa as mostly "beyond the reach of the state," self-organized by grassroots actors, and invariant across space. African land regimes and rural social structure have been almost completely invisible in political analysis, neither cause nor effect of anything. Readers who *are* familiar with African land regimes may conceptualize them in ways that differ strongly from the analytics proposed here.

Land tenure regimes have built state authority in the rural areas, fixed populations in rural territories, and organized rural populations into political collectivities that are subordinated to central control. Chapter 2 argues that these institutional configurations vary across subnational jurisdictions in ways that can be grasped in terms of a conceptual distinction between neocustomary and statist land regimes.

Chapter 3 develops the hypotheses that are tested in the remaining chapters. It provides evidence of rising competition for land and proposes that this be modeled as giving rise to *redistributive* conflict. This is a break with early New Institutional Economics and development-economics approaches to property rights change in Africa. Earlier work viewed rising land values as an impetus to incremental and voluntary recontracting of property rights that would gradually lead to Western-style land markets and private property in land. Contrary to expectations, land-related conflict now appears to be pervasive. It varies in intensity and takes on a myriad of forms. The argument here is that variations in conflict patterns are explained by land tenure rules that vary along the along the four politically salient dimensions that appear in Figure 1.1 (authority, citizenship, jurisdiction, and property). As the land tenure regime varies, so too does the political expression of land-related tension and conflict. Chapter 3 advances a series of deductive hypotheses about how variations in the structure of land institutions shape the political expression of redistributive conflict over land. A medium-N analysis of thirty-two cases appears here, establishing the plausibility of the general theory of institutional causes and political effects.

From this general theory, I derive and test hypotheses that cluster around three themes of particular interest to political science: ethnicity and ethnic conflict, state structure and variation therein, and elections and election-time conflict. The parts of the book are organized around these hypotheses.

Part II, "Ethnicity: Property Institutions and Ethnic Cleavage" (Chapters 4 and 5), argues that Africa's land tenure regimes *produce ethnic identity* and structure ethnic politics in subnational localities and jurisdictions, and do so in ways that vary across space as a function of differences in land regimes. Focusing on regions (jurisdictions) of high in-migration, the analysis shows that ethnic heterogeneity in itself does not predict how or whether ethnic identity will be an axis of land competition or whether government will side with ethnic insiders, ethnic outsiders, or neither in land conflicts. Comparative institutional analysis highlights the structuring effects of different land tenure institutions on the *formation* of ethnic groups, the establishment of *political and economic hierarchy* among groups, and the construction of *differential ties* to the state. The analysis reveals political effects that are invisible in analyses that see rural Africa as homogeneous and institutionless.

The analysis demonstrates the limits of studies that conceptualize ethnic identity as a purely ideational (subjective, cognitive) variable. It shows that in much of rural Africa, land institutions enforce and reproduce ethnicity as a state-imposed political status, channeling the tensions born of redistributive conflict in the rural areas along the lines of this political (ethnic) cleavage. Although this does not preclude consideration of ethnicity as a cultural force or a cognitive resource for individuals, we can go far beyond ideational theories in explaining why, how, and when ethnic difference constitutes a salient political cleavage and line of political mobilization in rural Africa.

Part III, "Political Scale: Property Institutions and the Scale and Scope of Conflict" (Chapters 6, 7, and 8), argues that land tenure regimes, by defining the jurisdictional scale of land-allocation authority, determine the political scale and scope of land-related conflict. The chapters identify the land regime conditions under which redistributive conflict over land is likely to be repressed by local authorities at the level of the extended family, when it is likely to be bottled up or repressed within the confines of an "ethnic homeland," and when it is likely to "go national" by finding expression in the national political arena. Only in the latter cases are aggrieved rural constituencies likely to join broader social coalitions that are mobilized for political action, including multiparty competition in the era of democratic transitions.

The analysis shows that African states are characterized by *heterogeneity of scale*. As in the federal systems studied by Schattschneider (1960) and Gibson

(2005, 2012), and in the "multilevel jurisdictions" of Indonesia described by Dik Roth (2003) and others, this results in the partial disarticulation of local political arenas from the national citizenship regimes, accountability mechanisms, and rules and processes of political representation that are inscribed in national constitutions. Mahmood Mamdani (1996a) is correct in arguing that this institutional disarticulation has been a structural feature of virtually all African states, including the apartheid state in South Africa. Part III describes these scalar effects, showing how they are produced by the political-economy rules that are inscribed in African land tenure regimes.

The effects for politics at the macrolevel are profound. Local-level control over land allocation and adjudication in the so-called customary land regimes works to insulate higher instances of the state apparatus from rural political unrest, including unrest born of land-related conflict. The so-called customary forms of authority repress redistributive conflict at the local level, channeling it along ethnic rather than class-like lines, and creating obstacles to the formation of political coalitions that transcend the boundaries of local ethnic jurisdictions. By contrast, where central states are themselves direct land allocators and adjudicators, land conflict transmits directly into the national political arena (it scales up to the national level). This is because the central state is involved directly as the author of the prevailing land allocation, creating a direct linkage or direct articulation between the local and national spheres of politics. This expands possibilities for the construction of national citizenship, but it also exposes rulers to the risks of mass mobilization, the formation of broad electoral coalitions, and class politics.

Part IV, "Multiparty Competition: Elections and the Nationalization of Land Conflict" (Chapters 9 and 10), argues that the effects of returns to multipartism on land politics have been mediated by variations in land tenure regimes. The land regime variable turns out to be key in identifying the conditions under which land-related conflict is likely to find expression in the national electoral arena, and why and where multiparty competition can open the door to wide-reaching redistributions of property rights.

Engerman and Metzer (2004, 2) write that sudden changes in the structure or locus of political control over a given territory can be expected to produce changes in the distribution of land rights. The analysis identifies the land tenure situations in which this effect is likely to be felt most acutely at election time. Where small-scale farmers' land rights hinge on a politically contingent relationship with an incumbent in the central government, the redistributive stakes of national elections can be very high. This is the mirror image of the situations described by Przeworski (1991) and Ordeshook (1993) when they wrote that credible private property regimes help stabilize electoral democracy by sheltering the "fundamental interests" of the average citizen from the vicissitudes of electoral politics. The vulnerability of the prevailing distribution of land rights to a shift in power at the top goes far in explaining the highly charged link between property conflict and elections in some African settings.

SIGNIFICANCE OF THE STUDY

We can learn much by studying how land conflicts vary in form and political expression in Africa. Analyzing property regimes, their variations, and how they are changing produces an understanding of the structures and processes by which rural Africa is governed and incorporated into the modern state. This study frames hypotheses about how variation in grassroots-level property relations shapes broader political dynamics. These hypotheses offer leverage in analyzing phenomena, such as voting behavior and political participation, ethnic cleavages and ethnic mobilization, patterns of distributive conflict, and rural unrest and rebellion that are very poorly understood.

Across much of Africa, farming and pastoral areas are under great pressure: economic, demographic, and environmental changes are straining prevailing political and social rules governing land access and land use. Returns to multi-partism and economic liberalization create new demands, risks, and openings. These pressures are having uneven and often unanticipated effects in rural Africa, often ramifying, spilling over, or scaling up to fuel macrodynamics that are of great interest to political science, and critically important in shaping national trajectories.

Tracking and attempting to explain these effects requires an understanding of the political-economy content of state institutions – formal and informal – at the local level. In agrarian society, land tenure regimes lie at the core of these political-institutional structures. This analysis points to the fact that in much of rural Africa, these local rules and institutions are, to varying degrees, nonliberal – in how they define property, in how they define citizenship, and in how they connect citizens to higher levels of the state apparatus. Hierarchical authority, both hereditary and bureaucratic, and ascriptive rights and entitlements go far in structuring access to land and other productive resources.[21] Patterns of resource access and control are not decided in an apparently neutral or apolitical marketplace. This is key to understanding why political liberalization and intensifying resource competition have heightened contestation over citizenship rights, entitlements, and the locus of legitimate political authority in many African countries, rather than dissipating conflict and fueling a smooth expansion of the political and economic market.

In tracing these processes, we also probe hypotheses about where, when, and how politicians try to suppress, amplify, or direct the momentum and tensions that arise from competition for land. Political entrepreneurs have often proved able to harness these processes for wider purposes, including state-building, economic development, rural political mobilization, the recruitment and organization of rebel groups, and electoral gain.

---

[21] Ascriptive rights are rights and entitlements assigned on the basis of membership in groups that individuals are assigned to at birth. See Mitnick (2006, 23), who explains that this kind of right has a "striking constitutive effect" on human identity.

This study is not the first to examine connections between state structure and land politics in Africa. There are excellent African land tenure literatures in social and economic anthropology, development studies and development economics, economic history, and the natural resource management field. Much of politics-centered work on African land tenure hinges on the problematique (or phenomenon) of legal pluralism. Legal pluralism points to the fact that in most (or perhaps all) African countries, there are unresolved legal contradictions between land policies and practices that recognize customary tenure on the one hand, and statutory land regimes that recognize formal-legal forms of land tenure (such as statutory freehold or private property) on the other. This study argues that various forms of legal pluralism must be understood, at least in part, as artifacts of state design, rather than as the products of error, delay, or failure on the part of governments that should be creating unified national property regimes. This makes it possible to see the political logics encoded in existing land regimes, and how rulers may use land rules strategically to gather and maintain power. This study also shows that the legal contradictions and sociopolitical conflicts that emerge from legal pluralism – including conflicts over citizenship, ethnicity, authority, and property – are not distributed evenly, or randomly, across space.[22] Rather, they distill in institutional configurations that differ across subregions, even within a single country.

Jean-Claude Willame (1997a, 40) captured this unevenness in the political geography of land tenure regimes in writing of "two different ways of governing territory in eastern Democratic Republic of Congo." I generalize this insight about spatial variation in land regimes, trace it to state-building strategies and logics, and show that it produces strongly varying political effects. Comparisons and contrasts that emerge in the cases allow us to draw out the broader political implications for understanding political conflict and political integration in African states and societies. By bringing property relations and property rights back into the comparative politics equation, the study unlocks new explanations for a wide variety of outcomes that have eluded analysis, or that have been attributed to idiosyncratic or purely ideational causes.

[22] For examples of such conflicts, see Geschiere and Gugler 1998, Joireman 2011, Lund 2008, and Onoma 2010.

PART I

PROPERTY RIGHTS AND
THE STRUCTURE OF POLITICS

CHAPTER 2

Land Tenure Regimes and Political Order in Rural Africa

> It is important to remember that the distribution of land is akin to the distribution of power.
> (Kiggundu 2007)
>
> *Les hommes sont beaucoup plus facile à contrôler en monde rural.*[1]
> (An Ivoirian economist, Abidjan, October 2011)

For political analysts working within the closely defined frame of formal political institutions such as legislatures and electoral systems, structures of government and social organization in rural Africa have been nearly indecipherable. In most of rural Africa, transparent forms of socioeconomic accounting – such as tax rolls, social security records, and land registries – are absent, incomplete, or outdated. The nature and distribution of asset holding are opaque. Formal institutions and opinion registers that would allow outsiders to identify competing rural interest groups, their representatives, and their policy preferences are few and far between. Latifundia and landholding aristocracies that are recognizable from afar are absent, giving rise to the stereotype of rural Africa as strongly egalitarian.

African governments themselves have often claimed that custom and tradition prevail where modernity is held at bay, and they have promoted the image of rural communities as existing in a premodern state of social equality and political inertia.[2] Most political analysts have not looked for or seen structural differentiation and institutionalized political forms in rural Africa; many seem

---

[1] It is much easier to control people in the rural areas.
[2] Absence of feudal relations of surplus extraction, and the strength of most households' land claims within their homelands – especially under conditions of land abundance – have served to deflect attention away from the land tenure regimes that create political hierarchy within rural localities.

to have simply assumed the absence thereof.[3] In public opinion polling and some election studies, for example, rural African voters are often modeled as ethnicity-driven individuals (or groups) who act in an unstructured and institutionless political space. Patterned outcomes, such as the persistent salience of ethnic cleavages in voting, the structure of patronage hierarchies, the scope and limits of state penetration of local life, and even outbursts of violent conflict, are thus often attributed to cultural and ideational factors – and especially to the exaggerated role of ethnic identity in political life. This bias in approach leaves the institutional and structural factors that shape rural political behavior largely uninvestigated and untheorized.

Reversing the dominant line of argument, this book argues patterned variation in rural outcomes is attributable to the structuring effects of rural institutions, both formal and informal, the state itself has worked to design and mold. The institutions at the center of the analysis are rural property regimes, or land tenure regimes (LTRs), that prevail in smallholder farming regions.

The first section of Chapter 2 begins with a simple argument about what these land tenure regimes are and are not. Africa's smallholder land regimes are defined as mostly authority-based (rather than predominantly market-based) property regimes. Some rough numbers show that in most African countries, very little rural land is governed under private property regimes that individualize ownership and allow land to be traded on open markets. Focusing on the smallholder land tenure regimes that prevail across most of Africa, I draw a distinction between *neocustomary* land tenure regimes and *statist* land tenure regimes.[4] These land tenure regimes are rooted in different modes of authority-based land allocation, and the distinction between them is the pivot point of our analysis.

The second section takes up questions of institutional origins and design and asks what sustains the land tenure regimes (LTRs) over time.[5] The origins

[3] Anglophone political scientists since the 1990s have veered away from analysis of institutions in African political systems in general and in the countryside in particular. Most of the political economy literature has focused at the national level and on patrimonial political networks that erode formal institutions. I return to this point in the book's Conclusion.

[4] The term "statist" invokes comparative political economy's notions of "statist development strategies" (as in Korea in the 1980s) or "statist" forms of economic regulation (as in France in the same era). It refers to situations in which the state's role in structuring the allocation of productive resources is direct and visible. In the neocustomary land regimes, by contrast, the hand of the state in structuring resource allocation is indirect and often "invisible."

[5] This book does not propose or test a full-blown theory of institutional origins or change, although it suggests how such a theory could be framed in strategic or contract-theoretic terms. That is, LTRs are institutional equilibriums formed as rulers seek to consolidate power at the national level and to establish routinized ways of governing potentially resistant or even rebellious social groups, whose capacity for collective action and value to central rulers (as food producers, tax payers, subjects, citizens, occupiers of strategic territory, etc.) varies over time and space. Herbst (2000) suggests starting points for such reasoning. The main purpose of this book is to conceptualize LTRs as political (and political-economy) institutions, conceptualize variation therein, and test arguments about institutional effects.

of today's land regimes lie in the efforts and strategies of rulers (colonial and postcolonial) to project authority over territory and to govern rural populations. Colonial rulers designed land institutions that defined administrative and political jurisdictions at the lowest levels of state apparatus. Through land tenure systems, the colonial rulers and their local allies codified and institutionalized relations of authority, citizenship, and property at the local level. In most countries, postcolonial rulers deliberately opted to modify but sustain these basic institutional configurations across most of the national territory. The third section develops the claim that in most postcolonial African countries, rural property regimes have played a critical role in creating and sustaining political order within national units. This section underscores the importance of rural land tenure regimes in structuring political authority in the rural areas, organizing the political incorporation of rural majorities into national political systems, and tying rural constituencies to government. Chapter 3 will argue that rising land values and land scarcities strain the sociopolitical hierarchies and interdependencies that are institutionalized in rural land regimes. Pressure on the land fuels the land-related tensions that drive the analysis in Parts II, III, and IV of the book.

MARKET-BASED AND AUTHORITY-BASED PROPERTY REGIMES

Some political economists juxtapose two ideal-type systems of resource allocation.[6] One is market-based systems of allocation, where land, labor, and capital are privately owned commodities that are allocated and combined mostly through the workings of competitive markets and price mechanisms. The second is an authority-based (or hierarchy- or politically based) system of resource allocation. In authority-based systems, market mechanisms are weak, economic resources are not traded as full commodities on open markets, and nonmarket actors such as political authorities exercise great influence over how (and by whom) land, labor, and/or capital are coordinated and combined in economic activity.[7]

In the real world, all national economic systems and property regimes are hybrids of these two. Some national economies are dominated by markets and private control over the means of production. State action remains mostly in the background of economic life. Others are strongly shaped by heavy-handed governmental and other authoritative controls over the economy. Since the 1990s or so, most governments have embraced the principle that markets can produce efficient and legitimate resource allocations in most sectors, and most political economists have walked away from ideological debates over the

---

[6] An ideal type is a hypothetical, abstract concept or analytic construct designed to stress particular elements that are common to a class of phenomena.

[7] Lindbloom (1977) offers an extended discussion.

market system per se. This does not mean that private property regimes and competitive markets prevail everywhere, however. The extent to which markets actually do allocate economic resources and assets must remain a *variable* in comparative political analysis.

In sub-Saharan Africa, most farmland and pastureland is not held as private property by titled individual owners. Most rural farm and pastureland is not fully commodified; it is not traded as a pure commodity on open and competitive markets. Although there are some exceptions, in the vast majority of cases, land rights are politically contingent and not exclusive to one person. In most places, permanent or outright transfers of ownership via sale are not recognized by law, even though informal commercial transactions in land rights are common and are becoming more and more prevalent.[8]

The vast majority of African smallholders do not have formal private property rights in the land they depend on for their livelihoods, well-being, and a place to reside. Legal markers of individual ownership rights – surveyed, registered, and titled land parcels – are rare. In Ghana, for example, a land titling and registration system was introduced in 1986, but as Kasanga and Kotey explained in 2001, "The process of registration is selective and, at the moment, only applies to the urban centres of Accra, Tema and parts of Kumasi.... [The title registration system has been in place for more than a decade. However], its impact has been negligible." In Ghana today and throughout the rest of sub-Saharan Africa, comprehensive national landholding registries and cadastres do not exist, and the institutional preconditions for imposing land taxes on family or peasant-scale farms are not in place.[9]

Writing for the World Bank, Deininger estimated in 2003 that only 2–10 percent of all land in sub-Saharan Africa is held under private title.[10] Table 2.1 compiles some country-specific indicators on this variable, affirming that this range is a good estimate of the extent of private property holding in African countries for which we have data. The African Development Bank's (2009, 9) observation about Cameroon captures much of the general picture: "Land certificates have been issued for barely 2% of the national territory." A 2005 study of Zambia reported a similar result, noting that "94% of all Zambian land is held in 'customary' tenure."[11]

Much of the privately registered and titled rural land in Africa is owned by large-scale commercial operators who engage in agribusiness or commercial ranching, not by the rural households that make up almost 70 percent of the

---

[8] By Alston and Mueller's (2005, 573) definitional scheme, these arrangements are not open-access systems, and they are not systems of fully specified private rights. They would be categorized under the heading of "a host of commons arrangements."

[9] Kasanga and Kotey 2001, 5. (South Africa is an exception.) This means that we cannot measure social stratification in the countryside by analyzing land title registries or tax records.

[10] Chimhowu and Woodhouse 2006, 346, citing Deininger 2003.

[11] Brown 2005, 79.

TABLE 2.1. *Land Registered under Private Title, by Country*[a]

Country	Percentage (est.)	Source
Senegal	5%	Often cited figure
Ghana	<20%	World Bank est. 2003b[b]
Côte d'Ivoire	1% (1987)	Club du Sahel 2006: 28
Côte d'Ivoire	2%	Norwegian Refugee Council 2009a
Cameroon	2%	ADB 2009: 9
Kenya	15% (of arable land)	Partners, "Joint Statement" 2005
Kenya	6.3% (of total land area)	Warner, K. 1993.[c]
Malawi	15%	Kandogo 2006
Malawi	8%	UNECA 2003: 2–3[d]
Uganda	20%	Businge 2007: 2[e]
Tanzania	2%	Liversage 2004[f]
Zambia	7%	Mbinji 2006[g]
Zambia	6%	Brown 2005
Zambia	3%	UNECA 2003: 2–3
Rwanda	<5%	Huggins, Kamungi, et al. :8
Burundi	<5%	Kiggundu 2008
Burundi	1%	Kohlhagen 2010: 69
DRC	<1%	Huggins, Kamungi, et al.: 8
Sudan	5%	Vermeulen and Cotula 2010: 905[h]
Mozambique	3%	UNECA, 2003: 2–3.
Namibia	44%	UNECA 2003: 2–3
Lesotho	44%	UNECA 2003: 2–3
Swaziland	27%	Rose 1992: 17
Botswana	5% (freehold)	Mathuba 2003; UNECA 2003: 2–3[i]
Zimbabwe	33%	Roe 1995
Zimbabwe	41%	UNECA 2003: 2–3
South Africa	72%	UNECA 2003: 2–3
Sub-Saharan Africa (SSA)	2–10%	Deininger 2003
"Most SSA countries"	<10%	Huggins, Kamungi, et al. 2006: 8

[a] These are rough estimates. Many sources are unclear about the denominator.

[b] This 20% includes both privately titled and state property (forests and parks).

[c] This is 1.5% freehold and 4.8% registered "other" trust land. Norton-Griffiths et al. (2009) estimate that 50% of all arable land is under customary tenure.

[d] UNECA (2003) figures refer to land under "private, freehold, or leasehold tenure" as percentage of national territory.

[e] Burns (2007) says that 62% of land (supporting 68% of the population) is under customary tenure.

[f] This source reports that 69% is governed as village land.

[g] Mbinji (2006) reports that 7% was under freehold until freehold was abolished in 1975. The 1995 Land Law says 93% of national territory is under control of chiefs.

[h] They write that about 95% of all land is de facto state owned.

[i] UNECA (2003) gives the figure 28% for freehold plus state land.

region's total population and 65 percent of its workforce.[12] Cross-national variations in land titling correspond roughly to cross-national differences in GDP per capita (if we remove a few outliers, such as Botswana, from the pool), but regime-type differences within Africa do not seem to be reliable predictors of variation in the extent to which governments have granted and enforced private property rights in land. In Senegal, considered in the 1990s to be one of the continent's most robust democracies, 5 percent or less of all land is under private title. Table 2.1 shows that percentages of land registered and held privately are higher in East and southern African countries where white settlers imposed private property regimes in some subnational jurisdictions during the colonial period (to protect their own landholdings).[13]

Legally, states themselves are the owners of all unregistered and untitled land, and the constitutions of some African countries vest the power to allocate land in the president. As land rights lawyers Liz Alden Wiley and Patrick McAuslan point out, the absence of formal or legal property rights in land for the vast majority of rural people means that the state is their landlord, or overlord. McAuslan writes that from a legal standpoint, most peasant farmers are "tenants at will" of the state. The lands worked by most African farmers (and pastoralists) are parts of "national domains" that are legally owned and managed by political authorities in the name of the state.

Two systems of authority-based land allocation are the focus of this analysis. In some places, governments administer the allocation and holding of rural property *directly*. This book refers to land regimes that fit this criterion as "statist" land tenure regimes and focuses on situations in which state agents are direct allocators of land.[14] In the clearest examples, the farmer may receive

[12] In two of every three sub-Saharan African countries, more than 60% of the total population lives and works in the countryside (see Table 3.1). Africa's urban-rural balance is almost the exact inverse of what is found in Latin America, where, in the year 2000, only about 25% of the population was living and working in rural areas, and 20% of the workforce was rural (WDR 2008). For figures on Western Europe, see Luebbert 1987.

[13] These states, including South Africa, Zimbabwe, and Kenya, inherited the British legal tradition, but British colonial inheritance itself does not explain the presence of private property institutions. Private property rights secured alienated land in French Algeria and Côte d'Ivoire. Difference in inherited legal tradition per se (between French civil law and British common law) does not appear to explain variation in the dependent variable examined in this book (i.e., forms of land-related conflict). The cases show that forms of land conflict can be constant across countries with different colonial legal traditions, vary across space within one country (i.e., with a single legal inheritance), and vary across countries with a shared legal tradition.

[14] The United Nations Economic Commission for Africa (UNECA 2003) typologizes African land regimes in terms of a distinction between "statutory" and "customary" law. Statutory tenure refers to land under "private, freehold, leasehold, and state land and other" arrangements. This study does not adopt the UNECA typology. Instead, my main empirical focus is on "state and other" tenure regimes on the one hand, and the neocustomary regimes on the other. These distinctions are not absolute, and some cases are hybrids. I develop a conceptual distinction between statist and neocustomary land regimes. Chapter 10, focused on Zimbabwe, argues for

a plot of land directly from a uniformed agent of the Ministry of Lands or from the local prefect or subprefect. In other places (in fact, across most of the national territory in most African countries), rural land is governed *indirectly*, through the neocustomary land tenure systems that have been shaped and codified by Africa's colonial and postcolonial rulers. Colonial and postcolonial governments have called these "customary" land tenure regimes, but I will use the term "neocustomary" to stress the fact that these property institutions often bear very limited resemblance to precolonial land rules and practices. In some places, they were even invented of whole cloth by colonial governors.

Under *both* kinds of land tenure regime, significant measures of hierarchical or authority-based control structures landholding, access to land, and land transactions. Political relationships involving hierarchy and dependency are insinuated into land-access and land-transaction relationships, even where informal (or "vernacular") markets in land rights exist.[15] This gives land-controlling authorities political leverage over land users. It also gives land users political arguments, and political avenues of defense, against market forces that threaten their access to land. Land tenure regimes create and institutionalize not only these vertical political inequalities and dependencies but also horizontal political inequalities. What are the implications of these arrangements for politics, democracy, and transitions to the market? How do patterns and politics of landholding influence voting patterns, identity politics, and patterns of collective action and mobilization? What are the implications for state structure and governing strategies? These are questions that this study seeks to address.

---

seeing private property in land as governed under a *type of* statist land tenure regime. This conceptualization emphasizes the extent to which private property holding is regulated and enforced directly by the state and state agents. It elides the (oversimplified) distinction between market-based and authority-based systems of allocation that is invoked early in Chapter 2. By looking at the Zimbabwe case, the study draws attention to the elements of "statism" that inhere in registered, titled, and transactable private property. As Engerman and Metzer (2004) argue, "statism" is particularly acute when we are talking about private property *in land*. A similar case could be made for some financial assets (think of government bonds, for example).

[15] "Vernacular" or informal markets in land rights exist in many parts of rural Africa (for rentals, pawning or mortgaging, share contracts, and so on). Usually the rights that are transferred fall short of what are considered full ownership rights in Western property law (Chimhowu and Woodhouse 2006, 346, 352). This is true in many areas of high market activity in land. As Sayonba Ouédraogo (2006, 22) says of transfers of irrigated lands located close to urban markets in Burkina Faso, land *is* sold, but these sales are *transactions dissimulées* that do not culminate in the definitive cession of property rights to buyers. Unofficial sales are common, but by definition, these are not enforced by the state. Sales are often redeemable by members of the seller's extended family, who are recognized as rights holders in land held under customary tenure. Land sales that are initiated by those empowered as "customary custodians of the land" are not classic market-based exchanges. They are more akin to a mayor selling off municipal property in a way that incites debates over use and abuse of authority, and debates over the scope of the market.

PROPERTY REGIMES AND POLITICAL STRUCTURE IN RURAL AFRICA

> Land has been an object of policy intervention from colonial times to the present, and *every spot of land in Africa* has a history of changing land policies and different forms of land politics. (Adams and Palmer 2007, 72, emphasis added)

Colonial administrations, independent governments, and actors at virtually all levels of Africa's social hierarchies have exploited the ways in which authority-based controls over land can be used to gather power over people and to structure and incentivize their political behavior.

Conquering European states claimed ownership or trusteeship of all land in the African territories. Where they wanted to use and exploit some of this land themselves (for urban development, government installations, mining, and the settlement of European farmers or ranchers), colonial authorities usually expropriated African landholders and users. In these places, farmers or pastoralists were forcibly expelled from their ancestral areas or from lands they claimed by other rights. Colonial states proceeded to allocate land access to users directly, either arbitrarily or under statute, institutionalizing the statist land regimes that figure prominently in this analysis.

Across most of Africa, however, the Europeans' main goal was *not* to expropriate existing users. The colonial powers did not seek to assert direct control over agricultural production, or to assert direct political control over the land. Rather, they sought to keep most of the population in the rural areas, subsisting and producing as farmers or pastoralists, and to control population mobility by fixing individuals and families within delimited territories designated as "ethnic homelands." To exert political control, the colonizers sought to take advantage of and accentuate mechanisms of social control that existed (or were presumed to exist) in "African tribal society." Institutionalizing the neocustomary land tenure regimes was rulers' main instrument for doing this. This involved defining, delimiting, or creating the "natural tribal communities" that were presumed to be the authentic African social form, fixing the boundaries of the microterritories that were designated as their ancestral homelands, and sharpening and codifying relations of political hierarchy within these geographic units. This transformed what the colonizers perceived as the vast and politically fluid (or decidedly oppositional) spaces of conquered Africa into the "governed spaces" of Africa under colonial rule.[16] It gave the colonial administrators the trusted local intermediaries (*interlocuteurs valables*) through whom they could govern the rural masses.

The neocustomary land tenure regimes were less costly to erect and enforce than the more invasive and overtly coercive statist land regimes. After the Second World War, the indirect-rule logic embodied in the customary land regime

---

[16] Watts 2004.

was the colonizers' preferred institutional choice across almost all sub-Saharan Africa – that is, wherever countervailing considerations did not create rationales for imposing the more costly (in terms of administration and coercion) statist land regimes.

The Neocustomary Land Regimes

In most of sub-Saharan Africa throughout most of the colonial period, land was abundant, and the colonial administrators' concern was not with managing land as a scarce resource. From the 1910s through the 1940s, the Europeans' main concern was to cement alliances with selected rural strongmen – chiefs, emirs, kings, elders, and other local rulers – who could serve as their agents or partners in ruling the countryside. To this end, territorial jurisdictions were delimited, and officially designated "customary rulers" were invested with wide-ranging executive and judicial authority to exercise within their official territorial domains. Sally Falk Moore (1991, 111) describes this process in the Mt. Kilimanjaro region of Tanganyika (today's Tanzania):

> The German colonial peace put a stop to the fighting [among several dozen politically autonomous chiefdoms on Mt. Kilimanjaro], hanged some chiefs, deposed others, and installed chiefs answerable to their colonial rulers.... Over time, the political arena was completely reorganized. What had been dozens of chiefdoms were consolidated into fewer and fewer [for the administrative convenience of the Europeans]. In both the German [1886–1916] and the British [1916–1961] periods, each chiefdom had a law court presided over by the chief.... The judicial role was an extension of chiefly administrative authority.... It served as an arm of the colonial government.

European colonial authorities' interest in *land tenure* flowed largely from their interest in establishing and enforcing these new forms of state-recognized authority over rural people.[17] Rules of land access were set to establish hierarchical relationships between the collaborating African elites and their subjects. Chanock writes that in the British colonies of Malawi and Zambia, the new systems of customary land tenure reflected the colonizers' vision of the customary rulers as petty monarchs with power to allocate land in their domains:

> Early administrators approached Africa with certain basics in mind.... An essential part of this picture was the model of land tenure, the basic features of which were that land was held in some form of communal tenure and could not be sold by individuals, and

---

[17] As Chanock (1998, 40) argues in an analysis of Malawi and Zambia in the early colonial period, land tenure systems were as much about imposing control over *rural populations* as about controlling land as an end in itself. Jean Schmitz (1991) makes the same point when he describes the sharply hierarchical systems of land control in the Middle Valley of the Senegal River in the 1980s as, first and foremost, a template for political and social order: control over land was a *pretexte* or mechanism for imposing control over people.

that all had a more or less equal right to land.... Rights in land were seen as flowing downward ... [and as] derived from the political authority, rather than residing in the peasantry. [It was] an essentially feudal model. (Chanock 1991, 63–64)

In Northern Nigeria, also under British rule, the colonial Lands Committee "quite literally 'invented' the idea of communal land tenure among Hausa communities in order to push through a particular type of colonial project" (Watts 1983a, 75).

Authority and jurisdiction under the neocustomary regimes
Although "some of the organizing concepts of precolonial land tenure systems continued to influence evolving patterns of land control" (Berry 1988, 58), state-recognized chiefs and the male elders or lineage heads who were often designated as their advisers were given wide powers to make up what colonialism recognized as customary land tenure. They used these prerogatives to extend their authority (and their landholdings). To extend Moore's Mt. Kilimanjaro example,

During the colonial period chiefs used their administrative powers gradually to appropriate increasing control over the allocation of unused land.... [By the middle of the colonial period, chiefs] actively interposed themselves in all land allocations and transactions. Hailey (1938, 848) cites a Chagga Native Authority regulation legitimating the transfer of land only if *made with the authority of the chief.* (Moore 1991, 113–114, emphasis in the original)

Land powers gave the customary authorities carrots and sticks that they used to govern their rural subjects. In the land domain, the customary rulers had the power to allocate unoccupied land; seize and reallocate land deemed not in use; cede land to the central government or at its behest; seize land they deemed needed for communal purposes; seize the land of people who did not pay taxes, fines, meet the corvée, or submit to conscription; force widows and divorced women to turn over land to their in-laws; force younger men to submit to the discretion of elders in deciding land disposition and use; dispose of inheritance cases; rule on other land disputes within and among families; authorize transactions or sanction individuals for land transactions (such as rentals) not deemed to conform to customary practice as defined by the chief and elders; and enforce colonial land-use policies (such as forced terracing or destocking). These prerogatives were supplemented by powers to tax, conscript, arrest, jail, and mete out justice (short of the death penalty). In all these ways, colonialism's political and economic institutions worked at the microlevel to impose and enforce the hierarchy of those who had administrative powers over the land, over those who worked the land or needed access to it. Writing of French West Africa, van Beusekom (1997) describes the land regime as a mechanism of social control prized by colonial officials.

Customary authority was conceptualized as "tribal authority" exercised by traditional rulers over tribes in their ancestral homelands. To put these ideas into practice, colonial officials had to designate officially recognized customary rulers, but this alone was not enough to impose a system of rule in the countryside. They also had to delimit territorial jurisdictions for the exercise of this form of authority and assign subject populations to rulers and territories. Mamdani (1996a) describes this process as "containerizing" African populations into separate ethnic cages.

With the help of anthropologists, colonial authorities undertook to draw jurisdictions that confirmed or expanded the geographic sphere of influence of some (trusted) customary authorities and reduced or eliminated the domains of other (often distrusted) local leaders. The size of jurisdictions was also adjusted to meet standards of bureaucratic expediency. The Gogo of Tanganyika, for example, were amalgamated into a new, hierarchically ordered chiefdom in the 1920s because British administrators deemed their existing political collectivities to be too small and too decentralized (Rigby 1977, 84).

These new jurisdictions were supposed to be tribal territories encompassing the ancestral homelands of the people (grouped into a tribe) who were subject to the authority of the customary (tribal) ruler. When reality did not fit the administrative map, reality was often adjusted. For example, the British in Tanganyika created a "Masailand" and in 1925 commanded that "all Masai are to be moved into the Masai Reserve." Those who refused to move were to "give up their claims to be Masai." Non-Masai finding themselves in the reserve were commanded either to become Masai or to move out: all communities were to "accept the citizenship of the tribes they were living among." The senior commissioner for Arusha District, Mr. Browne, quoted the late Governor Sir H. A. Byatt: "'They must definitively be Masai or not Masai.'"[18]

Administrative delineation of "tribes" and tribal identities was a precondition for attaching persons and groups to the chiefs who were to exercise personal authority over them. Chanock uses the term "new tribes" to distinguish the groupings recognized by the colonial state from precolonial territorial, identity-based, and political groupings.[19] Because customary law varied across the ethnic groups within one colony, it was necessary to assign a state-recognized tribal identity to each person in order to know, in the case of a dispute, claim, or infraction, *which* customary court and *which* customary law would apply. The working of the customary land tenure regimes was also predicated on assigning a clear ethnic status to each land user.

Official tribal homelands constituted the geographical/territorial arenas for the exercise of customary rulership and the operation of customary courts, land

---

[18] Tanzania National Archives (TNA), Mr. Browne, Sr. Commissioner Arusha District, Annual Report 1925, 18 January 1926, 11 (TNA, AB.31 [1925]. File n. 1733/1/36). Maasai is now the preferred spelling.

[19] Those not certified as official ethnic groups or tribes thus did not get their own homeland.

tenure regimes, and citizenship regimes.[20] Figures 2.1 and 2.2 are reproductions of colonial maps of tribal and chiefly territories. Van Binsbergen describes the first figure, originally published circa 1935 as "Tribal Territories of Northern Rhodesia":

For the African inhabitants of Northern Rhodesia, a...map was drawn up, clearly demarcating, and distinguishing by contrasting colours, the various "tribal" areas into which the territory was administratively divided; the assumption was that these divisions coincided with linguistic and cultural distinctions, thus reifying (through the binary opposition of ethnic names) cultural gradients that were in fact much more continuous, in most cases. Anthropologists used this map with the same enthusiasm as administrators.... The map was uncritically reprinted in post-colonial times by the Zambian Survey Department, the country's official producer of maps [as the Tribal and Linguistic Map of Zambia].[21]

The second figure, District of North-Kivu (Belgian Congo): Chieftaincy Jurisdictions, 1954 (Figure 2.2), is based on a land saturation map. It depicts political microterritories created by the colonial administration in what is now North Kivu Province of the DRC. Internal boundaries partitioned space, authority, population subgroups, and land. High variation in the population density scores of neighboring chiefdoms is an indicator of colonial authorities' attempts to restrict population movement across the jurisdictional boundaries.

Within these jurisdictions, the architects of Native Administration endeavored to organize colonialism's African intermediaries into hierarchies that could be managed and monitored in top-down fashion. These arrangements could also serve to channel information upward to European district officers.[22] Territorial jurisdictions were nested like Russian dolls, confirming rank not only of the chiefs but also of the jurisdictions themselves. A locale designated as the seat of a higher-ranking chief qualified for better administrative and social infrastructure, and the leading clans enjoyed elevated status. These territories and

---

[20] See Young 1994, 232–233. Groups without officially recognized homelands lost out completely and were pressured to "join recognized tribes." Recognition of a homeland can thus be seen as something valuable that some communities or peoples won from the colonial state, although, of course, they were dealing with the colonial government from a position of terrible disadvantage. In zones vulnerable to land expropriation by whites, such as northern Tanzania, state recognition of a homeland was a major political asset when it came to resisting (further) expropriation. See, for example, Spear 1997 on the 1951 Meru Land case.

[21] Manchester School Photo essay by Wim van Binsbergen, posted at www.shikanda.net/ethnicity/illustrations_manch/manchest.htm, 10 December 2009.

[22] In British Native Administration, the hierarchy ran from district officer to paramount chief, divisional chiefs, village chiefs, and sometimes ward chiefs. In French Africa, the hierarchy ran from commandant de cercle to cantonal chiefs, to village chiefs. Although "indirect rule" is associated with British colonial administration in Africa, the French also relied on this governing strategy. Chieftaincies were reestablished as basic administrative units throughout French West Africa in 1917. Thereafter, it was policy and standard procedure to subject Africans to African intermediaries who were appointed or confirmed in office by the French.

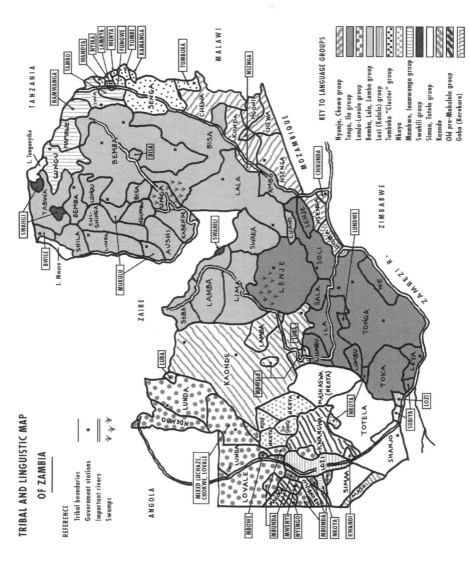

FIGURE 2.1. "Tribal Territories of Northern Rhodesia," circa 1935. *Source:* Survey Department of Zambia, reproduced in van Binsbergen 2006, adapted by K. Wyllys.

Level of Land Occupation
in the Masisi Territory (1954)

Source: Drawn from Map II, "District du Nord-Kivu: Carte de Saturation,
August 1, 1954," in Kivu, Regional Division of Agriculture, Bukavu.

FIGURE 2.2. District of North-Kivu (Belgian Congo): Chieftaincy Jurisdictions, 1954.
Source: Mararo, Stanislas Bucyalimwe, *Dialogue* n. 192, 1996, 90.

chiefly hierarchies constituted the basic administrative units and administrative machinery (the "local states") of rural Africa under colonial rule.[23]

This is the architecture of what Jean Schmitz (1991) called the "state constituted differently at different levels [or scales]" (*l'état à géometrie variable*). It was based on the coercive, formal-legal or bureaucratic, and secular authority of the colonial state at the very top levels. At the local levels, authority was nonsecular, hereditary, and neocustomary. Mamdani stresses that in the neocustomary jurisdictions, this institutionalized a form of authority that was, in essence, arbitrary. Because colonial administrative theory held that African custom was flexible and evolving, the customary authorities were given wide prerogative in defining the rules of customary land tenure flexibly and as they saw fit.[24] Personal rule unrestrained by codified principle or law was thus a

---

[23] Mamdani 1996a, 21–22. Lentz (2006) calls this the "native state."
[24] Colonial authorities resisted, until late in the colonial period, the formal codification of customary law (as implemented in customary courts) for fear that this would "freeze its natural development" (Chanock 1998).

deliberate feature of the colonial state in the rural areas. The result was the bifurcated form of state authority that Mamdani defines as the essential feature of the colonial state in Africa.

Property, in-migration, and citizenship under the neocustomary regimes

The customary land regimes were founded on the principle that the land encompassed within a chiefly jurisdiction (an officially delimited ethnic homeland) was the corporately held endowment of a descent-based community. Chiefs or other customary leaders were supposed to manage this corporate endowment on behalf of all members of the group. Membership in the descent-based corporate group was thus understood to confer a land entitlement. In John Bruce's (1988, 42–43) description of the generic features of indigenous land tenure systems prevailing in Africa, "all members of the community, a community most commonly defined by descent, are considered entitled to land. This will often be the case whether or not they are residents, and whether or not they are farmers.... The tenure system bases access to land on membership [in the community]." The political status of state-recognized membership in an official "tribe" or ethnic group thus became an asset in itself: it conferred a land entitlement.

In colonial (and postcolonial) Africa, some degree of ethnic heterogeneity has been a feature of many rural localities. The neocustomary land regimes imposed a distinction between those who had the economic right of land entitlement within the ethnic homeland and those who did not. Such distinctions became particularly salient where cash-crop production developed in zones of low population density, and in-migrants provided labor to expand the cash-crop economy. Those not recognized as members of the descent-based landholding group – referred to in English and French as strangers, outsiders, "acceptees," *étrangers*, or *allogènes* – were not entitled to land by birthright. Strangers could gain provisional access to it with the permission of certain community members, contingent on acceptance of their politically subordinate status within the community (and usually some kind of payment to the customary landholder). Under these political arrangements, a stranger could not "represent" the descent-based collectivity (because he or she was not regarded as a full member of the group) by holding community-wide political office or by participating in the interpretation and enforcement of local custom. As Painter and Philo (1995, 107) put it, customary authority created or reinforced "political system[s] of inclusion and exclusion" by stipulating who was considered a full citizen in the customary jurisdiction (with political rights and economic rights of membership) and who was not.

Across much of rural Africa, the definition of "who is a stranger" and the second-class citizenship status of strangers tended to harden over time. When land was abundant and labor was scarce, assimilation of strangers into the landholding collectivity (through marriage or investment of "sweat equity," for example) tended to be relatively easy.[25] As land became scarcer or as its political and economic value rose, boundaries of corporate lineages tended to be defined in more restrictive terms, and hierarchies of rights and dependency became steeper.[26] Institutionalization of colonialism's customary land tenure systems was itself a factor that worked to harden landlord-stranger distinctions. These relations create hierarchy in localities: in some rural districts of west and central Africa today, up to half of all farmers hold "derived rights" to land (i.e., conditional access granted to ethnic outsiders by permission of indigenous landholders).[27]

The customary land regimes also encoded sociopolitical hierarchy *within* corporate landholding groups. In much of Sahelian West Africa, for example, communities are structured by land-access hierarchies *among and within lineages*. Dahou and Ndiaye (2008, 61) describe lineage hierarchy in land systems in contemporary Senegal:

Inequalities in access to land can be explained by the way the land rights system works. It defines a hierarchy of access that privileges the settlement's founding families, then the non-founding families that have been established for a long time, and giving last place to new arrivals. Often, among families that are not members of the founding group, you find those that are marginalized in political decision making – including former slave families and casted groups – who gain access to good land only in very limited quantities. This discriminatory structure of access to the best land shows clearly that the hypothesis that "customary law is superior to other land systems when it comes to equity" does not stand up to analysis.

Colonialism's customary land regimes also recognized or imposed land-access hierarchies on the basis of gender and age, establishing and shoring up patriarchy at the molecular level of the lineage and family. The customary courts, for example, helped shore up senior males' (lineage or family elders) control over family lands, even as the commercialization of agriculture and the growing importance of off-farm incomes worked to erode the generational hierarchies.[28]

The customary land tenure regimes institutionalized property systems in which individuals and groups held *multiple and overlapping rights* in land (Berry 1988). Land was held corporately by members of a real or imagined

[25] Berry (1988) stresses that these social identities and the rights and entitlements they confer have sometimes been ambiguous and negotiable. Outsiders could sometimes be assimilated through marriage or labor contributions, by bequest, or on the basis of personal qualities or achievements. However, colonial and postcolonial rule, and rising land values, have often hardened the insider-outsider distinction.

[26] Austin (2005) and Chauveau (2000, 2001) show that shifts in balances of power between landlords and in-migrants can reflect changing factor prices and the changing land tenure strategies of the colonial and postcolonial governments.

[27] See Lavigne-Delville et al. 2002.

[28] In *Fathers Work for Their Sons* (1985), Sara Berry described such processes in southwestern Nigeria's cocoa-producing communities.

descent-based group (but farmed by extended households and families). Under the customary tenure principles, the descent-based community was seen as a nested hierarchy of social collectivities that ran from the encompassing tribe or ethnic group, to the major subgroupings by lineage or clan, and to hierarchically ordered household groupings at the molecular level of society. Layered and overlapping property rights bound individuals and groups to larger collectivities, thus creating and shoring up the social cohesion within tribes, lineages, and families that colonial rulers prized as the essence of "tribal society." Multiple and overlapping rights produced a multiplicity of interests in a particular piece of land: different rights to a given piece of land are held and exercised separately by different groups of people.[29] Communities as a whole gained a collective interest in protecting a land endowment in which each member, by the principles of customary tenure, could claim an entitlement. Lineages and clans held corporate interests in land, whether or not they were able to act as a group to "govern the commons" effectively.

A net effect of these property relations and rules was to create social cohesion and political hierarchy within (and sometimes across) the landholding communities that were the basic units of government under colonial rule.

The integrity of customary land tenure regimes as systems for enforcing hierarchical authority at the local level, and for enforcing the cohesion of descent-based groups, rested in large part on the principle of nonalienability of land. This is why colonial administrations sought to suppress land sales within the chiefly jurisdictions (Phillips 1989; Chimhowu and Woodhouse 2006; Rathbone 1993). They realized that the development of land markets would undermine chiefs' authority over land and over community members. The rulers also saw that the development of land markets would dissolve the hierarchically structured descent groups, headed by male elders, that they sought to reinforce as the basic landholding unit and the basic political unit (Goody 1980, 152).

Impetus for reproducing these arrangements did not come entirely from the state, however. In rural localities, the elite – chiefs and members of dominant lineages – had a long-term interest in defending their political prerogatives over land, even if they also often had short-term interests in strategic sales that would generate revenue (as Onoma 2010 and Berry 2013 pointed out in contemporary Ghana). At the grassroots level, there were smallholders and subordinate members of corporate landholding groups whose land rights were

---

[29] As Reyna and Downs (1988, 17) explain, "More than one person has valid claims to the same plot, either for the same or different purposes" – under rules of joint inheritance, for example. In addition, community members may retain rights to pasture and forage and to traverse a landholding, as well as reversionary rights to the land, should it fall into disuse or the landholder die with no heir.

threatened by the rise of markets (or by the possibility of expropriation by the colonial state, a chief, or a lineage head). Many of them developed vested interests in customary land rights, and in the principle that access to land in their ethnic homeland was a birthright recognized (if not always honored) by the state.[30] The customary structures also gave senior males authority over land farmed by women and youth, as well as claims to the labor of these subordinate household members.

Political independence did not put a halt to state-building in the farming regions of Africa. On the contrary, neocustomary land tenure regimes persist in a wide variety of forms as "chosen institutions" of postcolonial rulers. Most of the independent African governments sought to tap into the political potential inherent in customary land tenure and in customary authority over land allocation. Whether by constitutional dispensation, law, administrative or executive decree, or practice, most governments have confirmed the role of chiefs or other *autorités traditionnelles* in allocating access to farmland, and in adjudicating land-related disputes arising over boundaries, inheritance, and transactions. In addition, these same community-level authorities often retained prerogatives when it came to allocating access to shared resources such as community forests, water points, and pasture.

Explicit examples abound of deliberate and even muscular postcolonial state action to sustain and reproduce neocustomary forms of rule. The glossary of a 2009 African Development Bank report on land management in Cameroon gives a generic definition of "customary land law" that could have been taken straight from the playbook of high colonialism:

[Customary land law is] all unwritten rules which make up the customs of a people (as against statute law). Customary land law governs rights over land. It is the method of managing land and land-related rights in accordance with native customs. It varies from region to region and from one ethnic group to another and also over time owing to economic, social and political changes. (ADB 2009, Annex 2, 2)

The African Development Bank also reports that in Cameroon,

the customary land management method is still current. . . . Many Cameroonians are content with using customary or traditional systems to acquire land. Discussions with divisional and regional services revealed that "in actual fact, traditional rulers do not feel concerned [with the ambiguities of statutory law]; they even sell customary lands. . . . " The administration follows and regularizes the practices; . . . the traditional ruler settles people and the administration confirms the action. (ADB 2009, para. 4. 2. 6 and p. 10)

Ghana' s 1992 constitution makes chiefs owners and managers of stool and skin lands, which are lands attached to the chieftaincy as an institution and

---

[30] Chanock (1998, 235) makes this argument for parts of southern Africa that saw extensive development of labor systems based on outmigration of men from the rural areas: "there was a strong defensive element [to Africans' use of customary land tenure] where Africans anticipated further expropriations by settlers."

supposed to be held in trust for the members of the collectivity. To reconcile the concept of "ownership" with the chief's role as political representative, the constitution emphasizes that "those with responsibility for managing land must act in the wider interests of their communities."[31] In Benin, "customary laws were codified (accurately or not) by the French in *Le Coutumier du Dahomey* of 1931 ... which was still used in the courts until 1996. ... Land cases and inheritances cases [were heard in] "*la chambre traditionnelle des biens.*"[32] Postcolonial Kenya endorsed a more secular and bureaucratized version of customary land tenure in the former ethnic homelands, or what the colonial administration called "native land units":

> Native Lands Trust Boards [were] established by the Native Lands Trust Ordinance of 1938. At independence [in 1963], these native lands became trust lands, and were vested in county councils to hold them in trust for the benefit of all persons residing thereon. (Migai-Akech 2006)

In Sudan in 1994, the government *reinstated* "a system of local administration that relied on customary authorities, the old model inherited from British colonial rule. ... Once installed in office, state-recognized chiefs could use their power ... to allocate land [and] organize local militia (Reno 2010b, 329).[33]

Meanwhile, the notion of customary *rights* remains politically entrenched in most of rural Africa, where it is wielded for diverse purposes by the multiple actors – at all levels of state and society – who have a stake in the political prerogatives, protections, and promises it can provide. So it was that in Kenya, in the midst of raging debate over land tenure law in 2005, the Kenya Land Alliance declared that "the Kenyan customary concept of ownership of land still prevails."

> Since customarily no individual in a community owns land, land is owned by all collectively for the benefit of each and every member of the community. The result is that land relations in many parts of Kenya are still actualised on the basis of customary law. For instance, claims to land are still being made on the basis of customary law even where such land is registered under the Registered Land Act. Moreover, in practice, before Land Control Boards sanction any land transaction, they work with community elders to determine the different rights of the members of that community.... Customary lands are managed and controlled by the County Councils, which hold them in trust for communities (KLA 2005).[34]

---

[31] Article 36(8) of the 1992 constitution states: "The state shall recognize that ownership and possession of land carry a social obligation to serve the larger community and, in particular, the state shall recognize that the managers of public, stool, skin and family lands are fiduciaries charged with the obligation to discharge their functions for the benefit respectively of the people of Ghana and of the stool, skin or family concerned, and are accountable as fiduciaries in this regard." Kasanga and Kotey (2001, 1).

[32] Wing n.d., 21; see Wing 2012.

[33] Reno 2010, 319–341. Similarly, Forrest (2003, 213) writes of the "reestablishment of Mandjack kingships" in Guinée-Bissau after 1987.

[34] Kenya Land Alliance (KLA), Issues Paper n. 4, 2005a.

Postcolonial governments have been deeply and actively implicated in upholding and reproducing the institutions and political relationships embedded in
the (neo)customary land tenure regimes. It is incorrect to see customary land
regimes as informal in the sense of existing beyond the purview of the state, or
as subverting government efforts to administer the rural areas.

The Statist Land Tenure Regimes

Indirect rule through neocustomary authority has not prevailed everywhere
in colonial and postcolonial Africa. Within some geographically delimited
jurisdictions in every African colony, the state made itself the direct allocator, enforcer, and manager of rural land rights. Every student of African
history knows that in the white settler colonies of Kenya, Zimbabwe, South
Africa, Namibia, and Mozambique, colonial states alienated vast domains from
African land users, created separate administrative and political institutions
to govern these spaces, and assigned rights to arable and pasturable land to
European settlers or foreign companies for the creation of commercial farms,
plantations, and ranches. Less noticed is the fact that *postcolonial* African
governments have also assumed direct authority over land allocation, the management of land use, and land-rights adjudication in some strategic areas of
smallholder and peasant farming.

Both colonial and postcolonial governments have created schemes to resettle
African populations in new territory, to clear the way for other forms of land
use (including use by European settlers or agribusiness), relieve overcrowding
in densely populated districts, or establish peasantries on previously unfarmed
land.[35] Some of the best-known examples of postcolonial settlement schemes
are found in Kenya, where the government resettled more than 500,000 Kenyan
families on Rift Valley farmland in the 1960s and 1970s. In Côte d'Ivoire,
75,000 Baoulé displaced by construction of the Koussou Dam in 1970 were
resettled by the government in the western forest zone of the country. In postcolonial Rwanda, settlement schemes placed tens of thousands of families on
marshlands reclaimed by government, or on pasturelands that had been expropriated by the state. Governments have also asserted direct control over land
for the creation of cities, public works projects, transportation infrastructure,
airports, ports, agricultural research centers and demonstration farms, military
camps, and landed estates that can be given to political elites. They have cordoned off forest reserves, national parks, and game preserves, which become
off-limits to farmers and, often, most pastoralists as well.

In such areas, land authority is not devolved to state-recognized customary
authorities. The central state itself is a direct allocator and manager of land

---

[35] Amselle (1976, 24) refers to these as movements of rural African populations that were directed,
     oriented, or planned by the state. See Silberfein 1988b, 51; Adepoju 1982.

access and use. We refer to this type of land control regime as "statist" to underscore the directness of the state's role in allocating land and, thus, to distinguish this mode of land governance from the indirect rule arrangements that define the so-called customary land tenure regimes in Africa.[36]

Under colonialism, forcible displacement of settled farming communities or long-established pastoralists was a basic tool in the state's repertoire of techniques of territorial, resource, and political control. As Sara Berry has said, "Colonial officials resorted, time and time again, to moving people from one location and settling them in another.... Displacement was commonplace" (Berry 2002, 641). Kraler (n.d., 13) writes of Belgian Africa:

[There was a] wide policy of "social engineering," embarked upon from the 1920s onwards, over the course of which large numbers of people were displaced for various reasons, including the establishment of national parks, economic reasons (labor), on the grounds of public health (malaria and sleeping sickness), for administrative reasons (regroupment and villagization), and because of "overpopulation and landlessness."

Forced displacements often involved resettlement or relocation schemes of some sort.[37] Often, resettlement was an end in itself. Mafikiri refers to *migrations organisées* or *migrations officielles*, wherein states have directed movements of rural African populations into new territories to relocate displaced populations or to develop new agrarian frontiers.[38] In *Modern Migrations in West Africa* (1974), Samir Amin referred to such initiatives as state-sponsored movements of agrarian colonization. Receiving areas have sometimes been developed as actual *settlement schemes* in which the state itself built roads, demarcated and subdivided settlement areas, and assigned settlers to particular plots of land. As Mafikiri puts it, in-migrants are "administratively inserted" into localities or subregions.[39]

State-sponsored movements of agrarian colonization were promoted to relieve population pressure in high-density areas, control disease, increase agricultural production, assert political control over rural populations through creation of settled farming communities (the creation of peasantries), or clear the way for dams and reservoirs. John Kabera (1982, 183) provides some

---

[36] The analytic distinction between customary and statist land regimes can blur as, for example, when governments appoint new chiefs to rule over populations in government-created settlement schemes or when state-recognized customary authorities are pressured by government to settle strangers on customary land. Joireman (2011) notes that in the urban slums of Nairobi (on state land), the government appoints chiefs as local political authorities.

[37] Claassens (2005) comments that even the South African government spoke of "resettlement... of successive waves of people after forced removal from 'white' South Africa."

[38] Mafikiri Tsongo 1997. On 1940s and 1950s settlement schemes, see Kimble 1960, chapter 5. On cases of villagization (e.g., in Zambia, Angola, Mozambique, Ethiopia, Tanzania, Kenya), which may or may not involve the reallocation of farmland, see Silberfein in Silberfein 1998b, 51–69.

[39] Mafikiri Tsongo 1997.

examples in "Rural Population Redistribution in Uganda since 1900," which explains that resettlement schemes were common in colonial Uganda. They were aimed at combating tsetse fly and increasing agricultural production, relieving population pressures, and finding employment for youth. "Indeed, resettlement schemes in general were the vogue in population redistribution policies" (Kabera 1982, 199). Kabera elaborates:

Large-scale repopulation of the empty areas started in the 1940s aimed at relieving population pressure in certain densely populated parts of the country. Kigezi district, rather than other equally densely populated districts, caught the eyes of the government from the middle of the 1930s.... Enthusiastic agricultural officers and administrators [concluded that there were] land pressure problems.... [A] committee was set up within the Department of Agriculture in 1944 to locate immigration areas. Organized resettlement schemes started in 1946.... Thinly populated areas... were selected. By the end of 1954, 25000 persons had been resettled in north Kigezi; another 13000 were settled there between 1954 and 1961. Meanwhile west Ankole settled 8500 persons between 1951 and 1954. (Kabera 1982, 183)

Both colonial and postcolonial governments encouraged and facilitated the settlement of migrants on "state controlled agrarian frontiers,"[40] or on "new lands" opened up to smallholder farming by irrigation, swamp reclamation, tsetse fly eradication, borehole drilling (to create permanent sources of water), expulsion of pastoralists, or abandonment of properties by white settlers. As Table 2.2 shows, cases in point can be found in colonial and postcolonial South Africa, Rhodesia, Namibia, Kenya, Rwanda, Uganda, Tanzania, Nigeria, Ghana, Mali, Sudan, Ethiopia, Senegal, Belgian Congo/Zaire, and others.

In these situations, it is the state that regulates land access and land rights. The existing ancestral claims to land rights in zones of state-sponsored or enforced in-migration have sometimes been "fully extinguished" by formal decree of state authorities. Often, central authorities have simply *not recognized* ancestral claims or established user rights, thus giving practical meaning to the principle that a property right not honored by the state is no property right at all. There are places where prior users' ancestral rights have been subordinated, in the eyes of the state, to settlers' land-access rights, which are

---

[40] Médard (2009, 342) uses this term to describe the state-led clearing and settlement of the Chebyuk area on the southern slopes of Kenya's Mt. Elgon starting in the 1970s, 1980s, and 1990s, where "land allocations and access to forest resources are managed in neopatrimonial style." Some situations are more difficult to classify in terms of the schema proposed here. For example, there are situations in which the *pax colonial* (i.e., the end of the slave trade and suppression of local war and raiding) opened agricultural frontiers that were then "colonized" or repopulated by African settlers through processes that were not organized by the state (i.e., the state itself did not assert control over the settlement process). This seems to have been the situation in parts of the Middle Belt of Nigeria, especially the area south of Jos (see Appendix), where neither state authority nor state-recognized neocustomary authority was strong from the 1940s to the 1980s.

TABLE 2.2. *Settlement Schemes and State-Sponsored Zones of Agrarian Colonization: Examples*

Country	Scheme Name	Timing	Purpose	No. of People	Land Area	Sources
Sudan	Gezira, 1926–present	Nationalized in 1950	Development of irrigated cotton schemes (wheat)	100,000 tenants and 400,000 wage workers[a] (1980); 120,000 tenants (2000)	1,000,000 hectares[b]	Abdelkarin, 1986; Babikir and Babikir, 2007: 336
Kenya	Million Acres and other smallholder schemes	1960–1980	Peasantization	500,000 (1970)	900,000 ha. (1979)	Oucho 2002: 51, Leys 1975:75.
Kenya	Coastal (incl. Haraka) schemes	Late 1960s–1980s	Relieve landlessness	70,790 families (as of c. 2007)	351,000 ha (c. 2007)	Rep. of Kenya, Min. of Lands, 2009: 2
Côte d'Ivoire	Kossou Dam, AVB and coffee-cocoa schemes in SW	1970–1976	Resettle those displaced by dam	75,000 displaced, of which 4,000 to SW.[c] 63 new villages constructed.	1,500 km² flooded	Lassailly-Jacob 1986, AVB 1971
Ghana	Volta River Authority Resettlement	Mid-1960s	Resettle those displaced by Volta Dam (Akosombo)	80,000 displaced from 700 villages consolidated into 52 new villages	8,500 km² flooded	Ninsin 1989:179
Senegal	Senegal River Delta, SAED[d]	1965–1990s	Irrigated rice cultivation, peasantization	10,000–15,000 households	10,500 ha developed by SAED (1975)	Dahou 2004
Mali	Office du Niger	1940	Settlement of irrigated lands	12,000 (1940); 42,000 (1975); 325,000 (1988)	1,000,000 ha. [88,000 irrigated] (2005)	Crowder 1968: 321; Colvin 1981: 272; van Beusekom 1997; Diawara 2011
Tanzania	Ujamaa villages	Mid-1970s	Villagization	50% of national pop. (~5–8 million persons) relocated to 8,000 new villages		Maro and Mlay 1982; Massaro 1998

(*continued*)

TABLE 2.2 (*continued*)

Country	Scheme Name	Timing	Purpose	No. of People	Land Area	Sources
E. DRC (Congo)	MIB,[e] N. Kivu schemes	1937–1955	Relieve overcrowding in Rwanda, peasantization	85,000 (1955)	350 km² (35,000 ha)	Mathieu et Mafikiri Tsongo 1999: 24
E. DRC (Congo)	UNHCR[f] resettlements	1959–1963	Installation of Rwandan Tutsi refugees	100,000		Mathieu et Mafikiri Tsongo 1999: 44
Rwanda	Official *paysannats*	1960s–1970s	Reclaim swamp and pasture, relieve land pressure	~450,000 (1976, est.)	72,000 ha (1970); ~160,000 ha (1976, eastern regions)	Gotanegre, Prioul, Sirven 1974: 94; Olson 1990: 23; Verwimp 2011
Burundi	*Villages de la Paix*	2003+	Resettle returnees, ex-fighters	16 villages (2010), ~30–300 families (est.) each	Throughout national territory	IRIN reports; IRIN 5 August 2010
Cameroon, SEB[g]	SEB Sodecoton ventures	1978–1992	Promote cotton cultivation, peasantization	~19,000 (SEB), 33 new villages		Seignobos 2006, Jua 1990: 22
Ethiopia, Afar Region	Awash Valley Authority	1962–1991	Pastoral sedentarization, cotton farming	13,000 ha (1985)		Harbeson 1978, Said 1997, Hundie 2006, Rettberg 2010
Zimbabwe resettlement areas	Model A-C Schemes	1980–1989	Settlement, peasantization	54,000 families (1990) (80% on Model A schemes)	3,000,000 ha, most as Model A schemes	Kriger 2007:75

[a] Includes settled and seasonal wage laborers.

[b] 100 ha = 1 km².

[c] The Société pour l'Aménagement de la Vallée du Bandama (AVB) master plan originally called for resetting 65,000 persons in the SW. Only 4,000 went under the auspices of this plan. Many followed later, under ad hoc arrangements (Lassailly-Jacob 1986: 334).

[d] Société d'Aménagement et d'Exploitation des Terres du Delta du Fleuve Sénégal (SAED).

[e] Mission pour l'Immigration des Banyarwanda (MIB).

[f] United Nations High Commission for Refugees (UNHCR).

[g] Project Sud-Est-Bénoué (SEB).

granted and guaranteed by the central state. This may make the ethnic insiders, or autochthones, "involuntary hosts of uninvited guests."[41] At the extreme, they may believe that they have been expropriated outright by the state and its clients. Settlers, for their part, are vulnerable if the state withdraws its protection, as Jewish settlers on Israel's West Bank understand only too well.

Statist land tenure regimes create structures and relationships of political control over farmers that differ greatly from those prevailing under the (neo)customary land tenure regimes.

The in-migrants are *beholden to the central state* for land access, rather than to a customary chief, local landlord, or other indigenous host. Writing of settlers on Mali's Office du Niger irrigation scheme, for example, Robert Pringle (2006, 49) describes the position of the settlers vis-à-vis the state: "Because the *colons* [peasant settlers] from what is now Burkina Faso had no traditional rights to the authority's [i.e., Office's] previously vacant lands, they – and their dependents – remained uniquely vulnerable to central control." This dependency finds legal expression in the fact that farmers on peasant settlement schemes have rarely received private title to their land.

Just as the customary land regimes have had their stakeholders and defenders among land allocators and users, so too have the statist land regimes. Farmers whose land rights have been granted directly by state authorities, without appeal to the customary land regimes, have a vested stake in the central government's authority to allocate land, and in the national principle that "citizens have a right to live and hold land anywhere."

POSTCOLONIAL POLITICAL ORDER AND AUTHORITY-BASED CONTROLS OVER LAND

> A common saying in Burkina is that elections are won in the countryside, but that power is lost in town. (Hagberg 2002, 227)

> Our relatives back in the rural areas are much more exposed [than we are] to the pernicious pressure of the administration and the zealots of the rotten PDCI regime. (*La Voie*, n. 390, 7 janvier 1993, 10)

The drive to establish and maintain rural social and political order has shaped the character of national politics, state structure, and economic policy in ways that scholars of contemporary African politics have often not recognized. Crawford Young captured the image of the African colonial state as *Bula Mutari*, "the rock crusher," but the same colonial administrations were haunted by fears of rural uprisings, revolts, food shortages, and general disorder. Colonial authorities were explicit in crafting land and labor policies to suppress unmonitored rural population mobility and to thwart the rise of landlessness and full proletarianization. The customary land tenure regimes were created largely in

---

[41] Shack and Skinner 1979, 5.

response to such fears – that is, to fix populations on the land within clearly demarcated territorial jurisdictions and to tie them to chiefs who were trusted agents of the colonial state. Expelling unemployed or "floating" Africans from the cities and forcing them back to their assigned Native Authorities was a routine tool of population management under colonial rule. Colonial authorities also used law, regulations, and chiefly authority to suppress the development of land markets. Commodification of land raised the dreaded specters of the "detribalized African," peasant indebtedness, rural class formation, and political radicalization.[42]

Neocustomary land tenure was a solution to the problem of governing the rural areas – but one that was never complete or truly stable. This is partly because colonial subjects sometimes resisted the new political and economic institutions (as when they rejected the administrative chiefs), and partly because the Europeans caused turmoil and aroused opposition as they extracted revenue, resources, and labor. They taxed, conscripted, imposed corvée, and used coercion to prop up the colonial chiefs. They promoted export crop production, imposed or forbade particular farming techniques, forced ordinary farmers and other colonial subjects to build roads and railways, and expropriated farmland, forests, water, and pasture. Colonial histories are punctuated with the record of antitax revolts, antichief revolts, and myriad other forms of rural resistance against colonial impositions and extractions, both overt and covert. Nigeria's Abeokuta antitax revolt of 1918 was an organized uprising of 30,000 persons (Falola 2009, 89–94). Rural insurgencies in Kenya and Cameroon in the 1950s were the stuff of colonialists' nightmares. These radicalizations and mobilizations were not targeted at the European colonial rulers only. In parts of southern Ghana, Guineé, Rwanda, Kenya, and Tanzania, antichief mobilizations fueled the nationalist movements that eventually drove the colonial powers from Africa.[43] In 1967, Herbert Weiss argued that rural radicalism had probably been a much more important force in African nationalism than previous scholarship – which had emphasized urbanization and rural-to-urban migration – had allowed. The second wave of independence, from 1975 through 1980, was also propelled by rural political mobilization, this time in the form of peasant guerrilla wars in Angola, Mozambique, Guinea-Bissau, and Rhodesia/Zimbabwe.

Independent Africa has also known its share of rural revolts and uprisings against local authorities and central regimes. Examples include peasant uprisings and revolts in western Nigeria in 1968–1969 and in the parts of the Niger Delta region today, in western Côte d' Ivoire in 1970, and in Burundi in 1972 and 1988. The Mulelist rebellion of the early 1960s in Congo/Zaire, the Casamance secessionist movement in Senegal starting in 1982, and the rural insurgency that brought Museveni to power in Uganda in 1986 are also cases in

---

[42] See, for example, Phillips 1989; Throup 1988, 73, inter alia.
[43] Weiss 1967, 58, 199-200, inter alia; see also Mamdani 1996a.

point. "Small rebellions" that fly under the radar of most outside analysts can provoke harsh political repressions and decades of smoldering hostility toward national rulers and ruling parties.

Leaders of the newly decolonized African states – including Kenyatta, Nyerere, Nkrumah, Senghor, Adhidjo, and Mugabe – felt the hot breath of the rural masses on their necks as they undertook to consolidate power. An immediate priority was to demobilize and build political frameworks to contain (*encadrer*) the peasantries that helped thrust them to nationalist victory. These efforts have not always been successful, as the record of failed states, civil wars, and coups demonstrates, but this underscores the point: to govern African countries and remain in power, national rulers have had to design ways to secure rural acquiescence, elicit compliance, and maintain social order in the rural areas.[44] They have built and shored up institutions, including rural property institutions, to stabilize relationships, enhance their credibility, and vest interests in postcolonial political order.

Early postcolonial state-building projects were largely about demobilizing and reasserting control over rural populations. Almost everywhere, restraining the arbitrariness of chiefly prerogative and eliminating taxes extracted by chiefs were initial steps in this process (often following similar initiatives undertaken by the colonial administrations in the 1950s, for the same reasons). Rural development programs were targeted at key ethno-regional constituencies. Even more ubiquitously, governments made aggressive efforts to promote smallholder access to land. Most African leaders relied on the expansion of livelihood opportunities for the rural masses through the extension of peasant farming onto "free land" – land that was unmortgaged, untaxed, and not bought and sold on the market. Through access to land, better access to markets, and the removal of many restrictions on the mobility of labor, rural majorities were incorporated into postcolonial political and economic systems. Hugon (2003) describes the Ivoirian model of development as based in large part "on migration of rural populations toward pioneer fronts." Olson (1990, 133) reported that the spread of smallholder production to previously uncultivated land accounted for most of the 65 percent increase in land surface under cultivation in sub-Saharan Africa during 1950–1976.

Members of growing populations could establish new households and take their chances as farmers, hoping for subsistence at least, and perhaps cash incomes from commercially oriented production. Established households could expand production and possibly cash inflows. Economic possibilities in the 1960s and 1970s were buoyed by the availability of land in many long-settled rural areas, the open land frontier in many places, and high world prices for the African export commodities produced by peasant farmers, including cotton, cocoa, coffee, and tea. Most African governments have implicitly or explicitly

---

[44] See Azam 2001 and Azam and Mesnard 2003 for contract-theoretic conceptualizations of this problem. See also Nye 1997.

acknowledged what one Tanzanian land officer in the summer of 2011 called "the right of citizens to have access to land to meet their basic needs," even if governments have often not honored this.[45] Many have deployed this principle cynically or opportunistically in expelling the unemployed from the cities in coercive "clean sweeps" or "back to the land" programs, following colonial precedents.

Angelique Haugerud (1993, 185–186) in an analysis of Kenya observed that the expansion of smallholder agriculture was "the soft development option" of the 1960s and early 1970s. This surely holds for most countries. The state's interest in preserving the viability of smallholder agriculture, including the extensive model of expansion (opening new lands) on which it is based, "accord[ed] with its interest in preserving social order." Writing in the early 1990s, Bruce, Migot-Adholla, and Atherton still assumed that unused arable land was abundant in most parts of sub-Saharan Africa (1994, 256).[46]

The geographic expansion of smallholder agriculture happened largely through nonmarket channels and relationships. That access to land was politically mediated, through authority-based relationships, made land a political as much as an economic asset. Those in strategic land-allocation positions have been either neocustomary authorities whose land powers are recognized and (in many places) sustained actively by national political leaders, or direct state agents, such as uniformed settlement scheme officers, land officers, or district officers.

Postcolonial governments reformed and modified chieftaincy institutions, but few abolished them. Most African rulers undertook to subordinate the (neo)customary authorities more firmly to the center. Chiefly hierarchies were usually decapitated at the subdistrict level of government, removing the most influential and visible of the chiefs and placing lower-ranking customary authorities under the watch of district officers and prefects. Some governments actually created chieftaincy as a local institution where this had not existed before (such as in farming districts of the Rift Valley of Kenya). Others formalized hierarchies of neotraditional authority through constitutions, law, or decree, as noted earlier.[47] Many independent governments incorporated neocustomary authorities into new (or enhanced) local government institutions such as rural, district, or town-level councils. This could restrain or dilute chiefs' prerogatives – especially in matters not related to farmland and pasture – but

---

[45] Author's interviews in Babati District, Manyara Region, Tanzania, July 2011.

[46] In Kenya as in Senegal, Burkina Faso, Nigeria, Cameroon, and Tanzania, the so-called new lands were often taken from pastoralists.

[47] For example, "Cameroon's chieftaincy decree (law) of 1977 provides for three classes of chiefs: first-class chiefs, who enjoy the allegiance of two second-class chiefs within an administrative division; second-class chiefs, who claim the allegiance of two third-class chiefs within an administrative subdivision; and third-class chiefs, whose jurisdiction is restricted to villages or sections of towns or cities. The law defines chiefs as auxiliaries of the state, which authorizes their appointment, ranking, and emoluments" (Eyoh 1998, subsection 1).

usually did not undermine them completely. Central governments and ruling parties extended their influence in the localities in ways that usually preserved chiefly or neotraditional authority in both form and substance. Land allocation and land-dispute adjudication often remained arenas of neotraditional practice, giving chiefs, *lamibe, marabouts,* and other so-called customary or neotraditional elites powerful levers of influence over the daily lives and political options of rural people subject to their authority.

Chieftaincy and other forms of neotraditional authority were thus institutionalized at the lowest levels of territorial administration throughout most (but not all, as I have argued) of rural Africa. Postcolonial rulers incorporated neocustomary authorities into hierarchical patron-client networks that reinforced the center's ability to incentivize and monitor their behavior. Chiefs and other neocustomary leaders often remained the gatekeepers, political brokers, and local strongmen they had been under colonial rule, mediating local citizens' access to land and local justice, and brokering access to opportunities (and exposure to risks) posed by government.[48]

In most countries, the exceptions to this rule were found in subnational jurisdictions – the enclaves, zones, territories, regions, districts, settlement schemes, or project areas – that were subject to statist forms of land control.[49] Here, state power and authority were not mediated through neocustomary elites; there was no "cloak of tradition" to legitimate postcolonial order. State agents such as district officers, prefects and subprefects, land officers, agricultural extension officers, cooperative officers, and party cell leaders administered directly. Modernization, development, nation-building, and the quest for order itself were the justificatory ideologies of power.

Social Contracts: Acquiescence, Elections

For all the "urban bias" in African economic policy, the fact remains that most governments have consistently relied on the rural hinterlands as bastions of political and electoral support. Rural votes have been critical to the legitimacy of one-party rulers and to the survival of competitive authoritarian regimes – they count, whether they express compliance, acquiescence, or active support. As in Latin America in the 1920s, the rural constituencies in sub-Saharan Africa have consistently played the role of offsetting the electoral weight of urban populations that tended to be more volatile, mobilized, liberal, and leftist. Edward Gibson (1997) and Mick Moore (1997) wrote that rural electoral coalitions delivered national majorities in Mexico, Argentina, and Sri Lanka in the late

---

[48] Bierschenk and Olivier de Sardan 2003, 164.

[49] Colonialism's customary authorities were usually abandoned by postcolonial regimes when local opposition to chiefs fueled autonomous forms of rural political mobilization (as in key regions of Kenya, Tanzania, and Guinée in the 1950s), making chiefs more of a liability than an asset in imposing local order.

1980s and 1990s. Large literatures on electoral politics in agrarian societies locate mechanisms that help produce these outcomes in the land-related prerogatives of local elites and local government officials: land prerogatives are political levers that are used to mobilize and discipline rural voters.[50] Such relationships are stark in much of rural Africa.

The electoral potential of customary authority was evident early on. Many chiefs mobilized electoral blocks for the nationalist parties. Apter noted in the 1950s that "traditional forms of social organization were a kind of 'natural' mechanism for mobilizing rural voters [and] traditional government was ready-made party machinery.... [Politicians] could use traditional methods to maintain solidarity."[51] Although the colonial chiefs were reviled in some places, in other places chiefs and other rural political authorities contributed to nationalist victories and were rewarded as allies of postcolonial rulers. This was the case in central Senegal, eastern and northern Côte d'Ivoire, northern Ghana, northern Cameroon, and Sierra Leone. In the Zerma and Hausa zones of Niger, where chiefs supported Rassemblement Démocratique African (RDA) militants, RDA leaders "were thus forced to accommodate those responsible for their political victory."[52]

Most postcolonial rulers have counted on neocustomary elites, whose power over farmers is underwritten by their land prerogatives, to deliver the votes of rural communities at election time.[53] Where direct state agents have given peasant farmers land or permission to occupy land, the terms of ongoing access to land are often similarly subject to the prerogative of political authorities. Authority-based property relationships serve as a powerful lever over the political behavior of those who depend on access to land for livelihoods and a place to live.

Return to electoral competition in many African countries after 1990 renewed and even heightened the salience of rural territories as critical power bases in national politics (Geschiere and Gugler 1998, 312–313). Incumbents faced with electoral challenge, often for the first time in a generation, turned to rural voters in efforts to stave off urban-based opposition and prodemocracy movements. Moi in Kenya, Rawlings in Ghana, Diouf and later Wade in Senegal, Bédié in Côte d'Ivoire, and Biya in Cameroon, to name a few, invested in

---

[50] See Huntington 1968; Leveau 1985 on Morocco; Kazemi and Waterbury 1991 and Waldner 1999 on the Middle East; Anderson 2006 on Central America; Moore 1997 on South Asia; and Vellema et al. 2011 on the Philippines. There is a vast literature on Mexico under the Partido Revolucionario Institucional (PRI). See, for example, Fox 1994, Magaloni 2006, and Eisenstadt 2011. In post-Communist Eastern Europe, ex-Communist leaders maintained ties with rural districts that continued to provide political support long after liberal social movements had defeated Communism in the cities (Tucker 2006).

[51] Apter, Ghana 1955, 1972, 2nd ed., 340–341.

[52] Lombard 1967, 260. See also Wallerstein 1967, 500–506.

[53] As Magloire Somé (2003, 238) says of postcolonial Burkina Faso, "The chiefs understand that the intellectuals go to them for electoral purposes and for nothing else."

mobilizing rural voters in their bids to counter urban reform movements and retain their hold on national office.

The strong rural biases in many of Africa's electoral systems reinforce this argument. Samuels and Snyder (2001) found Africa and Latin America to be the two world regions with the highest levels of electoral malapportionment. Of seventy-eight countries worldwide, five of the ten most malapportioned are in Africa, magnifying the electoral weight of rural constituencies at the expense of urban voters. In Kenya in the 1990s, for example, each rural vote outweighed votes from the most populous urban jurisdiction by a margin of more than 2 to 1.[54] This was convenient for the incumbent: As the Kenya Human Rights Commission reported in 1998, in the wake of violent and bitterly contested national elections, support for the government was minimal in the urban areas.[55]

A rural bias is also evident in significantly higher rural voter turnout rates in many elections, a tendency that runs directly counter to modernization theories that predict that city dwellers' higher incomes and education levels will drive up their political participation rates. In Mali, one of the poorest and least-developed countries in the world, for example, turnout rates in the 2002–2007 elections averaged almost twice those in the capital city, Bamako.[56] Writing about Côte d'Ivoire in the early 1990s, Fauré flagged the same discrepancy: "It is noticeable the participation rate in the urban areas is significantly lower than that in the rural areas." For him, this was at least in part a result of local pressure and monitoring of citizens' voting behavior: "Networks of political domination in Africa are frequently strongly hierarchical and personalized, often forming a monopoly at the level of the local community" (1993, 325). The lack of competitiveness of most rural jurisdictions that Fauré alludes to is a staple observation in most Africa election studies. From a party system perspective, rural constituencies often look like one-party states, where, as Schattschneider (1960, 83) says, "Elections are won not by competing with the opposition party, but by eliminating it."

The ability of those in positions of political authority to offer land access or land tenure security in exchange for political compliance has constituted a source of political leverage over rural communities and rural voters. This arrangement has served as the core of an implicit social contract between rulers and much of the rural poor: ordinary people have been subject to the political

---

[54] Maupeu (2003, 159) writes that "the KANU regime has governed the country by denying the cities.... This phenomenon has become even more accentuated in the era of multipartism." See also Barkan 1995.

[55] KHRC 1998, 18.

[56] Wing 2010, 97. In Benin, "the scope of action enjoyed by the political parties... is largely restricted to the major urban centers" (Bierschenk and Olivier de Sardan 2003, 164). Wantchekon (2003) reported that in democratic Benin from 1996 to 2001, 92% of the country's eighty-four electoral districts were not competitive.

hierarchies anchored in land control in exchange for access to land. Neocustomary land tenure regimes have also created strong land-related incentives for individuals and families to invest in rural kinship networks and membership in ethnic groups that claim property rights in state-recognized rural homelands. Statist land tenure regimes tie land users to the state agents who grant them access (or turn a blind eye to illegal use of state forests, watersheds, parks, etc.). Urban-rural straddling (one foot in the city, one foot in the countryside), now a structural feature of livelihoods in most African economies, guarantees that many city dwellers retain a strong stake in defending the land entitlements, property claims, and political relations that support families' access to land in the rural areas.

Political order rooted in these property-cum-political ties has been partial and contingent. Africa's political, economic, demographic, and environmental changes since the early 1990s have revealed many of these contingencies, destabilizing what often appeared to be self-sustaining – even natural – forms of rural political order. Analyzing these processes and figuring out what they reveal about state structure and political order in Africa is what motivates this study.

Conclusion

Land tenure regimes of both neocustomary and statist character structured the political incorporation of rural communities and peasants into expanding national orders, albeit in different ways and with different political consequences for state-building, ethnic politics, rural political mobilization, and electoral dynamics. Authority-based controls over land have provided postcolonial rulers with the means (material resources and selective incentives) and the institutional infrastructure (in the form of political hierarchies and governed spaces) for establishing politically mediated access to livelihoods for large majorities. These arrangements tie rural populations to national governments and into national political economies. Rulers have had an interest in sustaining the authority-based controls over land because these help them stay in power. The prevailing property regimes in land reduce the political autonomy of land users and rural communities, give rulers control over resources to be used as patronage (or punishment), and underpin bargains with local strongmen who are tied to national rulers. The "rural masses" are, for the most part, tied to neocustomary leaders, microterritories, and land entitlements. Nested within larger ethnic territories or "homelands," these ethno-territorial groupings bargain and compete against each other for benefits that national rulers can provide.

The land tenure institutions that are the focus of this analysis are core products of the colonial and postcolonial state-building projects. Rulers have not designed these institutions in a political vacuum, or with complete autonomy. Rulers themselves are under pressure to avoid widespread rural discontent, to sustain local deference to local authority, and to avoid famine. They seek to fragment political opposition and deflect redistributive pressures away from the national elite. When it came to designing and redesigning land institutions, rulers' autonomy was limited by the capacity of rural populations to withdraw their acquiescence and thus destabilize the political order that state-builders sought to create.

By the 1990s and 2000s, strain on established land tenure institutions – be they of the neocustomary or statist variety – had become endemic and widespread. It arises from demographic pressure, environmental stress, and rising land values, and it heightens the stakes of land-related politics. These pressures are at work across wide arrays of rural settings that differ along dimensions that have been of interest to political scientists, including level of economic development (extent of commercialization of agriculture), ethnic makeup, colonial legal tradition and institutional inheritance, and national regime type. This opens the analytic possibilities pursued in this study.

CHAPTER 3

Rising Competition for Land

Redistribution and Its Varied Political Effects

> Property arrangements vary a great deal in the way they tie peasants to the prevailing society and hence in their political effects.
>
> (B. Moore Jr., 1966, 476)

In most of sub-Saharan Africa for most of the twentieth century, land was not the scarce factor of production. *Labor* scarcity was considered the most important factor in shaping patterns of land use and agricultural practice, and it was a key factor in shaping land tenure regimes and the organization of rural society. As land has become scarcer relative to labor (or has gained in commercial value for other reasons), sociopolitical arrangements institutionalized in the statist and neocustomary land regimes have come under great strain. Actors' interests and incentives, and balances of power among actors, are shifting. These changes find social and political expression in struggles over social obligations and entitlements. They also give rise to challenges to existing forms of authority over land.

Part I of this chapter discusses the phenomenon of rising pressure on the land. Part II traces social science debates about the expected effects of growing land scarcity for smallholders, identifying puzzles that become tractable, I argue, when land conflict is viewed as *redistributive* conflict. Part III proposes a model of African land tenure regimes and how they vary. Part IV deduces hypotheses that have to do with how land tenure institutions structure the social and political pressures arising from redistributive conflict over land.

RISING COMPETITION FOR LAND

Many regions of sub-Saharan Africa that can sustain rain-fed agriculture are now densely settled. The land frontier has closed or is closing. Between 1950 and 2000, the continent's rural population nearly tripled, increasing from 156 million to 430 million.[1] Rural population growth continent-wide, and in most African countries, is projected to continue to be substantial through 2025 and beyond, even with high rates of urbanization.[2] In Kenya and Tanzania, rural populations are expected to increase by 10 million persons between 2010 and 2025. In Uganda and DRC, rural populations are expected to increase by 20 million over the same period.

As of 2008, rural areas continued to support more than 60 percent of the national population in two-thirds of all sub-Saharan African countries. This level of ruralization is roughly comparable to that of most of western Europe circa 1850, and to most of Latin America circa 1900. Between 1970 and 2000, average levels of rural population density increased by nearly 50 percent in sub-Saharan Africa. Twenty African countries experienced increases of over half, and in eight countries, rural population density more than doubled. The reality of this is seen in the southern Malawi districts that Pauline Peters studied in the 1990s: "There is no longer unused land on which new villages can establish themselves.... [There are] much larger numbers of people seeking uncultivated land than there is land available" (2002, 173, 175). In some pockets of East Africa, rural landlessness is pervasive.[3]

Table 3.1 provides a country-level overview, showing increases in rural population density during the 1970–2005 period for all but eight of the forty-three countries for which we have World Bank data. The same data for 2012 show continuing increase in the absolute size of the rural population in every single country of continental sub-Saharan Africa except Botswana.[4]

Until the early 1980s, development theorists and many other observers believed that urbanization would solve the land problem. Urban transition models that were derived from the economic history of the West predicted that as agricultural productivity rose and as industrial employment expanded, young people would leave the countryside to make their livelihoods in the cities. Incomes would rise, and through investment and innovation, capital would substitute for labor in agricultural production. Yet contrary to these

---

[1] Tabutin and Schoumacker 2004, 505.

[2] Heller 2010, citing The United Nations Development Project.

[3] Jayne, Mather, and Mghenyi 2010. There are no simple relationships among rural population density, agricultural productivity, and demand for land: production techniques, investment, and off-farm livelihoods shape productivity of land and labor, and/or demand for land. Although Africa Development Indicators (ADI) show a real increase in per capita value added in agriculture for most countries during 1970–2000, most African agriculture is rain fed and rates of fertilizer use are low. The only non-island nations of sub-Saharan Africa in which irrigated cropland was more than 10% of the total in the mid-2000s are Sudan (11.4%) and Swaziland (26%) (ADI and WDI 2008). Olson (1990, 133) stresses the large extent to which increase in production has come from extension of the amount of land under cultivation, as does the World Bank (2010, 7, figure 1.1).

[4] Cape Verde saw a decrease. In 2012, both South Africa and Zimbabwe show a net increase over 2008 (WDI 2012). The 2010 data for rural population as a percentage of the total show a decrease of about 1% or less for all countries in Table 3.1.

TABLE 3.1. *Rural Population and Population Density over Time*

Country	Rural Pop. 2008 (% of total)	Rural Pop. Density (RPD) 1970	RPD* 2005	RPD % Change (1970–2005)
Congo, Dem. Rep.	66.0	222.9	595.3	167.0
Zambia	64.6	60.1	141.8	136.0
Ethiopia	83.0	204.8	480.9	134.8
Niger	83.5	34.4	76.7	123.2
Senegal	57.6	131.3	269.6	105.3
Uganda	87.0	233.1	469.1	101.3
Burundi	89.6	364.8	732.5	100.8
Swaziland	75.1	253.9	482.3	89.9
Congo, Rep.	38.7	154.9	290.3	87.4
Kenya	78.4	288.9	536.3	85.6
Guinea-Bissau	70.2	202.3	374.8	85.2
Lesotho	74.5	256.5	460.4	79.5
Tanzania	74.5	178.9	317.0	77.2
Central African Republic	61.4	76.9	134.4	74.9
Namibia	63.2	92.3	160.8	74.3
Togo	58.0	93.5	150.6	61.0
Chad	73.3	112.4	180.5	60.6
Nigeria	51.6	151.6	237.7	56.8
Madagascar	70.5	289.0	451.9	56.4
Mauritius	57.5	479.1	717.4	49.7
Zimbabwe	62.7	184.1	261.2	41.9
South Africa	39.3	93.2	129.4	38.8
Cameroon	43.2	100.9	136.5	35.2
Liberia	39.9	280.3	377.5	34.7
Equatorial Guinea	60.6	169.8	227.5	34.0
Somalia	63.5	297.3	393.4	32.3
Botswana	40.4	161.6	207.9	28.7
Cote d'Ivoire	51.2	224.3	282.5	26.0
Angola	43.3	178.3	224.4	25.8
Malawi	81.2	344.1	420.7	22.3
Sierra Leone	62.2	516.5	588.4	13.9
Sudan	56.6	103.8	112.4	8.3
Guinea	65.6	471.8	502.7	6.5
Burkina Faso	80.4	231.9	235.2	1.4
Mauritania	59.0	353.4	353.2	−.1
Mozambique	63.2	319.6	305.7	−4.4
Benin	58.8	196.3	185.2	−5.6
Rwanda	81.7	700.2	634.8	−9.3
Ghana	50.0	378.4	281.1	−25.7
Mali	67.8	242.7	168.1	−30.7
Gambia, The	43.6	307.7	213.0	−30.8
Gabon	15.0	200.0	65.1	−67.4
Eritrea	79.3	–	572.8	–
mean	62.5	231.1	328.8	47.2
std. deviation	15.8	138.7	178.2	50.8
N				43

*RPD = Rural population per sq. km of arable land (WDI 2008).
Source: WDI, 2008, 2010.

expectations, urban growth in Africa has not relieved pressure on the land. Tabutin and Schoumaker (2004, 505, 508) argued that in the 1990s, "most urban growth appear[ed] to stem from natural growth rates" rather than from massive rural-to-urban migration that might have been expected to relieve land pressure in the rural areas.[5] Demand for access to farmland and pasture continues to grow, and growing numbers of people seek access to land for subsistence and a place to reside.

The collapse of Africa's developmentalist project and the adoption of Structural Adjustment Programs in the 1980s and 1990s slowed or stemmed rural exodus to the cities, and thus contributed to increasing land pressure in the countryside. In some countries, the demographic flow was *reversed*: unemployed adults returned to their rural home areas, pressuring families and local leaders for access to arable land.[6] Some governments resorted to ruralization or "rustication" as official policy in return-to-the-land campaigns, forcibly expelling youth and the unemployed from the cities to the rural areas and using land access in the rural areas as a social safety net of last resort. Some analysts wondered whether Côte d'Ivoire and Zambia were undergoing a process of deurbanization. Others wrote of the re-ruralization or re-peasantization of social groups who had participated in the urbanization drives of earlier decades.[7]

Although there have been some gains in agricultural productivity since the 1970s, World Bank data show that increases in production are largely attributable to extension of the amount of land under cultivation.[8] This has not kept up with rural population increase, however. The result is "a steady decline in the ratio of arable land to agricultural population. In Kenya, Ethiopia, and Zambia, for example, this ratio is about half as large as it was in the 1960s."[9] Today, average landholding size per household varies widely by region, locale,

---

[5] They cite some analysts who believe that up to three-quarters of urban population growth in the 1990s was attributable to natural increase of the urban population itself. Rates of rural-to-urban migration increased in most countries after the early 2000s.

[6] See Tabutin and Schoumaker 2004, 505, 508.

[7] Tabutin and Schoumaker 2004, 508; Moyo and Yeros 2005, 27. "Rustication" campaigns have a long history in modern sub-Saharan Africa. Under the Nyerere government in Tanzania, people were repatriated from the city to rural Ujamaa villages in the 1970s (Maro and Mlay 1982, 180). The Houphouet regime in Côte d'Ivoire carried out a *"retour à la terre"* campaign in the 1990s (Babo 2010). Bierschenk and Olivier de Sardan (2003, 150, 155) write of a spontaneous "urban exodus" as unemployed graduates and school dropouts returned to their native villages in Benin, and Ferguson (1999) writes of Zambia's copper-belt workers who lost their jobs and "returned home" to villages that some had never lived in.

[8] From about 1960 to 2000, tripling of the population of households engaging in agriculture in sub-Saharan Africa was accompanied by an approximately 50% increase in the amount of arable land under cultivation (Jayne, Mather, and Mghenyi 2010, 1385, citing FAO data on households for 1960–2000.) Olson (1990, 133) stresses the large extent to which increases in production have come from extension of the amount of land under cultivation, as does the World Bank (2010, 7, fig. 1.1, on cultivated land area between 1961 and 2007).

[9] Jayne, Mather, and Mghenyi 2010, 1385.

and household. It generally ranges from about 1–10 hectares (2.4–24 acres), but in many, many places there is evidence of growing rural inequality, shrinking farm size, shortening fallow periods, and declining use of purchased inputs due to poverty.

Against this backdrop, since the 1990s, rural sociologists, anthropologists, economists, and land rights experts have observed "evidence of increasing land pressure and increasing conflict" (Berry 2002, 638). Although land-related conflict per se is not a novel phenomenon, what *is* new is its growing pervasiveness, its intensification, and the acceleration or compounding of the forces that produce it. The International Institute of Environment and Development (IIED) wrote that "in sub-Saharan Africa, competition over land has increased in frequency and severity in the last decades. The reasons for this are multiple, and essentially linked to the increased scarcity of land caused by demographic pressures and to the higher land values determined by agricultural intensification and commercialization."[10] Sara Berry offered this overview of the process:

In most countries, the causes of increasing competition and contestation over land have been similar. Rapid population growth, environmental degradation, and slow rates of economic development that leave many people dependent on small-scale farming, livestock raising and foraging have transformed Africa from a continent of land abundance in the first half of the twentieth century to one of increasing land scarcity by its end. (Berry 2002, 639)[11]

Land rights specialist Liz Alden Wily echoed this assessment in 2001, reporting that "tenure problems are reaching a crisis point more or less all over Africa for often similar historical reasons."[12]

Modernization theories and the prevailing institutionalist theories of land-rights transformation did not predict Africa's rising tide of land-related conflict, and so far, they have not provided much leverage when it comes to understanding the patterns and politics of contemporary struggles over land in Africa. Development economics and the New Institutional Economics (NIE) predicted that rising demographic pressure will promote the gradual commercialization of land and the commodification of property in peasant economies. Although this literature is well developed in African studies, much of the Africa evidence does not conform to the theoretical expectations. Many analysts have argued that gaps between theory and evidence point to the fact that the politics of these processes are very poorly understood. Practitioners find themselves in the

---

[10] Cotula, Toulmin, and Hesse 2004, 14. See also Yamano and Deininger 2005 and Deininger and Castagini 2006.

[11] Berry (2002, 639) stresses that "effective demand for land varies widely, of course, from one locality to another.... In many rural areas, low levels of productivity and widespread poverty have kept land values low even in the face of scarcity."

[12] Wily and Hammond 2001, part 6.

same boat. In a 2004 report on land rights in Africa, the IIED complained that we have little understanding of the political dynamics of land conflict.[13]

PROPERTY RIGHTS TRANSFORMATION: FROM SMOOTH CONTRACTING TO REDISTRIBUTIVE CONFLICT

> Even if only half the children stay here, there is not enough land. (A farmer in Kiru Valley, Tanzania, 19 July 2011)

Theoretical debates on the politics of changing property rights and empirical research from Africa both suggest ways of conceptualizing the problem at hand. Existing work also helps frame the need for new theory. From the 1970s through the early 1990s, development economists working in Africa endorsed the view that the existing (neo)customary[14] regimes would evolve over time, gradually becoming more like Western models of private property. Early New Institutional Economics property-rights theory, following the work of Douglass North, suggested how this can work. With rising populations and the commercialization of agriculture, landholders are expected to intensify production, invest more, and reap higher returns. As this happens, they are expected to demand better specified, more exclusive, and more transactable land rights. Land rights in Africa are expected to gradually shed their multiple and overlapping character, and to shake off the social and political encumbrances that are characteristic of nonmarket property regimes. Through this process, land rights become more fully commodified and more *exclusive* (through annulment of the multiple and overlapping claims of many actors).

In a political world wherein everyone benefits from the productivity gains made possible by better-specified property rights, the demand for private property rights is expected to evolve spontaneously or endogenously as land users respond to changes in relative prices (and to technological advance). The neutral or rational state is expected to supply them.[15]

Ester Boserup (1965, 1981) is given credit for identifying such a scenario in West Africa. She and Polly Hill (1963) tracked this process among the prosperous cocoa farmers of southern Ghana, where agricultural intensification and the growing specificity and exclusivity of land rights seemed to go hand in hand.

---

[13] Cotula 2004, 17.

[14] As stressed in Chapter 2, "customary" and "custom" are legal and administrative terms that convey the impression – which is often partially or largely misleading – of strong continuity with precolonial practice.

[15] North and Thomas 1973 and North 1981. Demsetz (1967) predicted that this should happen only when the benefits outweigh the costs of demarcating and enforcing rights. See also Barzel 1997. Libecap (1996) traced the growing exclusivity of land rights in the development of mineral-rights law in the western United States. Alston, Libecap, and Mueller (1999) studied land registration and titling in the Amazon Basin. Rulers are supposed to have an interest in supplying property rights (to increase production that can be taxed) but do not always do so, as explored by Levi (1988), Sonin (2003), and Onoma (2010).

Boserup noted that this process would not be frictionless, and that government would be called on to handle the vast amount of litigation that land-rights change would produce.[16] There are many other examples of transition *toward* agricultural intensification and exclusive land rights in smallholder farming areas of sub-Saharan Africa, even if they rarely culminate in outright privatization. Platteau (1996, 524) writes that in many places, "customary tenure has evolved toward individual title or sales, or land under the control of nuclear families." Jean Ensminger observed that evidence from African cases

provides strong support for the proposition that *social norms and institutions respond in ways economists would predict* to exogenous changes in relative prices [due to population pressure, rising returns to commercial agriculture, and technological advance].... Under these conditions, property rights moved most quickly in the direction of exclusivity of some rights if not outright privatization. In many if not all cases, this was accompanied by *complementary changes in social norms and social organization*, which restricted the size and obligations of the kinship group. (1997, 168, 170)

And yet, "more classic commons or lineage land rights still prevail in most areas" (Ensminger 1997, 168, 170).

NIE's early vision of land-rights modernization as a smooth contracting process was reflected in the policy-oriented literature on Africa in the 1980s. In an early 1980s study of land-rights change in six countries, Bruce and Migot-Adholla (1994) concluded that as African farmers intensify production, land rights tend to move in the direction of greater exclusivity, commodification, and transactability. Bruce and Migot-Adholla argued at the time that this process was best left to evolve on its own. They saw state intervention to impose mandatory registration and titling as desirable only as a last resort in situations where land relations were highly conflictual.[17] Until very recently, this has been the prevailing wisdom. Most land experts believed that land-related conflict was rare and likely to result from idiosyncratic factors.

Just as these conclusions became conventional wisdom in much of the policy world, the theory-disturbing presence of rising land conflict and other anomalies began to fill the empirical record. Ensminger framed the "intriguing puzzle" of why more exclusive rights did not always develop under the hypothesized demographic and economic conditions, and why such processes sometimes seemed to be blocked or reversed, with "increasing numbers of societies backing away from... freehold land tenure" (1997, 165). This was the case even when government policy appeared to support movement in that direction. She noted the reversal of land-titling processes in Kenya.[18] Meanwhile, most

---

[16] Boserup as cited in Platteau 1996, 39. See Holden, Otsuka, and Place 2009.

[17] Bruce and Migot-Adholla (1994, 262) argue that government intervention in land-rights systems should be limited to the essentially post hoc role of *confirming* or facilitating processes already under way or nearly completed. See also Olson (1990) on the intensification arguments.

[18] On Kenya, see also Haugerud (1993), Shipton (2009, 156–157 inter alia), Alden-Wily (2003) and Onoma (2010). Berry (1988, 60) and Shipton (2009, 155) point out that in some places, land

African governments (colonial and postcolonial) have not granted and enforced private property rights in land, even where grassroots processes of land-rights commodification are under way.[19] There are many cases in which government has reversed or undercut movement toward more individualized and transferable land rights, either declining to legalize land sales, not enforcing land titles once they have been granted, or deferring to grassroots-level resistance to the alienation of land to outsiders.[20]

Equally unexpected was the upsurge in land-related conflict, mostly nonviolent and confined to the grassroots levels, but sometimes exploding into wider social and political arenas. Writing of West Africa, Paul Mathieu wrote in 1997 that "land conflicts are becoming more numerous and more violent."[21] Pauline Peters (2002, 173) critiqued earlier work that had focused on the fluidity and negotiability of land rights in African contexts, arguing that it had downplayed the zero-sum nature of many struggles over land access. Writing of southern Malawi, she observed that "conflicts over land are now more widespread and deeper (more wounding)." Platteau argued that in many places, we see land conflict that involves violence (1995, 524), but violence that does not lead to institutional change in the form of a narrower specification of land rights – it is violence without clear-cut resolution. Paul Mathieu (1997, 42) made the same observation, writing that violence erupts "without preventing more or continuing land conflict."

The empirical record of mounting conflict pointed to a canonical weakness in the contracting models of property-rights change that had informed much of the thinking about Africa: the contracting models did not anticipate or explain *conflict* over property-rights change. Neoclassical economics, at its core, assumes a neutral state (not a partisan one) and a social world without coercion, social hierarchy, and winners and losers.[22] The original NIE models did not factor in unevenness in the distribution of costs and benefits of property rights transformation and hence the *redistributive* character of property rights change. It is no accident that much of the original empirical work on the spontaneous or endogenous emergence of private property rights focused on situations in which organized society is absent (such as the "state of nature" or

---

rights are being diffused across larger collectivities or social groups, rather than concentrated in narrower groups.

[19] Phillips (1989), Shenton (1986), Firmin-Sellers (1996), Onoma (2010), and others homed in on this theoretical anomaly.

[20] Political scientists have tended to interpret these theoretical anomalies as evidence of the weakness of the state (Herbst 2000), coordination problems among rulers, or the self-interest of predatory rulers (Firmin-Sellers 1996 and Onoma 2010, following Levi 1988).

[21] Mathieu 1997, 42. However, see Hussein, Sumberg, and Seddon (1999), who wonder whether there is an actual increase in conflict (as opposed to just an increase in *observed* conflict).

[22] Critics of the Northian model, from Field (1981) to Brenner (1982), to Knight (1992), to Alston and Libecap (1999), have made this argument.

"the frontier") or on conquered territories where rights losers have been killed or driven away.[23]

Moves toward competitive models of property rights transformation have come both from within NIE and from its critics.[24] Ron Harris (2003, para. 24) summarized these theoretical innovations:

> New institutional economic historians began to realize that the law was not supplied passively by the state upon demand. [The second-generation models proposed that] economic change creates the initial incentive for a group to alter an institution, such as the property rights regime; however, such a legal change will affect other groups, and these might lobby, or litigate, in opposition to it. Such a model tries to account for the interaction, beginning with the economic change, through its effect on the value of the legal institution, say property rights, and its distributive effects on interest groups' gains and losses, through the legal and political process in the state that involves transaction costs – at times change preventing – to the change in property rights and back to its effect on economic performance.

Comparative political economy has been quick to embrace the challenge of theorizing institutional change, including change in property rights, as a redistributive process.[25] When the costs and benefits of institutional change are spread unevenly, the specter of change gives rise to political struggle between potential winners and losers. Dynamics of these processes not only shape outcomes but also illuminate the character, resources, and capacities of the collectivities and actors with interests at stake. Abandoning the assumption of state neutrality makes it possible to examine the nature and effects of partisanship (and narrow self-interest) on the part of those who grant and enforce property rights.

This study joins others in applying these theoretical innovations to the study of property rights and how they change in Africa. Firmin-Sellers (1996) and Onoma (2010) examine *rulers' incentives and capacity* to supply more secure and exclusive property rights in land. These authors try to explain why rulers have not supplied the multitudes of small-scale African farmers with secure, welfare-enhancing property rights. Their explanations focus on individual self-interest, fraudsters and spoilers among the elite, and/or elites' failure to agree on how to distribute the gains that would result from more exclusive and efficient rights. Herbst (2000) discerns a more strategic calculation in rulers' actions: the high up-front costs of broadcasting power across rural territory (compared

---

[23] This is how Locke saw North America on the arrival of the English, and how Libecap (1996) and Anderson and Hill (2004) envision the Wild West when miners and settlers arrived in the 1800s. Barzel (1997) imagines the establishment of North Sea mining rights in the same way.

[24] Harris (2003, para. 24) adds that "models of institutional change that account for all or most of the above factors were developed and empirically examined by several new institutional economic historians, including North, Barzel, and Libecap after the late 1980s."

[25] See Knight 1992; Weiner 1997; Acemoglu, Johnson, and Robinson 2005; and Haber, Razo, and Mauer 2003.

to the uncertain long-term benefits of doing so) shape rulers' choices when it comes to rural property relations, incentivizing them to accept the status quo.[26]

The arguments here draw on these intuitions but depart from earlier NIE-inspired work on land-rights change in Africa in two critical ways. First, I see existing land regimes as sustained when rulers have a collective political interest in maintaining the political controls – both indirect and direct – that states have imposed over lands used by smallholders and peasants.[27] This is the connection between "property and political order" that is invoked in the book's title and developed in Chapter 2. It opens the door to a more systemic analysis of land rights and land politics. The second departure has to do with interests within rural society itself. Rather than assuming a uniform interest among ordinary landholders in narrower and more exclusive rights, I center the analysis on competition and conflict among ordinary land users.[28] Heterogeneity among productive land users, and politics associated with socially uneven distribution of the costs and benefits of property-rights transformation, are at the forefront of this analysis.

So far, the redistributive dynamics of land conflict in Africa have resisted systematic comparative analysis. I believe this is largely because scholars of Africa have lacked the requisite analytic tools. Old and largely misleading ideas about basic equality in rural landholding in Africa and about the "free peasantry" have been impediments to theorization, as has the assumption that all prevailing land regimes create "insecure" rights (thus implying that any move toward greater security would benefit everyone). Africa's bad fit with models of rural class structure that are familiar from the study of Europe and the New World has also been an impediment to theorization. Existing rural property institutions in Africa have themselves seemed resistant to much comparative analysis: the land tenure systems have been seen as opaque and highly particular ("bewilderingly complex"), and although changes are under way, the direction of processes of change has remained largely indeterminate.[29]

---

[26] This argument about the costs and benefits of registration and titling resonates with Demsetz (1967). My understanding of "neocustomary LTRs" is different from Herbst's. He describes neocustomary land tenure regimes self-organized by rural peoples. Here, focusing on neocustomary tenure in *farming* regions (not the "vast ungoverned spaces" that fit best with a simple application of Herbst's model), I conceptualize these land regimes as institutions built and upheld by states and as part of state structure. See Chapter 2.

[27] For more general renderings, see Sonin 2003, Frye 2004. This book offers an analytic description of land tenure regimes but does not propose a full theory of institutions as equilibriums, or of institutional statis and change. Rather, it develops and tests a theory of institutional *effects*.

[28] This follows Knight (1992), 113 inter alia; Acemoglu, Johnson, and Robinson (2005); and others who focus on the uneven distribution of the costs and benefits of institutional change.

[29] Another factor could be the disciplinary conventions and theoretical commitments of the legal anthropologists, development economists, and land-rights scholars – social scientists who are most knowledgeable about African land rights systems. Most have not been drawn to the kind of structuralist generalization that can serve as a point of departure for such an endeavor.

This is the frontier we venture to cross in this study. Land-related competition and conflict is modeled (informally) as a type of redistributive conflict. Where land rights are multiple or overlapping, as in most of rural Africa, moves toward *more exclusive property rights* make terms of land access more restrictive. Growing exclusivity of rights entails a *loss, or curtailing*, of rights of some of the individuals (or categories of individuals) who held shares under the more inclusive rules of access that lie at the heart of the neocustomary land systems.[30] These are land rights losers. Winners are those who gain more exclusive (more individualized) control over land.

How does loss or curtailing of land rights happen? It can happen through the hardening of terms of land access for "second-class citizens" (women, juniors, casted persons, outsiders, or strangers), nonrecognition of the land claims of members of such groups, attempts to narrow the circle of kinship obligations, attempts to shrink the boundaries of common-pool resources or of the group with entitled access, commodification of land-rights transfers and labor exchanges within lineages and families, enclosures, and sales or rentals of land rights to outsiders, whether or not such transactions are formally recognized by the state.[31] A loss of rights or entitlement also occurs when adult children discover that there is no family land for them to farm on their own account, no "unused" community land for them to clear, and no land to inherit. These are processes of restriction of access, narrowing of entitlement, and exclusion.

As a redistributive process, the specter of change in the direction of more exclusive and transactable rights creates political friction. Perceptions of growing land scarcity, and movement toward more exclusive land rights, can be expected to generate conflicts between potential winners and potential losers. In organized society (as opposed to the state of nature), these changes necessarily implicate those wielding political authority: authoritative actors are often simultaneously parties to such conflicts, conflict adjudicators, and enforcers of redistributive outcomes. These political dynamics are the focus of this study. Land-related competition and conflict among smallholders is understood as shaped by "bargaining" among actors who are embedded in institutional arenas that structure hierarchy, distribute power unevenly, and create or foreclose avenues for political action.

This reasoning raises the following questions about situations of land competition and conflict: Who are the (potential) winners and losers in conflicts over land rights, especially when some users seek more exclusive rights over land? What forms of coercive authority are they subject to, and to what forms

---

[30] As Chanock (1998, 235) puts it, with the breakdown of lineages and families as corporate landholding groups in colonial Zambia and Malawi, *conflict and injury* were experienced as the circle within which obligations were acknowledged was narrowed.

[31] Chimhowu and Woodhouse (2006, 346, 352) define vernacular land markets as involving the commoditized transfer of land within the framework of customary tenure.

of authority can they appeal? What partisan rationalities shape the strategies of property-rights adjudicators and enforcers, and whom do these biases favor? How does the bargaining power of potential losers vary across settings, and what are their options? How do patterns of conflict and outcome vary across space and time? Developing answers to these questions reveals much about not only land-related conflict, but also the political arenas in which land politics plays out.

HOW LAND TENURE REGIMES STRUCTURE LOCAL POLITICAL ARENAS: A MODEL[32]

> Actual tenurial situations [are] in a sense the social structure of rural communities. (Goody 1980, 152)

The political and social tensions aroused by moves toward more exclusive land rights are refracted through different types of local institutional configurations, producing variations in the forms of conflict by which land rights are won, renegotiated, defended, eroded, or lost. In agrarian localities, these institutional configurations are land tenure regimes.

Our dependent variable is the form or political expression of land-related conflict in a particular locality or rural jurisdiction (in a given time period). Patterned conflict is conceptualized as emerging between parties that share different positions in the structured political order that governs land access and allocation. As land grows scarce or increases in commercial value, some actors will seek more exclusive land rights.[33] That is, they will seek to curtail the access rights of some claimants, or to exclude some claimants completely. Potential losers can be expected to try to avoid or minimize their losses. These processes are modeled as *redistributive conflicts* that involve (potential) winners and losers. It is not necessary to assume teleology or unidirectionality in the outcomes of these process.[34] More exclusive land rights are a possible outcome of these conflicts, but stalemate, reversal, and more or less even distribution of the costs of change are also possible outcomes.[35]

---

[32] "Model" refers to a causal theory modeled informally in simple, visual form as a diagram, as in Table 3.2.

[33] Or, the goal can be a change in interpretation of existing rules. I do not assume that land conflict per se is new, that it does or will affect all regions or locales, or that it only increases over time.

[34] In what is now Kenya's Central Province, for example, the level or intensity of competition for land has fluctuated over time, with the closing of a land frontier (circa 1910, with European land expropriation), opening of the land frontier (1920–1940s, with land available to "squatters" on settler farms in the Rift), closing (1950s, with technological change that reduced settlers' demand for African labor, leading to expulsion of some African farmers from the European-owned farms), and opening (with the 1960s and 1970s settlement schemes).

[35] Berry (1988) and Amanor (1994) have argued that population pressure in some parts of southern Ghana has led to the diffusion of land rights (more and more claimants for each holding),

Land-related conflicts are structured by local institutional configurations. Conflicts take place within territorial jurisdictions and implicate land-allocation authorities as allocators, adjudicators, and/or enforcers of rights.[36] Within jurisdictions, actors' strategic options are shaped by prevailing citizenship regimes, which define actors' land rights, political rights, and the distribution of power among actors. This formulation allows us to differentiate land-related conflicts in terms of the locus, character, and jurisdictional scale of the land-allocation authority that is implicated in the conflict; the social identity of the group most likely to suffer the loss or curtailing of land rights; and the political options of the (potential) losers.

Each dimension of the land tenure regime is envisioned as a "parameter" or structuring feature of the local political arena. Building on Chapter 2, we model land regimes as constituted by rules about property, authority, jurisdiction, and citizenship, and *as differentiated along these dimensions*. Land regimes – understood as practiced institutions (following Ostrom 2005) – define a locus of political authority over land rights at the local level, a territorial arena, social groups with different land rights and interests, and the distribution of political and economic powers and rights among them. These arrangements frame the political arena in which land rights are contested.[37]

The sections that follow describe each structural dimension in turn and then generate hypotheses about the land-related conflicts that emerge in political arenas so constituted.

Locus of Authority over Land

Intrinsic to any property regime is specification of a locus of authority over rights enforcement and rights adjudication.[38] Where authority lies is a matter of fundamental importance in defining the shape of the local political arena and the dynamics of land politics. Table 3.2 draws a distinction between local and central authority over land.

---

rather than concentration and growing exclusivity of rights. This may be a sign of failed attempts by some to make land rights more exclusive.

[36] This study does not explicitly consider conflicts between territorial jurisdictions.

[37] Berry (1988, 1993), Ribot and Peluso (2003), and others have argued for more processual and less structural conceptualization of African land regimes. Here we are sacrificing the process-based view for a theoretical model that makes it possible to compare structural attributes of local settings as they vary across space. I argue along with Tarrow (1994) that structuralist models are pregnant with implications for the contingent, recursive, and processual aspects of politics, including issue framing, the shaping of political identities, and repertoires or routines of political discourse, action, and leadership. See also Tarrow and Tilly 2007.

[38] When subjects look to a ruler to allocate, enforce, or adjudicate property claims, the position of the authority wielder is confirmed and reinforced (Ribot and Peluso 2003; see also Joireman 2011, Sikor and Lund 2009). If control over an asset is not enforced by a third party wielding legitimate coercive power, then it is not held as property; it is merely a possession (Hafer 2003).

Local authority over land: The neocustomary land regimes

The customary land regimes, as defined and described in Chapter 2, are artifacts of colonial and postcolonial rule. Most postcolonial African governments
recognize customary land regimes in national constitutions, statutory law, executive or administrative decree, and/or administrative practice. In one way or
another, most contemporary African governments endorse – in law or administrative practice (or both) – the land-allocation and adjudication powers of
"customary authorities" (chiefs, traditional authorities, elders) within most
rural jurisdictions. In prevailing justificatory ideologies, the legitimacy of their
power derives from local (prestate or nonstate) sources. Authority derived from
religion, ancestral ways, or age-old tradition is not expected or required to be
fully delimited or fully specified in national statutory or constitutional rules.
Paradoxically, it is defined in law and practice as at least partially *informal*.
This is the basis of Mamdani's (1996a) criticism of neocustomary rule as inherently arbitrary. The critique applies to neocustomary authority even when it is
nested within a democratic republic.

Colonial indirect rule embraced the administrative principle and justificatory
belief that state-recognized customary authorities are authentic representatives
of "ethnic communities" indigenous to the chief's territorial jurisdiction. Postcolonial governments have not broken completely with this idea – it legitimates
their continuing recognition of (embrace of) customary authority and justifies
the idea that state-recognized customary authorities "represent" the ethnic
constituencies living in ethnic homelands.

I propose to conceptualize authority structure within this category of land
tenure regimes (LTRs) as differentiated along a continuum that runs from
decentralized (family) to centralized (e.g., chieftaincy) authority structures.
Strongly centralized and thus hierarchical chieftaincy institutions of significant geographical scope have been shored up in some parts of modern Africa.
Prime examples are the Buganda, Asante, and Mossi chieftaincies/kingdoms in
Uganda, Ghana, and Burkina Faso respectively, and the *lamidats* of northern
Cameroon. In these places, the local political arena is structured with reference
to a hierarchy of chiefs and subchiefs, each with a territorial jurisdiction and
all answerable, in principle, to a central, paramount authority. The customary
land tenure regimes give these chiefs a prime role in allocating unused land in
their jurisdictions. An example is the Asante (Ashanti) case in the 1940s, when
chiefs played a prominent role in allocating unoccupied land to in-migrants.

In most of rural Africa, the local or customary forms of land authority are
not steeply hierarchical. Authority over land is decentralized. In many places,
lineages that are recognized as "indigenous" to a particular jurisdiction have
consolidated land rights that cannot be easily revoked by customary authorities
such as chiefs. In these situations, lineage heads are land-allocation and land-
adjudication authorities, and they make land decisions by negotiating with the
dominant members of their extended families. They may have prerogatives to
rent land or sell (or provisionally sell) land-use rights, but the sale of the land

itself is usually considered illegitimate and not recognized by government as legal. When land rights have been consolidated at the level of households, land authority is even more decentralized and dispersed. A case in point is landholding in the Kisii region of Kenya, where lineage rights were disaggregated and invested in household heads by the government's land registration policies of the 1960s.

Under the customary land regimes (wherein local authorities govern land allocation within state-recognized jurisdictions), the locus of political authority over land can shift over time. Whereas chiefs have wide prerogatives over the allocation of common, unoccupied, unused, abandoned, or "vacant" land, lineages and families that are considered members of the descent-based community have strong land rights vis-à-vis chiefs over land that they are *using*. As lineages and families consolidate user rights over more and more land within a jurisdiction, "unused" land becomes scarce, and power over land shifts from chiefs to lineage heads, and then perhaps to the heads of nuclear families.[39] As Souleymane Ouédraogo (2005, 70–75) explained for northern Burkina Faso, land chiefs in the old Mossi villages have "no role" anymore, because all the land is now under lineage control. This process of decentralization of neo-customary authority over land is also visible in Ghana's Ashanti Region (see Chapter 7). Even in situations such as these, however, chiefs may retain land-dispute adjudication powers as well as the power to reclaim land (revoke land rights) "for public use" and the power to veto the alienation of land to outsiders.

Central state authority over land: The statist land regimes
The central state itself is the direct allocator and adjudicator of land rights in some places. Here, central governments may extinguish all ancestral or customary rights and not recognize the rules or practices of the customary tenure. This is the case in most places where land was expropriated from Africans and given to European settlers. As we saw in Chapter 2, it is also the case in many state-engineered settlement schemes and in national parks, urban areas, and forest reserves.

Where state agents exercise direct land-allocation and land-adjudication authority at the local level, a statist (or state-administered) land regime prevails. The locus of authority lies at the center of the national political system – the locus is "central," or national. The authority of these actors emanates from the central state, not from an appeal to local norms, customs, or ancestry.[40]

---

[39] We can thus infer that if there is little unoccupied land in a jurisdiction that is under customary authority, then families and lineages will have consolidated land-use rights at the expense of chiefs.

[40] A third possible ideal type, or category, is land administration and allocation by representative local government (e.g., popularly elected local government). We treat empirical cases of this type of regime as a hybrid form of the first two, on the basis of the hypothesis that these institutions tend to *take on the biases* of the land administration systems that they are supposed

By this reasoning, a private property regime is a particular variant or subtype of a statist land regime. Land is allocated primarily by the market (rather than directly by state agents), but market allocation takes place under rules and regulations established and enforced directly by the central state. The state itself defines and implements the rules governing transactions and enforces contracts and rights.[41]

Territorial Jurisdiction

This dimension of the land tenure regime refers to the territorial jurisdiction of the actor who grants and enforces land rights. Jurisdiction defines the geographic scope and boundaries of authority, conceived of in terms of territorial-political scale (e.g., restricted to a locality in the case of village chiefs; coterminous with the national unit in the case of central government). A territorial jurisdiction can thus be local, provincial, or national. In this analytic framework, the scale of territorial jurisdiction and the locus of authority are mutually constitutive and encoded jointly in the land tenure regime.[42]

Where the locus of land authority is local (i.e., in the customary land regimes), its jurisdictional scope is confined to the administrative unit that

to improve on or supersede. This means that within a given country, one would expect the political character and workings of local government land administration (decentralized land administration) to vary across space, partly as a function of variations in the preexisting (or underlying) land administration systems (see Boone 2003a, 2003b; Ribot 2004). This is a hypothesis. In concrete cases, analysis must remain open to the possibility of democratization of either the local state or the central state and open to incremental moves in these directions.

[41] As argued previously, this study considers private property regimes to be one type of statist LTR, since the state itself is the direct maker and enforcer of the rules governing land transactions and landholding. I employ this reasoning in the case of Zimbabwe (Chapter 10).

[42] See Sack 1986. In land politics, jurisdiction can be politically salient in ways not captured in this discussion. One could draw a tripartite distinction between territorial jurisdiction, functional jurisdiction, and jurisdiction over persons. *Territorial jurisdictions* can vary in terms of how unambiguously they are delimited by the central state, how they nest into administrative hierarchies of neotraditional and national government, and the extent to which they are recognized by key actors as setting the boundaries of (enclosing) legitimate territorial domains and social groupings. Where the boundaries of territorial jurisdictions are not clear or are contested, rights holders in neighboring or nested territorial jurisdictions (e.g., different chieftaincies) can hold competing rights to the same piece of land. Meanwhile, a single territorial jurisdiction can comprise *functional jurisdictions* exercised by different authorities. These functional divisions can be well specified, ambiguously delineated, or contested. Lund (2008) tackles such situations in showing that in parts of northern Ghana, rival land claimants can appeal to competing authorities, each of whom claims functional jurisdiction over land allocation (e.g., a land chief versus an administrative chief). Similarly, central actors and local actors may claim *competing* functional jurisdictions (e.g., does the central state have jurisdiction over land-rights allocation in a given locality?). Finally, within a given territorial jurisdiction, *jurisdiction over persons* can be fractured between different authorities, as in the millet system of the Ottoman Empire or in other situations where Islamic law applies only to Muslims living in a given territorial jurisdiction. The different kinds of jurisdictional disputes are not mutually exclusive: they can be compounding.

is supposed to delimit the territorial domain of the "natural community." As Chapter 2 argues, colonial states demarcated territorial jurisdictions for the express purpose of defining the domains of local-level customary or neo-traditional authorities. These jurisdictions were conceived as homeland areas (ethnic territories, tribal areas) for the members of the group deemed to be indigenous to that area (tribe, *tribu*, or *race indigène* in colonial terminology). Indirect rule created nested hierarchies of jurisdictions and customary author-ities within these tribal homelands. The "village and its hinterland" was the basic unit of territorial administration within the governing hierarchy of the colonial state. Customary authority within this unit would be incarnated in and exercised by the village chief.

Most postcolonial states have retained these basic principles and structures of territorial jurisdiction, redrawing some boundaries and reordering some hierarchies to serve their purposes. They often have abolished chieftaincy at the paramount or cantonal levels, but not at the more local levels.

Sometimes authority within the territorial units has been fully secularized through the abolition of state-recognized customary authority as well as its territorial bases (i.e., the administrative units based on chieftaincy hierarchies, all the way down to the most local level).[43] In these places, the central state has imposed direct rule. The jurisdiction of the land-allocating authority in these cases is thus "national," in the sense that the central state operates on a national scale, within the national-level institutions (e.g., constitution) that define the national political arena.

Citizenship

Citizenship regimes define the boundaries of membership in a political community.[44] Under the neocustomary land regimes, "local citizenship" is highly salient political status. It denotes inclusion, or membership, in the descent-based group considered to be indigenous to the region or locality.[45]

---

43 This *would be* the case in Kenyan settlement schemes. The title "chief" is often used but does not have any customary connotation.

44 The question of membership in the political community is, as Benhabib (2002, 413–414) argues, prior to all others. She points out, quoting Michael Walzer's *Spheres of Justice* (New York: Basic, 1983), that it is the first social good that needs to be allocated – all other rights and privileges flow from this.

45 For a political critique, see Jacob and Le Meur 2010 and Ribot 2004, 70. Membership itself is a socially constructed status, not a biological given. The restrictiveness of this status has varied by place and has tended to become stricter over time (first with the imposition of colonialism's land regimes and later with rising land values). See Lentz 2000. Compare this to the modern concept of national citizenship, defined by Scott (1998, 32) as a uniform, homogenous citizenship status prevailing through an integrated legal sphere, built on the abstraction of the "unmarked citizen." Scott defines this as a technology of government born of the modern era.

Status as an indigene, autochthone, or son-of-the-soil is the basis of membership in the community and thus local citizenship rights. This confers a land entitlement and political rights within the local political arena. Non-members are considered outsiders or "strangers" who have no land entitlement and who are politically subordinate in the local arena. As discussed in Chapter 2, the local citizenship regimes embedded in neocustomary land tenure are segmented in this way, and are also ranked (or stratified). They ascribe differential political status and rights, and differential economic rights, to different categories of citizens. Distinctions are drawn between superior and inferior lineages, and on the basis of age, other markers of seniority, and gender. Personal achievement and wealth can also matter, but citizenship status remains salient.

By contrast, the citizenship regimes that are enshrined in the constitutions of the national states encode the principle that all citizens of the national state are governed under national law.[46] This citizenship regime establishes a *direct connection* between the national state and the citizen. Under the statist LTRs, a direct agent of the central state – such as a prefect, land officer, settlement scheme officer, or forestry officer – allocates land directly to an individual user and sees to the enforcement of this land allocation. The land user is the direct subject of the central state – he or she is in a political relationship unmediated by neocustomary authority. Land users are drawn into the national jurisdiction (national political arena) through the land tenure relationship that makes them dependent on central authorities as land allocators (or enforcers).

In zones of high in-migration in modern Africa, citizenship regimes are highly salient in structuring social and political inequality around land: citizenship regimes determine "who is entitled" to land, and "who has the authority to decide." Answers to these questions differ markedly across space, depending on whether the rules of land access are defined by a neocustomary land regime or a statist land regime. Focusing on the locus of authority, these situations can be described as follows:

In-migration under local authority

In modern Africa, where in-migration has occurred under local authority and neocustomary LTRs, it has been hard for in-migrants to acquire permanent land rights.[47] Most have remained subject to the political authority of customary chiefs, other local chiefs, lineage heads and elders, and *autorités traditionnelles*. In these situations, in-migrants thus constitute a stratum of second-class citizens (or foreigners, strangers) in the local polity. By dint of this subordinate

---

[46] National citizenship can also be graduated across population groups, as, for example, in Rogers Smith's (1999) account of citizenship in the U.S. context.

[47] "Modern Africa" refers here to the era of consolidation of the authority of the colonial states and their systems for governing the countryside.

citizenship status in the neocustomary political order, their land rights are restricted and vulnerable. The modal case is one in which the in-migrant receives contingent access to land in exchange for political deference to the local land-holder (along with a payment in kind or in the form of labor services). In some regions of West and Central Africa, as many as half of all farmers in a given locality may hold contingent or "derived" land rights under these sorts of arrangements.

In-migration under central authority

Some modern in-migrations have been sponsored directly by the central state under statist LTRs. In these situations, it is the state that gives land access and land rights to in-migrants who are "administratively inserted" into localities or subregions.[48] Where this happens, the in-migrants are beholden to the central state, which is the author of their "insertion" into the locality and the guarantor of their right to land access, and not to their local hosts or landlords. If the in-migrants come from another part of the same country, they will point to their status as citizens of the national polity to legitimate and secure their land claims.

Citizenship dynamics in zones of state-sponsored in-migration in Africa revolve around an inherent structural contradiction. Where the state has inserted settlers alongside an established farming population, there is often a politically salient tension between migrants who owe their land access to the central state and claim land rights under a national citizenship regime, and an autochthonous population that claims ancestral rights to land in that locality.[49]

State-sponsored in-migration or colonization does not always encroach on the rights of an established farming population, however. In sub-Saharan Africa's largest irrigation schemes (including the Gezira Scheme in Sudan and the Office du Niger scheme in Mali), there is no strong tension between state-granted rights and settled agriculturalists' claims to ancestral rights.[50] Because

---

[48] Mafikiri Tsongo 1997.

[49] Partly this reflects a deep political contradiction of the modern state's own making: if the state has delimited and enforced "customary jurisdictions" throughout most of the country, then devaluing or refusing to recognize ancestral claims in one particular jurisdiction imposes a costly and unfair penalty on those whose can claim that the government has swept aside their customary rights.

[50] One would thus expect that if there were high competition for land on these schemes, then it would take the form of competition *within* families that hold state-granted rights, or perhaps *between* the state and such families. In the Office du Niger (ON) until the late 1990s, however, the presence of vacant land translated into low levels of competition among smallholders for land. The leasing of state land to large-scale international investors in the ON in the 2000s created a new dynamic. In these circumstances, small-scale farmers are likely to claim rights against the state and outsiders on the basis of user rights or citizenship rights (or perhaps inheritance), but not ancestral rights or neocustomary rights (defined here as rooted in state-recognized neocustomary authority) per se.

state-financed irrigation projects "opened" the land to farming, settlers on the new schemes did not encounter a critical mass of established farming communities that claimed ancestral rights. In such cases, settlers often *did* displace pastoralists. Pastoralists have been notoriously disadvantaged in their efforts to defend their claims to natural resources against modern governments that have, over the past century, systematically favored agriculturalists.

Losers' Options: Choices in Structured Settings

This study explores the politics produced by rising pressure on the land, perceptions of rising land values, and awareness of (growing) land scarcity for smallholders. Where property rights in land are multiple and overlapping, as discussed in Chapter 2, land scarcity and rising land values give those in a position to exclude, enclose, or encroach on the rights of others heightened incentive to do so. Land pressure thus creates the possibility that land-access rules and land rights will become narrower and more exclusive. This can create the specter of redistribution of land rights and heighten the possibility of zero-sum conflict over land. How (potential) land-access or land-rights losers *respond* to this real or impending loss of land access or rights is critical in producing the different forms of land-related conflict that are at the center of this study.

Losers' options are shaped by the political scale of the arena in which they are fighting to defend their land rights (local or national), the nature of the political authority to which they must appeal (customary or statist), and their own citizenship status. Hirschman's (1970) exit-voice-loyalty typology is a useful starting point for specifying these options in a way that highlights situational factors "that produce a dominant reaction mode."[51] Land-rights losers, or those threatened with loss, can respond with exit (out-migration), loyalty (taking the loss but maintaining prevailing relationships), or voice (pursuing redress or restitution through collective action in a political arena, by way of threats, protest, resistance, voting, etc.). Weapons-of-the-weak strategies such as witchcraft or subversion may also be employed as hybrid strategies combining elements of exit, loyalty, and voice.

When the cost of voice is very high, loyalty and exit are likely to be the dominant reaction strategies. Loyalty, or acquiescence and staying put, becomes a more acceptable option when the cost of exit is high. Voice is less costly and thus more likely when actors have political rights and influence within the decision-making arena.

---

[51] Exit, voice, and loyalty strategies can operate together, as when loyalty and a sense of efficacy incentivize an actor to use voice to try to reform the status quo, and the volume, level, or strength of voice is shaped by strategic calculations (Hirschman 1970, 31, 33, 108). Bierschenk and Olivier de Sardan (2003) adopt this framework, as do Hall and Gingerich (2004, 32) in describing political strategies that are shaped by a varieties-of-capitalism framework.

Exit, voice, and loyalty responses are shaped not only by actors' preferences but also by the institutions that channel and aggregate responses. Hirschman (1970, 43) argues that "the balance between exit and voice depends on the existence of institutions and mechanisms that can communicate complaints cheaply and effectively."

Following this logic, African land tenure regimes can be understood as made up of local-level political and economic institutions and mechanisms that shape the strategic options of individuals and groups who are (or at risk of being) on the losing end of processes that can produce more exclusionary land rights. Land regimes generate incentives for, and constraints on, exit, voice, and loyalty that vary not only across space but also across different groups of actors in a given setting. These aspects of socioeconomic structure help produce the varied patterns of land-related conflict that can be observed in Africa today.

Meanwhile, I recognize that some highly informed analysts have argued that African land regimes differ so much and so intricately that each can be thought of as sui generis – land rules "only apply in the groups where they have developed."[52] This study abstracts from this diversity to achieve greater analytic purchase on the problem of comparison across space and time. These simplifications may even suggest new ways of understanding the very forms of multiplicity and ambiguous transformation that are at the center of many existing analyses of land politics in Africa.

HOW LAND REGIMES STRUCTURE REDISTRIBUTIVE CONFLICT OVER LAND: HYPOTHESES

Rising competition for land will lead some rights holders to seek more exclusive land rights – this is the theoretical expectation. This produces redistributive tensions, which find expression in varying forms of land competition and conflict. These variations are the object of the present analysis.

The main argument is that under different land tenure regimes, redistributive tensions will find expression in different forms of land-related conflict. Each dimension of the land regime constitutes a parameter, or structuring element, of the local institutional context: this local context structures actors' responses to the specter of land-rights loss. Some testable hypotheses emanate from this theoretical foundation.

The **authority** variable points to the institutional position of the land-rights authority, who is expected to respond to the emergence of land-related conflicts in ways that help defend or increase political authority already achieved. Locus of authority over land is either local (neocustomary) or central (exercised by agents of the central state), and is thus inextricably linked to the **jurisdictional** scale of land-related conflict. Under local authority, the land-politics arena is

---

[52] This expression is from Reyna and Downs (1988, 10–11), but they would have agreed that patterns are visible in land relations and land regimes.

local. Neocustomary land regimes are built on segmented and ranked **citizen-ship** orders, in which low-ranking in-migrants (ethnic outsiders, or strangers) have the weakest land claims and are likely to be land-rights losers under conditions of high competition for land. Where the central government has sponsored in-migration, in-migrants' land claims are based on national citizen-ship, and the government that granted the land rights to the settlers is expected to defend these rights. Under this land tenure regime, the most likely land-rights losers are those who claim rights on the basis of indigeneity. The **in-migration** variable taps into the salience of the indigene-stranger distinction under local land authority and under central authority. The **competition for land** variable runs from low to high and indicates the intensity, within a given locality, of conflict-fueling pressure toward growing exclusivity of rights.

Under conditions of high competition for land, divergent institutional con-figurations at the local level will produce different kinds of politics. We hypoth-esize that under the following land tenure regimes, land-related conflict among smallholders will assume these forms:

I. In areas of high in-migration where land allocation is under the con-trol of neocustomary authorities, in-migrants (strangers) are likely to be the main land-rights losers. There will be indigene-stranger tensions and conflicts, focused on the local authorities who are decision mak-ers. Strangers will be the bearers of land-rights grievances, but they are unlikely to have access to a political arena where they can voice those grievances. Strangers will tend to be the land-rights losers. They have few options other than to exit. They may be expelled. Land-related conflict will appear as localized ethnic conflict (or discrimination) over land.

II. Where high in-migration has taken place under a statist land tenure regime, rising competition for land will find political expression in ten-sion between state-sponsored settlers and indigenes. Indigenes will be the land-rights losers. Their grievances will be focused on the central state and at the regime that is the author of the prevailing land alloca-tion. Central authorities can be expected to back those they have settled on the land: settlers with whom they have a patron-client relationship. Land-related conflict will find expression in the national political arena and in the guise of ethnic grievances.[53] The hypothesis is that this will not happen under the other land tenure regimes.

A couple of specific variants of hypothesis II are of particular interest to political science.

If the central authorities hold a political monopoly, as in an authoritar-ian regime, they can raise the cost of voice by using political repression

---

[53] Following Bates (1989, 47).

against those with grievances. Acquiescence becomes more likely. If, however, central authorities permit overt, legal contestation for control of the central state (as in national elections), then the cost of voice is lower. Voice is more likely, and more likely to be effective.

An attribute of central authority is that although its locus and scale are fixed (i.e., at the national level), its political character can change over time. This can happen through decolonization; incumbent turnover resulting from war, coup, revolution, or elections; or a shift from monopoly rule to a situation of legal contestation for state power. If the link between central authorities and in-migrants (settlers, or "strangers") *has been broken* by regime change at the national level, the new regime may either continue to back the settlers or switch sides.

If rival elites are in overt competition for control over the central state, as in situations of multiparty competition (or war), the political rivals may have incentives to appeal to rival groups of land claimants (settlers and indigenes, or ethnic outsiders and ethnic insiders). In this situation, politicized land conflict can find overt expression in the national political (electoral) arena. Our hypothesis is that this is unlikely under other land tenure regimes. In these situations, incumbent rulers are likely to back the settlers whom they themselves have implanted and protected in the past.

III. In areas of low in-migration where the locus of land authority rests with local lineage heads and elders and land competition is high, competition for land will play out within families and lineages. Subordinate members will tend to be the land-rights losers. Within the family, there is not a political or public arena in which to protest injury or voice grievances. Losers in this situation will therefore not have a voice option. They will usually be constrained to opt for loyalty (accept a hardening of terms of land access) or exit. They may employ weapons of the weak, such as subversion or witchcraft. Land-related conflict will take the form of "domestic conflict" and appear nonpolitical. It is unlikely that land-related conflict will find expression in any of the other forms specified here.

IV. If, however, chiefly authority is being exerted over land-rights allocation in these situations (as where chiefs are "taking back" land from autochthonous families), then there *is* a political arena that may be a forum for voice by farmers whose land rights are threatened. If this arena is not closed by repression, then the stage is set for land-related conflict that takes the form of a debate on chiefly accountability. The hypothesis is that this will play out as a political debate over accountability within the arena of the chiefly jurisdiction. Such a pattern of conflict is unlikely under other land tenure regimes.

V. The theoretical model generates a hypothetical situation in which central states are land allocators in situations of low in-migration and high competition among smallholders for land. In reality this configuration is improbable, because (a) central states have usually become directly involved in land allocation precisely to foster in-migration or to displace smallholders, and (b) in places where indigenes are densely settled and in-migration is low, customary regimes usually prevail. However, where a state has gone far in displacing customary or ancestral rights in jurisdictions where local populations are considered indigenous, the central state authority will be directly implicated in mediating land-rights conflicts among indigenes. They can be expected to use voice to express grievances in the national arena if it is open enough to permit that.[54]

Table 3.2 captures the variations in land tenure regimes that are discussed in this chapter, and summarizes my arguments linking institutional causes to political effects. It deals only with situations of high or rising competition for land.

Reading the table from top down, we evoke the salience of the citizenship variable first by drawing a distinction between cases of high and low in-migration. This captures the extent to which in-migration has been a factor in the local expansion of agricultural production. Where there is in-migration, there is usually ethnic heterogeneity.[55] In these situations, the citizenship regime establishes hierarchy between the ethnic insiders and the ethnic outsiders. Under the neocustomary regimes, the ethnic are politically dominant. Under the statist land tenure regimes, ethnic outsiders dominate politically as long as their land claims are enforced by the central state.

Columns then draw distinctions according to the locus (nature) of authority over land, which ranges from local (i.e., neocustomary forms, ranging from family-level to chieftaincy-level authority over land) to national (i.e., the statist form). We assume for the purposes of this schema that jurisdictional scale and the locus of authority are jointly determined: where the family head is the land

---

[54] This configuration exists in parts of Tanzania, in Mbulu District for example. See Boone and Nyeme, in preparation, and the Appendix. This land tenure configuration opens the door to easy state concessions of land to large-scale foreign investors. Central state authority is likely to be the focal point of conflict between citizens who are land users and the foreign "outsiders" invited in by the government. Such competition for land would, by hypothesis V, find political expression in nationalism and in demands that the national government give priority to the rights of citizens. This analysis does not give sustained consideration to these situations, however, since we are concerned mostly with land-related conflict *among smallholder farmers* in situations of rising competition for land.

[55] Some caveats and exceptions appear in Table 3.3.

TABLE 3.2. *Smallholder Land Tenure Regimes: Expected Forms of Land-Related Conflict (with High Levels of Competition for Land)*

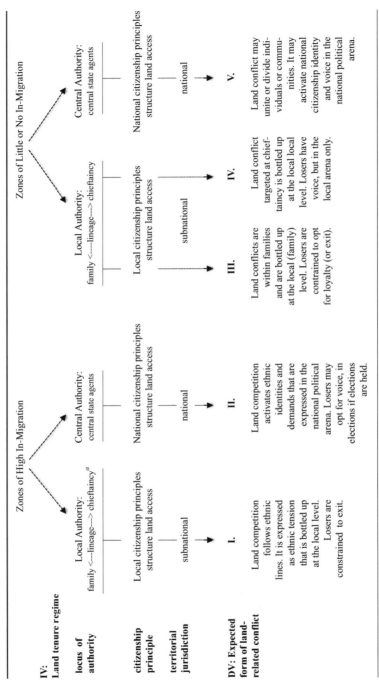

IV: Land tenure regime	Zones of High In-Migration		Zones of Little or No In-Migration	
locus of authority	Local Authority: family <——lineage——> chieftaincy[a]	Central Authority: central state agents	Local Authority: family <——lineage——> chieftaincy	Central Authority: central state agents
citizenship principle	Local citizenship principles structure land access	National citizenship principles structure land access	Local citizenship principles structure land access	National citizenship principles structure land access
territorial jurisdiction	subnational	national	subnational	national
DV: Expected form of land-related conflict	I.	II.	III. IV.	V.
	Land competition follows ethnic lines. It is expressed as ethnic tension that is bottled up at the local level. Losers are constrained to exit.	Land competition activates ethnic identities and demands that are expressed in the national political arena. Losers may opt for voice, in elections if elections are held.	III. Land conflicts are within families and are bottled up at the local (family) level. Losers are constrained to opt for loyalty (or exit). IV. Land conflict targeted at chieftaincy is bottled up at the local local level. Losers have voice, but in the local arena only.	Land conflict may unite or divide individuals or communities. It may activate national citizenship identity and voice in the national political arena.

[a] Chieftaincy or other forms of the neocustomary. The family-chieftaincy variable captures a continuum that runs from narrow family groups, to lineages and clans, to chieftaincy.

allocator, for example, the territorial jurisdiction is the family's land domain. Where the central state is the land allocator, the territorial jurisdiction of the land allocator is the national territory.

Hypotheses I–V predict political effects of these variations in land tenure regimes. Each hypothesis is multidimensional, incorporating arguments about ethnicity, scale, and elections.

EVIDENCE, FINDINGS, AND COUNTERARGUMENTS

Challenges of Inference and Measurement

Challenges of inference and measurement arise in conceptualizing "land-related conflict" as an outcome variable (a dependent variable). In the analysis of rural politics in Africa and elsewhere, many conflicts that have land-related dimensions are chalked up to other causes (e.g., family and interfamily feuds, thefts, ethnicity, chieftaincy disputes, religion, disputes over jurisdictional boundaries and borders, ideology, and even pure party politics).[56] It may also be that conflicts springing from one cause (e.g., a dispute over locus of authority at the local level) develop land-related dimensions later or over time. Most land-related conflict is of the nonviolent, low-intensity kind.[57] And it is surely the case that sustained and large-scale conflicts – and perhaps all violent conflicts – are traceable to multiple causes, including those that are purely idiosyncratic or contingent.

In undertaking to study land-related conflict in a comparative perspective, one confronts not only conceptual and inferential challenges but also measurement problems. No database on "land-related conflict" exists; there is no standard measure of land-related conflict that is used to collect data across regions or countries or over time. We do not know how many disputes, injuries (physical or other), or deaths have been caused by land-related conflict in Africa over time, or how many cases involving land disputes would have been taken to court if courts had existed everywhere and people had used them. We do not know how many youth, women, elderly people, members of subordinate lineages, or strangers have been driven off or kept down by land-related conflict, or how many episodes of election-related violence grew out of, or were stoked by, land disputes. Information we have about land-related conflict is "mainly case-based, partial, and not systematically comparable."[58] The challenge is to construct cases in ways that make comparison possible, and that allow analysts to discern patterns that provide a basis for evaluating hypotheses derived from this theorization of the problem.

---

[56] See Herring 2003.
[57] As discussed by Tettey et al., n.d., following Yamano and Deininger 2005.
[58] Crook and Sverrisson 2000: 22. See also Gerring 2004.

Cases: Selection and Coding

Cases were selected on the basis of availability of information, the quest for clear variation on all dimensions of comparison, and a hypothesis-testing logic. I attempted to zero in on situations with evidence of rising competition for land, and enough information to frame the local history and present patterns of land politics as a "case."[59] Constructing cases requires finding information on political and settlement history, local sociopolitical organization, land allocation and farming practices, and the insertion of the locality into the wider political-economic system. I have selected cases about which there was enough information to assign a clear value on two or more attributes of the land tenure regime, as well as information on the dependent variable (in order to see if the hypothesized effects are present in these situations).

Coding the cases in terms of the study variables is a task of descriptive inference that is not always straightforward. There is no World Bank, Freedom House, or UNFAO database of land tenure attributes of regions, districts, prefectures, or voting constituencies in sub-Saharan Africa. Available information is highly uneven in its spatial and temporal coverage. It comes mostly from site-specific work done by researchers across the range of social science disciplines, who employ highly variable concepts, units of analysis, time frames, and notions of causality and measurement.[60] Six of the cases draw on my own fieldwork and research in national archives.

Table 3.3 typologizes the case studies according to the land regime variables. The main horizontal division of Table 3.3 separates cases of low pressure on the land (low land scarcity) from cases with high pressure on the land (high land scarcity, or high land values). This allows for a full specification of the contrast space. In most of rural Africa for most of the twentieth century, pressure on the land was low: land was not the limiting factor of production, and land was not considered to be scarce. Even today, this is true in many places. Yet high or rising pressure on the land has become a pervasive reality, affecting zones of smallholder agriculture across much of sub-Saharan Africa and driving or heightening the forms of land-related competition and conflict that are the focus of this analysis. The table captures this variation in the intensity of pressure on

---

[59] Several context-specific indicators tap into the underlying concept of rising land values, rising competition for land, and growing land scarcity for smallholders. These include agricultural intensification, shorter fallows, shrinking plot size, shrinking land per capita within households, emergence of landlessness or near landlessness in the rural areas, increasing frequency or prices of land-rights sales or rentals, and so on.

[60] Fortunately, comparative work undertaken at the level of the units of analysis employed here has been sponsored by IIED (see Cotula et al. 2004), the World Bank (see Bruce and Migot-Adholla 1994), La Coopération Française (through GRET), ACTS in Nairobi, and the IRD Unité de Recherche n. 095, "Regulations Foncières, politique publique, logiques d'acteurs" (see, for example, Jacob and Le Meur 2010). Other scholars have also proposed structured comparisons of local-level land tenure situations (Platteau 1996, Boni 2005, Berry 1993, Bierschenk and Olivier de Sardan 2003, Bruce and Migot-Adholla 1994, Lund 2008, Onoma 2009, and others).

TABLE 3.3. *Land Tenure Situations and Cases: Typology*[a]

	Zones of In-Migration		Little or No In-Migration	
	Local, Neocustomary Authority: Family < – – – Lineage – – –> Chieftaincy[b]	**Central State Authority:** Central State Agents	**Local, Neocustomary Authority:** Family < – – – Lineage – – –> Chieftaincy	**Central State Authority:** Central State Agents
	1.	2.	3.	4.
Low competit. for land	• E. Côte d'Ivoire • Central Senegal, 1940s	• Office du Niger, Mali • N. Kivu, DRC, 1950s • SEB schemes, Cameroon, 1970s	• Upper/ Middle Senegal River Valley, 1960s • S. Niger, 1980s • Wa, Ghana	• Gezira, Sudan[c]
	5.	6.	7.	8.
High competit. for land	• Baoulé, Côte d'Iv. • Western Burkina • Western Ghana Ashanti 1960s [– Periurban Kumasi] • SEB/Rey Bouba Cameroon 1990s	• Rift Valley, Kenya • SW Côte d'Ivoire • much of Rwanda • Kibungo, Rwanda • Zim, commercial areas • N. Kivu, DRC • Plateau St., Nigeria[e] • Babati, TZ	• Kisii, Kenya • Central Province, Kenya • Ruhengeri, Rwanda • Enugu, Nigeria • Rural Ashanti, 1980s • Central Senegal • Periurban Kumasi[d]	• Giting, TZ, 1980s+[3] • Iraqw homeland of Mbulu district, TZ.

[a] Cases refer to present era, circa 1990 to the present, unless otherwise noted. See the chapters and Appendix 1.

[b] i.e., chieftaincy or other forms of neocustomary authority.

[c] Cells 4 and 8 are improbable situations; there are no clear-cut empirical examples in this study. Gezira could be placed in cell 2. In the Giting area, no farming community claims land on the basis of ancestral rights; almost all are 1950s in-migrants whose occupation of the area, well established since the 1980s, is uncontested. The *citizenship politics* are similar to those in cells 3, 4, 7, and 8.

[d] In periurban Kumasi, competition for land can involve local citizens or outsiders.

[e] In Nigeria's federal system, this refers to the Plateau State government.

79

the land, which is important to our argument. The thirty-two cases that appear in Table 3.3 constitute our "medium-N" set. Of these, twelve are more fully developed in Chapters 4 through 10.

The next step is to together information on both sides of the causal equation. The next three tables code the cases according to the land tenure regime (LTR) characteristics and land-conflict attributes I have identified. This provides leverage on the causal hypotheses that emanate from the theory. Cases are identified by country and subnational jurisdiction, and years (columns 1 and 2), and by LTR type according to the "locus of authority" variable (column 3). Fuller accounts of each case, along with the sources of information on which the categorizations and codings are based, appear in the chapters and the Appendix.

For each case, the presence and level of in-migration is noted (column 4). Level of in-migration is signaled by an estimate of in-migrants as a percentage of the local population (where this information is available). In-migration can occur under all land tenure regimes, and the theory proposed here does not explain its presence or absence. What varies across LTRs in the theory proposed here are the authority and citizenship rules that define the nature and terms of land access for in-migrants. These rules define the character of the indigene-stranger relationship, and they go far in shaping the forms of land-related conflict and competition that emerge in particular settings (cases). Column 4 indicates the character of this relationship (in-migrants as settlers, sharecroppers or share contract holders, wage laborers, returnees, or land buyers or renters). Column 5 codes cases by level of land competition (or "pressure on the land"), another variable that is exogenous to the rules about authority, jurisdiction, citizenship, and property that make up the LTRs.

On the outcome side of the causal equation, the tables code cases for three features of the dependent variable – that is, the form of land-related competition and conflict – that are determined, I argue, by the land tenure regime. Column 6 identifies the category of land users most likely to be on the losing side of the redistribution of land rights that can result from rising competition over land.[61] Column 7 is losers' strategy in the face of possible or real loss of land rights, denoted in terms of exit, voice, or loyalty/stay put. Column 9 is the form of land-related conflict, defined as the presence or absence of ethnicized land conflict and the political scale at which it plays out.[62]

Column 8 describes the intensity of land-related conflict in each case, even though the theory laid out in Part I of this book does not make predictions

---

[61] In agrarian society, land-related conflict within families is ubiquitous and generally plays out in the day-to-day politics of family life. This is coded as "the" form of conflict when it appears to be the predominant form of land-related conflict within a locality. I realize that this form of land conflict can co-exist and interact with the others, even though these interactions are not theorized in this study.

[62] Information in square brackets means that the coding decision was too hard to call or that criteria did not fit the case.

about this aspect of land politics. "Conflict intensity" is a very rough descriptor of different conflict situations, and can be read as follows: *High-intensity* land conflict disrupts all normal functioning of the region or locality, usually involving overt violence with significant numbers of casualties and population displacement. *Medium-intensity* land conflict attracts the attention of national administrative authorities (such as prefects and *sous-préfets*) and land-rights researchers. *Low-intensity* competition and conflict is woven into the ongoing functioning of the locality.

Table 3.4 contains the statist LTR cases, in which land-allocation authority is exercised directly by the central state. Table 3.5 contains the neocustomary LTR cases in which land authority is vested in hierarchically-structured local states and exercised by chiefs. Table 3.6 captures the neocustomary LTRs in which land authority is most local and most decentralized, and exercised by lineage heads and family elders. General patterns that appear within and across these three tables support our arguments. The main argument is that across different LTRs, rising pressure on the land (growing land scarcity for smallholders, and/or rising land values) will produce widely divergent political effects. The tables reveal a pattern of correlation between LTR type and forms of land-related conflict.

Under statist LTRs and conditions of high in-migration (Table 3.4), ethnic insiders are the land-rights losers, and they are targets of central-state repression. The high cost of voice biases outcomes toward the less costly options of loyalty/stay and exit. Some cases are divided into two time periods, which appear as two rows of the table. This captures change over time: openings to multipartism lowered the cost of voice for land-rights losers.

Under neocustomary LTRs that are centered on chieftaincy (Table 3.5), by contrast, when pressure on the land is high, the ethnic outsiders bear the brunt of exclusion. The local political arenas centered on chieftaincy or other forms of neocustomary authority offer little room for land-rights losers to express voice, as captured in Table 3.5. Land conflict is bottled up at the local level; state agents avoid direct involvement.

Table 3.6 is a set of neocustomary LTR cases in which land-allocation authority is exerised by lineage heads, elders, or household heads. Here, when pressure on the land is very high, in-migration is low. Mounting competition for land creates pressures and incentives for some people to seek more exclusive or exclusionary definitions of land rights. The losers in these situations will tend to be low-ranking members of families – youth and women – who will generally not have a political venue in which to seek redress. The land tenure regime works to keep conflict highly localized and contained within the family. Those threatened with the loss or narrowing of their land rights will be pressured to exit or simply remain loyal.

Comparisons and contrasts presented in the three tables also make it possible to rule out some alternative theories and arguments about land conflict, and to qualify and confirm others. The array of cases presented in Tables 3.4

TABLE 3.4. *Statist Land Tenure Regime Cases*

1. Case	2. Years	3. Locus of Land Authority	4. In-Migration (% Pop.)	5. Land Competition	6. Losers of Land Rights	7. Losers' Strategy	8. Conflict Intensity	9. Form of Land Conflict
Rift Valley Prov., Kenya	1960s–1980s	state	high (50%), settlers	high	ethnic insiders (indigenes)	loyalty/stay	medium	ethnicized conflict, losers repressed by state
Rift Valley Prov., Kenya	1991+	state	high (50%), settlers	high	ethnic insiders indigenes	voice	high	ethnicized conflict in national electoral arena
N. Kivu, DRC (Masisi)	1950s–1980s	state	high (50%), settlers and investors	increasing	ethnic insiders indigenes	loyalty/stay	medium	ethnicized conflict, losers repressed by state
N. Kivu, DRC (Masisi)	1990–1994	state	high (50%), settlers and investors	high	ethnic insiders indigenes	voice	high	ethnicized conflict in national (provincial) electoral arena
SW Côte d'Ivoire (Center-west)	1950s–1980s	state + lineages	high (~50%), settlers	increasing	ethnic insiders indigenes	loyalty/stay/ voice	medium–high	ethnicized conflict, losers repressed by state
SW Côte d'Ivoire (Center-west)	1990s+	state + lineages	high (~50%), settlers	high	ethnic insiders indigenes	voice	high	ethnicized conflict in national electoral arena
E. Rwanda and *paysannats*	1960s–1970s	state	high (60%), Hutu settlers	high	Tutsi (expelled in 1959–1963)	forced exit in 1962		ethnicized conflict promoted by state
E. Rwanda and *paysannats*	1990–1994	state	high (60%), Hutu settlers	high	Tutsi expelled in 1962	voice	high	ethnicized (electoral/military) conflict in national arena

					"voice"		
Zimbabwe, commercial farms	2000–2010	state	med (20%), white farmers + workers	medium	black Zimbabweans identified as losers	—	high	ethnicized (racial) conflict inflamed by government in national elections
Plateau State, Nigeria	1960s–1970s	ambiguous: frontier zone	high (90%), Christian settlers	low	no clear losers in frontier zone	—	—	—
Plateau State, Nigeria	1990s	state: Jos State gov.	high; new in-migrants are Muslim settlers	high	firstcomers vs. newcomers		high	ethnicized (ethno-religious) conflict with sporadic state involvement
N. Tanzania, Kiru Valley	1990+	state: national government	high (99%), large landholders, workers, smallholders	high	smallholders, youth, land-poor families	exit, voice	medium	"indigenous Tanzanians vs. outsiders" tension; some in national political arena
N. Tanzania: Mamire, Babati District	2000–present	state institutions: elected local bodies	high; 90%, state-sponsored settlers	medium	poorer or less influential persons?	loyalty, exit	low	individual/family conflicts, adjudication through state institutions (land tribunals)
Gezira Scheme, Sudan	1960s–present	state	med (20%), wage labor	low	—	—	low	—
Office du Niger, Mali	1950s–present	state	high (90%), settlers	low	—	—	low	—
Senegal River Delta	1970s–1980s	state	very high, settlers	low	—	—	low	—

TABLE 3.5. *Neocustomary (Chiefly) Land Tenure Regime Cases*

1. Case	2. Years	3. Locus of Land Authority	4. In-Migration (% Pop.)	5. Land Competition	6. Losers of Land Rights or Access	7. Losers' Strategy	8. Conflict Intensity	9. Form of Land Conflict
Western Burkina Faso	1990s	village chiefs, lineage heads	medium (~30%), land borrowers	medium-high	ethnic outsiders/in-migrants	exit	medium	conflict follows ethnic lines; confined to local level; strangers submit to local authorities
Senegal R. Valley (Upper and Middle)	1990s	chief-like *autorités traditionnelles*	(...), land borrowers, renters, graziers	medium	ethnic outsiders/in-migrants	exit	medium-low	conflict follows ethnic lines; confined to local level; strangers submit to local authorities
N. Cameroun, (*terroirs d'immigration*, SEB)	1960–2000s	chiefs displace the state in the 1990s	med (29% in Touboro), settlers	medium	ethnic outsiders prevented from gaining more secure land rights	loyalty/exit	medium	conflict follows ethnic lines; confined to local level; ethnic outsiders submit to chiefs
N. Cameroun, Maroua area	1960s–2000s	chiefs	(~30%), settlers	medium	ethnic out-group pressured to submit to chiefs	loyalty, some voice	medium	conflict follows ethnic lines; confined to local level; ethnic outsiders submit to chiefs
Ashanti Region, Ghana	1969	chiefs	~30%, share contract holders and laborers	medium	ethnic outsiders	exit	medium	conflict follows ethnic lines; confined to local level; outsiders submit to indigenous landholders
Periurban Kumasi (Ashanti Region), Ghana	2000+	chiefs	[investors and speculators, outsiders or locals]	high	indigenous landholders, properties reclaimed by chiefs	voice	medium	conflict between chiefs and citizens of the chieftaincy; confined to local arena
Western Region, Ghana	1990–2000s	chiefs (and state)	med (~30%), share contract holders, land buyers	medium	ethnic outsiders' rights are narrowed	exit, loyalty	medium	conflict follows ethnic lines; confined to local level; ethnic outsiders submit to chiefs
Sikasso, Mali	2000s	chiefs	low (...), returnees, settlers	low	no conflict?	–	–	–

Note: ellipsis (...) for "no estimate."

TABLE 3.6. *Neocustomary (Lineage/Family) Land Tenure Regime Cases: Land Conflict Indicators*

1. Case	2. Years	3. Locus of Land Authority	4. In-Migration (% Pop.)	5. Land Competition	6. Losers of Land Rights	7. Losers' Strategy	8. Conflict Intensity	9. Form of Land Conflict
Kisii, Kenya	1970s–present	family	none	high	family members	exit, stay	medium	intra-family; domestic gender and generational conflict
NW Rwanda, Ruhengeri and Gisenyi	1980s	family	very low	high	family members	stay, exit	medium	intra-family tension
Central Province, Kenya	1960s–present	family	very low	high	lineage/family members	exit, stay	low–medium	intra-family; generational and class-like tension
Ashanti, Ghana (not periurban)	1970s–present	lineage/family	very low	medium	lineage/family members	exit, stay	low	intra-family; domestic gender and generational tension
Eastern Côte d'Ivoire	1990s+	lineage/family	low	medium	lineage/family members	exit, stay	low	intra-family; domestic gender and generational tension
Central Côte d'Ivoire, Baoulé region	1990s–present	lineage/family	low-medium (10?), sharecroppers and wage labor	medium	family members and ethnic outsiders	family members exit, stay; outsiders exit	low	intra-family; generational; ethnic outsiders pressured to exit
Enugu, SE Nigeria	1980s	family	low	high	family members	exit, stay	low	intra-family
Groundnut basin, Senegal	1980s–present	family/lineage	low	medium–high	family members	exit, stay	low	intra-family

85

through 3.6 suggests that high competition for land – i.e., situations of demographic stress and land scarcity for smallholders – does not, in itself, explain
the form that land-related conflict may take, or whether it will produce any
form of overtly political land conflict at all. For example, rural population densities in Kisii in western Kenya were close to those prevailing in much of rural
Rwanda in the early 1990s. In the Kenya setting, land conflict remained bottled
up within families, whereas in Rwanda, it fueled tensions in the national political arena that politicians manipulated in a nationwide electoral struggle and
genocidal campaign. This confirms arguments made by Kahl (2006), Homer-
Dixon and Blitt (1998), and others that demographic increase and resource
competition do not, in themselves, predict or explain the emergence of overt
conflict over resources, or the social or political form that it will take.[63]

Empirical material summarized in the three tables also makes it possible to
discount arguments that take the presence of a weak or failed state as a general
cause, or predictor, of land-related conflict. Some of the most striking national-
level episodes of land-related conflict have taken place in some of sub-Saharan
Africa's most effective and institutionalized states. Côte d'Ivoire, Kenya, and
Zimbabwe are cases in point. North Kivu, the DRC region plagued by pervasive
and violent land conflict, is one of the richest zones of the country and, under
the Mobutu regime (1965–1997), it was one of the most intensively governed
(Lemarchand 2002). In these cases, land-related conflict has contributed to
state decay or decline, rather than the reverse.

It is also possible to discount the spatial hypothesis, generated by a literal
application of Herbst's (2000) power-projection theory, that land conflict is a
symptom of states' inability to project power into remote regions, especially
in countries with difficult geography.[64] On the basis of the twenty-four cases,
remoteness from the capital city does not appear to be a good predictor of
land conflict or the form it takes. Land conflict in its various forms happens
both in remote regions (North Kivu of the DRC, northern Cameroon) and in
those closer to capital cities (southwest Côte d'Ivoire, the farming districts of
Rift Valley Province in Kenya). This means that *proximity* to the capital city
(and, thus, the presence of higher land values, more pervasive government propaganda, or more information-rich environments) also does not predict which
regions will experience overt land conflict, or the highly politicized form of
land conflict that plays out in the national political arena. As the examples just
noted suggest, politicized election-time land conflict has developed in remote
and proximate regions alike.

---

[63] As Homer-Dixon (1998) argues, the effects of demographic and/or environmental stress are
mediated by social, economic, and political institutions and relationships (which may themselves
be implicated in the causes of environmental stress).
[64] Hechter (2008, 45–48) also writes of the effect of proximity and its opposite, remoteness, on
state form. Remoteness raises the costs of transport and communications.

Cases presented in the tables also provide leverage on a modernization hypothesis. Higher levels of wealth or education of the citizenry do not produce forms of land-related conflict that are focused on the "modern" state as opposed to the "customary" chiefs. In Ghana, the Ashanti Region is home to some of the wealthiest and best educated rural populations in all of sub-Saharan Africa. In the periurban areas of the regional capital of Kumasi, a city of over 2 million people in 2012, chiefs remain the central actors in local land politics. In these localities, land conflict finds political expression in calls for chiefly accountability, rather than in collective demands for central government intervention to redress land grievances.

No effect of variation in colonial institutional heritage across the former British, French, or Belgian territories is picked up in these comparisons and contrasts. Extensive development of smallholder commercial agriculture is a feature of French, British, and Belgian institutional inheritance. In four of the ex-British cases (Western Region and Ashanti Region of Ghana, Rift Valley and Kisii Districts of Kenya), land tenure regimes are decidedly nonliberal, and we observe the full range of outcomes on our dependent variable. Violent conflagrations around land in Kenya's Rift Valley and in Zimbabwe – zones where private property regimes in land were established under colonial rule – fly in the face of the argument that one institutional legacy of the British was stable, probusiness property regimes. In these cases, one cannot say that the positive effects of the liberal institutions left behind by the British were swamped by larger negatives in the macroenvironment: the property regimes themselves were very close to the epicenter of far larger conflicts. Neocustomary land tenure regimes were part of the institutional structure of French and Belgian colonial rule (as in northern Cameroon, western Burkina Faso, the Senegal River Valley, and Rwanda), just as they were in British Africa.

Comparisions across this array of cases offer leverage on some of the more nuanced arguments about how rural property regimes in Africa cause and shape the character of land conflict. Platteau (1996) and others have focused on legal dualism – the coexistence of overlapping systems of partly contradictory rights (customary versus statutory) – as a factor that goes far in defining the character and frequency of land-related conflict, and that also makes its resolution more difficult.[65] Cases presented in Tables 3.4 through 3.6 all fit the legal dualism mold in one way or another, making it possible to refine this argument. First, these case studies suggest that legal dualism per se is not always a factor shaping the character or denouement of land competition and conflict. If state-recognized customary authorities are in firm control of land allocation, regardless of the presence or absence of statutory ambiguities, they can often exclude, expel, or take away acquired rights. Rights losers may not have any legal or legitimate venue to protest or appeal. This may suppress the

[65] Platteau in Drèze and Sen, eds., 1995, 526, 531.

open expression of land conflict in the political arena (bottling it up at the local level, as in Ashanti Region in 1969 and in the Senegal River Valley today), rather than fuel it.[66] Second, different situations of legal dualism, depending on the character of the underlying land regime, produce different political effects. Where indigenous lineage heads are securely ensconced as land allocators, legal dualism may aid and abet nativism in land politics (as in western Burkina Faso). Where central states are land allocators, legal dualism may fuel anti-government mobilization on the part of those who see state agents as usurpers of their land rights (as in western Côte d'Ivoire).

Parts II, III, and IV of the book employ case material to test and refine the hypotheses and arguments proposed in this chapter. Rather than the more conventional strategy of walking straight through a sequence of case studies to illustrate and probe each of the five hypotheses summarized in Table 3.2, I have organized the hypotheses and empirical chapters around three analytic problems in political science. These center on ethnicity, political structure and scale, and elections.

Part II examines the institutional determinants of *ethnicity and of patterns of ethnic conflict* over land. The argument is that land regimes in modern African states produce ethnicity and structure ethnic relations in the rural areas. Focusing on regions of high in-migration, we contrast the political effects of rising competition for land in zones of local land authority (lineage and chieftaincy) with the political effects of such pressures under a statist land tenure regime (where the central state allocates land directly). Illustrative cases and counter-factual reasoning generate support for Table 3.2's hypotheses I and II regarding ethnic lines of cleavage, and rulers' partisanship in land-related conflicts. The analysis is a critique of studies that take ethnicity as an ideational variable, or the functional equivalent of an individual preference in behavioral research. Following Mamdani (1996a), I argue for reconceptualizing ethnicity as a state-assigned citizenship status, stressing its material dimension and incentivizing effects by showing how ethnic status confers a material entitlement within a subnational jurisdiction (or ethnic territory) that has been delimited by the state.

Part III tests the argument that land tenure regimes, which define the scale of land-allocation authority, determine the *political scale and scope* of land-related conflict. This part of the book pits Table 3.2's hypotheses I through IV against each other, generating support for the argument that the locus of land-allocation authority determines the political scale of land-related conflict. The various forms of neocustomary authority bottle up or repress redistributive conflict, including land conflict, at the local level. Under statist land regimes, by contrast, central states are themselves direct land allocators and adjudicators. Land-related conflict transmits directly into the national political arena (scales up to the national level) because the government is implicated

---

[66] See Joireman 2011.

so directly. I argue that these scalar effects are products of intentional state design.

Part IV examines forms of land-related conflict that play out in the national political arena, providing concrete instances of the causal logics laid out in hypothesis II. We develop the argument that the effects of *returns to multipartism* on land politics have been mediated by variations in land tenure regimes. Examination of five cases shows how the statist land tenure regimes create institutional mechanisms and political alignments that can channel land conflict into national electoral contests. Earlier chapters lay out contrasting cases and explore counterfactual scenarios that bolster support for the argument.

PART II

ETHNICITY

Property Institutions and Ethnic Cleavage

> Ethnic labels "code people according to their relation to property."
> (Ojalammi 2006, 1)

There is an image of rural Africa as settled by small, culturally homogeneous communities, but for much of the continent, it is a misconception. As Berman et al. note in *Ethnicity and Democracy in Africa*, ethnically homogenous localities and regions are "increasingly hard to find" (2004, 12–13). In-migration is a pervasive dynamic across land-abundant, labor-scarce parts of rural Africa, and in certain regions and districts, this has been the case for much of the past century. The chapters in Part II of this book show that within jurisdictions of heavy in-migration, Africa's customary and statist land tenure institutions channel tensions around land scarcity into political form as *ethnic* cleavages, claims, and conflict. And as land regimes vary, so, too, do the character and structure of ethnic conflict over land.

Under the so-called customary land regimes, in-migration and settlement in ethnic jurisdictions that have been defined by the state has often been organized through "landlord-stranger" relationships. The newcomers are defined as strangers or outsiders. They assume the subordinate status of clients, tenants, sharecroppers, or guests of the customary landholders. Yet as Cotula, Toulmin, and Hesse (2004, 22) write, "landlord-stranger relations are breaking down in much of Africa" under the pressures of the current era. A widespread source of pressure on these relationships is population pressure on the land. As competition for land intensifies, "a common response is to restrict outsiders' access to those resources."[1] The Senegal River Valley, where ethnic strangers have been gradually marginalized over time, provides a case in point: "An immediate upshot of the growing scarcity of land is that stranger farmers

---

[1] Platteau 2002, 8–9.

are being increasingly denied their rights of access to land, especially to plots of relatively high quality.... Similar events have occurred in many places in sub-Saharan Africa, and violent conflicts have resulted in not a few cases" (Platteau, 2002, 8). Ethnic strangers are not always the losers, however. Under statist land tenure regimes (LTRs), local power configurations are inverted.[2] In southwestern Côte d'Ivoire, for example, the Houphouet regime (1957–1993) systematically favored the ethnic strangers and protected them against the challenges of indigenes (or autochthones).[3] There has been "massive [and] particularly effective administrative protection of in-migrants to the [Ivoirian] coffee and cocoa zone."[4]

This contrast captures the two different patterns of land-related conflict that are the focus of Part II of this study.[5] In one, ethnic insiders retain the upper hand. Land conflict finds political expression in "silent violence" against politically subordinate ethnic outsiders, who experience localized dispossession or exclusion from land access. The ripple effects of these exclusions are confined to the local level. In the other pattern, the relations are inverted. A state-backed outsider or stranger group has the upper hand: ethnic insiders harbor resentment against the stranger community, as well as against the government that favors and protects the outsiders. Land conflict finds expression in highly politicized ethnic claims that scale up because they are targeted at the central state.

In analyses of ethnic conflict in another setting (urban ethnic riots in India), both Varshney (2002) and Wilkinson (2004) suggest that spatial variation in the character and political trajectory of interethnic tensions is a clue to their causal dynamics. This turns out to be true for rural Africa as well. Geographic unevenness in the form and structure of ethnic tensions in rural Africa directs our attention to local-level political variables that vary across space, and especially to the institutional arrangements that structure the distribution of political and economic rights.

---

[2] This argument holds for statist LTR wherein ethnic insiders claim land on the basis of firstcomer rights. Under some statist LTRs, no farmers claim firstcomer rights over other farmers. This is often the case where pastoralists have been displaced to make way for peasant settler groups. See for example the Tanzania cases in the Appendix.

[3] Indigene, autochthone, ethnic insider, and son-of-the-soil are used here as synonyms, although in some texts and settings, there are significant differences in meaning. Autochthony is the most primordial idea of group connection to the land.

[4] Chauveau 2000, 105.

[5] This analytic framework thus stands in contrast to earlier treatments of African land tenure regimes that emphasize fundamental *similarities* across these derived rights regimes (for example, Lavigne-Delville et al. (2002) take southwestern Côte d'Ivoire and western Burkina Faso as essentially the same). Here, we argue that the locus of authority over land allocation – which is tipped either in favor of the state or in favor of local authorities such as chiefs or lineage heads – constitutes a critical difference in the political character of landlord-stranger relations and in the political expression of the land tensions that run along the landlord-stranger divide. This distinction is highlighted in Fearon and Laitin 2011.

Our argument is that Africa's land tenure regimes cleave rural society along the lines of state-recognized ethnic identities, ensuring the political and economic salience of these ascriptive status markers by imposing differential rules of land access, landholding, and land adjudication on ethnic insiders on the one hand, and ethnic outsiders on the other. The LTRs also create political hierarchy between these two groups, defining who is likely to lose land rights under conditions of growing scarcity. And they structure the political options open to those who are threatened with loss or erosion of their land rights. Evidence in support of these claims is found in the empirical record: different land tenure regimes produce strikingly different patterns (forms) of land-related ethnic politics. The so-called customary regimes create and impose a political hierarchy between landlord and stranger groups that is almost completely inverted in the regions of statist (state-administered) land tenure.

HOW LAND REGIMES PRODUCE ETHNICITY

Neocustomary land tenure regimes – defined as land regimes that institutionalize state-recognized customary authority over land and the primacy of nativist claims to land – produce and sustain ethnicity.[6] Their land allocation and adjudication rules ensure that ethnic identity is a valuable asset: it provides an entitlement to claim land in one's ethnic homeland. In localities with high in-migration and land scarcity, the customary land tenure rules make the difference between ethnic insiders and ethnic outsiders a highly salient – often the *most* salient – socioeconomic and political cleavage in agrarian communities. As Robert Bates argued for the case of Kenya in the 1960s (1989, 47), the prevailing arrangements ensured that economic interest in land assumed political form in the guise of ethnic claims. Under these rules, ethnic identity is valorized and enforced through everyday landholding rules and practices, working to ensure that these ascriptive distinctions do not fade away. Although some might have expected that rising land values would fuel the melting-pot effect anticipated by modernization theory, the customary land tenure regimes have actually worked to produce the opposite effect. The value of ethnic indigeneity increases over time as land in one's ethnic homeland grows scarce (Geschiere and Gugler 1998).

---

[6] I will not argue that land relations and claims are the sole constitutive force in generating politically salient ethnicity. Rather, I stress the fact that *assigning users* to particular (state-recognized) ethnic categories is a requirement for the functioning of the neocustomary land tenure regimes. (I recognize that there are fine gradations of ethnic identity – a subclan identity, for example – that are not state recognized but that can be significant in the workings of the land regime.) My point in these chapters is not to argue that land competition "activates" ethnic identity, although I recognize that this can happen. I am stressing the ethnicity-producing and -reproducing effects of the LTRs.

The neocustomary or quasi-customary land tenure regimes assign land-access and land-use rights to *classes of users* on the basis of their *ethnic status*.[7] The customary tenurial and tax regimes rest on a basic distinction between two categories of land users: "natives" and "nonnatives" of a given ethnic homeland. As Stephano Boni (2005, 82) explains in the case of western Ghana, classifying each farmer's ethnic membership is necessary for the implementation of the tenurial and taxation regime. Recognized membership in an ethnic group is a requirement of all individuals wishing to obtain or defend a land right on the basis of *birthright*. In this sense, ethnic identity functions as a political and legal status that determines the terms under which a person may gain access to property. Governments themselves enforce and reproduce these status designations by recognizing and upholding the customary land tenure regimes that enshrine the primacy of indigeneity-based land claims within state-designated ethnic homelands. In-migrants to these jurisdictions are often referred to in official parlance as strangers, acceptees, *allogènes, alloctones*, newcomers, guests or tenants of local "hosts," or, in the jarring Nigerian variant, "internal foreigners" (Kraxberger 2005). Paul Blanc (1962, 122) was thus correct when he wrote in the early independence years that in Côte d'Ivoire, respecting the national slogan "We are all Ivoiriens" would have required radical changes in the national land tenure regime. It would have required an ethnicity-blind system of control over land, which the country, to this day, does not follow.

The basic political character of sub-Saharan Africa's statist land tenure regimes lies in their rejection (or nonrecognition) of these principles. In supplanting land claims based on indigeneity, the statist land tenure regimes promote the coalescing of group identities along the lines of a native-settler distinction, and the crystallization of nativist ethnic identities rooted in a sense of political and economic "marginalization with regard to land" (Médard 1996). Land tenure relationships defined by, and institutionalized in, the statist land regimes are the foundation of (1) indigenes' shared position vis-à-vis the settlers or "ethnic outsiders" and (2) their shared position as holders of land grievances against the state. As under the neocustomary regimes, under the statist regimes, land tenure rules are *the point of reference* in the development and polarization of ethnic status. Without the implication of the land questions, we cannot explain why one particular ethnic distinction rather than another becomes the axis of both political hierarchy and economic competition, or why local society cleaves along a particular ethnic axis rather than fragmenting into a mosaic of identity groups.

HOW LAND REGIMES STRUCTURE ETHNIC POLITICS

Both neocustomary and statist land regimes create political hierarchy between indigenes and strangers, albeit in radically different forms. Under the

---

[7] They also assign such rights based on age, gender, lineage, and political status within the local political arena.

neocustomary regimes, *ethnic insiders* exercise political dominance. These LTRs establish local hierarchies in which ethnic outsiders are in a position of structural disadvantage. Outsiders' land rights are weaker than those of natives, and access is contingent on permission granted by a local political authority or member of the landowning community. Outsiders are thus in a weak position when it comes to defending acquired land rights under conditions of rising competition for land. Under the neocustomary regimes, where lineages and chiefs retain control over land allocation, land-related conflict that runs along ethnic lines tends to confirm local political hierarchy.[8]

Under the statist regimes, the political dominance of ethnic insiders is ignored, suppressed, or extinguished – in these places, *ethnic outsiders* are very likely to hold the upper hand as long as they are tied (via patron-client relations) to the patrons in the central state who granted them land rights.[9] These differences are at the root of the very different forms of ethnicized land conflict that emerge under these two different institutional arrangements.

What happens under conditions of rising competition for land? In chieftaincy- and lineage-centered land regimes, strangers are likely to be squeezed. They are likely to see their rights rolled back or to be expelled, and they have few if any avenues of recourse through the use of political voice. Ethnic insiders can use their politically privileged positions to reallocate land rights to themselves. By contrast, under most state-administered land regimes, the balance of power between indigenes and strangers is reversed. Where the central state is the allocator of land, it is highly likely that "ethnic strangers" are the ones who have received land rights from the state. As land competition intensifies, sitting governments are likely to defend the land allocations that they themselves have made. State authorities will usually protect outsiders who are their clients. In these situations, ethnic insiders (aka indigenes or autochthones) are likely to be the land-rights losers and to suffer state repression if they protest.[10]

Part II develops the argument that variations in the character and political denouement of ethnic tension are traceable to variation in land tenure regimes. Chapters 4 and 5 compare land politics in six regions of high in-migration,

---

[8] There are hybrid cases: Jos Plateau, Nigeria, is an example. In the rural areas of Jos region, who is the land-rights allocator? See Appendix.

[9] State-administered land regimes, which prevail in circumscribed jurisdictions within many national territories (but are still the exception rather than the rule), are imposed precisely to achieve the effect of expunging, displacing, or suppressing indigeneity-based claims to land. Such land tenure regimes have been established in some of sub-Saharan Africa's most extensively commercialized zones of smallholder agriculture.

[10] This is exactly the prediction that Fearon and Laitin (2011) make in a study of "sons-of-the-soil" conflicts in Asia. How the state is implicated (on whose side) goes far in determining the political dynamics and character of interethnic relations set in motion by rising economic competition between groups. Where the state backs the indigenous, conflict is likely to be local and muted, and in-migrants are likely to exit under pressure. Where the state backs in-migrants, the situation is more combustible: the state is set up for confrontation with indigenes. On the effects of regime change, see Part IV of this book.

allowing us to instantiate these claims and to juxtapose positive cases to cases that can serve as counterfactuals. Table II.1 summarizes the arguments. In all the cases, the land regimes delineate a hierarchy of user groups and code them by ethnic status. The land institutions themselves go far in explaining why land-related competition runs along group lines, why these are *ethnic* lines, and, thus, why they fuel the potential for ethnic conflict. The institutional set-ups go far in explaining why tensions born of rising land values or land scarcity are likely to find *political expression* as tensions between ethnic insiders and ethnic outsiders, rather than as tensions running along the lines of class (owners versus workers), access to capital (capital-poor owners versus investors), farm size, or wealth. And by structuring the local political arenas, land regimes structure losers' options and, thus, patterns and forms of ethnic conflict that may emerge as land grows scarce.[11] Table II.1 captures the argument that is the centerpiece of this analysis: that the neocustomary land regimes (the top half of the table) and the statist land regimes (lower half of the table) produce very different effects. Who is likely to lose land rights under conditions of rising competition for land? Which group is the national government likely to align with in local-level redistributive conflicts over land? What are losers' options? Answers differ systematically across the two sets of cases.

It is true that ethnic identity might "melt away" in urban settings if individuals were to sever their ties to the countryside and be absorbed into the melting pots of the metropolis, as it does in Jan Vansina's (1982) depiction of the struggles of urban life in 1960s Kinshasa in "Mwasi's Trials."[12] This could also happen in the American Wild West or parts of the Amazon Basin, where individuals and nuclear families carve out frontier settlements in the near absence of social hierarchy and the state. Such conditions, however, are rare in the farming areas of sub-Saharan Africa: the job of colonialism's state builders and mapmakers was to *eliminate* the "no-man's-lands" and "ungoverned spaces" that were devoid of state-recognized territorial authority. Across most of their domains, colonial rulers delimited and institutionalized chiefly jurisdictions (ethnic homelands), which were governed indirectly via the intermediation of the so-called customary authorities.[13] Most postcolonial states chose to invest in and reproduce these arrangements, which serve as mechanisms of social control that can defuse mass politics and cross-jurisdictional political mobilizations and, as long as things are going pretty well and rainfall is good, support the livelihoods of most of the rural population.

---

[11] We do not discuss forms of ethnicized conflict over land that can take place between jurisdictions, in disputed territory between jurisdictions, or in the empirically rare (in Africa) cases of conflict among farmers in "no-man's-land."

[12] Or, new ethnic identities with new material bases and politically salient meanings could emerge.

[13] Institution-building was most intensive and complete in farming regions.

TABLE II.I *Land Regimes and Ethnic Politics: Overview of Cases*

Case	Land Access Granted to...	With Rising Competition, are In-Migrants' Land Rights Lost or Eroded?	National Gov. Sides With:	Losers' Options
(Neo)Customary authorities allocate land to:				
Ghana: Ashanti, 1930s-1960s	Outsiders (sharecroppers or *abusan*)	Y	Ethnic insiders (landlords)	No voice
Western Ghana: Sefwi and Wassa Amenfi, 1950s–2000s	Outsiders: buyers and farm-sharers	Y	Ethnic insiders (landlords), with brief exceptions.	No voice except under brief periods of populist national leadership
W. Burkina, old cotton zone, 1960s–1990s	Strangers: in-migrants	Y	Ethnic insiders, autochthones (hosts)	No voice
Central state allocates land to:				
Côte d'Ivoire, SW and Gagnoa region, 1940s–1990	Strangers: tenants, (buyers?)	N	Strangers (*allogènes* and *étrangers*)	Voice meets with repression
Kenya Rift Valley farming districts, 1960–1990	Settlers, ethnic strangers	N	Strangers (former squatters and "black settlers")	Voice meets with repression
E. DRC, N. Kivu, 1950s–1990	Settlers from Rwanda	N	Strangers (*étrangers*)	Voice meets with repression

CONTRA RIVAL THEORIES OF ETHNIC IDENTITY AND POLITICS

This argument represents a challenge to ideationalunderstandings of ethnicity and ethnic politics that have come to prevail in much of political science. Many political scientists, having rejected primordialist theories of ethnic identity, have accepted the view that ethnic groupness (group identity), however arbitrarily it may have been constructed in the past, acquires a life of its own as an ideational force in the present.[14] By this reasoning, ethnic identities are so slow changing that they remain salient shapers of politics *even after* they have outlived the political calculations and needs that brought them into existence. Ethnic identity thus becomes an independent variable in a behavioralist's tool kit – it is a source of individual preferences or values. As Kalyvas explains (2006, 365), the group or groupness becomes epiphenomenal to individual motives. Posner (2004, 2005) argues that these individual motives or preferences may find political expression in ways that are shaped by elections and electoral rules, but he does not undertake to explain *why* ethnicity per se is salient in postcolonial politics, or more salient than class, religion, region, gender, or generation.

A view from the rural areas, home to 60 percent of sub-Saharan Africa's population, belies visions of ethnic identity as prepolitical, purely ideational, and nonmaterial, and supports a far more institutionalist read. Neocustomary land institutions exert a powerful *constitutive effect on ethnic group formation* by making membership in an ethnic group compulsory or "required" for those seeking access to land, or seeking to retain access to land, on the basis of birthright or inheritance. To claim a land entitlement, one cannot opt out of membership in a particular political collectivity – usually one recognized by the state (i.e., the ethnic group rooted in a rural jurisdiction). It follows from this that the value of ethnic membership or attachment may increase as the value of land rises or is pushed up by the perception of scarcity.

Africa's neocustomary land rights are thus an instance of what Mitnick (2006, 23) calls an ascriptive right, or an entitlement that is assigned on the basis of membership in an ascriptively defined group. Mitnick (2006, 23) argues that such rights have a striking constitutive effect on human identity, and this is one point we wish to emphasize here. The state-backed neocustomary land tenure regimes that organize access to land in most of rural sub-Saharan Africa lay out one set of rules of land access for ethnic insiders, and another for outsiders. These rules impose a land-rights and land-access hierarchy that, in the neocustomary jurisdictions, makes ethnic insiders the politically dominant group.

The ethnic identities, categories, and boundaries that we observe in rural political arenas are largely produced and reproduced in and through everyday practices of land control and administration. When land competition runs along ethnic lines, this is not the spontaneous effect of local actors' informal cognitive

---

[14] See the critique developed by Brubaker and Cooper 2000, 9, 12 inter alia. Some scholars want to escape the charge of essentialism while still embracing the methodological convenience of taking ethnicity as fixed and exogenous to politics. Chandra (2012) identifies this same problem, and proposes ways to transcend it.

maps of social affinities, trustworthiness, or preference affinities. Rather, the channeling of land competition along ethnic lines is, more than anything, *an institutional effect*. Ethnic politics can thus involve not only contestation over access to resources but also contestation over rules and institutions – that is, over the criteria by which access to productive resources and livelihoods will be assigned, and over who will decide.

To take ethnic identity as exogenous to politics in general – and to the rural property regime in particular – is to deny what is often at stake in ethnic politics in these settings.[15] It also denies what is eminently political about conflicts over land. Governments make these depoliticizing moves when they brand land-related conflicts as "tribal disputes," thus implying that group rivalries and rural grievances predate modern politics and have nothing to do with the modern state or political economy. This semantic maneuvering was on display in 2000–2002, when the Sudanese government depicted the violence in Darfur as the expression of "local tribal disputes."[16] Political science need not fall into the trap of defining ethnic identities as prepolitical. It is one thing to see like a state, and another to be misled by one.

[15] Chanock (1998, 236 inter alia) points this out. Gramsci (1971, 149) makes the same point when he suggests that political questions become insoluble when disguised as cultural ones (as cited by Harvey 2005, 39).

[16] Srinivasan 2006; see also Reno 2007.

CHAPTER 4

Ethnic Strangers as Second-Class Citizens

> In the Senegal River valley, the local Haalpulaar ("Toucouleur") communities have become concerned that land will not be available in sufficient amounts for their children and grandchildren. As a result, they have started closing access to the good inundable lands . . . located near the river for all strangers and immigrant farmers.
>
> (Platteau 2002, 8)

> No matter how long one has stayed in the area, a migrant is still a migrant.
>
> (A son-of-the-soil, western Ghana, July 2009)

The customary land tenure regimes (LTRs) assign differential property rights and citizenship statuses to ethnic insiders and ethnic outsiders. These arrangements *impose* an ethnic status on land users and confirm hierarchy between the two groups. Where customary authorities at the local level (chiefs or lineage leaders) control land allocation and adjudication, ethnic outsiders or in-migrants are in a position of socioeconomic and political subordination. This hierarchy goes far in defining who is likely to lose land rights as land access becomes more exclusive: the customary land tenure regimes focus growing pressure on strangers. Rising demographic, environmental, and commercial pressures tend to result in the withdrawal or scaling back of in-migrants' land access. Political rules encoded in the customary land regimes also go far in structuring the political options of those threatened with this form of exclusion. In most such situations, the local political arena offers migrants very few avenues of recourse or appeal, and only ad hoc channels of access to the national administration. The subjugating effect on in-migrants is visible not only in matters concerning land per se but also in issue areas and political dynamics that do not concern land.

Cases examined in this book show not only that this effect is visible across an array of cases but also that the effect of the LTR variable holds across cases that differ along other political and economic dimensions. Customary regimes' subjugating effect on ethnic outsiders is visible in former French colonies, where indirect rule was elaborated as a colonial administrative and ideological template later, and with less ideological zeal, than in British Africa. The effect is visible in democratic, well-governed states such as Ghana, as well as in violent and often-arbitrary dictatorships such as Cameroon today (examined in Chapter 7). It is present both in subsistence zones, such as the upper Senegal River Valley, and in zones of highly commercialized agricultural production, such as Ashanti, and in zones proximate to national centers as well as in more remote zones, such as western Ghana and western Burkina Faso. And in none of the cases of land politics under the so-called customary regimes examined here do national-level politicians seek to use land-related conflict to mobilize "ethnic outsiders" as a voting constituency.

Chapter 4 considers three cases that fit this pattern, making it possible to see the causal mechanisms that produce political effects. Two within-case counterexamples provide occasion to extend the argument and probe it using counterfactual reasoning. The first is spatial: in Comoé Province in western Burkina Faso, a more statist LTR prevails, offering a clear contrast to the customary land tenure regime in the old cotton zones of Banwa, Houet/Tui, and Boucle de Mouhoun Provinces, which are the main focus of our analysis. The in-country contrast is useful in underscoring variation in the land regime across jurisdictions within one national unit, and in considering some possible causes of regional variation in the government's rural institution-building strategies (although we do not attempt to account for that variation here).[1] A second counterexample is temporal: in western Ghana, the government's commitment to a chieftaincy-centered land regime has wavered over time, first under Nkrumah and then in the first years of the Rawlings regime. In both periods, however, Ghanaian government reverts to its central tendency: the role of government in shoring up the chieftaincy-centered land allocation system in this region in the post-Nkrumah years, and in the later Rawlings years, is clearly visible. The Ghana cases help counter the argument, advanced by Herbst (2000) for example, that the customary land tenure systems exist beyond the reach of the state, or in spite of it.

ETHNIC HIERARCHY IN WESTERN BURKINA FASO

> Land tenure issues increasingly become the sites of ethnic conflict. (Gray and Kevane 2001, 584).

Since the 1960s, western Burkina Faso has been a zone of high in-migration and extensive state efforts to promote the expansion of cotton production.[2]

---

[1] On this question, see the discussion of historical contexts in Chapter 2 and Boone (2003a).

[2] There was a wave of in-migrants in the early 1960s, and another major inflow from the central plateau during the Sahelian drought starting in 1972. On government investment in smallholder cotton production in this zone, see Gray and Kevane 2001, 575.

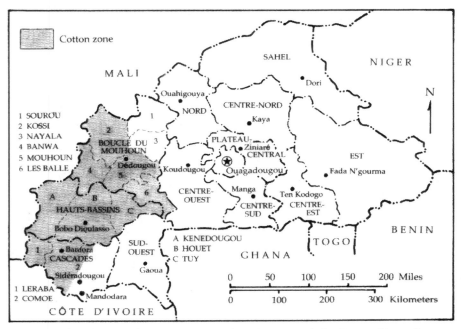

MAP I. Burkina Faso: Administrative Divisions (2001) and the Cotton Zone. *Sources:*
Hien in Kuba, Lentz, and Somda, eds., 2003; Paré 2001), drawn by John V. Cotter.

(See Map 1.) Today it is the most heavily populated part of the country.[3] As the
land frontier has closed and competition for land has increased in this region,
local tensions have escalated. The potential for land-related conflict is high,
and conflict is frequent and sometimes violent. In this part of Burkina Faso,
"land scarcity has indeed led to open conflict over land" (Gray and Kevane
2001, 583). The most visible land conflicts run along the fault line of ethnicity.

In-migrants settled in Banwa, Houet/Tui, and Mouhoun Provinces, the
established cotton-farming areas of western Burkina Faso, thirty or forty years
ago. The Bwa and the Bobo are considered to be autochthonous to this region.
Most of the in-migrants are Mossi, from Burkina Faso's densely populated
central plateau. The Mossi are the largest of the country's ethnic groups (about
40 percent of the national population), and the group that has historically been
very influential in national politics. In the areas that are the focus of this analysis, they can make up anywhere from less than half the residents of a locality
to 80 percent in some villages.[4]

---

[3] Paré 2001, 1. Population density is around forty to fifty people per square kilometer, rising to a
hundred in some places. See also Gray and Kevane 2001.

[4] The 80% figure is for Banwa village in Kouka Department (Banwa Province), a village of 10,000
people in 1998 (Paré 2001, 4).

In-migration and a doubling of the population growth rate in this region from 1975 to 1985[5] has closed the land frontier that existed a few decades ago. As Paré describes it, in many localities in Banwa, "there is no spare land left" (2001, 5). Zougouri and Mathieu write of "a crucial lack of available land" in their research site, a village of 5,000 persons in Houet Department, about 60 kilometers northwest of the regional capital, Bobo-Dioulasso (2006, 5).

As indigenous lineages find themselves in need of land that is farmed by in-migrants, they are forcing out many of the most vulnerable of the migrants who settled in these areas thirty or forty years ago.[6] Gray and Kevane (2001, 583) write that "in [the village of] Sara, Bwa farmers have expelled Mossi migrant farmers from an entire village area . . . us[ing] threats of violence. . . . In the end, . . . it was sorcery that convinced Mossi farmers to abandon their fields. . . . In several neighboring villages, land conflicts resulted in violence and murder."[7] Lavigne-Delville and Toulmin (2002, 108) explain that in the established cotton-farming region of western Burkina Faso, such practices are now commonplace: "the process of withdrawing land from migrant farmers has become so widespread, it seems futile to attempt to halt it."

Political Structure under a Neocustomary Land Regime

This is a classic example of a landlord-stranger land tenure regime in which land access is structured along the lines of an ethnic hierarchy that institutionalizes the primacy of ethnic insiders. In-migrants to the established cotton-producing region have neither statutory nor customary rights to land. They are basically "land borrowers" in informal, open-ended relationships with landowning families.

In the period of land abundance in the 1960s and 1970s, indigenous families found it advantageous to lend land to migrants. The presence of migrants helped domesticate wild land, expand village size and agricultural output (and thus importance in the eyes of the state), and increase the size and status of lineages and their clientele,[8] and until 1986, migrants paid head taxes directly to the administrative chiefs. Migrants owed ritual payments (usually in kind) to

---

[5] Gray and Kevane 2001, 575.

[6] Gray and Kevane (2001, 583) write that poorer, land-short, and younger farmers "used political discourse (infused with the language of ethnicity)" to halt strangers' attempts to strengthen their rights to the land.

[7] Paré (2001, 1–2) writes that now there is "demographic pressure and land scarcity in this region, to such an extent that cohabitation between indigenous and migrant communities . . . has become fraught with difficulty, disrupting social relations and putting a brake on agricultural growth."

[8] In the colonial period, chiefs extracted labor and taxes from those within their territorial jurisdictions, both indigenes and in-migrants. This gave them strong incentives to extend the territorial limits of chieftaincies to firmly encompass the migrant communities in hinterland areas and to starkly define chieftaincy boundaries (Lentz 2003, 125). Chiefs collected head taxes from indigenes and migrants until this imposition was abolished by Sankara in 1986 (Harsch 2009, 267).

"hosts" in exchange for land access, and they assumed a variety of social obligations to host families and communities, including the obligation to be present
at, and contribute to, weddings and funerals, offer services to the "patron"
family when called on (including occasional labor services), and express deference to the hosts (Paré 2001). Zougouri and Mathieu (2006, 7) explain that
autochthonous landholders see land used by migrants as "reserve land" that
they could legitimately reclaim under a wide variety of conditions, including
when the landholding family deems that it needs the land, when land tilled by
a migrant falls into disuse or is not properly maintained, when migrants do not
honor social obligations to the patron or the host community, or in the case of
quarrels (including quarrels among women and children) or other disruptions
of local harmony.

Migrants in western Burkina Faso cultivated their farms over three or four
decades, often over two generations. Gray and Kevane write that many migrant
farmers in Houet/Tui Province had farms of six hectares in the mid-1990s, often
about half of which was planted in wheat and cotton, and that most farmers
used animal traction and owned cattle.[9] By all appearances, they believed that
the longer they farmed a single tract continuously, the more secure their land
claims would become, as would have been the case in most savannah-region
societies in precolonial times, when political identities were more fluid and
assimilation into local communities was easier. Those with resources to invest
employed land-use strategies aimed at making their farms less vulnerable to
withdrawal by the local hosts or patrons.[10] These included tree-crop planting,
investing in manuring rather than allowing the land to lie in fallow, and other
forms of agricultural intensification.

The drama of recent decades is the undoing of these landlord-stranger relationships, a process that has entailed the apparent reversal of incremental
changes that seemed to be leading to greater security and autonomy (vis-à-vis
patrons or *tuteurs*) for the in-migrants. This is a process of redistribution of
property rights that is happening *within* village jurisdictions, on the basis of a
principle of autochthony. It is led by indigenous families who exert their will
through threats, pressures, and sometimes even acts of violence, which remain
low on the political and administrative radar screen and are usually politically
"silent." Political tension seems decentralized, tamped down to the village level,
and lacking organized expression. Prefects try their best to keep things this way.

Although migrants sometimes appeal to the departmental-level administrative authorities for redress, the prefects try to maintain their distance.
They "intervene only lightly in the tenure terrain... [and have] little desire
to enforce outcomes. [The state] is very hesitant to use its power in settling

---

[9] Gray and Kevane 2001, 577. Household size in Banwa, Kouka Department, runs from eight to
    fourteen people or more (Paré 2001, 4).
[10] See Mathieu, Lavigne-Delville, et al. 2003, 5–10. See also Gray and Kevane 2001, who focus
    on tree planting and agricultural intensification as strategies aimed at securing migrants' claims
    over the land. On assimilation in the precolonial period, see Lentz 2003, 123, 131.

land disputes."[11] Kevane and Gray write that the main strategy of the state agents was to try to avoid violence by discouraging land takings that happen "without warning." Most migrants who are victims of land withdrawals "don't do anything [to resist]."[12] A pattern of social and political deference to the local landlords, or *tuteurs*, was captured in Paré's observation that "migrants have difficulty expressing themselves in front of their indigenous 'patrons'" (Paré 2001, 3).

Colonial Origins of Ethnic Territories and Land Hierarchies

The ethnic hierarchies built into the customary land tenure regimes of western Burkina Faso are not cultural artifacts external to the state. They do not exist in spite of the state. Kuba and Lentz (2003) stress that although Burkina Faso's ethnic categories were not invented out of whole cloth by French colonial state builders, they were institutionalized as markers of political status, containerized in fixed territorial jurisdictions, and politicized by colonial authorities. A land-access hierarchy was carved into the national map and administrative grid by French colonial authorities, who delimited chiefly cantons as ethnic territories or homelands. Within these ethnic homelands, land was ruled to be held as the communal patrimony of the ethnic group deemed to be autochthonous to the (new) jurisdiction. In the so-called acephalous societies of western Upper Volta, "the village," including its hinterland of farmland, bushland, and forest, was defined as the basic territorial, political, and administrative political unit. It was viewed as a natural community based on descent, constituted by lineage hierarchies, and represented by an administrative chief appointed by the French. Within village territories, land chiefs allocated land domains to the leaders of the autochthonous lineages or clans.

In the village territories of western Burkina Faso, these lineages and sublineages now exercise the power to allocate and reallocate land. Cantonal chieftaincy as an institution was always contested in western Burkina Faso, and this institution was suppressed throughout the national territory by Thomas Sankara in 1984, at the start of his three-year tenure as head of state.[13] However, the outlines of the ethnic territories delimited by the cantons – and

---

[11] Gray and Kevane 2001, 584. See examples of intervention by *préfets* in Paré 2001, 18; Jacob 2002, 12. Paré and others write that the role of local government is growing, however. This reflects growing land pressure, the rising frequency and temperature of land-related conflict, and the increasing resort to "new transactions" that involve straight cash transfers or "new actors," such as urban professionals or bureaucrats who are interested in obtaining land in exchange for cash. Gray and Kevane (2001, 585) also observe that state agents were increasingly obliged to respond to local conflicts and threats of violence but argued that they did so on an ad hoc, case-by-case basis so that their positions could shift "as local power balances fluctuate."

[12] Zougouri and Mathieu 2006, 5.

[13] See Somé 2003, 241. Sankara also abolished the head tax that the administrative chiefs had continued to collect (from both migrants and autochthones) in the postcolonial period (Harsch 2009, 267).

viewed almost as land concessions by the colonial state – have been kept alive in the boundaries of postcolonial *départements*. So it is that in Karaborola (Comoé Province), for example, "Karaboro farmers claim [land] rights as firstcomers, as well as those granted through the colonial legacy (Karaborola *canton*)" (Hagberg 2003, 128).

Within the ethnic homelands, land tenure has remained under the control of the autochthonous land chiefs, lineage heads, and sublineage heads despite the 1984 Réorganisation Agraire et Foncière (RAF), which formally abolished traditional land relationships and declared that the land belongs to the user. The RAF, modified in 1991 and 1996, is not applied by local prefects, who are the highest-ranking administrators of the departments.[14] Paré writes that "real power over land is held by the main indigenous lineages and increasingly, by lineage segments and families.... Traditional [land] management systems remain omnipresent" (2001, 4, 23; see also 16, 17).

Land tenure institutions are foundational elements of local political order in the old farming zones of western Burkina Faso, where in-migrants and autochthones "differ sharply in terms of [land] tenure status,"[15] with in-migrants occupying positions of clear political and social subordination to autochthones. Administrative chiefs, land chiefs, and heads of indigenous lineages dominate the local political arena, with power and influence that is not confined to land affairs. These leaders are often recognized by the postcolonial state as the wielders of "*droits modernes 'administratifs'*" (modern administrative prerogatives) at the local level.[16]

Beyond Land Politics

The customary land tenure regime in the old cotton zone of western Burkina Faso imposes social subordination, economic vulnerability, and the norm of deference toward indigenous hosts on the ethnic strangers who have in-migrated over the past thirty to forty years. This hierarchy is also visible in patterns of political representation, political recognition, and access to local office. Carola Lentz (2003) observes that in the post-1990 years in Sisala, a province in center-west Burkina Faso (on the border with Ghana), political posts in local government and elected positions at the national level have all been occupied by members of the ethnic groups claiming to be indigenous to the area (or more precisely, to have "arrived first"). Mossi and Dagara in-migrants seem to have "voluntarily renounced" these positions. The element of coercion that is inherent in the property relationship contributes to the reproduction of this political order. Lentz (2003, 129) notes that "in a few cases, the land chiefs and chiefly families have made it known in unambiguous terms that any

---

[14] See Hagberg 2003, 128, 137 n. 187; Lentz 2003, 130; Gray and Kevane 2001, 584; Mathieu, Lavigne-Delville, et al. 2003, 25, 29.
[15] Gray and Kevane 2001, 579–580.
[16] Jacob (2002, 8), writing of Boromo, capital of Balé Province, in Région de Boucle du Mouhoun.

initiative on the part of migrants that was aimed at obtaining any of these [local government or elected, national-level] posts would put migrants' access to land at risk." J.-P. Jacob (2002) recounted a similar episode involving a Mossi hamlet that was established under the authority of local *tuteurs*, or hosts, whose seat of power was the administrative village of Boromo. ("Hamlet" is an official term designating a settlement not recognized by the government as an administrative unit.) When the Mossi tried to achieve political autonomy from their indigenous *tuteurs* by gaining official recognition from the government as a *village administratif*, the *tuteurs* threatened to expel them from their land. The prefect disengaged from the situation, "allowing a form of 'customary administration' to prevail" (Jacob 2002, 12).

The indigene-migrant line of tension in western, southwestern, and center-west Burkina Faso does not seem to find expression in the national electoral arena. In the 2005 presidential elections, at a time when land-related conflict cut deep along the indigene-stranger cleavage, no opposition candidate gathered more than 4.5 percent of the vote in the western or southwestern provinces (or in any other province).[17] Today's ruling party, the Congrès pour la Démocratie et le Progrès (CDP) of Blaise Compraoré, commands a powerful Ministry of Territorial Administration and Decentralization and is viewed as being strongly and squarely aligned with "traditional chiefs," who function as "the vote brokers [*grands électeurs*] who guarantee his election to office" (Somé 2003, 242). Burkina Faso's tradition of civil mobilization and protest is largely confined to Ouagadougou and the regional capitals.[18] Magloire Somé (2003) sees this as a legacy of the overthrow of Sankara, who stood for peasants and the "land to the tiller" principle and against traditional authority.

This means that the tensions between ethnic insiders and ethnic outsiders in the established western cotton zone, acute as they are, do not find expression in the formal institutions of political representation at the national level, including in party politics. (Re)distributive struggles over land are bottled up at the local level. The central state seems intent on confirming the land-control powers of local, autochthonous lineages and relying on local power structures that uphold "indigenous primacy."[19]

A Counterexample

A counterexample provides support for the argument that links institutional cause to political effect in the old cotton zone of western Burkina Faso. In the

---

[17] Harsch (2009, 276–277) notes that claims related to ethnicity or "indigenous primacy" did show up in some inter- and intraparty conflicts in 2001 and 2007, most evidently in fighting among ruling-party factions in Bobo-Dioulasso, the capital of "le Grand Ouest."

[18] On votes in the 2005 elections, see africanelections.tripod.com/bf_detail.html#2005_Presidential_Election (accessed 23 February 2010). On the Ministry of Territorial Administration, see Santiso and Loada 2003, 412. On chiefs, see Kirwin 2009, 23; Harsch 2009. On urban protest, see Hagberg 2002, Harsch 2009.

[19] This term is used by Harsch 2009.

newer zones of in-migration in Comoé Province (in Sidéradougou and Man-godara Départements, south of Bobo-Dioulasso), murderous conflicts between farmers and herders broke out in 1986 and 1995, provoking the high-profile intervention of politicians and the national army to quell violence and man-age its aftermath.[20] In Sidéradougou and Mangodara, land-related conflict met with direct, translocal, and high-profile government intervention to impose a solution that accommodated the needs of the agropastoralists, who are in-migrants and considered to be ethnic outsiders in these jurisdictions. This is the opposite of the form of land conflict observed in the old cotton zones of the western region, where conflict is low-intensity and local, state agents try to remain aloof, and ethnic insiders predominate.

These differences are registers or correlates of the statist character of land management in Sidéradougou. This is a pioneer zone that was opened up to migrants in the early 1980s. A Sidéradougou Agro-Pastoral Manage-ment Scheme was delimited in 1979, precisely to encourage and manage in-migration. Hagberg (2003, 128) describes this zone as one of the few in which the RAF was actually implemented.

A key difference between the cotton-zone conflicts discussed earlier and the Comoé conflicts is that the protagonists in the Comoé conflicts were mainly Fulbe (Peul) in-migrants who *carried out their agropastoral livelihoods on a supra- or translocal basis.* Their pasturelands and grazing spaces transcended the preexisting village administrative units of this zone. Competition between herders and farmers over pasture and access to watering sites fueled land-related tensions in this region. To create political infrastructure for governing the rural areas in Sidéradougou, where the preexisting (neo)customary tenure regime upheld the village territories of the longer-established Goin and Sénoufo agriculturalists, the national government created new institutions. First, it encouraged the agropastoralists to *organize politically on a supralocal level* into an Association de Chasseurs et d'Eleveurs, and a Syndicat d'Eleveurs de Bobo-Dioulasso, which were recognized by the state as corporate bodies. Sec-ond, the government implemented the RAF, which went far in circumscribing and eroding village-level land authority and inserting state authority directly into local land-use politics. The fact that the central state (via the national army) intervened directly to suppress conflict is a register of the difference between the form of land conflict in Comoé Province, on the one hand, and the form of land conflict in the old cotton zone, on the other. It is consistent with our theoretical expectations about the how statist land tenure regimes shape the character of the central government's implication in land-related conflict.

---

[20] This section is based on the work of Hagberg (1998, 2003), who analyzed these episodes in Sidéradougou Department and Mangodara Department in Comoé Province. He contrasts the character and structure of politics in these jurisdictions with politics in neighboring Karaboro, where a (neo)customary land regime is in place (2003, 128).

Conclusion

Neocustomary land tenure regimes similar to those prevailing in the old farming zone of western Burkina Faso structure similar patterns of ethnic hierarchy and ethnic relations in many parts of West Africa. In these situations, demographic pressure and land scarcity often produce resource competition that runs along ethnic lines and often leads to the gradual or abrupt exclusion of ethnic outsiders. However, under the neocustomary land regimes, such landlord-stranger conflicts rarely develop into conflict in which the government is implicated directly, as party or even mediator. Ethnic strangers are second-class citizens, and they can pay the price of their subordinate status through the loss of access to land they may have been farming for decades. The threat of revocation of land access by local authorities and landlords – or even expulsion – hangs like a sword of Damocles over their heads, working to enforce a political subordination to ethnic insiders that is visible in the patterns of associational life, voting patterns, and the circumscribing of ethnic strangers' political rights in the local political arena. In Burkina Faso, the central government under Blaise Compraoré has acted to reproduce and confirm the hierarchical structure of the local political arena by upholding the so-called customary land tenure regime for as long as it can, wherever it can, and by relying on those who wield authority over the land as its local agents.

EXPULSION OF ALIENS FROM GHANA'S COCOA REGION

> [In the 1969 election, there was some] threatening of share-croppers and cocoa laborers with dispossession or unemployment if they voted the wrong way. . . . The reality of the threat was indeed confirmed by the explanation given by an N.A.L.[21] organizer of the small forest wards in which this did prove successful: that the main landholdings in the area were under the control of strong party supporters. (Dunn, 1975, 188)

The vulnerability and subordination of "strangers" under a chieftaincy- and lineage-centered land regime were clearly visible in Ashanti Region of Ghana at the end of the 1960s. Ashanti Region was the home of some of the most elaborate structures of indirect rule in all of colonial Africa. It became a zone of in-migration in the 1920s and 1930s, when land was abundant and cocoa production expanded northward. In this era, Asante chiefs and subchiefs exercised wide-ranging, state-sanctioned prerogative to allocate access to "unused" land within their territorial jurisdictions to strangers. Strangers entered into sharecropping contracts (*abusa* contracts) and turned over tribute to chiefs, and a

---

[21] National Alliance of Liberals was Gbedemah's party; Dunn (1975, 169) describes it as an uneasy reincarnation of Nkrumah's Convention People's Party (CPP).

share of their proceeds to landlords.[22] In-migrants also worked as laborers on large chiefly estates carved out of the landed domains ("stool lands") that the chiefs were supposed to hold in communal trust.[23] Asante lineage heads with large tracts did the same. One source reported that in the 1960 census, in Ashanti Region about one-fifth of all farmers and two-fifths of all workers were non-Akans.[24] Many sharecroppers and laborers in the cocoa sector were from the savannah and Sahelian regions to the north, including northern Ghana.[25] (Map 2.)

By the 1950s and early 1960s, multiple lines of land-related tension were evident within Asante society. As poorer families and youth found themselves facing land pressure, tension emerged between chiefly authorities and these subordinate members of Asante society over sharecropping and the allocation of land for subsistence farming to migrant cocoa farmers and laborers. Share-cropping and wage contracts with outsiders allowed chiefly authorities and wealthy lineage heads to profit from landlord-stranger relationships, but as land became scarcer, many perceived that these deals came at the expense of Asante youth and families who needed access to land.[26] Social tensions over land access thus ran along indigene-stranger lines, class-like lines (sometimes visible along the chief-commoner divide), and intergenerational lines.

These tensions were evident in the intense electoral mobilizations of the nationalist era (Allman 1993, Beckman 1976). In their battles with Kwame Nkrumah's Convention People's Party (CPP), Asante elites were able to exploit their client relations with stranger groups for political ends in order to magnify their own political and economic power.[27] As Mikell (1989b, 181) explains in the case of Ahafo, strangers "could usually play no role in the political process [but] their interests were carefully bound up with those of the chiefs from whom

---

[22] Berry 1993, 111–113; Berry 2001, 154. The share paid to those controlling the land was normally one-third from 1920 to 1940 and one-half after the Second World War, as land became less abundant (Amanor 1994, 45).

[23] On the long-standing tension between stool land and a chief's private land, see Austin 2005, 351–353, 533 n. 94. He says that after the 1940s, it became more accepted that the chiefs themselves were owners of farms.

[24] Schildkrout 1979, 186–187. Addo (1970, 22) writes that 65.6% of the cocoa farmers' workers were aliens (by the 1960 census). Regarding the weight of immigrants in the cocoa sector, Addo (1969, 29) (from the Ghana Census) reports that about 18% of all cocoa *farmers* and 40% of all farm *laborers* were immigrants.

[25] See Amanor 1994, 44–45; Mikell 1989b, 159; Addo 1970.

[26] There was land scarcity in Ashanti in the late 1930s (Austin 2005, 398, 442–445). As Austin explains, the availability of fresh land to the West (Sefwi Wiawso) and northwest (Ahafo) meant that people could always out-migrate to create a farm somewhere else. Even debtors who lost their farms in Ashanti in the mid-1940s could move westward and start over. Out-migration surely defused land-related conflict in Ashanti itself. Austin also notes (2005, 446) a long transition since the 1950s toward more intensive forms of agriculture in the western districts, "reflect[ing] the progressive exhaustion of the forest rent."

[27] See Mikell 1989b, 173–174. She notes that the CPP "proceeded to banish or exile many of the more critical Hausa, Mossi, and Yoruba leaders who opposed the CPP."

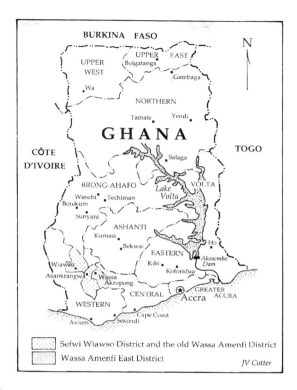

MAP 2. Ghana

they had acquired land." The CPP, for its part, launched "an assault against strangers" (Mikell 1989b, 174). It also exploited divisions within Asante society by pitching its progressive and populist appeals to Asante youth and commoners.

In 1969, in an economic climate of inflation, unemployment, and food shortages, there was a massive expulsion of "aliens" without residence permits from Ghana. Many thousands of cocoa sector farmers, including many on *abusa* sharecropping contracts, were forced off the farms and out of the country.[28] The expulsions happened in the wake of the Busia government's Alien Compliance Order of December 1969, but they cannot be attributed solely to it. The 1970 order targeted non-Ghanaians in urban retail business and the informal

---

[28] The November 1969 order was a Compliance Order, calling for enforcement of the Nkrumah administration's Aliens Acts of 1963 and 1965. Ghana's 1966–1969 National Liberation Council had also declared that aliens "in retail and other minor trades would be asked to leave the country to allow the indigenous people to take over" ("Aliens and Trade," *Ashanti Pioneer*, 13 November 1969). The anti-alien measures came at a time of falling cocoa prices and "a sudden increase in unemployment in 1965" (Addo 1970, 25, 37). See Beckman 1976, 218–222, on the catastrophic crisis in the cocoa economy.

sector, where large numbers were engaged in petty trade.[29] Foreigners working on cocoa farms were explicitly exempted from its mandate.[30] Yet in the weeks and months that followed the Compliance Order, there was a large-scale exodus of non-indigenous workers and sharecroppers from the cocoa sector. The expulsions "crippl[ed] the cocoa economy by depriving it of labor,"[31] bringing about what Lavigne-Delville et al. describe as "a massive shift in land and labor relations in the cocoa sector."[32]

This exclusion of stranger farmers and laborers appears to have been the result of opportunistic actions taken by local notables, village-level chiefs, local families, and youth in many localities of southern Ghana, including the cocoa regions of western Ashanti and Ahafo, who seized the occasion of the Compliance Order to push sharecroppers and laborers off the cocoa farms. Some local chiefs may have seized the chance to take back stool lands that were farmed by strangers, some of whom had grown prosperous and perhaps less dependent on, or deferent to, local authorities.[33] It appears that in some cases, the anti-foreign agitation itself provoked the strangers' departure. In other cases, the outsiders may have fled as the result of the "molestation of farm laborers [by] people who wanted to take over their food farms, since very little food was grown by the local population in mature cocoa areas."[34] The *Ashanti Pioneer* ran reports of such incidents, including Ministry of Interior warnings against "molesting farm laborers in the rural areas."[35] Adomako-Sarfoh (1974, 152) reports that two years later, when a new military government proposed to review policy to encourage a new inflow of migrants to the cocoa sector, "many youth demonstrated against the return of the aliens."

This case is important for present purposes for what did not happen. The *Ashanti Pioneer* does not mention public mobilizations of any kind, lawsuits against land-controlling authorities, or organized violence in the rural areas of Ashanti or neighboring Brong-Ahafo or Western Regions in late 1969 or early

---

[29] The main targets of the order were urban-based Nigerians, Syrians, "Gaos," and Sierra Leoneans.

[30] On this exemption, see Peil 1971, 226, see also 212–213 inter alia; Adomako-Sarfoh 1974, 139; Addo 1969, 36 n. 2; Beckman 1981, 153; and "Police Probe Alien Bribe Report," *Daily Graphic*, n. 6010, 28 January 1970.

[31] Mikell 1989b, 194.

[32] Lavigne-Delville et al. (2002, 82) report that "several hundred thousand sharecroppers and migrants were expelled." They seem to be counting both Ghanaians and non-Ghanaians expelled from the cocoa sectors. Peil (1971, 206, 208) reports that "over 100,000 aliens" were expelled. Adomako-Sarfoh (1974, 138) reports that by June 1970, 213,750 aliens ("mostly Mossi") had left Ghana. Many of these were not in the cocoa sector. It seems that the facts of this episode are not well known.

[33] See Beckman 1976, 157. Boni (2005, 113) reports that in Sefwi, the Omanhene took over property of non-Ghanaians who were forcibly repatriated.

[34] Peil 1971, 228. Such incidents were discussed in *Ashanti Pioneer*, "The Wanted Aliens," 29 January 1970.

[35] "Government Warns: Don't Molest Aliens," *Ashanti Pioneer*, 9 December 1969.

1970. There is no sign in the *Ashanti Pioneer* or in secondary accounts that the paramount chiefs of the region took a stand on the expulsion issue, or that the police or military were called on to enforce the order in the rural areas.[36] The Busia government, elected in 1969, had its electoral stronghold in the Ashanti and Brong-Ahafo Regions. While not at all hostile to chiefs, it catered to most Akan urban business and professional interests (which appear to have been in the lead as the intended beneficiaries of the Compliance Order).[37] Rural land and rural indigene-stranger questions do not seem to have figured into the 1969 campaign.

Departure of ethnic outsiders from Ghana's main cocoa region in 1969 and 1970 appears to have been a process that conforms to some of the general lines of our hypotheses. Economic pressure in the countryside – including land pressure, especially when it came to land for food crops – found expression along the lines of an indigene-stranger distinction that was carved into society by the land tenure regime. Land regimes in this region left ethnic outsiders with no recognized moral claim to landed property, even property that had been farmed by *abusa* sharecroppers for many years (or to houses or other improvements on the farms). Their subordinate and nearly rightless status was evident in the political arena: strangers lost their access to land and their investments, they were not protected in any way by government, and the expropriation of these people did not surface as an issue that was contested in public. There seem to have been no spokespersons to publicly defend the rights of the "outsiders," to attempt to organize them politically, or to mobilize better-protected groups on their behalf.

That some (perhaps many) of the land-access losers were surely Ghanaian nationals makes these silences even more pregnant with political meaning.[38] Busia's government order targeted "aliens," but this official, English-language term has a legalistic, justificatory connotation that may disguise what might well be classified, in other settings, as intercommunal or ethnic strife in the rural areas. A clear and stark distinction between non-Ghanaians and non-Akans probably did not exist in Ghana's cocoa-producing areas in 1969–1970. Although many of those expelled from the rural sector were surely seasonal laborers from neighboring countries, many were sharecroppers who had been

---

[36] There was much action by the police in Kumasi to quell looting and, later, to round up foreigners. See, for example, "Aliens Hunted Down," *Ashanti Pioneer*, 16 January 1970, and "More Aliens Rounded Up," *Ashanti Pioneer*, 20 January 1970. There were also raids to round up foreigners in Eastern Region in January 1970 (see *Ashanti Pioneer*, 1 and 2 January 1970).

[37] Mikell 1989b, 194; Mikell 1989a, 463; Nugent 1999, 289–290.

[38] Schildkrout (1979, 186–187) writes of "northern laborers" in terms that conflate the Ghanaians and non-Ghanaians among them. Addo (1970, 22) appears to deliberately conflate the terms "immigrants" and "immigrant tribes" when discussing the cocoa sector. See also Austin 2005, 420–424 and Berry 2001, 153. Abdul-Korah (2007, 77) reports that "Zachariah and Nair [1980] have estimated that of the in-migrants in the Brong-Ahafo Region in 1960, 40.9% were from northern Ghana" (emphasis added).

in Ghana for many years or decades, or were even born there. It is highly likely that some of those evicted from the cocoa farms, both laborers and share-croppers, were Ghanaian nationals from the north, given that northerners of diverse national origins (Ghana, Mali, Burkina Faso) were likely to share some distinctive northern ways (e.g., adherence to Islam) and be undocumented. One chilling *Ashanti Pioneer* report about the "alien hunt-down" in Kumasi underscored this ambiguity: "Policemen ... questioned any person whose external features resembled an alien about his real country of origin.... Anybody who could not produce his traveling document or permit was whisked away."[39]

An aspect of this case that is not anticipated in the analytic framework laid out in Chapter 3 is the public silence of the powerful Asante chiefs in the 1969–1970 alien expulsion episode.[40] Given their authoritative role in the neocustomary land tenure regime, why did the chiefs not publicly back the expulsions, or publicly condemn them? Perhaps the chiefs kept a low profile because the anti-outsider sentiments expressed populist tensions in agrarian society that could threaten their legitimacy and authority. The interests of large and prosperous landholders (many of them from the chiefly establishment) who engaged in-migrants as laborers and sharecroppers may have conflicted with the interests of the youth and land-poor who stood to gain from expulsion of the ethnic outsiders.[41] This suggests that there may have been a class-like dimension to these conflicts in the more densely populated areas of Ashanti. The public silence of the chiefly elite may mean that the larger landholders and agricultural employers decided to let the ethnic outsiders take the brunt of popular frustrations over poverty and inequality, rather than to enter the political arena openly in defense of the in-migrants who had contributed so much to the profitability of their cocoa plantations in the 1940s and 1950s. And chiefs at all levels of the Asante hierarchy may have viewed the expulsion of the ethnic outsiders as an opportunity to renew their authority over communal lands.[42]

[39] "Aliens Hunted Down," *Ashanti Pioneer*, 16 January 1970. The *Pioneer* also reported that the Nkrumah administration had explicitly exempted Burkinabè migrants from carrying traveling documents or work permits ("Let Them Go, But ...," *Ashanti Pioneer*, 28 November 1969). Burkina Faso was called Upper Volta at the time.

[40] With respect to Ashanti Region per se, this may also be partly because the dependence on in-migrants was declining by the mid-1960s, in contrast to the heavy dependence on migrant labor in western Ahafo by this time.

[41] Some Ghanaian farmers petitioned the Ministry of Agriculture, requesting that the government suspend the order in the case of cocoa laborers, "on the grounds that the year's cocoa crop would be destroyed without the assistance of the Northerners" (Schildkrout 1979, 186–187). On 21 January 1970, the *Pioneer* reported that "the Ghana National Farmers Union approached the Regional Chief Executive of Ashanti for the right to recommend alien farm laborers to be issued residence permits" ("Farmers' Union to seak [sic] right").

[42] See earlier episodes of chiefs' attempts to restrict cocoa planting (1937–1943) and the concern that cocoa crowded out food crop production (Austin 2005, 327–332, 349–350, 354). The

LAND TENSIONS IN WESTERN GHANA

The only option available for [migrant] farmers is submission.[43]

In western Ghana, as in the two cases discussed earlier, ethnic identity is not a self-designation that is voluntarily and opportunistically embraced or set aside. Rather, it is a political or legal status that can determine the terms under which one may or may not own property and what rights one has to speak and to be represented in the local political arena. In chieftaincy-centered land tenure regimes, classifying each farmer by ethnic status is necessary for the implementation of the local tenurial and taxation regime. These land regimes rest on a distinction between two basic categories of land users: citizens of the chieftaincy and strangers. The hierarchy so established leaves the outsiders in a position of structural disadvantage in defending acquired land rights (even property held under land title). In Ghana's Western Region, as in the other Chapter 4 cases, this disadvantage becomes more evident under conditions of rising competition for land.

Settlement and Cocoa History

Western Ghana is the country's newest cocoa frontier. (See Map 2.) As open forest land was exhausted in eastern Ghana and in Ashanti, and as the cocoa economy declined in those regions, waves of in-migrants from these regions pushed into Western Region, beginning in the 1950s. Logging companies cleared the way by laying roads and chopping down vast swaths of forest.[44] Cocoa output increased rapidly. By 1984–1985, the west was producing more cocoa than Ashanti Region. The new millennium saw large increases in cocoa output in the west. In 2003–2004, this region produced twice as much cocoa as Ashanti.[45]

Cocoa production came to Western Region when population densities were low, at a time when indigenous populations had little interest in export-crop production. Akan chieftaincies – first in Sefwi, where the largest of three Akan chiefdoms is Sefwi-Wiaso, and then to the south, in Wassa Amenfi paramountcy

expulsion of the aliens reaffirmed the stranger versus citizen distinction. It underscored the strangers' lack of secure claims and reaffirmed the local citizenship status of those who held customary, heritable, land-use rights.

[43] Interview in Twi by Dennis Duku with indigenous local community leader in his forties, July 2010, Wassa Amenfi East. Boone and Duku 2012.

[44] The expansion of cocoa production over more than a century has thus cut a counterclockwise path across the southern part of the country, starting in the original cocoa areas of the southeast, heading in a northwesterly direction into the Ashanti Region, continuing the northwesterly course into the Brong Ahafo Region, and then cutting southward into Western Region. This process has displayed some dramatic variations in land tenure regimes, relationships, and conflicts as the cocoa frontier has moved through space and time. See Hill 1963, Amanor 1994, Berry 1993, 2001, Austin 2005, and Boni 2005.

[45] For 1984–1985, see Addae-Mensah 1986, 48; for 2003–2004, see Teal, Zeitlin, Maamah 2006, 11.

and Juabeso-Bia District – allowed outsiders to purchase land-use rights to what were sometimes vast tracks of land.[46] Some in-migrants thus acquired possession of land in exchange for cash. Some entered into farm-sharing contracts[47] with chiefs and chiefly families with the understanding that land access so acquired would transform into a right akin to freehold title, which could be passed on to the in-migrant's heirs.[48] Landholdings of migrants were often surveyed by professional surveyors, and transactions were documented.[49] Properties so acquired were often subject to continuing payment of a land tribute to the office of the chieftaincy. Addae-Mensah (1986, 37) notes that "individual ownership of land by migrants is much higher in this region than in Ashanti," where outsiders gained access to land via sharecropping arrangements rather than through purchase.

By the 1970 census, 53 percent of the population of Wassa Amenfi was born outside the district. Studies from the 1990s reported that somewhere between one-third[50] and two-thirds[51] (by locale) of all farmers in this district were in-migrants, mostly from Ashanti Region or Eastern Region of Ghana. Many sources from the mid- to- late 1980s and early 1990s reported that *most* of the cocoa farms, and most of the larger farms, in Western Region were owned by non-indigenes.[52]

Rising Land Pressure

As commercial production spread in Western Region, indigenous farmers – commoners and subjects of the Sefwi and Wassa chiefs – also became cocoa

---

[46] Some early land contracts conveyed thousands of acres of land. Some purchases went to land-buying companies (groups of farmers who pooled their money) (Boni 2005, 92–93, 171–172). "Wasa" appears as an alternate spelling in some official and scholarly sources.

[47] In the 1950s, "these early contracts declared that once the chief's part [of the new farm – often one-third] was handed over, the tenant acquired exclusive bona fide property except for timber and mineral resources." Boundaries were "typically vague"; nonetheless, "it is most likely that often large tracts, on the order of some hundreds or even thousands of acres or, in local terminology, a few 'square miles,' were conveyed" (Boni 2005, 93). According to Addae-Mensah (1986, 35–36), 58% of the migrant farmers in Wassa held land under outright purchase.

[48] Boni 2005, 92. On farm-sharing contracts, see Takane 2002, 18–21, 100; Austin 2005, 423.

[49] Benneh 1988, 6; Alhassan and Manuh 2005; author's interviews with agents of the Customary Land Secretariat and farmers in Wassa Amenfi, 11–15 July 2009.

[50] Alhassan and Manuh (2005, 10) estimated the migrant population of Wassa Amenfi District as 40% of the total in 2000. About one-third of the population is made up of settler (in-migrant) farmers.

[51] Migot Adholla et al. write (1994, 106) that in Wassa, 33% of the farmers are indigenous and the rest are mostly Ashanti migrants. An early 1960s study reported that in the New Suhum area of Wassa, "98.6% of land was cultivated by migrant labor" (Amanor 1994, 46). Wassa Amenfi District had a population of 234,000 in 2000. The population of Western Region was 1.9 million (Alhassan and Manuh 2005, 11, 11 n. 15).

[52] Addae-Mensah 1986, 48; Migot-Adholla et al. 1994, 106. Benneh (1988, 6) notes that "Wassa citizens' farms are known to be smaller than those of the migrant farmers."

producers. They often found themselves in competition for land with in-migrants, who continued to buy parcels and larger tracts of land from chiefs who were willing to alienate communally owned land to outsiders in exchange for payment.[53] As land pressure increased in the west and as virgin forestland grew scarce, this region emerged as a hotbed of land conflict.[54] J. Addae-Mensah captured the locals' sense of indignation:

[My] Wassa-Amenfi study has shown that the youth who enjoy customary freehold or usufruct are finding it difficult to obtain land for farming on their communally-owned land due to the reckless alienation of interest to stranger settlers. [In] areas where sale of land for farming is rampant, most of the forest has been sold outright to wealthy strangers including aliens to cultivate. The indigenous citizens have been faced with shortage of farmland to grow their annual foodstuffs. The feeling of alienation is usually exhibited in the distribution of farmland which is titled in favor of the non-members of the land owning communities. Instances could be found where hungry farmers have illegally been encroaching upon reserved forest to grow foodstuffs. (1986, 37–38)

George Benneh (1988, 4) made the same observation: "Youth are becoming alarmingly aware of the rate at which they are losing land to strangers."

By the 1980s, chiefs were also feeling the pinch. Boni (2005, 109–110) explained that pressure on them came from two sides. On one side, chiefs suffered declining revenues. Revenues declined "because with the exhaustion of the forest, there were no longer interests to alienate, and because the chiefs failed to receive the expected revenues from the annual cocoa tribute." On the other side, chiefs were accused by their subjects of betraying their communities by selling off the communal patrimony of stool lands, which are supposed to be held in trust for members of the autochthonous community.[55]

Responses to Rising Competition for Land: Narrowing of Strangers' Land Rights

In response, the chiefs of Wassa Amenfi and Sefi-Wiawso have sought to reassert authority and control over land that they ceded to migrants in earlier decades.

---

[53] Boni 2005, 68–70, 85. He explains that chiefs often took an initial sum plus yearly agricultural tribute.

[54] Boni 2005, 2. Migot-Adholla et al. (1994, 104) wrote that "in Wassa, the heart of Western Region, land markets are [now] inactive because they are constrained by supply." Forty-five percent of farmers reported that it was impossible "obtain additional land for their children." They reported population density of 30 persons per square kilometer for the Wassa area around 1990, with median farm size in 1987 as 13.3 hectares (cocoa plus food crops, sometimes in several parcels). Alhassan and Manuh (2005, 10) wrote that "with increasing population and land scarcity, tenants and indigenes compete for scarce land. There are pronounced land use conflicts among tenants and indigenes." For Western Region as a whole, Addae-Mensah (1986, 42) gives the 1984 population density as 46 per square mile, representing a 131.4% increase over the 1970–1984 period. He reports the 1984 Brong-Ahafo average as 70 persons per square mile. This is yet another example in which the region or district with the most overt land-related conflict is *not* the most densely populated region.

[55] Boni 2005; Addae-Mensah 1986; Alhassan and Manuh 2005, 26–28.

Exploiting their positions as "both land guarantors and judges,"[56] chiefs have "attempt[ed] to reclaim prerogative from the tenant/settlers."[57] The 1980s and 1990s were marked by a rising perception on the part of migrants that they were being swindled and defrauded by chiefs who reneged on contracts and demanded increasingly arbitrary extractions.

In Sefwi-Wiaso in 1986 and 1987, outsiders who had acquired land via purchase in earlier decades saw their property invaded by local youth trying to take back land claimed by local citizens, sometimes with the encouragement of the chiefs.[58] In the face of periodic episodes of land-related violence, some in-migrants fled the region. Sefwi-Wiawso earned a reputation as "a chiefdom marked by chronic host-migrant conflict."[59]

Boni (2005, 2) explained that "in recent decades, with the exhaustion of available virgin forest, struggles have intensified as land pressure has become a growing concern." Migot-Adholla et al. picked up on these tensions in a comparison of three commercial farming areas of Ghana in the late 1980s: they found that land parcels in their Western Region study site (in Wassa) were twice as likely to be affected by land disputes as parcels in the other two regions. They observed that migrants in Western Region "may suffer from extreme levels of tenure insecurity" and that "the protection of migrants' [land] rights is an extremely sensitive political issue.... In the case of Wassa, uncertainties over the rights of migrant farmers versus the autochthones remain unresolved."[60] Uncertainty and tension put migrant farmers at a clear structural disadvantage: in 2003, more than 90 percent of all land disputes were settled outside the courts – that is, among farmers themselves or by chiefs. Court judgments are usually left to the winner to enforce (Alhassan and Manuh 2005, 28, 30).

Migrants' structural political and economic disadvantage was evident in the harassment of stranger framers, and in arbitrary extractions from them by local chiefs. Such dynamics are visible in social processes that produce and enforce political hierarchy at the village level. In July 2009, we spoke to a migrant farmer whose cocoa plantation, founded in 1975, was located on the lands of a village about 5 miles from Wassa Akropong.[61] He described his recent experience:

Yes, land is becoming scarce around here and there is tension between locals and migrants. For one thing, the chiefs now take more, such as charging us more for holding

---

[56] Boni 2005, 109–110; see also Benneh 1988.

[57] Gov. of Ghana, Report of the Committee on Tenant/Settler Farmers, May 1999. See also Benneh 1988, 5.

[58] Boni 2005, 103–104, 119.

[59] Fred-Mansah 1999, 953.

[60] Migot-Adholla et al. 1994, 111, 115. They found that 9.5% of all parcels in the Wassa site were affected by land disputes. The other two study sites were Ejura, 100 kilometers north of Kumasi, and Anloga, 150 kilometers east of Accra, on the Atlantic coast. On litigation, see also Benneh 1988, 5–6.

[61] He had 18 acres under cocoa in a region wherein average farm size in Wassa District (circa 1990) was 13.3 acres. Migot-Adholla et al. 1994, 104.

our traditional [Ewe] festivals in this area. The chiefs overcharge us. It has become worse recently; perhaps chiefs are more in need of money than they were before. (Field notes, 14 July 2009)

In Western Region of Ghana, rising pressures on the land and indigene-migrant tensions have not produced large-scale or sustained ethnic violence, or unidirectional movement toward strong private property rights. Rather, land competition and land-related tension has produced the steady erosion of the land rights acquired by in-migrants in earlier decades. As Boni (2005, 99) put it, their "titles have weakened over time."[62] Although outsiders have not been expelled en masse from Sefwi-Wiawso or Wassa Amenfi, or excluded from land access, the reassertion of autochthonous land rights has been the clear trend since the late 1980s in Sefwi-Wiawso, and since the late 1990s in Wassa Amenfi. "Now the same chiefs [who granted land in earlier decades] are saying that they never sold the land outright, but gave it for use for a limited time."[63] Chiefs have forced migrants to renegotiate titles to establish new terms more favorable to indigenes or chiefs, taken back land from the heirs of in-migrants who have passed away, sought to reappropriate uncultivated portions of parcels sold to outsiders, sought to repossess land that migrants had sublet to third parties, prohibited in-migrants from selling land to which they hold title, not recognized land titles acquired through the purchase of land from indigenous landholding families (rather than from chiefs), and not honored titles that do not bear the signature of the paramount chief himself.[64]

This process gained momentum in 2003, when Wassa Amenfi became one of several pilot districts of Ghana's national Land Administration Project (LAP), which aims at the registration of what are officially recognized as customary land rights. A Customary Land Secretariat was established in the district capital, Wassa-Akropong, seat of the Wassa Amenfi paramount chieftaincy. It was to gradually take over and extend the work that had been handled in the nearby office of the Stool Lands Administrator.[65] In the paramountcy in Wassa-Akropong, one divisional chief (who also served as secretary to the Omanehene) and another palace official explained the goals of the land registration process (not yet fully under way):

[62] Boni finds that in Western Region, "chiefly prerogatives have expanded over the years ... [and these are imposed even on strangers] who acquired their title decades ago, on more liberal terms" (2005, 106).

[63] Alhassan and Manuh 2005, 33.

[64] Boni 2005, 103–104 inter alia; Takane 2002, 40 (for Bepoase, which is in Wassa Amenfi); Addae-Mensah 1986.

[65] As the LAP coordinator in Brong-Ahafo Region, Sandy Anthony Mensah put it in an interview published in the *Ghanaian Chronicle* in 2007: "'Traditional authorities should be ensuring that people do not become landless in their own communities. ... The tenure rights of customary freeholders must not be compromised.' He stressed that the new Customary Land Secretariats were to strengthen customary land administration, and that as administrative units, they were 'owned by land-owning communities,'" "Stool Lands Revenues Are Not Solely for Chiefs," *Ghanaian Chronicle*, 12 September 2008, posted at AllAfrica.com (accessed 1 May 2009).

We plan to have all migrants registered as tenants on 50 year leases, counting from when the farm was created, even if they purchased the land from a local family. The terms of the new lease will be between the chief and the tenant. We [the chiefs] will reclaim land if we find any lapses, cheating, or fraud [such as under-declaring the size of the parcel] in the original agreements, or any sub-lets, or if we find the land is under-used ... or if royalties to the stool have not been paid. We plan to renegotiate all the tenancies. ... Everyone feels that land scarcity is coming. (Field notes, 13 July 2009)

Through this process, migrants who acquired title via what they thought was "outright purchase" in the 1950s, 1960s, or 1970s are designated as "tenants." Many of them will find that these retroactive tenancies have already expired and will thus require renegotiation with the chiefs.[66] The chiefs' assertiveness reflects the force of government backing. Agents of the Customary Land Secretariat encourage migrants to resurvey their land, telling them that this process will protect their parcels from future litigation.[67] Some stranger farmers with large holdings are encouraged to make concessions to land-hungry Wassa citizens by entering into farm-sharing arrangements with land-poor locals (through *abunu* contracts).

A member of the Wassa Amenfi East District Assembly (DA) – an indigene – offered these observations on this process:

The chief claims that all stranger farmers who have stayed on their land for more than fifty years should come and renegotiate a new agreement. The new agreement costs between 1,500 and 1,800 cedis. Those who fail to do so would forfeit half of the land. ... This is unconstitutional because the chief is taking advantage of obsolete by-laws of the traditional council. ... [Yet] the respect given to chiefs in the area has made it impossible for any protest on this matter. The only option available for farmers is submission. (Interview with indigenous local community leader in his forties, 27 July 2010, Wassa Amenfi East, north of Dikoto Junction)

In Western Ghana, in a chieftaincy-centered land regime, rising land competition finds social and political expression in tension that runs along the indigene-stranger cleavage. In part, this reflects systematic efforts on the part of chiefs to deflect the blame of indigenous Wassa communities from the chiefs themselves, who are held responsible for selling land to outsiders in the first place. By accentuating immigrants' subordinate political status and the provisional nature of

---

[66] Interview, Customary Land Secretariat/Land Administration Project (CLS/LAP), Akropong, 11 July 2009. As Addae-Mensah explained in 1986 (36), "Non-members of the landowning community would prefer to acquire farmland by outright purchase to enter into land tenancy arrangements with landlords. The latter agrarian status is usually regarded as a subordinate status for the tenants." The CLS/LAP in Wassa-Akropong covers the entire Wassa Amenfi Traditional Area, not just the (new) Wassa Amenfi East District.

[67] From on-farm interviews with eleven in-migrant farmers (three male spokespersons did the talking), 14 July 2009, Wassa-Akropong hinterland. They believe the CLS/LAP representatives are agents of the central state. However, the divisional chief explained that the CLS/LAP staff is paid by the paramountcy, and that they are former employees of the Office of the Stool Lands Administrator.

their land rights, chiefs deflect blame onto strangers, weaken the claims of "outsiders," and reassert and reaffirm the chiefs' own power and legitimacy.

The Making and Remaking of the Central Government's Commitment to the Chiefs

Chiefs in this region have not always been successful at this, however. This case is instructive because it provides stark evidence of the role of *central government* in shoring up (or eroding) the customary powers of Ghana's traditional chiefs. Rarely in contemporary Africa is the hand of the state in the making of the customary authority so obvious.

Nkrumah-era legislation strengthened the position of migrants throughout southern Ghana by weakening the *abusa/abunu* systems of crop and farm sharing.[68] The coup that overthrew Nkrumah in 1966 reversed these reforms. Boni (2005, 97, 100) writes that the 1966 coup "was celebrated with jubilation by most of the Sefwi chiefly establishment.... After the repeal of Act 109 [the Rents Stabilization Act of 1962], chiefs regained what they considered their 'customary prerogatives.'... From the 1970s onward they sought "to re-appropriate portions of uncultivated lands granted to tenants." In this they were helped by Ghana's 1979 constitution, which "consolidated communal land tenure systems ... by guaranteeing the institution of chieftaincy."[69]

In the 1980s, the political pendulum swung from the chiefs back to the migrants. In 1986, the Rawlings government again "tried to secure tenants' land rights [by] stimulating the registration of agricultural titles." Migrants in Western Region, strengthened by the regime's backing, confronted the Sefwi Traditional Council, which, "acting against the [Rawlings's] PNDC," had passed new regulations that increased extractions against migrants. Violence ensued as "Sefwi chiefs sent villagers to dispossess strangers" (Boni 2005, 107, 115, 119). The conflict provoked central government intervention in the form of an investigative committee (the April 1987 Asare Committee), which authored a report that was "sympathetic to the tenants." Boni (2005, 100) writes that "the chiefs appeared defeated, but continued to exercise considerable authority locally and maintained their privileges with regards to land rights and tenants' taxation. The issue gradually moved off the government's agenda."

The most recent chapter in this story is the introduction of the LAP, approved by the national government in 1999 and introduced in Wassa Amenfi in 2003. It clearly affirms the land authority of chiefs and primacy of autochthonous communities' land rights, "seeking to protect landholding communities and

---

[68] Ninsin 1989, 167–170; Gov. of Ghana, "Report of the Committee on Tenant/Settler Farmers, May 1999. Benneh (1988, 5) mentions the 1962 Rent Stabilization Act, amended in 1963, repealed by the military government in 1966.

[69] Ninsin (1989, 176–177) describes a general pattern in Ghana since the late 1960s "of frantic attempts ... to revest communal lands in the appropriate authorities, and conserve them." The Aliens Compliance Act of 1969 can be read as contributing to this.

their descendents from the risk of losing land or becoming tenants on their own land."[70]

In-migrants' capacity for collective political action seems to have peaked in the mid-1980s. This is when the central government took the migrants' side in their confrontations with the chiefs. Migrants in Sefwi formed a settler farmers' union to "protect tenants and oppose [the Sefwi Traditional Council's initiative]" (Boni 2005, 119). There was also an Association of Stranger Farmers of Wassa Amenfi in 1985 (Benneh 1988, 6). An in-migrant who arrived in Wassa Amenfi in the 1970s, now an employee of a cocoa-purchasing company, remembered the story this way:

A group was formed in 1984 by the settler farmers in the area, mostly from the Ashanti Region. Their main aim was to unite all the stranger farmers in the area of fight for their interest in terms of land rights. However, the chiefs saw the threat they would pose and therefore made efforts to persecute the leaders. [The chiefs'] agenda succeeded, leading to the demise of the Tenants Farmers Association (Interview in Wassa Amenfi East District, July 2010).

These organizations appear to have atrophied in the wake of government action to defuse the 1987 crisis.[71]

Western Ghana as a Political Anomaly

The hand of the state in *reinforcing* customary authority in the late 1960s, and again in the late 1990s onward, is particularly obvious in this case compared to the cases in which the government's role is less visible (as in Western Burkina Faso and the Ashanti Region in Ghana). Why is the hand of the postcolonial state in shoring up customary authority so visible in Western Ghana? And why did Ghana's national government side with "ethnic strangers" in Western Region in the early 1960s and again in the 1980? Even under Rawlings, this never happened in Ashanti, where the same kind of neocustomary land tenure regime prevails. The Ghanaian government's sporadic willingness to side with in-migrants in Western Region represents an anomaly for our theory, which predicts that in chieftaincy-centered land regimes, the government will uphold the primacy of chiefs and the primacy of indigenes' land rights.

These questions about temporal and spatial variation help isolate the role of national political forces in producing neocustomary authority at the subnational level in Ghana. Temporal variation in the western Ghana case tracks national-level struggles over chieftaincy. Postcolonial Ghana has been the theater of overt and sustained struggles over whether (and if so, how)

---

[70] Ouédraogo et al. 2006; Alhassan and Manuh, 2005, 18–20.
[71] While several of the nineteen randomly selected DA members we interviewed (Boone and Duku 2012) recalled the formation of migrant and tenant farmers' associations in the mid-1980s and the tumultuous clashes with chiefs that ensued, all the interviewees said that no migrants' organizations exist now. In their view, strangers caused the 1984–1986 conflicts by cheating on their land boundaries and resisting chiefs' attempts to survey the land properly.

to shore up the chieftaincy-centered land regimes inherited from colonialism. The Nkrumahist-tradition regimes (Nkrumah and early Rawlings) have been populist and nationalist (centralist) and have leaned toward curbing chiefly prerogative, whereas the Danquah-tradition regimes have been eager to invest in chiefly power and regional prerogative. Ghanaian political scientists would be the first to point out that this tension reflects more than mere ideological difference (see, for example, Ninsin 1989). In part, conflicting preferences over the land-controlling powers of chieftaincy grow out of the divergent interests of different segments of Ghanaian society. The regional cleavage pits migrant-accepting regions where chieftaincy is strong, such as Ashanti, against migrant-sending regions where chieftaincy is weak, such as Volta and the north. Class-like tensions align the interests of peasants, tenants, migrants, workers, and commoners against those of the elite, who are often large landholders or wielders of land prerogatives.

What is at stake is who controls the land and, thus, how to allocate the wealth that has come from the land in the form of revenues from timber, cocoa, gold, and periurban real-estate development. Conflicts over whether chieftaincy should be strengthened or weakened in Ghana have been highly structured and sustained and, thus, particularly visible, but such conflicts are not unique to this country. Analogous battles also mark the history of Senegal (where they were concentrated in the 1958–1962 conflict between Senghor and his prime minister, Mamadou Dia), Burkina Faso (where they came to a head in the Sankara Revolution of 1983 and the Compaoré counterrevolution), and Uganda (in battles to curb the power of Buganda), to mention a few notable postcolonial cases.

The spatial dimension of struggles over the neocustomary in Ghana points to cross-regional unevenness in the local dynamics of neocustomary authority and also to the national-level stakes of the game. That contests over chieftaincy have been played out more overtly in Ghana's Western Region than in Ashanti Region is partly a reflection of the fact that in Western Region, the balance of power between chiefs and migrants is less overwhelmingly tipped in favor of the chiefs. Chieftaincies in Western Region are less centralized, less politically influential, newer, smaller, and less strategically positioned in national politics than their Ashanti Region counterparts. And in the early stages of development of the cocoa economy in the west, the western chiefs also conceded more extensive land rights to ethnic strangers than did the chiefly elite in Ashanti and Brong Ahafo. Western Region chiefs are thus more open to challenge from migrants and more vulnerable to challenge from national-level leaders like Rawlings, who are interested in taking a stand against chiefly prerogatives and excess. These factors combine to make the Western Region a *subnational stage* on which Ghana's political and policy debates over chieftaincy and land have been played out in particularly visible ways.

In Ghana's Western Region, processes of competition and contestation over land trend in favor of strengthening chieftaincy and confirming indigenes' land rights. The losers are ethnic strangers, who see their land rights constrained and eroded. This conforms with our hypothesis about how land rights will evolve under chieftaincy-centered land regimes with (a) high in-migration, and (b) high competition for land. This case does more than provide support for the hypothesis, however. It advances the analysis by highlighting the role of central government in the process. Both the ebb and flow in the intensity of these contests between chiefs and outsiders in Ghana's Western Region, and the *overall directionality* of the process are influenced by national-level events and developments in Ghana.

Strangers' Marginal Political Representation in the Localities

In Wassa Amenfi today, migrants are "strongly networked"[72] within some localities, but not across localities. In many communities, ethnic outsiders do have a spokesman who represents them in their relationship with the village chief (i.e., the chief who exercises jurisdiction over the village territory in which they are settled).[73] Yet where this is the case, the ethnic outsiders are dealing only with the most local of chiefs rather than with higher-ranking chiefs, district administrative authorities,[74] or politicians or party organizers representing either the west or the migrants' home regions. This suggests that the ethnic outsiders accept a definition of local authority structure, and of their place within it, that puts them at considerable disadvantage vis-à-vis the chiefly hierarchy and indigenous westerners. In Ghana's presidential elections, in-migrants in Western Region vote freely at polling stations near their place of residence and tend to vote for parties based in their home regions (as they do in Brong-Ahafo and Ashanti Regions).[75] In village- and district-level political institutions, however, migrants are in a subordinate position. In the critical domain of land affairs, chiefly authority trumps democratic representation. In property affairs, migrants are heavily constrained to choose loyalty over voice.

This argument found support in a qualitative survey conducted for this study in 2010. We interviewed nineteen District Assembly members in Western Region: ten from Wassa Amenfi East District Assembly (WAEDA) and nine from Sefwi Wiawso District Assembly (SWDA). This sample represented 27 percent of all assembly members for the two districts.[76] Ghana's District

---

[72] Alhassan and Mensah 2005, in 18 July 2009 interviewees, said that in their locality, this was not the case.

[73] Interviews in Accra, 1–10 July 2009; Western Region interviews July 2009 and October 2009. On networking among migrants, see also Alhassan and Manuh, 2005, 18.

[74] Where chiefs or chiefly jurisdiction is weak, disputants do call on the district administration. See Berry 2001, 180 on Sekeye.

[75] Boone and Duku 2012. Arthur (2009, 59, 69) reports that in Western Region, the New Patriotic Party (NPP) and the National Democratic Congress (NDC) each received 47% of the vote in the first round of 2008 presidential elections.

[76] There are three DAs in the Sefwi Wiaso Traditional Area (i.e., within the jurisdiction of the SW Paramount Chieftaincy).

Assemblies were created by the Rawlings government in 1989 to replace the old District Councils. Two-thirds of the members are elected in formally nonpartisan local elections; the remaining one-third of the DA is appointed by the president. District Assemblies were originally billed as partially democratic organs of decentralized administration, but because of their limited powers and lack of budgetary autonomy, they have not lived up to the high expectations that attended their inauguration.[77] They represent the lowest-level instances of the modern state, in both its administrative and its democratic incarnations.

Interviews aimed to find out whether the most decentralized instance of Ghana's formally democratic state worked to counterbalance or circumscribe the role of chiefs by intervening directly in the allocation of farmland in Wassa Amenfi and Sefwi Wiawso Districts. If the DAs were found to be active in the land-allocation matters, then the argument about the predominance of chiefs as allocators of farmland would be at least partially undermined. Interviews also asked whether in-migrants were represented on the DA, and whether the DA was a forum open to those seeking to protect or advance the land-related interests of migrants.

Information gathered in these interviews squared with other evidence to confirm that in Western Region (1) the functioning of decentralized and semidemocratic local government does not impinge on the land prerogatives of chiefs, (2) DAs are not forums for the airing of landlord-stranger issues or tensions, or for the political organization of "stranger populations" seeking voice in the local political arena, and (3) in many localities, the landlord-stranger hierarchy is embedded in the unit committees, secular village-level institutions that mobilize voluntary labor for public works.[78] When it comes to land politics, the landlord-stranger hierarchy is well entrenched at the district and village levels.

All the nineteen District Assembly members confirmed forthrightly that in their areas, chiefs own stool lands and handle land matters having to do with farmland, especially issues arising between strangers and indigenes. Seventeen of the nineteen believed that chiefs *should* be allowed to handle land matters. Here are some of their comments:

Land cases involving migrant and indigenous farmers are usually dealt with by the chiefs because they are the custodians of the land. The Customary Land Secretariats are doing well. . . . Farmland matters are lodged at the chief's palace.

Before the creation of the WA District, chiefs were responsible for handling farmland disputes and this has not changed. I do not see why the DA should usurp this role played by the chiefs. . . . [This is because] the lands are for the chiefs and not the DA.

---

[77] As one interviewee put it, "The agenda of the DA is set by the central government and the DA is only there to rubber-stamp it" (Wassa Amenfi East, July 2010). This resonates with academics' conclusions. See Crook 1994, 339, 355–357; Kasanga and Kotey 2001, 9; Crawford 2008, 132; Ofei-Aboagye 2004, 753.

[78] See Boone and Duku 2012 on the unit committees.

It is only the chief and his elders who handle [land] matters, or the courts if the chief proves incapable of resolving it. . . . The DA does not discuss indigene-migrant disputes because the chiefs have been doing a good job in that direction. . . . Land here is very scarce.

It is not in the interest of peace for the DA to settle land disputes because this is the realm of the chiefs. Chiefs control the land. The LAP has enhanced the chiefs' role.

The most peaceful way to live in the district is for the migrant farmers to respect the traditional laws regulating land.

Two District Assembly members interviewed for this study, one migrant and one indigene, disagreed with the majority of the interviewees on this point. They argued that the government of Ghana should remove discrimination against migrants in land policy. One said, "For peace and fairness to reign in the area in terms of land management, laws should be enacted which eliminate all forms of discrimination against stranger farmers. The current procedure for acquiring land discriminates against the migrants and until this is done away with, peace will be an illusion."

The one DA member we interviewed from a neighboring district, an in-migrant from Volta Region, also argued against the status quo, saying that "the government should enact a law which makes it possible for any Ghanaian to purchase land in any part of the country."[79]

Conclusion

Under chieftaincy- and lineage-centered land tenure regimes, social groups claiming to be autochthonous, or firstcomers, are in a strong position to assert and retain local political dominance. When competition for land becomes more intense, members of the land-controlling community are likely to try to restrict strangers' ability to access land, to harden the terms under which strangers can access land, or exclude them altogether. When central states vest land-allocation powers in chiefs and the heads of autochthonous lineages, strangers are likely to have little recourse. In the absence of a politically neutral arena in which farmers can voice claims regardless of their ethnic status, and in the absence of a supralocal land-rights enforcer that recognizes their acquired rights, outsiders lack a political venue and leverage to use in seeking redress. They may experience the loss of land access under these conditions. This does not necessarily happen as the result of *overt* land-related conflict or defeat in an overt political struggle. It may be experienced as a kind of "silent violence" that plays out through the routine workings of structural power relationships in society.

[79] From an October 2010 interview conducted in Twi by Dennis Duku.

CHAPTER 5

Ethnic Strangers as Protected Clients of the State

> During the time of Houphouet, the Baoulé were installed in our territory *par force*! In the case of any issue or complaint, the Baoulé would summon the *sous-prefet* to come and persecute us.
>
> (FPI cadre, Abidjan 16 October 2010)

Although ethnic heterogeneity is a pervasive feature of much of rural Africa, the local political structures that organize interethnic relations vary a great deal across space. Such variation produces different forms of local hierarchy, different avenues and venues for political representation (or subordination) of ethnic outsiders, and different imbrications of the state in local-level power relations.

Where the state itself is the allocator of land rights, the political character and dénouement of land-related conflict are likely to contrast starkly with what we have observed in the customary land tenure regimes (LTRs), where local-level customary authorities (lineage heads or chiefs) control land allocation and adjudication. In zones of in-migration governed under statist land regimes, the central government itself has organized the in-migration and settlement (the "implantation") of ethnic outsiders. These are cases of the *migrations organisées* or *migrations officielles*, where state power has been used to "administratively insert" settlers into the locality.[1]

As in the cases of in-migration under customary authority described in Chapter 4, a relationship of political subordination, or patron-client linkage, ties ethnic strangers to the land-granting authorities. Where statist land tenure regimes prevail, however, the in-migrants *are beholden to the central state*

---

[1] Mafikiri Tsongo 1997.

rather than to a local landlord or host community. Land users may be acutely aware that legally and practically, the power to allocate and revoke land access lies in the hands of district officers, land board officers, local agents of the ruling party, or even the president himself. Such land-allocation power constitutes a potent political resource for national rulers.

In localities organized around statist land tenure regimes, what happens when land competition grows more intense? Our argument is that land competition will ignite political dynamics that are quite different from those observed in the chieftaincy- and lineage-centered land regimes. Where the state-administered (statist) land regimes prevail, state agents are the architects of the prevailing land allocation. The political rationales and institutional structures of the customary tenure regimes do not deflect land grievances and conflict into the "customary" institutions and channels of conflict suppression. Central authorities cannot hide behind the claim that land politics lie beyond the scope of their authority. In these situations, state agents are on the front lines of any effort to defend or revoke outsiders' land-access rights; they are the political focal point of land-related conflict that pits strangers against indigenes. Our working hypothesis is that central authorities will defend the land rights of settlers whom they themselves have installed – that is, those in control of the state will defend the land rights of their own clients.[2]

In the three cases presented here, settlers depend on the central state to enforce their land claims against indigenes.[3] We examine southwest Côte d'Ivoire before 1990, the Rift Valley of Kenya in the Kenyatta era, and eastern DRC before 1990. In stark contrast to the cases described in Chapter 4, in these cases, ethnic tension over land does *not* result in the tightening of indigenes' control over the land. Instead, the central state defends the in-migrants. This is manifest in administrative or other coercion to protect settlers in local disputes, pro-settler favoritism in the allocation of state services, legal support for in-migrants' land rights (for example, through documentation), and/or political repression against those attempting to assert ancestral claims. In all three cases examined here, this balance of forces persists *as long as those who have made the land grants retain control over the central state* – that is, in the one-party monopoly era of the 1960s, 1970s, and 1980s. Part IV shows how these political alignments have been overturned in the post-1990 era of multipartism.

---

[2] Cases that do not seem to fit the rule invite extensions of this argument. Uganda's Museveni first protected and patronized the Rwandan Tutsi settlers living in southern Uganda, when they assisted in his bid for national power, and then kicked them out. He did, however, help them find another place to go, thus offering a "side payment" to minimize or offset the political penalty that we would expect a ruler to incur when he abandons clients. That the Tutsis were nonnationals is also a salient factor.

[3] Ensminger (1997, 175 n. 5) noticed the presence of such power configurations.

SOUTHWESTERN CÔTE D'IVOIRE: STRANGERS IMPOSED "BY FORCE!"[4]

> The state used a combination of intimidation and incentive to persuade local populations to allow increasing numbers of migrants to break new land. . . . Chiefs, sous-prefets, and prefets were in charge of passing on instructions [to local families] to receive and accommodate migrants in search of land. (Marshall-Fratani 2006, 20)
>
> The Houphouet regime supported the migrants "against indigenous landowners." (Koné 2002, 25)

Transformation of densely forested southern Côte d'Ivoire into one of the world's leading coffee- and cocoa-producing regions was a process that spanned most of the twentieth century. In this region, the farming frontier moved from east to west. The Ivoirian southwest – or more precisely, the center-west region that lies between the Badama and Sassandra Rivers – opened up to "massive influxes" of migrant farmers in the 1930s. In-migrants were encouraged, promoted, and protected by the state as a vanguard of settlers who would drive forward the development of the *économie de plantation*, or smallholder plantation economy, in this region. Around the time of Côte d'Ivoire's independence in 1960, about half the population of the center-west – and perhaps an even larger percentage of the population of coffee and cocoa planters – was made up of ethnic strangers. (Map 3.)

Processes of land appropriation by outsiders in the Ivoirian southwest and center-west were defined by what was an essentially statist land tenure regime, rather than one in which chiefs or lineage heads retained prerogative over the giving and taking back of land. The qualifier is necessary because the land regime in this part of the Ivoirian forest zone had a mixed character: within an essentially statist land regime, lineage and household heads often retained some residual or symbolic prerogative over land allocations and over some in-migrants. By contrast, in a purely statist regime – as, for example, in the farming districts of Kenya's Rift Valley – state authorities claim to have extinguished the land authority of autochthonous communities.

The purpose of this section is to show how an essentially statist land tenure regime was established through conquest, law, coercion, and administrative pressure in center-west and southwestern Côte d'Ivoire. We also want to see if rising perceptions of land scarcity produced the predicted political effects.

French Conquest and Imposition of Direct Rule

French conquest of the zone was achieved via a scorched-earth strategy of physical and social destruction that was not complete until 1913. The defeated indigenous people of what was then a sparsely populated zone were

---

[4] I am referring to the center-west region (with Gagnoa as its main urban center) and the southwest.

MAP 3. Côte d'Ivoire

"regrouped" into administrative villages along the road axes and near surveillance posts (or they fled into the forest) and eventually placed under the authority of cantonal chiefs appointed by the French. By colonial administrative ideology, the new cantons and cantonal chieftaincies were supposed to encompass populations with some historical or cultural commonalities, but no one pretended that these territorial jurisdictions or the administratively defined "ethnic groupings" of this region represented precolonial nations or political/territorial entities.

In the 1920s, to stimulate the *mise en valeur* (putting to use), and especially the development of export-crop production in this region, the colonial administration began settling "African strangers" in new farming communities that were located along the roadways and protected by the colonial state.[5] In the 1930s, the colonial administration gave tracts of land to French *colons*, who

---

[5] Dozon 1985, 280, 286. Zolberg (1964, 41) wrote that in 1933, "the government encouraged the creation of colonization villages in the west by Baoulé and Malinké from savannah areas. These pioneer farmers [were given various incentives].... Most important of all, they were exempted from forced labor."

relied on forced labor mobilized by the colonial authorities to develop their own cocoa and coffee plantations.[6] The European plantations were a clear failure by the late 1940s. By that time, the colonial administration had switched strategies. After the Second World War, the state encouraged thousands of Baoulé farmers from eastern Côte d'Ivoire, and thousands of farmers from the savannah regions to the north (northern Côte d'Ivoire, Mali, and Burkina Faso), to emigrate to the western forest zone to establish small-scale coffee and cocoa plantations. Many were settled at "administrative initiative."[7] The indigenous population was considered too few in number and too backward to lead the smallholder revolution that was transforming the west.[8]

The French state claimed eminent domain over all land in the colony. In western Côte d'Ivoire, Félix Houphouet-Boigny's postcolonial regime embraced this authority without reservation. It had every interest in sustaining and supporting the processes of land pioneering in the west that filled state coffers with coffee and cocoa revenues. In 1962, Houphouet proclaimed that "the land is for the one who farms it" (*la terre est à celui qui la met en valeur*). This famous dictum assured established in-migrants in the center-west and southwest that land rights acquired under French rule would be upheld by the postcolonial state. More important for the future of the postcolony, it also encouraged new waves of immigration.

In the localities, a powerful prefectural administration and the heavy presence of state agents from the line ministries, especially the Ministère de l'Agriculture (Minagri) Service Dominial, enforced Houphouet's marching orders on the ground. In the center-west and southwest of Côte d'Ivoire, independence accelerated the rhythm of "the massive alienation of land to outsiders." By 1975 or so, strangers made up half or more of the population of the Divo and Gagnoa regions.[9]

Microlevel Dynamics of a Statist Land Regime in the Ivoirian Center-West

In the regions around Gagnoa and Divo, starting in the 1930s, autochthonous Bété and Dida became coffee and cocoa farmers themselves. On the lands

---

[6] In 1941, twenty-two expatriate planters, with average holdings of 150 hectares each, produced 55% of Divo Department's total output (Hecht 1985, 321–322). There were 150–200 expatriate-owned plantations in Côte d'Ivoire in the 1940s.

[7] Blanc 1962, 114, 117. He reports that these concessions (*"installations sans contrat"*) were contested by those in neighboring autochthonous villages in the late 1950s, as French authority waned.

[8] "Smallholder revolution" is Hecht's (1985) term. On the Bété's being seen as backward, see Dozon 1997, 790.

[9] "Marching orders" is from Dozon's (1985, 258) *mot d'ordre*. Strangers made up 64% of the population of Divo Department in 1975 (up from 6% in 1945) (Hecht 1985, 323). In the region around Gagnoa in the late 1970s, strangers accounted for almost half of the population (Dozon 1985, 28).

surrounding their villages, they created small plantations in village territory that was under the control of local lineages. Villages themselves were state-sanctioned administrative entities under the authority of a local chief. In the days of rapid expansion of export-crop production in this region, the central government encouraged and pressured autochthonous villages and lineage heads to cede "unused" or uncultivated village land to outsiders.

Local families were told that the state would not back up their desire to hold on to land that they did not cultivate (Lewis 2003, 3). Dozon explains that by granting land-use rights to ethnic outsiders or strangers, a household head was able to establish or confirm his "land-granting authority" over the area in question – and, thus, the family's right to demand payments and some social deference from the newcomer. Paradoxically, then, the act of granting outsiders access to land seems to have offered autochthones better prospects for retaining some rights over the land than did simply leaving it unoccupied and, thus, likely to be seized by either the state or a neighbor.[10] State agents encouraged in-migrants to enter into informal written contracts to document their transactions with Bété and Dida landholders. State agents often witnessed these contracts themselves. Later on, state agents were called on as dispute adjudicators, and they usually decided on behalf of the ethnic strangers when disputes arose over autochthones' attempts to reclaim the land.

In parts of the center-west and southwest, the government took land unilaterally on the grounds that it was unused or underused, and reallocated it to agricultural settlers. Most notoriously, in the late 1960s and early 1970s, Baoulé farmers who were displaced by the construction of the Kossou hydroelectric dam (near Yamoussoukro) were resettled on state-run settlement schemes in the Gagnoa region. Dida villagers complained to Barbara Lewis in the late 1980s that in these settlement schemes, "no *tuteurs* [autochthonous hosts] were recognized – the settlers were under the protection of the presidential umbrella" (2003, 6). Other Kossou Dam displacees were abandoned by the parastatals and "left on their own to colonize the forests of the south."[11]

Indigenous farmers and villagers did have incentives to make land available – at least provisionally – to ethnic strangers, especially when cash and labor seemed scarcer than land. Many Bété and Dida household heads exchanged lineage lands for lump-sum cash payments (land for cash). Baoulé settlers often acquired land in this manner. The Baoulé in-migrants tended to establish their plantations and autonomous village settlements (*campements*) on the

---

[10] Chauveau and Richard, in a study of the center-west, add an argument about economic pressure: by drawing resources out of agriculture (by tapping the coffee-cocoa export circuit), the state forced peasants to expand their farms or sell land in order to ensure simple reproduction of the household unit (1977, 518).

[11] Lassailly-Jacob 1986, 334–341. Declassification of protected forests was another mechanism for ceding lands directly to ethnic outsiders (or to politically well-connected individuals) (Chauveau 2000, 104–105).

remote limits of the Bété and Dida village territories, thus asserting a degree of social independence from the autochthonous communities that the latter would sometimes come to regret.[12] Seeds of discord were inherent in the nature of these contacts: had the land itself been sold? Or just the right *to use* the land? Or perhaps the buyer owned the trees he planted on the land, although not the land itself. Such sales were often viewed by the autochthonous families (often retrospectively) as redeemable. In deals with in-migrants, "sellers" often obliged buyers to make ongoing gifts or payments to the family that had made the land cession, thereby acknowledging its residual authority over the land.[13] These transactions generated funds that were often used to finance special life-cycle events, such as funerals and marriages, and thus help sustain the cohesion of the extended family and the authority of the lineage head.

Bété and Dida lineage heads also granted land access to strangers in exchange for labor. Deals of this sort were usually transacted with in-migrants from the north (northern Côte d'Ivoire, Mali, Burkina Faso) generically referred to as "Dioula." These in-migrants usually settled in Dioula quarters of the established villages and worked on the autochthones' cocoa and coffee plantations. In exchange for labor, they kept a share of the harvest. Many were also given access to expanses of land to create their own plantations. As was the case with the land-for-cash contracts, these arrangements often obliged the stranger farmers to make ongoing payments to the autochthonous hosts (in this case, in the form of bags of coffee or cocoa, food crops, or cash). Some laborers and sharecroppers did eventually escape these positions of social dependency through outright land purchases (Dozon 1985, 280–281).

Exchanges that were *individually* rational for the indigenous Bété and Dida in the 1940s and 1950s became less so over time. A collective irrationality became more obvious as a "tragedy of the commons" effect took hold: as the land frontier closed, the balance of power in the indigene-stranger relationships tended to shift in favor of the ethnic outsiders.[14] Ethnic strangers tended to own the largest plantations in the region,[15] to be more prosperous, and to have better access to labor. They were more likely to have invested in off-farm activities

---

[12] Dozon 1985, 28, 290–299.

[13] Hecht (1982, 1985), who worked in the Dida areas around Divo, stresses the relative absence of contracts involving such ongoing payments. However, Barbara Lewis, working in this area in 1988–2002, stressed locals' expectations of a continuing stream of goods and services from strangers (2003, 3). Dozon's (1985, 291) analyses in the Bété region also highlighted the existence of such contracts.

[14] Hecht 1985, Dozon 1985.

[15] In his work in two villages near Gagnoa, Dozon found that around 1975, autochthones' plantations averaged about 2 hectares in size, while ethnic outsiders' plantations averaged 4 hectares. Of the ethnic outsiders, the Baoulé were much better off: their plantations averaged 6 hectares. Of those with 6 to 10 hectares planted in coffee and/or cocoa, the ethnic outsiders (Dioula and Baoulé) were clearly more numerous than the autochthones (Dozon 1985, 293–294).

such as trade and money lending. Under prevailing norms and conventions, as long as their farms were under tree crops, their claims to the land were secure. And most important for the purposes of our analysis, the central state was on their side.

As autochthonous families ran out of land to offer to strangers, and as their power over the ethnic strangers declined, the complementarity that had helped smooth out and support indigene-stranger relationships began to erode. Families responded to these shifts by seeking ways to extract new payments from the strangers, recover land, or limit further land cessions. Such actions fueled tensions not only between the indigenes and the ethnic outsiders but also between the indigenes and the local agents of the central government.

I consider the land tenure regime in this region to be essentially statist (rather than archetypically statist) because local land-allocation authorities (lineage and household heads) did retain some residual and ritual land prerogatives over the lands surrounding their villages. These residual powers eroded over time, however. My characterization of the land regime in the region squares with that of Chauveau, who described Ivoirian state intervention in the allocation of rural land in the southwest and center-west as "massive" and "direct." He points to the "particularly effective administrative protection of Ivoirian and non-Ivoirian in-migrants in the West."[16]

Land Conflict under a Statist Land Regime

Land-related tension and conflict assumed political form in ways that are predicted by the statist character of the land regime. Jean-Pierre Dozon (1985, 255, 302–303) has argued that an ethnic consciousness among the Bété – a colonial-era social agglomeration of more than seventy tribal groupings with no shared language[17] – was produced in reaction to the "massive land alienations" that had been encouraged and supported and, in some places, carried out by the state. Bété consciousness, centered on the ideology of autochthony, was forged in large part in opposition to a state that was seen as the architect of this dispossession.[18] Parallels with the case of the Kalenjin in Kenya's Rift Valley (discussed later) are strong.

As in the cases considered in Chapter 4, the land tenure regime in southwestern Côte d'Ivoire structured the lines and character of ethnic tension. Although society in the Ivoirian center-west and southwest is a mosaic of different

[16] Chauveau 2000, 104–105.
[17] Dozon 1985, 17–21, 29, 29 n. 8, 85. Dozon explains that *"pays Bété"* or Bété territory was a colonial reality, corresponding to an administrative province. The small tribes of this area were regrouped into provincial subunits designated as cantons. Cantonal chiefs selected by the French were not indigenous to the areas in question. Not all the "Bété factions" shared a mutually intelligible language. See also Dian 1985, 83.
[18] Chauveau and Dozon 1987, 231–233 inter alia.

peoples, ethnic tension runs along the line that distinguishes the autochthones from all others. And as in the earlier cases, in southwestern and center-west Côte d'Ivoire, the land tenure regime went far in defining how ethnic tension found political expression. However, the similarity ends there. In the Chapter 4 cases, indigene-stranger competition played out mostly within frameworks of economic and political hierarchy as they were constituted within local jurisdictions. Land-related conflict produced few if any ripple effects outside the localities. By contrast, in the Bété region around Gagnoa, land-related conflict has found expression in autochthones' attempts to seize a share in *state* power – by gaining political representation at the national level – in order to limit the cession of land rights to strangers.

National-level space for organized political contestation among civil society groups first opened in Côte d'Ivoire in the 1950s. Dozon explains that from this beginning, land-related grievances of autochthonous people around Gagnoa took directly political form by targeting the structures and policy orientations of the central state. In the late 1950s, the main political rival to Houphouet-Boigny's SAA-RDA was the Mouvement Socialiste Africain (MSA), a political party with a regional political base centered in Gagnoa. Adrien Dignan Bailly led the party.[19] He was a Gagnoa son-of-the-soil, a member of the Territorial Assembly since 1945, and winner of the 1956 Gagnoa municipal elections. In the Gagnoa region as in other parts of Côte d'Ivoire, Houphouet's political formation (later to become the PDCI) embodied and symbolized the land-pioneering and commodity-brokering Baoulé and Dioula "bourgeoisie" that was nurtured by the rise of the postwar Ivoirian plantation economy.[20] The MSA gathered momentum as an expression of civil society in reaction to this offensive thrust. Part of the MSA program "concerned the regulation of [in-]migration and the ceding of land; . . . it was not the presence of *allochtones* [ethnic strangers] per se that was objected to; rather, it was the . . . colonization of the region by *allochtones*."[21] The 1956–1957 elections for Territorial Assembly were marked by numerous clashes between MSA and RDA supporters in the center-west, where support for the rival parties tended to follow along the autochthone-stranger distinction in the localities. In one clash, an RDA politician from Daloa was attacked and killed while campaigning in a village near Gagnoa. The RDA declared an election victory. The MSA claimed that the vote had been stolen.

---

[19] He was also leader (as of 1946) of the Ivoirian branch of the fiercely anticommunist SFIO (Section Française de l'Internationale Ouvrière), which received the support of the postwar colonial administration until the PDCI and RDA broke with the French Communist Party in 1950. On this, see Dozon 1985, 257–258, 337, 341–344. The MSA was the Ivoirian antenna of the SFIO.

[20] The SSA-RDA (Syndicat Agricole Africain-Rassemblement Démocratique Africain) was the precursor of the Parti Démocratique de Côte d'Ivoire (PDCI).

[21] Dozon 1985, 343; see also 351.

After a turbulent and repressive first decade of independence, land grievances in the center-west again provided fuel for a confrontation between southwestern autochthones and the state.[22] In 1970, in the period preceding elections for the renewal of local PDCI secretaries, subversive tracks circulated in the rural areas around Gagnoa. They aimed at discrediting the upcoming election on the grounds that the Houphouet government had shut down any possibility of legal opposition, and sought to mobilize a grassroots opposition to challenge the regime. A response materialized on 26 October 1970, when several hundred planters from around Gagnoa, led by Nragbé Kragbé (alt. Kragbé Gnagbé), formed a kind of peasant army of villagers armed with hunting rifles and machetes and marched on Gagnoa in an attempt to "seize power."[23] Dozon (1985, 345–348) recounts how the rebels occupied the city center, including government and municipal buildings and the headquarters of the ruling party, roughed up some government agents,[24] and proclaimed the formation of a République d'Eburnie. A flag was hung on municipal buildings, a constitution was promulgated, and Nragbé Kragbé proclaimed himself head of state and announced the formation of a government. Article 10 of the *Loi organique* (foundational law) of the new state read, "Land is the exclusive property of the tribes. They may cede land to the state for the greater good (*l'utilité publique*). The state may not dispossess the tribes."[25]

The Gagnoa gendarmerie and the Ivoirian army began the killing in short order. It lasted several days. The gendarmerie first cordoned off and went into the Bété quarter of Gagnoa ("symbol of opposition to the RDA") to mete out repression, and then continued in the rural areas to the east and south of Gagnoa, especially the canton of Guébié, the epicenter of the rebellion. Although no official death tally was ever made, "if commentaries are to be believed, the death toll varied between several hundred and several thousand" (Dozon 1985, 345). Marshall-Fratani (2006, 10, 21) said that 4,000 were killed in October 1970. Strozeski (2006,1) reports that between 4,000 and 6,000 Bété

---

[22] "The region of Gagnoa was the theatre of multiple incidents between *autochtones* and *allochtones* [indigenes and settlers]" in the 1960s (Dozon 1985, 344). In the 1963 repression of suspected regime opponents (the *complot manqué*), hundreds of Bété were arrested, and two subprefects from the Gagnoa region were imprisoned (Dozon 1985, 258).

[23] Dozon 1985, 345. In 1985, Dozon saw this as a kind of separatist movement (347). Korinman, however, argues that the objective of the movement was enlargement to include the entire country: the objective was "a march on Rome/Abidjan" (2005, 11). See also Gbagbo 1982 and Gadji-Dagbo 2002.

[24] Gadji-Dagbo (2002, 91) says that a Bété policeman ("a collaborator") was murdered.

[25] "Historical Document: Proclamation aux tribus d'Eburnie; Loi organique de l'Etat d'Eburnie," *Outre-Terre*, n. 11, 2005, 265–268. Dozon underscores that this version of facts did erase the history of land sales by autochthones (chiefs, lineage heads, household heads), who had contributed to the collective tragedy of the commons. However – and this is presumably what Gnagbe Kragbé had in mind – the coercive authority of the state could have been used to solve or contain this problem, as it has been in the Western Region of Ghana since the 1990s.

farmers were killed in these events.[26] This trauma is remembered by the Bété as the Guébié genocide.

The Ivoirian government depicted the Gagnoa rebellion as an atavistic tribal uprising, but this rendering of the situation lies about the modalities of the conflict and covers up what was at stake. The rebellion's leader, Nragbé Kragbé, was a native of Guébié canton and a graduate. He had been arrested and incarcerated in Abidjan in 1967 for attempting to form an opposition party called le PANA (Parti National Africain). According to Dozon (1985, 347–348), Nragbé Kragbé saw the Eburnie Republic as representing the populations of the western forest zone (*l'ouest forestier*) – including the various Bété subgroups or factions, the Dida, the Krou, and also, apparently, the Mande groups of the Gouro and the Dan – in their grievances against the Houphouet regime. As Dozon (1985, 347–348) wrote, Nragbé Kragbé's political program "called for not only a spectacular augmentation in the [official] purchase price of coffee and cocoa,... but also the departure of the *migrants allochtones* (whose presence was denounced as an act of internal colonialism and the land cessions as acts of theft)." Ruth Marshall-Fratani (2006, 10) provides this except from the Gagnoa manifesto: "Our lands, our most precious possession, were torn from us by force by the Akans, led by Houphouet-Boigny with the treacherous collusion of the Dioula and a handful of our own people.... The hour has come to recuperate our land."[27]

The Gagnoa uprising was repressed in ways that stoked the very grievances that had produced it in the first place.[28] In the wake of the mass killing, villages around Gagnoa were destroyed and populations were regrouped by government order. Expansion of the *économie de plantation* continued at full force. Autochthones' perceptions of growing land scarcity and their attempts to reappropriate land from in-migrants caused many local conflicts. Many of these were attended to by state agents from the prefectural administration and the Ministry of Agriculture, who took as their guiding principle Houphouet's rule that "the land is for [belongs to?] whomever is farming it." Many analysts report that state agents systematically protected the outsiders' acquired land rights against indigenous farmers' attempts to reclaim land or to reassert landlord prerogatives.[29] As Mariatou Koné (IIED 2002, 25) put it, the Houphouet

---

[26] Gadji-Dagbo (2002) says that Houphouet himself exaggerated the number of deaths (claiming that 4,000 were killed by the state) to discourage other would-be subversives.

[27] These lines may be from the 1966 Parti Nationaliste manifesto. See *Outre-Terre* 2005.

[28] Dozon reported that the repression itself provoked some reprisals on the part of autochthones against allochthones (that is, indigenes against settlers), especially Baoulé settlers, which led many Baoulé to return to their home region (1985, 345–346, n. 29, 348).

[29] Chauveau 2000; Lewis 2003; Dozon 1985, 303–304. Meanwhile, in 1974–1976, government planners sought to "nationalize" control over *bas-fonds* (marshy depressions) in the Gagnoa Region, which the parastatal SODERIZ (Société pour le Développement de la Riziculture) wanted to develop for rice growing.

regime supported the migrants "against the indigenous landowners." This resonates with what Barbara Lewis (2003, 6) heard from Dida villagers in 1988: they said that "the administrative officials would always rule in favor of the Baoulé.... Houphouet had made it clear that no harm should come to 'his' Baoulé." The large, heterogeneous Dioula population in the center-west and southwest was also viewed by many autochthones as enjoying the economic advantages of state patronage and protection. Many Dioula prospered as plantation owners, licensed traders in the coffee and cocoa export circuit, and money lenders and in business (e.g., retail, hotels) in the towns of the southwest.

The 1980s were marked by the indigenous population's growing perceptions of land shortage, along with their keen awareness of their multiple disadvantages vis-à-vis outsiders.[30] A drastic decline in world market prices for coffee and cocoa compounded the disadvantages of the autochthones. Côte d'Ivoire's larger economic crisis (and the structural adjustment policies adopted in response) produced unemployment in the cities and waves of returnees to the rural areas. Government policy encouraged this through a *retour à la terre* (back to the land) program, which exhorted youth to return to their villages of origin and take up farming. Many returnees, "forced to confront the loss of land they believed to be their birthright," sought to reclaim land that had been ceded to ethnic outsiders by their fathers and uncles.[31] Others tried to find ways to extract more labor, larger payments, or gifts from the stranger farmers. "Land shortage became an increasingly contentious issue [in the center-west] in the 1980s" (Lewis 2003, 8). Minagri officials intervened frequently and directly to protect the in-migrants' acquired rights.[32]

The record of the Houphouet regime, which ended with his death in 1993, confirms our expectation that in indigene-stranger land conflicts, the central authorities will side with the in-migrants whom they have implanted. Houphouet's government consistently sided with the Baoulé and Dioula stranger farmers who had been settled in the southwest under its encouragement and protection. This is the exact opposite of outcomes observed in the cases considered in Chapter 4, in which central governments sided with indigenes – the Asante chiefs and landowners, Wassa and Sefwi chiefs, and the autochthones in western Burkina Faso – in their efforts to retain the upper hand in land relations with strangers.

---

[30] Dozon 1985, 287; Dozon 1997, 794. On labor shortages facing Bété farmers, see Dozon 1985, 283, 295, 301. By the 1975 administrative census, the Gagnoa area was the most populous part of pays Bété, with average rural population density of fifty-five persons per square kilometer. To the northwest of the city of Gagnoa, this figure reached eighty. Average population density in Côte d'Ivoire (for 1971) was eighteen inhabitants per square kilometer (Dozon 1985, 28, 28 n. 7). See map in Dozon 1985, 8. On the "false plot" of 1982, the repression of which targeted the Bété, see Dozon 1985, 20–21, 349.

[31] Lewis 2003, 8.

[32] Lewis 2003, 8, 22–23, 37, writing of the Dida. Dozon (1985) observed similar pressures among the Bété of Gagnoa.

In southwestern Côte d'Ivoire, the stranger farmers were political clients of the PDCI party-state in every sense. In-migrants received particularistic benefits (land) and club goods (protection) through the sponsorship of the party-state. In return, the ethnic outsiders – including both Ivoirian citizens such as the Baoulé and members of ethnic groups from northern Côte d'Ivoire, and the noncitizen Dioula from Mali and Burkina Faso – constituted a solid base of political support for the ruling party in a region where the autochthonous population was clearly an oppositional force. This support, especially at election time, "was a civic thank-offering by the immigrants to Houphouët-Boigny for his hospitality" (Crook 1997, 222).

KENYA'S RIFT VALLEY SETTLERS

> The government owns the Rift.
> (Church pastor in Eldoret, November 2008)

Conflicts over access to land in Kenya's Rift Valley have marked all stages of Kenya's national history and shaped each critical juncture. The statist land tenure regime prevailing in the farming districts of the Rift has defined political and economic relationships around land, structuring patterns of competition, conflict, and political hierarchy in the rural areas.

As in the case of southwestern Côte d'Ivoire, rules of land allocation and access inscribed in this statist land regime, and the land-related conflicts that have ensued, have themselves been powerful *promoters* of a shared ethnic identity among those harboring land-related grievances against the state. Shared ethnic identity developed among those who were *losing out* in the transformation toward more exclusive land rights. This shared ethnic identity was used as a tool for political mobilization and as a justificatory ideology for advancing land claims against the national government and against the state-backed settlers.

This section holds constant the uncompetitive character of the national government by concentrating on the period of ascendance and incumbency of the Kenyatta regime, the government that made the early postcolonial land allocations in the Rift. In competition between indigenes and settlers over land, central rulers sided with the settlers. Chapter 9 varies this parameter by considering what happened in the Rift Valley districts in the 1990s, when the move to multipartism opened up broad-based competition for control over the national government.

The Statist Land Regime in the Farming Districts of the Rift Valley

The colonial state expropriated much of what is now Rift Valley Province from the Maasai and other peoples indigenous to the Rift. The British proclaimed direct jurisdiction over what it designated as Crown Land in the Rift

Valley in 1904. Through law and force, the colonial state extinguished ancestral rights throughout the Scheduled Areas of the central Rift and declared this zone – about 3 million hectares of farmland – off-limits to African land proprietorship.[33] This is the part of Kenya that came to be known as the White Highlands (or Kenya Highlands). Colonial authorities allocated often vast land tracts to white settlers from the 1910s to the late 1940s, often by sale or on 999-year leases.[34] To create and operate farms, estates, and ranches, these white settlers needed access to African labor. To obtain it, they provoked and encouraged the in-migration of African laborers from Kenya's densely packed reserves, especially the Kikuyu reserve, where population pressure and the development of commercial agriculture created intense competition for land. In the White Highlands, many of the Africa workers on the European-owned farms and estates resided as "squatters" on small parcels of land that they farmed on their own account. By the 1930s, some 100,000 Africans worked and lived in the Scheduled Areas as squatters. (Map 4.)

The rest of Kenya (except the coastal strip) was divided into ethnic homelands (called native or African land units, or reserves), which were "reserved" for members of the state-recognized ethnic groups that the colonial government designated as indigenous to those areas. In the reserves, the colonial administration fashioned the customary land regimes wherein state-backed or appointed chiefs allocated land to (or confirmed the holdings of) members of the ethnically defined communities designated as their subjects. Land in the native land units was "reserved" for members of the titular ethnic group, with the colonial architects of the ethnic homelands providing for the possibility that African outsiders would gain land access as "acceptees" into local ethnic communities. The opposite land tenure regime prevailed in the so-called Scheduled Areas of Kenya that were reserved for white settlement and ownership.

Colonialism in Kenya culminated in violent confrontation. The bloodiest aspects of the protracted decolonization struggle centered on efforts of the colonial regime and the British government to expel squatters from the Rift and suppress African demands for land in the Scheduled Areas, and on the violent struggle within the densely populated Kikuyu reserve for land rights, political voice, political power and chiefly accountability. The guerrilla movement known as Mau Mau (which emerged in 1952 and called itself the Land

---

[33] Leys reports that the conventionally cited figure for land area of the White Highlands, that is, the Scheduled Areas, was 7.6 million acres (or 3 million hectares), 3 million acres of which was farmland and the rest mostly ranchland (1975, 63 n. 2, 85 n. 61). See also Odingo 1971, 187.

[34] Most of the settlers were South African or British. Most of the mixed farms in Uasin Gishu District were 2,000 acres in the 1940s, of which about half would be devoted to wheat and maize and half to grazing (Klopp 2002, 277). As Klopp reports, this area was known as the "breadbasket of Kenya." European mixed farms around Nakuru were generally smaller (e.g., 400 acres in Londiani).

MAP 4. Kenya

Freedom Army) was largely made up of squatters, former squatters, workers on Rift properties, and landless Kikuyu. It demanded that the state recognize African farmers' claims to land in the Rift that they had cultivated (as squatters), the end of the white man's monopoly over Kenya's best and least intensively used farmland, and political and economic rights within the native reserves (especially Kikuyuland).[35] During the 1952–1956 state of emergency, under which the colonial government repressed and defeated the Mau Mau, some 32 Europeans and an estimated 50,000 Africans were killed, thousands at the hands of the British.

In 1960, the European monopoly on the White Highlands was suppressed, and over the next decade, most of the European-held "mixed farms" were sold to the British government or the African successor state.[36] The two centerpieces of Kenya's decolonization settlement were (1) the establishment of a

[35] See Furedi 1989; Kanongo 1987; Berman and Lonsdale 1992a; Berman and Lonsdale 1992b; Harbeson 1973, 146.
[36] See Leys 1975. The mixed farms had depended for their economic survival on subsidies from the colonial state. On the opening of the Highlands, see Harbeson 1973, 93–95.

land tenure system in the former White Highlands that would define the locus of authority over the allocation of this land, and (2) allocation of these lands among competing African claimants.

A central drama in the drafting of the national constitution of Kenya from 1960 to 1964 was the struggle to redesign the institutions governing access to land in the Rift. The Kenya African Democratic Union, or KADU, championed the interests of the collection of peoples who had lost land rights in the colonial expropriation of much of the Rift in the early 1900s and advocated for a federal (Majimbo, or regionalist) constitution. The constitution would return expropriated lands to indigenous peoples, giving ethnically defined regional governments considerable political autonomy – including political control over land allocation – within jurisdictions that would be constituted as ethnic homelands. In effect, KADU wanted to *replace* direct control of the central government over land in the contested Rift districts with a locally controlled land regime in which ethnic elites would be in charge of land matters, and in which indigeneity would be honored as the first principle of land access.[37] The dominant political party, Kenyatta's Kenya African National Union (KANU), took the opposite stance. It insisted that customary and ancestral rights had been extinguished in the former Scheduled Areas, and insisted on retaining central government control over land allocation in this zone (that is, a statist LTR). The principal goal was to build institutions that would structure the development and expansion of an open land market – open to all Kenyans regardless of their ethnic identity – in this part of the country. KANU and the British were also intently focused on the goal of taking advantage of the "land frontier" that had opened up in the Rift in order to relieve the excruciating land pressure, mostly among the Kikuyu, that was so manifestly fueling radical nationalism in Kenya.

The line of cleavage that pitted the Majimboists of KADU against the dominant (and winning) KANU had an "ethnic guise," but it was not a line that followed ethnic identities per se. (At the time, Kenya had forty state-recognized ethnic groups, almost half of them with a stake in the Rift.) Rather, the line of cleavage that divided Kenyans was the distinction between prospective land-rights losers and land-rights winners. On one side were those who had lost once (in 1905–1950) and stood to lose out again under a postcolonial statist LTR in the central districts of the Rift. On the other were those who stood to benefit from state-administered land allocation and open land markets in the central Rift Valley – two mechanisms that were both understood as means for transferring land rights to non-indigenes. Multiethnic coalitions formed along this axis.

---

[37] Under the Majimboist constitution, this kind of land regime would have been put in place nationwide. Only in the farming districts of the Rift and parts of Coast Province, however, would this have meant "switching" from a statist to something closer to a neocustomary regime. This was precisely the goal of the Majimboists.

Allocation of Land under the Kenyatta Regime

The statist land tenure regime established in the Rift Valley farming districts by the colonial state was perpetuated and elaborated by the KANU government after independence. From 1960 to 1966, approximately half of the former White Highlands (Leys 1975,116) – 3–4 million acres – was purchased by the state, mostly from departing European settlers. Government allocated about half of this (approximately 1.5 million acres) directly to smallholders through settlement schemes between 1960 and 1975. More went to smallholders in the late 1960s and 1970s through the state-financed and -sponsored establishment of private land-buying companies, bringing the total acreage allocated to smallholders up to about 2.2 million acres by 1984.[38] Much of the rest of the land so acquired was transferred in the form of large estates to high-ranking members of the Kenyatta regime, entrenching their status as an economic as well as a political elite. The government itself retained some land as state-owned property (in the form of the Agricultural Development Corporation farms, for example).

This process established large zones of African smallholder farming throughout what had been the White Highlands. The statist character of the land tenure regime was clearly visible in the institutional framework and procedures that organized this process. This same set of institutions constituted a political-economy framework for governing people within these territories. The land regime structured political authority by placing land recipients in a relationship of direct economic dependency on agents of the central state (unmediated by so-called traditional or customary authorities). State actors gained considerable economic leverage over these African farmers, and this translated into power to influence their patterns of political participation. In the jurisdictions under the statist land tenure regime, no customary or ancestral rights, claims, or hierarchies were recognized by the state in either the economic or the political domain. Recipients were welded into a solid and politically decisive multiethnic constituency for the leading party, KANU.

Very different land tenure arrangements prevailed in the postcolonial jurisdictions (districts) that were created out of the former African reserves. In these territories, the new Kenyan government upheld land rights that the colonial state had recognized as customary, including the practices of ethnic exclusivity and gender hierarchy that customary land allocation implied. The Kenyatta government institutionalized the land-allocation and adjudication powers of

---

[38] Oucho (2002, 151). Leys (1975, 89–90) wrote that about 40% of the old mixed-farm area became settlement schemes and that about 60% (2 million acres, he says) was sold as large farms, many of which were group-owned (as land-purchase cooperatives). Most assessments converge around the finding that about 3–4 million acres, or about half of the old Scheduled Areas, was settled by African smallholders by the end of the 1970s. On large holdings, see Leys 1975, 89–90.

senior male community members by vesting these in postcolonial county councils, and by upholding them in everyday land-administration practice.[39] These
political choices enhanced the land prerogatives of household heads at the
expense of the colonial chiefs in the farming areas of the former reserves. Kisii
district, discussed in Chapter 6, is a case in point. Examples can also be found
throughout the rest of Nyanza Province and in the long-settled farming areas
of Central Province.

For smallholders, there were two main routes of access to government-
allocated land in the Rift: the settlement schemes and the land-buying
companies.

Land transfer programs of the 1960s created a total of 123 smallholder
settlement schemes.[40] Most were either 5,000-acre "low-density schemes"
designed for commercial farming, or 10,000-acre "high-density schemes"
designed for subsistence farming.[41] Land was allocated in average parcel sizes
of 20 to 40 acres (8 to 16 hectares) in low-density schemes that were intended to
be run as businesses and generate commercial returns. In high-density schemes
where the creation of a stable peasantry was the government's goal, the average landholding size was 10 to 15 acres (4 to 6 hectares) in areas with good
farming potential, and 27 to 40 acres (11 to 16 hectares) in less favorable areas.
Through this process, the government by 1970 had established about 500,000
people on the land, out of a Kenyan population of 11.2 million. Oucho (2002,
151) reported that by 1984, 2,198,000 acres had been allocated through a total
of 278 settlement schemes.

Before 1963, most of the land for smallholders was allotted on an ethnic
basis. One mechanism for accomplishing this was redrawing the boundaries of
the ethnic reserves (by the 1962 Carter Boundaries Commission) to incorporate
parts of the former Scheduled Areas into the ethnic homelands. For example,
through an adjustment of the Rift Valley/Western Province boundary, land
allocated through the Muhoroni settlement scheme "for the Luo" was incorporated into the new Western Province, comprising the old Luo reserve and
intended as a Luo "sphere of influence" (see Harbeson 1973,148, 237, inter
alia). Similarly, the boundaries of the new Central Province, comprising the
Kikuyu reserve and reconfirmed as the "Kikuyu sphere of influence" under the
new designation, were drawn to incorporate the Kinangop Plateau lands that
were allocated under the Nyandarua District schemes "for the Kikuyu." The
same goal was achieved by creating settlement schemes on land *contiguous*
with the homelands of ethnic groups deemed deserving (in need) of additional
land, and designating these lands as expansion areas for the members of that

[39] Coldham 1984, 63–64.
[40] Von Haugwitz 1972, 12.
[41] See Odingo 1971, 200–201.

group. Yet another mechanism that reproduced the link between ethnic entitlement and land access was the creation of settlement areas in the former Scheduled Areas that were specifically designated "for the Luo" or "for the Luyha" or "for the Kipsigis." (See Etherington 1963, 24–25; Harbeson 1973, 266–267.) Until 1963, local and regional leaders picked the settlers for these ethnic schemes.

After 1963, with the independence of Kenya, most of the regionalist provisions of the Majimbo Constitution were gutted. The political and institutional shift in the balance of power had three main effects on land allocation: (1) the idea of making ethnic schemes contiguous to the ethnic "homelands" was dropped; (2) multiethnic schemes, and schemes that implanted settlers "not of the surrounding ethnic community," were created in Rift Valley Province districts, in the heartlands of the former Scheduled Areas; and (3), the balance of power among those involved in selecting settlers and administering the schemes shifted from local or regional political leaders and provincial administrators to an agency of the central government, the Department of Settlement (which included nearly sixty Peace Corps volunteers), which ran the schemes directly until 1966.[42]

Harbeson argues that "KADU [had] wished...to prevent the central government from introducing into the settlement schemes settlers of ethnic groups different from those that inhabited the remainder of the region" (1973, 155), but that KANU had won out on this and had "remove[d] features of the Majimbo constitution that provided for separate administration of the land program" (1973, 165).[43]

These were the terms and conditions under which most of the Rift Valley Province settlement schemes were created. As Robert Maxon explains, by 1969, Kericho and Nandi Districts in the reconstituted Rift Valley Province now had both high density and low density schemes within their borders. The period of intensive settlement on the Kericho and Nandi schemes was 1963–1967, with most completed by 1969. High and low density schemes in Uasin Gishu and Trans Nzoia Districts drew settlers from Nyanza, Western, and Central Provinces as well as from within Rift Valley Province.[44] The Burnt Forest area, which became a zone of mostly Kikuyu settlement schemes, was purchased by the state in 1965.[45] Many settlers on the Uasin Gishu and Trans Nzoia District schemes were Kikuyu who had previously been employed on European farms in these areas.[46] By 1971, one-sixth of the total land area of these two districts had been converted into settlement schemes (i.e., 100,000 hectares of a total

---

[42] Harbeson 1973, 154–156, 234, 253.
[43] See also Odingo 1971; Bates 2005, chapter 1; Anderson 2005.
[44] Maxon in Ochieng', ed., 2002, 294–295.
[45] C. Bryson Hull, "Ghost of Moi," Reuters, 11 January 2008.
[46] Etherington 1963 (see also van Haugwitz 1972, 16; Leys 1975, 73).

of 607,000 hectares).[47] Meanwhile, by 1971, more than 125,000 hectares in Nakuru District were under settlement schemes (Odingo 1971, 193). According to Oucho's figures, the number of African land allottees in Rift Valley Province increased more than sixfold from 1968 to 1979, from 5,350 settlers (allottees) to 34,253.[48]

State officials – political appointees, politicians, and civil servants – were in direct control of the allocation of plots to individual household heads, who were selected one-by-one, often on the basis of individual applications. According to Berman and Lonsdale (1992b), politicians were reluctant to concede too much of such a valuable patronage resource to the former squatters who had formed the backbone of the nationalist insurgency, and who claimed to have earned land rights on the basis of their own sweat equity. The allocation of land on the schemes was governed largely by the political needs of an emergent class of politicians who "wanted strong constituencies of support" which could be built up in part by establishing relations of clientage with settlers on the state-sponsored schemes.[49] The gateway to access to these "new lands" was selection by the government's land boards, and access to state financing.

Harbeson describes the security of tenure on these schemes:

The actual titles to the lands are held by the Central Land Board and are to become the possession of the settlers only when they meet their financial and developmental obligations [to pay for their plots, financed on a 30-year government loan at 6 percent rate of interest, and farm according to conditions laid out in a Letter of Allotment]. The settlers ... have no legal recourse in case the settlement administration tries to recall loans or repossess plots. . . . The settlers are in reality tenants on sufferance of the settlement administration. . . . [Their] security of tenure is substantially *less* than that of the Africans involved in the land-consolidation programs [in Central Province] and even of those who have access to land according to traditional rules of tenure. (Harbeson 1973, 282, 283, 284–285)

Rates of loan repayment on the schemes were low, and eviction of defaulters was rare.[50] In some cases, President Kenyatta himself intervened to offer repayment relief. Land titles were not issued to individuals who had not paid off their government loans. Often, no individual titles were issued to members

---

[47] Odingo 1971, 188. Note that the Haraka Schemes were settled in 1966–1970 and the Shirika (or Cooperative) schemes were settled in 1970–1976.

[48] In Central Province, the number of settlers increased by about 60% in the same period (from 14,734 to 23,898 persons) (Oucho 2002, 155). In August 1964, Kenyatta announced a new Two Million Acre scheme to resettle 200,000 families on 10- to 15-acre plots, covering the whole of the remaining mixed-farm area. "By 1970, the pressure of landlessness made a further project of resettlement politically inescapable" (Leys 1975, 83–84).

[49] Berman and Lonsdale 1992b, 460–461.

[50] On repayment rates, Harbeson 1973, 300–301; von Haugwitz 1972, 67–73; Migot-Adholla et al. 1994, 129–130; Ensminger 1997, 182. On the low incidence of eviction of defaulters, see Leys 1975, 79. On repayment relief, see Harbeson 1973, 300–301.

of cooperative societies who received state financing to purchase shares in group farms.[51] Transferability of rights was restricted: sale of land on the settlement areas had to be approved by the Land Control Board, which "operated paternalistically to protect people from becoming landless."[52] Membership in the state-organized agricultural cooperatives was "nearly universal" (Harbeson 1973, 286; von Haugwitz 1972, 16; Bates 1981). These features of land rights on the schemes kept alive the direct, political tie between the rights holders and the state.

In the late 1960s and 1970s, the Kenyatta government also encouraged the formation of semiprivate land-buying companies. Land-buying companies purchased or leased farms or estates in the former White Highlands from the government, often from the Settlement Fund Trustees (SFT), and then subdivided these holdings among individual (family) shareholders. Many ordinary Kenyan citizens, mostly groups of Kikuyu and Luo coethnics but also groups from other ethnicities, acquired land in the Rift by purchasing shares in the land-buying companies.[53] For example, the Owiro Farm in Songhor Location, in Tinderet Division of Nandi District (Rift Valley Province), was bought by a group of Luo from a European named Evanson with money contributed by them and bridging finance from the Agricultural Finance Corporation.[54] Objections by Nandi politicians (starting in the late 1950s) about government-assisted settlement of non-Nandi in what they viewed as the "Nandi sphere of influence" were systematically overridden.

Onoma (2010) explains that the processes of creating and running the land-buying companies was sometimes very politicized. Around Nakuru, for example, the SFT acquired estates and then sold them to land-buying companies headed by high-ranking members of the Kenyatta regime, some of whom had received state financing for this purpose.[55] The Akiwumi Report (1999, 138, 147, 60) cited the case of a member of parliament who represented Laikipia West Constituency and, later, Molo Constituency, in both Nakuru District, who owned private finance companies that provided loans for settlers to obtain plots on properties that he himself had acquired from the government and that lay in his own electoral constituencies.[56] Those who settled the land in this

---

[51] See, for example, Akiwumi Report 1999, 62–63 and 210 on the lack of title deeds. Page 210 deals with Trans-Nzoia schemes.

[52] Ensminger 1997, 188. More generally, see Migot-Adholla et al. 1994, 127.

[53] Berman and Lonsdale 1992b, 460, see also 460–463; Leys 1975, 74–75. On the move away from the idea that the Rift settlement schemes would be used mostly to alleviate Kikuyu land hunger, see Wasserman 1973, 137; Harbeson 1973, 149; Gisemba 2008.

[54] Akiwumi Report (1999, 76).

[55] As explained in the Akiwumi Report (1999, 138). Some were financed through private mortgage companies owned by prominent politicians.

[56] This MP, Dixon Kihika Kimani, "wields a lot of influence in the two areas, largely because of his past role in assisting the majority of the residents to get land there" (Akiwumi Report 1999, 160).

way often became the political clients of those who controlled the land-buying companies.

In 1975, Colin Leys (1975, 228; see also 84) presciently identified the key political stakes in the land-allocation process: the land patronage, the rising stakes as land grew scarcer, and the sharpening of the distributive struggle:

> The final stages of the British-financed buy-outs of mixed farms [from 1970 on] were marked by a significant blurring of the boundary between "settlement" and large-farm transfer [as LBCs or cooperatives], the President regularly "handing over" large farms to hundreds of assembled people at well-publicized ceremonies. This served the purpose [inter alia] of keeping hope alive among the constantly renewed ranks of the land-less.... The major difficulty which this policy presented was that it did involve further large-scale immigration of Kikuyu onto land in the Rift Valley which was regarded by the various Kalenjin tribes as traditionally theirs. At first this problem was muted, but in the second half of the 1960s it began to dawn on everyone that the amount of mixed-farm land still available for purchase in the Rift Valley was limited, and the question was, who would get hold of it?

As under feudalism in Europe and under the customary land regimes in Africa, in the statist LTRs there is a blending of land authority and political authority. In the case of the early Kenyan settlement schemes described by Harbeson, this could be either an asset or a liability for the government. Settlers could credit the Kenyatta regime for their good fortune in receiving land allotments, but they could also use their direct tie to the state to send messages of protest. For example, nonservicing of government loans on some of the early settlement schemes was sometimes interpreted as a statement of political protest against government policy (see Harbeson 1973). With the political closure of the mid-1960s, the political autonomy of farmers on the state-allocated plots of land was further constrained. State agents could pressure and monitor settlers directly through the clientelist relations that tied settlers to the political patrons who sponsored their access to the land schemes, or to settlement-scheme administrators and the party men who ran the cooperatives (as described by Bates 1981 in *Markets and States in Tropical Africa*).

Agents of Kenya's powerful provincial administration ruled these districts with a heavy hand, participating in the management of the schemes, sitting on the Land Control Boards, and keeping a tight political watch on populations.[57]

The National Citizenship Regime in the Rift

In the Rift Valley, the postcolonial government of Kenyatta imposed the basic principle that access to government-allocated lands – through settlement schemes, the LBCs, or transactions authorized by the local land boards – was open to all Kenyans (even if particular schemes and deals were structured

---

[57] See Mueller 1984 on 1960s elections. See also Branch and Cheeseman 2006.

around ethnic patronage or favoritism). In the former Scheduled Areas of the Rift, the principle of *national* citizenship prevailed, rather than the customary land tenure principles that had legitimated political authority and land entitlement in the reserves under colonial rule and that remained salient in these jurisdictions after independence. With the defeat of Majimboism in 1964, many of the settlement schemes and LBCs in Nandi, Kericho, Bomet, Uasin Gishu, and Trans-Nzoia Districts were constituted as "intertribal entities," either formally or de facto when allocation was done without regard to ethnicity.[58] Many of the schemes became intertribal entities over the course of the 1960s, 1970s, and 1980s, through land transactions (including land sales) and the creation of new families. These arrangements stood out as highly distinctive in the Kenyan context. James Scott (1998, 32) defines "national citizenship" as a technology of government born of the modern era – it is defined as a uniform, homogenous citizenship status, prevailing throughout an integrated legal sphere and centered on the abstraction of the "unmarked citizen." The antithesis is the society of subject populations clustered into ethnic groups and ethnic homelands.

The national, economically liberal principle that "Kenyans have the right to live anywhere and own property anywhere" had limited practical meaning in jurisdictions in which neocustomary land tenure regimes remained strong and salient – that is, in former native reserves such as Kisii and Central Province, wherein the "titular nationality" asserted a group entitlement to land and remained the overwhelming majority of the population.[59] Yet the principle of national citizenship was enforced with government muscle in the settlement scheme areas of the Rift and the state-controlled lands in Coastal Province. KANU's position in the 1960s, as voiced by the party chairman, was "that there should be no tribal boundaries and that land should be obtainable anywhere."[60] By Kenya's 1962 census, 43.5 percent of the population of Rift Valley Province had not been born in that jurisdiction.[61] By the end of the 1960s, ethnic strangers were a majority of the population of Nakuru District.

Losers and Ethnogenesis

The Majimboists lobbied and maneuvered for the restoration (creation) of ethnoterritorial spheres of influence that would have considerable political

---

[58] See Gisemba 2008.

[59] This remained true in spite of land registration of the 1960s and early 1970s. See Chapter 3's references to the Kenyan land registration experience and Chapter 6 on Kisii.

[60] As reported in a 19 November 1960 letter from the Kakamega District Commissioner to the Settlement Board. KNA, PC/NZA/4/14/9, Correspondence.

[61] Ominde 1968, 122, 124. He compares this to 11.18% in Central Province and 4.61% in Nyanza and notes that "the African districts within Rift Valley Province [i.e., ex-reserves such as Nandi and Kericho] attracted a very small part of the inflow." Only 1.6% of the Nandi District population was not born there.

autonomy vis-à-vis the central government, including political control over land. They were defeated by the nationalists organized by KANU in 1963 and 1964. Under Kenyatta, the KANU government used its land powers to open the Rift to settlement by peoples and persons who were not recognized by the state as indigenous to these jurisdictions, and who did not claim ancestral or customary rights in these areas.

The main land-rights losers in this process were members of groups claiming ancestral or precolonial rights over the former Scheduled Areas of the Rift. These people had been pushed behind the White Highlands boundary line by the colonial state. Under colonial rule, they were categorized into state-recognized ethnic groups (the Nandi, Kipsigis, Maasai, Tugen, Elgeyo, Samburu, Marakwet, Sabaot, Pokot, Terik, Turkana, and so on), which were recognized as corporate entities with state-recognized land rights in the Tribal Trust Lands, or "reserves," that flanked the White Highlands (see Lynch 2008). Almost 75 percent of what became the White Highlands was claimed by the Maasai, and the rest by the more populous agropastoral groups who lived on "the western side of the Rift and the low-lying sides of [Lake] Victoria/Nyanza."[62]

State authorities at the time (both colonial and Kenyatta's KANU government) argued that the ongoing development of more exclusive land rights in the Rift, especially the exclusion of predominantly pastoral peoples from the central farming districts, did not impose much opportunity cost on the affected populations. They pointed to low population densities in zones supposedly most suitable for pastoral livelihoods and possibilities for agricultural intensification on family farms in the reserves (Harbeson 1973, 189–190).[63] While this argument may have been plausible for some parts of the Rift in the 1960s, demographic increase and the extension of large landholdings in the central Rift made it completely implausible by the late 1970s. For the peoples claiming precolonial and ancestral rights to land in the central Rift, the perceived costs of this loss did not decrease, or become less onerous, over time. Demographic and environmental stress in the former reserves, and a slowing (by the early 1980s) in the expansion of non-farm employment, sustained and increased demand for farmland and pastureland in the central Rift.

---

[62] Berman and Lonsdale 1992a, 20.

[63] One obvious exceptions was the case of the Nandi. Nandi leaders had complained of overcrowding in the Nandi reserve since the 1930s, and "the Nandi" had received an allotment of Scheduled Areas land (structured into a settlement scheme within an expanded Nandi District) in 1962 and 1963, supposedly to relieve population pressure. Because they claimed much of Uasin Gishu District, and because parts of the future Nandi District were turned into multiethnic settlement schemes controlled directly by the central government, the addition of land to Nandi District in 1962 did not resolve the land-rights conflict as far as many Nandi were concerned. The Nandi situation is discussed later in this chapter. See also Klopp 2002.

The substantive basis for the rise of a "Kalenjin" ethnic identity lay in the shared interests of those who lost land rights through the imposition and workings of Kenya's statist land tenure regime in the central Rift. Political leaders invested initiative and effort in building a common defensive front or alliance against land-rights expropriation by the state. They sought to rectify not only the loss of land per se but also the loss of *political control* over land.

The name Kalenjin came into use as a group designation in Kenya among World War II servicemen and ex-servicemen and students in the elite East African high schools in Nairobi and Kampala in the 1940s.[64] When Moi led the effort to amalgamate the political organizations of the state-recognized tribes of the western Rift in early 1960, he called the umbrella group the Kalenjin Political Association. When the colonial ban on supralocal political parties was lifted, KADU was founded as a political vehicle to promote the interests of this group. The centerpiece of KADU's political platform, and the glue that held together its constituent elements, was the goal of securing an institutional dispensation that would allow these groups to assert political authority over Rift Valley lands abandoned by whites and/or owned by the central government at the time the new constitution came into force. By the time of the February 1962 Lancaster House constitutional negotiations, "the rifts between KANU and KADU were ... 'deep and deeply felt.' ... [In the talks,] Moi would repeat that 'the people of Kalenjin were prepared to fight and die for their land'" (Anderson 2005, 556).

Kalenjin first appeared as an official ethnicity on the Kenyan census in 1979, Moi's first year as president. Moi promoted Kalenjin identity in the 1980s and 1990s as an ethnic designation to transcend the narrower, older colonial-era identities of Nandi, Kipsigis, Elgeyo, Tugen, and so on (Médard 1996, 69, 73). The same "historical marginalisation with regards to land" was the grist for the Moi regime's attempts to mobilize an even larger political coalition around the KAMATUSA identity (Kalenjin-Maasai-Turkana-Samburu) in the 1990s.

This ethnic consciousness of being Kalenjin was rooted in the native-stranger distinction. In very large part, it was produced by the land tenure regime. To paraphrase Ley's counterfactual reasoning (1975, 203), the form of ethnic consciousness and mobilization that developed in Kenya was not the consciousness of "all the people of each tribe as having a common grievance against all the people of other tribes." If that were the case, tribalism in Rift Valley land politics "would not have had its most striking characteristic, namely that it was almost wholly a consciousness of being either Kikuyu or not Kikuyu." By the 1990s, it would be more accurate to refer to a cleavage that separated the Kikuyu-led coalition of people claiming the land as settlers and squatters from

---

[64] Anderson 2005, 551 n. 10; Klopp 2002.

the countercoalition of peoples claiming land on the grounds that these were their ancestral homelands.

Land Conflict under the Statist LTR

Under the statist LTR in the Rift, the predominance of the settlers' land claims was grounded in, and enforced by, the coercive and law-making powers of the national government. Rulers backed the land tenure of the in-migrants they sponsored, as they did in the case of southwestern Côte d'Ivoire under Houphouet.

This pattern was visible in the unfolding of land conflicts around the Rift Valley settlement schemes under both the late colonial regime and the Kenyatta regime. Anderson (2005, 552, 556) writes of "Kalenjin fear of Gikuyu colonization of the Rift" in the 1950s. By 1961, the outcome the Rift Valley indigenes feared was taking shape. In August 1961, the *East African Standard* reported on conflict over settlement projects that were already under way: people from Central Province "were being intimidated and told not to enter into settlement schemes," but Mr. Lipscomb, chairman of the Settlement Board, said that "desire for land would overcome intimidation.... Mr. Blundell [minister for agriculture] said that the schemes would go on."[65] The Kenyan government's Official Commission of Inquiry into the ethnic violence of the 1990s made frequent references to earlier "land clashes" that were quickly extinguished by the police or the provincial authorities, such as those that expressed "prophetic tensions" around Nakuru in 1961, and violent clashes in Narok West between newcomers and Maasai in 1967. A dispute over the Buru Farm in Kericho District dated back to 1972, when the government settled Luo farmers and defended them against local hostility.[66] Throup and Hornsby (1998, 188) mention 1984 clashes between Nandi and Luhya in Kapkangani, describing these as "similar to the outbreak of violence in Nov. 1991 on Miteitei Farm" (where locals claiming ancestral land rights mobilized in attacks aimed at the expulsion of settlers) but note that the 1984 clashes were "quickly ended by the local administration."

Our argument is that statist land regimes channel land-related conflict into the national political arena. This dynamic is starkly visible in the conflicts over Rift Valley lands: grievances were targeted at the central state. In the years following Kenya's independence, avenues and forums for the overt political expression of these grievances were shut down. At the subnational level, localities were ruled by pro-KANU chiefs and KANU party bosses right down to

---

[65] Kenya National Archives, "Settlement Schemes: Land Development and Settlement Board Papers," 1962 [PC/NZA/4/14/9] clipping from *East Africa Standard*, 8 September 1961.
[66] Akiwumi Report 1999, 116, 96–103, 163–164.

Kenya's smallest administrative jurisdictions (the sublocations).[67] The Provincial Administration ruled the districts with a heavy hand.[68]

At the national level, KADU, the voice for the political defense of land rights that had been lost to the state, was snuffed out in 1964 when it dissolved in a merger with KANU. Moi became vice president of the republic and receded into the shadowy corridors of power.[69] Kenya became a one-party state in 1966. The assassination or imprisonment of Kenyatta's most visible and popular ex-comrades in 1969 (Mboya and Odinga) contributed to the steady closure of the national political arena. The land grievances of people claiming to be indigenous to the Rift, which had been widely aired in national political forums in the late 1950s and early 1960s, were repressed.[70] In Hirschman's terms, the "voice" of Rift Valley land-rights losers was silenced. Their menu of practical political options was effectively limited to exit and loyalty.

The highly visible political trajectory of Jean-Marie Seroney is one of the exceptions that help prove these rules. Jean-Marie Seroney was an MP from Nandi District, where bitter land disputes and negotiations between the native Nandi and the central state had been ongoing since 1919.[71] Long-standing grievances were fueled by the official settlement programs of 1960–1966, in which properties within the Nandi reserve that had been expropriated by the state in 1919, as well some expatriate-owned sugar farms in the southern part of Nandi District, were reacquired by the government and redistributed to Kenyan settlers with no ancestral claims to Nandi land. Jean Seroney, born in Kapsabet in 1925, was elected MP for Nandi North Constituency (Tinderet) in 1963 on a KADU ticket. He became deputy speaker of parliament, and, not silenced

---

[67] For a glimpse into KANU organization at the sublocation level in the Rift, see the Kiliku Report 1992, 61. Barkan and Chege (1989, 447) argue that whereas Kenyatta had come to rely on clientelist networks centered on loyal bosses, Moi had invested in the revival of the district and local-level KANU organizations in the 1980s.

[68] See Barkan and Chege 1989, Branch and Cheeseman 2006, Bates 1981.

[69] On the land side of the deal, see Leys 1975, 229.

[70] In addition to KADU itself, there was another public forum for the expression of these demands and grievances: it was the audiences and hearings held by the 1962 Kenya Regional Boundaries Commission, which had been broadly sympathetic to historical claims to land and the need for "expansion areas." It was guided by the principle of "taking into account tribal affinities and historical claims" in accordance with people's wishes to "avoid domination by others" (4).

[71] After 1904, the British pushed the Nandi out of land they had won from the Maasai in the 1880s. A "reserve" was created for them on the Rift's western flanks. In 1919, the state expropriated about 17% of this land area (the Nandi Salient/Kipkarren area) – the Carter Commission (1933, 272) described it as "some of the best agricultural land in the country" – to create a Soldier Settlement Scheme for European World War I veterans. In the early 1930s, some 8,000 Nandi living on alienated land were considered squatters. In testimony to the 1933 Carter Commission, "the Nandi at Kapsabet regarded the question of the Kipkarren farms as a serious grievance" (Carter Commission 1933, 271, 277; see also 270–275; map on 492). On the Nandi situation, see note 157, this chapter, and Ellis 1976.

by the KADU-KANU merger in 1964, Seroney carried forward his mandate of "protesting the invasion of their [Nandi] ancestral lands by settlers."[72] He published the Nandi Hills Declaration in 1969, denouncing Kenyatta's sale of Nandi land to non-Nandi, branding the settlement schemes "Kenyatta's colonization of the Rift," and laying claim to all land in the district for the Nandi.[73] For this Seroney was charged with sedition, convicted, and fined. Still serving as the Nandi North MP, he was imprisoned in 1975 for denouncing the postcolonial land allocation to non-Nandi settlers. He remained in detention until the end of the Kenyatta regime in 1978.[74] The Seroney episode was one of the landmark cases of high-level political repression of the Kenyatta years, and as Walter Oyugi (2000, 7) points out, "The matter [Saroney had raised] never died and erupted in the fiery clashes of 1991 and 2. It recurred in 1997 and 2002."

A more famous victim of land-related political repression in Kenyatta's Kenya is J. M. Kariuki. Kariuki gained huge popularity by denouncing in parliament the unfair land distribution policies of the Kenyatta regime, and for accusing Kenyatta of allocating the lion's share of state-owned Rift Valley land to his own cronies rather than to the poor, including those who had actually fought for Kenya's independence. Echoes of earlier fights within Kikuyuland over dispossession within the reserve, and fights of national scope over who was entitled to Rift lands, ran through his discourse.[75]

The Moi Government in the 1980s

When Kenyatta died in 1978, Vice President Moi inherited the presidency and proceeded to use all the machinery of government, including the land-allocation and land-adjudication powers of the state, to consolidate his position.

The first step in this process was the 1981 presidential edict that subdivided the Rift Valley land-buying companies "to undercut those who were using them as a springboard for electoral politics" (Gisemba, 2008, 5; see also Onoma 2010). This worked to dissolve the political clienteles of some of Moi's

---

[72] Oyugi 2000, 7.

[73] See Leys 1975, 229–230.

[74] Harbeson (1973, 238, 238 n. 45) notes that Maasai politicians also voiced land grievances, also targeted at the central government, but did so within elite circles. "The Maasai claimed several thousand acres of Nyandarua on the grounds that this land had previously been theirs.... The Maasai, including the Maasai assistant ministers in government, continue to express their dissatisfaction and resentment over this whenever the opportunity presents itself.... [They] do not hesitate even today to embarrass their cabinet colleagues by reasserting this claim."

[75] Kariuki, an ex–Mau Mau fighter and Kenyatta's personal secretary from 1963 to 1969, was elected a member of parliament from Nyandarua North constituency in 1974. He was assassinated in 1975 in the most notorious political torture and murder of the decade. He is remembered for arguing that "Kenya has become a nation of 10 millionaires and 10 million beggars." See Githinji 2000.

immediate rivals: Kikuyu barons of the ancien régime. Land politics in these localities was drawn out of Kenyatta-era machine politics and into the courts (and the market).[76] Accelerating processes of registration, titling, and negotiation of mortgages in the smallholder areas had two political effects that are important in the present analysis. First, these processes increased the profile and expanded the role of the courts in land processes, notably in settling ownership disputes and processing foreclosures. Second, the new spurt of land registration and titling raised the temperature of indigene-settler tensions in disputed areas. Registration and titling are legal markers of the growing exclusivity of land rights. These changes mark a critical (although not irreversible) step in the state's institutionalization of land enclosures and land markets. In at least some of the settlement scheme and LBC areas in the Rift, renewed impetus toward titling, along with the end of the Kenyatta government – which was widely regarded as the patron of the Kikuyu settlers – added new urgency to efforts to secure official recognition of land claims by both settlers and indigenes.[77]

In the late 1980s, Moi undertook to reassert the ruler's political prerogative in land allocation by constraining the role of the courts and markets in allocating land rights. The provincial administration was his instrument of choice.[78] Ensminger (1997, 190) quotes the *Daily Nation* of 21 June 1989 as saying that Moi "argued that it was unfair to take land cases to courts," and that as a result, more land transactions "are being moved out of the courts and back to the local land boards [provincial administration plus "elders"].... [Land cases are moved] from the courts to the local level." This was formalized in a 1991 presidential decree wherein "President Moi ordered that all land foreclosures must be approved by the provincial administration, a more cumbersome process than the courts" (Ensminger 1997, 189). Henrysson and Joireman reinforce the point: under Moi, the courts were discouraged from carrying out their jurisdiction over land issues as Moi maintained a patronage system through land allocation.[79]

Meanwhile, Moi used the sweeping land-allocation powers of the office of the president to begin to reallocate land to his own core constituencies in the

---

[76] Ensminger (1997, 189) says that "in the late 1980s, an increasing number of mortgage foreclosures were making it into the popular press."

[77] Throup and Hornsby (1998, 198–199) note that registration and titling (replacement of communal deeds with individual titles) was under way in several settlement areas in the late 1980s – 1991, and that one goal of the 1991 attacks on settlers (discussed in Chapter 9), was to drive out settlers before this process could be completed.

[78] On the provincial administration under Moi, see Barkan and Chege 1989; Throup and Hornsby 1998, 37–38; Branch and Cheeseman 2006.

[79] Henrysson and Joireman 2009, 49, citing Okuro 2002. On the displacement of the courts from the land-allocation and land-dispute adjudication processes in the 1950s and 1960s, and the role of provincial administration in this domain, see Coldham 1984, 63–65. Coldham argues that "the main reason [for this] was probably political" (63).

Rift Valley.[80] From 1986 on, government forestlands became a *caisse noire* of patronage resources that were used to cement elite alliances and build political support for Moi among the Kalenjin constituencies he needed as a mass power base.[81] Evictions of Kenyatta-era forest squatters and the declassification of new forestland opened a land frontier that Moi used to settle thousands of Kalenjin families. The Kikuyu owner of a small residential plot located between Turi and Molo in Nakuru District told me that "most Kikuyu were expelled from the Mau [Forest] in the 1980s. Kalenjin moved in. Many were allowed to settle [in the Mau Forest area] south of Njoro. They clear-cut and started farming."[82]

Our theory predicts that under statist land tenure regimes, governments will protect settler communities *they themselves have implanted* (but not those settled by their political rivals in earlier eras). Moi's 1980s forest evictions of Kikuyu squatters – the most politically vulnerable of the farming communities settled under the patronage of the Kenyatta regime – were the first real evidence that the Kenyatta-to-Moi power shift could indeed produce this effect (i.e., the disowning of settlers). Once the new Kalenjin-coalition communities were settled in government forests, they became dependent on the political favor and protection of regime dignitaries, just as their Kenyatta-era predecessors had been.[83] New state purchases of land, including the 1980s acquisition of a large parcel in Kipkabus, Uasin Gishu District, from the Lonhro subsidiary EATEC, gave the government direct control over new lands that could be

---

[80] Leys (1975, 229) mentions Moi's personal sponsorship of settlement schemes for Kalenjin after 1966. On Moi's efforts to dynamize the Kalenjin bloc after 1980, see Lynch 2006, 2008. Lynch (2008, 543) notes that the various Kalenjin subgroups formed the majority in twenty-eight of fifty constituencies in Rift Valley Province. Klopp (2002) flags class and other divisions within the Kalenjin bloc.

[81] Southall 2005, 149, summarizes Ndungu Report findings on forestland.

[82] He added that others were settled on ADC farms acquired by (Moi ally and minister of roads from Buret) Franklin Bett (interview, Molo, 16 November 2008). As one victim of 2007–2008 election violence put it, the Mau forest evictions of 1986 "were the start of all these problems." They were evicted from forests around Londiani, Njoro, and Elburgon. "Then, this land was given to Kalenjin" (interview, Eldoret, 18 November 2008). Another interviewee added that Kalenjin were settled in the 1980s in the Anabkoi and Singalo Forests (Timbaroa, 17 November 2008).

[83] In the 1990s, the period covered in Chapter 9, the Moi government allowed large numbers of Kalenjin squatters to settle in the Anabkoi and Singalo forests of Uasin Gishu District in forest reserve areas that were often adjacent to the preexisting settlement schemes and LBC farms. In the run-up to the 2002 elections, vast tracks of the Mau forest reserve were cleared for settlement. In 2001, 27.3% of the southwest Mau Forest Reserve (22,797 hectares) was degazetted and settled. In addition, 54.3% of the eastern Mau Forest (35,301 ha) was degazetted in 2001. The Mau excision "was challenged in court and orders were given to stop it, but settlement went ahead and most of the area is now settled." (UNEP/KWS 2008). The Ndungu Commission Report (2004) stated that about 39% of the officially gazetted forest had been illegally excised (according to aerial surveys) and recommended that most of the illegally allocated land be revoked. Degazetting may have happened *after* the actual settlement of farmers (i.e., as a post hoc ratification).

allocated in statist fashion to settlers: "Through sponsored economic mobility and political patronage, [the EATEC property] was allocated to members of the Kalenjin community."[84] The discretionary power of the state over land, exercised through the president's office and the Ministry of Lands, was also used to allocate large farms and vast estates to members of Moi's ruling clique.[85]

As Gisemba (2008, 5) summarized it, "In the best practices of political patronage, Moi used state forest, and demonstration and research farms owned by parastatals such as the Agricultural Development Corporation (ADC) and Kenya Agricultural Research Institute (KARI) to reward loyalists drawn largely from his community."

Conclusion

The case of the Rift is useful in building our argument about the political effects of *variation* in LTRs. The (neo)customary and the statist LTRs structure the relationship between ethnic insiders, outsiders, and the state in two very different ways. The so-called customary regimes are structured to favor ethnic insiders' land claims over those of ethnic outsiders, and governments, in opting to invest in the so-called customary tenure regimes, have opted to bolster the putatively customary authority wielded by "traditional authorities," elders, or chiefs. In direct contrast to this, in all three of the statist LTRs considered in this chapter, *settlers'* land claims trump those of people claiming ancestral rights.

"FORCED COHABITATION" IN EASTERN DRC

> The local population never accepted the implantation of Rwandans on their
> ancestral lands (*terres autochtones*).
> (Mathieu and Mafikiri Tsongo 1999, 44)

Eastern Democratic Republic of the Congo (DRC) (formerly Congo, then Zaire), especially the areas closest to the lakes, is a zone of high in-migration.[86] (Map 5.) From low population densities in the mid-1800s, the eastern edges of the Kivu region became, over the course of the next century, the most densely populated areas of the country.[87] Mountain districts of Kivu (*le Kivu montagneux*) – including the North Kivu zones of Masisi and Rutshuru, the epicenter of the land-related conflicts analyzed here, and the South Kivu areas around the city of Bukavu – reached population densities of 108 inhabitants per square kilometer in 1990. Mathieu et al. report that real population densities in the

---

[84] Gisemba 2008, 4–5. EATEC is the East African Tannin Extract Company. See also Klopp 2002.
[85] Klopp 2000, Southall 2005.
[86] Willame (1997a, 40) explains that the west side of the Great Lakes was seen as a frontier zone (or as "uninhabited" – see Rugenena Mucyo 1996).
[87] Vlassenroot and Huggins 2005, 118, 140.

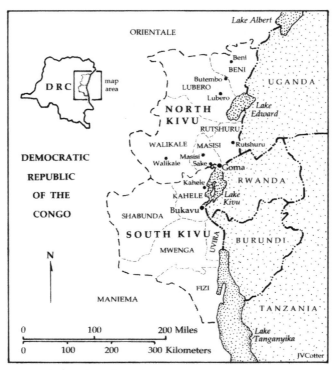

MAP 5. Eastern DRC: North and South Kivu

peasant farming areas of Masisi zone in 1990 (that is, excluding large ranches
and commercial estates that dominate the countryside in parts of North Kivu)
were around 300 inhabitants per square kilometer – "scarcely less than those
prevailing in neighboring Rwanda."[88] (These are about the same as the population densities observed in Kisii, in western Kenya. See Chapter 6.)

Steadily intensifying pressure on the land reflects at least three forces at
work in North Kivu Province, the focus of this analysis.[89] First is the history of

[88] Mathieu and Mafikiri Tsongo 1999, 27; Mathieu, Laurent, Mafikiri Tsongo, and Mugangu
1999, 13.

[89] Until 1988, North Kivu was one of four administrative subdivisions (*sous-régions*) of Kivu
Province (one of eight Zairian provinces). In 1988, North Kivu became a province in its own
right, with Goma as the capital. (See Roland Pourtier 1997, 34.) North Kivu is a territory of
59,483 sq. km, 37% of which is covered by parks, forest reserve, lakes, and mountain peaks.
Masisi zone is a jurisdiction of 4,737 sq. km. North Kivu's population circa 1992 was 2.274
million; South Kivu's population was 2.303 million (de Villiers with Omasombo-Tshando 1997,
61).

"massive population displacements"[90] in the Great Lakes Region, which has produced both state-coerced and spontaneous migrations of populations (from Rwanda, mostly) into the mountainous areas of Kivu. Second is the process of concentration of landholding, via forceful expropriations of communal and peasant land by the state, which began in the Belgian colonial period and accelerated greatly in the 1970s. Third is a high rate of natural population increase (about 3.1 percent per year) for North and South Kivu as of the early 1990s.[91]

J.-C. Willame (1997, 44) writes that rising population density and land scarcity, coupled with extremely feeble rates and forms of development of alternative livelihoods, gave the region a *conflictualité potentielle* (conflict proneness) that was already evident at the time of independence in 1960. As argued at earlier points in this study, however, scarcity alone does not predict whether, when, where, or how social conflict over resource access will find expression in the political arena.

Ethnic heterogeneity is a striking feature of society in North Kivu, but this does not tell us how rising pressure on the land will find political expression, as demonstrated in the assembled case studies in Part II of this book. Of a North Kivu population of about 3 million in 1993, 1.6 to 2 million persons – by varying estimates 30–50 percent,[92] 50 percent,[93] or almost 60 percent[94] of the total – were considered non-autochthonous and of Rwandan origin, and known locally as Banyarwanda. Of these, about 80 percent were Hutu and about 20 percent were Tutsi,[95] although this distinction was not always politically salient in North Kivu.

The autochthonous population itself was not unified under a single ethnic institution or identity. Under colonial rule, the autochthones had been categorized, grouped into territorially circumscribed administrative jurisdictions called *chefferies* (chieftaincies) and placed under the authority of chiefs named and recognized by the Belgian authorities. In the early 1990s, the population of North Kivu was officially classified as 40 percent Nande (aka Banande, predominant in Beni and Lubero jurisdictions in the northern parts of the province)

---

[90] Mafikiri Tsongo 1997.
[91] On rate of the population increase, see Vlassenroot and Huggins 2005, 140–143.
[92] Mathieu, Laurent, Mafikiri Tsongo, and Mugangu 1999, 13; Mathieu and Mafikiri Tsongo 1999, 24–25.
[93] Tegera 1995, 398–399; Prunier 1997, 43. Prunier gives the corresponding figure for South Kivu (for 1990) as 20%.
[94] Kabamba and Lanotte 1999, 125–126. The Rwandan-origin population of North Kivu appears to have doubled from 1955 to 1970 (from 175,000 to 335,000) as a result of both natural increase and an influx of Rwandan Tutsi refugees during 1959–1963), and doubled again (or tripled) from 1970 to 1994 (to between 700,000 and one million). From Mathieu and Mafikiri Tsongo 1999, 28.
[95] Rugenena Mucyo 1996, 38.

and 3 percent Hunde (Bahunde, regarded as autochthonous in Masisi zone), with smaller groups, including the Nyanga, making up the remaining 6 percent (Tegera 1995, 398–399). The ethnic population mix varied across the five administrative jurisdictions of North Kivu Province. In the early 1990s, in the zones of Masisi, Rutshuru, and Walikale (the three zones closest to Goma, the provincial capital), Banyarwanda were considered to be about 65–70 percent, 25 percent, and 14 percent of the population, respectively. Percentages for the Rwandan-origin population approached zero in the northern zones of the province.[96]

Mafikiri Tsongo uses the term "administrative insertion" to describe the process by which the modern state organized the in-migration of peasant farmers to the Kivus from the 1930s to the 1950s. He and his coauthors describe the resulting social configuration of modern North Kivu as a *cohabitation imposée*, in which autochthonous groups were forced, first by the Belgian colonial state and then by the Zairean state, to accept the presence of immigrant farming populations in provinces marked by growing shortages of new land for smallholders.[97]

Focusing on the Masisi, Rutshuru, and Walikale zones, we see a clear case of a statist land tenure regime, even though the central authorities, from the 1920s to the end of the Mobutu regime in 1997, sought to maintain the screen or buffer of chiefly authority between themselves and peasant farming populations in these jurisdictions. The first section of this analysis makes this argument in tracing three successive eras of state insertion of settlers into rural society in the Kivus. The second section analyzes the political regulation of land in this part of Congo/Zaire, asking whether the statist land tenure regime produced political effects consistent with the hypotheses set forth in Chapter 3. Focusing on questions of ethnicity during the period of one-party rule under Mobutu, we ask: Does the indigene-settler distinction produce (new) ethnic identities, as we saw in the case of the Bété in Côte d'Ivoire and the Kalenjin in Kenya, and a new ethnic cleavage *along the line defined by the land regime*? As rising land scarcity raises the specter of exclusion for some, are the indigenes (that is, the autochthones) the land-rights losers, and does the shape of the local political arena foreclose the political option of voice? Do state-backed ethnic outsiders retain the upper hand? Are land politics projected into the national political arena, as we would predict, given the statist nature of the land tenure regime?

Chapter 9 studies the effects of Zaire's political opening and aborted "transition to democracy" in 1990–1994 on the struggle for and against state-allocated land rights in North Kivu.

---

[96] Mathieu, Laurent, Mafikiri Tsongo, and Mugangu 1999, 13; Mathieu and Mafikiri Tsongo 1999, 24–25; Pabanel (1991, 36), citing dubious official estimates; Guichaoua 1989, T. 1, 151.

[97] Mathieu, Laurent, Mafikiri Tsongo, and Mugangu 1999, 14, 15 inter alia.

Three Eras of State Insertion of Settlers into the Kivus

1. *The Mission pour l'Immigration des Banyarwanda (1937–1955)*

The Belgian colonial state made vast concessions in the Congo to private companies, including the Comité Spécial du Katanga and the Comité National du Kivu, which was granted an 800,000-hectare concession in Kivu.[98] In the 1930s, the colonial state developed a policy of "transplanting" Rwandan peasants in Kivu, both to relieve overpopulation in Rwanda and support the development of commercial activities, especially plantation agriculture.[99] The task was charged to the MIB. This agency took charge of more than 150,000 hectares in Kivu, of which 35,000 (or 350 square kilometers,[100] or 7 percent of Masisi's total area) were designated for *lotissement* (division into lots) and the creation of settlement schemes for immigrant Rwandans. From 1937 to 1945, the MIB forcibly transplanted some 25,000 Rwandans to Gishari (Masisi zone, west of Goma), then a sparsely populated highland area.[101] Immigrants were "installed" on plots of 2.5 to 5 hectares[102] that were laid out along lines cut by roads and that were supposed to provide for households' subsistence needs and a small cash income. From 1949 to 1954, another 60,000 Rwandans (15,000 families) were officially "imported" to North Kivu. The "assisted migrants" settled in the collectivities of Mushali and Bwito (in Rutshuru) and Washali and Mokoto (in Masisi zone). Willame (1997a, 41–42) refers to MIB displacement and relocation protocols and writes that in Rutshuru,

the same policy of displacement and relocalization of Rwandan-origin populations was undertaken. Here, it involved the clearing-out [*vider*] of territory to make room for European coffee growers (60–70 ha per *colon*) and for the creation...of the Parc de la Virunga. Here also, populations were transplanted into *paysannats* [settlement schemes], where Banyarwanda and members of the Nande ethnic group [whose traditional area lay farther to the north] lived together at the end of the 1950s, and where farmers were obliged to grow coffee.

---

[98] The CNKi (Comité National du Kivu) chartered in 1928, was dissolved in 1960 and replaced by the Service des Titres Immobiliers du Kivu (Bukavu). Mathieu and Mafikiri Tsongo 1999, 47, 48. The size of the concession was reduced to 400,000 ha in 1943 (Willame 1997a, 40).

[99] See Newbury 1988, 143–144, 159–161, 166–167. She mentions that some of the "transplants" had been displaced by expropriations in Rwanda. Newbury explains that after World War I, an influx of Europeans settled near Lake Kivu. They created coffee, tea, and quinine plantations. By 1929, there were 943 European settlers in this part of Belgian Congo. See also Guichaoua 1989, 31. Some of the Rwandans were sent to the Congo's Katanga province to help develop a workforce for mining companies. Of the Rwandans who immigrated to Congo under l'Immigration des Banyarwanda (MIB) auspices, the colonial authorities classified 70% as Hutu and 30% as Tutsi (Willame 1997a, 42).

[100] Mathieu et Mafikiri Tsongo 1999, 24.

[101] Newbury 1988, 143.

[102] Kraler n.d., 13.

The MIB was in charge of the "technical and political problems (vis-à-vis the local chiefs)" associated with these waves of settlement.[103] "Everything was planned down to an extraordinary level of minutia": formalities on arrival, political organization of the immigration zones, land tenure rules, salaries to pay to workers, infrastructure to be built by the new arrivals (Willame 1997a, 41).

During the same period, some 30,000 unofficial immigrants arrived from Rwanda, especially during the 1949–1953 famine in Rwanda. From 1953 to 1955, more immigrants arrived, still encouraged by the colonial authorities. The newcomers spilled out beyond the limits of the "attributed zone" of Gishari, and occupied lands "to the west in Washali-Mokoto, and in the direction of Walikali."[104]

The settlement programs that were engineered along what Guichaoua (1989, 309) calls Rwanda's *"l'axe d'émigration forcée vers le Congo"* (axis of forced emigration to the Congo) were considered successful. By the time of Congo's independence from Belgium, Kivu was home to about 85,450 of these official in-migrants, plus their offspring, plus many informal or spontaneous in-migrants, creating a Rwandan-origin population of about 200,000 persons. Mathieu et al. (1999) write that most of the Banyarwanda population of North Kivu traces its roots in Congo/Zaire to these colonial-era migrations.[105]

2. High Commission on Refugees

From 1959 to 1963, some 100,000 Rwandan (Tutsi) refugees were installed in what are now North and South Kivu Provinces, especially in the territories of Kalehe, Kabare, Uvira, Goma, and Masisi, by the UN High Commission on Refugees.[106] "The customary chiefs considered the implantation of several refugee camps as an outright expropriation of land."[107] By Reyntjens and Marysse's (1996, 18) count, this refugee inflow brought to about 300,000, the number of Kinyarwanda speakers installed in Kivu since 1920. These migrants were "settled by the national and international authorities. To gain access to

---

[103] Guichaoua 1989, 309.

[104] Paternostre de la Mairieu 1972, 177; Mathieu and Mafikiri Tsongo 1999, 24. Pabanel 1991, 33 explains that Washali-Mokoto was considered "full Bahunde territory."

[105] Mathieu, Laurent, Mafikiri Tsongo, and Mugangu 1999, 14. Some Kinyarwanda-speaking populations in the Kivus have a different history. A Rwandan population in what is now the Bwisha collectivity of Rutshuru zone of North Kivu Province was established in the 1700s. See Pottier 2002, 19; Pottier and Fairhead 1991; Reyntjens 1994, 140; and Willame 1997a, 43 (who said in the 1990s that the Bwisha collectivity was the most ethnically heterogeneous part of North Kivu). Another Rwandan-origin population was established in South Kivu in the 1890s; they came to be known as the Banyamulenge. And in 1925, there was a forced migration of Rwandans into Kivu, toward Rutshuru and Masisi, to clear the way for the creation of the Parc National des Virunga (Guichaoua 1989, 309).

[106] The first refugees (1959–1960) came to Ihula and Bibwe, under the UNHCR and in cooperation with the local authorities, but were later dispersed (Tegera 1995, 397).

[107] Mathieu and Mafikiri Tsongo 1999, 44.

land, the refugees did not negotiate directly with the existing land authorities and the local level" (Mafikiri Tsongo 1997, 184). The "forced welcome" of the Rwandan Tutsi refugees was viewed by local populations as yet another *cohabitation imposée.*

3. Centrally Imposed "Acquéreurs"

Nationalization of all foreign-owned properties in Zaire in 1973 transferred a dazzling array of assets into the hands of the Mobutu regime: mines, plantations, real estate, factories, businesses. In a process of "Zairianization," these assets were handed out to regime clients who came to be known as *acquéreurs* (acquirers).[108] In the Kivus, Mobutu transferred ownership of ranches and plantations to members of the Rwandan elite, a group he had cultivated as a base of support in eastern Zaire and as a counterweight to politicians and administrators claiming to represent autochthonous communities. These land transfers were confirmed via the issuance of private titles to the new owners – a move designed to confirm the extraction of these properties from the realm of customary land rights, land claims, and local authority and to locate the titled properties squarely in the domain of statutory law and under the direct jurisdiction of the central state. The Rwandan-origin *acquéreurs* of the 1970s included Rwema Bisengimana, Mobutu's chief of staff, who received the biggest of all the estates, the Osso Ranch, around 1975. In 1980, a 230,000-hectare concession in the territory of Walikale was granted to the Cyprien Rwakabuba, a Rwandan and longtime Mobutu-regime insider (member of the MPR Comité Central). The concession was later revoked in response to flaming protest and official complaints in Kinshasa.[109] Vlassenroot and Huggins (2005, 135) report that since 1973, an estimated 90 percent of the former properties of the Comité National du Kivu has been transferred to Banyarwanda.

From 1979 onward, the process of privatization of land via purchase and titling in Kivu seems to have assumed a more commercial and politically decentralized character. Many wealthy individuals were able to grease the regional and local levers of power to acquire large landholdings in Kivu or acquire titles to land they had staked claim to in earlier periods. Members of the Rwandaphone elite who had arrived with the early 1960s wave of refugees were very conspicuous among these "cosmopolitan bourgeoisie businessmen and property owners," especially in Masisi.[110] The World Bank and other external funding agencies played a role in this process by encouraging and financing the development of extensive forms of "modern ranching" (one head of cattle per hectare) in the Kivus. Mathieu et al. point out that these vast ranching concessions absorbed little labor, created few employment opportunities, and

---

[108] See Young and Turner 1985.

[109] Willame 1997a, 57. MPR was the Mouvement Populaire de la Révolution, Mobutu's ruling party.

[110] Mathieu and Mafikiri Tsongo 1999, 27.

created few multiplier effects for the regional economy.[111] Peasant populations were expelled to clear the way for grazing animals.

In 1991, Mobutu gave a 20,000-hectare estate in Walikale to Juvenal Habyarimana, the president of Rwanda.[112] The Habyarimana family also had ranches in Masisi. In 1989, 58 percent of the land under title in Masisi was owned by 512 families, of whom 503 were immigrants "installed under Mobutu on land expropriated in the 1970s from the Belgians."[113]

The Political Regulation of Land: 1930s–1990

Conflicts over land and the regulation of land access have been endemic in the eastern part of Kivu since the 1940s. Our argument is that the particular character of these conflicts – the main line of social cleavage, the balance of power between the antagonists, the ethnic identities mobilized in land politics, the political target of land grievances – is determined by the land tenure regime. The direct role of the central state in the allocation of land is the decisive variable, as it has been in the cases of southwestern Côte d'Ivoire and the farming districts of Kenya's Rift Valley. Chapter 9 argues that this is why *the electoral arena* became a theater of land-related conflict in 1991–1994.

As the theory would predict, in North Kivu the political advantage of the settlers over the indigenes rises and falls along with the power of the central state. We track this effect by tracking the region's politics – never separable from land struggles – over four time periods: the Belgian colonial period, the "deregulatory aftermath of independence" period, the high-water mark of the Mobutu regime, and the onset of the decline of the Mobutu regime.

The Central State and Chieftaincy, 1930–1960

In the 1930s, the Belgian colonial authorities decided to apply an administrative strategy of indirect rule in Kivu. In North Kivu, the Belgians' version of "customary authority" was based on the *droit de autochtonie*, or the principle of indigeneity (firstcomer status), "divided almost exclusively" between the groups deemed by the Belgians to be preeminent in the area: the Hunde, Nyanga, Nande, and Tembo.[114] This process created an explicit political hierarchy among and within the population groups of the region, and linked land rights to membership in official chieftaincies. These arrangements gave the holders of the land rights so secured a stake in making sure that outsiders and newcomers respected the official chieftaincies and chiefly authority.

---

[111] Mathieu, Mafikiri Tsongo, and Mugangu 1999, 89.

[112] Willame 1997a, 65.

[113] Vlassenroot and Huggins 2004, 3. Mafikiri Tsongo (1997, 194) says that 75% of all arable land in Masisi is occupied by Banyarwanda. The figure "58 percent of titled land" is from Mathieu and Mafikiri Tsongo 1999, 52.

[114] Tegera 1995, 398. See Kraler n.d., 6. Callaghy writes in 1984 that the important Bahunde chiefdom was the direct descendant of a precolonial ministate (1984, 382).

So it was that in the mid-1930s, to obtain land for Rwandan families transplanted into the Congo, the MIB had to negotiate the purchase of tens of thousands of hectares of land in Masisi and Rutshuru from customary chiefs whom the Belgians themselves had recognized and confirmed in office. Sources note that in Masisi, the legitimate Hunde chief was imprisoned at the time of this transaction; that local populations had never recognized the *acte de cession* signed by the Bahunde chief, Kalinda, as a permanent transfer of land rights to outsiders; and that the conditions under which the Rwandans were settled in North Kivu had been contested by the autochthones from the start.[115] Pottier writes that signing these "lease agreements" for the resettlement of Rwandans was also difficult in Rutshuru because some colonial plantations had already been created in that area, "and there was confusion of land rights between plantations and the new immigrants."[116]

In an attempt to "naturalize" the Rwandan immigrants in Masisi and create an administrative jurisdiction isomorphic to the chieftaincies already in place, in 1940 a Belgian district commissioner created a "Rwandan chiefdom" to govern and represent the newcomers. A jurisdiction of 350 square kilometers was carved out of Kishali lands in Hunde territory and designated "the autonomous chiefdom of Gishari."[117] (See Figure 2.2.) A Rwandan chief (a Tutsi), chosen from among the immigrants, was appointed. Pottier (2002, 20) writes that Rwandan chiefs were also appointed in some other jurisdictions where the "assisted migrants" had settled. These measures were contested, however. In 1957, the governor general of the Belgian Congo abolished the Rwandan chiefdom of Gishari and integrated it into the Hunde chiefdom.

Over time, the in-migrant population spilled out of its original jurisdictions and into territory governed as "indigenous circumscriptions" under colonialism's default model of customary land tenure.[118] "As lands allocated by the colonial state became saturated, new immigrants sought land from the local chiefs. This required them to pay a regular *redevance* [payment or fee], and submit to the political authority of the local autochthonous chiefs.... The land remained the property of the indigenous chief [but use rights could become more secure over time]."[119]

As the land frontier in North Kivu closed and unoccupied land became scarcer, social and political tension intensified. As the end of colonial rule

---

[115] Mathieu and Mafikiri Tsongo 1999, 43–44; Pottier (2002), citing Pabanel (1991, 33), say that the original transaction was a lease agreement and that Kalinda received 29,600 Belgian francs as compensation.

[116] Pottier 2002, 26, citing Fairhead 1989, 12.

[117] See Pabanel 1991 and Mararo 1996, 89–91. This was the size of the MIB concession, so these might have been coterminous. Some sources report that the Gishari chiefdom was created in 1939.

[118] This was the official term. See Pole Institute 2003, 7.

[119] Mathieu and Mafikiri Tsongo 1999, 40.

approached, "land conflicts soared" (Kraler n.d., 14), and local populations
were "more and more hostile over the colonial state's land allocations."[120]
Land competition, and competition for the political authority to define land
rights, created a clear line of division in North Kivu. It pitted those who
could claim land rights on the basis of "citizenship" in an autochthonous
chieftaincy against those whose land rights were derived from direct allocation
from the central state (in this case, from the colonial administration's land
allocations, administered in some cases by "immigrant chiefs" appointed by the
Belgians).[121] The coexistence of a neocustomary land tenure regime and a statist
land tenure regime was a legacy of Belgian rule. In some areas, the two different
land tenure regimes were in force in adjacent territories (or even governed
adjacent properties, as was the case where commercial ranches abutted peasant
farming areas). In other areas, the two land regimes were superimposed one
over the other, as when administratively inserted immigrants were placed under
the authority of the Hunde chiefdom in the late 1950s.

After 1966, under Mobutu, the statist character of the postcolonial land
regime became uniformly predominant throughout Masisi and Rutshuru, with
the chief-administered land regime a vestigial residue that appears to have
served mostly to administer peasant areas and facilitate direct state expropriation of peasant lands.

"The Deregulatory Aftermath of Independence": 1960–1966[122]

The years 1960–1966 were a period of open confrontation over these issues,
pitting autochthones against the transplants in a struggle over *le pouvoir foncier*
(literally, land power). The Banyarwanda population of the Kivus looked to
a strong central government to enforce their claims to citizenship, their right
to exercise political power, and their land rights. They threw their weight
behind strong nationalist (Lumumbist) or moderate, regionwide (i.e., noneth-
nic) political parties in 1960–1964[123] and pushed for the maintenance of large
political jurisdictions in Kivu that would dilute the power of "ethnic politicians" with small territorial bases. They also pushed for liberal definitions
of Congolese citizenship that would include most of the Rwandan-speaking

---

[120] Willame 1997a, 40. See also Pabanel 1991, 33–34.

[121] According to Mathieu and Mafikiri Tsongo (1999, 39–40), the indigenous population held
that (1) the sale of use rights was limited to the colonial period only and that rights should
return to the domain of customary authority on the departure of the Belgians; and (2) the immigrants should be dependent politically on the authority of the chiefs. Immigrants, however,
believed that the colonial administration had given them inheritable rights to the land they had
settled.

[122] This phrase is from Pottier 2002, 26, citing Fairhead 1989, 15.

[123] The Banyarwanda supported the regional party CEREA (Centre de Regroupement Africain),
which won a "crushing majority" in North Kivu and a little less than half in Kivu-Maniema
in the 1960 elections. Willame 1997a, 46–47.

population. Banyarwanda politicians held ministerial positions in both the national and provincial governments.[124]

Politicians representing the most numerous of the autochthonous groups, by contrast, saw colonialism's end as an opportunity to try to lighten the weight of oppressive central rule, to establish smaller administrative-cum-political jurisdictions in which the highly localized territorial bases of their power and their small but cohesive ethnic constituencies would acquire maximum political value, to assert "autochthony" as the criterion for citizenship (and, thus, political power and representation in the postcolonial state), and to reassert traditional, chieftaincy-based rights over land. As Mathieu and Mafikiri Tsongo (1999, 45) write, "The goal of the autochthonous political elite was to control power and scarce resources (land), and to mobilize the rural masses around the problem of occupation of land and territory by immigrants." To be credible, the autochthonous leaders themselves had some credential polishing to do: Hunde and other chiefs who were blamed for complicity in the 1937–1955 "invasion" of Kivu by Rwandans scrambled to reestablish their nativist bona fides and to show that they were capable of defending the interests of the autochthones. Through the subdivision of some local jurisdictions (chieftaincies), the administrative reach of some of the most compromised chiefs was reduced.[125]

Willame argues in *Banyarwanda et Banyamulenge* (1997a, 44–50) that the Rwandan-origin populations sought political protection and advantage in deterritorialization strategies.[126] That is, they relied on – and, therefore, invested in – strategies that established their political influence (and the security of their property claims) in nonlocal or supralocal political arenas. Deterritorialization aimed to put the Rwandan-origin population "above and beyond"

---

[124] Willame 1997a, 47–48. He notes that Celestin Rwamakubu was minister of mines in the (new) provincial government of Kivu Central in 1963, Cyprien Rwakabuba was minister of education of the provincial government of Kivu, and that Marcel Bisukiro was named by Lumumba as minister of external commerce in the national government.

[125] One result is the November 1961 division of the (Ba) Hunde chieftaincy (Masisi) into two, in response to demands of the Bashali, whose territory was the locus of massive installation of Rwandans under the chieftaincy of Kalinda. The Bashali argued that Kalinda had betrayed the Hunde by giving so much land to the Banyarwanda. They now demanded the right to secede from Kalinda's jurisdiction and manage their own territory. The Bahunde chieftaincy was divided into Bashali (four *groupements*) and Banyungu (nine *groupements*). Rutshuru was divided into Bwisha and Bwito. See Mathieu and Mafikiri Tsongo 1999, 46.

[126] The case can be made for both North and South Kivu, but it seems that the so-called Banyamulenge have more consistently pursued a two-track strategy: both reinforcing their links to the center *and* trying to secure formal/legal recognition in customary idiom (as would be the case if they were to gain their own jurisdiction/chieftaincy). It is true that there have been moments when some Banyarwanda populations of North Kivu have also sought formal-level parity with autochthonous groups via the establishment of their "own" administrative jurisdictions, most notably in 1947, 1963–1964, and 1993.

the territorially bound authority of local chiefs, and outside of restrictions that defined political and property rights in terms of autochthony. This seems fully consistent with the fact that at the time of independence, at the microlevel, the land claims of most of the Banyarwanda were pegged to the authority of the central state.[127] In this regard, their situation was structurally similar to that of the Rift Valley settlers and the strangers in southwestern Côte d'Ivoire, who were also bearers of a national vision of citizenship and dependent on a strong central state.

Land-related conflict between the Rwandan-origin immigrant populations and the autochthones in North Kivu was projected onto the larger stages of electoral and legislative politics in the 1960–1966 period. Control over the lucrative commercial circuits that linked eastern Congo to Uganda was also at stake. The political strength of the Banyarwanda ebbed and flowed, largely as a function of changes in the political strength of the central government.

With the end of colonial rule, autochthonous leaders went on the political offensive immediately. "Autochthones voted with their feet and entered the Banyarwanda settlements to reclaim their 'inheritance.' Throughout Kivu, those who considered themselves to be rightful inheritors of the land began to (re?)claim what they considered to be their inalienable ancestral land."[128] In Rutshuru, autochthonous politicians campaigned to have Banyarwanda declared to be noncitizens.

Yet Rwandan-origin populations *were* recognized as citizens in the new Congolese state. Banyarwanda politicians and constituencies – already about half the population of North Kivu[129] – were well represented in the 1960 and 1962 provincial assemblies of Kivu, where they carried a regionwide political party to victory. They "jostled for political power" with autochthonous elites in provincial elections and in the assembly.[130] Political discourse was structured around the stranger-versus-indigene cleavage and dominated by the debate over "the Rwandans' massive infiltration of Kivu."[131]

The Rwandan-origin politicians were unable to block the *démembrement* (dismemberment) of Kivu into three "provincettes" in 1963, but they were well represented in the Central and North Kivu Assemblies that were created as a

---

[127] Mathieu, Laurent, Mafikiri Tsongo, and Mugangu (1999, 18) draw these same connections: "for Rwandans in general, the procedures and logics of modern law [modern land law] clearly represented the only possible route to the securing of their land rights that they so desperately sought.... For them, to accept the logic of autochthony would have necessarily meant dependency, precariousness, and the risks of very real and growing economic exploitation at the hands of the local chiefs."

[128] Pottier 2002, 26, citing Fairhead 1989, 15.

[129] Mathieu, Laurent, Mafikiri Tsongo, and Mugangu 1999, 18–19. The Hunde were probably already a minority in Masisi. Chrétien (2003, 342–343) estimates that in the 1960s, half the population of North Kivu (and one-fifth of Sout Kivu's population) was of Rwandan origin.

[130] Pottier 2002, 26. Willame (1997a, 47 n. 26–27 inter alia) draws on the Comptes Rendus (minutes) of the 1962 meetings of the Assemblée Provinciale du Kivu.

[131] Willame 1997a, 47–48.

result. A *"Rwandais"* of Rutshuru presided over the Assemblée Provinciale of Kivu-Central, and Banyarwanda were disproportionately represented in the assembly and controlled strategic positions therein. Willame (1997a, 47–49) explains that in North Kivu in 1963–1964, the Banyarwanda went head-to-head with the Banande elites in the struggle to establish political dominance. Banande politicians were determined to control the new Assemblée Provinciale. Banyarwanda leaders tried to ally with two smaller groups, the Bahunde and the Banyanga, to check their ascent.[132]

In 1964, the tide turned dramatically, although temporarily, in favor of the autochthonous groups: the central government passed a law restricting citizenship and its attendant rights to those who traced their ancestry to groups established in the national territory before 1908. This disenfranchised almost the entire Banyarwanda population of North Kivu. One direct consequence was that Banyarwanda chiefs were replaced with Hunde chiefs throughout Masisi.[133] "This loss of power for the Banyarwanda resulted in a loss of property: houses, shops, cattle, and plantations were all (re?)claimed by autochthones"; [much] "became the property of the Hunde authorities."[134]

The "Kanyarwanda revolt" or Kanyarwanda movement of 1962–1964 developed in this context, when central state authority was at its lowest ebb. In 1963–1964, with the 1965 legislative and national elections in view, Banyarwanda populations attempted to free themselves from the authority of the local chiefs by securing a separate administrative zone for themselves.[135] This attempt was brutally repressed by the Goma territorial authorities, with the help of the national army. Many of those implicated as leaders or active MNC/Lumumba or CEREA partisans were murdered. Some of the "Rwandan" leaders were arrested and transferred to Léopoldville (Kinshasa) for "disobedience during an electoral period" or for sabotaging an election. In October 1965, the North Kivu Assemblée Provinciale passed a *résolution-loi* authorizing the expulsion of all Rwandans from the region, citing "collusion with rebels."[136]

The military coup of 25 November 1965 put an end to Congo's First Republic. Mobutu, now in control of the national government, undertook to bring

---

[132] See also Tegera 1995, 399, and Pole Institute 2003.

[133] Willame 1997a, 50; Pottier 2002, 26–27.

[134] Before and after the "[much]" are from Pottier (2002, 26–27) and Willame (1997a, 50), respectively.

[135] See Willame 1997a, 51.

[136] Willame 1997a, 51. See also Memorandum des Communautés Hutu et Tutsi du Nord-Kivu, 25 avril 1993, 5–6. Rugenena Mucyo (1996, 35) dates the arrests and violence to the period after the May 1965 election and attributes them to the *"truquage des elections au profit des seules Hunde"* (election fraud that advantaged the Hunde alone). MNC/Lumumba was the Mouvement National Congolais/Lumumba. On CEREA (Centre de Regroupement Africain), see earlier note.

Kivu, "one of the most ungovernable of regions of the Congo," under central control.[137]

High-Water Mark of Central State Authority: 1972 to circa 1980

Under the Mobutu dictatorship, the authority of the Zairian state, as it was renamed in 1971, was reasserted at the expense of political localisms and democratic forms of representation. Willame (1997a, 52) writes that the coming to power of Mobutu "saved the 'Rwandans' installed legally or illegally in Congo."

Mobutu cultivated Rwandan-origin politicians and businessmen as a political and economic elite in North Kivu and as regime insiders in Kinshasa. Those associated with the 1959 expulsion of Tutsi from Rwanda were especially favored.[138] Many analysts describe this strategy as exemplary of Mobutu's general modus operandi, which was to ally with political leaders "whose ethnic groups were small or who had an ambiguous status" (1) as part of a divide-and-rule strategy in the regions, and (2) to block the assent of ambitious politicians who might "aspire to national leadership or threaten the central government" (Pottier 2002, 27). This strategy had the effect not only of stabilizing the status and acquired land rights of Rwandan-origin populations in Kivu but also of greatly benefitting the Rwandan-origin elite.

The provincial governments, which had provided a base for the rise of autochthonous politicians in the Kivus, were abolished. A hierarchical provincial administration linked directly to the central state imposed control, and the colonial *chefferies*, microterritories at the bottom of the political-administrative ladder, were assimilated into it. Some chiefs were named zone commissioners, and most became grassroots agents of the ruling party, the MPR. Callaghy (1984, 383–384) describes how the fusion of administrative/coercive and chiefly authority in Masisi promoted the economic and political fortunes of the chiefly Kalinda family (known for Kalinda's collaboration with the Belgians in installing the Rwandans in Masisi) and helped the regime control the Bahunde population.[139] Many observers have described the process of

---

[137] Willame 1997a, 45–46, 49–51. See also Mathieu et Mafikiri Tsongo 1999, 49–50. Willame underscores that the North Kivu political struggles were not connected to the Mulelist rebellion, which was centered in South Kivu and Maniema. Rwandaphone populations in South Kivu supported the central government, by now under the control of Mobutu, in its repression of the Mulelists in South Kivu.

[138] Willame 1997b, 90–91. Worthy of mention are Bathélémy Bisengimana, leader of the Rwandan students' association in the 1960s, who became director of Bureau du Président de la République, 1967–1977, and Cyprien Rwakabuba, who became a member of the Comité Central of the MPR.

[139] Callaghy (1984, 387–389) notes that recentralization of the Bahunde chieftaincy "prevented the secession of Bashali," which had regained its autonomy in 1963–1967. The family of Mwami Kalinda Miteetso established a corrupt feudal enclave. Callaghy describes the Rutshuru chieftaincy of Mwami Ndeze Rubago II in the same terms.

centralization of power under Mobutu as a reversion to the colonial model of government.

The most important collective gain for Rwandan-origin populations was the 1972 citizenship law. This law retroactively granted citizenship to all Rwandan immigrants living in Congo as of 1950, thus reconfirming their rights to political participation, political representation, and property holding – *"principally those rights relating to land access"* – within the state of Zaire.[140]

For all practical purposes, the 1972 law conferred almost blanket citizenship to all Rwandan-origin groups in Kivu, given the administrative difficulties of distinguishing the pre-1950 from the post-1950 immigrants, the fact that no census or registration of Zaireans and non-Zaireans in Kivu was undertaken after 1972, and the ease with which one could purchase citizenship papers in eastern Zaire.[141] With passage of this law, *"Masisi literally changes owners"* as the Rwandan population, almost 70 percent of the total, becomes the politically recognized majority (Willame 1997a, 54). Pottier (2002, 27) notes the flip side: the new law "harmed the interests of North Kivu's autochthonous groups, especially the Nyanga and Hunde, who overnight had been turned into minority groups." Banyarwanda reclaimed some lands that had been seized in 1964.

Shortly thereafter, two political changes occurred that further strengthened the role of the central state in allocating land in Kivu and that redounded to the benefit of the Banyarwanda elite. The first was Zairianization (nationalization of properties) by decree. This inaugurated a process by which lands that had been allocated by the Comité National du Kivu were nationalized and transferred to clients of the regime. In North Kivu, most of them were Banyarwanda.

The second was the 1973 land law – the so-called Loi Bakajika de 1973 – which legalized private ownership of land by Zairean nationals (only), through processes implemented and enforced by the central state. P.-J. Laurent describes this law as "giving the state monopoly land powers" (*monopole foncier*) and opening the door to the "massive intrusion of the Zairian state into land questions in Kivu."[142] In legal terms, the 1973 Loi Bakajika created the foundation for an open land market. In practical terms, it was a tool that was used to bring about a virtually unrestricted state-engineered transfer of land from the peasant

---

[140] Emphasis added. Mathieu, Laurent, Mafikiri Tsongo, and Mugangu 1999, 18. This is Law 72–002 du 5 janvier 1972, granting citizenship to those in Congo in 1950 and for the next ten years. Reyntjens and Marysse (1996, 27) and others note that the law seems to be the result of the personal initiative of Bisengimana, who explained to the Conseil Legislative that Rwandans "deported" to the Congo by the Belgian authorities deserved to have citizenship rights. See also Mugangu 1999, 202.

[141] Mathieu and Mafikiri Tsongo 1999, 25.

[142] Laurent 1999, 75, 77; see also 74–78. Young and Turner (1985, 288) report that the Bakajika Law was adopted and voted on by both houses of parliament in 1966, stipulating inter alia that all public land was a domain of the Zairian nation-state. The 1973 land laws must have been an extension of this.

(or neocustomary) sector to individuals and firms whose rights were derived directly from the central state ("private owners").[143] Mathieu and Mafikiri Tsongo (1999, 36, 38) explain this by saying that the 1973 land law integrated all state agents with land-allocation powers into a single corrupt, clientelist hierarchy: from the president himself to the minister of land affairs, to the regional governors appointed by the president, to the regional land registrars (in the offices of the Conservation des Titres), to the local chiefs.

This strong imposition of central state authority in the 1966–1980 period was the sine qua non of the third wave of administrative insertion of regime clients into the rural territories of North Kivu. Banyarwanda members of the Mobutu-era elite acquired large landholdings in North Kivu, both through land grants from Kinshasa and through land purchases.[144]

Purchase and titling were arranged through regional administrative authorities and the chiefs, whose reputation for corruption and venality soared after 1973. Under the 1973 land law, "the local chiefs became administrative agents in the state-controlled system of land registration, cadastration, and concession-granting."[145] They were thus empowered to sell "communal lands" out from under small farmers, forcibly expel families from their villages and farms, and pocket the proceeds. After 1973, the chiefs of Kivu became more powerful vis-à-vis their subjects/clients, with enhanced powers to arbitrarily allocate, repossess, expropriate, reallocate, and sell land. These changes accentuated their role as tools of the central state.

Vlassenroot and Huggins (2005, 142) note that growing land scarcity for smallholders strengthened the political hold of the neocustomary authorities over local populations, even as these actors became less legitimate in the eyes of the people they both oppressed and claimed to represent. The land-to-person

---

[143] On the nature of these private rights (under *concession perpétuelle ou ordinaire*, subject to *mise en valeur effective des terres*), and the "confused and indeterminate" status of peasant/customary rights under the 1973 law, see Mathieu and Mafikiri Tsongo 1999, 33–36, 47; Vlassenroot and Huggins 2005, 131–135.

[144] Séverin Mugangu (1999, 203) points out that Rwandaphone elites were also among the prominent beneficiaries of Zairianization measures at the national level, most notably in the telecommunication and information sectors. As he suggests, the Rwandaphone elite's complicity in the Mobutu regime's excesses helps explaining why backlash against them emanated from the center of the political system as well as from the eastern provinces.

[145] Mafikiri Tsongo (1996, 185) and Vlassenroot and Huggins 2005, 131, 134, 142. See also Van Acker 2005, 89–90; Tull 2003, 437. A subsequent development, Loi 82–006 du 25 February 1982, made the *chefferies* "entités administratives décentralisées dirigées par des chefs coutumiers" (decentralized administrative entities led/directed by customary chiefs). Mathieu and Mafikiri Tsongo (1999, 37) say that this increased their powers. They write that the chiefs tried to *prevent* the registration (titling) of land in their domains, which would have afforded their subjects a little more protection against arbitrary chiefly authority. Other observers note that when chiefs *did* sell land, they made money but their power was reduced (because lands were removed from their control). Pottier (2002, 27) adds that in some cases, autochthonous chiefs sold land that Banyarwanda Hutu (the most vulnerable and least politically useful of their clients) had been cultivating for decades.

ratio for the mountainous region of Kivu as a whole declined by 62 percent from 1958 to 1990 (from 2.2 hectares per person to 0.81 per person), with about half of this decline occurring by 1970.[146] A general trend toward food insecurity in the Kivus – including famine in the Bwisha collectivity in 1984 and food shortages throughout the region in 1989 – is evidence of a pervasive economic insecurity that would be linked to restricted access to livelihoods, including small-scale farming, in a region with few viable alternatives to agricultural production.[147] "Widespread rural landlessness" or "acute" landlessness meant that many North Kivu families lived in deep poverty.[148] Conditions for much of the poor peasantry in the mountainous parts of Kivu, both autochthones and in-migrants, became increasingly desperate from the mid-1980s onward. At the same time, these people witnessed the enclosure of vast territories, described by some observers as latifundia, by powerful estate owners and ranchers.[149]

Cracks in the Mobutu Regime: 1981–1991
The opening for the autochthonous political elite in Kivu Province began to appear with the early signs of Mobutu's loosening grip on political forces in Zaire. Mugangu (1999, 203) dates this process to the 1977 Shaba rebellions and the early stages of crisis in Zaire's monolithic political system. The late 1970s saw a slight political liberalization. This opened the door to a backlash at high levels of government against the Rwandaphone elite, as well as "growing opposition among autochthonous Zairois in Kivu to the collective granting of citizenship rights to Rwanda and Burundian immigrants."[150]

In June 1981, parliamentarians in Zaire's third legislature (1977–1982) passed Loi 81–002, which annulled and retroactively revoked the citizenship rights granted to the Rwandan-origin population in 1972.[151] Mobutu promulgated the law promptly "to gain the sympathy of the parliamentary malcontents" (Mugangu 1999, 203).

---

[146] Vlassenroot and Huggins 2004, 2; Kraler n.d., 14.
[147] Van Acker 2005, 83; Pottier and Fairhead 1991, 466–467; Vlassenroot and Huggins 2005, 140–141.
[148] Vlassenroot and Huggins 2005, 140–143.
[149] Mathieu, Mafikiri Tsongo, and Mugangu 1999, 89; Mafikiri Tsongo 1996, 193.
[150] Mathieu and Mafikiri Tsongo 1999, 53. The winds were shifting in the late 1970s. Bisengimana lost his post as Mobutu's chief of staff in 1977. In Kivu, a concession of 230,000 hectares in Walikale (one-tenth of Walikale, and a densely populated area) allocated to C. Rwakabuba in 1980 (i.e., to Le Group Rwacico) was withdrawn in the face of official complaints by this zone's deputies who were residing in Kinshasa (Mathieu and Mafikiri Tsongo 1999, 52).
[151] In February 1981, the Comité Central of the MPR established a commission of inquiry into citizenship. By the 1981 law, citizenship was reserved for those demonstrating an ancestral tie to the pre-1885 populations of Zaire. Rwandan immigrants could apply for Zairian citizenship individually. In the nationality debates, the general tendency of the anti-Rwandan camps was to lump all Rwandaphones together. Mathieu and Mafikiri Tsongo 1999, 25, 53; Willame 1997a, 57–61.

In the most contested zones of Masisi and Kalehe, autochthonous politicians, now with the hope that the central state's levers of power could be deployed to their political advantage, "demanded that properties allocated to Banyarwanda be recuperated by the state and redistributed to nationals."[152] In the localities, some politicians riled up peasants against owners of large farms and plantations. A census was announced to provide a legal basis for using state authority to dispossess those determined to be noncitizens and to determine who had a right to vote and run for office. Elections loomed on the horizon.

However, no "identity census" was ever taken in North Kivu, the provincial elections scheduled for 1987 (then pushed back to 1989) were therefore not held in this province, and there were few if any actual dispossessions of *acquéreurs* in the 1980s.[153] The balance of power at the national level was decisive for outcomes in North Kivu: Banyarwanda elites appointed by the central government continued to control the strategic positions within the North Kivu territorial administration. Over the course of the 1980s, dispossession of smallholders, and political and administrative corruption in the land sale and titling processes, reached hitherto unseen proportions.[154] Land conflict in the Kivus intensified. Localized violence broke out (especially in Masisi), sometimes prompting intervention by the province's churches or local NGOs.[155] The conflict also found expression at higher levels of the political system: in petitioning North Kivu's administrative authorities and, for a few, in legal struggles in the courts of Goma.[156] Even so, some local actors remember this as a period of relative calm before the storm that was unleashed with Zaire's transition to multipartism, starting in 1990.[157]

Land politics and land institutions defined the main line of political cleavage in North Kivu in Congo's early postcolonial era, and again with the quickening of political competition in the late 1980s. The settler-versus-native distinction was imposed by the statist land tenure regime (or developed with reference to it), and the ethnic identities of Banyarwanda and *autochtone* aligned along this axis. Banyarwanda meant "Kinyarwanda-speaking," Tutsi and Hutu. "*Autochtone*" was a coalition of Hunde, Nandi, and others who carried the burden of what Claire Médard (1996), writing of the Kalenjin in Kenya, called their "historic marginalization with respect to land." In facing

---

[152] Mathieu and Mafikiri Tsongo 1999, 53.

[153] Willame 1997a, 59–61. South Kivu also failed to hold elections in 1987. Pabanel (1991, 37–38) writes that in 1980, 1982, 1987, and 1989, Hunde and other autochthonous politicians protested the granting of administrative and political posts in North Kivu to Banyarwanda.

[154] Meanwhile, more and more smallholders were forced to sell their land in the economic crisis of the 1980s. Willame 1997a, 64–65.

[155] Churches and local cooperatives sometimes mediated these conflicts (Vlassenroot and Huggins 2005, 142). See also Willame 1997b on churches and NGOs in the wake of the 1993 land-related violence.

[156] See Mafikiri Tsongo 1997.

[157] Memorandum des Communautés Hutu et Tutsi du Nord-Kivu, 25 avril 1993, 6.

the central state, the line of cleavage between these two megagroups, or ethnic coalitions, was the division over the legitimacy of the statist land tenure regime in North Kivu.

Conclusion

By defining political and economic relationships around land, land tenure regimes go far in determining patterns of competition, conflict, and social hierarchy in rural areas. The political effects of the statist land tenure regime prevailing in southwest and center-west Côte d'Ivoire, the farming districts of the Rift, and North Kivu were quite different from those that emerged under the customary tenure regimes considered in Chapter 4. Under the statist land tenure regimes, in complete reversal of the patterns observed where neo-customary authority over land prevails, ethnic groups claiming ancestral or customary rights to land have been the main land-rights *losers*. As a result, land-related conflict took political form as discourses of ethnic revindication launched against the national government, rather than as local-level subordination or repression of ethnic outsiders by their indigenous landlords or hosts. The structure of conflict in the Rift Valley during the Kenyatta years was thus similar to that observed in south-central and southwestern Côte d'Ivoire under the Houphouet regime, and in the Eastern DRC under Mobutu, where statist land tenure regimes also pitted indigenes against the state.

In the cases considered in this chapter, ethnic demands did not follow lines formed by the mosaic of different ethnic identities found in each locality, and violent clashes were not concentrated along the geographic boundaries dividing the homelands of "rival" ethnic groups. Rather, conflict that was expressed in ethnic terms *followed the lines of a political-economic hierarchy inscribed in the land tenure regime* – that is, a hierarchy that granted and enforced settlers' land claims over those of indigenes. An ethnically diverse coalition of indigenes found itself on the losing side of a competition against the ethnically diverse coalition of those who came in and settled under the patronage of the state. The land tenure regime created a line of cleavage around which new ethnic identities coalesced: "Kalenjin" in Kenya, "Bété" in Côte d'Ivoire, and *autochtones* in the eastern DRC. And because the state itself was the author of the prevailing land allocation, land-related conflict was channeled straight into the national political arena, where land-rights losers found voice as aggrieved ethnic constituencies.

PART III

POLITICAL SCALE

Property Institutions and the Scale and Scope of Conflict

> The quarrels and disputes have the effect of turning family members into
> "strangers," or those who do not belong on family land. Often accusations of
> witchcraft accompany the final rupture when a family sub-group is driven out of
> the area, thereby ceding the family land to those who remain.
> (Peters 2002, 158)

> The problem around here is that when the town reaches your land, the chiefs
> take it and there is nothing you can do. You are just on your own. People are
> angry, but there is nothing they can do because they are committed to respect
> for chiefs. Yes, people should band together to resist, but they do not.
> (Assemblyman in periurban Kumasi, 21 July 2009)

> The government and Hutu extremists purposefully politicized the land
> issue. . . . Claims to land by returning Tutsi were used to cast Tutsi intentions as
> an attempt to capture the state and reclaim scarce land from Hutu. . . . This
> resonated with poor rural Hutu who were concerned about the security of their
> own land rights.
> (Bigagaza et al. 2002, 73)

Mahmood Mamdani describes African states as "bifurcated states" that institutionalized two different modes of state-society relations: a civic, republican mode for the urban areas, and an authoritarian, nonliberal mode for
the rural areas. As Mamdani's analysis suggests, a subnational rural jurisdiction in which chiefly authority holds sway is not a miniature version of a
national arena organized around a republican form of government. Although
local units are nested into a national hierarchy, the modes of political representation, association, participation, and contestation that prevail at different levels of the system are not necessarily the same. Where a chiefly jurisdiction is nested into a national administrative hierarchy, the character and

procedures of the national state are at least formally bureaucratic, secular, and constitutional, whereas at the local level, the character of public authority and government is at least partially hereditary, neocustomary, and nonsecular. African political systems are thus marked by what Schattschneider (1960) and Gibson (2005, 2012) have described as *heterogeneity of scale*.[1]

This argument extends to the domain of land tenure institutions and land politics. Differences in the scale of land-allocation authority are associated with differences in what Max Weber would have seen as the form of authority, including modes of allocative and adjudicative decision making, modes of legitimation and accountability, and modes of coercion or repression.

The scale of land-allocation authority also sets parameters that work to delimit the political scope of conflict. Schattschneider defined scope as "who is involved"; it refers to the inclusiveness or exclusiveness of political struggle.[2] As the scale of land-allocation authority varies, so too does the scope of representation and accountability in land politics. Where a village chief has full authority to allocate land, the political scope of a land-related conflict that involves members of the community is likely to be restricted to the village's members and residents.[3] The more explicitly statist the land regime, the larger the possibilities for expanding the political scope of conflict to include the citizenry at large.

Variation in the scale of land-allocation authority produces differences in the scale, scope, and political expression of land-related conflict. These variations are the focus of Part III of this book. The key differences are captured in the introductory epigraphs. Conflict *within* the extended family is evoked first. In the land conflicts in southern Malawi described by Pauline Peters, the scale is extremely local; the territorial and social scope is highly restricted; representation, decision making, and accountability are *familial;* and repression is essentially domestic (as captured in the term "domestic violence").[4] This differs

---

[1] Gibson uses the term "regime juxtaposition" to describe heterogeneity in regime type across levels of government.

[2] Schattschneider 1960, 4–10. Scope may affect the balance of forces in a conflict. In small conflicts, the relative strengths of the contestants is known in advance. People are not apt to fight if they are sure to lose. "One way to restrict the scope of politics is to localize it" (Schattschneider 1960, 10).

[3] As noted in Chapter 2, this study does not consider interjurisdictional land conflicts explicitly. However, it follows logically that the *political scope* of such conflict could encompass both communities.

[4] We assume that in agrarian society, family-level conflict over land is ubiquitous. This is the residual form of land-related conflict – it is visible as the *predominant* form of land-related conflict in situations where neither chiefs nor the state are present as land authorities (and are thus not present to take the heat of land-related tensions). Where chiefs or the state *are* land allocators, lineage and family conflict over land coexists with the other forms of land-related conflict identified here. In the case of southwestern Côte d'Ivoire (Chapters 5, 8), family-level land conflict was deflected or partly defused when youth's anger at their elders was redirected to target ethnic outsiders.

from land-related conflict that invites or activates contestation over the powers of *chieftaincy*, as in the Ghana case invoked in the second epigraph. In these settings, there is potential for expanding the scope of land politics to encompass members of a descent-based landholding (multiclan or ethnic) community. Decision making is oligarchic, although it may be tempered by norms calling for wider consultation (or some legal constraints). Legitimacy and accountability discourses refer to historical precedent and to preservation and welfare of the landholding community. There is a "public arena," but it is confined to what Mamdani called "the local state" – that is, the local jurisdiction in which chiefly authority is constituted, performed, and possibly legitimated. This local public arena may or may not be open to participation and accountability politics. When the state itself is the direct allocator of land rights, as it was throughout much of Rwanda (the case invoked in the third epigraph), the scale and character of politics look very different. An actor with a national jurisdiction, the national government, is the land-rights allocator. It exercises a form of authority that appeals to a republican or nationalist mandate and to a national citizenry for legitimacy. The scope of politics expands because actors throughout the national space can refer to these mandates in attempts to make demands or call rulers to account. Repression is carried out via organs of the national state. The scale and scope of the conflict are "national."

The basic proposition of Part III is that there is a correspondence between the scale of land-allocation authority and the scale and scope of land-related conflict. This is not only because ontologically, power and resistance (or ruler and ruled) are mutually constitutive categories – it is also an institutional effect. These differences in the scale and scope of land-related conflict reflect differences in land tenure regimes (LTRs) and in the local political arenas that they structure and uphold. As Schattschneider puts it, "The structure of government molds the conflict system" (1960, 14).

Table III.1 describes these differences schematically, on a continuum running from the local scale to the national scale (as denoted in the column on the far left). This provides a heuristic for conceptualizing and analyzing variation across space (and time). Reading across the rows, the table summarizes the general argument. Where authority to allocate land is lodged in the family or lineage, and the jurisdictional scale is thus at its most local, the character of authority (mode of decision making, mode of exercise of coercion, and form of accountability), the form of citizenship and political representation, and the scope of politics are all cast in ways that place land politics outside the domain of authority of the national state. Under the chieftaincy-centered land regimes, the net effect is similar (with land politics practiced largely as if it were beyond state purview), but the modes of authority and representation, and the scope of politics, are different. The statist regimes create a completely different configuration in authority relations, citizenship rights, and the potential scope of politics. In real situations, of course, categories can blur, as the concept of a continuum suggests. The discussion is not exhaustive, but the conceptual

TABLE III.I. *Locus and Scale of Land Authority: Implications for Politics*

Locus of Authority Over Land Allocation	Jurisdictional Scale of Land Politics	Authority: Mode of Decision Making	Authority: Character of Coercion	Authority: Form of Legitimacy/ Accountability	Citizenship: Mode of Representation	Scope of Politics (social boundary)	Land Issues and Statutory Authority	Part III Cases
Family/ lineage	Most local or micro	Private or familial	"Domestic"	Traditional/ patriarchal	Familial (patriarchal)	Restricted to family or clan	Outside of statute where family and land law are "customary"	Kisii, Kenya
Chief, chieftaincy	Chiefly jurisdiction or "local state"	Oligarchic, autocratic, or aristocratic	Extralegal or customary	Customary, enacted in a local public sphere	Ethnic citizens represented by "customary" notables	Restricted to ethnic citizens	Outside of statutory authority and judicial purview to a large extent	N. Cameroon; periurban Kumasi, Ghana
Central state	Potentially national	Use of state institutional mechanisms; republican institutions	Waged by the state, legal or not	Republican (secular, nationalist), enacted in a national public sphere	National citizenship	Potentially expanded to national citizenry	Within statutory or constitutional prerogative	Rwanda

repertoire extends to patterns of conflict that are not considered explicitly in these pages.[5]

This concept of political scale resonates with that employed by J.-P. Jacob (2002, 12, 22–26), who invokes it in identifying a situation not anticipated by the argument developed here. Jacob observes that in western Burkina Faso, several arenas of land conflict were visible when villagers "exported" a conflict onto the official scene by going to the local administration to seek redress for grievances against local landholders, the presumed local *maîtres territoriaux* (local territorial masters). Jacob explains, however, that the villagers did not achieve much success. The local prefect preferred to avoid larger troubles by pushing the dispute back down to the neocustomary level, and deferring to the local elite. This outcome conforms to the expectations of the heuristic model proposed here.

We expect the scale and scope effects that are visible in the land-politics domain to be visible in other aspects of rural political organization and mobilization (e.g., the nature of patron-client relations, patterns of associational life, patterns of electoral mobilization or rebel recruitment). And as Chapter 1 argues, the more agrarian the society, the more these arguments are expected to hold. The more agrarian the society, the more the land regime is expected to define the character of the local political arena writ large.[6]

HOW THE SCALE OF AUTHORITY PRODUCES POLITICAL EFFECTS

This introduction to Part III lays out the general argument, which is then developed across a series of case studies in Chapters 6, 7, and 8. The discussion here begins with the chiefly jurisdictions because these stand in clearest opposition to the unified state that political science usually takes as its default model of state structure.

Chiefs as Land Allocators

Under the customary land regimes that prevail in most settings, land-related conflict is deflected, or channeled *away*, from the formal political arena. Where chiefs exercise wide authority in allocating land and adjudicating disputes,

---

[5] I do not analyze interjurisdictional conflicts (as between chieftaincies) or conflicts between a landholder and an actor who does not fall under the political jurisdiction of the authority enforcing the landholder's rights. Meanwhile, it is true that there can be high levels of legal pluralism within jurisdictions, as there is where forum shopping between neocustomary and statutory venues and authorities is common. See, for example, Bierschenk and Olivier de Sardan on Benin (2003, 158). Such situations are not featured in the present study. Here we parse these issues conceptually and focus on variation across space in the character of the rules and their effects. The extent of dualism or hybridity could be taken as a variable.

[6] On the deagrarianization debate, see Bryceson 2002; Ontita 2007, 70–76, 199.

land-related issues that concern the public are bottled up within the chiefly jurisdiction and contained in a local public sphere that is nonliberal, non-democratic, and largely disconnected from the national political arena.[7] State structure in the neocustomary jurisdictions deflects the focus of land-related conflict downward into localities that have weak structural connections to national political institutions and the national arena.

This occurs for three reasons. First, to the extent that the customary author-ity has formal jurisdiction (functional as well as territorial) over land allocation, land politics is placed at least partly outside national statutory law. These cus-tomary authorities are not fully subordinated into the national administrative hierarchy. Therefore, citizens cannot hold them accountable under national law for their decisions in the land domain. Second, land allocation carried out by the customary authority is supposed to be conducted on behalf of members of a "natural community" that is structurally and legally differentiated from the national citizenry (as is the case where ethnic status is formalized by the state). This natural community is supposedly represented by and within local chiefly jurisdiction.[8] Third, land administration is carried out by subnational authorities who operate, at least partially, informally – that is, by personal rule (with low levels of standardization, bureaucratization, and overall trans-parency, including in record keeping, and largely outside of restraining laws), employing multistranded forms of leverage over those under their authority. As Schattschneider (1960, 14–16) argues, informality restricts information and, thus, possibilities for public scrutiny and wider public intervention. In these ways, the customary land tenure systems work to enforce localism, "to nar-row the scope of politics," and to keep land conflict "dampened down" to the subdistricts and *sous-préfectures* that correspond to chiefly jurisdictions.[9] The effect is the *opposite* of incorporation of land politics into the national political arena.

Land matters that are formally subject to chiefly discretion can, in principle, be contested by community members in a neocustomary public sphere. The cases examined in Chapter 7 show that the political character of this local state can vary widely – from arbitrary, violent, and despotic in some of the *lamidat* chieftaincies of northern Cameroon, to more open and relatively more restrained and rule abiding in Kumasi, the seat of the Asante paramount chief-taincy in Ghana. Our arguments about the scale and scope of land-related conflict hold in both situations, with strong reverberations for other spheres of politics, such as elections.

---

[7] The image of land conflict as "bottled up" at the local level is Bierschenk and Olivier de Sardan's (2003, 116).

[8] Sack 1986, 131.

[9] As Fearon and Laitin (1996) argue, mechanisms of in-group policing can manage conflict by containerizing it, confining conflict to the local level and a bounded territorial unit, and restricting its social scope. This dampens possibilities for conflict escalation. The quoted phrase is from Schattschneider 1960, 14–16.

My argument is that these scale and scope effects are *effects of state structure*, rather than simply effects of the poverty or remoteness of rural localities, the parochialism of the inhabitants, or cultural factors "endogenous to the constitution of the rural self" in terms of caste, language, or ethnicity (Varshney 1995, 4–5).

Indirect rule was very clearly a defensive rampart built and maintained by colonial administrations as a defense against the specter of mass politics. Today's customary land regimes continue to produce these demobilizing and collective action-impeding effects. Localization and segmentation of political arenas is antithetical to mass politics (Sack 1986, 78, 131). Customary jurisdictions fragment peasantries across space, facilitating divide and rule. Within jurisdictions, communities are often segmented along the lines of citizenship status (along the indigene-stranger distinction). And among citizens of the local state, groups are ranked according to the status distinctions of lineage, age, and gender. Such structures impede the formation of class-like and translocal alliances in the rural areas. It is therefore not surprising that Karuti Kanyinga et al. (1994, 20) find that in rural East Africa in the 1990s, associations of civil society tend to coalesce around established local notables, rather than as an alternative to them: "Individuals often face obstacles in building autonomous bases of organization that undercut or threaten established authority, hierarchy, and already-existing lines of local alliance."

Indirect rule produces the very weakest possible form of political integration. While it helps insulate the center from pressures from below, it invariably spawns agency problems that weaken central authority (Hechter 2000, 58). Both effects have been seen as liabilities by different (and sometimes opposed) constituencies – that is, by those pushing for democratization of local political arenas as well as by those seeking to enhance the effectiveness of the center. Pursuit of these ends has led most African governments since the late 1940s (both colonial and postcolonial) to embrace "modernization of the chieftaincy" as a formal goal, as argued in Chapter 2. In most countries, this has meant deeper integration of the chieftaincy into the national *administrative* hierarchy. Some countries abolished all levels of chieftaincy except for the most local (village chief), thus replacing higher-ranking chiefs with direct state agents such as prefects or district officers. In many countries, it is the formal duty of a district commissioner to "oversee" the chief, or the chief may be appointed by the president or a regional governor.[10] In some places, especially since the 1990s, governments have sought to integrate chieftaincy directly into the national political hierarchy[11] or to establish a structural linkage between the office of chieftaincy and a secular organ of government at the local level, such

[10] Subjecting the chiefs to closer supervision and reporting requirements is sometimes called "bureaucratization of the chieftaincy."
[11] An early example is election of the Chagga chiefs in the 1950s in what is now northern Tanzania. See Sally Falk Moore 1991.

as a District Council, which could be elective, appointed, or (more commonly) a combination of both. There is great variation in the formal structure of such institutional arrangements, the extent to which central governments have actually endeavored to achieve the official goals of state redesign, and the practical effects of institutional innovation.

Change over time is not always in the direction of stronger central control or greater democratization. In southern Ghana, in both Ashanti and Western Region, the government is working to enhance chiefs' role in land allocation and adjudication via reforms of land administration that further institutionalize their positions. In northern Cameroon, some chieftaincies have become more powerful *and more despotic* over time. In many places, formal decentralization programs have worked to augment the social, economic, and political capital – including the land-related powers – of customary or neotraditional actors within local jurisdictions (Ribot 2004; Bako-Arifari and Laurent 1998; Boone 2003). We expect such variations to be visible in the land-politics domain, where they will have implications for the shape and character of the public sphere, losers' rights and protest options, and the scope of political conflict.

Lineage and Family Heads as Land Allocators

In the customary land tenure systems with very localized or weak chieftaincies (or no chieftaincies), control over land is lodged in lineages, clans, or families who are recognized as members (citizens) of a descent-based landholding collectivity. If political hierarchy that is anchored in control over land extends only as far as the lineage or family, then hierarchy in these situations is truncated in scope and height. The sociopolitical unit may comprise from ten to forty persons – perhaps more or fewer, depending on time and place.[12] Authority structure within these microjurisdictions devolves into something almost akin to authority within the "private sphere" of the family in market society (before the recognition of women as full legal persons) and may be only remotely connected, or not connected at all, to an overarching public arena centered on chieftaincy. Here, the scale of land politics among smallholders is at its most local, and its scope is at its narrowest. Male elders may exercise wide discretion over land allocation in a political arena that affords little or no public space for overt contestation of their decisions. Within this restricted sphere, however, structures of authority may be still be strongly hierarchical, as manifest in stark political inequalities among adult members of the household by gender, family status, or age (as well as by achievement).

---

[12] For example, Paré (2001, 4–5) reports that in western Burkina Faso (old cotton area), household size ranges from eight to fourteen people or more. A hamlet in Koukra Department has households of ten to fifteen persons per holding. Writing of the Gambia in the 1980s, Robertson observed that the total number of persons in a three-generation household (courtyard) could exceed a hundred (1987, 220).

As the jurisdiction of land authority shrinks to cover smaller groups of people and smaller land units (through the process of parcel fragmentation via inheritance, for example), a destructuring of political authority over land occurs. At the extreme, this dissolves away the land-related social structures that produce political effects – it works to dissolve the ability of lineage elders to dominate the local political arena and associational life within it. Although individuals are thus freer to engage in collective action around land issues that affect smallholders within the jurisdiction, there is no collective (public) form of authority over land for them to target and hold accountable.

As Pauline Peters (2013) points out, smallholders in these settings are highly vulnerable to encroachment or expropriation by wealthy insiders or by outsiders who are beyond the reach of the (local land) law. In this study, I do not analyze conflicts between a landholder and an actor who does not fall under the political jurisdiction of the authority enforcing the landholder's rights. This means that the analysis does not explicitly consider the case of a smallholder in a neocustomary land regime whose land is expropriated by a minister in the national government. That is a type of conflict that cannot be processed within existing political institutions. It represents a kind of systemic political failure: the fictive sovereignty of the neotraditional sphere in land matters has been violated, but because of the disarticulated structure of the state, the injured parties have no institutionalized avenue of recourse. Politics cannot scale up through institutional channels.

The Central State as Land Allocator

Where statist land regimes are in place, the land allocators are state agents. In the ideal-type situation, relationships between state agents and land users are unmediated by chiefly or lineage authority. Land allocation happens at state directive and at the hands of state officials. Direct institutional connections to the central state bring contestants into direct contact with the central government. Grievances can be targeted at the central state, and "contestants can move from one level or scale of government to another in an attempt to find the level at which they might try most advantageously to get what they want" (e.g., from very local, to regional, to national) (Schattschneider 1960, 10). Where local populations are not under the politics-dampening control of customary authorities aligned with the center, a barrier is removed. Conditions for the emergence of mass politics (in the form of cross-ethnic, class-like, or populist coalitions) are improved.

These scale and scope factors thus create the possibility for mass politics and for "nationalizing" the scope of conflict (Schattschneider 1960; Gibson 2005). It is not surprising that in most places, African governments have sought to limit the risks of such confrontation or challenges by propping up the local authority of customary leaders who are beholden to the center, or by building heavy political machines to short-circuit political mobilization in localities, as Bates described in *Markets and States in Tropical Africa* (1981).

Statist land regimes open central governments to political opportunities and dangers. Direct rule allows the state fuller control over land use and, thus, may promote faster spread of export crop production (as was the case in southwestern Côte d'Ivoire, explored in Chapter 5), or more direct control over production processes and techniques (as in the Office du Niger irrigation schemes in Mali). These arrangements also allow the central state to use land as a patronage resource. Land users who have received land from government authorities, but who have no formal title or access to neutral courts to enforce this claim, depend on politicians and state officials for protection of their land rights. This can be a political asset for power holders, as it was, for example, in the Northwest Province of Cameroon, where Mbororo graziers were caught in "predatory patronage relations" with the high-ranking administrative officials who controlled their access to rangeland (Hickey 2007, 86, 98).

Yet here, too, there are liabilities and risks for rulers. As Michael Hechter points out (2008, 58), this structure of government can provoke local resistance, given that one purpose of direct rule is to redistribute power from local to central authorities. And by establishing direct channels to the center, direct rule leaves the center more exposed to local challenge. Unlike chiefs, local-level state agents cannot hide behind the veil of customary authority that screens off the local political arena (structurally, legally, politically, and ideologically) from the national polity.

PROBING THE ARGUMENT

These variations produce macroeffects that shape national political systems as a whole. Neocustomary land tenure systems can buffer the central state from resource-related competition at the local level (at the cost of limiting the reach, accountability, and capacity of the state). They also compromise the quality of national citizenship regimes. Meanwhile, statist land regimes can bring land-related conflicts directly onto the national stage by making central state authorities the target of land-related grievances. This opens the door to expanding the scope of conflict in ways that may strengthen regime opponents, and/or create opportunities for building political coalitions that transcend the boundaries of local jurisdictions.

Part III uses four cases to demonstrate that variation in the character of land tenure regimes is visible in variation in the scale and scope of land-related conflict, and to trace the causal mechanisms and processes by which land tenure regimes (LTRs) produce these scale and scope effects. As in earlier chapters, the focus is on conflicts that emerge in situations of rising competition for land among smallholders.

We develop these arguments through a series of structured comparisons, working up the hierarchy of scale. In Chapter 6, land-related conflict is most restricted in terms of scale and scope. This is the level at which LTRs vest allocation and adjudication authority in lineage and family heads. The Kisii district of western Kenya is a case in point: there is virtually no in-migration, land is under the control of extended and nuclear families, neocustomary authority above the household level is extremely weak, and land pressure is as acute as it is anywhere in rural Africa. Chapter 7 considers two cases of land-related conflict that pivot around chieftaincy: land politics in the chieftaincies (or *lamidat*) of northern Cameroon and in the chieftaincies on the periurban fringes of Kumasi, the capital of Ashanti Region in central Ghana.[13] Chapter 8 looks at land dynamics under a statist regime, offering a new perspective on Rwandan state structure and political dynamics in the years that preceded the 1994 genocide. There are strong parallels with the cases of southwestern Côte d'Ivoire and the Rift Valley of Kenya (Chapter 5), where statist land tenure regimes also channeled land conflict into the national political arena.

Part III supports the main argument with cases in point and within-case counterfactuals. To demonstrate the limits of rival explanations, it is necessary to invoke the larger range of cases considered in this book. A modernization argument would predict that land-related conflict is more likely to become a national political issue in democratic countries with stronger and more effective states and wealthier citizens. In the cases of Western Ghana and Ashanti Region of Ghana, however, modernization-theory expectations do not hold. Land conflict in the two Ghanaian regions, one wealthy (Ashanti) and both fairly democratic (Ashanti and Western), tends to "stay local." Our cases also contradict the argument that land politics "goes national" only in situations of state collapse. Rwanda in 1990–1994 and Kenya in the 1990s are two strong states that were racked by land conflict that played out on the national stage. Eastern DRC in the early 1990s is also a case that runs against the argument that land conflict surges in conditions of state collapse. As René Lemarchand (2000) explained, when North Kivu emerged as an epicenter of conflict, it was one of the most intensively governed regions of the country. We can also discount an explanation that predicts that land politics "goes national" only in small countries, where transportation and communication grids are tighter and the countryside is less remote. Southwest and center-west Côte d'Ivoire and eastern DRC are cases in which local land conflicts reverberate on the national stage, but neither country is small and tightly knit. Finally, we can discount the argument that chieftaincies are the focal point of land conflict only in small, poor, weakly integrated countries. Chieftaincies are strong focal points of land conflict in parts of Ghana, Uganda, and Cameroon – all countries that are not small, weak, or poor by African standards. In Ghana and Uganda, chieftaincies are strong in the wealthiest and most developed regions of the country.

---

[13] The Ghana case also considers the phenomenon of *downward shift* over time in the scale of land-allocation authority in rural Ashanti, as extended families consolidate control over farmland at the expense of chiefs (a change over time that is also visible in several of the other cases considered in this study, including western Burkina Faso and Kisii). The extraction of lands from the communal domain contributes to the growing exclusivity of land rights.

CHAPTER 6

Land Conflict at the Micro-Scale: Family

> The truth is that we are at a turning point. Today, . . . no reserve of land
> remains, so any accumulation of land can only take place by a redistribution
> within the village community. . . . A new chapter in the history of peasant
> societies in Niger is beginning to be written.
>
> (Raynaut 1988, 235–236)[1]
>
> Pressure on the land is overwhelming.
>
> (Ontita 2007, 37)

The Kisii region of western Kenya has one of the highest rural population
densities in all sub-Saharan Africa. Landholdings were consolidated under the
control of Gusii lineage heads during the colonial state-formation period of the
1920s and 1930s. In the 1960s, the government broke up the clan-based or lineage holdings and registered land in the names of patriarchs who presided over
extended families composed of their wives (often two or three), children, and
grandchildren. During the next five decades, Gusii elders divided the original
landholdings (often 40–50 acres in size) among their sons who have, by now,
subdivided the land again. In this region of Kenya, the land frontier is closed.
High population growth rates, combined with the low rates of increase in
off-farm and national employment opportunities, have placed "overwhelming
population pressure on the land."[2]

This is a region experiencing classic "agricultural involution" as described
by Clifford Geertz: rates of increase in the productivity of labor are falling as
families invest more and more labor for declining returns on ever-shrinking
land parcels. Kisii is an example of a neocustomary land tenure regime (LTR)

---

[1] Cited by Pauline Peters, 2013.
[2] Okoth-Ogendo and Oucho 1993, 194. Population growth rates for Kisii were 4% per annum
for 1969–1979, 2.7% for 1979–1989, and 3.1% for 1989–1999.

centered on lineage- or family-based authority over land, in a situation of acute land scarcity and high ethnic homogeneity. In these respects, it is similar to areas featured in some of the best-known studies in the African land-politics literature, including Kojo Amanor's (1999) studies of Akim region of Ghana, Pauline Peters's study of southern Malawi (2004), André and Platteau on northwest Rwanda (1998), Fiona MacKenzie on Meru (1998), and a long tradition of work on Kenya's Central Province (Berman and Lonsdale 1992, for example).

In these situations, as Amanor puts in (1999, 139–140), the lineage or family becomes an arena of conflict over the allocation and appropriation of land. Struggles are internalized within extended families and are fought over attempts to narrow the social boundaries of the family. As competition for land increases, land-rights losers tend to be family members with subordinate land rights and less standing in the political hierarchy of the lineage – notably women (especially single women, including widows), youth, and marginal family members such as adoptees. Those excluded from land access have very few options for protest through voice (public or collective action aimed at seeking remedy) within the highly constrained field of action that is the family or lineage.[3] Land-related conflict tends to play out as interfamily and interpersonal struggles that often run along generational and gender lines and tend to culminate in either exit, in the form of out-migration, or loyalty (hanging on, even in a worsened position) on the part of losers. Individual birthright and ancestral-familial rights to land are the standards by which the morality of such dispossessions is judged, rather than by the kind of ethnic claims, claims against the state, chieftaincy-centered claims, or class-based claims that are observed in other settings.[4]

In places such as Kisii, discourses of loss are likely to be framed in terms of the interpersonal or family crimes of dishonesty and betrayal, rather than in terms of collective grievances of wider social and political scope. Overt violence in land-related conflict, to the extent that it exists, plays out on the interpersonal level as domestic violence, homicide or threats thereof, or witchcraft. In the Kisii case, we see clearly the hand of the central state in creating land-control institutions that produce these apparently apolitical or subpolitical forms of land conflict.

---

[3] The salience of what Bierschenk and Olivier de Sardan (2003) call the *arène politique villa-geoise* (village-level political arena) is a variable affected by the extent to which a multilineage collectivity holds and manages corporate assets (such as a village forest, lake, or unused land). Without these, we would not expect authority over land to be lodged at the translineage (village) level. See Olivier de Sardan (1999) on the "unfindable" public sphere in southern Niger villages in the 1990s.

[4] Here we borrow from Berman and Lonsdale (1992b), who showed how the morality of individual accumulation where class-formation processes are under way can be pitted against the moral principle of collective solidarity as represented in the ideology of "tribe."

WESTERN KENYA: KISII

The customary land tenure regime in Kisii (which has undergone successive subdivision as a postcolonial administrative unit[5]) has been crafted by the state over time. A century ago, the British delimited Gusiiland as an ethnic territory or province for the peoples inhabiting the region. In 1933, the colonial government recognized this territory as a "reserve" (or reservation) for members of what it recognized as the Gusii tribe, and designated Musa Nyandusi of the Nyaribari clan as paramount chief.[6] Boundaries delimited subterritories belonging to each of seven extended groupings that the British considered to be Gusii subtribes or clans. (See Map 6.) This became Kisii District in the administrative restructuring of 1961–1963, when some land excised from Kenya's so-called White Highlands was added to the district "to relieve population pressure" in the Gusii reserve.[7] The seven clan territories of "old Gusii" became the seven locations, or administrative subdivisions, of the new district.[8]

It was under the Swynnerton Plan land registration campaigns of the 1960s that the British and then the Kenyan government proceeded to register landholdings in the Kisii reserve in the names of Gusii extended-family heads, or elders.[9] This move put an end to the clan-based struggles over the territorial boundaries of lineages that had dominated land politics in the 1950s,[10] and effectively dissolved suprafamilial structures of control over land, labor use, and agricultural production. However, contrary to much of the conventional wisdom about the adjudication and titling process, the goal of government was neither to extinguish nor to render obsolete what it saw as the customary structures of family control over land, exercised through politically reliable elders.[11] A system of land control that revolved around political considerations, social hierarchy, and social obligation was confirmed.

The Land Adjudication Committees that registered land in the names of Gusii extended-family heads in the 1960s were *composed of elders chosen by the district officers.* The committees were tasked with deciding disputes over

---

[5] Kisii District was divided into Kisii and Nyamira (North Kisii) in approximately 1989. In 1995, a Gucha District (aka Ogembo District, or South Kisii) was created. In 2007, several new districts were created, including Borabu, which was hived off of Nyamira.

[6] Carter Commission, Kenya 1933, 351, para. 1379. As the commission notes, the Crown did not divest itself irrevocably of its rights over such land (369, para. 1454); Lonsdale 1977.

[7] Great Britain, Kenya Regional Boundaries Commission, 1962, p. 7.

[8] Maxon 2003, 11. The locations are divided into sublocations that are administered by chiefs and subchiefs who are appointed by the Civil Service Commission. They serve under district officers, who in turn answer to district commissioners. See Ontita 2007, 13.

[9] Reserves were renamed "Trust Lands" in June 1963.

[10] Orvis 1997, 78.

[11] This point is well developed with respect to land registration in several other Kenyan provinces. See Shipton (2009) for Luoland, Haugerud (1993) for Central Province, and Mackenzie (1998) for Meru.

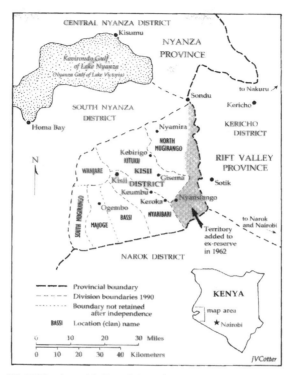

MAP 6. Kenya's Kisii District with Local Jurisdictions (c. 1990). *Source:* Maxon 1989, 28; Maxon, 2003. *Note:* South Mugirango and Wanjare were merged after independence, as were Majoge and Bassi.

boundaries and hierarchies of land claims, as well as engineering agreements on parcel swaps and trades to consolidate scattered family holdings into compact tracts. This was an eminently political process of distribution and redistribution of assets and authority, and the government saw it as such. As the Lawrance Commission of Inquiry explained in 1966, the Adjudication Committees displaced the "African Courts" hitherto empowered to hear land disputes in the reserves, including in Kisii. Complaints about this from Nyanza Province were dismissed on the grounds that "speed in reaching a final decision is an essential ingredient of the adjudication process and the courts certainly cannot provide this."[12] The job of the district officer and the Kisii elders selected to sit on the Land Adjudication Committee was not to create land markets and promote

---

[12] The Republic of Kenya Lawrance Commission Report (1966, 47–48, see also 159) pointed out with consternation that the land adjudication processes in the former reserves worked to deepen and confirm ethnic groups' claims to land. See also Coldham 1984.

maximum efficiency of land use but rather "to adjudicate on and determine in accordance with native law and custom the claims of individuals in rights to land."[13]

This process helped cement the link between Kenya's powerful provincial administration and the Gusii elders and chiefs who would, for the next fifty years, wield land prerogative at the local level as dispute adjudicators in the Kisii district. It also succeeded in creating family holdings rather than individual holdings and, in this sense, recognized and vindicated the corporate claims of extended families – entrusted to, and managed by, family elders (Okoth-Ogendo and Oucho 1993, 199). These arrangements gave family heads control over the allocation of access rights to what were, in practice, corporately held properties.

So far, this has ensured that interfamily hierarchies and relationships, rather than market forces, are the dominant force in the allocation and reallocation of land in the former Kisii reserve.[14] Family holdings have been subdivided among wives and sons according to the claimants' understanding of custom, leading to extreme land fragmentation. Within a generation or two, most holdings were far below the minimum required for subsistence. In Nyanmira (formerly North Muriango), one family's story unfolded this way:

Issac's cousin's husband said that his father had about twelve acres. This was divided equally between his two wives, the first of whom had four sons, one of whom got a plot elsewhere. So three brothers divided the six acres among themselves, with Issac's cousin's husband getting two acres. They had ten children, five of whom are sons. One of the sons was educated by Issac's family, and this fellow now has a job at a bank. That job supports Issac's cousin's family. Today, though, they have not yet had anything to eat.... Issac's cousin-in-law does not know anything about the land ever being adjudicated and registered. He does know that his sons will insist that the land be subdivided among them. (Field notes, Nyamira District, 17 March 2009)

Okoth-Ogendo and Oucho (1993, 199) found a very high incidence of land disputes in Kisii in the 1970s, with evidence of "continuous vindication of indigenous tenure rights," especially the "access rights of those whose livelihood depends or could conceivably depend upon [land access]."

[13] Republic of Kenya Lawrance Commission Report 1966, 48. Ontita (2007, 37) also says that the chiefs selected the settlers for the Sotik Settlement Schemes that were attached to Kisii District, doing so "on the basis of political patronage and considerations."

[14] Norton-Griffiths (June 2008, 7) wrote that "90–95% of the land in 'Kisii' is under private freehold tenure, defined as titled or with issue of title in-process." Maxon (2002b, 298) reports that by the end of 1980, 93% of registerable land in Nyanza Province had been registered, and individual titles distributed. We do not dispute this, but rather seek to stress Okoth-Ogendo and Oucho's 1993 finding, which is that there was "continuous vindication of indigenous tenure rights long after the technical aspect of the government-sponsored tenure reform had been completed in the district" (1993, 199). They note by way of contrast that de jure arrangements approaching "classic freehold" characterized land purchases on the nearby Sotik Settlement Scheme (198).

PRESSURES TO MOVE TOWARD MORE EXCLUSIVE LAND RIGHTS

Population pressure on the land in this part of Kenya is often described as very high or extreme.[15] From a region of low population density in the 1930s (Maxon 2003, 54), Kisii region is now the most densely populated part of Kenya. Population increase has sustained the intensification of agricultural production, but this seems to have culminated in a process of agricultural involution rather than steady movement toward the commercialization of land and output. Maxon (2003, 237) describes how "Gusiiland was swept up in Kenya's agrarian revolution of the 1950s" as farmers planted maize, wimbi (millet), and coffee, the region's most important cash crop in the 1950s and 1960s. Tea and pyrethrum were important as cash crops in the 1970s and 1980s. By the 1990s, however, the market for coffee and pyrethrum had collapsed,[16] and tea, maize, and other food crops (beans, bananas, and wimbi) predominated. Because of subdivision, most holdings had shrunk to between 0.5 and 2 acres by the 1980s,[17] with much or perhaps most land on the smallholdings devoted to family subsistence needs. Okoth-Ogendo and Oucho (1993, 201) found at the end of the 1980s that 83 percent of farm families in Kisii had holdings of less than 0.73 acres. Even then, holdings were "nowhere near [large] enough to feed a family."[18] Agricultural involution and creeping proletarianization were one side of processes of social differentiation that were observable within the district itself. A small minority of relatively prosperous Kisii families (almost all with access to salaried off-farm income) was able to hire-in labor and obtain use rights to relatively more land per household, often through informal purchases of scattered land fragments.[19] Orvis (1997, 101) found that "a growing number of households is destined to become effectively landless within a decade or so."

The stresses of land pressure and economic distress contributed to an exceptionally high incidence of land disputes in this part of Kenya.[20] Even though most land parcels in Kisii were adjudicated and registered by the government in the 1960s, the vast majority of land disputes are not processed through the court system (which would offer access to rule of law, lawyers, and appeal

---

[15] Okoth-Ogendo and Oucho (1993, 194) give an average population density of 304 persons per square kilometer for Kisii in 1969, rising to 395 in 1979. Nyang'au (2002, 5) reports a population density of 690 persons per square kilometer for Kisii/Gucha District.

[16] This was due to both collapse in world market prices and corruption in – and then dismantling of – the parastatal marketing boards. (Nyang'au 2002; Ontita 2007, 28).

[17] Silberschmidt 1992, 240; see also Maxon 2002, 297. Okoth-Ogendo and Oucho (1993, 202) report that "export crops (coffee, tea, pyrethrum) occupied less than 25% of the agricultural land in the district" at the time of their study. Maize can be sold or consumed by the household.

[18] Silberschmidt 1992, 240.

[19] Orvis 1997, 97–101, 150 inter alia. See Murton (1999) (cited by Orvis 1997, 122), who makes a similar argument for Machakos.

[20] Okoth-Ogendo and Oucho 1993, 199.

to higher levels of the judicial system). Instead, as Coldham (1984) notes for all the former reserve territories of Kenya in the 1980s, even disputes on registered land were adjudicated by a district officer and a Panel of Elders. Coldham presents this as evidence that the government was committed to relying on the administrative machinery and political support of the old Native Authority system and unwilling to turn land matters over to the courts.[21] In the 1990s, Orvis (1997, 78) found that "because formal resolution [of land disputes] is prohibitively expensive, local elders generally settle these matters by holding an informal hearing at the site of the dispute. . . . Given that few formal records are kept, maintaining good relations with the local elders remains important." In 2009, Henrysson and Joireman concluded that this was still the process for small cases,[22] most of which involve division of land among members of extended families.

This adjudication process invests most authority in land dispute matters in "elders," themselves lineage and family heads, most of them heirs of the individuals whose names appeared on the original registration documents. By reinforcing this channel of dispute resolution, the government gave disputants no practical avenue or forum for appeal that could supersede or escape these intensely local and personalized venues, which were centered on patriarchal authority and appeals to "custom."

In Kisii, intensely competitive struggles to gain or retain land rights result in highly uneven and conflict-ridden processes of redistribution, resulting in both socioeconomic differentiation and exclusion. Those highly vulnerable to the loss of land rights are individuals and family subgroups who have secondary rights (such as adult women and their children, if there is no husband), junior sons, and others who are unable to prevail in these struggles.[23] Losers have few options other than to resign their land claims and exit (out-migration) or to adopt a strategy of what Hirschman might have considered to be loyalty (staying put and trying to adapt to loss of land rights). This is accompanied by high levels of social conflict within families and extended families, and social instability within localities.[24]

---

[21] Coldham 1984, 59–71.

[22] They note that the provincial administration can also get involved. Most of the land-dispute case studies in Ontita (2007) concern land division within families. See, for example, 143, 266, 272.

[23] A growing proportion of the population can be excluded from land even without a secular trend toward the individualization of land rights. There can be more and more people with rights in a given parcel, even as effective landlessness affects a larger and larger proportion of the population. See Orvis 1997, 93–94.

[24] Bierschenk and Olivier de Sardan (2003, 116) say that "the more usual solution is that of loyalty, e.g., 'bottling up', which leads to conflicts continuing to fester underground. This promotes the spread of rumour, suspicion, and accusations (of witchcraft, inter alia), which were constantly encountered in all the villages surveyed."

FORMS OF LAND CONFLICT IN KISII

The Kisii region has known high rates of out-migration since the 1930s, when it was incorporated into the colonial economy as a labor reserve. Development of the coffee economy in Kisii seemed to have stemmed rates of exit in the 1960s, but by the 1970s Kisii was once again a zone of net out-migration to other parts of Kenya. Many analysts link some of this emigration to land pressure in Kisii itself.[25] Orvis (1997, 94) says that in the poorest Kisii households, "poverty drives members (especially daughters) out." More closely documented at the microlevel are the processes by which people are pushed out of agricultural livelihoods and into less desirable situations in informal-sector occupations, whether in Kisii or elsewhere in Kenya. The poorest respondents in Orvis's Kisii study were people without viable farms who had been pushed into marginal informal-sector niches in services or commerce.[26] Women who are unmarried, children born out of wedlock, younger sons, and returning out-migrants may be excluded completely from land access.

Echoing Pauline Peters's findings for rural Malawi, Edward Ontita concluded that "recent field evidence [including his own] indicates that divestiture in social relations does occur" as families shed ties to kin, and landless young people forgo marriage.[27] Orvis (1997, 107, 74) found that often, there is a lack of assistance to poor households "even from very close relatives" and that there was a growing population "of young men and women who are not gainfully employed, in school, or married" and thus had no visible prospects for ensuring their economic survival.[28] Within marriages, polygamous marriages, and extended families, even where sharing and solidarity are present, there can be acute conflicts over land access and use, land transactions (selling off parts of parcels), inheritance, control over cash revenues from tea farms, and the search for other ways to get money.

Struggles over land and other family resources produce stresses that find expression in many forms of conflict, including high rates of intrafamily

---

[25] Okoth-Ogendo and Oucho (1993, 194, 196) date net out-migration to the early 1970s.

[26] Orvis 1997, 74 inter alia.

[27] Ontita 2007, 74 inter alia. Silberschmidt (2001, 663) writes that "in Kisii...the form and content of the marriage contract have changed. Many men and women in my study live in more or less informal or passing unions."

[28] In the wake of the expulsion of many Gusii people from Rift Valley farms in the election-related violence of 1991–1992 and 2008, local newspapers reported that many returned to their original homes in Kisii. Relatives accommodated some of the returnees, but in 2008, and perhaps other years as well, "quite a few [were] rejected by relatives due to overstretched resources which included land, food, and shelter.... One returnee, 81 [years old] and the father of 10, says his aging brothers in Gusii have rejected him, leaving him with nowhere else to go.... [Another man] has also been rejected by his uncles, who argue that his father...had no land" (Angwenyi Gichana, "Famine Fears as 50,000 People Return to Gusiiland," *Daily Nation On Line*, 1 March 2008, reposted at Kisii.com [accessed 12 March 2009]).

violence. Kisii "is in a process of fundamental socioeconomic transformation and proletarianization. Gender antagonism and domestic violence have escalated, often resulting in men killing their wives and vice versa. Persistent rumors about men being poisoned by wives circulate. In recent years, the district has become known for its witch hunts and witch burnings."[29] Orvis (1997, 89, 87) mentions witchcraft as a pervasive Gusii concern in a context of rising poverty and heightened clan conflict, with "wealthier households" as a "particular target of witches." In the wake of one very bad month in Kitutu Chache constituency, in which fifteen people were killed and fifty-three houses torched in witch huntings, one local newspaper explained that "the majority of the victims were elderly women between 75 and 85.... [An] inquiry revealed that some of the incidents were caused by family jealousy, love triangles, and long-standing land and business disputes."[30] Ontita (2007, 24, 266) selected similar words in describing village discourse on failure and success in his Nyamira study site as dominated by "jealousy and witchcraft." Meanwhile, the Kisii districts have the highest homicide rates in Kenya and famously high rates of alcohol abuse among men.[31] Silberschmidt's surveys uncovered that "a surprisingly large number of men thought that they might be... killed by their sons" (1992, 247). "The extent to which criminality and violence may emanate from conflict over resources or struggles to make a living in difficult circumstances has been a thread in research on the Abugusii" (Ontita 2007, 33).

   This chapter argues that in the old Kisii divisions, a region with no in-migration and where authority over land is invested in household heads, the LTR works to define the *family itself* as the arena of land-related conflict. Although the family is surely an arena of land conflict in all agrarian societies (peasant societies), our argument is that under the type of LTR that we see in old Kisii, the family is virtually the *only* arena. In areas where there has been high in-migration, by contrast, "new land can be found" by targeting strangers (as bluntly put in an anti-stranger pamphlet circulated in Kericho Town before Kenya's 2007 election).[32] Also presenting a clear contrast to what we observe in Kisii are areas where the state allocates land directly to particular land claimants. Under statist land regimes, the government itself and government policy are ready targets and rallying points for those with land grievances. The Kisii case presents a distinctive type of outcome, structured in large part by a

[29] Silberschmidt 2001, 662. Ontita (2007, 33) mentions that Levine (1980) claimed that crime and violence in Gusii, especially against women, was the highest in British Africa (Ontita 2007, 33).

[30] Leo Odera Omolo, "'Sungu Sungu' Gangsters Killing Innocent People in Kisii Must Be Stopped by the Government," African Press International (API) (daily online news channel), 21 June 2008 posted at africanpress.worldpress.com (accessed 10 May 2009).

[31] See Silberschmidt 1992, 247; Ontita 2007, 198–200.

[32] Nation Team, "Nyache Backers' Assault on ODM," *Daily Nation* (Nairobi), 22 October 2008, posted at www.nation.co.ke (accessed 3 March 2009).

land regime in which strangers do not hold derived rights in land, and in which the state itself does not appear to be the direct author of the prevailing pattern of land allocation.[33]

In Kisii, we see the progressive breakdown of local political space (domains of collective decision making centered on the management, use, and allocation of corporately held land) into narrower and narrower arenas of decision making, resource allocation, and social hierarchy. These narrower and more localized political arenas are riven by generational and gender conflicts, as well as divisions running along the lines of success or failure within families. Where exclusion from access to what are considered to be "corporate landholdings" is near absolute (where deagrarianization,[34] or what Orvis defines as proletarianization, are realities for families or individuals), the social and political bonds of hierarchy, obligation, and dependence begin to dissolve away. At this extreme, the politically structuring effects of relations of production and land access disappear. In Kisii, some effects of these processes are visible in the wider political domain, and in electoral politics in particular.

Conclusion: Beyond Land Politics

From the 1960s through the 1980s, Kisii lined up squarely behind the ruling party, KANU, and the Kenyatta regime that held power in Nairobi. Kisii's tie to the center was assured and personified by local political baron Simeon Nyachae, member of parliament from Nyaribari Chache. He was the son of Gusii paramount chief Musa Nyandusi. Continuity with the politics of the colonial Native Authority was strong and, I would argue, surely rooted in part in a postcolonial land tenure regime that upheld the authority of clan heads and elders who were loyal to Simeon Nyachae and the ruling party. Politics in Kisii revolved around clan and interclan competition, and within constituencies, bloc voting by clans was the norm.[35] The region as a whole remained a secure KANU stronghold.[36] A full generation later, in 2008, the cumulative effects of the old political structure's gradual splintering in this region were clear. In the December 2007 elections, the Kisii vote was split among the three leading presidential

---

[33] In other situations, family-level conflicts might be partially displaced by blaming strangers for land scarcity or be exported out of the household to a wider political arena (a lineage arena, a chieftaincy arena, or the arena of national politics). In Kisii, such family conflicts "have nowhere else to go."

[34] Ontita 2007, 33, 70–76; Orvis 1997.

[35] Ontita 2007, 24; Joshua Araka, "Fortunes Change as Power Base Shifts in Gusii Politics," *Kenya Times*, 20 April 2008, 7; and Joshua Araka, "Have Gusii MPs This Time Started on the Wrong Footing Once Again?" *Kenya Times Web Edition*, 30 March 2008.

[36] Throup and Hornsby (1998, 204) describe the Gusii (Kisii and Nyamira) as a swing constituency in 1991–1992. In 2002, the Gusii voted as a bloc for Simeon Nyachae, the presidential candidate for FORD People. A close associate of Kibaki, Nyachae lost his seat as MP for Nyaribari Chache in a "humiliating defeat" in the December 2007 election (see Araka, "Have Gusii MPs," note 48, this chapter).

contenders, with rich-poor divisions visible across constituencies,[37] and a bitter generational cleavage evident within them. Some youth militias, often rough and sometimes violent, coalesced around the opposition Orange Democratic Movement (ODM) party. As Bernard Calas (2009, 172–173) describes it, "In a number of areas [within Kenya], the generational dimension of the election was finally expressed clearly. Thus, in Kisii land, where the same number of MPs was elected by both sides, scenes of violence during riots at the beginning of January [2008] involved pro-ODM youths hunting down and threatening their elders whom they blamed for supporting [KANU's] Kibaki, considered a dishonest elder."

Some sources reported that the police themselves patronized and deployed the Chinkororo and Kisungusungu youth militia to check the pro-ODM militia and harass journalists.[38] Evidence of progressive decomposition of sociopolitical structure in Kisii also emerged in Tom Wolf's analyses of the 2007 parliamentary vote: the ten Kisii constituencies evidenced unusually high degrees of party fractionalization, with winners garnering an average of only 28.7 percent of the votes in their constituencies.[39]

For present purposes, the significance of these facts about elections in Kisii lies in how strongly they differ from voting patterns observed in parts of rural Africa where "either most people in a community vote, or most do not, and electoral participation is a communal activity."[40] It is possible to find many places in rural Africa where, as Fauré (1993 44) puts it, "lines of political domination are ordinarily strongly hierarchical, personalized, and monopolistic at the level of the community and the territory." The argument advanced in this book is that where such local cohesion exists, we expect it to be associated with hierarchical structures of control over access to livelihood resources, including

[37] In particular, the Sotik settlement scheme areas that had been attached to the old Kisii reserve in 1962 were wealthier and were tied to the old Kenyatta regime coalition, through which they had gained access to land in the settlement schemes in the first place. They supported the Kibaki coalition in December 2007 (Calas 2009). The opposition gained much more support in the poorest areas of the old Kisii reserve. The pro-ODM militias were raised in the old Kisii districts. As an interlocutor in Borabu division (17 March 2009) explained, there are "only old people and their workers" in the richer settlement scheme areas – the young people, including the males, are in school or working as professionals in other parts of Kenya (or abroad). In 2007, South Mugirango elected the ODM treasurer, Omingo Magara, as MP. North Mugirango/Borabu elected a KANU MP.

[38] See IRIN, "Kenya: Armed and Dangerous," 22 February 2008. (See also "Kenya Corruption and Warlords Revealed," posted at kenya-thieves-warlords.blogspot.com/2008/01/chinkororo-and-kisungusungu.html, 28 January 2008 [accessed 25 November 2009.])

[39] According to Wolf's analysis of the 2007 voting in Kisii ("Ethnic Mobilization versus Political Parties"), six of the ten Kisii constituencies were among the 12% of all Kenyan constituencies that were won with 29% or less of the vote, and the seventh was won with only 30% of the vote. The eighth and ninth were won with only 34%, and the last with 40%. Some news accounts do underscore the continuing salience of clan politics at the county council level. See Araka, "Have Gusii MPs."

[40] David Simon 1999, 25.

land. These can concentrate local authority to an extent and on a scale necessary to produce political cohesion in voting. Local clientelist networks rooted in land-access relationships are a mechanism by which economic dependency at the microlevel can be translated into political (including electoral) effects. In Kisii, such land-control institutions are very weak, very narrow in scope, or absent; the effects of this are visible in Kisii's highly *fractionalized* voting patterns. Kisii voting patterns are also useful in disproving the assumption that ethnic identity itself is what produces community cohesion at the local level, and also contradicting the stereotype that ethnicity trumps all in African elections, especially in the rural areas.

CHAPTER 7

The Local State as an Arena of Redistributive Conflict

Chieftaincy

> What is interesting about the Ghana case is that it is a counterfactual: Ghana
> has seen extensive local conflict, often linked to questions of traditional
> chieftaincy and land. But these conflicts have remained localized and have never
> infected national politics to the point of igniting civil wars like those we have
> seen in other countries. [What specific elements] in the politics or the structure
> of the Ghanaian state... have made it possible to isolate the national political
> sphere from infection by violent conflict at the local level?
> (Camara et al. 2007, 14)

This chapter focuses on politics at a scale that has been mostly invisible in
political science analyses of Africa: the scale of the "local state" constituted
by chieftaincy. Our argument is that redistributive conflicts generated in these
arenas are tamped down at this level, and this is a result of state-building
strategies chosen to produce this very effect. For national political systems
as a whole, the effect is to weaken the possibilities for building larger social
coalitions, shorten the reach of national institutions, strengthen and reproduce
ethnic identity as a political status that individuals are constrained to assume,
and diminish the national public sphere.

The analysis in this chapter focuses on land politics in northern Cameroon
and the Ashanti Region of Ghana. Variation across these two settings (and
across both space and time within each region) provides considerable leverage
on the main hypotheses and creates opportunities to refine some aspects of
the argument. Chieftaincies in both regions are strong by African standards,
corresponding in part to the extensive land-allocation powers of the so-called
customary authorities in the most visible of the *lamidats* of northern Cameroon
and in Ghana's Ashanti Region. They define what Mamdani (1996a) calls
"local states," and constitute local public spheres in which membership in
these local polities is performed and reproduced. Within these public spheres,

populations subject to the land-allocation authority of the neocustomary elites are audiences for the performance of chiefly power.

The contrast in the political character of the local state across these two settings shows that chieftaincies vary in their openness to participation, voice, and the exercise of accountability mechanisms. Chapter 2 argued that to a very large extent, the customary land tenure regimes (LTRs) and the forms of customary authority that they define are the *products* of modern state-building exercises. A general implication of this claim would be that one source of variation in the political character of the chieftaincies is difference in the political character of the national governments that confirm and uphold them. Although we do not test this proposition here, it rings true for the cases examined. In democratic Ghana, the local public sphere constituted by chieftaincy in Ashanti offers some open space for debating and contesting the exercise of chiefly power, even though local collective action does not always produce the desired results. In authoritarian Cameroon, the most notorious chieftaincies are as violent and repressive as the national government itself.

The Ashanti Region case tracks a shift over time in the scale of land authority and land-related conflict. Chiefs' power to allocate unused land has dwindled along with the availability of unused land. The land frontier in rural Ashanti has closed, largely as a result of growth in the number of persons claiming land on the basis of birthright. Lineage- and family-centered forms of neocustomary authority over land now prevail in the rural areas of this region. In the periurban areas, however, chiefly power has been asserted strongly in the past decade or so. Chiefs assert the right to reclaim lineage and family farmland when it is need for urban expansion – a practice honored by the state. This form of eminent domain has opened up a new land frontier for chiefs and sparked a wildfire of conflict between landholders and chiefs over the exercise of this neocustomary prerogative.

Cases presented in Part III focus on scale effects. The Ashanti case concentrates on politics among local chiefs and the citizens of those chieftaincies. In the case of northern Cameroon, land politics revolves around the kind of ethnic hierarchy between landlords and land users that the reader encountered in Chapter 4. One specificity of the northern Cameroon case is that the politically dominant stratum justifies its land prerogatives on a right of conquest, rather than on the firstcomer or ancestral claims that are invoked by landlord groups in the Chapter 4 cases.

NORTHERN CAMEROON: STATES WITHIN THE STATE

The lamidats of Cameroon's three northern provinces are chiefly jurisdictions.[1] They dominate politics in a region that holds 30 percent of the national

---

[1] That is, Far North or Extrême Nord (Maroua), North or Nord (Garoua), and Adamaoua (Ngaoundéré). Together they hold 30% of the national population (Teyssier et al. 2003). This analysis focuses on the Far North and North.

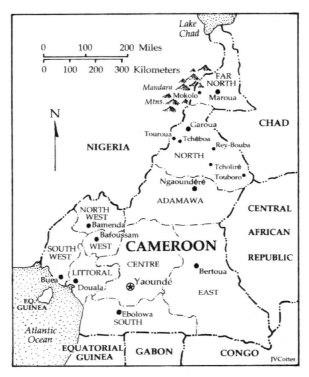

MAP 7. Cameroon

population. (Map 7.) In the most important Peul[2] lamidats, chiefs' (*lamibe's* [sing. *lamido*'s]) vast powers over land access and adjudication are matched by their heavy-handed domination of rural political arenas.[3]

Northern Cameroon's most powerful lamidats are often described as "states within the state," especially in terms of the authority and autonomy they exercise vis-à-vis the civil administration in the rural areas. These political entities trace their origins to the Islamic emirates created around the time of the Peul conquest of the animist peoples of this region in the early 1800s. The new Peul kingdoms and aristocracies "overthrew diverse socio-political structures of the

---

[2] They are also called Fulbe, or Fulani.
[3] By contrast, in Northwest Province of (anglophone) Cameroon, also known as the Bamenda Grasslands region, under the 1974 land ordinance inter alia, the state took control of rangelands from the local chiefs, or *fons*, resulting in the chiefs' "loss of control over this crucial political, material, and symbolic resource to the state" (Hickey 2007, 93, n. 26, citing Fisiy 1995). Fisiy (1992, 288–289) offers a comparison and contrast of Northwest and Southwest Provinces that parallels the kind of comparative analysis developed here. There is also variation *within* the North. Moritz et al. (2002), for example, wrote about the Diamaré plains of the Far North, where *lamibe* (chiefs) lost land prerogatives with devolution and the creation of national parks.

various 'pagan' populations of the region"[4] and established their hegemony. Indigenous peoples of the region, subject to raids and taxation, were driven into mountain refuges. The well-irrigated plains and valleys of what is now northern Cameroon were left to the predominantly pastoralist subjects of the new rulers.

Colonial rule "erected a [political] superstructure above the lamidats" but did not destroy them. Both the German (1903–1915) and the French (1915–1950s) administrations were driven by "the desire to preserve structures that [could] be useful to the colonizer."[5] *Lamibe* were forced into clientelistic dependence on the French, but the most powerful and cooperative among them preserved great autonomy, including their own taxation systems, police, and armies within their territorial domains (Taguem-Fah 2003). The postcolonial governments of Ahmadou Ahidjo (1960–1982) and Paul Biya (1982–present) "embraced and subordinated" the lamidats and the Peul elite of northern Cameroon, adopting "the same strategy as the colonial administration . . . and using them as local conduits of central power" (Taguem-Fah 2003, 281).[6] Today there are about fifty such lamidats or chiefly jurisdictions in northern Cameroon, varying in territorial scope, autonomy, and closeness to the regime in the national capital of Yaoundé.[7] The Peul lamibe are appointed "from aristocratic families" by the central government. The most influential of these form a "regional plutocracy that pulls strings at the national level" (Taguem-Fah 2003, 277). The Cameroon government relies on these strongmen to control the rural populations of the north.

From the 1950s to the 1990s, the "traditional aristocracy" of what is now North Province (Province du Nord) seems to have been a willing partner of the modern state in schemes to promote the settlement of agriculturalists on land in some of the "unused" plains and valleys of this region. For the central state, these were potential *terroirs d'immigration* that could be used to "decongest" the densely populated regions of the Far North and to promote cash-crop

[4] Taguem-Fah 2003, 269. The new provinces in what is today northern Cameroon were subsidiaries of the Peul empire of Sokoto (Seignobos 2006, 3).

[5] Taguem-Fah 2003, 272–273.

[6] Ahidjo reduced the size of the lamidat jurisdictions (except in the case of Mayo-Rey, which remained a "vast department, of a land area greater than Belgium") (Seignobos 2006, 4). Biya also reduced the size of the northern jurisdictions, except for Rey Bouba.

[7] The lamidats differ along several dimensions, including ethnic character and position within the hierarchy of lamidats of the North. From the mid-1920s, the French created some non-Peul cantons which "liberated" some indigenous groups from Peul domination. Other non-Peul cantons, or lamidats, were created later, and were politically subordinate to the Peul lamidats under Ahidjo and (in parts of Northern Province at least) under Biya. See Tassou 2008, 6 on the Lamidats de Mokolo and Matakam-Sud, and Schilder 1994 on the Mundang lamidat of Kaele. The land-related powers of the non-Peul lamibe ruling over autochthonous agriculturalists in their "home territories" in southwestern Far North Province would be far weaker than those of the Peul lamibe. The political fallout of Biya's purge of members of the northern elite who were closest to Ahidjo, and who moved into the opposition after 1991, was also uneven.

(especially cotton) production in state-sponsored project zones. The lamibe extracted tribute from many of the agriculturalists newly settled within their domains (through taxes, fines, and payments in kind in the form of food crops and, in some cases, labor services) and received premiums from the parastatals for increasing cotton output within their jurisdictions,[8] expanding not only their sources of revenue but also their clout as rural strongmen and allies of the central administration. Chiefs and notables also became large planters themselves (Boutrais 1978, 71 n. 2, 4). Taguem-Fah (2003, 277) writes that with the state-sponsored development of cotton production in the lamidat of Rey Bouba, "the lamido enriched himself by distributing land, collecting royalties, and other advantages."

The territorial reach of the lamidats is considerable, even after divisions engineered by successive state administrations to ensure their manipulability. The largest one, not subject to subdivision since the midcolonial period, is the Lamidat of Rey Bouba. Its 36,500-square kilometers territory coincides with the modern department of Mayo-Rey and is larger than Belgium.[9] The *lamido* has a private army of several hundred, along with a phalanx of territorial representatives (*dogari*), whom he appoints directly.[10] The Lamidat of Tchéboa covers 4,000 square kilometers and 50 villages and is controlled by a lamido with a militia of 30 guards, and 10 lesser chiefs.[11]

The land regime is the institutional and political foundation of the Peul lamibe's power over rural populations. Lamibe and their subchiefs, the *chefs de canton*, are allocators and adjudicators of land used by farmers and pastoralists in northern Cameroon.[12] The literature on this region often describes their powers in this domain as nearly absolute, although the weight of their extractions and the solidity of the chiefly hierarchies varies across jurisdictions.

Postcolonial land politics in this region revolves around gaining and securing access to lands controlled by these neotraditional, state-backed authorities. The dynamics in the lamidats governed by the Peul chiefs can be described in terms of how they play out three analytically distinct (but interrelated) land-use situations.

Three Land-Use Situations

The first land-use situation is that of the Peul/Muslim pastoralists and agropastoralists who, in the neocustomary political order, are regarded as the natural

---

[8] Schilder 1994, 141–142.
[9] Seignobos 2006.
[10] Article 19 (1995, 11) reported that the population of the department/lamidat was 180,000. About 20,000 had come into the Sodecoton/SEB scheme by 1990.
[11] Article 19, 1995, 16.
[12] It seems that the jurisdiction of the *chef de canton* (second-class chief) is the *sous-préfecture*.

subjects of the Peul aristocracies of the region. Their claims to land on the vast plains of this region are founded on a right of conquest and Peul political hegemony.[13] They are governed by hierarchies of chiefs within the lamidats and pay land and cattle taxes directly to these authorities. Nomadic pastoralists must negotiate access to rangeland within each of the lamidats and pay grazing and cattle taxes to the lamibe (Moritz et al. 2002). Herders, graziers, and agropastoralists face pressure from environmental stress, population increase, and shrinking pasturelands, due in part to "immigration of peasants" into their territories, and the creation of forest reserves and national parks in northern Cameroon. Progressive development of agropastoralism among Peul with long-established land claims, and sedentarization of pastoralist communities who are considered to be "outsiders," complicates land-use patterns and contributes to rising competition for land.[14]

Second is the situation of the autochthonous agriculturalists of northern Cameroon. Predominantly food-crop farmers, their ancestors were subjugated and displaced from the plains by Peul raiding and conquest. Many established themselves as subsistence farmers in the Mandara Mountains that form the western boundary of this region (thus they are often called *montagnard* peoples). Under the pressure of taxation under the French and the postcolonial regimes and with population pressure, growing numbers have descended to the foothills and plains, where they must negotiate land access with the Peul authorities (and find accommodation with pastoralists).[15]

A third situation is that of in-migrants in the state-managed project zones of northern Cameroon.[16] Many of these "administratively inserted" agriculturalists are from the mountainous regions of Cameroon's North and Far North Provinces (from the *montagnard* ethnic groups). In some of these zones, the parastatal agency Sodecoton has demarcated parcels of land and allocated them to users.[17] In the schema developed in this book, this land regime has to be categorized as statist. However, the statist character of land administration in the project zones is attenuated by the strong presence of the lamibe and lesser

---

[13] The Peul are considered by the autochthones to be *allogènes* who rule and occupy territory by right of conquest. See Tassou 2008, 10, n. 7.

[14] Kossoumna-Liba'a 2003. In keeping with our focus on agricultural land users, we do not deal further here with pastoralists such as those in the Logone River floodplains (see Moritz et al. 2002).

[15] The Peul lamidats claimed authority over autochthonous agriculturalists in the southwestern part of what is now the Far North and extracted tribute. The Germans reinforced the lamibe's hold over these people, but the French "liberated them from the Fulbe" and governed them under separate administrative jurisdictions. See Schilder 1994, 143–144; Roitman 2005, 136–138, 142.

[16] Some of the irrigated development schemes are called *"perimètres de colonisation"* by Jua 1990, 22.

[17] See Seignobos 2006. Sodecoton, established in 1974, is successor to the colonial-era CFDT (Compagnie Française pour le Développement des Textiles).

neocustomary chiefs, who are, in many such situations, able to impose *lamidale* (i.e., of the lamidat, or chiefly) land taxes and other routine extractions on in-migrants. Sodecoton project zones in the Rey Bouba and Tchéboa lamidats seem to be at least partially *nested* – not only territorially but also politically – within the Peul lamidats. In Rey Bouba, the lamido was implicated in the creation of the Sodecoton Sud-Est-Benoué (SEB) project zone and, in the 1990s and 2000s, he exercised political prerogative in governing and taxing farmers in these territories.[18] Taguem-Fah (2003, 286) and Seignobos (2006) write that the state agents assigned to work within the lamidat of Rey Bouba – including prefectural administrators and Sodecoton employees – are treated by the Biya regime as political subordinates or auxiliaries of the lamido.

Rising Competition for Land

Rising competition for land is felt throughout the northern provinces. In the Far North, autochthonous populations (Mafa, Mofu) have long practiced terracing and other advanced forms of agricultural intensification on the mountain slopes, where their claims to land are based on indigeneity (autochthony). High population pressure in these areas dates to the 1930s and 1940s.[19] Gonné and Seignobos (2006) write that this has intensified in recent decades, producing two related effects. First, population pressure fuels intensifying struggles within the Mandara Mountain farming areas, both within and between families, leading to exclusion of those considered "less autochthonous" than others. Second, it heightens the need for farmers to seek land in the foothills and on the plains from the Peul land authorities, especially the *chefs de canton* who serve under the lamibe. "This has become necessary to secure a modicum of food security."[20] Land saturation in the foothills and adjacent plains has made land access extremely competitive and expensive. *Chefs de canton* demand land tribute of 10 percent of the harvest. These charges are compounded by rising rents and transaction fees charged by Peul agropastoralists who occupy the lands. According to Gonné and Seignobos, demand for land is so high that many tracts are subject to multiple transactions (i.e., rented to more than one user for the same purpose), engendering frequent and sometimes violent local conflicts. Conflicts drive claimants into costly adjudication processes controlled by the chiefs and their dignitaries, making land seekers who have no

---

[18] The Sud-Est-Bénoué project received the first migrants to the *sous-préfecture* of Touboro in the mid-1980s. See Seignobos 2006, 7–10. Teyssier et al. (2003, 6) report that in the Sodecoton zones in Rey Bouba, settlers are not sheltered from taxation by the lamido.

[19] Van Santen (1998, 404) reports population densities of 400 per square kilometer in the late 1980s in Mafa communities in the Mandara Mountains above Mokolo, as well as the presence of landlessness. See also Haller 2001; Boutrais 1978.

[20] Gonné and Seignobos 2006, 16. See also Boutrais 1978.

state-recognized land rights (and no legal recourse) "subject to arbitrary judgments orchestrated by the cantonal chiefs."[21]

Farther out onto the plains, in the rural areas within about a fifty-mile radius of the provincial capital of Maroua in Far North Province, there is also strong demand for farmland. In these areas, attempts by Peul landholders to sell land to non-Peul – including Guiziga – buyers[22] generate multiple lines of land-related conflict. Heirs of the Peul sellers often attempt to reclaim family lands, generating disputes that open the door to costly mediation by the lamidale authorities, especially *chefs de canton*. According to Gonné and Seignobos (2006, 16), the cantonal chiefs attempt to defend Peul/Muslim control over the land by blocking sales and sanctioning village chiefs who tolerate such sales. This positions them to prey on disputants by extracting adjudication fees, and also to take advantage of eventual renters from whom they demand tribute. "The Guiziga cultivators are powerless in the face of the hierarchy of Peul authorities who control the land" (Gonné and Seignobos 2006, 16).[23]

In some areas, rising competition for land is a legacy of the state-sponsored colonization projects.[24] This is observable in the Touboro area of the Rey Bouba lamidat. In-migrants whose installation in the zone was sponsored by Sodecoton (1985–1990) are now seeking land in areas beyond the limits of the original projects.[25] The autochthonous Mbum people of the area are subjects of the lamido; they are governed at the village level by autochthonous chiefs who can be removed from office by the lamido. According to Seignobos (2006), Mbum people have responded to rising competition for land in their home areas by intensifying their agricultural production techniques (moving away from the shifting practices of the earlier era) and seeking to secure their rights to village territories.[26] By these processes, both the Mbum and the in-migrants are drawn

---

[21] Teyssier et al. (2003, 10) write that payments needed to tip an arbitration over a parcel of less than 1 hectare in size could reach 500,000 to nearly a million CFA francs in the late 1990s.

[22] They are identified by Gonné and Seignobos (2006, 16) as a conquered people displaced or forced into tribute-paying status by the Peul conquest.

[23] Moritz et al. (2002) argue that in the Longone River floodplains farther east, close to the Chad border, the Peul lamibe's powers over the land have weakened since the 1970s. See also Schilder 1994.

[24] Kossoumna-Liba'a (2003) reported that the rate of population growth in the Northern Province was 5–6%, and that in-migration accounted for half of this.

[25] From 1985 to 1990, 19,000 in-migrants from the Far North were resettled in 33 new villages in Mayo-Rey, around Touboro, under the Sud-Est Bénoué project. Many or most were Tupuri or Mafa. This is Cameroon's "most important *bassin d'immigration*" (Seignobos 2006, 4, 6). Gonné and Seignobos (2006, 18) report that since 1997, "the traditional chiefs of the North have been against any further/new *migration encadrée* (state-sponsored and -planned immigration)."

[26] In this lamidat, the lamido controls the appointment and removal of village chiefs. In Mbum areas, village chiefs are Mbum. Representation is by communal grouping. On land-use conflicts around Touboro, see Seignobos 2006, 7–8; Teyssier, Hamadou, and Seignobos 2003.

more tightly into the embrace of the lamido and are more fully exposed to the Peul chiefs' extractions and political machinations. Like the other lamibe, the ruler of Rey Bouba profits not only by extracting land tribute and in-kind taxes but also by granting permission to use the land (*autorisations d'occupation* and *autorisations d'exploitation*) and mediating disputes that emerge between communities of land users.[27]

Farmer-herder competition and tension is also pervasive in northern Cameroon. The land tenure regime makes chiefs the pivotal actors in mediating this kind of competition as well. In many situations, pastoralists, agropastoralists, and farmers are sharing spaces (within the lamidats) that are single jurisdictions under the authority of one ruler. Kossoumna-Liba'a (2003, 5) provides an example in an examination of land politics in the lamidat of Tchéboa (45 kilometers from Garoua). He explains that throughout much of North Province, growing populations of both people and livestock place tremendous pressure on resources. In Tchéboa, the lamido has hosted the settlement of Mbororo communities of sedentarizing pastoralists, and allocated them lands.[28] Sedentarization dovetails with the state's efforts to promote cotton cultivation in the province. It serves the lamido's interests because settlers pay the *zakkat* (the lamidat tax or *fiscalité lamidale*), and because their presence adds clients to the chief's power base. With the resulting densification and intensification of land use, conflicts between established Peul agropastoralists and the cattle-owning in-migrants are inevitable. Kossoumna-Liba'a reports that in the Tchéboa localities he studied, farmer-herder conflicts are frequent but not violent, and that government agencies operating in this zone rely on the chiefs to structure and mediate relations between the in-migrants and the longer-established Peuls. For the most part, the lamido does so by using his power to allocate land, impose fines, confiscate animals, and settle cases.

In-migrants form a politically subordinate stratum in the villages. They are taxed more heavily than the other residents, obliged by the lamido to contribute to social works such as the building of training centers and schools "from which they derive no benefit," and not allowed into positions of authority over local institutions such as cooperatives.[29] Even so, the authority of the lamido "has not provoked any outflanking attempts [*n'incite d'ailleurs pas à des débordements*]" (Kossoumna-Liba'a 2003, 6).

---

[27] Moritz et al. (2002) write than in the Longone River floodplain, the chiefs and lamibe profit so much from disputes that they have little incentive to see them attenuated.

[28] Herders need dry- and wet-season pasture, as well as migratory corridors that link grazing areas. They feel their spaces shrinking as more lands come under cultivation and as forest reserves and game parks are made off-limits. One solution is sedentarization or partial sedentarization. Border politics (with Nigeria, Chad, and Central African Republic) can also drive people out of established areas and into new ones.

[29] Kossoumna-Liba'a 2003, 6. Meanwhile the lamido "plays the migrants against the autochthones when the autochthones oppose him" (Gonné and Seignobos 2006, 18). Boutrais (1978) makes the same observation.

Land Conflict under a Chieftaincy-Centered Land Tenure Regime

In the rural areas of northern Cameroon, the LTR positions the chiefs as the pivotal authorities in land conflicts. Land matters are handled in a "juridical void" (Kossoumna Liba'a 2003, 2) – the central state has "abandoned rural land administration to the chieftaincies" (Teyssier et al. 2003), willfully allowing the lamidale authorities to exercise wide-ranging power in this domain. Lamidale authorities retain a hand in land matters even in areas that were "colonized" by the central administration. Seignobos (2006, 17–19) suggests that in some such areas, chiefly prerogative has increased over time, especially in the 1990s as the Biya regime cemented alliances with northern chiefs. In the Sodecoton project zones around Touboro in the Lamidat of Rey Bouba, for example, the administration is backing out of land tenure matters, leaving these to the lamido and his enforcers, the *dogari*.[30] Gonné and Seignobos (2006, 16) underscore the weakness of state intervention in land matters throughout the North, with prefectural agents "preferring to leave land affairs, too complex and recurring, to the traditional chiefs.... The administration is quick to turn anything having to do with *le foncier* (land tenure) over to the lamibe." Land users find themselves without any administrative support (*tutelle administrative*).[31] In some areas, when small-scale land conflict breaks into open violence among land users, the prefectural authorities and gendarmeries intervene on an ad-hoc basis, but they do not resolve the underlying tenure disputes, which are referred back to the neocustomary authorities.

Many critics report that the Cameroon government allows the lamibe and other chiefs to employ organized violence openly against their subjects in land matters and in other political affairs (Article 19 1995, 1997; Amnesty International 1997, 2009). In some lamidats of Far North Province, and the Rey Bouba and Tchéboa lamidats of North Province, chiefs hold opponents and dissidents shackled in private prisons in their palaces or in the homes of notables and dignitaries. Article 19 (1995, 16, 19) reported that in Tchéboa in 1994, the lamido threatened and detained members of a village who attempted to resist his demand that they perform compulsory labor in his fields. The same lamido was responsible for detaining, beating, and robbing seventeen opposition-party activists who tried to campaign in the lamidat that same year. Deaths resulting from such beatings and detentions have been well documented. It is not that the civil authorities are absent in this region or that the abuses are invisible to the central government. On the contrary, in many of the documented cases, citizens have gone to local administrative authorities (especially subprefects) to request protection from the violence of the lamido and have been refused.

[30] In this area, the lamido's enforcers, the *dogari*, are strongly present in land matters (Teyssier, Hamadou, and Seignobos 2003).
[31] Gonné and Seignobos 2006, 18. On the 1974 land ordinance and the unrealized possibility of registration of rural landholdings, see, for example, Fisiy 1992.

The chieftaincy-centered LTR prevailing in the rural areas of northern Cameroon has given the Peul lamidal authorities strong control over extensive "open plains" and wide pioneer fronts, as well as over settled agriculturalists. In contexts of intensifying competition for land, there is, as Boutrais puts it in his 1978 study of agricultural development in the Far North, a "hardening of the land tenure regime" (84–87). Peul authorities have opportunities to reinforce their control over land and to become more predatory in their dealings with agropastoralists and peasant farmers. These local strongmen control land adjudication and the allocation of open land, and profit from both kinds of transaction. It is extractions that occur through these mechanisms, rather than the outright expulsion of farmers from the areas that they have cultivated (as, for example, in the cases examined in Chapter 4), that seem to be the focal point of land-related politics in the settled farming areas of the northern plains.

In these situations, conflicts over surplus appropriation and land rights are centered on the use of chiefly authority and play out in institutional arenas that are structured around chieftaincy. Within these arenas, the scope of citizenship rights and channels of access/voice are extremely limited. In-migrants to the lamidats, including *montagnard* peoples who have become landless or nearly so in their "home areas" and must negotiate access to land on the plains, are in the worst position: they cannot claim land on the basis of autochthony, and they also cannot invoke the "right of conquest" that is used to justify Peul occupation of the plains. They are vulnerable to landlessness, to exploitative dealings, and to being relegated, by lack of political clout and citizenship rights in the local state, to marginal and less productive lands (Boutrais 1978). Pastoralists who have lost or never had the protection of strong lamibe have also lost rights to rangelands (Moritz et al. 2002).

The political arrangements prevailing in these jurisdictions go far in limiting the political options of land-rights losers and potential losers, as well as those of anyone subject to the predatory practices of the chiefs. Rights conferred by national citizenship appear to be barely relevant in the rural political arenas defined by the Peul lamidats. In northern Cameroon, according to Gonné and Seignobos (2006, 18), "civil society exists in the cities, but it barely exists in the Peul jurisdictions." This rural-urban contrast can be framed as the logical extension of a theory that identifies rural land tenure regimes as the foundation of democracy-stifling political relationships in the rural areas.

Land politics is visible in both submission and resistance to chiefly authority. Throughout much of the region, most land users submit to the lamidal authority and extractions. At least since the 1950s, there does not seem to be a pattern of rural revolts or uprisings against the lamibe.[32] In-migrants who access land directly through the lamidal authorities are tightly constrained by the structure

---

[32] See Bah 1974 on the 1920 insurrection that tore apart the lamidat of Ngaoundéré.

of the political situation in which they find themselves. The predicament of the sedentarized pastoralists who have settled in the villages in Tchéboa shows why: They "are taxed heavily and fined often, which they do complain about, ... but each one has an interest in respecting the established rules to avoid being summarily expelled from the area and forced to leave behind everything they have, as has often been the case" (Kossoumna-Liba'a, 2003, 6). Seignobos notes that in Rey Bouba, some land users who cannot bear the lamido's extractions flee the lamidat. They resettle under the jurisdiction of less heavy handed chiefs, or along the roadsides in neighboring provinces, where they can be closer to the national adminstration. Gonné and Seignobos (2006) emphasize that farmers from the highland ethnic groups who seek land on the plains, including sedentarized pastoralists (such as the Mbororo who settled in Tchéboa), have no rights to land in the lamidats.

There is some overt contestation of the lamibe's land powers, however. What Seignobos and others call *la course à la sécurisation foncière* – the "rush to make landholdings more secure" – appears to be a visible expression of resistance to chiefly authority in this region. Securization aims not only to preempt another user's claims but also to decrease chiefs' prerogatives when it comes to dispute adjudication and extracting fees and other payments from land users. In this sense, it is eminently political.

Gonné and Seignobos (2006, 16–17) write that around Maroua, rising competition for land, rising land values, and escalating land-related disputes fuel the questioning of the land-adjudication powers of the Peul authorities, which "tends to take on political overtones." If Mofu and Guiziga elites "begin to demand land on the plains as *their lands*," as Gonné and Seignobos suggest that some are doing, then this could be taken as the stirrings of a subversive impulse aimed at diminishing the authority of the Peul chiefs.[33]

The key fact is that many aspects of these land-related struggles are targeted at, and fought out over, the institutions of chieftaincy. This channeling effect of the land tenure regime is visible in multistranded attempts coming from literate farmers and outsiders to contest or neutralize the cantonal chiefs' ability to intervene in land transactions and disputes. In the rural areas around Maroua, literate farmers, the Catholic Comités Doicésians de Développement (CDDs), and human rights organizations have moved in this direction.[34] The Peul elites have responded by struggling to retain their prerogatives in the property rights domain (Gonné and Seignobos 2006).

---

[33] Emphasis added.

[34] One strategy the CDDs have promoted is use of written documents that record land transactions that are witnessed by neutral parties (use of so-called *petits papiers*). Although these documents do not have legal standing, the aim is to reduce disputes. Maroua is now an urban agglomeration of 400,000 people.

To this end, the neotraditional authorities have been known to unleash violence against subversives, agitators, and those who question their authority. Article 19 (1995, 17) reports this case:[35]

> Bakari Madi, a 61-year-old resident of Mindif, a village in Far North Province, was, he alleges, detained and tortured for having challenged the lamido's authority. He was among other things shackled to a wall in his home for about six months by local dignitaries after having accused the lamido of stealing his land.... He was [also] detained by the lamido for two months in 1992 for attending an SDF meeting [political party meeting] at which he criticized the ruling party.

Bakari Madi sought to bring suit against the lamido in court, but "the Public Prosecutor is reported to have announced ... that the case cannot go forward without the approval of Cameroon's Minister of Justice" (Article 19, 18). Just as E. E. Schattschneider would have predicted, the national authorities worked to "containerize" conflict within the rural jurisdiction, thus limiting possibilities for expansion of the scope of conflict.

Chiefs and the government administration work together in repressing civil society organizations in Far North Province, especially in restricting their reach into the rural areas. In a report entitled "Impunity Underpins Persistent Abuse" (January 2009), Amnesty International described continuing government repression of the Mouvement pour la Défense des Droits de l'Homme et la Liberté (MDDHL), including the arrest of two MDDHL members for going into Ndoukoula District to gather information on human rights violations (including land-related cases such as the Mindif case just described). The procurator general in Maroua

> had reportedly instructed the district administrator, in writing, to arrest human rights activists who visited the district. MDDHL informed Amnesty International that [their group] was accused of involvement in local disputes among the population, including disputes about land and hereditary rights.... A[n] MDDHL member was detained for several months in Mokolo in Far North Province [Lamidat of Tchéboa] (Amnesty International 2009: 15–16).

This fits a general pattern of repression in the rural areas of Far North and North Provinces.[36] Article 19 (1995, 1) reports that

---

[35] The same source reports other beating and floggings by lamido palace guards in Far North Province, including the case of a mother who was flogged for trying to get her fourteen-year-old daughter back from the lamido of Pouss, who had decided he wanted to marry the girl. "The mother fled to a hospital in Maga (near Pouss) for treatment after her flogging, but the doctor refused to treat her" (Article 19 1995, 18).

[36] Schilder (1994, 24) reports that the chief/lamido Kakiang Abubakar, ruler of Kaele canton since 1955 and local party boss for Presidents Ahidjo and Biya, "prevented a militant group of young men of the opposition party from entering Kaele town" during the presidential campaign and election of 1992.

attacks on government critics and opposition parties are widespread in [those] rural areas where support for opposition parties is strong, and gross violations go unreported in either the national or the international press. The government frequently uses bans on political activity, restrictions on freedom of association, intimidation, and arrest to curb opposition activities outside the main urban areas.

In Rey Bouba, there have been attempts to partially insulate some small-scale farmers from chiefly authority by reducing the scale, scope, and frequency of land disputes. The strategy hinges on better demarcation of village territories (and parcels) and the development of alternative dispute resolution mechanisms that can "fly beneath the radar" of the lamidal authorities. This is not a head-on assault on the status quo. Indeed, it is the *opposite* of a more transformative strategy that would aim at scaling up and widening the scope of politics by seeking to expand farmers' access to national administrative, judicial, and political institutions. An internationally funded research project (attached to Sodecoton)[37] spearheaded a land-demarcation project aimed at securization of user rights in the Touboro area in 1997–2001. The project positioned 57 site markers and demarcated 212 kilometers of boundary lines. Both autochthones and in-migrants cooperated, and some even requested demarcation of areas not included in the original pilot area (Teyssier et al. 2003, 6). The political implications of these initiatives were not lost on the lamido of Rey Bouba. In 2004, the lamido, Bouba Abdoulaye, died and was replaced by his son, whose guards tore up the boundary markers with the battle cry "*On ne coupe pas la terre du Baaba!* (One does not cut up the lamido's land!) (Seignobos 2006, 4–5).

Meanwhile, the lamido has waged all-out war on local challengers, including rivals within the local aristocracy[38] as well as opposition party representatives who might seek access to peasants (especially those with land-related grievances against the lamido), attempt to expand the scale and scope of conflict, and outflank the local state. In the legislative elections of 1992 and 1995, opposition candidates were systematically persecuted and forbidden from campaigning in the lamidat. Several opposition candidates and election workers were killed by the lamidal authorities. Even so, three opposition candidates won constituencies centered in the jurisdiction's main towns. Among those

---

[37] The DPGT project (Développement Paysannal et Gestion de Terroirs, 1994–2002) was developed in association with l'Institut de Recherches pour le Développement (IRD, France), funded by the Agence Française de Développement (AFD), and attached to Sodecoton (Teyssier et al. 2003, 14).

[38] The 1990s opposition party Union Nationale pour la Démocratie et le Progrès (UNDP) is strong in the north. Party leader Maigari Bello Bouba was a high-ranking member of the Ahidjo regime and briefly served as prime minister under Biya. He went into exile after the alleged coup plot of 1984 and returned to lead the UNDP in 1991–1992, was elected as a Bénoué MP in 1992, was incorporated into Biya's government in 1997, lost his seat in 2002, and was reelected UNDP president in 2007. Defections to the government, starting in 1994, split the party. See Amnesty International 1997, Article 19, 1995, 5–6.

killed was Adama Haman-Daouda, who was elected to parliament from Rey-Bouba constituency and later died from a beating by the lamido's guards.[39] In 1997, the legislative electoral results in this lamidat were annulled. One Sodeco-ton employee from Touroro who was an opposition party member was chained within the confines of the lamido's palace for two years – a fate that has befallen other personal and political opponents of the lamibe. Article 19 (1995, 12–14) reported that seventy opposition party members were detained in the lamido's private prisons in 1992. In Rey Bouba, the lamido has also sought to strengthen his hold at the grassroots level by removing autochthonous chiefs from power. This incited resistance from villagers that was violently repressed by the *dogari*. In 1993, 300 armed guards of the lamido fired on a crowd of unarmed villagers at Mbang Rey, killing 20. "Several hundred people reportedly have fled from the villages of Touboro and Mbang-Rey since these incidents" (Article 19, 1995, 12; Amnesty International 1997).

The Biya regime has been the traditional authorities' ally in local repression against those who challenge the authority of the lamibe, whether they are engaged in opposition politics, land politics, or resistance to extractions of other kinds. "Government authorities not only have failed to stop the illegal actions by traditional authorities against opposition activists but also have intervened to thwart attempts of victims to bring traditional authorities to court" (Article 19, 1995, 3).[40]

Although the transition from the Ahidjo regime to that of Biya in 1982–1984 culminated in the political purge of personalities most closely associated with Ahidjo's Northern Bloc, it did not alter the state's reliance on the structures and authority of chieftaincy to govern and control the populations of the north.[41] Teyssier et al. (2003, 4) report, "A deal was made: The chieftaincies benefited from a blank check to administer their territories as they wished . . . as long as they remained faithful to the regime and demonstrated this at election time." Chiefs have remained *les gardiens des urnes* (guardians of the ballot boxes), as they were during the Ahidjo regime. The nature of land regimes in the Peul jurisdictions goes far in explaining the reproduction of their power over time.

Land-related conflicts that might otherwise play out in a national system of courts or in the national political arena (in legislative struggles and party

---

[39] Article 19, 1997. In the municipal elections of 1996, 99.5% of the electors in Mayo-Rey department voted for the ruling party, the RDPC (Rassemblement Démocratique du Peuple Camerounais). To most people, this was an indication of the power of the lamido, not of loyalty to the president. "Fear and power were closely connected in Cameroon" (Hansen 2003, 217).

[40] See F. Pigenaud 2011, 74–75 for the update.

[41] On the tumultuous transitions of 1982–1984 (end of Ahidjo regime) and 1991–1992 (transition to multipartism), see Schilder 1994, 159–162, 222–226 inter alia. See Takougang and Krieger (1998, 169–174), who analyze the struggle over the privatization of Sodecoton in 1993–1997, which brought a coalition of powerful northern regional interests into the open.

politics, for example) are fought out within local jurisdictions, where the mechanisms, coercive practices, and idioms of neotraditional rule are employed and contested. This LTR produces a national-level effect: land-related struggles are bottled up at the local level and contained within the *structures lamidales*. The chiefs in the populous and politically strategic northern jurisdictions vigorously resist any attempts to breach these ramparts, and the central state backs them up in this.

These arrangements subvert or preempt the possibility of rural democracy.[42] And as Skrowneck (1982) suggests of extreme devolution of power in the United States in the nineteenth century, it weakens the national judicial, representative, and administrative institutions.

CONFLICT REPRESSED WITHIN CHIEFTAINCIES: PERIURBAN KUMASI, GHANA

> Four elected Assemblymen said they were completely exasperated by the chiefs but did not see any way to speak up or do anything about it. (Field notes, outskirts of Kumasi, June 2009)

In the Ashanti Region of Ghana, as in most of southern Ghana, the power to allocate unused land and authorize the sale of land is vested in the chiefs. Early in the colonial period, British authorities delimited the Asante chiefs' territorial jurisdictions and codified their powers to allocate, control, and dispose of land within these domains. The institution of stool lands (lands controlled through the Akan chieftaincies) developed as the linchpin of British indirect rule in Ghana. The British realized that chiefly prerogatives over land could be wielded to restrain the development of land markets, thus allowing the chiefs to retain authority in the rural areas and political leverage over their subjects.[43]

These arrangements are the cornerstone of a postcolonial political and legal framework for governing southern Ghana that has allowed chiefs to extract tribute, rents, revenue, and profits from stool lands and also to accumulate properties on their own account – sometimes at the expense of their subjects and the communities they are supposed to represent. The ultimate vesting of

---

[42] Tassou (2008) cites this news report by Alawadi-Zelao, which appeared in the *L'Oeil du Sahel*, n. 207, July 2008, 11: "In this part of Cameroun [North and Far North Provinces], the residences of the chiefs are usually transformed into polling stations. Only the ballots of the ruling party are distributed to the population (illiterate and gullible) who execute the voting act under the pressure of a team of representatives of the lamido who do their best to terrorise the masses in a rigged political game [*un contexte politique de 'concurrence déloyale'*]."

[43] "In the Gold Coast, land sales had commenced at the turn of the century and had been given judicial recognition [by the colonial state]. The West African Lands Committee, however, in 1912 took the view that the sales of land were inconsistent with African customs which should be enforced.... After 1917 neither the administration nor the judiciary would enforce sales by Africans" (Noronha 1985, 27, 31). See also Phillips 1989.

land in the stools also gives chiefs political leverage over both stool citizens and in-migrants within their jurisdictions. Ever since the 1920s, much of the conflict over land rights and political authority in southern Ghana has centered on the rights and prerogatives of chiefs.[44] National governments, with a few short-lived exceptions (discussed in Chapter 4), have chosen to ally with chiefs and to keep land-related redistributive politics bottled up at the level of the chieftaincies.

Closing of the Land Frontier and the Downward Shift in the Scale of Land Politics in Rural Ashanti

The rise of a peasant-based export economy in Ghana dates to the second half of the nineteenth century. By 1911, the territory was the world's leading cocoa supplier. In-migration to clear forest and establish farms on "new land" provided much of the labor to fuel this process. In Ashanti Region, the expansion of cocoa production was driven forward by an *abusa* sharecropping system, under which migrant farmers asked local chiefs and lineage heads for permission to cultivate stool lands. In exchange, migrants paid tribute to the chiefs, and a share of the harvest (one-third or one-half) to the landholder.[45] As described in Chapter 4, in Ashanti Region from the 1920s through the 1940s or so, the virgin land opened up to cocoa cultivation was stool land under the control of chiefs. Chiefs allocated land for cocoa farming to migrants, established their own cocoa plantations on stool lands, and granted holdings to families and lineages within their jurisdictions. This added to the chiefs' wealth, economic clout, and political power.[46]

Lineages in this region, including those of the lower-ranking chiefs, expanded their landholdings and land claims by developing cocoa plantations, often through sharecropping arrangements with outsiders and through the use of hired labor. Full citizenship rights in the Akan polities meant that they had strong rights to lineage farmlands: they did not pay land tribute to chiefs (unlike

---

[44] A World Bank report from the early 2000s estimated that more 80% of Ghana's total land area is held under some form of customary authority.

[45] All or part of the land tribute was claimed by the paramount stool treasuries in Ashanti Region. The paramount chief remitted a share to subordinate chiefs. Tribute-paying migrant farmers constituted perhaps 20–40% of all cocoa farmers in Ashanti and Ahafo Regions circa 1960, and thus represented an important source of income for chiefs and stool treasuries at the time (see Schildkrout 1979, 187–188; Apter 1972, 163).

[46] See Allman 1993, 37; Austin 1987; Phillips 1989; and Kay 1972. Ghanaian law gives chiefs the right to allocate virgin land within their jurisdiction – that is, to lease it to nonmembers of the community, to revoke leases (as in the termination of *abusa* sharecropping arrangements), or to sell usufruct rights to community members (which transforms the land into lineage land rather than private property). Because the land itself is supposed to be communal, proceeds from leasing and sales are expected to be used on behalf of the community.

strangers), and the stool could not easily claim or reallocate their land.[47] Families and individuals also purchased land from the stools, and these properties tended to become assimilated into lineage holdings over time. These lands can be mortgaged, rented, or leased, and use rights can be sold, with the chief's permission and payment of a transaction tax to the stool. Yet because holdings are lineage or family assets, rather than individually held assets, transactions are often encumbered by family members' claims. Chiefs are pivotal in dispute adjudication when conflicts cannot be resolved within families, especially in cases of interlineage or interjurisdictional disputes.[48]

As the amount of lineage-held land within the Asante jurisdiction expanded, the amount of unclaimed virgin land under the full (direct) discretionary control of the stool diminished. By the mid-twentieth century, the land frontier was closing in what is now Ashanti Region. Very little unclaimed rural land was left for the chiefs to allocate.

Chapter 4 examined the ramifications of these changes for landlord-stranger (interethnic) relations in Ashanti and Western Regions. The expulsion of aliens from the rural areas of Ashanti Region in 1969 almost surely reflected, in part, the frustrations of Asante youth facing a shortage of land to farm on their own account. This can be inferred from the fact that, in some areas, gangs of youth appeared to act unilaterally to chase migrants off the farms. And with land saturation, the pioneer front shifted to the northwest and west, producing waves of in-migration to Brong-Ahafo and Western Regions, where chiefs allocated land to strangers (including Asante land seekers), as chiefs had done in Ashanti Region in earlier decades.

In rural Ashanti Region, end of the land-pioneering era altered the scale and character of land politics. During the colonial period, chiefs' appropriation of communal land to create what were, in effect, their own private plantations had elicited much resistance by the citizens of the Ashanti stool. Chiefs' eagerness to allocate land to migrants was also contested when this conflicted with stool citizens' own demands for land.[49] Destoolments – the act of removing chiefs

47 If the stool asserted eminent domain, the family "has a right to expect compensation" (Berry 2001, 179). Lineage lands in Ashanti are often described as held under customary freehold, with the caveat that they are difficult to transfer outside the family. However, in periurban Kumasi today, chiefs and some local state officials insist that lineage rights are *only usufruct rights for farming*. This represents a narrowing of the meaning of lineage land rights.
48 Crook (2008, 131–132) elaborates: Chiefs run "'customary courts' for the settlement of land and other disputes. Most customary landholders are, therefore, still very much dependent on chiefly and local or family institutions to uphold their right of access to land, and for protection against unlawful dispossession of their customary landholdings."
49 Amanor explains: "As chiefs had alienated significant areas to migrants for cocoa farming in the early 20th century, creating land shortage problems for commoners, the local peasantry blamed the chiefs directly, rather than entering into internecine conflict with the migrants" (2005, 104). In cases considered in Chapter 4, chiefs responded to such pressures by excluding migrants (or

from office by a Traditional Council on charges brought forth by elders – usually on the grounds of criminality or abuse of power – were common from the 1920s onward, and often took place in the context of growing resentment of chiefly elites seen to be exploiting their land prerogatives for self-enrichment. Jean Allman described these land-related tensions as they found expression in the 1950s in widespread support among commoners and youth in Ashanti Region for Kwame Nkrumah's Convention People's Party. The CPP scaled up, or nationalized, conflict between chiefs and commoners in Ashanti Region by positioning itself as the enemy of the chiefly establishment in this region (in part by attacking the chiefs' land prerogatives).[50]

Over the course of the 1950s and 1960s, the scale and scope of land politics in rural communities *shifted downward* from the arena of chieftaincy to the arena of the extended family. This was a result of the consolidation of lineage control over most land in the established cocoa-growing areas, and the expulsion of many of the strangers from this region in 1969. The overthrow of Nkrumah in 1966 also put an end to the national-level wrangling over the land prerogatives of the chiefs that had been a leitmotif of state-building under his administration.

In Ashanti Region in recent decades, competition for farmland between citizens of the chieftaincies has taken place mostly within lineages and over access to lineage lands (much as in the Kisii region of Kenya, as discussed in Chapter 6). Parcel sizes are shrinking, and families feel the pinch of the land constraint. There are incentives and pressures to narrow the scope of claims and entitlements to family land.[51] The investments in social relationships analyzed by Sara Berry (2001) can be read as microstrategies aimed at warding off such exclusion (or at gaining advantage) by maintaining diversified portfolios of kinship-based entitlements to land access. Amanor's writings (1994, 2010) on land politics within the tight confines of family arenas in Akwampin in Eastern Region offer a more structuralist look at what appear to be essentially the same processes. Amanor describes the narrowing of the circle of entitlement and obligation within extended families, and creeping commodification of relations among kin in a region where families hold strong title to land.[52] Uncles who are unable or unwilling to allocate land to their nephews, for example, try to hire them as sharecroppers or laborers instead.

---

hardening the terms by which they gained land access) in conditions of rising competition for land.

[50] Allman 1993. This was a radical move that is not anticipated by our theorization of the problem. That Nkrumah ultimately did not succeed is perhaps a register of the political riskiness of this move. See Chapter 4 and Boone 2003.

[51] On land shortage and rising land values, see Amanor 1999. On shrinking size of parcels held by family members, see Takane 2002.

[52] In Eastern Region in the first half of the twentieth century, chiefs sold land outright; in Ashanti Region, this did not happen. Baryeh (1997) implies that, for this reason, periurban land conflicts are more acute in Ashanti Region than in Eastern Region. See also Onoma 2010.

TABLE 7.1. *Changing Locus and Scale of Land Conflict in Ashanti Region*

Timeline:	1940s–1950s	2000s
Urban/ periurban:	In central Kumasi, the state (Lands Commission) controls land administration.	In periurban areas, land "conversion" and leasing produces conflict within chieftaincies, centered on chiefs' land authority.
Rural:	Chiefs' allocations of land produce conflict within chieftaincies, centered on the chiefs' land authority.	Families have consolidated land rights in old cocoa areas. Land conflict is generational. Tensions play out at the family level.

Struggles over chiefly allocations of virgin land are no longer the dominant form of land-related conflict in Ashanti Region. Contestation over the use of chiefs' land-related powers has not disappeared, however. It has emerged as the most prominent form of land conflict in subjurisdictions where the chiefs *retain or can gain* wide-ranging land prerogatives.[53]

Where chiefs' prerogatives over land allocation are strong, we anticipate that competition for this resource will produce land-related conflict that plays out in the local political arena defined by chieftaincy, is community-wide in scope, and targets chiefs. There is clear evidence of this cause-effect relationship in periurban jurisdictions around Kumasi, the regional capital, a fast-growing city with a population of almost 1.5 million in 2005.[54] With the backing of the state, chiefs have been able to assert an interpretation of existing law that allows them full discretion over the decision to convert farmland to potential urban use, thus annulling the lineages' and families' usufruct rights and "merging" the plot with stool land under the direct control of the chief (Baryeh 1997). With urban sprawl and suburbanization, much of the roadside and village land around periurban Kumasi has become vulnerable to potential conversion. A resident of Ejusu explained it: "When the town reaches your land, your farm becomes the property of the chief."[55]

These transformations have produced change over time in the geographic locus of chieftaincy-centered land conflicts in Ashanti Region. Table 7.1 summarizes this argument. In rural areas, where chieftaincy was deeply implicated

[53] Berry (2001, 154, 180–183) analyzes interjurisdictional disputes, farmer-herder, and indigene-migrant conflict on the Afram Plains, one of the last pioneer fronts in Ashanti Region.

[54] Contestation over the scope of chiefly prerogative in matters concerning timber and mining concessions, which pay royalties to the stools, is also prominent. De jure regulatory authority over forestland has been vested in the central government since 1962, with about 30% of the proceeds from timber concessions reverting to the stool, paramount chief, and now, local District Assemblies.

[55] Interview near Ejusu and Juaben, assemblyman, 21 July 2009.

in land conflicts in the 1940s, conflict now plays out mostly within extended families (although chiefs may adjudicate disputes). In metropolitan Kumasi, the central government controls land administration now as in the past, but *periurban* Kumasi has witnessed a dramatic change. As chiefs reassert powers over periurban land, the periurban areas have become the locus of struggles over the chiefs' land authority.

Land Struggles in Periurban Kumasi

In the customary land tenure system that the Ghanaian government has institutionalized in Ashanti Region, family and lineage land rights are *usufruct rights for farming*. These rights are secure from confiscation by the stool as long as the land is dedicated to this use. Lineage rights are not exactly freehold rights in this LTR, however: the usufruct is "superimposed" on the a stool's ultimate ownership of the land (allodial title), which is recognized in the Ghanaian Constitution. Put differently, in Ashanti Region, the hard reading of the customary LTR is that family owns the crops, but not the land on which the crops are growing. Stools retain direct control over all land transactions involving outsiders (noncitizens of the stool), and nonagricultural use of lands to which the stool holds allodial title.

An estimated 98 percent of land in the urban fringes of Kumasi (about a forty-kilometer radius from Kumasi center) constitutes stool land in this ultimate sense.[56] Yet by the 1990s, very little of this was vacant communal land available to the chiefs to reallocate for farming purposes (as is the case throughout most of the old cocoa zone of southern Ghana). Janine Ubink (2008, 157) explains: "Now,... the only way that chiefs can make money from land is to cancel out the usufructuary rights of the citizens." In periurban Kumasi, this is precisely what some have done.

Chiefs can decide to "convert" a parcel or tract of land to urban use (residential or commercial). When this happens, the lineage or family usufruct right that was granted for farming is lost, and the land "is easily merged under absolute stool management.... Plots are subsequently allocated by the chief on the advice of elders," usually to a lessee who pays market rates for the land, and often without consent or recognition of the former usufruct holder (Baryeh 1997, 16). This constitutes a process of expropriation of family and lineage land rights that is rampant in periurban Kumasi.

The 1990s saw an explosion in demand for land for building purposes in periurban Kumasi. (Map 8.) Rising population density, recovery from two decades of economic decline, urban sprawl, suburbanization, and improvement in the quality of the roads all fueled demand.[57] Land values rose, and plots in the periurban villages, tracts of farmland bordering town plots, and farms

[56] Baryeh 1997, 14–15.
[57] Berry 2001, chapter 4, 103–138.

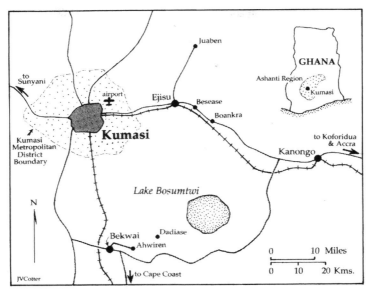

MAP 8. Periurban Kumasi, Ashanti Region, Ghana. (Drawn by John V. Cotter).

close to the roads became lands that could, on the authority of the chiefs, be converted for potential urban use. Decentralization measures enacted in 1993 cleared the way for rapid land conversion. At the request of the chiefs, the Town and Country Planning Department formulates a town layout (or plan) and demarcates plots for residential or commercial use. Newly defined plots are the chiefs' to allocate, even if they are occupied by the (former!) usufruct holder. As Sara Berry puts it, "This layout can serve as an instrument of dispossession" (2001, 134). Plots can be leased to outsiders, allocated to prominent community members such as subchiefs or lineage heads, or otherwise disposed of in return for revenues that go to the chiefs and stool treasuries. Such conversions are justified on the grounds that urban development generates revenues that can used for the benefit of the community as a whole.

Revenue generated by these land leases goes straight to the chiefs, who exercise wide discretion over the apportionment of those funds. The chief may keep all or part of the revenue, allocate some to the office of the chieftaincy (the stool), share some with village elders, offer some in compensation to the former usufruct-right holders, and/or devote some of the money to community improvement. Some villages have local plot-allocation committees that create a structure for community participation in decisions about land takings and leasing to outsiders, but these are created or disbanded at the discretion of chiefs. Ubink (2007, 11) writes, "Many chiefs are unwilling to explicitly account for stool land revenues, including chiefs who spend the money, as they should, on community development projects." She points to the case of the Jachiehene, "who was enthusiastically developing his village. . . . [He] not only abolished the local Plot Allocation Committee but stated outright that 'land in Jachie belongs solely to the royal family' and 'a chief does not need to account to anyone, only if things go wrong.'" Some chiefs argue straightforwardly that as land values rise, "communal lands that can be used in a more productive way should be brought back under chiefly administration" (Ubink 2007, 4).

Throughout the periurban region, families have lost farmland to residential development. Ubink found that most (58 percent) of the residents in the eight periurban Kumasi villages she surveyed in 2003–2004 had seen part of their land taken and reallocated as building plots (2008, 158). Some family heads had received some compensation in the form of a share of the revenue generated by the sale of the lease, but most had not. Ubink (2007, 2–3) finds that

> despite the fact that the chiefs are customarily and constitutionally obliged to administer the land in the interests of the whole community, they generally display little accountability for any money generated and most indigenous community members are seeing little or no benefit from the leases. The customary land users are only rarely – and then very inadequately – compensated for the loss of their farmland, and in most villages only a meagre part of the money is used for community development.

She reports that "[in one] research project it was found that of the 364 farms in peri-urban Kumasi taken away from community members for housing development, only 7% of farmers had received compensation, and most of those were related to the royal family in the village, as described in Kotey and Yeboah 2003: 21."[58]

This squares with our observations. Compensation paid for takings of family or lineage lands may go to male elders, but these individuals may not distribute the revenue to all family members who have claims to the parcel. In one periurban village with a population of about 3,500, the divisional chief entered a deal with the central government in 2003 to cede 400 acres of land for a major infrastructure project. All the revenue that came to the village as compensation went to the heads of the eight lineages making up the community, whether each lineage had actually lost land or not. The eight notables (lineage heads) did not necessarily pass shares down to family members or to those who actually lost their farms. "Some farmers who lost land received one cedi, or nothing."[59]

---

[58] Ubink 2007, 3, n. 4.

[59] Interviews with residents, 17–21 July 2009. In general, there is a double gender bias in these processes of expropriation: "Women farmers suffer the worst. They traditionally grow subsistence crops such as cassava, plantain and yam on land closest to the heart of the villages. But this land is most valuable to land developers. It is sold first." BBC World Service, "The Need for Agricultural Land in the City: Ghana," first broadcast 17 January 2001, accessed 12 May 2010. See also Baryeh (1997, 22), who writes that "youth and women are the worst affected."

Land-Related Conflict in and out of the Local Public Sphere

Conversion of farmland to an urban use in the periurban zone can involve the termination of family and usufruct land rights. It is a process that creates clear winners and losers. Hamidu Ibrahim Baryeh, a regional lands officer, did not mince words: "The current situation is a free for all affair and the winners are the most powerful in society such as chiefs, government officials, and rich men. The losers are the youth, women folk, and the disabled, thereby sowing the seeds of instability in the future" (1997, 23). Low-status lineages are also more vulnerable than more powerful lineages. Dispossessions can result in landlessness and homelessness, as Baryeh points out.[60] Also lost in many cases is the presumed right of the usufruct holder to receive some compensation.

These processes give rise to land-related conflicts that find expression in ways we would anticipate, given the nature of the land tenure regime prevailing in these jurisdictions. Land-related conflict plays out in the local political arena defined by chieftaincy, is often community-wide in scope, and targets the chieftaincy itself. Whereas exit (whether out-migration or exit from farming as a livelihood) and loyalty (acquiescence) are options for losers, chieftaincy creates a "public sphere" where contestation over loss of land rights can take the form of voice. Where voice is an option, land-related conflict can take explicitly political forms. This happens in periurban Kumasi. At issue are the scope and limits of chiefly prerogative over land. Do chiefs monopolize the power to decide to convert farmland to urban use? Do chiefs monopolize the right to allocate parcels designated for potential urban use and to lease converted land?[61] Do they control unilaterally the disposition of revenues so generated, even to the point of appropriating the funds?

Open contestation over the chiefs' land powers takes place both within and outside channels institutionalized in the local state that is represented by the stool. Protest and resistance take the form of contentious politics, including public denunciations, petitioning, demonstrations, and public attacks on chiefs' palaces, plantations, or cars. In some confrontations, chiefs themselves have been threatened, assaulted, or chased away. Ubink (2008, 158, 176) writes that all eight of her study villages have "witnessed various kinds of on going struggles and negotiations between the land-owning chiefs and their people, ranging from direct confrontation with the chief [including swearing and shouting at the chief at public village meetings] to bringing in other people or agencies, to more evasive techniques to 'get around' the chief."[62]

---

[60] "At Atasamanso it is estimated that 700 people have no place to farm and neither do they possess building plots. At Kyerekrom it was estimated that 90% of the adult population were landless... 100% due to the urban conversion process" (Baryeh 1997, 22).

[61] Baryeh (1997, 19) explains that "families are at loggerheads with chiefs over who has the right to sell agricultural lands converted for urban development."

[62] Similar confrontations happen in Accra. In the *Ghanaian Chronicle* of 11 August 2005 ("Asante Warns Ga Chiefs of Possible Youth Uprising"), Gabby Asumin reported that the president of

In the controversy over the loss of farmland to the "inland port" infrastructure project in Boankra, for example, those who had lost land took over a town meeting in protest.

At an emotionally charged meeting at the town on December 30th [2007], the land owners, clad in red and black attires, hoisted red and black flags in and at the entrance of the town and demanded that Nana Abena Afriyie [the Queenmother] should cough up the said amount given to her by the Otumfuo [the Asantehene] as compensation by the 8th of [January]. They claimed that they would make life unbearable for the Queenmother if she fails to release the said amount by the deadline. The secretary of the land owners association [said they would not allow] the Queenmother to rob them in broad daylight. When contacted, [the Queenmother]... said the land owners got everything wrong because by the dictates of custom, individuals do not own lands and that traditional authorities do so on their behalf.[63]

Ubink (2007, 6) tells of an even more extreme confrontation from 2003 to 2004:

In some villages there have even been large-scale violent uprisings of commoners against the chief. For instance in Pekyi No. 2, where the chief sold a large part of the village land to the Deeper Life Christian Ministry and then pocketed the money, the commoners chased both the chief and the church representatives out of the village, killing one of the latter in the process.

Some village communities have sought to appeal a chief's decisions by going up the chiefly hierarchy to the Asante Traditional Council or seeking the intervention of the paramount chief, and some have threatened chiefs with destoolment.[64] Baryeh, the regional lands officer, points to a few "best-practice" cases in which villages have successfully demanded the creation of Land Allocation Committees to include community representatives in decision making (alongside the chief and elders). This is not always a solution, however. Baryeh notes that in some localities, demands for the creation of such committees have been the subject of hostile confrontations between chiefs and local community members (Baryeh 1997).

the Ga-Dangme Council, Mr. K. B. Asante, "warned of a possible uprising against chiefs and elders of the Ga State by the youth who feel marginalized... by the reckless sale of lands without accountability. [The youth] lack places to lay their heads [while] their lands have been sold out." See Pinkston 2007, Onoma 2010.

[63] *Ghanaian Journal*, "Boankra Inland Port Threatened," Business Section, 4 January 2008, posted at www.theghanaianjournal.com/2008/01/04/boankra-inland-port-threatened/ (accessed 10 May 2010).

[64] Ubink mentions that some village Unit Committees have threatened the chiefs with destoolment (Ubink 2008, 159). Some Unit Committees have pushed for the creation of Land Allocation Committees or tried to mediate conflicts between chiefs and particular families (as in Boankra, for example, field notes, July 2009). These are instances of citizens taking advantage of the grassroots-level emanations of national representative institutions to try to impose some accountability on chiefs and democratize decision making.

Local landholders and communities do sometimes try to induce agents and institutions of the central state to intevene in land-related disputes. Aggrieved citizens appeal to the District Assemblies, implore the police to sanction unlawful behavior, petition powerful persons such as the minister of the interior or the head of state, demonstrate in front of government offices, and so on.[65] This was true in the Boankra case mentioned earlier. Citizens petitioned the Ejusu-Juaben District Assembly (unsuccessfully), took the scandal to the local press, and petitioned then-president John Kufuor and the speaker of parliament. These are instances of locals trying to "broaden the scope of conflict" by scaling it up to the national level, thus attempting to transcend the boundaries of the local political arena defined by chieftaincy.[66] Yet according to Ubink (2007, 6, 13–14; 2008b), the central administration generally tries to stay out of these cases, and the District Assemblies, which are representative bodies and local instances of the national government, rarely take action in land disputes. One assemblyman in periurban Kumasi explained the passive role of decentralized local government in land-related conflicts by saying that "the Assembly cannot do anything. Anyway, people fear the chiefs."[67]

Attempting to take chiefs to court is another way for citizens with land-related grievances (or other grievances against chiefs) to try to harness the power of national government to their cause. In Ghana, however, this is a slow, costly, difficult, and uncertain option.[68] The high cost of formal adjudication in these venues means that only high-profile cases actually end up in the court. In 2007, with an estimated 35,000 land-dispute cases backlogging the courts, using the formal legal system to attempt to defend acquired land rights was not a real option for an ordinary citizen.[69] It is also true that Ghanaian law and justice go very far in affirming the land-related powers and prerogatives of chieftaincy. Chiefs are more likely to win in court than lowly citizens who hold

---

[65] For example, in December 2005, in a conflict between local farmers and Fulani herdsmen on Kumawu stool lands (in the Sekyere East District in Ashanti; see Berry 2001, chapters 5–6), aggrieved farmers with a complaint against the chief, the Kumawuhene, and the Kumawu Traditional Council (the grantors of the grazing permits) "lodged a complaint with the District Assembly and the local police, hoping that the District Chief Executive would direct some energy into bringing the situation under control" (Freiku, *Ghanaian Chronicle*, 5 December 2005).

[66] See *Insight*, Wednesday–Thursday edition, 11–12 November 2002, 1; *The Graphic*, Wednesday, 18 September 2002, 1; *Ghanaian Times*, Wednesday, 13 July 2003, 1. It is noteworthy that the strategies employed did not follow routinized or institutionalized channels.

[67] Interview near Ejusu, periurban Kumasi, 17 July 2009.

[68] The Ghanaian court system is a formal channel of appeal for cases not resolved through the neocustomary institutions. Many high-profile cases are reported in the Ghanaian press.

[69] In his Ghana sample, Crook (2008, 142–143) found that about one in six households was involved in a land dispute related to unlawful sale, inheritance, dispossession disputes, family disputes, or disputes with another farmer (other than trespass). This places the 35,000 figure in some perspective. On this, see Alhassan and Manuh 2005, 28.

land under "customary law," especially given that the national constitution vests ownership of land in the stools.[70]

Ubink (2007, 6, 13–14) argues explicitly that so far, no Ghanaian political party in the current period has attempted to take up the issue of land rights, land law reform, or abuse of chiefly authority.[71] According to her, the entire Ghanaian central administration adheres to a "policy of non-interference" in chiefly affairs, in an attempt to stay on the good side of those who broker land and votes at the local level.[72] Her view resonates strongly with the conventional wisdom. When asked "Why is the government trying to please the chiefs?," one Besease assemblyman replied, "Because they have authority. Their authority is felt especially in the rural areas. They control the vote."[73]

Conclusion

In periurban Kumasi, the chieftaincy-centered land tenure regime works to tamp down the scale of land-related conflict, containerizing it within local jurisdictions. Very similar effects were observed in northern Cameroon. In both Ashanti Region and the strong lamidats of northern Cameroon, chieftaincy-centered land regimes are *impediments* to the processing of citizens' grievances through politywide political, administrative, and legal institutions. In both settings, ordinary citizens of the national polity may be subject, at the local level, to expropriation, intimidation, and the exercise of personal rule by local strongmen who wield extensive powers over the conditions of everyday life. And in both cases, this suits the interests of politicians and state administrators who operate at higher levels of the state apparatus and who rely on local strongmen to deliver the votes of their subjects *en bloc*.

Some land policy analysts point to "the Asante Model of Dispute Adjudication" – the process by which subjects of the Asante stools seek land dispute resolution via customary processes controlled by chiefs – as a positive example of how local actors can employ customary institutions to resolve land disputes without resort to costly formal procedures.[74] It is deemed by the World Bank

---

[70] Baryeh (1997, 19) reports that the chief of Mampongten in periurban Kumasi used the courts to defend his exclusive right to lease land for urban use against the demands of the usufruct holders (lineage landholders), who wanted to lease the lands in question themselves.

[71] However, as already noted, Nkrumah and Rawlings, at various times in their respective tenures in office, did seek to mobilize popular support by giving voice to ordinary people's frustration with chiefs.

[72] The Ghanaian government's 1999 land policy framework defines the policy direction of the Land Administration Project. It aims to confirm the land adjudication powers of local-level authorities. As these authorities are themselves implicated in land conflict, the reform initiative seems likely to heighten the stakes of larger struggles over how to maintain legitimate authority at the local level in a context of rising tensions over land rights and access to livelihoods. See Ubink and Amanor 2008.

[73] Local assemblyman, interviewed near Besease, 17 July 2009.

[74] Alden Wily 2003, 66; Camara et al. 2007, 14.

to work well in land matters. Others warn that this form of alternative dispute resolution often just bolsters the power and prerogatives of chiefs (Crook 2008, 131–132, 136; Ubink 2008). Both perspectives can be correct. It can be functional for the state to cordon off, or containerize, some spheres of social conflict, insulate the national-level political system from some social demands, limit the potential for mass politics, and localize and fragment political conflict. This can also work well for some local interests. Political science should be able to pick up these effects in voting patterns, public opinion, the quality of citizenship regimes, and the structural and ideological forms of the local (and national) state.

There are some important differences across these cases, however, and these are in part registers of *national effects* on subnational political dynamics. The cross-case differences we observe are consistent with what one would expect in comparing politics in a relatively democratic country (Ghana) with politics in a non-democratic country (Cameroon). In Ghana, national-level citizenship does protect villagers from the kind of wanton violence by chiefs that exists in the lamidat of Rey Bouba and some of the other chieftaincies of northern Cameroon. And in Ghana's Ashanti Region, access to political institutions that are polity-wide in scope, and that connect to national-level organs (such as Unit Committees, District Assemblies, the courts, civil administration, and political parties), is *formally* open to villagers.

Yet the main objective here is to focus on the structural similarity that is evident across these two cases. We have seen in periurban Kumasi (and in the Western Region case presented in Chapter 4) that even in Ghana, struggles over the land-related prerogatives of chieftaincy are very difficult to "export" to these other institutional forums. This is both because pro-chieftaincy national governments work to maintain the legal fiction of a "firewall" between chieftaincy and party politics, and because the national legal system defends customary law as a semiautonomous realm in which the secular courts and legislature exercise limited powers of lawmaking and legal interpretation. As Amanor explained it, "While the peasantry is also theoretically recognized via its elected representatives in the democratic process, this has limited impact on the land question, since land matters are recognized as the preserve of chiefs, not elected local councils" (2005, 105). For ordinary citizens, the practical impediments to appealing to the courts of the civil administration for redress can also be overwhelming, especially in settings where the exercise of power is clearly biased in favor of chiefs. When these factors are taken into account, the predicament of villagers living under chieftaincy in southern Ghana shows some structural similarities to the predicament of smallholders in the lamidats of northern Cameroon.

In the Chapter 7 cases, land competition and exclusion take place within political arenas that are *structurally disarticulated* from national political institutions of law, representation, and adjudication. To use Mamdani's term, land-related conflict is "containerized" at the political scale of the local state. This is an effect of property institutions that structure land politics within these jurisdictions, vesting the neocustomary authorities with wide authority over land. This land authority conveys into other domains of local political life. It gives the customary authorities considerable leverage over subjects – both ethnic strangers and the ethnic citizens of the chieftaincy – who hold or use land, need land, have land ambitions, are engaged in land disputes, or are thinking about land disputes they may find themselves in the future. In agrarian society, there is every reason to expect that neocustomary authorities' clout in property matters may influence local actors' calculations in other social and political matters, such as an individual's vote choice, decision to create or join a local civil society organization or lobbying effort, or decision to speak out or remain silent in the face of an instance of local corruption or human rights abuse.

A logical extension of this claim would be that in jurisdictions where chiefs have almost no land-related power, they are not the focal point of land-related contestation. Not only would we expect the local political influence of such "landless chiefs" to be greatly attenuated compared with the influence of chiefs who do exercise land-related powers, but we would also expect the chiefly jurisdiction to be weakly relevant (if at all) in structuring the scale of local politics.[75] Where chiefs are very weak in land matters but land markets are only partially or weakly developed, *other political modes* of land allocation are likely to remain highly salient: land-related politics will probably either scale down ("dissolve") into politics at the level of family or lineage, or scale up to the national political arena. Chapters 6, 7, and 8 present clear-cut examples of each type of situation.

---

[75] Berry (2001, 196) draws the contrast between Asante chiefs and Yoruba chiefs. In Yorubaland, "there are no lands attached to chieftaincy titles." This chapter has also drawn a contrast between rural and periurban areas of Ashanti Region.

CHAPTER 8

Land Conflict at the National Scale

Rwanda

> Those who only wanted to steal our land could have simply chased us out, as
> they did to our parents and grandparents in the North. Why cut us as well?
> (Tutsi survivor, interviewed by Hatzfeld 2005a, 137)

> The ruling elite manipulates land scarcity for its own advantage.
> (Bigagaza et al. 2002, 73)

In October 1990, second-generation exiles based in Uganda initiated an attempt
to forcibly claim the right of some 400,000 Tutsi exiles to return to Rwanda.
The Rwanda Patriotic Front (RPF) invaded northern Rwanda in October 1990
and made a drive for the capital, Kigali. The attack was repelled with the
help of the French. Shortly thereafter, in June 1991, the authoritarian one-
party state of Juvenal Habyarimana acceded to international pressure to open
the political arena to multiparty competition as it simultaneously sought to
ward off the RPF and consolidate its political control over the population.
The ruling party attempted to defend its political hegemony during a period of
multipartism and civil war by threatening the predominantly Hutu population
with the misfortunes that would befall them if the RPF leaders "and their
accomplices" were to take power, whether by force, through a peace accord,
or via the ballot box. Rwandan Hutu were instructed to fear massive killing of
Hutu, along with the destruction of their livelihoods and society as they knew
it, should the Tutsi gain control of the central state. The civil strife that raged
in Rwanda during 1990–1994 reached a crescendo in the state-directed murder
of approximately 800,000 citizens (about 15 percent of the total population)
in mid-1994, as the RPF swept toward and eventually overtook Kigali.[1]

---

[1] The toll from the final report of the 2001 census (cited by Eltringham 2006, 67) gives the number
937,000. These numbers are still the subject of debate and reanalysis.

Scholars interested in explaining the domestic context and stakes of this terrible implosion have pointed to land competition and land scarcity as critical background factors. A substantial literature identifies the Rwandan genocide as a resource-related conflict, at least in part, and points to land scarcity, land inequality, and hunger in rural Rwanda as contextual factors that are critical in understanding the horrific violence that was unleashed in 1993 and 1994.[2] So far, however, arguments that have focused on land scarcity per se or on the ethnic dimension of struggles in Rwanda over land (and over other assets and opportunities) have failed to make the case connecting *land conflict* to the larger political conflagration.

These arguments have been vulnerable to charges of overdeterminism (or ecodeterminism) on two counts. First, arguments focusing on land scarcity, or ethnicized competition over land, overpredict large-scale land-related violence, which is far rarer in Africa (and everywhere) than land scarcity, ethnic tensions over land, or even the two variables combined. All the extended case studies in this book are cases of land scarcity, and they show that overt violence is rare, even when land competition and conflict runs along ethnic lines. Second, the received analyses are overdetermining in the sense that they do not explain why land scarcity, and/or ethnicized land relations, contributes to national-level political conflict in some countries but not in others. This is the analytic problem targeted in Part III of this book. In this chapter, I argue that the link between land scarcity and the political character of the larger conflict that engulfed Rwanda in 1990–1994 lies in *political institutions* and, in particular, in the statist character of the land tenure regime (LTR).

Part III (Chapters 6, 7, and 8) argues that variation in the character of land tenure regimes is key in explaining variation in the political scale and scope of land-related conflict. The basic unit of analysis is the subnational jurisdiction. In some subnational jurisdictions, LTRs bottle up land conflict in local political institutions and allocation rules that are, in crucial ways and by design, "structurally disarticulated" from the national apparatus of state. In other places, LTRs link land conflicts *directly* to the national machinery of state. Under these statist LTRs, national institutions and national actors are directly implicated in conflicts concerning the redistribution of land rights.

This chapter argues that Rwanda's LTR is statist, and that this explains why and how land-related conflict in Rwanda was fused with the larger struggle for control over the national government. The statist land tenure regime inserted

---

[2] See Bigagaza et al. 2002, Huggins 2009, Lind and Sturman 2002, Percival and Homer-Dixon 1998, Gasana 2002. Philippe Hugon (2003, 118) has argued that the resource competition that contributed to explosive civil conflict in Rwanda has parallels in other African countries, such as Côte d'Ivoire. Uvin 1996 offers a nuanced account of the relationship between resource scarcity and conflict in Rwanda.

state authority directly into local land-access and land-use relationships in ways that created grievances and claims and directed these *against the central state*. This placed conflict over land allocation (exclusion) and the enforcement of land claims in the national political arena, producing the scale effect that is the centerpiece of this chapter. Control over the central state was the sine qua non of imposing outcomes in land-related conflicts in which the state was so directly implicated. In some parts of Rwanda, land tenure institutions also created microscopic relations of control and dependency that tied land users directly to political patrons in the central government and, thus, gave state agents leverage over land users. State agents used this leverage to elicit compliance and induce participation in pro-regime mobilizations. The statist land tenure regime connected the land grievances of some to the fears of landlessness of others, creating conditions for expansion of the scope of conflict.

The intention here is not to show that the Rwandan civil war and genocide were essentially about land: the 1990–1994 conflict over the central state, which pitted the regime against the RPF and the opposition parties, was not first and foremost about land, and land-related conflict was *not the fundamental cause* of the genocide. The main goal of the present analysis is to argue that because of the statist character of the land regime in Rwanda, land conflict and the more totalizing struggle for control over the state were inextricably intertwined. The particular character of land-related conflict in Rwanda – land grievances and claims targeted at the central state, central state agents' direct political instrumentalization of power relationships governing land access, the intertwining of land conflict and a struggle for control over the central state – was traceable to the statist character of the land regime.

Reciprocally, if the civil war and the state-led genocide in Rwanda did have something to do with land scarcity and ethnicized land conflict, then it is the political-institutional variables that account for this particular form of politicization – that is, the intimate intertwining of the issues of state control and land control. Contrasting cases presented in earlier chapters help support this argument. In much of Africa, land conflict is fueled by scarcity. It often runs along an ethnic cleavage (for LTR-related reasons that we have analyzed), but it rarely finds expression at the national political scale and is rarely fought out within (or over) the national institutions of the state. In the absence of a statist LTR, neither land scarcity nor ethnicized competition over land is expected to fuel land conflicts that play out in the national political arena. Material presented in Chapters 4, 6, and 7 enables us to consider these counterfactual scenarios.

Because of the statist character of the land tenure regime in Rwanda, land-related conflict was played out in the national arena, in the ways anticipated by the theory. Statist control over land allocation made peasant farmers' livelihoods depend on staying on the good side of the land-controlling authorities. The prospect of overthrow of the sitting regime represented a threat to

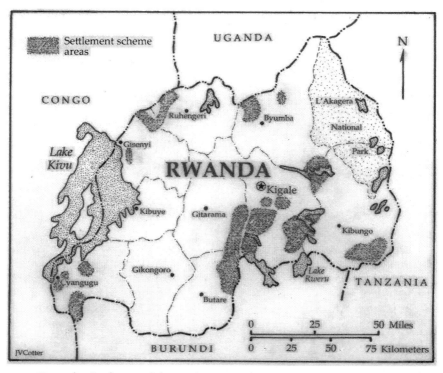

MAP 9. Rwanda: Settlement Scheme Areas, c. 1975. *Sources:* Gotanegre, Prioul, and Sirven 1974; Prioul and Sirven 1981. Drawn by John V. Cotter.

the incumbents' "land clients" (those who had received land grants or land access from government officials) who faced the risk of losing their land rights. Meanwhile, those who had been excluded from land access could support the effort to overthrow the sitting regime: they could hope that the new government would reward its supporters in the allocation of state-controlled land. Land calculations such as these raised the stakes of politics, and worked to structure political alignments and popular mobilization in the civil war and genocide.

This chapter has four sections. The first section identifies land tenure institutions in Rwanda as statist and traces their development over time. The second section zeros in on the role of land institutions in constituting state authority over land users at the microlevel. These relationships were starkest in the paysannat settlement scheme areas (Map 9). The third section links land tenure institutions to the scale and scope of the 1991–1994 conflict. The concluding section ties Rwanda to analogous cases that were presented in Chapter 5 and returns to our argument about the indeterminacy of land scarcity as a variable in explaining political conflict over land.

THE STATIST CHARACTER OF RWANDA'S LAND TENURE INSTITUTIONS

The precolonial state imposed its hegemony over much of what is modern-day Rwanda by asserting control over land, thus eroding the power of preexisting lineages and chieftaincies. The colonial state sought to manage population pressure through forced emigrations, forced conversions of pastureland to farmland, and forced antierosion and farming-intensification practices. Rwanda's move to political independence in 1959–1963 was marked by a paroxysm of violence and population expulsions, followed by land reallocations and state-directed rural-rural migrations, repeated again in 1973 around the time of the transition from the First to the Second Republic. The entire history of the twentieth century was marked by state projects to "redeploy," equilibrate, and balance the geographical distribution of the Rwandan population. The goals were to relieve and manage population pressure on the land, build political hierarchy, and establish and maintain the landed domains of the political elite.

In Rwanda, central state agents designed and manipulated land tenure institutions to structure the allocation of land between communal groups, within communities, and between families and individuals. Grievances and exclusions surrounding this, and the coercion and violence by which it was achieved, fueled the formation of the RPF and the pressures behind its 1990 invasion of Rwanda. At the same time, political claims and dependencies rooted in land tenure relationships gave postcolonial rulers deep roots in rural society, and levers of power within communities that could be used to influence the political behavior of members of ordinary farming families. These state-society connections help explain the national scale and scope of land-related conflict in Rwanda.

Variation across jurisdictions within Rwanda offers additional analytic leverage on the causal relationships that are the focus of this study. Spatial variation in the degree and intensity of state involvement in land expropriation and reallocation appears to correspond to local-level variations in the timing of the onset of genocidal violence in 1994, and suggests that some of the mechanisms by which ordinary people were mobilized to participate in the rulers' murderous designs were embedded in land tenure relationships.

Development of a Statist Land Tenure Regime under Colonial Rule

Catharine Newbury explains that in precolonial Rwanda, "the autonomous power of local chiefs was gradually undermined as the central state extended its authority" (1983, 258). She writes that during 1860–1895, "forms of land tenure under the direct control of central authorities replaced, in many parts of the kingdom," land tenure rooted in the rights of the "original occupants" and the associated rights of inheritance. The new forms of tenure for pasture and farmland "were based on acquiescence to the principle that the representatives of the central court had discretion to grant land" (Newbury 1983, 263). This process continued under colonial rule as the Belgians promoted the geographic extension of the Tutsi monarchy's authority and bureaucratization of the powers of the chiefs. Throughout much of modern-day Rwanda, these processes undercut lineage-based controls over land and even made inheritance rights subject to the arbitrary exercise of central authority.[3] The major exception lay in the northwest, in what are now the prefectures of Ruhengeri and Gisenyi. In this area, autonomous ("Hutu") polities resisted Tutsi domination until the late nineteenth century, and lineage-based systems of land control were never fully eradicated.[4]

The land tenure arrangements that developed in most of Rwanda under precolonial and colonial rule had macropolitical consequences. One was the weakness – or even absence – of the kinds of social institutions and neotraditional institutions that, elsewhere in Africa, may dilute or mediate the power of the central state.[5] In much of Rwanda, the central state exercised a form of unmediated power over rural producers. This helps explain the coerciveness and exploitativeness of state authorities, even at the local level, during the colonial period. It foreshadows the strong subjugation of communal authorities to the central state in modern-day Rwanda.

While chiefs appointed by central authorities governed Rwanda's population under colonial rule, privileged landholders and pastoralists linked to the Tutsi monarchy controlled vast domains. Their cattle grazed the pasturelands and fertilized the fields. Cattle-lending arrangements between pastoralists and cultivators secured the relations of political hierarchy that were woven through Rwandan society. In the mid-1950s, the Belgians pressured the Tutsi monarchy to agree to reforms that would expand cultivators' rights to own cattle, free of exploitative political obligations to an overlord. Many Tutsi landlords were able to compensate by tightening their controls over grazing land.[6]

As of the early 1950s, most of Rwanda's farming population was settled in the western highlands. Increasing population density and the scarcity of

---

[3] Newbury (1988, 133) writes that in the 1930s, "refusal to comply with any of the demands of the hill chief would expose a person to the possibility of losing his land. [For cultivators, this represented] a significant decline in security of tenure.... It was often in the interests of a chief to expel a local landholder and install others who then became directly dependent on the chief for land; the previous tenant had to move, hoping to obtain land from another chief elsewhere." See also Newbury (1988, 79–81) on "private land patrons" and the increasing predominance, under colonial rule, of "political land patrons."

[4] Van Hoyweghen 1999, 359; Newbury 1988, 183, 211, 290 n. 5, 6; Lemarchand 1970, 104–106. Lemarchand includes the territory of Byumba (Biyumba) in the "distinctive northern enclave," or "feudal enclave of the north," of "people we call 'Hutu' but who actually call themselves Kiga or Bakiga" (1970, 99, 116, 117).

[5] This point is made by Saskia van Hoyweghen (1999, 359, n. 14).

[6] Lemarchand 1970, 129, 131–132; see also Newbury 1988; Paternostre de la Mairieu 1972, 183–184.

uncultivated land in prime farming areas forced cultivators to move higher up on Rwanda's hillsides to less desirable and more erosion-prone land. Politically privileged pastoralists controlled large areas of land, including in the central plateau region, to graze livestock. To relieve population pressure on the land, the Belgian authorities began creating new settlement schemes for cultivators in the river valleys in the eastern periphery of Butare prefecture.[7] Farther to the east, the savannas bordering Tanzania were "reserved" as pasture for Tutsi livestock.

Inequality in access to land, the extractions by landlords, and the reassertion of "the lesser gentry's" authority over grazing land were central issues in late 1950s Rwanda and helped fuel the populist revolution that swept away the Tutsi elite on the eve of Rwanda's independence.[8] Lemarchand (1970, 131–132) writes that land access "has justly been regarded as a key issue in the background of the Hutu revolution." This assessment finds support in the words of Rwanda's future president, Grégoire Kayibanda, who rallied supporters in a political meeting in 1959, shortly before the "social revolution," by declaring that "our movement is for the Hutu group. We are here to restore this country to its owners. This is the land of the Hutus.... Who cleared the forest? Hutu did. So let's go! [*Alors!*]"[9]

In 1959–1961, a Hutu-inspired and Belgian-assisted coup led to the proclamation of a republic and installation of a new provisional government under Hutu control.[10] The victors abolished the Tutsi monarchy, usurped the Tutsi landlords, outlawed the institutions of land clientage, and smashed the political hegemony of the once-privileged Tutsi caste. Chiefs were killed or forced to resign, and refugees streamed out of Rwanda. Incursions by exiles were repelled in 1961 and 1963, followed by massive reprisals against the Tutsi and by new refugee flows out of Rwanda.[11] By mid-1964, about half of the Tutsi population had been killed or expelled (10,000 killed and between

---

7   A list of colonial-era settlement scheme *paysannats*, on which land was allocated in 2-hectare parcels, is offered by Paternostre de la Mairieu (1972, 177–179, 268): Shyogwe in 1953 (near Nyanza, also known as Nyabisindu, in Butare); Gakoma in 1953 (on the borders of the Akanyaru River, in Butare); Muhero-Ntyazo in 1954 (in Butare); Ntete in 1955 (in Kibungo); Bugarama in 1956 (in the Rusizi River valley); Gahanga in 1956 (in the Nyabarongo River valley); and Mbogo in 1956 (in the Akanyaru River valley). Schemes created in 1960 included Nyamata (in Bugesera), and Rukumberi (in Mirenge), "where some [78,000 by the government's count] of those displaced by the 1959 revolution were installed." An Office du Bugesera-Mayaga (OBM) opened on 31 August 1959. Anti-tsetse campaigns were required to open up some of these areas. Later projects were the Projet d'Aménagement du Nil-Nyabarongo, Projets Crête-Zaire-Nil (CZN), and the Projet Kigali-Est.

8   Lemarchand 1970, 131–132; Newbury 1988, 146.

9   From Pierre Erny 1995, 58, as cited by Mathieu 1997, 34.

10 See Lemarchand 1970, 85; Newbury 1988, 187–188.

11 There were ten invasion attempts between 1961 and 1971 (HRW 1993a, 2). Uganda-based Tutsi refugees' first military incursion into Rwanda was in 1963 (Prunier 1995, 52; Bigagaza et al. 2002, 54).

120,000 and 336,000 expelled). By the end of 1966 another 10,000 Tutsi had been killed.[12] There was another wave of killing and expulsion of Tutsi in 1973.

New Land Frontiers and State-Allocated Land Rights: 1960 to 1980s

These upheavals opened up new land frontiers in Rwanda that did not finally close until the mid-1980s. In the 1960s, lands of killed or displaced Tutsi landlords were parceled out among small farmers and impoverished peasants, most of whom came from south and central Rwanda, the regional support bases of the ruling Parmehutu Party.[13] J.-P. Chrétien wrote that the landhold-ings of 15,000 Tutsi victims of the December 1963–1964 repression "were redistributed by the préfets or bourgmestres to the [Parmehutu] party faith-ful" (1985, 159). River valleys formerly controlled by Tutsi pastoralists were settled by agriculturalists, and vast rangelands in the central plateau area and eastern Rwanda that had been reserved for Tutsi pastoralists were "liber-ated" and opened up to agricultural settlement.[14] Forest clearing, draining of marshes, and the conversion of about 300,000 hectares of pastureland to farmland[15] temporarily relieved land pressure in the highland areas of western Rwanda.

According to the Rwandan government, total farmland area in Rwanda "was increased by an estimated 50% in the years after the revolution [through 1970]," by the opening up of "political and private" rangelands, the allo-cation of land that had been "abandoned by political émigrés," extension of *paysannats* (the official settlement schemes), and the draining of marshes.[16] Rural-to-rural migration programs and state-sponsored resettlement developed as central elements of postcolonial Rwandan government land and agricultural policy.[17] The zones targeted were the central and eastern regions, the core areas of the old Rwandan kingdom and the pastoralist heartlands. According

---

[12] Head count of exiles (number range) from Eltringham 2006, 82. He quotes Bertrand Russell, who "described the 1963 massacre of Tutsi in Rwanda as 'the most horrible systemic human massacre we have had occasion to witness since the extermination of the Jews by Nazis'" (Eltringham 2006, 73–74). On 1966, HRW 1993a, 2.

[13] Jefremovas 2002.

[14] In 1963 the government also programmed the elimination of approximately one-half of Rwanda's total stock of cattle (Paternostre de la Mairieu, 1972, 183; Guichaoua 1989). Cattle were removed from areas targeted for settlement.

[15] André and Platteau 1998, 4, n. 4.

[16] From Paternostre de la Mairieu (1972, 320), who cites the Secrétariat d'Etat au Plan National de Développment, Rapport d'Exécution du Premier Plan Quinquennal de Développement Economique et Social 1966–1970, Kigali, 1971, 3. This figure may be in the ballpark. Olson (1990, 24) reports on studies from the mid-1980s that calculate average annual increase in area harvested, countrywide (1966–1983), to be 3.7%.

[17] Bigagaza et al. 2002, 74. In the southwest, paysannat schemes were created as places for commercial plantation workers to live, and thus were not actually designed for "peasants."

to Newbury (1983, 268), these were the regions in which Tutsi rule had been longest standing and most entrenched. Ford explains:

Beginning in 1962, the Hutu government began an aggressive campaign to open up "new lands" in once-banned areas in the Central Plateau and the Eastern lowlands.... [In the 1962–1971 phase of rural-rural migration,] the migrants' decision to move and choice of destination were heavily controlled by the government's effort to direct investment and migration toward planned "new settlements" called *paysannats* whose primary purpose was the expansion of export agriculture, particularly coffee and pyrethrum [and groundnuts] (1998, 183, 185).

From 1960 to 1967, the natural region of Mayaga (along the Akanyaru valley) and the historic region of Bugesera were colonized by Rwandans from the western highland areas. (See Map 9.) Mayaga received many in-migrants from Gitarama prefecture (Guichaoua 1989, Tome 1, 79), the home base of the Kayibanda regime.[18] Settlers received parcels of approximately 2 hectares on government-sponsored land distribution schemes, many centered on contract-farming arrangements in which settlers received credit and agreed to farm cash crops according to official specifications and schedules.[19] Beginning in 1961, the Fonds Européen de Développement financed schemes in these areas, including much of Kigali prefecture (around the city and south of Kigali itself). See Map 10 for Kigali and Kibungo prefectures, their subdivisions (the communes), and the historic regions of Bugesera and Gisaka in eastern Rwanda. Other schemes were financed by the Belgians, including in Icyanya and Rusomo (in the eastern part of Kibungo prefecture, near the Tanzanian border). In 1965, new colonization projects were opened up in Kibungo prefecture. Map 11 is a plan of the Paysannat de Muhero in Bugesera.

The process of land pioneering continued in the 1970s. It was targeted at parts of the country once reserved for pastoralists, formerly under the political control of the colonial-era Tutsi elite or designated as forest reserve. Uvin (1996, 10) reported that from 1970 to 1986, the amount of land available for cultivation jumped from 528,000 to 831,000 hectares, an increase from 1970 onward of 58 percent, two-thirds of which came from the conversion of pastureland to farmland.

After the July 1973 coup that ushered in Habyarimana and the founding of the Second Republic, and especially during 1977–1980, the colonization front moved farther east into Kibungo prefecture (in Gisaka), where the new regime offered *paysannats* to peasant settlers and large landholdings to political elites.

---

[18] Some Tutsi displaced during the 1959–1963 revolution were "reinstalled" in Bugesera in *paysannats* and camps for internally displaced persons (IDPs) (Guichaoua 1999, 315). Bugesera in the 1990s was a region with a large Tutsi population. Hatzfeld (2005a, 2005b) focuses on this region (Nyamata).

[19] A 1991 Rwandan government report notes that there is credit for farmers on the government-sponsored land distribution schemes (the *paysannat* area schemes), but that repayment rates are low (République Rwandaise 1991, 102–103).

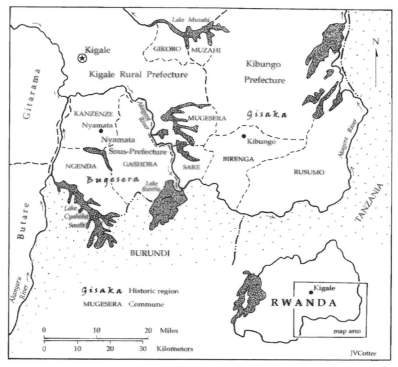

MAP 10. Eastern Rwanda, c. 1990

Guichaoua (1999, 315) wrote that compared to the land pioneering for the 1960s, *"la colonisation interne"* under the Second Republic assumed a more developmentalist thrust and was more explicitly aimed at relieving population pressure. Kibungo became the "receptacle *par excellence* of populations in search of land."[20] The total population of this prefecture increased by 69 percent from 1970 to 1978 (Olson 1990, 86). A new project called Kibungo II was created in 1980. In-migration was especially heavy from Ruhengeri and Gisenyi prefectures in northwestern Rwanda, the regional power base of the Habyarimana regime.[21]

The actual number of migrants to the *paysannat* settlement schemes – 80,000 families as of 1976, or about 450,000 people, representing about 10 percent of the Rwanda's population in 1976 – was *exceeded by* the number who

---

[20] Guichaoua 1999, 315. See also Ford 1998, 184. Although the extreme east is a region with irregular rainfall and less fertile land and, thus, less desirable overall for Rwandan agriculturalists, migrants to Kibungo were doing better than those who stayed in their home areas (as of the 1980s). See Olson 1990, 115–116.

[21] Ford 1993, 156; Guichaoua 1989, T. 1, 79; Olson 1990, 86.

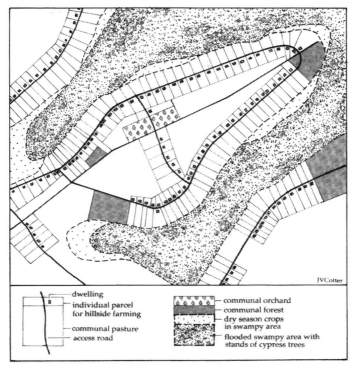

MAP 11. *Paysannat* Scheme (Paysannat de Muhero), 1978, Rwanda. *Source:* Adapted from Prioul and Sirven 1981; Planche XXIII.

settled outside the formal colonization schemes.[22] By this rendering, more than 20 percent of the total Rwandan population was farming in the areas of state-sponsored colonization by 1976. Jennifer Olson (1990, 23) explained that "although the schemes may have been the attraction for many people, they were soon full and migrants settled in surrounding areas." The hand of the government was ever present in these spontaneous migrations, however. One indicator of this is that in-migrants came in disproportionate numbers from politically favored areas of the country rather than disfavored areas (such as high-density Kibuye prefecture, with its large Tutsi population).[23] Another indicator is sensitivity of migration flows to "[government] announcements of

[22] Olson (1990, 23) reports that a total of 80,000 families were settled in the *paysannats* through 1976. If average household size in Rwanda is calculated at 5.7 persons (following May 1995, for 1990), this would be about 450,000 people out of a 1976 population of 4.2 million, or more than 10%. The 1991 population of Kibungo and Kigali-Rurale prefectures was 1.2 million (May 1995).

[23] Olson (1990, 82–84) explains that after 1978, only 30% of the cross-prefecture variation in out-migration rates is explained by population density per se.

settlement scheme land [that] focused in-migration to specific regions" (Olson 1990, 86). Official directives produced abrupt changes in the size and destination of the population flows. A precipitous drop in the number of in-migrants to rural Kigali prefecture in 1970 and 1971, for example, followed government announcements that free land was no longer available in that area.[24]

In the mid-1980s, the pioneer fronts closed: "Almost all the land in the East had been claimed and settled."[25] Once-large disparities in prefectural population densities had diminished markedly. By 1991, at the national rate of population increase of 3.5 percent, the 400,000 people settled on *paysannats* as of 1976 would have grown to about 650,000, representing almost half the total populations of Kibungo and Kigali-Rurale prefectures combined (1.4 million).[26]

LAND TENURE AND CENTRAL STATE AUTHORITY

These land tenure arrangements gave central authorities microlevel levers of influence over ordinary farmers, more so in the south and east than in other regions of the country, and more so in and around *paysannats* than in areas where community, lineage, and historical claims were stronger. In regions of post-1960 in-migration, land tenure arrangements may have heightened many ordinary farmers' stakes in the political status quo – that is, in defending the national government that had given them permission to use land to which they could claim neither birthright nor title, and perhaps even in defending the political positions of individual land patrons whose power was anchored in the Habyarimana regime and the ruling party, the MRND.[27]

Guichaoua (1999, 311) invokes the colonial-era ideal of the *paysannat* creating a "modern peasantry transplanted out of the traditional milieu and set down on lots in planned settlement schemes," thus creating *"centres ex-coutumiers"* (zones outside of customary control) more directly subject to modernizing influences and central government control. This vision would have appealed to postcolonial rulers. These relations of political control, rooted in the LTR, are the focus of this section of our analysis.

---

[24] Olson 1990, 64, 70.

[25] André and Platteau, 1998, 11, citing J. Olson.

[26] Not all *paysannats* were located in these two provinces, but most were. May (1995, table 2) gives population totals and densities by prefecture. The population densities, in ascending order, were Kibungo (213 inhabitants per square kilometer), Byumba (304), Gikongoro (356), Kibuye (393), Gitarama (427), Cyangugu (457), Kigali-Rurale (466), Butare (517), Gisenyi (540), Ruhengeri (560).

[27] The Mouvement Républicain National pour la Démocratie et le Développement. Several MRND Central Committee members were *bourgmestres* and *préfets* in the eastern regions. In 1993, many *bourgmestres* were removed by the multiparty government, but MRND officials were reelected in the eastern region. (Many of the ousted elites still controlled militias. See Rentjens 1994, 226).

Lemarchand wrote in 1970 that "the allocation of landed property previously owned by Tutsi" was a patronage resource used by local politicians to build up political and personal clientele. He calls this "the survival of feudal relationships" in post-independence Rwanda (1970, 275). Guichaoua writes that communal authorities allocated land to individuals in the zones of colonization just as they had redistributed the land of killed and displaced Tutsi elsewhere in Rwanda (Guichaoua 1989, T. 1, 55), and that these same communal authorities were responsible for adjudicating land disputes, organizing communal work, and *animation politique* (political education and mobilization). On the *paysannat* schemes, where migrants were resettled in "farming villages," farmers were linked to the central government not only through the usual hierarchical structures of the Rwandan ruling party and territorial administration, but also through the relationship of land patronage, credit dependency, and the other ties of contract farming.[28] In a 1982 study of a World Bank–funded *paysannat* scheme to settle 9,000 farming families on 51,000 hectares of savanna land in Mutara (Byumba prefecture), Lemarchand concluded that the project created a system of political patronage for the dominant Hutu group (at the expense of Tutsi pastoralists, who were forced to give up livestock and grazing area to make way for homesteaders).[29]

Some rough indicators of the extent to which Rwandan smallholders depended directly on the central state itself for permission to use land (long-term use rights) are available in the literature. Blarel (1994, 77, 78) reports that in 1988, between 40.4 percent and 46.7 percent of landholdings in Ruhengeri, Butare, and Gitarama prefectures were acquired through inheritance. Meanwhile, the figures for land acquired via "government allocation" or on *paysannats* were 9.9 percent, 16 percent, and 44.3 percent for the three prefectures, respectively. On average across these three regions, 15.5 percent of all land acquired in 1963 or earlier (that is, *before* the major land-settlement schemes of the postcolonial era) was allocated by government. Blarel notes "strong regional patterns" in modes of access to land, and this is indeed the case: figures for land acquired through government allocation were even higher in Kibungo and Kigali-Rurale, the main sites of the government-sponsored colonization schemes from 1963 to the early 1980s.

The use of the state's land-allocation powers shaped settlement patterns and created a complex topography of state-society linkages. It also went very far in defining patterns of inequality in the rural areas. According to Guichaoua (1989, 59), much larger-than-average landholdings were not a marginal phenomenon: some 182,000 landholdings (or 16 percent of an overall total of 1.1 million farms) accounted for almost half of all arable land in the country.

[28] See Guichaoua 1989, T. 1, 172–174; Paternostre de la Mairieu 1972.
[29] Lemarchand (1982) notes that political elites received land allocations on the schemes and established landlord-tenant relations with "settlers," who were thus more rural proletarians or sharecroppers than peasants.

These large holdings were concentrated in Kigali, Gitarama, Kibungo, Gikongoro, and Byumba prefectures – "regions of relatively recent settlement, where one saw the initial allocation [i.e., post-1960] of vast parcels."[30] High-ranking members of the Habyarimana regime were notorious for having acquired very large landholdings in northwestern, central, and eastern Rwanda since coming to power in 1973.

LAND INSTITUTIONS AND THE POLITICAL SCALE AND SCOPE OF CONFLICT

The RPF invaded northern Rwanda from Uganda in October 1990. A stated purpose of its campaign was to capture (a share in) state power in order to use it to restructure the state-imposed land allocations of earlier periods. An explicit objective was to engineer the resettlement of a refugee population of 480,000, representing about 7 percent of the Rwandan population.[31] The prospect of return of Tutsi exiles had negative land-related implications for many Rwandans, perhaps especially for those living on state-allocated and state-controlled land that had been expropriated from Tutsis or carved out of formerly Tutsi land domains. The Habyarimana government alluded to these land-distribution realities in its refusal to recognize the "right of return" of most Tutsi exiles, and in its broader attempts to rally ordinary Hutu around the ruling elite. Statist land tenure institutions and practices played a role in shaping patterns of political mobilization in the politics of 1991–1994, fueling a conflict that was national in both scale and scope.

Defining the Stakes of Victory and Defeat

In the multiparty competition of mid-1991 to 1994, most of the opposition to the ruling MRND government was painted as pro-Tutsi and pro-RPF.[32] As J.-P. Chrétien argues (2003, 321), "From 1991–1993, two logics were locked in a race against time in Rwanda: on the one hand, negotiation and democratization; on the other, war and ethnicist mobilization. The Habyarimana regime in fact pursued both strategies for three years."

Judging by their rhetoric and propaganda, militants of the Habyarimana regime, including the extreme hard-liners who executed the policy of genocide in April–July 1994, concluded that threatening ordinary citizens with the

---

[30] Guichaoua 1989, 59.

[31] From Bigagaza (2002, 58; see also 73). Negotiations that led to the Arusha Agreement included a protocol signed on 9 June 1993 (but later disowned by the two parties) that provided for repatriation and resettlement of refugees in Rusumo, Mugina, and Gashora, three communes with extensive *paysannats* (Rentjens 1994, 207–210).

[32] The new political parties engaged in peace negotiations with, and made concessions to, the RPF. The ruling party, the MRND, counted the CDR (Coalition pour la Défense de la République, a far-right Hutu Power party) as an ally.

prospect that they would *be killed* by pro-Tutsi forces was insufficient as a weapon to mobilize the masses. The need for a more context-specific and nuanced rationale for supporting the MRND government was perhaps highest in the period from June 1991 (the moment of opening to multipartism) to April 1994. Official observers, both French and American, and many academics as well, described Rwanda in this period as a country undergoing a "transition to democracy."[33] Human rights groups such as Human Rights Watch (HRW 1993a) were more skeptical. This period saw the entry of opposition party members into the Rwanda government and power sharing among the rival parties within the executive cabinet (April 1992), the election of an opposition-party prime minister, the election of non-MRND *bourgmestres* in 24 of Rwanda's approximately 145 rural communes in March and April 1993,[34] and the appointment of an opposition party representative as prefect of Butare. Meanwhile, the period was punctuated by seemingly productive negotiations with the RPF, marked by a cease-fire in March 1993 and the conclusion of a peace accord in August 1993. On April 6, 1994, Habyarimana was killed while returning from Tanzania, where he and a Rwandan team of negotiators, with strong opposition-party representation, had worked out a power-sharing agreement with the RPF. This agreement was supposed to lead to national elections in two years' time.

The 1992 through April 1994 period was also riddled by state-sponsored violence against opposition supporters and party leaders in Rwanda, as well as militia-led slaughters of large numbers of mostly Tutsi civilians. HRW (1999, 81) estimated that 2,000 people were killed in 1992 and 1993 by government security agencies and militias that had been raised, starting in 1991, by hardliners within the Habyarimana regime.

For Rwanda, 1991 to early 1994 was a period of multiparty competition in which the MRND tried to attack the opposition politically (while simultaneously preparing a "final solution") and mobilize the support of rural constituencies. The argument here is that in this political environment, the stakes of national-level political competition were framed by the ruling party and understood to varying extents at the grassroots level as land related, in part.[35] The ruling party argued that should it lose power, there would be a redefining and reallocation of land rights, to the detriment of its supporters and constituents, who were defined by the MRND as "the Hutu majority."

---

[33] See Prunier (1995, 154, n. 44) on French statements about the ongoing democratization in Rwanda.

[34] Limited elections (electoral consultations) were held in forty communes in March and April 1993 (HRW 1993, 19).

[35] The October 1993 government-led slaughter of 100,000 Hutu in Burundi had a ratcheting-up effect in Rwanda. Perhaps in October 1993, the argument that the RPF would kill Hutu peasants became more immediate and compelling than any land-related argument. Critical for my argument is that the Rwandan government emphasized the land-related implications of "Tutsi victory" so systematically over the course of 1991–1993.

In 1991, 1992, and 1993, the government's propaganda machines spewed rhetoric exhorting the population to "defend the gains [*les acquis*] of the Hutu revolution."[36] Regime propaganda referred explicitly to the land tenure relations that prevailed in the earlier period, warning that "Tutsi overlords" wanted to return to reestablish feudalism and to whip and enslave the Hutu. As Hintjens writes (1999, 261), the regime "claimed that 'democratization' was being used as a cover for the restoration of Batutsi hegemony and feudalism.... The old feudal order would come back to haunt the Hutu majority." The drumbeat of references to feudalism evoked the oppressive system of land-and-cattle clientelism that had deprived Hutu farmers of autonomy and land tenure security in the pre-independence period.

Government propagandists also referred explicitly to the allocation or distribution of land by warning that the purpose of the RPF invasion and of the attempts of Tutsi and their accomplices to seize power was to reclaim land that had been lost in the political convulsions of 1959–1963 and 1973. Alison Des Forges and the coauthors of the 1999 Human Rights Watch report emphasize this point. They write that propaganda about restoration of the old regime of Tutsi feudalism was a reminder that

should the Tutsi win, they would not just reverse the political changes of the [1959–1962] revolution but also reclaim all the property that had once been theirs, leaving many Hutu destitute. This argument carried great weight with cultivators who were working lands received after the expulsion of the Tutsi and who feared above all being reduced to landless laborers. (HRW 1999, 77–78)

Mahmood Mamdani's study of Rwanda (2001) centers on the question of why hundreds of thousands of ordinary citizens participated in the 1994 genocide. Mamdani seeks to identify the peasantry's stake in the Hutu government's fight for survival, rather than micro-incentives that drove action at the individual level. He argues explicitly that ordinary citizens believed they were defending gains of the 1959 revolution, which to them meant "free access to land and freedom of labor." "Control of land allocation passed to the majority [in 1959–1962].... It was a historical gain that was real, and remained so until the closure of the late 1980s. To the extent that the Bahutu masses partook directly in the genocide of 1994, they did so to protect the gains of 1959."[37]

Official ideology and propaganda established the moral foundations of Hutu rights to land and territory in Rwanda in the doctrines of indigeneity and democracy. By official history, "the Tutsi" were invaders and colonists from Abyssinia who had come to Rwanda in the 1400s. As nonindigenes, their claims to land had no moral foundation. Chrétien (2003, 305) writes that "the advent of 'democracy' in Rwanda in 1962–63 was depicted as the legitimate

---

[36] Chrétien 1991.
[37] Mamdani 1996b, 33. See also Mamdani 2001.

revenge of the 'autochthones,' the Bahutu, on the Batutsi, who were treated as a foreign minority."[38] By this logic, the Tutsi had "stolen Rwanda from its rightful inhabitants:" properties or territory they controlled in the pre-independence period were ill-gotten in the first place.[39] Democracy's doctrine of "majority rule" offered a modern and universal justification for reversing this historical legacy. This may have resonated at a very personal level with people whose livelihoods depended on land that had been liberated from the Tutsi a generation or two ago.

The question of land access remained squarely in the national political arena throughout the course of events under consideration here – it was a matter dealt with at the highest levels of state. Starting in the mid-1980s, Tutsi refugees organized to seek the right to return to Rwanda. They "were denied this by the [Habyarimana] government, officially on the grounds of population pressure and scarce land" in Rwanda (Bigagaza et al. 2002, 58). Uvin (1996, 14) characterizes this as part of "the [Habyarimana] regime's tradition of arguing that there was not enough land in Rwanda to accommodate the Tutsi refugee population." Uganda's parliament pressed the issue from the other side of the border: Uganda's 1990 Land Law denied noncitizens the right to own land, thus rendering the status of some 450,000 Rwandan refugees more precarious. The stated purpose of the RPF invasion of 1990 was to ensure the return of refugees to Rwanda, and this was indeed won in the 1993 Arusha Accords. A critical compromise in the Arusha Accords, however, underscored the salience of the land issue: Article 4 "relative to the repatriation of refugees" stipulated that "refugees returning after more than 10 years should not reclaim their lost property but instead be resettled in unoccupied land with government assistance to do so."[40]

Geographic Patterns of Mobilization and Microincentives

The foregoing discussion focuses on the land issue as it was framed in the national political arena, and on land-related propaganda that was disseminated nationwide by the MRND regime in 1991–1993. Now we show that a focus on land institutions and land tenure relations also helps explain why patterns of political mobilization in 1991–1994, including the April–July 1994 genocide, varied across space.

---

[38] See also Hintjens 1999.

[39] The quote is from HRW/Des Forges 1999, 72. On majority rule, see also Chrétien 1991.

[40] Burnet n.d. and Burnet 2003. It is not clear, however, what "unoccupied land" had been put on the bargaining table – perhaps Akagera National Park, which was in fact later used by the RPF-led government for the settlement of some refugees. The national park system covered 20% of Rwandan territory before 1994 (André and Platteau 1998, 4).

Many analysts of the events of 1991–1994 have noted regional unevenness in patterns of government influence and political mobilization.[41] The opposition parties were strongest in the central and southern regions of the country and weakest in the northwest and east. Conversely, the MRND was strongest in the northeast (the home of the ruling clique) and the east, and it is in these regions that the anti-Tutsi and antiopposition violence of 1991–1993 was concentrated. In April 1994, populations in the east were mobilized first for participation in the genocide. By contrast, in the south, citizens and many local-level state agents joined the violence late, killing reluctantly and with delay, and under threat of physical reprisal from state authorities.

Provisional data from Davenport and Stam offered a detailed analysis of this pattern: it shows that Kigali-Rurale (especially the southern half) and Kibungo prefectures were the first zones of widespread genocidal killing.[42] In these prefectures, genocide was carried out in many communes simultaneously, and in most communes by the end of April. According to this provisional analysis, in Kibungo the number of communes involved in genocide killings in the first week of the genocide (8–13 April 1994) ranged from 7 to 11, with an average of 8.5 each day, compared with the approximate ranges for Ruhengeri, Gisenyi, Gitarama, Butare, Gikongoro, Cyangugu, and Kibuye of between 0 and 3. The range for Kigali-Rurale prefecture was also high: slaughter was carried out in 4 to 7 communes each day for this first week of genocide. There was a concentration of contiguous communes, each the site of mass slaughter continuously over all seven days, in the communes south of the capital city. By contrast, the genocide began later in most other prefectures, and in most prefectures, mass killings were limited to only one or two communes during the month of April.

Straus's data for genocide onset dates by commune confirm this general picture (2006, 55–57, 256). So does the analysis of the Human Rights Watch team led by Alison des Forges, which focuses on the challenges the central authorities faced as they tried to expand the genocide from the east, where the killing started, to the center and south of Rwanda, "where opposition parties were stronger" (1999, 7, 10–12, 87). They explain that in some regions of the country,

authorities needed to do little more than give the signal for Hutu to begin attacking Tutsi. In other areas, such as central and southern Rwanda where Habyarimana's party

[41] See, for example, HRW/Des Forges 1999, 87 inter alia; Prunier 1995, 244 inter alia; Nkunzumwami 1999; Straus 2006; Davenport and Stam 2004; Verwimp 2011.

[42] Davenport 2004. "24 days: Rwanda Daily Victim Total by Commune, 4/6/94–4/30/94," with supporting figures on "Genocidal Activity," preliminary data collected by Davenport and Stam as part of a NSF-funded project entitled "GenoDynamics: Understanding Genocide through Time and Space." The provisional data were posted in 2004 and accessed in spring 2007 and spring 2008 (www.bsos.umd.edu/gvpt/davenport/genodynamics/data.htm). These provisional findings are consistent with patterns described by many other analysts.

had little standing, many Hutu initially refused to attack Tutsi and joined with them in fighting off assailants. Only when military and civilian authorities resorted to public criticism and harassment . . . injury, and threats of death did these Hutu give up their opposition to the genocide (HRW/Des Forges 1999, 11).

In much of the center and south, communal authorities were reluctant or obstructionist, and populations were slow to respond. In these places, mass killing did not begin until military and militia were trucked in from the outside to carry out government orders.

Several scholars have argued that economic desperation per se, as measured in regional land scarcity and regional differences in average farm size, does not explain the regionally uneven pattern of mass mobilization in the genocide. In Butare prefecture, where opposition parties were strong and with the highest population density per square kilometer of arable land,[43] populations and prefectural-level authorities resisted the government's calls to action. Local authorities and populations had to be pushed aside to allow the military and militia to do the killing. In Kibungo prefecture, by contrast, populations responded immediately to government calls to action. Here, population densities were the lowest in the country, the average landholding size was the largest, and average incomes were higher than they were in MRND rulers' homelands in the northwestern prefectures of Gisenyi and Ruhengeri.[44]

Straus (2006, 60, 61) shows that proximity to Kigali also fails as an explanation of regional variation in the timing and ferocity of the genocide. Proximity to the war front and Byumba prefecture, which had been ceded to the RPF by a cease-fire agreement in July 1992, also does not provide a compelling explanation for spatial variation in the timing of the onset of mass killings in the genocide. Killings in April were not widespread in Ruhengeri prefecture (compared to Kigali-Rurale and Kibungo prefectures), although Ruhengeri was located close to the front. Ethnic makeup of the prefecture is also a variable that fails to explain the timing and geography of mobilization for genocide: Kibuye prefecture, with the highest proportion of Tutsi population in the country (30 percent on the eve of the genocide, compared to the national average of 15 percent), was not among the first sites of widespread genocidal killing.

An alternative explanation for the pattern of mobilization focuses on land tenure arrangements. This variable goes far in accounting for the strength of the MRND government in the east, its main region of support *outside* Habyarimana's home base. The MRND regime's strong hold on the eastern region is a fact that is widely noted but that has yet to be explained in scholarly analysis of these events (see, for example, Straus 2006, 26). The character of

---

[43] Blarel 1994, 72–74 reports population density for Butare as 994 persons per square kilometer. Butare was the site of famine in 1989 and was receiving emergency food aid (beans and rice) from USAID in early 1994.

[44] Olson 1990. In 1988, Kibungo's average farm size was 1.95 hectares, compared with .77 hectare in Ruhengeri, for example.

the land tenure regime helps explain why the entire region to the south and east of Kigali – the Kigali Rurale and Kibungo prefectures featured in Map 10 – was under such tight control by MRND hard-liners, and why this region witnessed massive slaughter first and on the most widespread basis in the early phases of the genocide.

The areas of heaviest killing in the early days of the genocide were the areas that had been settled under the aegis and guiding hand of the postcolonial state. The *paysannats* concentrated in this region were MRND strongholds, and seats of ruling clique members who commanded political machines. In some cases, these political machines probably incorporated the workers and tenants on landholdings owned or controlled by the political strongmen themselves, creating political organizations structured more like feudal estates than modern political parties. International Criminal Tribunal for Rwanda records indicate that ruling clique members began to activate militia among landless youth in this region in 1992.[45] This is consistent with Reyntjens's (1994, 189) observation that the "Hutu Power" group was comprised of about fifteen persons who "already had local agents ready to carry out their orders: subprefects, prefects, and *bourgmestres*." Several of the Kigali-Rurale and Kibungo *bourgmestres* were in Habyarimana's inner circle or the MRND Central Committee.

Violence was early and sustained in Bugesera and Gisaka in concentrated zones of *paysannats* and the areas of heavy in-migration immediately surrounding the government-sponsored colonization schemes.[46] In these precise regions, the government's hold over rural populations was particularly strong, and local populations had strong land-related incentives for mobilizing to participate in a very bitter struggle for control over the central state.

In Kigali-Rurale south and Kibungo, Hutu governments had settled their own constituents on lands that had been "liberated" from Tutsi overlords. Hutu populations in these areas thus had particular reasons to be beholden to the nationalist Hutu governments that had given them land-use rights. Migrants to Kibungo prefecture were mostly from Gisenyi and Ruhengeri, and had thus been selected from among the MRND's core clientele, and may have been

---

[45] The army began training civilians in Byumba (Mutara) in January 1993 (Reyntjens 1994, 117–118).

[46] The Nyamata District of Bugesera was the site of a notorious slaughter of Tutsi in March 1992 that came to be seen as the precursor of the much wider genocide to come. The massacre took place in an area in which "large numbers of recent Hutu migrants from the Northwest had settled adjacent to groups of Tutsi resident there since the revolution" (HRW/Des Forges 1999, 89). Nyamata District was the geographic epicenter of the large *paysannat* settlement schemes in the southern part of Kigali-Rurale. Kazenze commune's *bourgmestre*, Fidèle Rwambuka, directed the massacres. Hundreds were killed and 15,000 were displaced (Verwimp 2011). Rusumo commune in Kibungo prefecture, site of Belgian-funded *paysannats*, was the theater of one of the most-remembered episodes in the Rwandan genocide. Here, Bourgmestre Sylvestre Gacumbitsi led attacks against the Catholic Church of Nyarubuye, in which 20,000 Tutsi were killed.

captured in the MRND political machine in particularly encompassing ways.[47] Meanwhile, because they were literally living on land forcibly taken from the Tutsi, in-migrants to Kigali-Rurale (south) and Kibungo prefectures also had particular reasons to fear that Tutsi would be back to "reclaim" land lost in 1959–1962 and in the 1973 wave of killings and expulsions.

Hutu peasants in the zones of in-migration would have been particularly exposed to social pressures exerted by the local-level agents of the state: in-migrants lacked historical ties to the region, robust lineage structures rooted in local landholding patterns, or historically rooted forms of associational life. They may have been less autonomous vis-à-vis the central state than their relatives who still lived in their ancestral home areas of Gitarama, Gisenyi, and Ruhengeri.

Land Reallocations Following the RPF Victory

When Tutsi refugees did return to Rwanda in the wake of the RPF victory, large numbers came to the eastern savannas and reclaimed lands lost in the 1960s and 1970s. Uvin (1996, 14) wrote that by May 1995, more than 700,000 refugees – mostly the children of the Tutsi refugees of 1959–1963 – had come back "mainly to the eastern plains their parents had abandoned, bringing with them at least as many cattle."[48] Guichaoua (1999, 332) writes that lands in the eastern prefectures were "colonized outright" by returnees and by the new governmental authorities, who set out to reinforce their hold across the entire national territory, especially in the nearly monoethnic provinces of the northwest, by implanting returnees "who could serve as footholds for the administration in overtly hostile communes." This also happened in the southeast: some 13,000 former refugees streamed in from Burundi and "evicted Hutu from the properties which they claimed had been theirs thirty years earlier."[49]

---

[47] Lemarchand, in discussing land issues in the 1959–1962 Hutu revolution, notes that neotraditional-type relations of land clientelage in the northwestern districts, which linked Hutu peasants to leaders of the locally dominant lineages (the *bagererwa-bakone* relationship), could be "easily activated for revolutionary purposes" (1970, 106). Similar relationships in secular form, established in the zones of new settlement, may have similarly been "easily activated" for political purposes in the early 1990s. Although relations of land clientage had proved difficult to sustain in Ruhengeri because of land scarcity and the increasing commercialization of land (van Hoyweghen 1999, 359; André and Platteau 1998), it may have been possible to re-create a more bureaucratic form of these relations in the settlement scheme areas, where political leaders' ability to grant land rights would have allowed them to establish patron-client relationships with settlers.

[48] Van Hoyweghen (1999, 362–363, n. 34) writes that many returning refugees, entering the country behind the RPF, remained in Kibungo prefecture, where "there was still land available" and where prefects basically forced peasants to give returnees their land. Kibungo's population rose from 279,000 in January 1994 to 790,000 in late December 1996. See D. Newbury 2005, 277 inter alia.

[49] Prunier 1995, 310.

HRW (2001b) documented an extensive pattern of forced "land sharing" (especially in Kibungo and Kigali-Rurale prefectures) and of farmers being forced to cede land to returnees who had spent a generation in exile.

CONCLUSION

Evidence from the Rwandan case conforms to the expectations of the model presented in Chapter 3. That model identified statist land tenure regimes as institutional arrangements that can link social tension over redistribution of land rights to national-level political processes and to the national political arena. Mechanisms linking a statist land tenure regime to these political effects appear clearly in the case of Rwanda from the 1960s to the early 1990s. Rulers' land-allocation powers were used in ways that produced land-related claims and grievances that were pinned on the central state. The statist LTR operated through patron-client linkages that bound peasants to state officials by relations of land dependency; government officials could use these as political levers to mobilize and manipulate grassroots actors in the 1990–1994 conflict. The analysis also sheds some new light on questions related to the geographical locus of mobilization of militia, the locus of the onset of the genocide, and geographical variation in the scale of the Hutu exodus from Rwanda.

Analogous Cases

A larger point is to show that the land tenure institutions that gave central state authorities such power over much of the rural population, and that were so effectively manipulated by the Rwandan political elite for partisan advantage in 1991–1994, are not unique to Rwanda. Similar land tenure institutions found elsewhere in Africa have also created potent opportunities for partisan manipulation.

The statism of Rwanda's LTR is not unique to this case. In southwestern Côte d'Ivoire and Kenya's Rift Valley Province, statist land tenure regimes established a direct institutional connection between local land users (and land claimants) and the central state. Similar institutional causes and political effects were at work in North Kivu Province in the DRC in the early 1990s. These cases are considered in Chapter 5 ("Ethnic Strangers as Protected Clients of the State"). In these places, national-level political authorities have made a Faustian bargain. They have gained direct and unmediated control over land allocation. Rulers can use these powers to manipulate farmers directly and to try to engineer changes in farming patterns and practices that are desired by the state. At the same time, this direct connection exposes them to the potential demands and revindications of those who have land tenure claims against the state.

The institutional causes, mechanisms, and some of the political effects that we observe in Rwanda are congruent with those identified in the Chapter 5 cases. A difference is that in Rwanda in the early to mid-1990s, land struggles were subsumed in a conflict that was more encompassing.

Land Scarcity and Political Conflict

In considering the role of land questions in the strife of 1990–1994, many analysts have focused on demographic and environmental stress, or land scarcity. Rwanda has some of Africa's highest rural population densities, with approximately 7 million people (1990) in a territory the size of Maryland (26,340 square kilometers). In the early 1990s, more than 93 percent of all inhabitants lived in the rural areas, and agriculture was the primary means of livelihood for 90 percent of the population.[50] Demographic pressure on the land has been a central political and economic fact in Rwanda since the 1920s, if not before, and land scarcity was clearly a source of acute social pressure and tension in the time period under consideration here.[51] As André and Platteau (1998) showed in minute detail, land scarcity contributed to poverty, insecurity, and social and economic desperation across large swaths of the Rwandan population. Competition for land at the microlevel fostered a climate of suspicious competition among neighbors and sometimes even among family members. Landlessness (combined with lack of alternative employment opportunities) also helped create the mass of unemployed and frustrated youth who were recruited as the brownshirts and foot soldiers for much of the 1990–1994 violence.[52] Prunier (1995, 142 inter alia) and many other observers have noted that the prospect of "inheriting" the land of people who had been murdered was also a powerful incentive motivating many of the militia members and ordinary citizens who were on the front lines of the genocidal violence in 1994.[53]

Yet the causal chain that links land competition and land scarcity to *political action of any kind* (i.e., whether narrow or wide in scope, and on the local, regional, or national scale) is very long indeed. It is weakened by the great

---

[50] Percival and Homer-Dixon 1998, 206.

[51] On demographic stress and land scarcity, see Olson 1990, 2–3, 20–22, 114. On shrinking farm size, land fragmentation, decreasing fallows, intensification, declining per capita food production, rising landlessness, and land transactions, see Blarel 1994, 73–74 inter alia. Olson also cites 1980s studies tracking increasing frequency of land disputes, land sales and purchases, and land rentals. See also André and Platteau 1998, Percival and Homer-Dixon 1998, Bigagaza et al. 2002.

[52] Olson's (1990, 119–120) 1988 household survey data showed that almost half of all household heads "saw no local opportunities for their children [in agriculture, because of land scarcity] and would advise them directly to migrate."

[53] This calculus is however inseparable from the larger political calculation. Land forcibly acquired would have little value if a postconflict government were unwilling to enforce the acquirer's property claim. Land's value as simple booty was close to nil; its value depended completely on the macropolitical outcome of the conflict – the structure of postconflict power relations.

indeterminacy of many of the possible causal connections.[54] The comparative material surveyed in earlier chapters of this work suggests how indeterminate these connections are. In sub-Saharan Africa today, acute land scarcity is far more common than violent land-related conflict, or national-level conflagrations with land-related drivers. Growing land competition and scarcity are common in many parts of the continent today, but land-related violence is not. Even the *acute* land scarcity that is visible in some parts of Rwanda is not unique to this case: Kisii in western Kenya is similar in the degree of demographic and environmental stress. Yet as Chapter 6 argued, land-related conflict in Kisii is suppressed (or bottled up) within the intimacies of family and neighborhood. This is the opposite of the Rwandan outcome. In Rwanda, land-related conflict did simmer within families,[55] *but the crucial fact for our analysis is that it also fused directly with national mega-conflicts* and found expression in political struggles of national scale and scope. The statist character of the LTR in Rwanda meant that land conflict would directly implicate state institutions, state agents, and the question of who controlled state power to allocate land.

[54] This indeterminacy is present even within the Rwanda case, where the highest population densities and arguably the most acute land (and food) scarcities in 1994 were in Butare prefecture – the prefecture most resistant to the *genocidaires'* April 1994 calls to action. Percival and Homer-Dixon (1998, 212) and many others stress this point.

[55] This is the main theme of André and Platteau (1998), who focus on the northwest.

PART IV

MULTIPARTY COMPETITION

Elections and the Nationalization of Land Conflict

> Alternatively, a rival with the support of the landless may replace the existing
> rulers and redistribute land in such a way as to give land to the landless.
>
> (North 1981, 116)

Debates and conflicts over land rights have played a powerful role in some of
the continent's most closely studied experiments with political liberalization –
including those in Kenya in the 1990s, Côte d'Ivoire since the mid-1990s, the
Democratic Republic of the Congo, Zimbabwe, and Rwanda (1990–1994). In
Kenya in 1992 and 1997, the incumbent regime of Daniel arap Moi stoked land
tensions in the Rift Valley to consolidate its electoral constituencies, disorganize
the opposition, and help strengthen the ruling party's hold on power. In Côte
d'Ivoire since the mid-1990s, national-level politicians have catered to south-
westerners' land grievances against immigrant farmers in order to mobilize the
electoral support of "true Ivoirians" in this region. In Zaire, Mobutu's National
Conference in 1991 opened the door for politicians in eastern provinces to
mobilize electoral constituencies around promises of land restitution. In Zimbabwe from the mid-1990s on, Mugabe played the land issue to the hilt to
bolster his nationalist and populist credentials, cement his hold on an electoral
base, and destroy the opposition. In Rwanda, too, an ongoing history of the use
of state power to impose, allocate, and reallocate land rights shaped patterns
of political mobilization in the period of multiparty politics from 1991 through
April 1994.

In these situations, land tensions and land questions helped fuel multiparty
dynamics by mobilizing voters in national-level electoral contests. Land issues
defined or deepened lines of partisan affiliation at the local level, providing
national-level politicians with highly salient issues they could exploit for electoral advantage, and helping kindle election-related strife. Voters in some significant constituencies were told – or believed – that the security of their access

to land would be affected by the outcome of a national-level (or, in the case of Eastern DRC, a regional-level) contest for state power. In all these cases, there were close connections between land-related conflict on the one hand, and competition for national-level elected office on the other. If we follow Kenneth Roberts's terminology in calling an issue "politicized" when it becomes an axis of electoral competition, then this phenomenon is "politicized land conflict."[1] Under what conditions does this happen?

MULTIPARTISM UNDER STATIST LAND TENURE REGIMES

Our answer is that the character of the land tenure regime (LTR) is a key explanatory variable. Under statist LTRs, the possibility of partisan alternation raises the specter of a *redistribution* of land rights. In these situations, settler populations are directly beholden to central authorities for their land rights. This makes them highly mobilizable by incumbents who have the power to enforce and renew their land tenure. For the same reason, settlers' land rights are vulnerable to power shifts (political dislocation) at the top of the state apparatus, including shifts that may result from electoral turnover. If rulers have extinguished or disregarded ancestral land rights of an indigenous (autochthonous, or firstcomer) community in order to implant that settler population, then rulers are likely to have created at least a latent constituency with land-rights grievances that they pin on the central state. Aggrieved constituencies' demands for restitution may be championed by political entrepreneurs who promise to redress the historical land grievances by overturning the work of the ancien régime. Under the statist land tenure regimes, settlers' land-access rights may turn out to be no more secure than the government that provided the land access in the first place.

The redistributive implications of elections under statist LTRs explain these upsurges of land-related conflict at election time. The move to multipartism encourages and allows those who have been on the losing end of the land competition, whose political options have been hitherto constrained to exit and loyalty, to opt for *voice*. Those who have benefited from the patronage of national-level incumbents have heightened incentives to support them – the incumbents are likely to be their protectors. The LTR thus defines *microlevel expectations* about the possible consequences of regime turnover. These expectations are a key link between structure, as defined by the statist LTR, and the agency of land claimants. Where settler-versus-indigene land conflict develops under a statist land tenure regime, multiparty competition can give national-level entrepreneurs incentives to mobilize constituencies for electoral battle.

Will political entrepreneurs seek to take advantage of the opportunity to mobilize voters with land grievances and politically contingent land rights? Politicians' move from opportunity to action depends on demographic and electoral-system variables that we do not explore systematically here. One

---

[1] Roberts (forthcoming). Mozaffar et al. (2003, 383) use the term "particization."

variable is the numerical significance of the voter population that can be mobilized around the land issue. Another is electoral rules that may determine a given population's electoral significance – at both the constituency and the national level.[2] A particular constituency's symbolic value may also matter. In the 31 October 2010 first-round presidential election in Côte d'Ivoire, for example, militants of the ruling Front Populaire Ivoirien (FPI) wanted to guarantee that President Laurent Gbagbo would win "100 percent of the vote in his home area."[3]

Multipartism raises the value of rural voices to politicians, and it should lower the cost of "voice" for those with land-related grievances. As Scott Matter (2010) notes in a study of land politics in Narok District, Kenya, the politics that ensue are a coproduction of those who need land access and those with the power to grant it.

The dynamics observed in these cases show that democracy's Third Wave in the 1990s not only rendered authoritarian regimes insecure, but also upset the property allocations that these regimes had authored and enforced. Where authority-based systems of resource allocation are pervasive in national economies, regime change can ignite redistributive conflict that reaches deep into society.

Table IV.1 depicts the partisan alignments over land issues that emerged in the cases considered in Part IV of this book. As hypothesized in Chapter 3, *incumbents defended the status quo* land allocations when they themselves were the authors of that distribution of rights. These incumbents were challenged by oppositions that championed land rights restitution. This alignment emerged under the Habyarimana regime in Rwanda in 1991–1994, the Mobutu regime in eastern DRC in 1990–1994, and the PDCI regime in Côte d'Ivoire (until 1998).

By contrast, incumbents *renounced* the land allocations of their predecessors in Kenya under Moi in the 1990s, and in Zimbabwe under Mugabe. These incumbents championed restitution and faced off against opposition parties that defended (or did not renounce) the earlier land allocations.

RIVAL ARGUMENTS AND COUNTERFACTUAL SCENARIOS

Cases developed in earlier chapters are counterfactuals that help support the argument here, which is that under multipartism, land conflicts structured

---

[2] If we had the data to run a regression analysis to test the argument that "under multiparty competition, high in-migration under a statist LTR increases the likelihood of politicized land-related conflict," we would have to specify these parameters to get a good test. It would also be necessary to code for the presence or absence of political entrepreneurs to organize collective action in the form of land-related conflict. The argument here points to social-structural and institutional parameters that *create conditions* for politicized (election time) land conflict, and shows that they are salient across an array of cases. Considering counterfactual hypotheses that are framed by the theory enhances confidence in the argument.

[3] Interviews in Abidjan, 20 October 2010.

TABLE IV.1. *Land and Partisan Politics: Case Summaries*

	Where?	When?	Defending Land Rights Granted by the Central State	Championing Restitution of Customary/Historical Rights	Scale of Conflict/Violence
Rwanda	National; eastern prefectures	1991–1994	Incumbents defend status quo (MRND defends gains of Hutu Revolution)	Opposition (RPF and opposition parties endorsing Arusha Process and Tutsi return)	~800,000 killed, 2 million displaced
Kenya	Rift Valley Province	1992–1998	Opposition defends status quo (inherited from Kenyatta regime)	Incumbents (Moi's KANU supports restitution demands in the Rift)	1,500 killed, 500,000 displaced
Kenya	National	2002+	Incumbent defends status quo (inherited from Kenyatta regime)	Opposition (Ruto-wing of ODM supports restitution)	1,000 killed, ~400,000 displaced
Zimbabwe	Commercial estate areas	2000–	Opposition defends status quo (inherited from Rhodesian government)	Incumbent (Mugabe regime expropriates non-indigenous estate owners)	4,000 farms expropriated; owners and ~300,000 farmworkers and families displaced
DRC (ex-Zaire)	N. Kivu Province	1990–1993	Ancien regime established status quo (colonial regime, Mobutu regime)	New players and political outsiders (autochthonous Hunde/Nyanga politicians)	~7,000 killed, 250,000 displaced
Côte d'Ivoire	SW region	1990–2000	Incumbents defend status quo (established by Houphouet regime)	Opposition (Gbagbo/FPI demand restitution)	~5,000 displaced (1995); 20,000 displaced (1999)
Côte d'Ivoire	National	2002–2010	Opposition defends status quo (Forces Nouvelles and supporting groups)	Incumbent (Gbagbo/FPI demand restitution)	~300,000+ displaced

by the statist LTRs are likely (i.e., more likely than land conflicts generated under the neocustomary regimes) to find expression in the arena of multiparty politics. Cases considered in Chapters 4 through 8 combine with the material presented in Chapters 9 and 10 to provide leverage on three rival explanations of land-related election conflict and election-time violence (1) that land scarcity itself causes violent land conflict, (2) that the ethnic heterogeneity of electoral constituencies is a predictor of the emergence of election-time land conflict, and (3) that this kind of politicized land conflict reflects the weakness of the central state. Cases developed in previous chapters (4, 6, and 7) provide evidence about the effects of multiparty politics on local jurisdictions under *non-statist* land tenure regimes.

Land Scarcity and Land-Related Violence

Does rising pressure on the land explain the election-time land conflict that developed in the 1990s in these five cases? In Chapter 8, we argued that scarcity does not explain the scale or scope of conflict in the case of Rwanda. This reasoning extends to the other cases presented here. Perceived land scarcity is present in all the cases we have considered so far. Scarcity per se tells us little about how the resulting social tensions will find political expression. Parts II and III of this book presented cases in which tensions over rising population pressure, shrinking landholding size, and the closing of the land frontier do not become an animating force in electoral politics or fuel election-time violence. The cases discussed in previous chapters help drive home the point that tensions arising from demographic stress are not necessarily stoked or harnessed by politicians for electoral advantage. In fact, in sub-Saharan Africa, they rarely are.

Ethnic Heterogeneity and Land Conflict

An even more pervasive line of argument attributes election-time land conflict to ethnic heterogeneity. Does the existence of ethnic heterogeneity in rural localities mean that land tensions, if they exist, are likely to find expression as ethnic conflict in the electoral arena? Each of the study zones examined in Chapter 9 is indeed ethnically heterogeneous. In each subnational jurisdiction of interest in Kenya, Côte d'Ivoire, and DRC, from 20 to 60 percent of the population is composed of ethnic strangers or in-migrants. In Rwanda, about 20 percent of the national population was classified as non-Hutu in the 1980s. In Zimbabwe, politicized land conflict targeted the white minority. Land scarcity and ethnic heterogeneity are simultaneously present in each of the cases examined in Chapter 9. In seeking to explain why politicized land conflict developed in these cases but not in all cases considered in this book, however, ethnic heterogeneity – alone or in combination with scarcity and land hunger – proves to be underdetermining. The co-presence of these two factors does not produce

politicized land conflict as we have defined it here in the cases of western
Ghana and western Burkina Faso. Fearon and Laitin (1996) suggested that
violent conflict is a *rare* feature of life in ethnically heterogeneous localities,
and our cases suggest that this is true in ethnically mixed, land-scarce districts
of rural Africa.[4] Where land-related conflicts over resource use divide communities along ethnic lines, they generally play out as highly localized affairs, as in
western Ghana, western Burkina Faso, and northern Cameroon. They do not
fuel the flames of partisan conflict in national-level electoral competition.

State Weakness and Politicized Land Conflict

A "state weakness" hypothesis holds that in Africa, national government
barely penetrates the countryside, and land tenure relations lie beyond the
reach of the state. This argument is made by Herbst in *States and Power in
Africa* (2000), for example. By this logic, multiparty competition would result
in land-related conflict where political liberalization takes the lid off long-
simmering intercommunal squabbles that were repressed by the authoritarian
state.

The land-tenure facts of the cases considered in Chapters 9 and 10 directly
contradict the central tenet of the weak-state hypothesis. In each case, the land
rights that were called into question were modern artifacts, created through
a recent history of deep state involvement in land tenure and land allocation. In each country, violence occurred precisely in the subregions where land
tenure relations had been the most intensively governed and structured by
the modern state. All the conflict-affected areas were zones of extensive commercialization of agriculture, marked by deep state involvement in structuring
factor allocation, including land allocation, and the strong administrative presence of the state. The statist LTR prevailing in these jurisdictions is itself a
prime indicator of high state penetration of the rural areas in these subnational
jurisdictions.

The ethnic heterogeneity in the case studies that we examine in Chapter 9, as
well as the racial heterogeneity of Zimbabwean society (Chapter 10), is largely
traceable to *state-sponsored movements* of agrarian settlement/colonization.
As analysts of central Africa have argued, the forcible and coercive "trans-
plantation" of populations creates a new *gestion d'espace* (i.e., a new way
of governing or managing territory) in which the modern state is the central and sometimes hegemonic arbiter. What Mathieu et al. (1999, 19) have
called "*cohabitations imposées*" in eastern Zaire/DRC structured land tenure
relations in ways that are largely isomorphic to the patterns we observe in
south-central and southwestern Côte d'Ivoire and in the farming districts of
Kenya's Rift Valley Province. In Rwanda, the postcolonial state redefined land

[4] On ethnic nationalism, see also Snyder's *From Voting to Violence* (W. W. Norton 2000).

rights and settlement patterns throughout much of the national territory, creating patterns of land clientelism and exclusion that fueled deadly struggles over state power. In Zimbabwe, the Mugabe regime presented itself as reversing land expropriations and a *cohabitation imposée* engineered by the colonial state. Mugabe positioned himself in 2000 as a revolutionary and a restorer of native land rights, producing forms of land-related conflict in Zimbabwe that resemble the politicized land conflicts that exploded in the other four cases.

Multiparty Competition under the Neocustomary Land Regimes

In most rural jurisdictions, the return to multipartism at the national level has *not* resulted in much electoral competition at the local level. And in the vast majority of rural jurisdictions, the land tenure regime is organized largely around neocustomary relations. These more ordinary or typical cases help support – by way of counterfactual reasoning – the argument advanced in Part IV, which is that politicized land-related conflict is more likely to emerge under the statist LTRs.

Material presented in previous chapters permits a close look at these contrast cases in which the statist LTRs are absent. Land conflict did not become an axis of electoral competition in Kisii, Kenya, providing us with an in-country contrast to the Rift Valley Province case study, considered here. And the cases of Western Region in Ghana, Ashanti Region's "expulsion of the aliens" in 1966, western Burkina Faso, and northern Cameroon suggest that even under multipartism, the neocustomary regimes repress land-related conflict at the local level. By the logic advanced here, if indigene-stranger conflict did emerge as an axis of electoral competition in a jurisdiction with a neocustomary LTR, then that would be an indicator of *the weakness or weakening of neocustomary authority* over land.[5]

---

[5] A subtler version of the argument holds that the effect is proportional to the *directness* of the state's intervention in land issues. In western Ghana (Chapter 4), an apparent anomaly for our theory was resolved by treating the directness of central authorities' hand in shoring up a neocustomary LTR as a variable (that is, as a continuous rather than dichotomous variable), and one that changes over time. Neocustomary LTRs in Sefwi Wiawso and Wassa Amenfi had a statist cast under Nkrumah and the early Rawlings regimes, creating institutional and political conditions for bringing land-related politics into the national arena. Nkrumah's immediate successors and the late Rawlings regime bolstered chieftaincy decisively, resulting in institutional arrangements that worked to push indigene-stranger land conflict out of the national political arena – an outcome that conforms to our theoretical expectations.

CHAPTER 9

Winning and Losing Politically Allocated Land Rights
Property Conflict in the Electoral Arena

> Unlike Kenyatta, who could give without taking away, Moi had to take away
> before he could give.
> (Mueller 2008, 188)

> When [opposition leader Laurent] Gbagbo comes to power, he will chase out all
> the strangers for us.
> (Lewis 2003)

Under what conditions do land-related tensions fuel partisan competition in the national electoral arena? This chapter offers a focused comparison of politicized land conflict in four countries: Kenya in 1992 and 1997, Côte d'Ivoire in the elections of the 1990s, Rwanda in 1991–1994, and Democratic Republic of Congo in 1991–1994. These countries differ in significant ways – in terms of size, level of economic development, colonial institutional heritage, and the presence or absence of a history of large-scale European land expropriations. Despite these dissimilarities, land politics became a divisive, explosive issue in the electoral arena in each country.[1]

Our argument is that politicized land conflict, as we have defined it, is traceable to the statist character of the land tenure regime (LTR) in each of these settings. In each country, election-time conflict exploded in jurisdictions where the central state itself was responsible for allocating land rights and where state authorities (past or present) had assigned land to their own clients or constituents *at the expense of* aggrieved communities claiming ancestral rights to land. A mechanism linking institutional cause to political effect in each case was the presence of a belief – fear or hope – among the voters that

---

[1] We employ a "most different systems" comparison – that is, an attempt to explain the emergence of a similar outcome in what seem to be very different cases. Cases presented in previous chapters allow us to examine counterfactual arguments.

the security/status of their land rights and claims hinged on the outcome of an electoral struggle for control over state power. The politically contingent nature of the ties that bound farming households to central authorities underlay these dynamics. Elections opened or heightened the possibility of a redistribution of land rights.

In these situations, the land tenure regime goes far in defining the stakes of competition. The land regime also defines an *axis of competition* (ethnic outsiders versus ethnic insiders, settlers versus autochthones, original inhabitants versus state-imposed settlers) in the local jurisdiction, as argued in Part II, as well as the *scale of the competition* (which is national, because the central state is the allocator of land rights and the author of the prevailing land allocation), as argued in Part III. Given the national scale at which the issue is determined, contestants have opportunities to widen the scope of conflict by allying with others who have grievances against, or are tied to, the same national authorities. While political liberalization expands such opportunities, political parties provide the actors and organizational resources to engineer alliances. The product in the cases examined here was politicized land conflict – that is, land conflict became an axis of electoral competition – that was played out in the national electoral arena.

KENYA: 1991–2010

> Members of the central Kenya communities displaced by the clashes believe they
> will regain their lands once Uhuru [Kenyatta, KANU nominee in 2002] takes
> over, something that cabinet minister William Ntimama, a key opponent of his
> nomination, has ruled out.[2]

The farming districts of Kenya's Rift Valley Province are some of the most productive and highly commercialized rural zones of sub-Saharan Africa. These districts – Nakuru, Trans-Nzoia, Uasin-Gishu, and Nandi – are territories with high in-migration and high ethnic heterogeneity, and with settlement patterns and land allocations authored directly by the central state. It is a region with an archetypically statist or state-administered LTR. It is also one of Africa's most conflict-ridden rural areas, with a long and bloody history of land-related struggles that find political expression in ways that conform to our hypotheses.

Chapter 5 examined this case. Land-related conflict pitted the dominant KANU party against the KADU opposition in 1960–1963. After 1963, party politics was squashed in Kenya, and the uncompetitive character of the regime at the national level was a constant from 1963 to 1990. The 1960s and 1970s were decades of consolidation of the Kenyatta regime, which sidelined those claiming ancestral land rights in the Rift Valley and "inserted" African settlers into Rift Valley farming districts.

---

[2] Peter Munaita, "Kenyatta and Moi: The Common Strand Running through Their Regimes," *East African*, 23 September 2002.

In the third decade of independence, the 1980s, a new governing coalition came to power under the leadership of Daniel arap Moi. Under Moi, the political pendulum swung back toward those who had been excluded and marginalized in the earlier period. The new regime worked to cultivate popular support and rural constituencies among the dispossessed Rift Valley communities who harbored land grievances against the Kenyatta regime. The Moi regime used the central state's land prerogatives in the Rift Valley to reward its own clients, who were encouraged by the regime to coalesce around an ethnic identity, Kalenjin-ness, that was centered on indigeneity (autochthony) in the Rift Valley.

In 1991, under pressure from within and without, Moi agreed to hold multiparty elections in 1992. He stood for reelection in 1997 and in 2002 (when he lost to Mwai Kibaki). In these elections, the Moi government mobilized its Rift Valley constituencies along an axis of competition that pitted the indigenes of the Rift Valley against settlers who had been implanted by the Kenyatta regime. Rift Valley politicians tapped into existing land-related tensions in which the central state was directly implicated as the author and enforcer of a contested distribution of land rights. With the return to multipartism in 1991, this land-related conflict found direct expression in electoral politics at the national level.

Run-Up to the 1990s Elections

From the mid-1980s onward, the Moi regime became progressively more active in using land allocation and the land-restitution issue as tools to forge a cohesive ethnopolitical constituency out of the Kalenjin groups and the other ethnocultural communities claiming to be native or indigenous to the Rift Valley. Political entrepreneurs marketed the KAMATUSA identity (embracing Kalenjin, Maasai, Turkana, and Samburu) (Lynch 2008). Key to this constituency-building effort was a shift toward the Kalenjin-coalition constituencies in the bias of government land allocation. Most notoriously, the Rift Valley forest reserves were plundered for this purpose, especially the Mau Forest reserves, but so were state properties such as Agricultural Development Corporation (ADC) farms, which were supposed to be devoted to agricultural research, and Settlement Fund Trustees (SFT) properties that were recently acquired or had not been divvied up in the earlier period.[3] At the same time, the Moi regime

---

[3] On the SFT acquisition and reallocation of land, see Southhall's 2005 summary of the Ndungu Report, and Gisemba 2008. On ADC farms allocated to Kalenjin-cluster groups in 1993, see Lynch 2006. Klopp (2000) stresses that at the same time, Moi regime barons acquired huge Rift Valley estates. Leading members of the Kalenjin ruling elite were notorious land-grabbers in Nandi and Kericho Districts, regions of "intense development of capitalist agriculture and increasing social differentiation, including landlessness caused by land-grabbing elites such as [MP] Biwott" (Throup and Hornsby 1998, 198–199).

encouraged those who had lost out or been dispossessed in the land-allocation politics of the 1960s and 1970s to air their grievances, and called into question the legitimacy of settlement schemes and land buying companies created under the patronage of Kenyatta. This underscored and heightened the political contingency of the prevailing distribution of land in the Rift.

Demographic and environmental stress heightened the tensions and stakes in conflicts over land allocation (see Kahl 2006). Closing of land frontiers in smallholder farming areas throughout Kenya gave many poor families few options for creating viable livelihoods in agriculture for their children. Drought and the sedentarization of pastoral people increased demands for farmland. Domestic legal challenge to the razing of forests, and international pressure to curb corruption and lawlessness at the pinnacles of the Moi regime, raised the costs of using the forest reserves as a new land frontier to settle Kalenjin farmers. These pressures made it harder for Moi to provide land for his own constituencies without directly attacking the acquired rights of those who had received land under Kenyatta. And as Klopp (2000) emphasized, it was convenient to scapegoat Kikuyu and Luo smallholders as illegitimate settlers in order to deflect the wrath of land-hungry Kalenjin away from the vast properties of Moi's own cronies.

Consolidation of private, formally-registered land rights in the hands of more and more Rift Valley settlers intensified the pressures. Onoma (2010) explains that in the early 1980s, Moi promoted the conversion of some Land Buying Company titles to individual title, in the effort to break patron-client links between smallholders and the politicians who had established themselves as land purveyors under Kenyatta. (See also Gisemba 2008.) One by-product of this process, perhaps unanticipated by the Moi regime at first, was heightened anxiety among those claiming rights to the same land on the basis of indigeneity. Throup and Hornsby (1998, 198–199) mention how these two dynamics – demands for restitution and the titling of "ill-gotten" land – formed a combustible combination at election time:

In several settlement areas, the process of land registration was underway [as provided for by precedent and by existing national land policy in Kenya]. Individual titles were being issued to local residents, replacing earlier communal [i.e., cooperative or company] title deeds. If Kikuyu, Abaluhya, Gusii, and Luo settlers could be driven out of the Rift Valley borderlands before the process was completed, small-holdings could be appropriated by their Kalenjin former neighbors and they would forfeit all claims to the land.

There were sporadic outbreaks of land-related violence in the Rift under the Moi regime in the 1980s, but these were contained and repressed by the provincial administration and security forces. For example, Throup and Hornsby (1998, 188) mention 1984 clashes between Nandi and Luhya in Kapkangani, describing these as "similar to the outbreak of violence in November 1991 on

Miteitei Farm [around Tinderet in Nandi District]" but point out that the 1984 clashes had been "quickly ended" by the local administration.

The 1990s Elections

The introduction of multipartism in 1991–1992 changed the incentives for Moi regime politicians. Multipartism also lowered the cost of voice for those with interests in advancing land claims on the basis of indigeneity. The opening of the national political arena brought questions of land distribution and redistribution, already squarely in the national arena, into the open.[4]

The statist LTR defined the axis of competition in the electoral battles in the Rift Valley. Here, elections were fought to decide who would gain control of the central state and, with it, control over the allocation of land for farming and settlement.

Leading members of the Moi government campaigned openly on a platform of chasing settlers out of the Rift and reallocating land to the regime's own supporters.[5] Starting in late 1991, peoples claiming to be indigenous to the Rift Valley, the Maasai and the Kalenjin coalition of smaller groups, were encouraged by ruling-party politicians to demand that settlers be dispossessed of their land and expelled from the Rift. Politicians dangled the tantalizing prize of restoring land in the Rift Valley to the "original owners" who had been twice denied – first by the colonial state in 1905–1920, and then by the ruling party of Jomo Kenyatta in the 1960s and 1970s.

Political rhetoric that pervaded Nandi, Nakuru, Uasin-Gishu, and Trans-Nzoia Districts dwelled on how land lost to the Europeans was never recovered, and how under Kenyatta, "black colonists" had been allowed to buy up land that rightfully should have belonged to indigenous communities. Grassroots political discourse was filled with loud denunciations of Kenyatta's land gifts. In Likia Location, in Molo Division, Nakuru District, for example, where "most land belonged to Kikuyus in the early 1990s ... local Kalenjin politicians reminded people of the past ownership of the land" and encouraged them to reclaim it.[6] In Narok, politicians rallied constituencies of "indigenous people" around the battle cry that the land titles of Kenyan settlers were worthless pieces

---

[4] See Mutua 2008, 78–79.

[5] Reintroduction of the "majimbo system of government" was an explicit part of this platform as articulated by KANU politicians in Kapsabet and Kaptatet rallies; majimboism was presented as an alternative to multipartism. (See Akiwumi Report 1999, 212, 223; Kahl 2006, 142–143.) The argument presumes that multipartism would take the presidency away from Moi and the "minority tribes."

[6] IRIN, "Kenya, Clashes, Elections, and Land – Church Keeps Watch in Molo," 19 July 2007, posted at www.alertnet.org (accessed 28 July 2007). This source quotes Keffah Magenyi, national coordinator of the Internally Displaced Persons (IDP) Network, a Kenyan NGO, as saying that in Molo, "where most land belonged to Kikuyus" in 1990, "90% of the [2007] IDPs are Kikuyu."

of paper that had been handed out by corrupt agents of the Kenyatta regime. Farmers who believed they had rightfully purchased land in Narok, or that they had responded straightforwardly to public policies providing incentives to settle in the Rift, were reduced to the status of land clients who had lost their patron and protector.

In 1991 and 1992, election-time pogroms targeted farmers on settlement schemes and in the land buying company areas. Hundreds were killed and thousands were driven off the land. The main victims of violence and displacement were rural families who had benefited from the Kenyatta-era land programs. Evidence describing these processes and the geography of the violence is abundant.[7] Local leaders who often had obvious links to higher-ups sponsored the formation of militias of "Kalenjin warriors" who attacked smallholder settlements, destroyed farm equipment and animals, burned down houses, and raped, maimed, and killed people. In these jurisdictions, mobilization patterns were shaped by prevailing patterns of effective authority over the land, with central-state agents and their local operatives often taking a leading role in organizing and spearheading the attacks.

The government's own investigatory committees, the Kiliku Committee (1992) and the Akiwumi Commission (1999), reported the details of many such cases. In Trans-Nzoia District, gangs incited by Kalenjin politicians invaded farms and drove off settlers, declaring that it was time for the native people to reclaim land that had been transferred to outsiders under Kenyatta. A notorious case from Kericho District (Kipsitet) was that of Buru Farm, noteworthy for the high-profile role of government agents, the explicitness of the government's claim to complete prerogative over the land, and the pre- and post-election time span of the violence. Occupation of Buru Farm by Luo had been under dispute since 1972. The Akiwumi Report explained that attacks by Kalenjin militia began in October 1991 in Nandi District and spread to Kericho District and Buru Farm on 5 November 1991. At Buru Farm, Kalenjin warriors were joined by armed policemen who helped them "drive out the Luo from land which the government had decided to settle them on." In December 1993, after the election, the Luo who had moved back to Buru Farm were forced out again, and their houses were bulldozed by armed policemen. They were told to leave "government land" and move to their ethnic homeland in Nyanza.

Approximately 1,500 people were killed, and as many as 300,000 displaced, by election-related violence that began in 1991 and continued throughout 1993 and 1994, with sporadic incidents in 1995 and 1996.[8] The geographic epicenter of this violence was the farming districts of the Rift Valley, much of it targetted

---

[7] There is, for example, Republic of Kenya Kiliku Report of 1992, the Akiwumi Report of 1999, HRW 1993b, Kenya National Council of Churches reports, and many secondary analyses, including Oucho 2002; Kimenyi and N'Dung'u 2005; Anderson and Lochery 2008; and the sources cited in Boone 2007, 2011.

[8] HRW 1993b. On the 1993 expulsions from Enoosupukia in northern Narok, for example, see Throup and Hornsby 1998, 542–543; Klopp 2002. On the timing, see Akiwumi Report

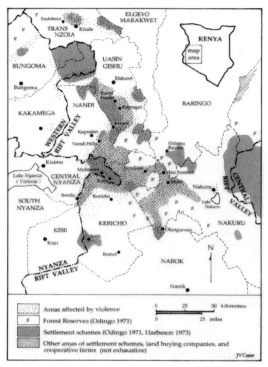

MAP 12. Kenya, Rift Valley Province: Areas Affected by Violence in 1990s Elections.
Sources: Odingo 1971; Harbeson 1973; Boone 2009.

at the settlement schemes and surrounding areas. Map 12 offers a rough picture
of the geographic pattern of election-time violence.

   Moi regime supporters moved into vacated farms and homes with the assistance and protection of the government. In some cases, land titles were issued
to the new occupants.[9] The politics of taking land in order to give it to regime
supporters was explicit.[10] As Kahl (2006, 146, 147–148) points out, "The
prospect of gaining access to land was used by KANU elites as a powerful
selective incentive to encourage individuals to drive away their neighbors."
Citing Jacqueline Klopp's dissertation on land politics in Kenya, he writes that
"cleared land opened up new resources to buy support through patronage and

   1999 and the National Council of Churches of Kenya, *The Clashes Update* for 1995 and
   1996.
[9] See Norwegian Refugee Council, Internal Displacement Monitoring Centre (NRC-IDMC),
   "Kenya: The Conflicts and Displacements Have Caused a Lasting Alteration of Land Occupancy and Ownership Patterns (1997–2000)," n.d., posted at www.internal-displacement.org,
   (accessed 12 August 2008).
[10] Akiwumi Report 1999, 73–79, 96–103.

raised the stakes in the fight for change. By effectively taking land claimed by others, [KANU MP and cabinet minister William Ole] Ntimama's supporters now had a stronger stake in maintaining KANU and Ntimama in power."

Because the land-politics battle was fought at the national level, *the scope of conflict* was also defined at that level, just as E. E. Schattschneider would have predicted. The struggle over land rights in the Rift Valley was woven almost seamlessly into partisan battles of national scope over whether President Moi would be confirmed in office in 1992.

Kenya's 1997 and 2007 national elections were marked by similar patterns of land-related violence.[11] In the 1997 elections, settlement scheme areas of Coastal Province were also sites of extensive land-related violence (Kanyinga 1998). The Norwegian Refugee Council (2004, 83) reported that the total number of persons displaced in the violence of the 1990s exceeded 500,000. When the Moi regime ended in 2002, there were still 350,000 internally displaced persons in Kenya.

The 1990s violence led to what many observers considered to be a deliberate and permanent reallocation of land in the Rift. As the Norwegian Refugee Council wrote:

A long-term effect of the violence is the lasting alteration of land occupancy and owner-ship patterns in the areas where "ethnic" clashes took place, and a significant reduction in the number of non-Kalenjin landowners, particularly in Rift Valley Province. The government has continued to pursue its politics of ... allowing and cooperating in the illegal expropriation of land owned primarily by Kikuyus, Luhyas, and Luos. [This] benefits the Moi government ... : it expects their [the beneficiaries'] political support by claiming to have got "their" land back. (NRC 2004, 92)

Kibaki's win in 2002 was not marked by violence, but the specter of land (re)distribution hung heavy over his election. The candidate promised land restitution or resettlement to the hundreds of thousands of IDPs who remained displaced from the 1990s violence.[12] As one local peace committee organizer said, "2002 was a time of change of guard in the political alignments and the displaced families felt they will be protected to enable them to return home."[13] And once in office, Kibaki's government began evicting tens of thou-sands of squatters from the Mau Forests, most of them members of Kalenjin

---

[11] Akiwumi Report 1999. On the rise of gangs, see Mueller 2008. See Boone 2011, 2012.

[12] The promises were not kept, however. The IDP Network, a Kenyan NGO, said in 2007 that most of the 400,000 they estimate to have been displaced in the 1990s land conflicts "remain landless" (IRIN, "Kenya: Clashes, Elections, and Land: Church Keeps Watch in Molo," 19 July 2007, posted at www.irinnews.org [accessed 1 August 2008]). As of January 2008, there were still fifty "volatile" IDP camps ("congested sites") in Molo, full of displaced people from Molo itself (IRIN, "Kenya: Concern over Molo IDPs as Camp Closures Continue," 24 January 2008 [accessed 1 May 2013]).

[13] "Kuresoi Analysis Report," 16 May 2007, posted at NRC-IDMC, www.internal-displaced.org (accessed 12 August 2008).

constituencies who had been settled during the Moi years.[14] Some Moi-era allocations of SFT land were also withdrawn. One example was the January 2005 revocation of 3,000 acres of SFT land at Kanyarkwat in Trans-Nzoia District, to the anger of Pokot farmers.

If a statist land tenure regime means that land politics will be played out at the national scale, then this should be visible not only in the electoral arena but also in other arenas of national-level politics. This is indeed the case. Land policy emerged as a lightning rod of conflict in the national political arena with creation of the Ndungu Commission by Kibaki in 2003–2004, the release of its findings in 2004, and the setting in motion of a land-policy reform process that was deeply intertwined with the struggle over the national constitution itself.

In April 2005, an article entitled "Kenyans Are 'Free to Live Anywhere'" appeared in *The Nation* (Nairobi).[15] It opened with "Kenyans have the right to live anywhere in the country, the Government has reaffirmed.... Kenyans have a right to buy property, reside, conduct business, live and die anywhere in Kenya. Kenya belongs to all Kenyans." The Kibaki government's position in 2002–2007 was an explicit repudiation of the so-called Majimboist political platform that was promoted by the Moi government in the 1990s and that had been promoted by the opposition party, KADU, in 1960–1963. Majimboism in both periods was, to a very large extent, about reasserting the primacy of indigenous land claims to the Rift. Battle lines in the geopolitically strategic Rift Valley Province in the 1990s and after 2000 largely followed the line of cleavage defined by this long-standing conflict over state-allocated land rights.

CÔTE D'IVOIRE: 1990–2010

> Just like Gbagbo, [Zimbabwe President Robert] Mugabe said to his people,
> "The land is yours!" (FPI official, Abidjan, 15 October 2010)

Chapter 5 traced the imposition of a statist land tenure regime in southwestern Côte d'Ivoire, and forging of the Bété ethnic identity in the crucible of what indigenous communities experienced as land-rights dispossession. Settlers in the Ivoirian southwest lived as protected clients of the state. These arrangements were a long-standing source of grievance in this region, finding expression in a 1970 uprising that was ruthlessly repressed by the regime, producing 4,000 deaths by the government's own count. Autochthonous communities' perception of their growing exclusion from access to land was heightened in the 1980s by the closing of the land frontier. Near social crisis resulted in the villages throughout the west when families were unable to offer farmland to

---

[14] See Kenya Land Alliance 2005b. "New Security Plan for Mau Forest," *The Nation*, 12 June 2005 reports that 30,000 were evicted from the Mau Forest.
[15] *The Nation*, 1 April 2005, posted at allafrica.com (accessed 31 March 2005). The Citizens' Coalition for Constitutional Change Model Constitution of 1997 included almost this exact clause (see Mutunga 1999).

sons and daughters who followed the government's instruction for unemployed youth to "return to the land." Many or perhaps most returnees found that their parents had ceded land (either willingly or under government pressure) to outsiders who now refused to give it up. Representatives of the central state – in the persons of the prefectorial corps, ruling-party politicians, the gendarmerie, and the president himself, who argued that "the land belongs to whomever is making it productive" – backed the settlers.

With Côte d'Ivoire's return to multipartism in 1990, this statist LTR defined the main axis of political competition across most of southwestern Côte d'Ivoire.[16] The focal point of the autochthones' grievances in southwestern Côte d'Ivoire was the legacy of land-rights dispossession under the Houphouet regime. The vehicle for the expression of these grievances was the Front Populaire Ivoirien (FPI), which inaugurated its electoral campaign in Gagnoa on the site of one of the mass graves from the 1970 Bété uprising.[17] The "consistent stance" of the FPI since the 1980s had been that indigenous Ivoirians should reclaim the land (HRW 2003). It attracted the support of most autochthones in the center-west.[18] After decades of repression, they found the cost of *voice* lowered dramatically by political liberalization. The political entrepreneur who was able to capitalize on their grievances was Laurent Gbagbo, professor of history at the national university, longtime democracy advocate and opponent of Félix Houphouet-Boigny, and native of Ouragahio, Department of Gagnoa, at the heart of Bété region.

Gbagbo's party drew a direct link between the question of party control over the national government on the one hand, and the question of distribution of land rights in the southwest on the other. The FPI denounced the Houphouet regime's distribution of voter cards to foreigners and individuals of "dubious citizenship," arguing that it was only the protection of the ruling PDCI that had allowed noncitizens and ethnic strangers – above all the Baoulé clients of the regime – to establish control over so much land in the regions of Gagnoa, San Pedro, and the far west, and only the electoral support of the foreigners that kept the PDCI in power. The core supporters of the FPI believed that overturning the PDCI regime at the national level would lead to a redistribution (restitution) of land rights, in their favor, in their home region.

On the other side of the political cleavage running through the region were the settlers, a category that included both ethnic outsiders from other parts of Côte d'Ivoire and non-Ivoirians from Burkina Faso and Mali. They had

---

[16] That is, the south-center around Divo and Gagnoa, the so-called *pays Bété*, that has been the focus of our analysis, as well as the southwest proper (San Pedro) and the Far West (Région des Montagnes).

[17] Lewis 2003, 15. These sites were used consistently. For an account of a Front Populaire Ivoirien (FPI) meeting at Gnagbodougou, one of the 1970 mass graves, see Franck Mamadou Bamba, "Gagnoa: Abou Drahamane [n. 2 du FPI] Sangaré dans le Guébie," *La Voie*, n. 1036 du 8 mars 1995, 3.

[18] Dozon 1997, 794.

gained access to land under the land-pioneering policies and practices of the Houphouet regime. Houphouet and his successor at the helm of the PDCI, Henri Konan Bédié, relied on the votes of these in-migrants, including the foreigners who had registered and voted for the ruling party since the 1960s, to guarantee victory in the 1990 (presidential), 1993 (legislative), and 1995 (presidential) elections in this region. The PDCI mobilized its voters in these regions with the threat that if the PDCI lost at the polls, they would lose their property. Chauveau underscored the land clientelism that bound the foreigners, especially, to the state:

[This was] the social pact between the non-Ivorian in-migrants and the party-state: they received protected access to land in exchange for their support for the PDCI.... The instruction to vote for the PDCI (*la consigne de vôte*) was tinged with the threat, for the Burkinabè, Maliens, and Guineéns, of expulsion from their land if the FPI took power.[19]

Land Threats and Promises in the 1990s Campaigns

Campaigning in the elections of 1990 and 1995, and in the run-up to the 2000 election, was saturated with land threats, land promises, and explicit invocation of past land allocations and grievances.

The PDCI under Houphouet in 1990, and under his successor, Bédié, in 1995, aligned starkly with the settlers it had implanted in the west, as predicted by our theory. The ruling party both backed the in-migrants (both non-Ivoirians and the Ivoirian ethnic strangers in the West) and threatened them with revocation of their state-granted land rights if they did not toe the party line. The FPI newspaper, *La Voie*, eagerly reported on such tactics, accusing the ruling party of threatening the foreigners in order to secure their votes and of fomenting tribalism.

The leader of the Burkinabè community in Bouaké, M. Zerbo Ousmane, was quoted in *La Voie* as saying that his community had received voter cards and voted for the PDCI in 1990. As Burkinabè leaders, "we were told by the PDCI mayor and the party notables to spread the word to our relatives at funerals, the mosque, and during baptisms and marriages that Laurent Gbagbo had come to kick us out."[20] *La Voie* profited from this testimony, using it to accuse the PDCI of relying on foreigners' votes to win the election.

The same source recounted ominous warnings that the PDCI directed at Baoulé (and Agni) settlers in the west who depended on the regime's protection. *La Voie* used this as grounds to accuse the PDCI of tribalism.

The PDCI's land threats seemed designed to keep the settlers in line: "In the 1990 municipal elections, the deputy of the Duédoué circumscription (and

---

[19] Chauveau 2000, 104, 111. According to Chauveau, foreigners' right to vote was officially revoked after 1990, but a large number still voted in 1995.

[20] See Tayoro 2003, 10.

former Minister of Mines), M. Paul Gui Dibo, reportedly told the peasants occupying a classified forest (where they had been farming since 1923), 'if you do not elect me, you will not have a single patch of grass to cultivate. I will take away all your land.'"[21] In the same vein, the FPI newspaper reported that in Grand Lahou, *allogènes gros planteurs* (Baoulé owners of large plantations) who were installed in the classified forest of Gô "live every day under the threat of expulsion. They are a voting constituency of the PDCI deputy and the mayor of the constituency of which they are not legally a part."[22] *La Voie* claimed that throughout the cocoa regions of the southwest and center-west, the PDCI rallied its electoral clientele by saying that "the Bété want to snatch away the Baoulés' holdings."[23] In the Baoulé and Agni villages around Gagnoa, the *La Voie* reporters quoted the PDCI barons as mobilizing settlers with the threat that "if the FPI takes power, the Bété will chase you out and take your property."

At Guibéroua, in the *campement* "Petit-Bongouanou," M. Joachim Yoro was come upon in 1994 while he was in the middle of telling the Akans (Agni and Baoulé) living in this *campement* that if they ever let the PDCI lose power, his own brothers [Yoro is a Bété PDCI cadre] would chase them off this land and off their plantations. He delivered this message in the presence of the third adjoint [deputy] of the mayor of Guibéroua, the *sous-prefet*, and the commander of the local brigade of the *gendarmerie*.[24]

The FPI described Baoulé settlers in the satellite *campements* around the Bété villages as "the hostages of PDCI politicians."[25] This captures our basic argument about the relationship between settlers and government under a statist LTR. The politically contingent nature of the settlers' land rights, and their dependency on the center, is a not-so-subtle constraint on their freedom of political action.

PDCI efforts on behalf of its clients in the center-west extended to arming Baoulé settlers in some localities.[26] According to *La Voie*, the PDCI never

---

[21] Felix Teha Dessrait, "Forêt classée de Duékoué – Conflit SODEFOR-Riverains," *La Voie*, n. 535 des 3–4 juillet 2003, 5.

[22] "Grand Lahou: Elections Générales: La question du Gô divise la classe politique," *La Voie*, 1037 du 9 mars 1995, 7.

[23] *La Voie*, n. 1171 du 23 août 1995, 3.

[24] César Etou and Bamba F. Mamadou, "Incidents survenus lors de l'élection presidentielle à Gagnoa," Guibéroua et Bayota: 10 morts, 10.000 déplacés dans un conflit stupide," *La Voie*, n. 1232 du 2 novembre 1995, 6–7, 10.

[25] Ibid.

[26] In 1990 and 1995, the PDCI also employed the "closed district" strategy of trying to prevent the opposition from campaigning in some rural localities, using the chiefs as their local enforcers in, for example, the Far West and around Béoumi. According to Freedom Neruda ("Sémien: C'était beau," *La Voie*, n. 389 du 6 janvier 1993, 10) on the occasion of an FPI rally in Sémien, a canton of nine villages in the *sous-préfecture* of Facobly in the far west, the chief of staff of PDCI dignitary Philippe Yacé visited all nine villages to "formally forbid the notables of Sémien to take part in the festivities. He asked them to not receive the outsiders (*étrangers*) who were about to invade the chef-lieu of the canton at the invitation of the FPI. To assume

denied that some party barons armed Baoulé settlers in the Gagnoa region and encouraged them to defend themselves against Bété attempts to expropriate their plantations in the 1995 elections.[27] Opposition press reports claimed that Baoulé militias were on maximum alert in the Gagnoa region in the run-up to the elections. Around Divo, by contrast, Barbara Lewis (2003, 24) observed in 1995 that most Baoulé thought their land rights were secure "because they were convinced that the PDCI would prevail" in the elections.

Reciprocally, the PDCI consistently accused Gbagbo of exploiting land conflicts in the west for *"fins politiciennes"* (narrow political ends). Gbagbo replied by pointing to indigenous westerners' long history of land grievances against the central authorities. He invoked the massive repression of the Bété in 1970 and referred often to the forced implantation in *pays Bété* of the Baoulés displaced by the Koussou Dam.[28] Gbagbo and other FPI campaigners and militants in the west vigorously voiced and endorsed the indigenes' (autochthones', or first inhabitants') claim to "rightful ownership" of the land and promised to restore these rights once in office.

They correctly perceived that the scope of conflict could be expanded to include other Ivoirian communities whose autochthonous land rights had been violated by the Houphouet regime. Gbagbo made these appeals in 1993 campaign rallies in Korhogo, where locals had tried to protest the government's decision to invite in Peul herders whose animals destroyed Senoufo farmers' crops.[29] He also employed these arguments in seeking votes around Béoumi, where the state had expropriated Baoulé lands for the construction of the Koussou Dam and irrigated farmlands on the shores of the new lake.

Meetings and rallies were held repeatedly on the sites of mass graves from the 1970 massacres of Bétés. In one highly publicized event in August 1995, Laurent Gbagbo attended the burial of the father of Kragbé Gnagbé (leader

their *indéfectible attachement* to the PDCI, [he] made them swear on their sacred fetishes." The reporter notes dryly that they did so "in villages that were not connected to Sémien by a paved road, while everyone milled around in the dirt and dust." On prefects denying FPI activists access to localities around Béomi, in the Koussou Dam area, see Aimé Mian Kadié, who wrote that "PDCI cadres seem to want to keep their regions closed indefinitely to the FPI" ("La difficile pénétration du FPI dans le Centre du Pays," *La Voie*, n. 390, 7 janvier 1993, 3). In May 1995, the FPI press reported that around Divo, the PDCI minister Kakpa Komenan "forces his way into villages to say, 'Do not receive Laurent Gbagbo and the other opposition figures. They want to create a war in Côte d'Ivoire.... If you think that Gbagbo is your messiah, your villages will not be electrified and will not benefit from water systems. And then, too bad for you, your sons who now work in government will be thrown out of their jobs" (*La Voie* du 1102, 29 mai, 1995, 5).

[27] "Tribalisation du débat politique: Le vrai danger qui manace la CI," *La Voie*, n. 1228 du 27 octobre 1995, 2.

[28] "Antipatriotisme, malaise de l'économie, problèmes fonciers: Laurent Gbagbo parle aux Ivoiriens," *La Voie*, n. 1803, 6 janvier, 1998, 2–4; "Foncier Rural: le gouvernement tarde à attaquer le mal à la racine," *Notre Voie*, n. 059, 14 juillet 1998, 4.

[29] Lazare Koffi Koffi, "La visite de M. Laurent Gbagbo dans le Nord," *La Voie*, n. 475, 20 avril 1993, 10–11). Gbagbo made three *grands tournées* in the north in 1993.

of the 1970 Bété uprising), who was interred alongside one of the 1970 mass graves.[30]

Gbagbo consistently denied any plan to expel all ethnic strangers, but he still invoked the power to do so, using his dual position as a Bété and as a member of parliament in the 1995 campaign to remind settlers that their land rights were vulnerable, whether the land was allocated customarily or by the state. In the early months of the 1995 campaign, when visiting one of the forty-four Baoulé *campements* in his own electoral circumscription of Ouragahio (Department of Gagnoa), Gbagbo said, "You see, I have been in power [as an MP] for five years and have not kicked you out; not a hair on your heads or a fingernail has been touched."[31] FPI reporters following the campaign expressed indignation that [non-Bété] PDCI politicians would promise to protect settlers "on Bété land, against the Bété people."[32]

In March 1995, the FPI, in alliance with the other main opposition party, the Rassemblement des Républicains (RDR), announced a boycott of the presidential elections, pointing to the government's refusal to withdraw its new, restrictive Code Electorale.[33] Around Gagnoa, members of autochthonous communities responded to FPI calls to disrupt the upcoming elections through a "*boycott actif.*" Long-simmering disputes over land ownership and political control of territory fused with the immediate struggle against the PDCI's attempt to use the uncontested elections to ratify its hold on power.

Violent confrontations between Baoulé and Bété villages ensued, coming to a head as FPI militants began to block local roads to prevent delivery of ballot boxes. In the electoral constituencies of center-west and southwest, Baoulé settlers were driven off their farms, and their *campements* were burned to the ground (Crook 1997, 235, 138; Chauveau 2000, 115). In Gagnoa, Guiberoua, and Soubre, 345 *campements* were looted and 233 were burned down. The government counted thirty deaths.[34] An estimated 5,000 to 7,000 Baoulé fled the "*tensions electorales*" of 1995 from localities around Gagnoa, Soubré, and communes in Tabou and Soubré Departments (including Buyo, Méagui, Grand-Zatry) of Bas-Sassandra Region.[35] There were also *affrontements* (clashes) in the far west. See Map 3.

---

[30] Robert Krassault, "Gagnoa: Père de Christophe Kragbé Gnagbé, François Kragbé Gnabé a été inhumé," *La Voie*, n. 1173, 24 août 1995, 3.
[31] Robert Krassault, "Accueil délirant our le député Gbagbo," *La Voie*, n. 995, 17 janvier 1995, 2. The number of "strangers' encampments" in this circumscription is from Krassault, "Tournée du Séc. Gen. du FPI à Ouragahio," *La Voie*, n. 992, 13 janvier 1995, 2.
[32] César Etou and Bamba F. Mamadou, "Incidents survenus lors de l'élection presidentielle à Gagnoa," *La Voie*, n. 1232, 2 novembre 1995, 6–7, 10.
[33] Crook, 1997, 229.
[34] "Machinations: Bédié élimine Gbagbo et Djény: Bilan des Affrontements," *La Voie*, n. 1245 des 18–19 novembre 1995, 3.
[35] Babo and Droz (2008, 752) report that 5,000 were displaced, but *La Voie* put the number at 7,000.

According to *La Voie*, two weeks after the election clashes, there were still 5,000 Baoulé in IDP camps in Gagnoa. The conditions of return to their plantations, as reported in the FPI press, were that the Baoulé settlers (a) live in the Bété villages, like the foreign migrants from Burkina Faso and Mali, rather than in the forest *campements* that the Baoulé in-migrants preferred because of the greater autonomy this provided them; (b) recognize the autochthones as customary landowners who never have and never will sell land; (c) disarm (turn in their hunting rifles) and disband their militia; and (d) submit to a local political order wherein the provincial administration and *forces d'order* function as neutral arbiters in the rural areas, rather than as patrons of the Baoulé and other in-migrants. "It would be a grave error to attempt to impose upon us, by military force, the presence of the Baoulé."[36]

Recognizing autochthones as landowners and the related acts of subordination – moving into Bété villages, disarming, and losing the protection of the administration – would mark a clear reversal of fortune for the settlers. Its logical consequence would be that settlers could be pressured into tenancy arrangements with those who had been restored as rightful landowners. *La Voie* reported that on Gbagbo's advice, the "leader of the Comité des réfugiés de Gagnoa, COREGA, responded to those who had driven them off the land by saying, 'We are ready to ask for pardon from the Bété landowners and to go back to our plantations.'"[37] By this point, however, the balance of power had tipped against them, and large numbers of Baoulé farmers were deciding to leave the center-west and southwest to return to their *villages d'origine*.[38] The FPI press did not hesitate to point out to the settlers that the PDCI had failed to send in the army to protect them.

Clashes between Baoulé and autochthonous populations simmered over the years leading up to 2000. The question of disarmament of the Baoulé in the west remained a burning issue.

Run-Up to 2000 Elections: Realignment along the Land Axis

Bédié won in 1995, amid this storm of violence and incrimination, a badly compromised election, the near collapse of the national economy, and fragmentation and disarray among the ruling elite.[39] By then the once hegemonic PDCI had lost its northern wing, centered on Korhogo, which had defected in early 1994 along with some key southern leaders and members of parliament,

---

[36] César Etou and Bamba F. Mamadou, "Incidents survenus lors de l'élection presidentielle à Gagnoa: Les conditions de retour," *La Voie*, n. 1232, 2 novembre 1995, 6–7, 10.

[37] "Le mensonge rattrapé," *La Voie*, n. 1239, 10 novembre 1995, 2.

[38] Babo and Droz, 2008, 754–760; Babo 2010.

[39] With the opposition boycott of the 1995 presidential race, Bédié won with 95% of the vote (with an official turnout rate of 57%). Legislative elections followed but were suspended in Gbagbo's constituency. The PDCI ended up with 146 deputies, the FPI with 14, and the RDR with 14.

including Philip Yacé, to form the Rassemblement des Républicains. What remained of the PDCI attempted to consolidate power by stoking antiforeigner and anti-Muslim sentiment, attempting to paint both foreigners and Ivoirian supporters of the opposition RDR with the same brush.[40] Simultaneously, Bédié and his ideologues repositioned the PDCI as the champion of "pure-blooded" Ivoirians who were supposedly autochthonous to a newly imagined geopolitical entity, Le Grand Sud (the Greater South).

In a massive expansion of *the scope of conflict*, the land ownership question, which had emerged "at the forefront of electoral preoccupations and arguments" (Chauveau 2000, 113), became "the main rallying point for those seeking to promote anti-foreigner ideology."[41]

The rallying point was a new Code Foncier, or land law, that tapped straight into the grievances of indigenous communities in the center-west and southwest. Proposed by the Bédié government in 1997, it was approved by a vote in 1998 and promulgated in 1999, one year before elections that were scheduled for 2000. In a complete PDCI realignment on the land issue, the new Code Foncier formally recognized customary land rights for the first time, unequivocally overturning Houphouet's dictum that "the land belongs to the one who is using it."[42] The new law provided for the registration and titling of most farmland, and restricted the right of land ownership to those who could prove they were true Ivoirian citizens.

The redistributive implications of the new Code Foncier were clear. The law undercut the acquired land rights of in-migrants to the forest zone and laid out legal procedures for formalizing the land rights of the autochthones.[43] The PDCI had pulled the rug out from under the settlers (that is, the strangers or ethnic outsiders) in the forest zone, abolishing the statist land tenure regime that had protected them.

In the words of the Burkinabé community leader in Bouaké who was quoted earlier, the Code Foncier "made a liar of Houphouet" and "broke the bones

---

[40] The RDR was forced onto the political defensive as the representative and political voice of "Le Grand Nord," which included not only the 14% of the Ivoirian population that actually lived in the north, but also the 33% of the southern population made up of Ivoirians who traced their ancestry to the north. By the 1998 census, 39% of the total Ivoirian population was Muslim. In the worldview of the propagandists of Ivoirité, they were outsiders, usurpers, and not "truly Ivoirian" (Bassett 2003a, 19).

[41] International Crisis Group 2003, 37.

[42] On 23 December 1998, the National Assembly reportedly voted almost unanimously for the new Code Foncier (Loi 98–750). Article 1 excluded foreigners from land ownership. The law stipulated that decentralized committees of elders at the local level could be called on to settle questions and disputes over ownership at the village level. In the center-west and southwest, this handed prerogative to local actors who were committed to defining citizenship in terms of autochthony.

[43] Chauveau 2000, 2002a, 2002b, 65; see also Koné 2002, 184. The law would also confirm Baoulé land rights over those of non-Baoulé in the *boucle de cacao* (cocoa-growing region), reinforcing Baoulé land rights over those of Dioula farmers in the Tiébissou area, for example. The government might have pointed to this as creating possibilities for compensation.

of the PDCI."[44] The theory laid out in Chapter 3 does not predict the ruling party's about-face on this issue: it predicts that the regime will align with the settlers it has implanted. One might argue, however, that Bédié had presided over the complete collapse of the old ruling party, and that his regime and that of Houphouet were the same in name only. By this reasoning, the theory's prediction would hold.

The question of autochthonous land rights had been championed by the FPI and had provided Gbagbo with an electoral base in the center-west, the geographic epicenter of land-related conflict in Côte d'Ivoire. With the Code Foncier of 1998, Bédié's government had seized on the property rights question as a wedge issue to reconfigure party alignments at the national level. It made possible the cooptation of the Bété and other autochthonous groups from the center and southwest into a coalition of *Ivoiriens de souche* (pure-blooded Ivoirians). At the same time, the Code Foncier split the opposition along the FPI/RDR divide into two irreconcilable camps, since many ethnic outsiders who held land in the west were Muslim RDR supporters. The Baoulé settlers whose land rights were contested at the village level were collateral damage, abandoned by a ruling group that had lost the will to defend them.

In May–July 1998, the government instructed members of parliament to participate in *tournées de sensibilisation* (awareness-raising or education campaigns) organized by the prefectoral corps in rural districts throughout Côte d'Ivoire. The announced purpose of the *tournées* of the sixteen delegations was to allow the MPs to "sensitize" themselves to the realities of autochthonous land rights and customary land practices. Babo and Droz (2008) wrote that in the center-south and southwest, PDCI politicians used these occasions to focus autochthones' land frustrations on the Burkinabès, Maliens, and Guineans rather than on their "Baoulé brothers."[45] This did not reassure all the Baoulé settlers, and the Code Foncier appeared to add impetus to their exodus from the region. Babo and Droz (2008, 758) reported that from 1994 to about 2000, 44 percent of the Baoulé migrants in the center-west and southwest returned to their villages of origin.

In 2010, FPI cadres referred to the 1998 Code Foncier as the "Loi Gbagbo."[46] This slip in remembering (for the law was sponsored by the Bédié regime) revealed an essential truth of the matter: the land code was built around the central plank of the FPI's political platform, and it gave indigenous (autochthonous) communities in the center-west and southwest much of what

[44] Paul D. Tayoro, "Centre: Bouaké: M. Antoine Konan Koffi (Maire de Bouaké) aux Etrangèrs: C'est le FPI qui a envoyé les policiers vous humilier," *La Voie*, n. 391, 8 Jan. 1993:10.

[45] The International Crisis Group (ICG) reported that in the far west, land-related tension between "authentically Ivoirien" Baoulé settlers and indigenous Guéré was higher than it was between Guéré and Burkinabè immigrants (ICG 2005, 11, n. 50).

[46] See also Koné 2006, 13.

they had been demanding since the late 1960s, if not before: state recognition of autochthones' ancestral land rights.

Aftermath

Barbara Lewis (2003, 29) wrote that "the picture of enormous amounts of Ivoirien property, already *'mis en valeur'* [in production] but vacant by the stroke of a legal pen, excited many Ivoirien villagers, both the presumed winners of the vacated lands and the losers." After passage of the law, local leaders, members of parliament, and youth groups mobilized autochthonous people to assert their newly sanctioned land-ownership rights. As Chauveau puts it, "Conflict broke out" after villagers were informed of the provisions of the new law (2000, 115). Gangs of villagers led by youth seized farms, burned homes, and destroyed the *campements* of those dispossessed by the new Code Foncier. The year following the passage of the Code Foncier was marked by the expulsion of tens of thousands of non-autochthones from the southwest and center-west. In 1999, in the most notorious incidents, some 12,000 Burkinabè farmers were driven out of Tabou in the southwest. Babo and Droz (2008, 755) report that the locals invoked the terms of the 1998 land law in justifying the expulsions. After Tabou, local-level "land clashes" then spread to Oumé, Gagnoa, and Daloa. An estimated 20,000 Burkinabè-origin farmers and farmworkers were expelled from the rural areas of the center-west and southwest over the course of 1999.[47] Authorities in Abidjan and the local police forces mounted tepid, restrained attempts to contain and mitigate the spread of violence (Chauveau, 2000, 116).

The decade ended with the 24 December 1999 coup d'état of General Robert Guéi, a westerner who led a corps of mutineers drawn from northern military and security units that had been disbanded by Bédié. Guéi organized national elections for 22 October 2000; embraced the nativist, southern ultranationalism of his predecessor; and disqualified Bédié and Alassane Ouattara from running in the election (the former on the grounds of corruption, the latter on the grounds that he was not a "true Ivoirian citizen"). Guéi ran for election against the only challenger left in the race, Laurent Gbagbo. In a violent, low-turnout election (with an official turnout rate of 37 percent) that was ultimately arbitrated by pro-Gbagbo military units, Gbagbo was declared winner.

In the first two years of the Gbagbo presidency, expropriations of the farms and crops of non-autochthones spread throughout the center-west and southwest, becoming commonplace and often violent. At the village level, locals acted on the knowledge that previous rules regarding the land rights of migrants "had been overturned" (Koné 2002, 28). Violent confrontations broke out in many

---

47 In fieldwork in villages in the center-west of Côte d'Ivoire, Strozeski (2006, 142) reported a fivefold increase in conflicts between indigenous Bété and immigrant Burkinabè households after the passage of the 1998 land law.

localities. In May 2001, in an attempt to clarify the situation, the Minister of Defense and Civil Protection in the new FPI government stated that the "land belongs to its owner *and not the person using it*" (Koné 2002, 31). It is clear that the FPI government was giving the green light to village-level displacements and land reappropriations.

By mid-2002, 100,000 Burkinabè were estimated to have left the country, with many additional thousands forced off the land and into refugee camps within Côte d'Ivoire. One source estimated that 300,000 Burkinabè were driven into Abidjan (NRC 2010, 31).

We have argued that the statist LTR defined the *political scale* at which the conflict over land rights in Côte d'Ivoire's center-west and southwest would play out. The argument about scale does not apply to electoral politics only. The national army's suppression of the 1970 Guébié uprising is one case in point. Another is the September 2002 attempted military coup against Gbagbo, mounted by northern and western soldiers who said they had taken up arms "to demand their Ivoirien national identity cards."[48] The frustrated putschistes then took over and occupied the northern half of the country. One well-placed FPI cadre underscored the land-related dimension of the crisis, saying that "as soon as they realized they'd lost their land rights, the Northerners took up arms [against the government]."[49]

With the country in a state of civil war, many additional tens of thousands of non-autochthones were driven from villages and farms in the center-south and southwest. The Norwegian Refugee Council reported that 158,000 Burkinabè were forced to leave Côte d'Ivoire in the first six months after the military coup.[50] As a cease-fire between the government and the Forces Nouvelles military-political coalition took hold in 2004, military operations gave way to a period of "no peace, no war." In the center-west and southwest, ethnic cleansing (via displacement mostly) and expropriation of farms orchestrated by local militias and village defense committees continued. It was often encouraged by municipal politicians and linked to the national-level FPI wheels and the FPI youth militia, the Jeunes Patriotes. They took control of plantations, villages, and roads using threats and violence to drive out non-autochthones and reclaim the land.[51]

The Marcoussis Accords "road map to peace," brokered by France and signed by Ivoirians in January 2003, called for revision of the 1998 land law to protect "acquired rights" that predated the enactment of the law, and amendment of the Code de la Nationalité to broaden naturalization provisions. The government did not budge. In late 2003, the International Crisis Group

---

[48] International Crisis Group, 2005, 17. With the assistance of France, Gbagbo and his government survived until December 2010.

[49] Interview, Abidjan, 15 October 2010.

[50] Norwegian Refugee Council 2009a, 10. See also Banegas and Otayek 2003.

[51] ICG 2003, 2004, 2005; HRW 2007.

reported that "the FPI promises its southwestern constituency that they will recover land in the wake of a campaign to identify true citizens and apply the 1998 law" (ICG, 2003, 38). Marc Yevou of *Fraternité Matin* explained that "land rights are also an issue upon which the FPI bases its objection to [the nationality code reforms contained in Marcoussis]. Those who would be nationalized would become land owners, because of their new status as citizens."[52]

RWANDA: 1991–1994

> One man in Cyangugu reported that in his region returnees have aggressively demanded all the holdings they say once belonged to them.... He assessed it in this way: "It is the victor and the vanquished.... You spoke yesterday, we speak today. That's how they take the land." (HRW 2001b, 50).

Rwanda is known to the world for the 1994 genocide, not for its failed "transition to democracy" of the early 1990s. Yet as noted in Chapter 8, these outcomes were layered one upon the other: what happened in 1991–1994 was an aborted democratization, a civil war, a power-sharing agreement gone bad, a coup d'état, a genocide, and a case of land-related conflict, all intertwined in a struggle for control of the central state. Kuperman (2001) captured this in describing President Juvenal Habyarimana's strategy in these years as a "two-track strategy" combining elections and the use of force.

Our theory predicts that when the growing scarcity and/or exclusivity of land rights is structured by the institutions of a statist LTR, it will generate land-related conflict that plays out at a national scale. By extension, when the national arena is opened to multipartism, land-related conflict will find expression in the national electoral arena. We predict that under these conditions, land conflict will be an axis of partisan competition, will meld with other struggles that target the central state to produce a broadening of the scope of conflict (as Schattschneider would predict), will pit state-backed settlers against those claiming land rights on the grounds of ancestral or firstcomer rights, and will align the sitting government with settlers (if that government is responsible for settling them). By this reasoning, the land-patronage relationship that makes settlers clients of the government is likely to be manipulated by state agents to *mobilize* settlers to throw themselves into the electoral fray.

These dynamics, in their rough outlines, are visible in the Rwandan case, even after making the adjustments necessary to account for Rwandan specifics, including the fact that the Rwanda Patriotic Front (RPF) was not a political

---

[52] Yevou 2004. See also Babo 2005, 34; Niada 2005. The government calculated that the changes proposed in the Marcoussis Accords would enfranchise 500,000 people, representing about 8% of the electorate. Finally, the Nationality Code was modified by 2004–662 of 17 décembre 2005, which was changed again by 2005–10/PR du 29 août 2005. Article 43 of 2004–662 reserved a preference in the liberal professions for Ivoirians.

party but an invading force involved in a high-stakes game with multiparty players. Drawing out these points of similarity shows how some broad features of the Rwanda conflict in 1990–1994 parallel features of politicized land conflict in the other situations considered in this chapter, as well as how these situations differ from the counterfactuals examined elsewhere in this book. I deal with Rwanda briefly here and refer the reader back to Chapter 8 for a more sustained discussion.

Land Grievances and Land Patronage under Multipartism and War

Chapter 8 described Rwanda's land tenure regime as starkly statist. The late colonial and postcolonial state exercised a very heavy hand in extinguishing hereditary land rights throughout much (perhaps half) of the arable land in the national territory, and in imposing top-down controls over land allocation and land access. The colonial state sponsored the transfer of hereditary rights to state-appointed Tutsi chiefs in much of Rwanda (Newbury 1988). With the Hutu revolution of 1959–1962, these powers were then transferred to the state itself. State appropriation and reallocation of the land of tens of thousands of Tutsis killed, exiled, or driven into marginal territories in 1959 and 1961–1966 (including the 1963 massacres) extended and deepened the statist character of the land tenure regime.[53] Rural development had the same effect. Paternostre de la Mairieu (1972, 320) cites official sources that claim that in the 1950s and 1960s, state-led land reclamation projects and programs to convert pastureland to farmland increased the amount of arable land in Rwanda by half.[54] Access to this land was allocated by the state, much by way of state-sponsored settlement schemes, the *paysannats*. In the 1970s, the process continued as much of the former pastureland in eastern Rwanda was converted to farmland and parceled out to users on large state-run settlement schemes.[55]

One product of these transformations was a huge refugee population – almost 10 percent of Rwanda's total population. These refugees demanded return to Rwanda. They also harbored terrible grievances against the state, on the basis of their experiences of genocide, executions, exile, expropriation of land and other property, political repression, and general discrimination. Another product of this history was a peasantry within Rwanda that depended, in one way or another, on permissive access to farmland legally owned by the state. This dependency was especially acute in the eastern prefectures, where much of the land was farmed within the tenure system of the state-managed *paysannats*, where some of the Habyarimana regime's most

---

[53] In 1959, between 40% and 70% of the Tutsi population (between 120,000 and 336,000 persons) fled to neighboring countries, and hundreds were killed. An estimated 180,000 were displaced within Rwanda (Eltringham 2006, 82).

[54] See Chapter 8.

[55] Bigagaza et al. (2002, 66) report that 18% of all landholdings acquired before 1963 or after 1978 were allocated by the state. This figure does not include land allocated by the state from 1963 to 1978, the years of Rwanda's state-sponsored settlement schemes.

militant local government officials controlled the commune that owned the land.

The issue of return of the Tutsi refugees had festered for decades. In 1966, the Government of Rwanda had issued an *arrêté presidentiel* (presidential order) foreclosing any possibility of recuperation of lands left behind by Tutsi refugees. The Second Republic did not recognize their citizenship status, thus precluding any grant of a "right to return" on those grounds.[56] Bigagaza et al. (2002, 58) wrote that toward the end of the 1980s, about 480,000 Tutsi refugees sought to return to Rwanda, but that the government had denied them this in 1980, "officially on the grounds of population pressure and scarce land." In 1986, the Habyarimana government agreed to accept some *economically independent* returnees. In 1989, a plan for repatriation of some Tutsi refugees in Uganda was being put in place.

The RPF invasion of October 1990, the central goals of which were refugee return and land restitution, changed the nature of the game, as Guichaoua (1998) put it, but it did not derail the political process aimed at negotiating refugee return. In the spring of 1991, in the wake of a political glasnost that began a year before, policy and judicial reforms helped restart the policy process aimed at reinstallation of Tutsi refugees. At the same time, opposition parties began to form semi-clandestinely.[57]

In June 1991, the one-party state of Juvenal Habyarimana ceded to international pressure to open the political arena to multiparty competition. For the next three years, it fought desperately to ward off the RPF and to consolidate its political control over a disaffected and restive population. The government consistently melded these struggles into one by painting the new opposition parties as accomplices of the invading army, and by painting itself as the defender of the Hutu peasantry and the gains of the Hutu Revolution.

The RPF was not a political party in Rwanda, but its political wing operated on the field of opposition politics, and its presence and strategies interacted with multipartism. The internal opposition parties maintained an ambivalent stance (or "uneasy relations," according to Guichaoua 1998) toward the political wing of the RPF.[58] They maintained an open negotiating stance with the RPF's political representatives. The Parti Libéral (PL) leaned toward the RPF and was strong in Bugesera and the eastern provinces, drawing on support of the Tutsi business elite and Tutsi populations who had been displaced to these regions in the 1960s. It was accused by the Hutu extremists of being the "internal branch" of the guerrilla army.[59] Military and political advances of the RPF could be used to give some leverage to the opposition as a whole. Opposition

---

[56] Guichaoua 1992, 24.

[57] Guichaoua 1999, 326; Reyntjens 1994, 106.

[58] That is, all the opposition parties except the CDR, a ethnicist, extremist party of "*Hutu pur et dur*" (pure and hard Hutu), associated with the antidemocratic wing of the MRND (Reyntjens 1994, 136).

[59] Reyntjens 1994, 127, 185. According to Reyntjens, the MDRP was also considered by some to be rather close to the RPF before its split in May 1993 (1994, 121–122).

members of the 1992 multiparty "government of transition" negotiated the Arusha Accords with the RPF, a process that began in late February 1993. The Arusha Agreement of August 1993 brought the RPF into a transitional government with five opposition parties in anticipation of general elections.

Signature of the Arusha Accords had a polarizing effect on the alignment of actors in the electoral arena. Those who believed that excessive concessions had been granted to the RPF coalesced around the MRND pole. The other (smaller) parties were associated more closely with the RPF, even though the RPF "refused to cooperate fully with the partisan opposition in a strategy that would lead to elections."[60]

By early 1993, military strategies had eclipsed and displaced the electoral process. The Rwandan army was gravitating out of civilian control and was engaged in raising a "popular army" by arming and training civilians. Guichaoua (1998) argued that after the Arusha Accords, the RPF itself leaned toward a military outcome (*un dénouement militaire*).

The story of violence-drenched struggles over political power is accompanied by a subtext that has to do with conflict over land control and access. Lemarchand (2000, 13) writes that with the first whiffs of the prospect of multiparty democracy in the south, violence against ruling-party officials spread in the areas of greatest land hunger and economic inequality. Acts of civil disobedience and land seizures targeted properties that had been given to local MRND authorities by the state, as well as land used by cooperatives and development projects. "In the process, hundreds of Hutu suspected of MRND sympathies were massacred; in return, possibly as many MRND opponents were killed in retribution by *interahamwe* youth gangs." Influential politicians mobilized *interahamwe* gangs to "protect their land from squatters, or 'liberate back' the lands that had already been taken over" (Lemarchand 2000, 13). In pre-genocide violence in Gisenyi and Kibuye prefectures, "elite Hutu exploited the grievances of the poor landless and turned them against their Tutsi neighbors while promising them the Tutsi lands in return" (Bigagaza et al. 2002, 12). Death squad activity targeted at regime opponents of all stripes started early in the multiparty era, when eventual defeat of the RPF seemed more certain and multipartism and refugee return were the biggest threats.[61] From 1990 to 1993, death squads were "directed by a group [close to the regime, and with local operatives at the regional and local level] attempting to put an end to the democratic process and negotiations aimed at ending the war and permitting the return of the refugees" (Reyntjens 1994, 189).

In its general outlines, the case also conforms to other expectations of the theory. Political opening in 1991 gave voice to Tutsi who had lost land rights in the preceding decades and had been forced to take the exit option.

---

[60] From the transcript of Guichaoua's 1998 testimony before the French Assemblé Nationale.
[61] Guichaoua (1999, 326) wrote that in 1992, Habyarimana considered the RPF "a defeated enemy."

Land-related conflict played out at the national level, where the scope of conflict expanded to include social groups, such as pro-democracy groups and the various opposition parties, that did not see the struggle for political reform in Rwanda in terms of the land issue. And as argued in Chapter 8, the role of land tenure institutions in *mobilizing constituencies* is visible both close up and from afar. At the microlevel, promises of land to be retained, gotten, or returned offered inducements for individuals to line up for or against the ruling party in the electoral arena. At the macrolevel, the role of land relations in structuring and mobilizing voting constituencies is visible in the geographic localization of the government's strongest bases of partisan support. The zones of densest and most intensive state-sponsored in-migration and settlement, Kigali-Rurale and Kibungo, were both ruling party strongholds and the zones of the earliest and most extensive mobilization of pro-government militias. The role of Rwanda's land tenure institutions in constituting the core RPF constituency – Uganda-based Tutsi exiles seeking to return – is also clear.[62]

The implications of the peace settlement spelled out in the Arusha Accords, which included a right of return for Tutsi refugees, would have had direct (negative) land-tenure implications for the many land clients of the Habyarimana regime. It is noteworthy that settlement of Tutsi refugees in eastern Rwanda had been discussed explicitly as part of the Arusha Accords negotiation process. Both settlers in the *paysannats* and Tutsi exiles had good reason to think that their land rights would be affected by the outcome of the struggle for control over the state. As Uvin (1996, 14) puts it, "The RPF invasion...ignited fears among Hutu peasants that the Tutsi would reclaim their lands, a fear that the government and Hutu extremists exploited ruthlessly." And as we saw in Chapter 8, this is exactly what happened when 700,000 Tutsi returned in the wake of the RPF victory in 1994.

How would actors' expectations about land redistribution have been shaped if Rwanda had followed the 1993 Arusha Agreement's path of multipartism and national elections? What could the political wing of the RPF have promised and delivered to its constituency had it competed in nationwide elections in Rwanda? Where would the RPF-leaning opposition parties have stood on the land issue, had they addressed this issue directly in a national election? Unfortunately, this alternative history will never be written, but as a thought experiment it helps bring the land-related aspects of the 1991–1994 conflict into sharper focus. It might have been easier to negotiate a power-sharing arrangement at the national level if control over state power had not been so directly connected to burning and divisive conflicts about the distribution of land.

---

[62] Guichaoua (1999, 324–325) underscores the disparate political and economic currents running through the Tutsi exile communities and the Tutsi groups inside Rwanda in the early 1990s. According to him, the land issue was central for the Tutsi in Uganda but not for the others. This probably goes far in explaining splits among the Tutsi groups over strategy, and reinforces my argument about the importance of land issues in explaining the denouement of this conflict.

EASTERN DRC: 1990–1994

> Since 20 March 1993, in the rural zones of Walikale, Masisi, and part of
> Rutshuru, a bloody conflict divides the Hunde, Nyanga and Tembo populations,
> holders of customary power over the land, and the Hutu and Tutsi groups who
> have been present on these lands for a long time, having been brought here in a
> migratory movement organized by the Belgian colonial authorities. (Muhonghya
> Katikati 1996, 47)

> Since the colonial period, the transplanted Rwandans have had troubled
> relations with the autochthonous tribes. . . . There is always a surge of conflict on
> the eve of elections. (Rugenena Mucyo 1996, 33)

In 1990, Mobutu Sese Seko opened the national political arena to multiparty
competition. A Conférence Nationale Sovereign (CNS) was held in Kinshasa in
1991 to serve as prelude to rounds of regional and national elections that were
expected by many to bring about the transition to a post-Mobutu order. These
changes at the highest levels of the Zairian state reverberated over a thousand
miles away, in North Kivu Province. The faltering of the Mobutu regime was
evident in the dislocation of political hierarchies that had structured Kinshasa's
control of North Kivu from the 1970s to 1990 and that had defined the locus
and uses of the state's *pouvoir foncier* in North Kivu for more than thirty years.

This section of the chapter argues that the *fin-du-régime* destabilization
of the political status quo, and the specter of electorally driven shifts in the
locus and uses of the land prerogatives of the state in North Kivu, ignited
a process of mobilization of local and regional constituencies. Constituencies
mobilized along lines defined by long-standing disputes over how state power
was used to allocate land. Settlers who had been implanted in North Kivu by
the state remained beholden to the Mobutu regime. They were challenged by
autochthonous groups who used the recent political opening to raise their voices
in opposition and to demand restitution of their ancestral lands. The ensuing
electoral- and land-related political violence in North Kivu province killed an
estimated 7,000 to 10,000 people and displaced 250,000 during 1991–1994.[63]

---

[63] The focus here is on 1990 to April 1994, and on what are known as the "ethnic clashes of
1992–1993," which opposed the autochthones and Banyarwanda in North Kivu. South Kivu,
by contrast, remained relatively calm. See Pottier 2002, 30, 49, 51. The case analysis ends
with the arrival of the Rwandan refugees/FAR in July 1994. As Pottier (2002, 51) explains,
"The refugee factor was not an add-on to the conflict scene, but rather a catalyst which
reconfigured that scene." Indeed, there is no *electoral logic* per se to the violent clashes *after*
July 1994, as the ex-FAR and *interahamwe* undertook to seize control of North Kivu (some
say to create a new "Hutuland" there). The refugees allied with the Zairois Hutu against,
mostly, the post-1959 Tutsi population, with the aim of seizing their large properties and
cattle (Mathieu and Mafikiri-Tsongo 1999, 61). Through this process, an initial (1990–1994)
cleavage between Banyarwanda/autochthones gave way to a four-way confrontation between
Hunde self-defense militias, Hutu armed bands reinforced or egged on by the ex-FAR, the
Forces Armées du Zaïre and elements hired by the Tutsi to protect their properties (ibid). The
conflict was internationalized in November 1996 with the formation of the (Alliance des Forces

The line of argument developed here contrasts with two alternative approaches to understanding political upheaval in Kivu in the early 1990s.

First, by focusing on the land dimensions of North Kivu's political trajectory, the present analysis stands in direct contradiction to the "weak state" explanation of the regional political crises in Zaire in general, and North Kivu in particular, in the early 1990s. Callaghy (1984, 338–342) and Herbst (2000), for example, would suggest that the Zairian state failed to penetrate its hinterland, or had never effectively reached its eastern frontiers (except to put down rural rebellions and local conflicts in the 1960s). This view emphasizes the weakness of the Zairian state and the enduring autonomy of traditional authority systems in the rural periphery. It suggests that as central state authority decayed in 1990–1994, we witnessed the anarchic resurgence of previously repressed, but basically autonomously generated, tribal and ethnic rivalries.

The present analysis contradicts this view by showing that a key variable in explaining the election-time mobilization in North Kivu, as well as the pattern of political alignment that ensued, is *the institutional reality of a statist land tenure regime that penetrated rural society at the deepest levels*. A key variable in explaining politicized land conflict in North Kivu – as in the cases of Kenya's Rift Valley in the early 1990s, Rwanda in the same time period, and southwestern Côte d'Ivoire in the 1990s – is the land regime centered on state-directed allocation and reallocation of land rights to favored constituencies. As in the other cases, where the central state is the direct author of the existing pattern of land-rights allocation, the prospect of regime change at the national level creates the possibility of sweeping reallocation of land rights at the local level. Constituencies mobilized along the lines of winners and losers in (possible) land reallocations, and the local-level stakes of national or regional contests were defined in land-related terms.

In a second approach to understanding the Kivu crises, land issues are at the very center of the analysis. Many close observers construct a causal chain that leads from the state-led commercialization of land (and corresponding enclosures which extracted land from the customary or peasant domain), to the rapid concentration of landholding in the hands of wealthy clients of the

Démocratiques pour la Libération du Congo-Zaïre (AFDL), supported and guided from Kigali and then Uganda, in alliance with the Banyamulenge of South Kivu. From 1998, the RCD (Rassemblement Congolais pour la Démocratie), mainly supported by Rwanda, took effective control of North Kivu in "the Second Kivu War," also known as the "Second Congo War" (Pottier 2003; Tull 2003; Hale 2005; Kabamba and Lenotte in Mathieu and Willame 1999, 138 inter alia; Autesserre 2010).

    Although the situation on the ground in the Kivus took a turn in July 1994, the national-level story of citizenship/land disputes in Kivu continued to play out on Zaire's national stage. In 1995, the Haut Conseil de la République adopted the report of the Commission Vangu, which reaffirmed the 1981 law affirming that "refugees and immigrants from Burundi and Rwanda" were not citizens and that any claims to property they may have had were not valid (Mugangu 1999, 208–211). Mobutu was overthrown by the AFDL and replaced by Laurent-Désiré Kabila in July 1997.

Mobutu regime from the early 1970s onward, to tenure insecurity, mounting contestation among smallholders over land rights, poverty, and widespread landlessness.[64] The resulting material and social desperation at the mass level was manifest in what Laurent calls *"les révoltes paysannes"* of 1992 and 1993. Using broad brushstrokes to identify the sources of conflict in Kivu, many observers have emphasized the link between land dispossession, food and livelihood insecurity, and political desperation. Pottier (2002, 34 inter alia) underscores the class element in the making of the 1990–1994 Kivu conflict.

The argument here differs in that it focuses less on the class-formation and food/livelihood-insecurity dimensions of the land story (which are acutely relevant to understanding politics in this case) and more on the contestation over the institutional locus of land-allocation authority. This is the variable that links this case to the others in this chapter. An advantage of the focus on land-allocation institutions and *pouvoir foncier* is that it generates a fuller explanation of the political form and political denouement of the land-related conflicts in Kivu in the early 1990s. In particular, it helps explain why land-related conflict in North Kivu in 1990–1994 became an axis of electoral competition and was centered on and ignited by electoral institutions and processes. The institutions that went far in defining the *political* character of land-related conflict in the multiparty era of 1990–1994 were those linked to state appropriation and allocation of peasant lands (and the use of the chieftaincy to serve the purposes of the central state). They were territorial rather than class based and were designed for the clientelistic allocation of land access. Whether the 1990–1994 land conflicts were but one chapter in a larger, ongoing story of struggles over land alienation and class formation in North Kivu is a question that remains open, however, as it does in the cases of Kenya, Côte d'Ivoire, and Rwanda, considered earlier in this chapter.

During Zaire's ill-fated "transition to democracy" in the early 1990s, conflict over land became entangled with electoral politics in North Kivu, as it had in the electoral period of 1963–1965. Chapter 5 described three eras of state insertion of new landholders into existing rural society in the Kivus. In this chapter, we trace the struggle for and against state-allocated land rights in North Kivu through the years of Zaire's aborted political opening, during 1990–1994.

The reach of the state in this province was felt not only in the domain of land tenure per se but also through the multiple tiers of a hierarchically structured administrative apparatus. Zaire's structures of provincial administration designated regional governors, prefects, *sous-prefets*, and chiefs and empowered them by giving them access to economic, administrative, and coercive powers of the modern state. Denis Tull (2003, 432) described the state in the Kivus as a "virtually omnipresent system of political domination.... Indeed, no Congolese could fail to note that he/she was a subject of the oppressive Zairian

---

[64] On the agrarian issues, see Pottier (2003, 2004); Vlassenroot and Huggins (2004, 2005, 7, 142); and Laurent 1999.

state." Governors and prefects named by Mobutu were powerful within their jurisdictions; their autonomy increased as the 1980s wore on, in the context of a weakening center.[65] Under the rule of the one-party state, provincial elites coalesced around and within Provincial Assemblies that linked them to the center and the ruling party, the MPR.[66] Regional elites were also well connected to the central organs of the state at its epicenter in Kinshasa, in the ministries, security services, and national assembly.

Kivu was a populous, resource-rich region, home to a landholding elite and wealthy commercial interests. It was also a region stirred by subversive currents and conflicts over how central state authority was used in the region, which had provoked repeated deployment of the national army and security services over the course of the postcolonial period. Regional politics were manipulated intensively from the center, largely according to a divide-and-rule logic that stoked competition between Rwandaphone and indigenous elites. Echoing an argument that Pierre Englebert made for Zaire/DRC as a whole, Tull (2003, 432) writes, "Political competition among indigenous and Banyarwanda elites never resulted in a challenge to the state, but rather in a struggle for access to resources distributed by the state." In the Kivus, the most prominent of these resources was land itself: "Mobutu's manipulation of land and nationality issues . . . long served as his principal instrument to divide and rule North Kivu" (Tull 2003, 432).

Politicized Land Conflict in North Kivu, 1990–1994

> Managing the political transition has been a question of life or death for many members of these groups [Banyarwanda groups, the Hutu of Masisi, the Hutu of Bwisha or Banyabwisha, the Tutsi]. (Mararo 2003, 167)

Zaire's would-be transition to democracy began in 1990, when Mobutu announced the end of monopartism under the MPR. By mid-1991, more than 130 political parties had formed, some the "legitimate offspring" of the MPR, some brand new, and others the descendants of long-established movements. A coalition of opposition parties, called the Union Sacrée, successfully demanded the holding of a sovereign national conference, or CNS, as a prelude to elections that would eventually be held at all levels of government.[67] The CNS opened in Kinshasa in August 1991. Pro-Mobutu parties and those that gravitated around them were able to destabilize the older and generally more liberal pro-democracy and civil society groups by promoting the principle of *géopolitique*,

---

[65] Willame 1997, 17.

[66] Elections of MPR-nominated candidates to these assemblies were held in 1982 and 1987. The Assemblées Provinciales were "mises en véilleuses" (closed for the time being) at the beginning of the transition in 1990. Elections of 29 October 2006 were supposed to bring them back to life.

[67] At one point, presidential elections were planned for 1994 (Van Acker 2005, 84).

whereby populations in each political jurisdiction of the Zairian state would be represented by their own *originaires* – that is, by authentically autochthonous leaders. *Géopolitique* was presented by its promoters as a Zairian form of federalism, but critics saw it as atavistic (at best) and destructive of national unity.[68]

The prospect of elections in Kivu – that is, of a shift in the locus of control over provincial administration and, thus, over land – ignited political mobilization. The Banyarwanda (Tutsi) elite that was ensconced within the MPR (and had benefited the most from the MPR political machine) organized the CEREA. It was a resurrected version of the 1960s political party that sought to establish a broad base of political representation for Banyarwanda throughout the Kivus. CEREA now sought a presence at the national level as well.[69] This elite could not make it on its own in the numbers game in North Kivu, however, and therefore "was less enthusiastic about the prospect of elections . . . because they feared losing them and along with the elections, the strong positions and enormous privileges obtained during 30 years of [Mobutist] dictatorship" (Mararo 2003, 162).

In the reawakening of electoral politics in North Kivu, Banyarwanda Hutu who had ambitions of their own confronted autochthonous politicians who rose up at both the national and provincial levels to take advantage of *géopolitique*, the new political dispensation gaining momentum through the CNS, which called for representation on the basis of ethnic and regional quotas.[70] This *géopolitique* promised to overturn twenty-five years of Mobutist policy of governing North Kivu through Banyarwanda allies (defined starkly as "*non-originaires*").[71] Emboldened Kivu politicians from the Nande, Hunde, Nyanga, and Tembo groups organized coalitions with national-level political parties championing the new "federalist" dispensation. The most important

---

[68] De Villiers and Tshonda 1997, 160–163. Many have noted that it served Mobutu's interests to stir up ethnic conflict and local disputes, "thus neutralizing any possibility of a broad front forming against the government in Kinshasa" and also weakening Zaire's nascent civil society (Prunier 1997, 42). See also Chrétien 2003, 342–346.

[69] CEREA was brought back to life by Rwakabuba and another 1960 party founder, Jean-Chrysostome Weregemere, an *originaire* of South Kivu. The idea was to regroup the Banyarwanda in this organization (Willame 1997, 62).

[70] Zairois playwright Lye M. Yola (1995, 33–34) satirized this *géopolitique*, mispronounced as "*zoo-politique*," as a system by which even access to apartment buildings in Kinshasa would be allocated by tribal quotas. Domestic animals, when their tribal identity was in question, would be classified by the identity of their owner.

[71] Autochthonous politicians from North Kivu had, until the CNS period, a weak presence on the national stage. They "were never very active or well-known, and some were even distrusted" (Willame 1997, 4). Cancellation of 1987 elections in the Kivus was a missed opportunity for them: politicians from other regions were able to take better advantage of Kinshasa politics from 1987 to 1990 (Mararo 2003). Vlassenroot and Huggins (2005, 145) write, "The democratization process set into motion a fierce competition between former members of the centrally-led patronage network and new political actors contesting their power position." Kabamba and Lanotte (1999, 101 and 101, n. 7) write that the CNS represented a "challenge to the Mobutu regime, the protector and promoter of the Banyarwanda Tutsi."

of these were UFERI,[72] a Shaba-based regionalist party led by Karl-I-Bond, and DCF/Nyamwisi, a party strongly linked to the Nande of the northern zones of North Kivu but with a geographic reach "from Goma all the way to Kisangani."[73] These alliances expanded the scope of conflict. Parties to a land conflict that was hardwired into North Kivu (and to Masisi, Rutushu, and eastern Walikale in particular) found common cause with politicians from other parts of Zaire's vast national territory.

Province-wide, Nande political entrepreneurs centered in Butembo had the upper hand. They rallied Hunde (in Masisi) and Nyanga (in Rutshuru and Walikale) populations around long-standing land grievances.[74] Chiefs who had long basked in the Mobutu regime's protection now scrambled to clean up their credentials as defenders of autochthonous land rights. They did so by scapegoating the Banyarwanda for land shortages, in some cases attempting to revoke land rights granted to immigrants in the earlier period, and intensifying the exploitation and abuse of the Banyarwanda subjects under their authority.[75] Van Acker (2005, 84) writes that this is when the autochthonous politicians of Kivu, some of whom had sat in the Zairian legislature as MPR appointees during the one-party era, "awoke to the need to establish a rural presence in order to rally voters."

Land restitution was the political issue that established a connection between these autochthonous politicians, the autochthonous chiefs, and their would-be constituencies.[76] Willame (1997, 4) framed it starkly: "The native agriculturalists of North Kivu (Bahunde, Batembo, and Nyanga)... now tend to associate 'democracy' with the recapture of what they deem to be their own land and property and the expulsion of those they regard as foreigners." Land was also the issue that provided the basis for alliances among the autochthonous groups, and that was invoked to drive a stark wedge between autochthonous and non-autochthonous groups. The statist LTR had thus provoked the emergence of a *common, transethnic identity among autochthonous groups* as land-rights

---

[72] L'Union des Fédéralistes et Républicains Indépendants (UFERI) was one of the three most significant parties in the Union Sacrée, created in September 1991, but was expelled from it in October 1991. In 1993 in Shaba, local authorities of this party launched a wave of violent ethnic cleansing against Kasai Luba (i.e., Baluba, most of whom had been "imported" into Katanga by the colonial authorities to work as miners). ("Zaire: IRIN Briefing Part I," 2/24/97; and "Zaire: IRIN Briefing Part V: Shaba," 3/19/97).

[73] Mararo 2003, 170–172. DCF/Nyamwisi, or Démocratie Chrétienne Féderaliste, was a Nande-dominant party with presence in government at the national level and member of the *regroupement politique* "les Forces de Renouveau." Its members/supporters assumed control of North Kivu provincial administration in 1991. See below.

[74] As Mararo (2003, 171) explains it, the Hunde were focused mostly on Masisi, while the Nande wanted to dominate the entire province.

[75] Vlassenroot and Huggins 2005, 146.

[76] "Reference to land rights became an integral part of these strategies [of political mobilization and extremist ethnic appeals]" (Vlassenroot and Huggins 2005, 145). They note that the decrease in the top-down flow of resources needed to feed patronage networks further accentuated the centrality of land as a political resource.

losers, and defined the axis of conflict in the electoral arena. Statist LTRs produced similar political effects in the other cases examined in this chapter. And in Zaire as in Côte d'Ivoire and Rwanda in the 1990s, national citizenship was a central bone of contention, precisely because a definitive ruling on this issue would settle the big questions: who had the right to vote, run for office, serve in the provincial assembly or administration (or at the national level), and own land. Nationality was thus a logically prior, although not separate, issue. As Jesse Ribot put it, the nationality question was wrapped around the land question.[77]

One of the first acts of the CNS was to exclude CEREA and all other Banyarwanda participants on the grounds of *nationalité douteuse* (dubious citizenship status). The North Kivu conference delegations, in which the Nande representatives predominated, mounted "diatribe after diatribe" against the domination and exploitation of the province by "Rwandan foreigners."[78] At about the same time, in an attempt to staunch the hemorrhaging of MPR influence in North Kivu, Mobutu replaced most of the North Kivu provincial administration with autochthones, relying on *"un homme sûr,"* Enoch Nyamwisi Muvingi, to manage this reversal of the twenty-five-year policy of appointing non-indigenous allies to executive posts in the region.[79] Mararo (2003, 156) explains that Nyamwisi used the opportunity to strengthen the implantation of his party, the DCF-Nyamwisi (an expression of the *mouvance présidentielle* in the region. In 1991, close allies of Nyamwisi were installed as governor (Jean-Pierre Kalumbo) and vice-governor (Miha Bamwisho) of North Kivu.

Mararo (2003, 163–164) argues that with these changes, CEREA and the forces it represented lost political and administrative control of North Kivu, and that in response, they embraced a nonelectoral strategy for regaining power. Closer to the grass roots in North Kivu, however, Banyarwanda Hutu groups mobilized around the cooperative society MAGRIVI (Mutuelle Agricole des Virunga, established in 1980) to use it as a vehicle for warding off the chiefs' new anti-immigrant offensives and protecting their interests in Kivu more generally.[80] MAGRIVI launched a campaign of resistance to the autochthonous

---

[77] Social Science Research Council Regional Advisory Panel for Africa, Workshop on Citizenship, University of Amsterdam, 20 September, 2003.

[78] Willame 1997, 63. He explains that the final report of the CNS took a moderate and cautious position on the nationality issue. It was approved over the opposition of a coalition of Nande-Hunde-Nyanga-Tembo delegates, which assembled at the CNS and had already contested the nationality of four delegates of Rwandan origin (Willame 1997, 64). On this, see Rugenena Mucyo (1996, 38), who thinks that the Banyarwandas' citizenship rights were basically endorsed by the CNS (finally).

[79] Basemba Emina, replaced in 1991, was "the last *non-originaire* gouverneur of Kivu" (Mararo 2003, 170).

[80] Willame 1997, 63–64; Pottier 2002, 28. Although no Kinyarwanda speakers were admitted to the CNS as political party delegates, a MAGRIVI leader, a Banyarwanda Hutu named Banzira, was admitted. He was the vice-president of North Kivu's "civil society" delegation at the conference. Mararo (2003) focuses considerable attention on divisions within MAGRIVI

chiefs (civil disobedience and some killings and house burnings). Hutu Banyarwanda in Masisi and Rutshuru were encouraged to refuse to pay tribute to
the chiefs and to refuse to recognize the chiefs' authority to grant, revoke, or
collect tribute on land rights.[81]

Outbreaks of election-related violence in North Kivu began in May–June
1991 as the "transition authorities" began preparations for a nationality census (*identification des nationaux*) in anticipation of communal and provincial
elections. This was a reactivation of a 1989 presidential ordinance calling for
a census and was "directed against the Banyarwanda population,"[82] which
made up 25 percent to 50 percent of the total North Kivu population and
about 70 percent of the population of Masisi zone. Banyarwanda communities,
with the encouragement of MAGRIVI, refused to cooperate with the census
agents, obstructed their movements in Masisi, and destroyed their equipment.
Armed groups destroyed the offices of the registration teams and threatened
them physically, forcing them to flee.[83] Violence escalated as chiefs and other
local authorities took action to suppress what they defined as a Banyarwanda
uprising. Laurent writes that for autochthonous populations, the stakes in
the looming local elections were very high: "In localities where immigrants
had become the majority, local (municipal) elections were interpreted by the
autochthonous populations as the [possible] consecration of their disqualifica-
tion [loss of authority] vis-à-vis the foreigners. Autochthones would be politically marginalized in the new, democratic institutional framework."[84] Tegera
(1995, 400) is more specific: "At the level of the rural collectivités in Masisi,
Rutshuru, and Walikale, the objective [of the autochthonous peasant communi-
ties] is the maintenance in place of the customary chiefs." These chiefs were, in
fact, appointed by authorities higher up in the provincial administration. By this
time they had (re)positioned themselves as the defenders of ancestral land rights.

Politicians campaigned on the issue of land restitution and sponsored the
recruitment of landless youth into ethnic *mutuelles*, or militias, to solidify their
presence at the local level. A group of Hutu and Tutsi Banyarwanda recounted
the period leading up to what became known as the 1993 Masisi war:

Even after 1981 [with the revocation of citizenship rights that had been granted to
Banyarwanda in 1972], hatred was not stirred up in North Kivu. It was the debates in
the CNS over the question of nationality that ignited the gunpowder and unburied the
hatchet. Adding to that were the conferences and meetings held [around the province]

between the Banyabwisha, for whom the problem of nationality was less acute than it was for
those implanted in 1937–1950 by the Belgians, and the Hutu of Masisi. On MAGRIVI, see also
Mathieu and Mafikiri Tsongo 1999, 54–55.
[81] Vlassenroot and Huggins 2005, 146. On the conflicts over whether payments to chiefs marked
permanent land sales or just the payment of tribute recognizing the chiefs' continued authority
over the land (and political authority), see Willame 1997b, 102. Here the debates look just like
those in southwestern Côte d'Ivoire in the 1990s.
[82] De Villers with Omasombo-Tshonda, 1997, 269.
[83] Mathieu, Laurent, Mafikiri Tsongo, and Mugangu 1999, 19.
[84] Laurent 1999, 81, 82.

by members of the CNS upon their return to Kivu, and those of the *mutuelles tribales des ethnies aggresseurs* [tribal associations of the ethnic groups that had gone on the offensive].[85]

Politicians promised to restore land expropriated by the central government. As Mafikiri Tsongo explained it,

> Certain leaders of parties that operate at the federal level [*parties à character fédéral*] do not hesitate to promise the Bahunde and Nyanga that they [the politicians] will help them get rid of the Rwandan immigrants who occupy their land, if they vote for them.... [Appealing to the land question was] the surest and easiest way to mobilize support among the autochthonous rural population.[86]

Laurent (1999, 80) makes the same point: politicians used "incendiary discourse that linked property rights to membership in particular ethnic groups," and "promised [local populations] land guarantees on the basis of their autochthony."

A major wave of violence swept North Kivu in April–September 1993, killing perhaps 10,000 and displacing 250,000.[87] Four features of this episode have haunting parallels with the 1990s land-related electoral violence that we have examined in Kenya, Côte d'Ivoire, and Rwanda. First, in the DRC, Kenya, and Rwanda, the provincial administration, with the support of local law enforcement agencies, was involved in planning, initiating, and coordinating violence.[88] Second, youth militias, including many landless youth linked to political parties, were vanguard perpetrators of violence. Third, the explicit purpose of the violence was to either maintain or overturn a land-rights order that was deeply politicized because it had been constructed by a partisan central government, and deeply contested because for smallholders, land scarcity was acute. And fourth, in all these cases, politicians mobilized ordinary people to vote for them and to participate in violence by promising to reward supporters with land freed up by expulsion of targeted groups.[89]

---

[85] Memorandum des Communautés..., avril 1993, 6. On the *mutuelles*, see also Gouvernement de Transition du Zaire, "Livre Blanc," 1993, 3.

[86] Mafikiri-Tsongo 1997, 193.

[87] Vlassenroot and Huggins (2005, 146; 2004, 3) estimate that 6,000–10,000 were killed and 250,000 displaced. Mathieu et al. (1999, 14) say that 10,000–14,000 were killed. The number 7,000 was offered by the Gouvernement de Transition du Zaïre, 1993.

[88] Laurent (1999, 78–79) draws a straight comparison between the 1993 "Hunde uprising" and the 1970 Bété uprising in Côte d'Ivoire, but this element – plotting by the provincial administration against settlers protected by the central government – which was very important in the case of Masisi, was missing in Gagnoa in 1970.

[89] Note also that the population's "ethnic mix" per se is not a predictor of the localization of the violence. Masisi, the epicenter of the violence, was 70% Banyarwanda – overwhelming predominance of one ethnic group should have made this an electorally noncompetitive jurisdiction (i.e., no need to fight). By a similar logic, there should also have been no conflict in Kalehe, where the Rwandan-origin population made up only 12% of the population. Even in Rutshuru, the Kinyarwanda speaking population was only 25% of the total – not enough to

In North Kivu, before the outbreak of the so-called Masisi war in April 1993, the new Kalumbo-Bamwisho provincial administration installed Nande administrators linked to the DCF/Nyamwisi at all levels of government, including in Walikale, Masisi, and Rutshuru. In these last three zones, where Banyarwanda populations were concentrated, Banyarwanda gendarmes and community-level administrators (*commisaires de zones assistants résidents*) were replaced with agents from autochthonous groups (i.e., Hunde in Masisi), and gendarmeries were reinforced.[90] Enoch Nyamwisi Muvingi, closely associated with Mobutu, was assassinated in his stronghold of Butembo on 5 January 1993, just a few weeks before Vice-Governor Bamwisho's tour of Walikale province set off the massacre of 1,000 persons at the administrative post of Ntoto.[91] Violence quickly spread to Masisi.

Identifying the geographic epicenter of the violence that raged in North Kivu provides support for our main argument, as it does in the cases of Kenya, Rwanda, and Côte d'Ivoire: land rights that had been allocated by the central government were the main bone of contention in this conflict. The Ntoto massacre took place in the Wanyanga chieftaincy of Walikale, where Banyarwanda populations displaced from Masisi in the late 1980s had moved in the hope of getting land from Nyanga chiefs.[92] It was followed shortly thereafter by massacres, house burnings, the cutting of rope bridges, and the burning of entire villages in Masisi, starting in Masisi town (the *chef-lieu* of the zone), and then concentrating on the Collectivité Bashali, the precise locus of the "administrative implantation" of Rwandans in 1937–1955.[93] (See Figure 2.2.) The other site of extensive violence in this period was the Bwito chieftaincy of Rutshuru.

make them much of a threat at the ballot box. It is true that province-wide, the Banyarwanda made up about 50% of the population, and that figure is a predictor of election-time violence. However, the Banyarwanda were deeply divided among themselves, along both ethnic and class lines. Even the Banyarwanda Hutu were divided between the Banyabwisha and Masisi groups.

[90] Willame 1997a, 65; Mararo 2003, 171–172. The Memorandum des Communautés (25 avril 1993, 7), tracing the "tribalization of the local administration" notes that in Masisi, one Capitaine Misingi, a Hunde-Nyanga, was placed at the head of the gendarmerie, displacing the civilian authority as administrator of the zone.

[91] Mararo (2003, 171), once again, gives us a close account of politics on the ground: While Kalumbo was focused mostly on Rutshuru and aiding the Nande advance there, Bamwisho was focused on Masisi and was more visibly engaged in grassroots politics. Bamwisho, "interested in the eventual change in the political landscape that would come if elections were held," sided actively with the Hunde and Nyanga. His family had been in a bitter land dispute with Cyprien Rwakabuba. See also Vlassenroot and Huggins 2005, 146.

[92] Vlassenroot and Huggins (2005, 145–146) say that the displacement of these Hutu Banyarwanda happened when Hunde chiefs sold their land to Tutsi Banyarwanda in the late 1980s. See also Mararo 2003, 153–154.

[93] The targets were mostly villagers, villages, and houses. Although most violence during this period was not targeted at large estates, some large holdings were attacked. One example was the *ferme diocésaine* of the Catholic Church of Goma, taken as an institution serving the interests of the Rwanda-origin population. See Mathieu and Mafikiri Tsongo 1999, 45. Herds of cattle were also targeted. These facts appear to link violence to the enclosure process – this

Rugenena Mucyo (1996, 33) noted that the target of the violence in these areas was *les transplantés* (the settlers).

Mapping the geographic pattern of territory *not* affected also helps support the argument that the intense politicization of land rights was focused on areas in which *the central government itself* was the lead author of the prevailing land allocations. South Kivu remained relatively calm during this period (before the arrival of the 600,000 Rwandan refugees in July 1994). The only major violence in South Kivu during this period was in Kalehe, another site of the colonial-era *paysannats* for Rwandans, where "*les transplantés*" were also killed or driven off the land during the April–December 1993 Masisi war.[94]

In May–June 1993, the Mobutu government deployed 500 troops from the Special Forces, and they reestablished order. Mobutu went to Goma himself. In late 1993 and again in February 1994, local NGOs undertook extensive mediation activities in Masisi, "bringing all parties together" in *Journées de Réflexion*.[95] And as Mararo (2003, 172, 173) recounts, because of the war, Governor Kalumbo was replaced by a new governor, Moto Mupenda, who was "less implicated in the land-related conflict." Mupenda was widely seen as the "candidate of the Tutsis." The central state appointed allochthones (ethnic outsiders), most of them members of CEREA and its associated *mutuelle*, UMUBANO, "in force." They assumed posts in the North Kivu government in Goma and on the ground in Masisi (including the Gishari chieftaincy) and Walikale. This was a dramatic comeback for the Banyarwanda Tutsi after their displacement from the administration in 1991: "The war thus permitted the Tutsi to recuperate the political momentum that had begun to slip away with the *remise en cause* of the MPR political machine" in this province (Mararo 2003, 173). As our theory predicts, the Mobutu regime continued to side with the settlers it had implanted.

This provincial administration was in place at the time of the July 1994 arrival of the Rwandan FAR, the *interahamwe*, and refugees. It was the group that handed over power to the RPF government when the Rwandan army arrived in Goma in 1996.

---

type of violence seems to have been more prevalent or a more distinct phenomenon in 1990–1992, preceding the outbreak of ethnic cleansing. See Willame 1997a, 66, 1997b, 100. The Memorandum des Communautés (25 avril 1993, 8) also reports cattle killings in 1992 and the names of villages attacked in Masisi during 9–22 April 1993. Willame (1997b, 100) mentions that the 1992–1993 period of violence included Lubero, a zone of acute land grievances and vast inequalities in the distribution of landholdings, resulting (at least in part) from the creation of huge ranches and commercial plantations, many owned by outsiders.

[94] Rugenena Mucyo 1996, 33. On land rights in South Kivu, see Muchukiwa 2004. It seems that the question of the legitimacy of the so-called Banyamulenge was not first and foremost a question of land occupancy. Arrival of the Rwandans – including much of the defeated FAR – from Cyangugu Province in summer 1994 changed the balance of power. In 1995, the provincial administration of South Kivu decreed that the Banyamulenge be expelled from South Kivu. This was one of the catalysts for the formation of the AFDL.

[95] Willame 1997a, 66–68; Willame 1997b, 100–104.

CONCLUSION

Open competition for control over the central state, as in the context of the post-1990 returns to multipartism in many African countries, can fuel expectations that a shift in the locus of control over the central state will produce a reallocation of land rights at the local level. We have argued that this is most likely to be the case in places where the central government itself is the direct allocator of land rights. This was the case in southeastern Rwanda, southwestern and center-west Côte d'Ivoire, North Kivu in the DRC, and the farming districts of Kenya's Rift Valley. Politicians can use these powers and prerogatives to mobilize supporters, weaken opposition, polarize social groups, and incite action on the part of those who depend on the central state to defend, grant, or restore their land rights.

In Africa today, rural territories governed through statist property regimes are less common than rural territories under the neo- or quasi-customary land regimes, but they constitute significant exceptions to the norm. The modern state has done the most to supersede customary land rights and to assume the role of direct landlord to peasant producers in some of Africa's most developed and commercialized agricultural zones. The state's role as direct allocator of land rights has been conspicuous in the settlement scheme areas of the Rift Valley of Kenya and in eastern Congo, in the zones of state-sponsored in-migration in southwestern Côte d'Ivoire, and throughout much of the national territory of Rwanda.

The general argument advanced here is that in rural political economies structured by this type of property regime, politicians seeking to mobilize electoral support can use land rights as a patronage resource. They can promise to reward supporters with land rights and credibly threaten to revoke the land rights of nonsupporters. Under some conditions (i.e., existence of electoral competition, presence of significant constituencies that can be mobilized around land grievances), politicians may have strong incentives to use land rights in just this way. The specter of property expropriation/reallocation can raise the stakes of electoral competition over the threshold at which the ordinary person "can afford to lose the election."[96] In extreme cases, these pressures can contribute to the breakdown not only of electoral processes but also of civil order.

---

[96] Przeworski 1991, chapter 2; Weingast 2002, 680; and Ordeshook 1993. Ordeshook writes that credible enforced private property rights are a limit on majoritarianism that works to lower the stakes of electoral politics in a liberal democracy. This can help stabilize liberal democracy as long as the general constitutional order, including the property regime, retains legitimacy. See also Riker and Weimer 1995.

CHAPTER 10

Zimbabwe in Comparative Perspective

> Mugabe was reelected president in March 2002 by 56 per cent of the vote. The Justice Minister called it a "runaway victory" that "was won on the issue of land."[1]

In Zimbabwe, a statist land tenure regime (LTR) produced land-related conflict that was, in many ways, isomorphic to the land conflicts observed in the cases considered in Chapter 9. The 1970s war of national liberation was undertaken in part to "reclaim and redistribute the land." It can be taken as an episode of land-related conflict that squares with our expectations about how statist LTRs structure land-related conflict.[2] More recently, during 2000–2005, the invasion, takeover, and expropriation of almost 4,000 white-owned commercial farms (under the so-called Fast Track land reform program) is an episode of politicized land conflict that also squares with our predictions about how and why statist land tenure regimes can bring land conflict straight into the electoral arena.[3] As in the cases examined in Chapter 9, the analysis of Zimbabwe concentrates on explaining the *form* of land-related conflict, defined in terms of the axis of competition, scale and scope of conflict, ethnicity effects, winners' and losers' political options, mobilizing structures, and how the government will align in a land conflict framed in "indigenes versus settlers" terms. In this

---

[1] *The Guardian* (UK), 14 March 2002. Violence and intimidation also played a role in Mugabe's win.

[2] The grievances of the colonial era's land-rights losers did find expression through "voice" in an earlier period – in the waging of the guerrilla war and the broader nationalist struggle against the Rhodesian state, and in independence in 1979.

[3] About 4,500 commercial farms existed in 2000.

case, the conflict was framed by the Mugabe government as pitting indigenous (African) Zimbabweans against white settlers.[4]

ELECTIONS AND EXPROPRIATIONS, 2000–2010

The Fast Track land reform is the main focus of this analysis. It was carried out in the context of election-time struggles for control over the central state, through a vast campaign of violence and intimidation. As in the other four cases examined in Chapter 9, key constituencies were told – or believed – that the allocation of land rights would depend on the outcome of the vote. The pattern of institutional cause and political effect observed in 2000–2005 land-related conflicts is congruent with the expectations of the theory laid out in Chapter 3, which links politicized land-related conflict to statist land tenure regimes, and consistent with the findings for the other cases presented in Part IV.

Some caveats are in order, however, for Zimbabwe does not fit our case-selection specifications perfectly. First, the conflict surrounding Fast Track did not involve competition among smallholders. Second, the Fast Track policy of land seizures was not a response to grassroots (smallholder) demands for the state to evict white farmers from these particular lands. Smallholders and landless people were making demands for land and agricultural support in the 1990s, but these were more general, less geographically localized, and less targeted at whites per se than the regime's rhetoric suggested. Development of multiparty politics in this case cannot be said to have given "voice" to aggrieved peasants who demanded restitution of white-owned commercial farms. Rather, as resistance to the Mugabe regime coalesced and a viable partisan opposition emerged in the late 1990s, radicals within the ruling elite – especially the leaders of the war veterans' organization and the black empowerment lobby – led the charge for abrogating the private property protection clauses of the 1980 constitution, expropriating the white commercial farmers, and redistributing the land to black Africans.[5]

With these caveats, Zimbabwe can be viewed as an instantiation of Part IV's more general arguments about why and how some land-related conflicts

---

[4] In fact, most of the whites who were affected were citizens, and many of the land-access losers were Africans – many were workers on the expropriated commercial farms, some of whom were not Zimbabwean citizens.

[5] Alexander (1994, 338) writes that "the revival of promises of land in the late 1980s and early 1990s was not a response to an upsurge in organized demands for land, but rather to the pre-election insecurity which ZANU(PF) felt when faced with disaffection over corruption and the economy." Moyo (2001) sees the roots of Fast Track in grassroots demands for land expropriated from Africans in the colonial era, although the 1990s grassroots agenda was, by several accounts, not targeted at white properties per se. Mugabe's February 2000 attempt to alter the national constitution to allow compulsory acquisition of commercial farms without compensation was defeated at the polls.

find expression in the electoral arena, and about how variation in the land tenure regime structures possibilities for politics. Zimbabwe also *extends* earlier arguments through an explicit consideration of a private property regime, a variant of a statist land tenure regime. The Zimbabwe case shows that under the private property regime, as under the other statist land tenure regimes, the security of property rights is tied directly to the security and credibility of the government that upholds and enforces them.

The case can be taken as either a "most likely" or "least likely" instance of our argument. Given the black/white *racial* dimension of land issues in Zimbabwe, the fact that land conflict emerged as a central bone of contention in a national-scale political contest has been seen by some as almost inevitable (i.e., most likely), given the bitter history of white settler colonization in southern Africa. This would make the Chapter 9 outcomes the unexpected ones, as there are no white landholders in those cases. Conversely, given the property rights that upheld the Zimbabwean commercial farmers' land claims were *private property* rights, the Zimbabwe case could be regarded the least likely to produce politicized land conflict of the kind tracked in Chapter 9. If one assumed that the de jure security of property rights would dictate the de facto outcomes, then Zimbabwe would be the anomalous case. Either way, the Chapter 9 and 10 cases work together to support the argument that land-related conflicts structured by statist land regimes are prone to election-time politicization, whereas those that develop under the neocustomary land regimes are not.

ZIMBABWE'S STATIST LAND TENURE REGIME

The role of the land tenure regime in structuring patterns of political conflict in Rhodesia (as the country was known before its 1979 transition to black-majority rule) and Zimbabwe is one of the most obvious features of national politics. Under colonial rule, about 40 percent of the national territory (15.3 million hectares, including most of the best-watered land) had been transferred to white farmers and ranchers. A small share of the national territory (less than 5 percent) was held as private property by black commercial farmers. Most of the rest (about 42 percent of total land area, or 16.3 million hectares, home to 51 percent of the population) was set up as "African reserves" (tribal trust land, later called communal areas), administered under colonialism through the indirect rule of neocustomary chiefs who were appointed or recognized by the state and who controlled land allocation within their jurisdictions.[6] With Zimbabwe's independence in 1980, the land held by the white commercial farmers was institutionalized as fully commodified private property protected

---

[6] Munro 1998; Alexander 1994; Laasko 2002, 343 inter alia; Roe 1995. Darbon (1992) refers to the ex-Tribal Trust Lands (TTLs) as the *secteur paysan*.

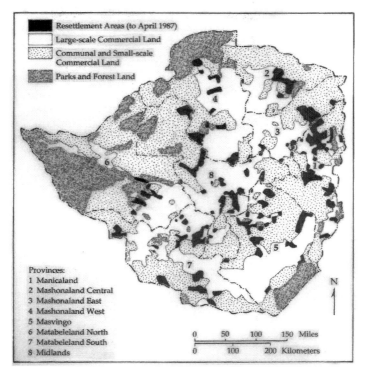

Provinces:
1 Manicaland
2 Mashonaland Central
3 Mashonaland East
4 Mashonaland West
5 Masvingo
6 Matabeleland North
7 Matabeleland South
8 Midlands

MAP 13. Zimbabwe: Provinces and Land Use Categories. *Source:* Zinyama 1998 (reused with permission), redrawn by John V. Cotter.

under the national constitution, as agreed in the Lancaster House Agreement that ended the nationalist war and white-minority rule.

In the first decade of independence, about 3.5 million hectares of formerly white-owned land was purchased by the Zimbabwe government and used to create settlement schemes for about 52,000 African smallholder families (Alexander 1994, 335). In the resettlement areas, the settlers were not given land titles. Land access was mediated through relations of state patronage, putting the settlers in a situation of structural dependency on state agents similar to that of settlers on Kenya's Rift Valley settlement schemes in the 1960s and 1970s.[7] A statist land tenure regime prevailed in these areas. (Map 13 outlines the land-use and administrative divisions circa 1990.)

The pivot of the present analysis is not the resettlement areas, however. The focus here is on the statist LTR in the commercial farming areas. A private property land regime is a species of statist land regime – its "statist" character resides in the fact that private property rights are recognized, enforced, and

---

[7] Roe (199, 834–835) explains that within rural jurisdictions, the land tenure regime defined the form of local government. Decentralized local government in the form of elected rural

adjudicated by the state. Under a credible private property regime, the state is constrained by law from arbitrary seizure and reallocation, and market mechanisms play a predominant role in allocating land. Weakening of such constraints expands the prerogatives of the state, accentuating the statist character of the land regime and heightening the political vulnerability of land-rights holders. This is what happened in Zimbabwe over the course of the 1992–2005 period. The government (a) adopted the Land Acquisition Act of 1992 to give the state a freer hand in compulsory acquisitions of land, (b) shifted land administration from the Ministry of Lands and Water to the Central Committee of the ruling party, ZANU-PF, in 1996,[8] (c) amended the constitution in April 2000 to allow the state to expropriate agricultural land without compensation to land owners,[9] (d) introduced Fast Track land acquisition and resettlement in 2000, and (e) removed individuals' right to challenge land expropriations in the courts in 2005.

The land regime defined the line of political cleavage in the rural guerrilla war in the 1970s – the nationalist guerrilla army fought in the name of dispossessed black Zimbabweans to reclaim land that had been granted to white colonialists. This was the line of political cleavage that Mugabe sought to reactivate and instrumentalize from about 1997. The statist character of the LTR made the central state itself the arena and agent of property allocation, thus locating land struggles at the *national scale* and making *control of the state apparatus* the key to land-rights redistribution. Under these conditions, revolution was a perfect instrument for undoing the land allocations of the colonial state, and in the late 1990s and 2000s, the Mugabe government cast its land policy as completing this revolutionary reversal. The scope and scale of the conflict were thus inherently national (rather than being bottled up at the local level). The commercial farmers, "in the attempt to assert and protect their interests, joined the wider calls for regime change [via electoral turnover],"[10] while all those with a land-related stake in the survival of the Mugabe government had incentives to line up on the opposite side of the political spectrum.

In the late 1990s and 2000s, the most visible organizational frameworks within which people were mobilized for collective action around land restitution were state organizations infused with a national identity and nationalist mandate. The most important of these were the Zimbabwe National War Veterans Association and ZANU-PF itself, the Mugabe regime's tool of mass mobilization. Correspondingly, the struggle against the commercial landholders (and

---

councils existed in the commercial farming areas. In the Communal Areas, indirect ("tribal") rule was the form of local government under colonialism. After independence, deconcentrated district councils dominated by ZANU-PF loyalists existed in the Communal Areas. In the settlement schemes, direct rule was the mode of administration. On the latter, see Kriger 2007.

[8] Selby 2006, 234. ZANU-PF is the Zimbabwe African National Union-Patriotic Front.

[9] This was done by act of parliament. The change had been rejected in the "no" vote on the February 2000 constitutional referendum.

[10] The scope of conflict was broad and included many without land-related stakes.

their farmworkers) was defined as a nationalist struggle against foreigners and aliens.

Opposition parties advocated for respect for the private property regime and against coercive land expropriations, and thus found themselves on the opposite side of a land-related conflict that animated electoral politics for a decade. When a viable opposition party, the Movement for Democratic Change (MDC), emerged in 2000, Mugabe painted it as successor to the colonialist ancien régime and as siding with the white settlers who had received land rights from the Rhodesian state.

LAND HUNGER

Land hunger, created or exacerbated by the expropriation and enclosure by European settlers of the territory's best land, is the backdrop to the story of land-related conflict in Rhodesia/Zimbabwe, starting from the middle of the twentieth century, if not before. Among the Mugabe regime's first major policy initiatives was the purchase of about 16 percent of the white-owned land, subdivision of the large tracts into 5-hectare plots, and settlement of about 52,000 families from the overcrowded communal areas.[11] Seventy percent of this initial wave of resettlement was accomplished during 1981–1983. Grassroots political pressure for more resettlement land waned over the course of the 1980s and then intensified in the early 1990s. Drought in 1992 was accompanied by new waves of land invasions. Chan and Primorac (2004, 69) write of a "squatting movement" that, by the end of the 1990s, affected not only white commercial farmers but also state, church, and black-owned lands. Localized farm occupations in 1998 contributed to the momentum for land redistribution. Moyo and Yeros emphasize land hunger and these farm occupations as an intensifying source of pressure on the Mugabe government, calling them "a grave threat to [the government's] legitimacy" (2005, 182).

The predicament of the rural poor, including the landless, was a backdrop to the politicized land conflict of 2000–2005. It helped keep the demand for land reform (redistribution) on the national agenda in the 1990s, fueled expectations for more land reform, gave state-led land redistribution broad-based political and moral legitimacy, and gave Fast Track reform its populist appeal. However, the Fast Track program was not a grassroots initiative driven by organized constituencies of small-scale farmers struggling with problems of land access (and landlessness). Fast Track farm takeovers of 2000–2005 happened at government initiative. They transferred land to many powerful ZANU-PF insiders and members of the military, as well as to the landless and land poor.[12]

---

[11] That is, by 1990. Selby (2006, 240) discusses the Rukumi Commission report of 1994, which described land pressure in the communal areas as "dire."

[12] The expropriated land was transferred to an estimated 5,000 Mugabe regime elites and approximately 160,000 smallholder families.

ELECTIONS

Land politics played a critical part in the electoral campaigns of 1990, 1996, 2000, 2002, 2004, and 2008. Mugabe used promises and plans of land acquisitions and state-sponsored resettlement to energize the party's rural supporters, and to secure the loyalty of ZANU-PF hard-liners, the military, and rural constituencies. The rhetoric and pace of invasions, expropriations, and reallocations increased steadily over the course of the 1990s, reaching a crescendo in 2000–2005 with Fast Track. After 2005, the main question was whether those holding state-allocated land would retain access to the land acquired through this process.

In September 1994, Mugabe promised to acquire an additional 5 million hectares (10.2 million acres) of land for resettlement, but embarked on wrangling with the British government over who was responsible for compensating farmers for land that was compulsorily acquired. By the time of the 1996 elections, economic recession and structural adjustment had upped the pressure on the government. The bad economy and austerity programs generated hardship, limited the government's ability to expand its patronage networks and to finance land acquisition and resettlement, and fueled discontent that ate away at the political hegemony of ZANU-PF. The regime's land rhetoric intensified. More land redistribution and promises thereof offered a way to "buy votes" in the rural areas, renew the regime's nationalist and revolutionary credentials, and respond to the rising pressure of radicals within ZANU-PF, who, after 1997, gained the upper hand over the moderates and technocrats within the ruling party and government.[13]

The central state's power to seize and reallocate commercial farmland became a focal point of conflict in the late 1990s. By 1997 and 1998, the government was tolerating and even supporting localized land invasions and promising to seize white-owned land as a way of threatening commercial farmers who were lending their support to opposition parties. "By mid-1998 thousands of blacks had occupied white-owned farms, encouraged by Mugabe's threats to 'take' the land and by war veterans, so-called veterans and ZANU-PF party officials."[14]

In 1999, a viable electoral contender emerged for the first time. The Movement for Democratic Change, a party built on the base of trade unions and the urban middle class, attracted much support from those ready for a post-Mugabe era. Kriger writes, "Once the MDC appeared as a contender for power, ZANU PF made land and race the centrepiece of its electoral mobilizing

---

[13] Jenkins 1997, 602; Brett 2005; Kriger 2006, 1163 inter alia; Kriger 2007; Selby 2006, 234.

[14] Boone and Kriger 2010, 179, citing International Crisis Group (ICG) 2004, xii. Alexander 2006 and Sachikonye 2003a emphasize the spontaneity of the 1990s land occupations. These lines and the next two paragraphs are from Boone and Kriger 2010 and were written by Norma Kriger.

strategy and initiated occupations of white-owned farms."[15] In the run-up to the 2000 election and the other elections of that decade, the Mugabe regime argued explicitly that the fate and future of land redistribution hinged on its ability to defeat the electoral opposition and silence critics who sought to curb the government's power to redistribute land.

The government lost a February 2000 referendum in which voters were asked to approve a revision of the constitution that would expand the powers of the executive branch, including the president's power to expropriate land without compensation. White commercial farmers had campaigned openly for a "no" vote, and encouraged their farmworkers – who numbered some 350,000, or about one-third of the formal-sector workforce in 2000 – to reject the constitution. Turnout for the vote was very low (about 25 percent). For the Mugabe regime, both the battle lines and the scale of the challenge ahead became very clear.

Within days of the rejection of the constitution, land invasions of white-owned farms started. They were spearheaded by war veterans, aided by unemployed youth, and received logistical support from party officials, the Central Intelligence Organization, police, and military.[16] Using commercial farms as bases, veterans with their supporters deployed violence and intimidation to punish white farmers and their workers for their "no" vote. At the same time, liberation war discourse, liberation-style *pungwes* (nighttime meetings), and violence were used in the communal areas to prevent the MDC from gaining ground in places where smallholder farming predominated. In April 2000, the overwhelmingly ZANU-PF parliament passed a constitutional amendment renouncing responsibility for paying compensation for compulsorily acquired resettlement land.

In the June 2000 parliamentary elections, ZANU-PF campaigned on the slogan "land is the economy, and the economy is land." The party promised priority in land redistribution to peasants, war veterans and the youth who had supported them during the war, former political prisoners and detainees in the struggle for independence, young agricultural graduates and other professionals, and indigenous businesspeople who demonstrated capacity for farming. The party highlighted its revolutionary nationalist credentials while portraying the MDC as a party of British puppets representing white interests and advocating a return to white rule. By the time of the election, 28 percent of all farms owned by Commercial Farmers' Union members (including black farmers) had been invaded.[17]

ZANU-PF won 62, and the MDC 57, of the 120 contested seats (30 out of 150 seats were guaranteed to ZANU-PF). Nationalist credentials and land

---

[15] Boone and Kriger 2010, 180.
[16] Boone and Kriger 2010, 181.
[17] Boone and Kriger 2010, 181, citing Harold-Barry 2004, 269.

redistribution won ZANU-PF votes, but violence, intimidation, and manipulation of electoral rules and processes also contributed to the party's wins.

In July 2000, the government announced the Fast Track land reform program, with the goal of acquiring 5 million hectares from commercial farmers by December. Fast Track laid out two resettlement models. The A1 model provided small-scale holdings for the poor and landless in the communal areas, reserving 20 percent of the plots for war veterans. The A2 model provided medium- and large-scale commercial farms "for those with agricultural experience and capital to develop the land and repay the cost of the farm as determined by the government." Land occupations became more formalized, and explicitly partisan committees made up of war veterans and ZANU-PF officials assumed control of the allocation of farms and plots.[18]

An official land audit reported in August 2003 that 6.4 million hectares of the 9 million hectares acquired between 2000 and 2002 – nearly double the initial 2000 goal – had been allocated. By February 2003, almost 5,000 farms had been acquired for resettlement.

Mugabe won the March 2002 presidential election that was held at the peak of this process.[19] In the campaign, the president had argued that MDC leader Morgan Tsvangirai planned to return the land to the whites, who were cast as alien imperialists. This point was driven home by preelection legislation that disenfranchised not only many (perhaps most) whites but also hundreds of thousands of commercial farmworkers by canceling their Zimbabwean citizenship. The Citizenship Amendment Act revoked Zimbabwean nationality from anyone of foreign ancestry who had declined to legally renounce the presumptive right to foreign citizenship. Revocation of citizenship in 2002 is said to have affected up to 20 percent of Zimbabwe's population, including the many farmworkers whose parents or grandparents had been born in Mozambique, Zambia, or Malawi.[20] They were an MDC-leaning constituency and had a material stake in the survival of the commercial farms. Manby (2009, 50) writes that in Zimbabwe, the "citizenship issue [was] tied to land redistribution." That is also true in Côte d'Ivoire, Rwanda, and the DRC. In all these cases, denial or revocation of citizenship was used not only to exclude groups from the political process but also to open the door to property expropriation.

By late 2004, about 1,000 ZANU-PF insiders had acquired large farms under the A2 schemes.[21] The names of judges, parliamentarians and their

---

[18] Chaumba, Scoones, and Wolmer 2003b, 603; HRW 2002, 3, 12, 16, 27, 29–30; Alexander 2006, 188–189. On the A2 schemes, Sachikonye 2003a, 240, cited in Boone and Kriger 2010.

[19] Mugabe was reelected with 56% of the vote to MDC leader Tsvangirai's 42%.

[20] Bernstein 2004, 213; Manby 2009, 40–50. The 350,000 farmworkers plus their family members totaled about 2.3 million people in a population of about 11.5 million. By 2002, the denominator, or total population figure, was changing: an estimated 3–4 million people had already been displaced.

[21] International Crisis Group (ICG) 2004, 109. The Zimbabwean NGO Justice for Agriculture (JAG 2008, 7) wrote that "this blatant system of patronage is a double-edged sword. Whilst the

family members, government ministers and their families and employees, and military officers were conspicuous on the lists of grantees. According to Kriger, there is no definitive information about who benefited from most of the A1 schemes, designed for smallholders. One study of a single ranch in Chiredzi District, Masvingo Province, found that a majority of settlers were twenty-five to forty-year-old young men who had left families in the communal areas where they had little or no land. A significant minority were single women household heads, usually divorcées or widows, who had no communal land. Kriger writes that without political connections and ZANU-PF loyalties, it was difficult to get land. "War veterans chose plots first."[22]

The MDC produced a policy document in January 2004 that attempted to spell out its political position on land allocation. "Hedging to avoid alienating the international community and to avoid the ZANU-PF charge that it [was] doing the bidding of white outsiders," the party argued that "the pre-2000 status quo will not be restored, [but that] the current status quo resulting from the fast track land grab will also not be maintained."[23] Chen and Primorac (2004, 74–75) wrote that the party accepted the land seizures as a fait accompli but endorsed a policy of compensation for expropriated property.

By 2004, more than 90 percent of previously white-owned commercial farmland had been transferred to black Zimbabweans (Oxfam 2004a). After ZANU-PF recaptured enough seats in the March 2005 parliamentary election to change the constitution, it continued to remove constitutional and legal constraints to the acquisition of agricultural land for resettlement. The party retroactively legalized the acquisition of land and removed the right to challenge land acquisitions in the courts, made it a criminal offense for a former owner or occupier to stay on the land without lawful authority (in the form of an offer letter from the lands minister, a state permit, or a lease), and authorized the courts to order the eviction of those on the land without that lawful authority.

Destruction of the white farming sector was virtually complete. In January 2007, a state-owned newspaper reported that the government had resettled 231,251 families on 10.7 million hectares.[24]

In the March 2008 presidential and parliamentary elections, ZANU-PF stressed the threat that the MDC would reverse the land redistribution. Forced into a runoff, ZANU-PF conducted a vicious campaign of violence and intimidation focused on both the urban and rural areas, and claimed that white farmers were returning to the country and ready to reclaim their land in the

---

new A2 farmers have been rewarded with the allocation of farms, they do not possess the title deeds for this land, and are thus in a precarious position. Any show of disloyalty can result in the immediate confiscation of their farm. This encourages and ensures their continued support for the embattled regime."

[22] Kriger cites Chaumba, Scoones, and Walmer, 2003b, 547 inter alia; Scarnecchia 2006, 227 (in Boone and Kriger 2010, 183).

[23] ICG 2004, 116.

[24] Boone and Kriger 2010, 183.

event of an MDC victory. An internationally mediated power-sharing deal was signed in September 2008, and the MDC and Tsvangirai entered the government in February 2009. The MDC accepted the outcome of the Fast Track land redistribution as irreversible.

CONCLUSION: PRIVATE PROPERTY AND THE HALF-LIBERAL INHERITANCE

Like Côte d'Ivoire, Rwanda, and Kenya, Zimbabwe circa 1990 was considered one of sub-Saharan Africa's most successful postcolonial states and national economies. Darbon (1992, 125) wrote that Zimbabwe was viewed as one of the rare agricultural success stories in Africa, thanks not only to the productivity of its commercial farming sector but also to the success of post-1980 policies targeted at developing the smallholder sector. At that point, Zimbabwe could perhaps have stood as proof positive of the claim, advanced by Acemoglu, Johnson, and Robinson (2001), and recently elaborated by Mahoney, that the British, being liberal colonizers, had successfully transplanted "features of themselves" (Mahoney 2010 23) in the form of private property institutions to their southern African colony, leaving a colonial legacy of pro-growth institutions. Zimbabwe's trajectory makes it possible to improve on these arguments in two ways.[25]

First, as the New Institutional Economics insists, institutional configurations such as Zimbabwe's private property regime circa 1990 may be best understood as a kind of contract or political equilibrium achieved through bargaining among social actors. Understood as a contract between property holders and rulers, the sanctity of private property would be no more credible than the state that was both party to and enforcer of the agreement.[26] And if the property institutions represented a kind of equilibrium, then as the power of the property holders declined (perhaps as a function of a decline in the value, to the ruler, of their ability to be productive and pay taxes in the long run), their ability to defend the integrity of the contract would decline as well. This reasoning points to the fact that a private property regime, such as property arrangements under statist land regimes in general (or any property regime for that matter), cannot be treated as a juridical absolute. Institutionalist theory drives home the point that no institutional arrangement will persist over time in the face of radical changes in the political conditions underpinning the original social bargain. Expropriations in modern European history are reminders of the fact

---

[25] To restate, in the private property variant of a statist LTR, the state is not the direct allocator of land (although the hand of the state in the primitive accumulation process may be very obvious as it is in Zimbabwe, and as it was for many Native Americans in the United States, for example), but the central state does enforce, adjudicate, and regulate land transactions directly.

[26] As Weingast (1995) pointed out, a state that is strong enough to protect/enforce private property rights is also strong enough to take them away.

that Zimbabwe's trajectory is not an exotic anomaly. The expropriations of the Jews in Nazi Germany and Vichy France (buildings, land, bank accounts, businesses, art, and so on), for example, involved similar disregard for the institution of private property.

Haber, Razo, and Maurer (2003) extended this point about the political manipulability and contingency of private property regimes by arguing that private property rights can be enforced *selectively* as private or club goods, with the resulting rents shared among politicians and asset holders. In an analysis of Mexico during 1876–1929, they showed that the regime of private property prevailed as institutional arrangement underpinned by a coalition of state elites and private asset holders *in a privileged sector*, rather than society-wide. This resonates with the analysis of African rural land regimes developed here: Haber et al. describe variation in the character of the property regime across subsectors within a national unit, and explain how these differences correlate with differences in the relationship between rulers and different asset-holding constituencies. Their description of selectively enforced private property institutions fits well with the property regimes for whites that prevailed under the colonial and apartheid rulers in sub-Saharan Africa. One can see how mass suffrage could destabilize a selectively enforced private property regime of the kind that Haber et al. describe.[27]

The manifest political vulnerabilities of the putatively neo-British property institutions in Zimbabwe and Kenya point to a second weakness of the Acemoglu, Johnson, and Robinson (2001) thesis, and a limitation in Mahoney's (2010) thesis. Property institutions not only assign ownership, they also organize the social relations of production and surplus appropriation. In Great Britain, liberal property institutions created both private property and the British proletariat, and then structured the *combining* of labor and capital in productive enterprise. Apparently liberal property regimes in British Africa did not do this for labor – in this sense, they could perhaps be described as half-liberal. They were thus fundamentally different, both as economic institutions and as political institutions, from the property regimes that were established in the colonial metropole. In the European settler colonies of Africa, private property in land was made productive through *illiberal*, repressive labor regimes.[28] Systems for labor use and control rested in part on the neocustomary land tenure regimes that were established in the so-called communal areas that

<hr />

[27] On this point, see also Sonin 2003 and Acemoglu and Robinson 2006.

[28] Arrighi (1970, 208) writes that Europeans expropriated land in Rhodesia simply by demarcating it. "Africans were generally allowed to remain on their ancestral lands upon payment of rent or commitment to supply labour services. Roder [1964, 51] has remarked on the 'feudal' character of these relations: 'The moment a man had pegged his farm, he regarded the African villagers on it as his serfs, who would have to work for him. The chief means of mobilising this pool of labour in the first years [after 1903] was the *sjambok* or hippohide whip, and after 1908 [it was] labour agreements which committed tenants to work several months, usually three, for the privilege of remaining on their ancestral land.'"

served as labor reserves. The neocustomary sector of these "dual economies" subsidized the reproduction of labor that was used on the commercial estates and plantations (and in the mines), and simultaneously excluded people from membership in a society-wide political community. Such arrangements radically foreclosed the possibility of organizing these political economies along liberal lines (in part through the mechanisms discussed in Parts II and III of this study). The political form of the settler colonies – the colonial dictatorships and apartheid regimes in South Africa, Rhodesia, and Kenya – is a key indicator of the fundamental illiberalism of the British colonial inheritance in these cases.

Predictably, all three countries have been torn by social conflicts that the inherited constitutional order could not contain. Part of the colonial constitutional inheritance in each case was direct insinuation of the modern state in property regimes that engender bitter distributive conflict. Even with the transformation of regime type in each country through decolonization, the dismantling of apartheid, and openings to electoral competition, conflicts over the inherited property regimes have been a wellspring of social tension that has found expression, in one way or another, in system-threatening political conflict and instability.

In Zimbabwe, the Mugabe regime after 1990 disowned the land allocations of its predecessor, the Rhodesian government, just as the Moi regime in Kenya disowned the land allocations of the Kenyatta regime.[29] Although most of those Rhodesian land allocations had been "laundered through the market" over time (as the saying goes in Kenya), they were treated by the Mugabe government as land grants as arbitrary as the most political of Kenya's settlement scheme allocations. This is a bracing fact, underscoring that even private property regimes are never fully or permanently depoliticized.

---

[29] In the other cases examined in Part IV (eastern DRC under Mobutu, Côte d'Ivoire until 1998, and Rwanda under Habyarimana), rulers backed the land allocations that their governments had authored.

Conclusion

Property Institutions in Political Explanation

This book has made four arguments about property institutions in rural Africa. First, they are created, enforced, and manipulated by states (both colonial and contemporary). Second, they are largely authority based rather than market based, and thus differ fundamentally from liberal forms of property. Third, they vary across space, providing the main analytic leverage point that we exploit in this analysis. And fourth, they have political effects – not only on forms of land-related conflict, but also on ethnicity and ethnic politics, the scale and scope of political competition within national territories, the politicization of local resource struggles, and electoral dynamics. This conclusion draws out ramifications of these arguments for comparative politics and African politics.

PROPERTY REGIMES AND COMPARATIVE POLITICS

Secure, credible private-property regimes are absent in many parts of the world. The field of comparative politics has yet to exploit the full implications of this fact. The "transitions to democracy" literature focused intently on the *political* effects of *political* institutions such as formal regime type and electoral rules, yet often ignored what classical political economy regarded as the institutional core of all economies: the property regimes. Transitions studies were built on the general belief that economic and political liberalization go hand in hand, and would work together to depoliticize property relations. Structural adjustment in the developing world and the fall of communism were believed to have liberated productive assets from political controls, weakening rulers and empowering individuals in society.

As Edward Steinfeld (2003) pointed out in a study of economic reform in China, these expectations rested on the assumption that markets exist "underneath" the heavy blanket of state regulation. This assumption is often incorrect. Asset holding, mobilization and use of labor, and transactions are often very significantly shaped by and embedded in nonmarket political and social relations.[1] In many places, political authorities wield control over valuable resources, including property and land-based natural resources, that people require for their livelihoods and well-being. Collectivities and social hierarchies can be embedded in shared ownership and control over resources. By omitting property regimes from their analyses, comparative politics scholars may miss the political-economy determinants of outcomes – electoral outcomes, clientelism, ethnic politics, territorial conflicts, regime type, strength or weakness of civil society – that they have attributed to other causes.

Legally enforced private property rights in agricultural land do not exist in much of the late-developing world, including most of sub-Saharan Africa and Asia, including China, and large parts of the post-Soviet world. Where rulers or their delegates allocate land to users, and where political authorities can revoke land rights arbitrarily, land is a politicized resource or political asset, rather than a politically neutral market commodity. Across much of the world, communities and households use land and natural resources to which they have no legal, enforceable title, or no strong political claim. Boundaries between private agricultural lands, communal land, and state lands are often contested or unstable, blurring distinctions between private and public resources and making use contingent on the forbearance of political authorities. Pastoralists often have no secure claims to the pastures and watering spots that they depend on – they comprise about 10 percent of the population of sub-Saharan Africa, and 5 percent in South and East Asia. Refugees, in-migrants, and minorities often lack any state-recognized access to property at all. Such situations are common in the developing world's expanding cities, where large populations live in illegal settlements on untitled and unregistered plots of land, as Hernando de Soto (2000) has emphasized.

In the post-Soviet countries, political relationships have guided the massive reallocation of state-owned assets. This has created vast opportunities not only for class formation at the commanding heights of the Russian economy (as the rise of the oligarchs has demonstrated), but also for state-building and the consolidation of political power through the strategic allocation of land in the rural areas of the post-Soviet republics.[2] In the Russian Republic of Dagestan, district governors control access to and allocation of as much as 70 percent of agricultural land, allowing political authorities to manipulate citizens' insecure land tenure to achieve political ends (Lazarev 2011). This shapes electoral dynamics in ways that are strikingly similar to what we have seen in some of the regions considered in this study. The competitiveness of elections is close to nil in Dagestan, leaders give and take land as reward and punishment, and the incidence of election-related political violence is high.

---

[1] Engerman and Metzer (2004) show that this is particularly true of land.

[2] Similar dynamics are visible in China. On state structuring of deployment of assets, including land, in China, see Whiting 2000.

When land and other assets are allocated via political hierarchies rather than through impersonal market relationships, voters, citizens, and businesspeople lack the *economic and political autonomy* that is a sine qua non of liberal democracy.[3] Those who do control access to livelihoods and assets have a source of political leverage over citizens that can be deployed to pressure or threaten voters in subtle ways. By contrast, in settings where market relations predominate, the ability of political elites and politicians to assign control over land, labor, and capital is greatly attenuated, and the direct political leverage of political elites over individual citizens is also greatly attenuated.

Where property regimes give political authorities wide discretion over the allocation of valuable resources, the resulting politicization of economic relations heightens the stakes of politics.[4] Control over the state and political office is more valuable than it would otherwise be, because the state allocates resources and decides who holds the strategic gatekeeper positions in the economy. In elections, the prospect of an opposition victory can raise the specter of widespread redistribution of assets, setting in motion political dynamics that are difficult to contain within the parameters of electoralism.

Boix (2003) suggested that in agrarian society, regardless of the property regime, asset holding will be considerably more politicized than is the norm in the industrialized democracies. For Boix, democracy is unlikely in these settings, and unlikely to be stable when it does emerge. Because asset mobility in agrarian society is low (landed property cannot be moved beyond the reach of state, as financial capital can), property holders are especially vulnerable to pressures for expropriation and redistribution. By Boix's reasoning, it is almost axiomatic that an enfranchised poor majority in an agrarian society would use the power of the ballot box to press for access to land. The structural feature of the economy that makes asset holding particularly vulnerable to state-engineered redistribution (immobility of land as an asset) will tend to push politics beyond the bounds of liberal democracy and toward other ideological and institutional forms. Such pressures for state-engineered redistribution are visible at the subnational level in the cases examined in Part IV of this book. Under statist land tenure regimes, victory in elections translated directly into the power to reassign land rights. Land conflict is played out in the electoral arena. This is consistent with Boix's general intuition. Elections in these agrarian settings are *overpoliticized* when judged by liberal democracy's ideal, wherein control of economic assets is separated (in formal terms, at least) from control of elective office.[5]

In a liberal nation-state, the property regime, land markets, and labor markets are national in scope, and reinforce and are upheld by a national

---

[3] McMann (2006) and Junisbai (2009) have made this argument for post-Soviet republics.

[4] Weingast 2002; Ordeshook 1993; Robinson and Verdier 2002, 3–4.

[5] When the illusion of separation, or formal separation, fails (as it often does in established democracies such as the United States), this erodes the legitimacy of the system.

(unified) citizenship regime. Comparative politics scholars often assume that these arrangements are in place when they analyze late-developing and transition economies, especially in countries that have formally embraced market democracy. Land ownership, labor, and capital are assumed to circulate freely throughout the national space, disassociating political collectivities from particular territories and detaching persons and capital from particularistic local norms and social controls. In fact, these conditions often do not hold. Where these integrating institutions are weak or absent, subnational territories may begin to resemble political enclaves, fiefdoms, or "mini states." Citizenries may be ranked and segmented by territorially specific economic rights in ways that *produce* the ethno-regional cleavages that are often taken as purely ideational or ideological artifacts. Political authorities may allocate and "gatekeep" access to markets and productive resources, and regulate movement of persons and assets, in ways that citizens in more fully developed market societies may find difficult to image. Clientelism can be a response to the power relations embedded in these institutional settings, rather than a mindset, or a response to one-off appeals or incentives. These political causes and effects are likely to be invisible when property regime variables are omitted from analysis.

ECONOMIC INSTITUTIONS AND DEMOCRACY

The Congolese politician Wambia-dia-Wamba (1991, 58) wrote, "There is nothing liberal or bourgeois about the organization of the state's authority in the rural areas." The chapters of this book have shown that this is true in much of Africa in at least three ways. Each runs through the property regimes that govern access to land. First, access to land is often very significantly encumbered and conditioned by political obligations and relationships, rather than allocated mostly through impersonal markets. Under the land tenure regimes that prevail in most of rural Africa, there is a low degree of *formal separation* between economic and political power. Sovereignty, administrative authority, and high political status often confer power to allocate property. Political authorities – be they state agents or quasi-customary leaders – wield considerable latitude in deciding how land is allocated, who keeps it, whose rights can be taken away, and who wins in ordinary land disputes. Second, under the customary land regimes, minorities or residents who do not have ancestral links to the area are second-class citizens without full social, economic, or political rights in the jurisdictions in which they reside. This contradicts the liberal ideal of formal-legal equality of all citizens throughout the national space, and the principle of a unified citizenship regime. Third, the state, rather than protecting individual rights (Durkheim defined this as the primary job of the liberal state[6]), is constituted in the rural areas by institutions that enforce *group* rights. The

[6] Giddens 1971.

neocustomary regimes have reinforced the land-based communal identities that were fixed in place under the Native Authority system and other forms of indirect rule. Under the neocustomary regimes, collectivities, not individuals, are the molecular unit of landholding and the basis of many of the politico-administrative relations that tie localities to the state.

Observations about what land tenure regimes "are not" are only points of comparison to other property regimes. A main contribution of this study has been to argue that Africa's rural land tenure regimes are *constitutive of certain kinds of political order*. Land tenure regimes go far in defining (a) the character of the relation between the landholder and the state, (b) relations among members of territorially-defined ethnic communities, and (c) relations among (members of) different territorially based ethnic groups. These are the authority, property, citizenship, and jurisdiction dimensions of land regimes that were introduced in Chapter 3. Viewed abstractly, they constitute basic elements of constitutional order at the local level. Linkages between farming populations and central rulers are embedded in (largely defined by) these aspects of rural land tenure regimes. Implications for liberal democracy and other kinds of politics are multistranded.

Will Reno (2011) observes that although African states have been ineffectual in many ways, they have generally been very *effective* in controlling the mobilization of rural citizens. Many of the institutional and political-economy mechanisms by which this has been accomplished are linked to land tenure regimes. The prevailing property regimes work to impede autonomous mobilization within and across ethnically defined communities, reduce the scope of politics, and make farmers vulnerable to the exercise of local authorities' administrative and land prerogatives. They impede strategic coordination across rural constituencies, blunting possibilities of broad-based anti-regime or anti-incumbent mobilization.[7] By mediating rural residents' access to national institutions of representation and the judiciary, the neocustomary LTRs have worked as a barrier or filter to the direct participation of rural citizens in national politics. By segmenting communities along communal lines and shoring up hierarchy within them, the neocustomary land regimes have also worked to containerize land politics in ethnic jurisdictions, tamp down the scale of politics, and reproduce ethnicity as the basis of politics. These arguments about tamping down politics and the containerization of politics are reinforced (by way counterfactual) in studies of the "nationalizations" of politics that can happen under the statist land tenure regimes. Statist land tenure regimes provide institutional channels for politics to scale-up to the national political arena, and to expand the scope of politics to across constituencies. Under the statist regimes,

[7] This can be taken as a particular instance of a more general phenomenon flagged by Bueno de Mesquita and Downs (2005), who attributed the persistence of authoritarianism in modernizing countries such as China to regimes' ability to impede strategic coordination among potential regime opponents.

property relations are acutely politicized and connected to political hierarchies of national scope.

Politics in these settings are not devoid of ideological, programmatic, and policy content, in contrast to what some political scientists who study Africa have suggested. Those who assert that African political parties and elections are non-ideological or non-programmatic may be looking for the right-left political spectrum that defines ideology in liberal nation-states. In many African settings, however, much political competition may have to do with *whether* key features of liberal order – private property in land, national markets in land, unified citizenship regimes, and unmediated relationships between the state and individuals – are desirable as ends in themselves, and if not, what alternative arrangements politics should seek to institutionalize. Politics can revolve around the assertion or defense of entitlements rooted in non-liberal visions of political order (such as the right to land in an ethnic homeland).[8]

For example, the principle that Kenyans [or Cameroonians, or Ghanaians, or Ivoirians] have the right to live and own land anywhere in the country, articulates a liberal idea of national citizenship. It stands in direct challenge to the political and economic integrity of ethnic homelands. The liberal citizenship principle may serve the interests of those who have the financial resources to buy land, and political confidence that the state will enforce their property rights. Yet the principle of open land markets and of undifferentiated national citizenship may represent a threat to those who are poor, who do not trust the central government, and who do not think they can protect their interests in court. These are programmatic issues that can electrify constituencies and generate intense mobilization, including around elections. Analysts may miss these programmatic and policy-relevant drivers of popular action if the very issues at stake – legitimacy of the market, individualization, national citizenship, private property – are assumed to have been already settled.

Will the state enforce land sales that have taken place as "informal transactions" in the past? Will government protect customary and neocustomary entitlements? If the authorities will not uphold these economic rights, then what others will they offer? Politics played out in these registers resonate in the deep structures of contemporary African states and society. They are intensely programmatic and ideological, often in ways that suggest the absence of a liberal consensus around individual property rights and fully open markets for land, labor, and capital. This is evident not only in the electoral arena in some countries, as we saw in Part IV, but also in policy and political debates over land law reform. Debates over land law reform that are playing out in many African countries raise programmatic and ideological issues – indeed, fundamentally constitutional issues – having to do with not only the scope of markets, but also citizenship, state structure, and the character of state authority. Policy debates

---

[8] This argument is framed in Zeurn's *Politics of Necessity* (2011), which explores the tension between substantive and procedural ideas of democracy in South Africa.

around land law have often been widely participatory, and also socially and politically divisive. In many countries these debates are ongoing and have been inconclusive.[9]

PATRIMONIALISM VERSUS BARGAINED INSTITUTIONS

The idea of rural society in Africa as politically unstructured underlies much theorizing about African politics. Its counterpart is formless conceptualizations of the state. The term "neopatrimonialism" – widely employed in the comparative politics literature to describe African political systems – implies lack of institutionalization, centralization of power in the hands of a supreme ruler, and government through personalized, shifting networks.[10]

In comparative studies of regime type, the African state is often taken as an example of patrimonialism in near ideal-typical form. Africa is held up as the model of what government looks like in the absence of institutions. Once "institutionless Africa" is accepted as a descriptive claim, then, almost by definition, politics revolves around belief, identity, and trust and distrust. Ethnicity takes on an exaggerated role. As a prescriptive matter, institution-*building* becomes an urgent priority, and calls to build new and stronger institutions take on a voluntaristic ring. In the absence of vested interests in an established institutional order, lack of will to build institutions can look like the main barrier to positive change.

The arguments in this book reverse this image of African states and rural societies as unstructured and institutionless. I have proposed a model of rural society as structured by land tenure institutions, and argued that these land regimes are products of the state-making and institution-building strategies of modern rulers, both colonial and postcolonial. This understanding of rulers' strategy contradicts the image of rulers as focused only on power games among an elite, or motivated only by short-term self-interest. It derives from a model that sees all rulers, including rulers in Africa, as constrained by the need to elicit compliance from subjects and citizens (Moore, Jr. 1966, North 1981, Levi 1988, Nye 1997), and reinforces the claim that rulers in Africa pursue state-building strategies that are shaped by the societies they seek to govern.

Colonial and postcolonial rulers in Africa confronted the challenge of creating governed space and eliciting compliance. They have been aware of African populations' capacity to resist overrule, extraction, and land dispossession, and thus their capacity to raise the costs of governing and heighten the risk of disruption and failure.[11] Rulers have worried about ungovernability, unrest, rebellions, revolts, assassinations, uprisings, and rural exodus to the cities.

---

[9] On land law reform debates, see Boone 2007, 2012. See also Shivji 2006; Manji 2001, 2006; McAuslan 1998; and Joireman 2011.

[10] See Gazibo and Bach 2012, Pitcher, Moran, and Johnson 2009, Woods 2012.

[11] Obviously, rural populations have not always succeeded in resisting dispossession.

Cities have presented an entirely new set of challenges; they have been even harder and costlier to govern.

A historical sensibility that is attuned to these dynamics sees cooperation and acquiescence as surrendered by subjects "in exchange" for rulers' restraint, or for provision of some palpable good or service. By the same logic, pure coercion and predation are strategies of rule that are too costly for most rulers to impose over most of the population most of the time. These intuitions underlie the bargaining models of states and social contracts that have emerged from both the sociological tradition and the economistic tradition of theorizing about state formation in Africa (Nugent 2010; Bates 1989, 2008; Azam 2001).

In Africa, agrarian society's productive capacity, combined with its capacity for disruption, has led governments to create and uphold smallholder land tenure regimes in most places. These worked to secure rural acquiescence, provide livelihoods and a social safety net, limit population mobility, and underwrite rural elites allied with the center. Where states wanted to promote peasant (household) production of agricultural commodities and tax part of the wealth so generated, government provided public goods, and regions were more intensively governed. The latent power of multitudes of small-scale land users has been a check on the rapid and wholesale commodification of land rights, enclosure, and massive expropriation. Where government has accommodated rural interests, rulers' legitimacy and electoral strength has derived largely from political bases in agrarian society, and from governing networks that run through provincial elites whose power is rooted in part in authority over land. Africa's newest country, South Sudan, provides fresh support for this claim: the new Sudan People's Liberation Movement (SPLM) government, in the wake of its victory, is seeking the allegiance of local communities by promising to respect their territory and land rights.[12]

If rulers' dominant strategy has been the pursuit of rural governability through the upholding of smallholder land tenure regimes, then this goal has been alloyed with others. Other goals include using statist land controls to solve other pressing political problems and to make land grants to the postcolonial elites (as in the case of Kenya's Rift Valley), achieving more rapid increases in agricultural production and productivity by supporting large-scale commercial agriculture, exploiting mineral and forest resources, creating national parks and other zones that would be off-limits to smallholders and pastoralists, and constructing dams and reservoirs. Rulers have not always been successful in achieving rural political stability in the face of these often competing objectives, but they have succeeded in most places for most of the postcolonial

---

[12] Badiey (2013) explains that the previous government of Sudan often dispossessed these groups, creating grievances that helped fuel demands for southern autonomy. In the new South Sudan, diasporic groups want *national* citizenship rights, whereas many local communities are demanding *ethnic* rights. This mirrors a programmatic and ideological tension evident in many of the land cases examined in this study.

period (often sustaining smallholder land tenure regimes at the cost of other objectives).

This era may now be drawing to a close, however. Land frontiers have closed or are closing. Pressure on the land widens cleavages in society that run along the lines of power relations, economic inequalities, ethnicity, generation, and gender. Neoliberalism and fiscal austerity have done away with many of the old ways of targeting government spending on rural localities. Economic liberalization also quickens markets. In these contexts, land politics often comes to the fore, framing stark questions about the terms of social contract – past, present, and future – between African governments and rural populations.

ETHNICITY AS AN INSTITUTIONAL EFFECT

Robert Bates (1983) wrote that ethnic identity was employed by individuals and groups in competition for the benefits of modernization, such as jobs and schools. His argument can be broadened to include land. Most African states exercise administrative prerogatives to give and take the land of ordinary smallholders – these prerogatives are often and perhaps usually unrestained by the application of law. Under the neocustomary land tenure regimes, ethnic identity has been a criterion by which governments and their local agents (neocustomary authorities such as administrative chiefs) allocate access to land. Deep politicization and ethnicization of this resource are built into the institutional infrastructure of most contemporary African economies and states. Part II of this book draws out this argument and its implications for ethnicity and land politics.

Much contemporary political science takes ethnic identity as a preference or ideology, constructed in a distant past and now acting as an ideational force in the political world. Work on African politics often adopts this approach. In top-down instrumentalist theories of ethnic politics, ethnic identity is often taken as a latent attribute of public opinion that is activated opportunistically by elites, most conspicuously in electoral campaigns in bids for political support. In studies of political behavior, ethnic identity is an ideological or cognitive resource, a preference, or emotional attachment held by individuals. It is essentially prepolitical or nonpolitical until it is activated by elites or mobilized in situations of competition among groups. This study argues that this is a truncated understanding of ethnic politics.

My argument is that when it comes to understanding ethnic politics in Africa, ethnicity is better understood as a juridical status, or a state-recognized or even state-imposed political identity, which operates through state processes. In rural Africa, ethnic identities are grounded in the legal infrastructure of the state, and in the political-economy institutions that allocate access to resources, including farmland. Ethnicity is embedded in the practiced rules that allocate resource entitlements and govern excludability. Strong evidence for this is found in the structure and workings of contemporary land tenure regimes.[13] The neocustomary land tenure regimes have a powerful constitutive effect on the formation of both individual identities and political groups, and they work to structure the coalescing and expression of popular demands on the state. Like the minority identities imposed under Soviet rule, ethnicity in Africa corresponds to internal administrative-territorial divisions established by the central state. And, as under the Soviet system, the system of ethnic classifications was used for "distributing political and economic resources and resolving disputes."[14] Ethnicity and ethnic institutions are institutional-political designations and technologies of rule that states use to govern populations.[15]

A logical implication would be that where there are no ethnic homelands, and where customary authority is not institutionalized in state procedures, there is no politically salient ethnicity. Research in 2011 in the western districts of Manyara Region, Tanzania, provides some empirical support for this proposition.[16] Customary land tenure, defined as supporting ethnic claims to land in an ethnic homeland that is at least partly administered by state-recognized customary authorities, is extremely weak in Tanzania. This is due to the government's choices, starting in the early 1960s, to suppress chiefly jurisdictions throughout all the national territory, *not* to recognize ethnic territories, and to build secular, bureaucratic structures of local government and land administration throughout the country.

Neocustomary land tenure as I have defined it here is basically nonexistent in Babati District and in the eastern part of Hanang District of Manyara Region. In the ethnically heterogeneous localities of these districts, ethnic claims to land and the use of ethnicity discourses in conflicts among small-scale farmers are absent from the public arena.[17] Ethnicity has low salience not only in land politics but also in the civic realm in general. Other researchers have observed similar forms of local politics in rural districts of central Tanzania. Rising pressure on the land heats up farmer-herder competition, but this involves groups who mobilize along occupational lines, as agriculturalists and pastoralists, rather than along ethnic lines. Projected onto the national stage, the implication is that the low salience of ethnicity in Tanzanian politics is traceable in part to the near absence of state-recognized ethnic homelands and ethnicity-based land

---

[13] Mamdani (2006a) makes this argument.

[14] Luong 2002, 17, 52.

[15] This does not mean that ethnicity cannot *also be* a form of identity or ideology, a valued cultural referent, or a political resource. Indeed, it can be all these as well and is often reproduced as such by the institutions and governing practices of the state. As Knight (1992, 81) argues, beliefs and ideologies can be derived from existing institutions and rules.

[16] See Boone and Nyeme, under review.

[17] The case of pastoralists in Hanang District is a partial counterfactual that helps prove the rule – the homeland claims of the Barabaig are present but not deployed overtly as such in political discourse. Rather, they are advanced as claims by pastoralists (against farmers) or as the claims of indigenous people. See the Appendix on these cases.

entitlements. This argument stands in contrast to explanations of ethnicity's low salience in Tanzanian politics that focus on cultural factors (such as the use of Swahili as a lingua franca) or ideological variables (e.g., rulers' socialist ideology) that do not, in fact, strongly differentiate Tanzania from its neighbors in the region.[18]

ETHNICITY AND CLASS POLITICS ENTWINED

Political economists have been preoccupied by questions about the *directionality* of change in African property regimes. In the 1980s and 1990s, New Institutional Economics (NIE) provided considerable support for the argument that land rights would, in the face of rising land values and demographic pressure on the land, "endogenously" evolve toward more exclusive and individualized forms, moving ever closer toward classic private property rights in land. Governments were expected to support this process, or even lead it, as more exclusive and transactable rights would induce private investment, more efficient use of land, higher productivity, higher output, and the generation of more taxable wealth. In this scenario, land would be gradually freed from political and social encumbrances associated with neocustomary tenure. Government, for its part, would surrender its old forms of social control over rural land users, and the sphere of individual autonomy would expand. Via this process, control over land would be depoliticized, land markets would develop, ethnic groups would disintegrate, and social classes would develop. A new kind of African state would emerge.

The reality, however, does not look much like this. Movement toward more exclusive property rights is not experienced by people as a Pareto optimal process in which everyone becomes better off. Transition away from Africa's more inclusive land rights systems looks and feels more like a *redistributive* process. It involves a narrowing and thinning of the systems of "multiple and overlapping rights" that structure landholding and productive relations around land. This process creates winners and losers. Governments, for their part, have not been eager to supply private property rights in land. Government itself would lose direct and indirect political controls over rural land users.

Property rights change involves the exercise of political authority and coercion on the part of partisan rulers, and can produce acute social strain. Across the regions of smallholder production in sub-Saharan Africa today, it is difficult to discern a clear trajectory of change in these processes. The quickening of informal or "vernacular" markets in land rights (which Chimhowu and Woodhouse (2006) define as commercial transactions within the frameworks of

---

[18] Swahili is also a lingua franca in other countries of the subregion. Zambia's Kenneth Kaunda also embraced socialism strongly, as did Uganda's Milton Obote. A refined and improved version of the ideology argument could zero in on how Julius Nyerere's ideology shaped his regime's institution-building choices and strategies in land tenure and administration.

customary land tenure) destabilizes land-use relationships established in earlier periods, but rarely extinguishes preexisting land claims and authority relationships. Markets in use rights can promote the emergence of denser and more complex systems of multiple and overlapping rights, rather than the freeing of land from social and political encumbrance.[19] Berry (1988) and Amanor (1994) observed that in some parts of southern Ghana, property rights are becoming more diffuse and socially embedded, rather than more exclusive, transactable, and concentrated in the hands of market-driven actors. Morcellation of rights is what seems to be happening in Kisii, in western Kenya. Several of our case studies have shown that land markets can develop and then be undone. In center-west Côte d'Ivoire and western Ghana, land markets that developed in the 1960s and 1970s have now been suppressed as the original owners have, with state backing, moved to reclaim land that was sold off in earlier decades. Under Fast Track land reform in Zimbabwe, the government has dismantled estates and ranches held under private title and used much of the land to create a peasantry that will be tied to the state.

Land-related conflict is widespread and increasing in many places, sometimes fueling larger political struggles, as in several of the cases tracked in this study. Meanwhile, top-down land law reform initiatives, such as those promoted by the World Bank as part of second-generation Structural Adjustment reforms, have often been highly contentious, are often stalled in political processes and legislative circuits, and often difficult to put into practice.

The complexity of these processes is surely because contracting and recontracting around property rights takes place within nested hierarchies of political-economic institutions that bind landholders to ranked and segmented communities, to "local states," and to central governments. A main goal of this book has been to depict structure and variation in these institutional configurations in Africa. This has made it possible to connect the study of local property regimes to broader, more institutionalist understandings of regime type and political order, and also expose political dynamics in Africa that have so far escaped comparative and scaled-up analysis.

From this perspective, some of the larger political stakes and strains of property rights transformation in rural Africa come into focus. For governments, the stakes in agrarian transformation are double edged. Governments are ambivalent or hesitant in the face of pressures to enforce and accelerate the full commodification of land. The prevailing land regimes anchor their power in the rural areas, structure rural constituencies and state control over them, and give rulers expansive powers over land management and land allocation. For farmers and populations in the rural areas, growing exclusivity and transactability of land rights is also double edged. Full commodification of land erodes communal solidarities, and exposes individuals and collectivities even more fully to the compulsions and risks of the market. Because of

---

[19] Onoma 2010, Pelissier 2006, Ouédraogo 2006.

the redistributive implications of these changes, they divide communities and families.

This book tracks *political processes* that are set in motion by rising pressure on the land. Social-structural hierarchy and cleavages, and authority relations (state and nonstate) rooted in control over property, go far in structuring conflicts over enclosure and the growing exclusivity of land rights. This study has documented the mobilization of political solidarities and, especially, of ideologies of communal solidarity in efforts to channel and contain the dislocative effects of the growing exclusivity of land rights.

These efforts often force the costs of change onto the politically weakest local residents. In ethnically heterogeneous zones under the neo- or quasi-customary land tenure systems, the costs are imposed on in-migrants or ethnic outsiders who do not have full citizenship rights in the local state. This is the case in western Burkina Faso, western Ghana, and northern Cameroon, which are examined in Chapters 4 and 7. Ideologies of communal solidarity can also rally groups around attempts to demand restitution of lands that have been brought under direct state control in the past, as in parts of Kenya, Côte d'Ivoire, the DRC, Rwanda, and, arguably, in Zimbabwe (examined in Chapters 8–10). Where there are few ethnic outsiders, low-status family members (women, especially widows, and youth) are extremely vulnerable to loss of land rights, as seen in the Kisii study in Chapter 6. Communal solidarities that exist at the molecular level of the clan or family can become narrower and more exclusive.

Communal solidarities and ideologies may also be mobilized to resist land expropriation and enclosure by wealthy and powerful outsiders.[20] Tanzanians refer to such outsiders in generic terms as "investors." Burkinabè analysts write of "new actors" in the land domain. Kenyan land rights advocates refer to them as land grabbers. Often these outsiders are foreign investors and wealthy nationals (often politicians or urban professionals) who have no historic connection to the locality. Locals' best defense against such encroachments may be the invocation of community members' rights to the land in their ethnic homeland. This defense is available as a legitimate discourse for claim making where national governments themselves have institutionalized the ethnic homelands, justifying their non-democratic and non-national character on the grounds of protecting livelihoods and communities that are intrinsically bound to a particular territory. In these situations, asserting ethnic claims to land and territory can be an act of what O'Brien and Li (2006) call "rightful resistance."[21] Ethnic claims can work as part of a

---

[20] This has not been tracked in this study; I have focused mostly on land-related conflicts among established smallholders or peasant farmers. It is noteworthy that primitive accumulation by ethnic outsiders and large-scale land grabbers often happens under the statist land tenure regimes, where rulers exercise direct control over land allocation. Ethnic claims in such jurisdictions have already been attenuated or legally "extinguished," and national governments have a freer hand.

[21] O'Brien and Li follow Scott 1976 and Thompson 1963.

moral economy of resistance to land expropriation and the unfettered workings of the market. In zones of statist land tenure, by contrast, governments can often move with a freer hand to transfer land to outsiders. They
can claim that ancestral or customary rights never existed, are long extinguished, or were never recognized by the state (as the Office du Niger zone in
Mali).

From this perspective, it is not surprising that in the results of recent Afrobarometer surveys, Carolyn Logan (2010) found that Africans support their
chiefs.[22] The finding seems to fly in the face of social science that denounces
chieftaincy and finds administrative chiefs and other neotraditional authorities to be undemocratic, and sometimes opportunistic and exploitative (Munro
2001, Ribot 2004). Chapter 7's case studies support such judgments. Yet our
analysis of African land tenure regimes also goes far in explaining the apparent
paradox: without chiefs, there is no chieftaincy; without chieftaincy, there is no
neocustomary land tenure to uphold one's right to claim land in one's ethnic
homeland as an entitlement, a birthright. This makes chiefs a crucial link in
many smallholders' last line of defense against loss of land.[23] It is also true –
and true for the *same reasons* – that those with chiefly powers are some of
the most notorious land-rights predators in rural Africa. Jack Knight (1992,
208) said that recourse to the power of the state is a mixed blessing for the
weak because they are likely to end up on the losing side of the relationship.
This seems to hold in African jurisdictions where smallholders depend on the
state-like powers of neocustomary authorities to honor and enforce their land
rights. It also seems to hold under statist land regimes, where power shifts at
the top may lead to a redealing of the cards at the local level.

In conflict and change in Africa's rural property regimes, class formation
dynamics and ethnicity dynamics are often entwined. This often happens in
the very ways that Michael Mann described in *The Dark Side of Democracy*
(2005): ideologies of ethnic solidarity can capture class-like distributive conflict and the sense of exploitation, channeling these social strains into conflict
that runs along ethnic lines.[24] The rights of a (poorer) neocustomarily defined
community can be invoked to trump the claims of (richer) ethnic outsiders who
may have established larger landholdings, mobilized more labor, and invested
more capital than most of the indigenes. In many of the regions examined

---

[22] Logan uncovers spatial unevenness in support of chiefs. This is an indicator – partly an effect, I
would argue – of the very unevenness in the character of land regimes that we have analyzed here.
These logics are not unique to Africa. Tucker (2006) applied standard models of voter choice
to formerly Communist countries of central Europe and found that apparently anomalous
regional voting patterns were largely explainable in terms of the uneven effects of economic
liberalization. Economic liberalization produced winners and losers, and in the rural areas that
had largely lost out in these processes, voters stuck by the ex-Communist leaders who promised
to protect them from the full brunt of market forces.

[23] See Mamdani (1996a, 169), who also invokes Chanock (1998).

[24] See also Amy Chua, *World on Fire* (2004).

in this study, ethnic outsiders are among the biggest landholders, even if not all strangers are wealthy. As Chauveau and Colin said of south-central and southwestern Côte d'Ivoire, "The strangers have become richer and richer, while local farmers are struggling."[25] Similar tensions are expressed in western Ghana, where many of the largest plantation owners are ethnic outsiders. In some communities, citizens have begun to debate the legitimacy of ownership of large parcels by individual families, thinking "the land is too much for one person" and wanting to redistribute a portion of it.[26] In these settings, class-like tensions clearly animate land politics.

Yet prevailing land tenure regimes and political institutions channel these social tensions and anxieties along the lines of the ethnic insider/outsider distinction, rather than along class-like lines. The muting of class politics at the local level (and the national level) is at least partly an institutional effect. Local processes of class formation are developing within the context of nested hierarchies of institutions that reproduce ethnicized politics within and across the microterritories that segment and fracture the national political arena.

That ethnic politics often trumps class politics an institutional effect. The institutions themselves are sustained in part from below, as just noted. The main point of this book, however, is that these institutions are created and sustained from above. They serve the interests of politicians and rulers who seek to avoid the politicization of the extreme economic inequalities that divide the "ethnic communities" they seek to mobilize. Klopp (2002) writes of the land barons of the Moi regime in Kenya in the 1990s, who scrambled to save themselves from the wrath of the landless in the Rift Valley (including those displaced by the land grabbing of Moi and his inner circle) by deflecting antagonism onto ethnic outsiders, Kikuyu smallholders, and "land stealers" who had in-migrated from other parts of Kenya.[27] Ethnicity is thus a wedge that deflects and blunts class tensions. These arguments and institutions are not always effective, but they fuel and structure politics.

SCALE EFFECTS IN POLITICAL EXPLANATION

Comparative politics gives analytic primacy to *national-level causes* (such as resource dependence, regime type, GDP per capita, colonial institutional inheritance, ethnolinguistic diversity) of *national-level effects*, such as the quality of democracy, regime stability, or the outbreak of civil war. These formulations omit subnational variables on both sides of the explanatory equation.[28] When

[25] Chauveau and Colin 2010, 94–95.
[26] Alhassan and Manuh 2005, 16.
[27] A similar dynamic was starkly obvious in Rwanda in the early 1990s. Much of the Catholic Hutu elite embraced anti-Tutsi ideology in part to deflect class-based resistance to local forms of exploitation, including the church's seizures of land, and to quash radical and prodemocracy tendencies within the churches (Longman 2010, 211–228, 299–305 inter alia).
[28] Bates points this out (2008, 133 inter alia). See also Gibson 2012.

scale does shift to the subnational level, Africa-focused political science has tended to conceive of subnational-level institutional and political factors as invariant across space. These analytic strategies sometimes obscure as much as they reveal.

This book inverts the usual logics by focusing on structure and variation across local jurisdictions. It identifies spatial variation in land tenure regimes and in the local political arenas in which they are embedded (in the character of local authority, political hierarchy, property-holding rules, citizenship rules, and rules structuring options for those seeking to protect their access to productive assets). Part III extended the argument by analyzing the heterogeneity of scale that is feature of state structure in much of sub-Saharan Africa, and that is visible in land institutions and land politics. Heterogeneity of scale produces disarticulation in the body politic that works to containerize political conflict at the local level, and to impede rural citizens' access to the formal, national institutions of state – be they administrative, judicial, or representative. It is also a structural impediment to translocal political organizing and mobilization.

Analysts of comparative politics could probably agree that there is variation across countries in the extent of (a) spatial unevenness in the character of political institutions and (b) of heterogeneity in the political character of governing institutions at different scales of a national political system (Caramani 2004, Barkey 2008). These are features of political systems that can be taken as variables in cross-national analysis. In African countries, this territorial unevenness is striking.[29] A major argument of this book is that heterogeneity across space and scale is highly salient in understanding the character of national political systems and the dynamics of political representation.

The present study has specified a new variable for political analysis in Africa – that is, structure and variation in local jurisdictions – and opened avenues of research that target the causes and effects thereof (both national and local). One result, I hope, has been to expose the ecological fallacy in the suggestion that in Africa, the local is a microcosm of the national. The standard practice of generalizing about the local on the basis of national-level attributes is based on the assumption – usually unscrutinized – that top-down influences are determinant, and that they exert effects evenly across the national space. In studies of democratization and democratic regimes in Africa, for example, a rarely questioned assumption is that if a government is democratic "at the top" (with national leaders selected by competitive elections), then it is equally

---

[29] This is part a reflection of the agrarian character of national political economies, as well as the weakness – or partial and uneven effects – of "nationalizing" effects such as industrialization (Caramani 2004), central state provision of social services (Chhibber and Kollman 2005), and national regulatory apparatuses (Skowneck 1982). Many African countries are also very large (Sudan, DRC) and/or span starkly different ecological zones (because of the size, shape, and location of the African continent), as is the case for the coastal West African countries, for example, which span the coastal, forest, and savanna zones, each supporting different social forms and systems of production.

democratic, if not more so, in the localities and constituencies where government is smaller and closer to the people.[30] By the same reasoning, breakdown of the national government is presumed to produce anarchy at the local level. The cure for this is power sharing at the top, which is expected to quell disorder at the grassroots.[31] Public opinion data that is gathered and compared across subnational units – provinces, districts, or constituencies – is supposed to represent the views of citizens who are all operating under the same political rules and within the same institutional framework. Indeed, in comparing the views of citizens across regions or jurisdictions within one country, public opinion analysts argue (often explicitly) that they are controlling for, or *holding constant*, institutional effects. Conflict studies have long relied on national-level aggregates, implicitly assuming that "country-level measures are . . . representative for the circumstances in the conflict areas."[32]

The analysis here shows that rural jurisdictions cannot be assumed to be miniature versions of the national (or institutionless), and that they are not all the same. There can be large differences in the political character and structure of institutions across local jurisdictions within the same country. Some local political arenas are repressively hierarchical and may disenfranchise important groups of citizens, even if this is not visible or at work in national-level institutions. Similarly, as emphasized in Part II, second-class citizenship status – more or less discriminatory and repressive in its effects – may be pervasively imposed on "ethnic outsiders" in jurisdictions organized around neocustomary forms of authority, even if such rules do not exist and are not operant at the national level. And as argued in Part III, many "local states" bottle up local conflict, impeding the upward transmission of citizens' demands and blocking access to national systems of representation and justice that are supposedly open to all. Political contestation over ideology or policy that plays out at this scale of politics is unlikely to find open expression in a national party system.

The typology of land tenure regimes proposed in this book identifies political-institutional variables by which local political arenas can vary significantly, both across time and space. It suggests criteria for defining and selecting cases in studies that (a) use subnational data to generalize about national-level

---

[30] Boone and Duku (2012) take on this argument explicitly. Schattschneider (1960) rejected this "national" hypothesis for the United States. See Gibson 2012 on Argentina, Mexico, and the United States.

[31] As Autesserre (2010) argues, by this reasoning, a peace settlement or power-sharing deal at the summit of the political system should produce peace in the localities. However, this has not happened in Eastern DRC in the 2000s. As she explains, this is because many of the drivers of conflict in Eastern DRC are local and land related.

[32] Buhaug and Lujala (2005, 415) identify this problem. Goldstone (2003, 43) puts it this way: "Let us say explorers are surveying a large territory. . . . If the territory has substantial local variations [or] if the territory has six or seven distinctive zones, then sampling may just produce confusing or inconclusive results, leading observers to image a fictitious 'average' character that actually obtains nowhere."

characteristics and processes, (b) test arguments about institutional and social structural effects on political outcomes, such as the arguments about the effects of variation in LTRs advanced here, and (c) employ subnational data in cross-national comparisons.

Regional and subnational dynamics also shape the character and fate of nations. This is the most important *substantive* defense of the analytic perspective developed in this book. Scholars of elections, civil wars, and other subnational phenomena in Africa increasingly acknowledge this, but generation of knowledge about subnational dynamics in Africa has not kept up with the demand. This is not only because of the lack of data per se. It is also because of a lack of conceptual tools for seeing and theorizing about subnational politics.

ELECTIONS AND CIVIL WAR

Although studies of elections and civil war often shift to the subnational scale, subnational-level variables are usually conceived as nonpolitical or as exogenous to politics. The variables invoked most often have to do with population density, natural endowment (e.g., the presence or absence of lootable resources), or ethnic makeup. Ethnic makeup itself is usually treated as if it were part of a country's natural endowment, fixed in the prehistory of the modern state, or an immutable inheritance of colonialism. In such work, local-level political, institutional, and social structural variables are *undetected and undetectable*. Formal and informal institutions at the local level – and the political processes they cause and structure – remain invisible. Analysis thus misses the role of subnational ʻinstitutions, including political-economy institutions such as land tenure regimes, in structuring bottom-up forces that can culminate in national outcomes of great interest to political science.[33]

In national elections, repressive local-level institutions and authority structures help produce victories in national elections that would be unattainable if electoral participation played out freely throughout the national space. Many African incumbents who have lost elections in the cities have won the national vote by dominating the countryside. Scholars who track electoral dyanmics on the ground have written of rural territories that are monopolized by incumbent regimes in electoral contests, and rural "safe areas" that are off-limits to opposition parties (Bekoe 2012). Kenya in the 1990s was notorious for incumbents' "zonal policies" that aimed at preventing the opposition from campaigning in constituencies that the ruling party needed to win. Kenyan lawyer and pro-democracy activist Willy Mutunga wrote in the late 1990s that the incumbent regime of Daniel arap Moi retained power because it "monopolized access to the grassroots.... The Moi-KANU regime rightly regards this monopoly as the

---

[33] Elinor Ostrom (2005) has emphasized the importance of microdynamics that are necessary aspects of larger processes.

last bastion of its political power" (1999, 7–8).[34] Land tenure institutions and the authority relations they uphold help explain where and how ruling parties create and hold these bastions of electoral power in the countryside.[35] Case studies featured in the chapters show that these effects can be highly uneven across space, drawing some rural constituencies directly into national politics while isolating or suppressing others. These dynamics are striking in all the subnational political jurisdictions examined in this study. Land institutions also structure cleavages and alliances within jurisdictions, helping to account for electoral alignments that define politics at the local level, and that sometimes scale-up to national politics.

Beatriz Magaloni (2006) argued that in Mexico, rural voters are easier to surveil and monitor, cheaper to buy off, and easier to punish than most other social groups or constituencies. Guillermo O'Donnell (1993) made a similar observation about rural zones of low republicanism in Brazil and elsewhere in Latin America. These observations hold for much of Africa, and the institutional factors highlighted in the foregoing analysis go far in producing or reinforcing these subnational and microlevel effects.

Africa's "new" regional and civil wars are subnational phenomena, and they often produce massive national-level effects. Local conflicts over land and territory are increasingly recognized as important bottom-up drivers of protracted, destructive, and traumatic wars in the DRC, Côte d'Ivoire, Sudan (Darfur and South Sudan), Somalia, Liberia, and Sierra Leone.[36] A new wave of country-focused scholarship, epitomized by the work of Séverine Autesserre (2010) and Kjrin Peters (2011), identifies land tenure battles, interjurisdictional conflicts over land, and struggles arising out of agrarian social relations as drivers of protracted wars and civil strife in the Eastern DCR and Sierra Leone. The broader field of conflict studies, however, has yet to incorporate subnational institutional and social-structural factors into analyses of the origins and dynamics of civil wars in Africa.

Institutional and agrarian factors remain, at best, at the margins of analysis in the exploding literatures on civil war in Africa. Large-N studies have relied mostly on national-level aggregates, such as national wealth and poverty scores and demographic structure, but country-level measures can be misleading. Recently, large-N studies have turned toward geographic data that is available at the subnational level. Using GIS, scholars have mapped terrain, rainfall,

---

[34] Mutunga was appointed chief justice of Kenya in 2011.

[35] See Conroy-Krutz 2009, Harding 2010. On the rural bias of postcolonial state-building in most African countries, see Chapter 2 and Rabinowitz 2013.

[36] Crawford Young (2002, 537) lists seven post-1975 cases of destruction of national regimes by insurgents from the rural periphery or the rural areas of neighboring states: Uganda (1979), Chad (1990), Liberia (1990), Ethiopia (1991), Somalia (1991), Rwanda (1994), and DR Congo (1997). The cases of Sierra Leone (in the 1990s) and South Sudan (2011) could be added to this list. See also Joshua Forrest 2004. Land issues have been central in all of these.

census data, locational variables, and the presence of natural resources – all features that may help explain why a given locale or region is conflict prone, or likely to be the theater of prolonged conflict. Institutional and social-structural variables (including factors related to agrarian political economy) have remained absent, however. Blattman and Miguel's 2010 review of the literature on the causes and effects of civil war barely mentions institutional factors, and does not consider social-structural factors on either side of the causal equation.

For conflict studies and African studies, the challenge is to see these local-level agrarian and institutional variables, and to incorporate them into analysis. They often turn out to be critical in explaining why these conflicts develop, become so protracted, and unfold with such ferocity that they seem to devour local communities from within. Such factors are also critical in explaining why localized armed conflict can be immune to high-level power-sharing deals that reorganize relations within national political institutions: high-level deals often do not resolve subnational conflicts over power and resources that stoke and sustain conflict on the ground.

The subnational institutional analysis featured in this book speaks directly to these challenges. The land tenure regimes that are the center of the analysis embed community structures, local hierarchy, and authority relations that *often serve as local templates for these conflicts.* Land tenure regimes define (a) jurisdictions; (b) social hierarchies, cleavages, and solidarities; and (c) scale dynamics that are critical to understanding these local wars and how they fuel the flames of national (and international) conflicts.

Ethnic jurisdictions such as chieftaincy jurisdictions are often the territories within which local grievances, armed group mobilizations, and combatants' political and military strategies are organized. Discrete microterritories are sites of "local states" of varying scope, coherence, and autonomy vis-à-vis the center. The political-economy meanings and salience of such jurisdictions have been spotlighted across the case studies in this analysis. War at the local level may consist largely of defense of, conquest of, and displacement from these territorial jurisdictions (rural microterritories). Contrary to what many outsiders might suppose, the boundaries of the relevant territorial units are usually *not* hidden or shrouded in local folklore. Rather, they are almost always those that have been delineated or recognized by the contemporary state. Militia and rebel groups are organizing within territorial units that are artifacts of state-building processes. This is the true of the Mai Mai militia in eastern DRC, and of the insurgencies in Liberia, Sierra Leone, and South Sudan (Autessere 2010, Peters 2011, Reno 2007, 2010). Local jurisdictions are spaces within which relationships around territory, authority, citizenship, and resource access develop, are reproduced, and can be destabilized and challenged. Such aspects of local political structure can be key to understanding conflict and unlocking possibilities for managing it.

Social hierarchy, cleavage, and exclusion within these local arenas are often defined by control over agricultural land and labor, and access to water and pasture. These power relations can generate the grievances that create fertile ground for the mobilization of rebels and militia. Peters and Richards (1998) show that in the ethnicized microterritories of rural Sierra Leone, as in much of rural Africa, youth and in-migrants are politically subordinate and the most vulnerable to economic marginalization and exploitation. Recruits into local militia and rebel groups were mostly likely to be drawn from precisely these groups (see also Humphreys and Weinstein 2008). As local social conflicts layer and overlap, they expand in scope and scale up. Marginalized youth and ethnic outsiders are drawn into movements with larger political agendas, creating the combustible mixes of grievance, ambition, displacement, and occupation of territory that can fuel and sustain devastating civil wars.

Local hierarchies and exclusions rooted in agrarian social relations also shape the internal organizational structures of rebel groups, and help explain how rebels treat civilians. Richards (2006) and Peters (2011) show that the Revolutionary United Front (RUF) rebels in Sierre Leone waged violent campaigns against local land-allocating elites and members of the locally dominant lineages. Reno (2007, 2011) argued that in South Sudan, patterns in rebel group organization and treatment of civilians (predatory versus protective behavior) are better explained by institutional variables that operate at the local level – that is, by the territorial and hierarchical organization of local patronage structures, and whether and how these are linked to the central state – than by the presence or absence of lootable resources or rebel ideology (two factors that have been the focus of much contemporary analysis).[37]

Scale dynamics can be critical in the causal equation, as Reno shows. The position of provincial elites in local and national power hierarchies goes far in determining their degree of dependency on national politicians, and the extent to which local militia are tools of actors who are battling for position in the central government.[38] The most autonomous provincial elites will be least constrained by peace settlements signed in the capital city.[39] Reno's arguments dovetail with the analysis of scalar effects developed in Part III of this book.

A politics of space and scale directs analysis to how territorial boundaries within countries shape political possibilities, and how political institutions can vary with political scale. Subnational institutional configurations differ across space, shaping variegated patterns of mobilization, representation, and incorporation across national territories. Working to discern these spatial and scalar

[37] Reno 2007, 333, 2010. See also Weinstein 2007, Chauveau and Richards 2008.
[38] This is true when armed groups form with state encouragement and support, as in the *janjaweed* in Darfur or the progovernment militia in parts of Sierra Leone.
[39] This was the case for the autonomy-seeking armed rebellions in Senegal's Casamance, and the Sudan People's Liberation Army (SPLA) in southern Sudan.

patterns turns out to be necessary for solving many of the empirical and theoretical problems that are central to the preoccupations of political scientists focused on Africa, including problems having to do with ethnic politics, elections, and civil war.

Africa's colonial and contemporary rulers have used political territory *strategically* in efforts to create political order. Like the rulers of the Ottoman Empire, the USSR, and modern China, rulers in Africa have viewed national territory as geopolitical space. They have employed the option that Robert Sack (1986) calls "nonuniformity of territorial units" to promote the differential incorporation of territories into national political systems and economies. Construction of land tenure regimes – territorially-bounded, varying across space in their political character and structure, and filtering access to national-level state institutions – has been a cornerstone of these projects. Social and territorial boundaries that are embedded in land tenure regimes have worked to fragment, containerize, and layer constituencies in ways that constrain possibilities for system-wide conflict. This institutional geometry creates space and scale effects that find expression in localisms and regionalisms whose repercussions are felt throughout national territories.[40]

EPILOGUE: RISING PRESSURE ON THE LAND

Africa is changing from a continent with open land frontiers into one of widespread and intensifying land pressure and scarcity. As this happens, rural land tenure regimes come under strain. Because the territorial and institutional underpinnings of state authority are partly grounded in these land regimes, land tensions and land-related conflict destabilize established forms of political order. Ties that bind farming populations to the state weaken, clients abandon patrons, new patrons emerge, ethnic identities rise and fall in value, chiefs accumulate, landlords squeeze tenants, investors appear, women push back, strangers rise up. Understanding these processes in both their micro- and macro-aspects is a first-order task for scholars of African politics. They connect closely to many of the political phenomena that have long been at the center of scholars' preoccupations – the salience of ethnicity in politics, clientelism and patrimonialism, the possibility of democracy, electoral dynamics, civil society strengths and weaknesses, and civil war.

There are multiple constraints on rulers' ability, capacity, and perhaps even willingness to sustain the land-based political relationships that have been the focus of this work. This book has focused mostly on one limit: the resource constraint that lies in the limited availability of arable land to accommodate the growth of rural populations. Yet forces producing more pressure on the

---

[40] This is a path to exploring the contours and effects of state structure in polities that, in their internal segmentations and boundaries, resemble empire as much as they resemble unitary nation-states.

land are complex and complexly interrelated. Demographics interact with natural endowment, technology, and the socioeconomic and political factors that produce population mobility. Now as in the past, some of Africa's most heavily commercialized farming and ranching zones are affected by declining soil fertility and erosion (themselves the result, in part, of insufficient or inappropriate technological change and investment). Many localities and regions must cope with in-migration from zones of declining productivity and land shortage. Climate change compounds and aggravates these processes. Farmers and pastoralists respond to drought, desertification, flooding, or salinization by seeking access to new land. Political conflict can also drive in-migration to farming and pastoral areas: in 2004, Africa's refugee population stood at seven million.[41] These processes fuel competition for land. Urbanization drives up periurban land values in ways that can upend existing patterns of land use and access.

Liberalization has opened the door to new foreign and domestic investors who are interested in land deals (for farming, mining, and building). National governments are now eager to offer such deals, sometimes with little regard for the user rights of small-scale farmers. In Tanzania since about 2004, the government has leased hundreds of thousands of hectares of land to Saudi, North American, and Chinese companies. The government of Ghana leases tracts to American and Chinese companies for gold mining, clearing the way for them by displacing farming communities. In Ethiopia, hundreds of thousands of hectares have been leased to foreign agribusiness. And in many (probably most) African countries, land acquisitions by rich and powerful elites have accelerated in era of neoliberalism and multipartism.

Demographic increase, urbanization, environmental degradation and climate change, and structural adjustment and economic liberalization are macrotrends that have *sustained and increased demand* by smallholders and pastoralists for access to new land and pasture and, at the same time, worked to *reduce the availability* of land to small-scale farmers. Economists, demographers, and environmental experts report that "rural populations are expanding and land availability is contracting."[42]

As competition for farmland and pasture rises across many parts of sub-Saharan Africa, the social contracts that tied farmers to the state – offering access to land in exchange for political acquiescence – come under strain. In many rural districts and localities, the old social contracts have worn out completely. The resulting strains find political expression in a myriad of ways – in intensifying distributive conflicts, struggles over entitlements and citizenship rights, and heightening conflict over authority and jurisdiction. These arguments often focus on control of land. In very concrete ways, the future of African states and the character of their economies are at stake. At the same time, land-related conflict reveals, in its patterns and dynamics, outlines of

---

[41] Tabutin and Schoumaker 2004.
[42] Bryceson 2002, 735.

the economic and political institutions that have been invisible in much of the scholarly work on African politics. By tracing the structure and workings of these institutions and rules, the analysis offers a potentially powerful tool for seeing state structure and state effects in processes that have hitherto remained mostly beyond our analytic reach.

APPENDIX

Land Politics Cases and Sources

Case (Abbreviation)	Country	Time Period(s)	Sources
Western and SW Burkina Faso	Burkina Faso	1990s+	Kuba and Lentz 2003; Paré 2001; Gray and Kevane 2001; JP Jacob, 2002; Mathieu et al., 2003; Zougouri and Mathieu 2006

This west African savannah zone experienced high in-migration in the 1960s and 1970s to the zone north of Bobo Dioulasso, and in the 1980s and 1990s to the zone south of Bobo Dioulasso. Rural development schemes since the 1970s have promoted cotton production and encouraged the inflow of farmers, but land tenure has remained under the control of the autochthonous administrative chiefs, land chiefs, and lineage heads. As land has become scarce and transactions have become more commercialized, autochthonous landowners (patrons, sponsors, *tuteurs*) and autochthonous "parent villages" have been withdrawing their previous land loans from migrant clients and guest communities, sometimes using the threat of violence or sorcery to dislodge migrants. The local administration tries to head off violence, but has not challenged landholders' right to take back land. The losers are in-migrants; their main option is to exit or negotiate a compromise with the landholders (e.g., allocation of another parcel elsewhere, a grace period before leaving, or cash payment to the landholder). The average population density for the long-established cotton zone is 40–50 persons per square kilometer, rising to 100 in some places (Paré 2001, 1). See Chapter 4.

CAMEROON CASES

Case (Abbreviation)	Country	Time Period(s)	Sources
North Province and Far North Province	Cameroon	1970s–2000s	Seignobos 2006; Gonné and Seignobos 2006; Teyssier et al., 2003; Kossoumna-Liba'a 2003; Article 19 1995; Moritz et al., 2002; Taguem-Fah 2003, Tassou 2008

Here, neotraditional authorities *(lamibe)* exercise extensive powers over land within chiefly juridictions *(lamidat)* that often coincide with departmental and *sous-prefectural* level administrative divisions. Competition for land is intense among user groups of different political status vis-à-vis the land allocation authorities. Peul agropastoralists, descendants of conquest groups, are the privileged clients of the Peul *lamibe*. Those recognized as autochtones (that is, as the original inhabitants of this region) are relegated to inferior status and must seek permission from chiefs to gain access to farmlands within the *lamibe's* jurisdictions. Official settlement scheme areas are treated as a separate case (described next), although the two LTRs overlap in territories in which land authority has shifted over time from the chiefs to the state bureaucracy and back. See Chapter 7.

SEB settlement schemes, Touboro and Touroua areas	N. Cameroon	1970s–1990s	See sources for N. Cameroon

In the 1970s, there was low competition for land in these zones. In-migrants (mostly from Far North Province) were encouraged by the state to settle in North Province in cotton-producing schemes of the parastatal Sodecoton (in the SEB schemes in the Lamidat of Rey Bouba (the area near Touboro town) and the Lamidat of Tchéboa (including the area near the towns of Touroua and Mokolo). The state worked hand-in-hand with the *lamibe* who served as as administrative auxiliaries and political allies of the central authorities. In the settlement scheme areas, the state ceded greater land prerogatives to the *lamibe* over time. As land grew scarce, mounting landlord-stranger tensions were mediated by the *lamibe*. The neocustomary elites have benefited from the presence of taxable in-migrants and from the fees the *lamibe* charge to mediate land disputes. See Chapter 7.

CÔTE D'IVOIRE CASES

Case (Abbreviation)	Country	Time Period(s)	Sources
Abengourou/Agni region	E. Côte d'Ivoire	1970–2000	Boutillier 1960; Chauveau and Dozon 1987; Gastellu 1989; Diaby 1997; Colin, Kouamé, and Soro 2007

Land rights of the indigenous population were gradually specified as the commercialization of agriculture progressed from the 1920s onward, with indigenes retaining the upper hand over in-migrants, who established themselves as tenant farmers. Terms of tenancy contracts with in-migrants changed over time to reflect market pressures, risk, and cost of labor. The central state has affirmed this process but has not led or imposed. Indigenous losers have responded with out-migration; migrants exit when pressured to do so.

Case (Abbreviation)	Country	Time Period(s)	Sources
Southwest and Center west (Gagnoa region) RCI	Côte d'Ivoire	1970–2000	Dozon 1985; Hecht 1985; Lewis 2003; Chauveau 2000, 2002a; Koné 2002; Woods 2003; HRW 2001a; Babo 2005; Boone 2009

In-migration that was encouraged by the Houphouet regime and backed with administrative muscle allowed settlers to gradually acquire and solidify land use rights, to the growing consternation of the sons-of-the soil, or "original inhabitants." With the turn to multipartism, politicians Bédié and Gbagbo appealed for support among these aggrieved constituencies by offering not to recognize the acquired land rights of the in-migrants. This political movement culminated in a 1998 law that explicitly revoked land rights acquired by nonindigenes. See Chapters 5 and 9.

Case (Abbreviation)	Country	Time Period(s)	Sources
Baoulé region (Bouaké Dept.)	Central Côte d'Ivoire	1990s	Babo 2010

This is a zone with high population density, land scarcity, and high competition for land. Indigenous (autochthonous) lineages and families control the land. In the late 1990s, in-migrants were pushed out to make way for Baoulés who were returning to their home areas, having been pushed out of the export-crop-producing zones in the center-west and west.

DEMOCRATIC REPUBLIC OF CONGO CASES

Case (Abbreviation)	Country	Time Period(s)	Sources
N. Kivu	DRC	1950s; 1990s	Mafikiri Tsongo 1997; Mararo 1997; Vlassenroot 2004; Mathieu and Willame 1999; Prunier 1997; Van Acker 2005; Autesserre 2010

In-migration was sponsored by the Belgian authorities. Settlers' land rights and status were confirmed under the Mobutu regime in the face of opposition by indigenes. Politicians and agents of the provincial administration who were empowered with reintroduction of multipartism in the early 1990s did not respect settlers' acquired land rights, setting the stage for highly politicized land-related conflict between settlers and sons-of-the-soil (the autochthonous groups) in the 1990–1994 period. The main theater of this conflict was North Kivu Province, but it did reverberate at the national level (as expected in the case of a statist LTR). See Chapters 5 and 9.

The land-to-person ratio for the mountainous region of Kivu as a whole declined by 62 percent from 1958 to 1990 (from 2.2 hectares per person to 0.81 hectare per person), with about half of this decline occurring by 1970 (Vlassenroot and Huggins 2004, 2).

GHANA CASES

Ashanti Region	Ghana	1940s 1960s–1980s+	Allman 1993; Austin 1987, 1988, 2005; Adomako-Sarfoh 1974; Berry 2001; Amanor 1994, 1999; Alden-Wily 2003; field notes

Under colonial rule, chiefs gradually secured increasingly concentrated and exclusive control over stool lands, retaining the upper hand in adjudication processes throughout Ashanti Region. Terms of in-migrants' land access hardened over time, as manifest in the 1966 "expulsion of aliens" from parts of rural Ashanti. With the closing of the land frontier in the rural areas by the 1970s, if not before, family rights over land were consolidated at expense of the chiefs. See Chapters 4 and 7.

Periurban Kumasi (Ashanti Region)	Ghana	2000+	Ubink 2007, 2008; Ubink and Amanor 2008; Crook 2008; field notes

When "the town reaches your [rural] property," it becomes land that belongs to the chief. In periurban areas, chiefs reassert control over land that is held by families. They may protest, but the arena of chieftaincy politics is their main forum for voice. See Chapter 7.

Case (Abbreviation)	Country	Time Period(s)	Sources
Western Region	W. Ghana	1980s–2000+	Boni 2005; Benneh 1988; Addae-Mensah 1986; Alhassan and Manuh 2005; Migot-Adholla et al. 1994; field notes

This is a chieftaincy-centered land regime with high in-migration (since the 1950s) from the Ashanti and Eastern Regions of Ghana. Many in-migrants purchased land from chiefs in the 1950s, 1960s, and 1970s, and some obtained titles. As competition for land intensified in the 1980s, indigenous westerners pressured chiefs for land. Chiefs sought to bolster their own land powers, revenues, and local authority by scaling back land rights conceded to outsiders in earlier decades. Outsiders have not been expelled or "excluded" en masse, but they have been incrementally excluded from ownership (loss of land rights), and some have actually lost land. The role of central government in producing this trend is clearer in this case than it is in many similarly structured situations.

Migot-Adholla et al. (1994, 104) report a population density of 30 persons per square kilometer (1990), and median farm size in 1987 of 13.3 hectares.

See Chapter 4.

Wa District	NW Ghana	1980s–2000s	Wilks 1989; Lentz 2006; Primavera 2005 (on neighboring Lawra District)

In the Upper West Region (UWR) of Ghana (savannah dry grassland), paramount chieftaincies have claimed jurisdiction over land use; their authority layers over that of local land chiefs (aka earth priests) representing founding lineages, some of whom in-migrated during the past 150 years or so. Population growth rate and density in UWR are low by Ghana standards (1.7 percent from 1984–2000; 31 persons per square kilometer on average, in 2000), and commercial agriculture is limited. More than 80 percent of the UWR population is rural. In the current period, there is low in-migration to the rural areas and high out-migration to the mines and farms of southern Ghana.

In Lawra District, where population densities are almost 2.5 times the regional average (83 persons per square kilometer in 2000), there is more commercial farming than in Wa District. Here, there is firstcomer and in-migrant tension, with groups dividing along the lines of micro-identities linked to earth shrines and settlement history. In Nandom paramountcy, conflict erupted between local Dagara and Sisala land and village chiefs and their communities in the early 1980s (Lentz 2006, 242–247). Redistricting in 1983 moved the jurisdictional boundaries of land chiefs, precipitating the reclaiming of farms from those who, due to movement of administrative boundaries, became strangers in places they had lived for a long time.

Wa District (now Wa East, Wa Municipal, and West, comprising 40 percent of the UWR population) is among the poorest in a poor region. In this part of UWR, centralized chieftaincy (the Wa chieftaincy) predated British colonial rule, and there seems to be less of a history of politicized rural-to-rural migration than in Lawra District. There is, however, much farmer-herder conflict in Wa East and Wa West.

KENYA CASES

Case (Abbreviation)	Country	Time Period(s)	Sources
Rift Valley Province (farming districts)	Kenya	1970–2000	Odingo 1971; Harbeson 1973; Migot-Adholla, Place, and Oluoch-Kosura 1994; Berman and Lonsdale 1992a, 1992b; Harbeson 1973; Throup and Hornsby 1998; Klopp 2001, 2002; Boone 2008, 2012; field notes

Land expropriated by the colonial administration was reallocated to nonindigenes by the Kenyatta regime in the early 1960s in the face of opposition by "original inhabitants." The Moi regime, exposed to multiparty competition, sided with those land-rights "losers"; Moi championed the revendications of those who were reclaiming their ancestral land rights in the Rift. Many holders of land rights acquired under the statist LTR were expropriated in 1992–1997. See Chapters 5 and 9.

Kisii district	Kenya	1960–2000	Okoth-Ogendo and Oucho 1993; Silberschmidt 1992; Orvis 1997; Ontita 2007; field notes

Authority over land in the old Kisii District (the former Kisii reserve) was lodged in families at the time of land adjudication in the 1960s. Family entitlements were confirmed. Since then, an informal land adjudication system centered on elders helps to shore up the family as a landholding unit. High population pressure on the land has produced extreme fragmentation of land units. Okoth-Ogendo and Oucho (1993, 201) found at the end of the 1980s that 83 percent of farm families in Kisii had holdings of less than 0.73 acre. Women, youth, unmarried people, and those born out of wedlock are among the front-line losers. Out-migration from the area is high (exit) and land-related conflict is turned inward, into the family. By contrast, in the Sotik Settlement Scheme area, what many analysts describe as a classic freehold LTR prevails. This area was added to the Kisii district upon the recommendation of the Kenya Boundaries Commission in 1962.

Okoth-Ogendo and Oucho (1993, 194) give an average population density of 304 persons per square kilometer for Kisii in 1969, rising to 395 in 1979. Nyang'au (2002, 5) reports a population density of 690 persons per square kilometer for Kisii/Gucha District.

See Chapter 6.

Case (Abbreviation)	Country	Time Period(s)	Sources
Central Province	Kenya	1950s+	Berman and Lonsdale 1992a, 1992b; Kitching 1980; Mackenzie 1998; Haugerud 1993; Throup 1988; Migot-Adholla, Place, and Oluoch-Kosura, 1994

This is a region of ethnic homogeneity, family control over land, very few in-migrants, land hunger provoked by population pressure, and a long history of class-like tensions. With rising pressure on the land in the colonial Kikuyu Reserve in the 1930s and 1940s, first tenants and then subordinate lineages and family members faced exclusion from access to land. Land hunger and land-related conflict reached a point of crisis by the late 1940s, contributing to the land-related tensions that fueled the Mau Mau revolt. Land tenure reforms of the 1950s consolidated and registered smallholdings, excluding many marginal land-rights claimants.

Population density in Nyeri District, a zone of high agricultural potential, was about 400 persons per square kilometer in the mid-1980s (Migot-Adholla, Place, Oluoch-Kosura 1994, 120–121, 125). In 1988, most parcels in Nyeri were about 1 hectare; the trend is for parcels to shrink over time. Many studies have determined that land titling did not clear the way for the full commodification of land. Rights tend to diffuse within families rather than become more individualized. The incidence of boundary-related land disputes is very high.

MALI CASES

Office du Niger	Mali	1920s–1990s	Colvin 1981; van Beusekom 1997; Pringle 2006; Diawara 2011; Camara, 2013

The territory that was claimed by the French colonial administration for the creation of the the Office du Niger was a sparsely populated area lying to the west of the more densely populated inner Niger Delta. With the construction of the irrigation scheme in the 1930s, the land was leased to tenant cultivators brought in by the colonial administration from other parts of what is now Mali and Burkina Faso. This basic land tenure model persisted (with modifications) through the 1990s. See Camara 2013. State control over the land has been entrenched and is not contested by groups claiming antecedent historical or customary rights. Land allocation and dispute adjudication processes are statist in nature, and conflicts among smallholders are handled by Office du Niger administration. Circa 1988, there were approximately 325,000 persons on smallholdings (3.7 hectares per family) in the zone of controlled irrigation, which covered 88,000 hectares of the one million hectares controlled by the Office du Niger (Diawara 2011).

Case (Abbreviation)	Country	Time Period(s)	Sources
Sikasso	Mali	1990s–2000s	Doujara, Bélières, Kébé 2006; Camara et al. 2007; Camara 2013

In this zone of southern Mali (Sénoufo and Minyaka zones) comprising the *cercles* of Sikasso, Koutiala, and Kadiolo, cotton production is promoted by the parastatal Compagnie Malienne pour le Développement des Textiles (CMDT). Land is controlled by autochthonous lineages. Sikasso is the poorest of the three *cercles*. Around Sikasso, the average size landholding was 10 hectares (of which 10–20 percent was planted in cotton) in 1994–2003; average household size was 14–18 persons. There is a land frontier (perhaps expanded by crisis in the cotton sector affecting this zone in the late 1990s and 2000s) that is shared uneasily with herders. Malians expelled from southern Côte d'Ivoire after 2002 returned to the Sikasso area, and *maîtres de la terre* and *chefs de village* (land chiefs and village chiefs) allocated land to indigenous returnees (and other in-migrants). According to Camara et al. (2007), most land conflicts between established families and the returnees and in-migrants – along with farmer-herder conflicts – are mediated locally by traditional procedures and traditional authorities, including imams. Over the course of the 2000s, however, secular authorities may have established a larger role in conflict adjudication in the cotton zone.

NIGER CASE

S. Niger	Niger	1950s–1980s	Olivier de Sardan 1999; Miles 1994; Lund 1998; Raynaut 1977, 1988

Raynaut (1988, 222) described the southern Niger zone of rain-fed agriculture as covering 8 percent of the national territory. The center and eastern parts of this region (Maradi, Zinder) are Hausa-dominant zones. In these parts of southern Niger, hierarchies of administrative chiefs have been the backbone of territorial administration. When land frontiers were open in the Maradi area, a situation lasting until the 1970s or so, religious and village-level political/territorial chiefs gave their consent to cultivators seeking to clear new land and/or found new villages. Lund (1998) describes the deep implication of village chiefs – who are subordinate to cantonal chiefs – in land dispute adjudication in the 1980s and 1990s. Cases occasionally scaled up for adjudication by canton chiefs. At the cantonal level, *sous-préfets* and *préfets* were also present. As land has become scarce, lineages have decomposed into family-centered units of production and landholding. Olivier de Sardan (1999) notes that there is a great deal of farmer-herder conflict in zones of land pressure, which chiefs and the *sous-préfets* have attempted to manage.

NIGERIA CASES

Case (Abbreviation)	Country	Time Period(s)	Sources
Enugu area, Anambra, Imo State	SE Nigeria	1980s	Okafor 1993; Martin 1993, Goldman 1993; Chukwuezi 1999, 2001

These are zones of "Iboland" with family control over land, high competition for land, and few in-migrants. It is a zone of out-migration from agriculture. Family farms are largely under individualized control. The region is characterized by a process of agricultural involution or "stagnation" (Okafor 1993, 352): agricultural intensification is accompanied by soil degradation, shortened fallows, declining yields, and food deficits. A class of landless adult males has emerged. Chukwuezi 1999 describes a process of de-agrarianization.

Family landholdings almost always total fewer than 2 acres (0.81 hectare) per household, with median farm size half of that (Chukwuezi 1999).

In 1988, Imo State population density was approximately 430 to 520 per square kilometer, with the "Igbo heartland" reaching densities of more than 1,400 persons per square kilometer, "probably the most densely populated rural areas of sub-Saharan Africa" (Goldman 1993, 253). A 1991 figure for Anambra State is 571 (Chukwuezi 1999, 11).

Plateau State (Jos area, Kofyar)	Nigeria	1970–2004	Netting 1968; Netting et al. 1993; Stone 1998; Isa-Odidi 2004; Mang 2008, 2009; Harnischfeger 2004

From the 1940s onward, Koyfar people indigenous to the highlands near Jos ("highland Kofyar") moved down into the Benue Valley and settled. This part of the Benue Valley was essentially a frontier zone in both the political and the economic sense. There was no established "local state" in the areas into which the Koyfar agriculturalists migrated, and the in-migration of Kofyar agriculturalists was not initiated, organized, or spurred on by the central state. Until the mid-1970s, processes of agricultural intensification were under way and the land rights of the recently Christianized Kofyar settlers were generally being consolidated. They were land rights "winners" in a context in which there was no clearly identifiable group of "land rights losers." In the mid-1970s and 1980s, these Kofyar agriculturalists began to face competition from Muslim pastoralists who began migrating into the Benue Valley in ever larger numbers (in response to drought and demographic stress elsewhere). The Muslim pastoralists came with the encouragement of the state-level authorities – they were "state-encouraged in-migrants," but in the 1980s the state government did not appear to be protecting them very well, or enforcing their right to be Plateau State as a matter of policy. Muslims also migrated into the nonfarming sector, and along with other small groups (for example, the Pan), attempted in the 1980s and thereafter to carve out some land rights. In 2004–2006, there were many violent clashes between these groups as the Kofyar, the first wave of in-migrants, undertook to defend their land rights against the newcomer groups they defined as "non indigenous" to Plateau State ("a Christian state"). The land-related ethnic divide conflated with a religious divide.

In the early 2000s the central government did not seem to have sided definitively with any of the contending groups. Local and state-level politicians took competing sides in the violent clashes over land.

RWANDA CASES

Case (Abbreviation)	Country	Time Period(s)	Sources
Kibungo/ *paysannat* settlement schemes	E. Rwanda	1970–2000	St. John 1971; Lemarchand 1982; Olson 1990; Imbs and Bart 1994; Imbs 1997; HRW 2001; Prioul and Sirvin 1981

Once a pastoral zone, expropriation of Tutsi in the early 1960s cleared the way for creation of a zone of settlement schemes under direct control of the central state. Olson (1990, 19, 22) reports average landholding size of 1.95 hectares in 1998. Landholding sizes were larger and population densities were lower in this region than throughout the rest of Rwanda. Kibungo was largely emptied out in 1994 and then resettled under the Kagame regime. See Chapter 8.

Case (Abbreviation)	Country	Time Period(s)	Sources
Ruhengeri (and Gisenyi)	NW Rwanda	1980s–early 1990s	André and Platteau 1998; Van Hoyweghen 1999, Lemarchand 1970; Newbury 1988; Blarel 1994; Ford 1993

The northern and northwestern regions of Rwanda (Ruhengeri and Gisenyi) were zones of high competition for land, family control over land, and few in-migrants. This was President Habyarimana's home region. André and Platteau reported a high and rising incidence of quasi-landlessness, acute inequalities, and intense land-related conflict within the core of families in Gisenyi, a region in which "customary tenure based on lineage ownership is stronger than in other regions of Rwanda" (1998, 20, n. 22). The kind of statist LTR that prevailed in much of eastern Rwanda and on the *paysannat* settlement schemes was absent in most of northwest Rwanda.

Population density of Ruhengeri District was 313 persons per square kilometer in 1978, with average landholding size of 0.77 hectare in 1988 (Olson 1990, 19, 22). May (1995) reports population density for Ruhengeri of 560 persons per square kilometer. The national average population density in the early 1990s was 300 persons per square kilometer (Imbs and Bart 1994, 259).

SENEGAL CASES

| Senegal River Valley, Upper and Middle Valley | Senegal | 1960s; 1980s and 1990s | Adams and So 1996; Platteau 2002; Crousse, Mathieu, and Seck 1991; Dahou 2004 |

This was a zone that saw little in-migration of farmers in the 1960s, and low pressure on rain-fed land. Lineage authority over floodplain and rain-fed land was strong. However, 1970s drought and the development of irrigation in the 1970s and 1980s (through both artisanal and large-scale statist projects) fueled the rise of more intense competition for land both within indigenous communities and between indigenous communities and in-migrant agropastoralists. In-migrants often saw their land-rights rolled back.

| Senegal River Delta | Senegal | 1970–1990 | Dahou 2004; Faye 2006; Crousse, Mathieu, Seck 1991; Rodenbach 1999; Boone 2003 |

A statist land tenure regime provided the institutional infrastructure for the state-directed in-migration of settlers in the 1970s and 1980s. The Delta was transformed into a zone of rice cultivation by the Société Nationale d'Aménagement et d'Exploitation des Terres du Delta (SAED), starting in 1965. The state controlled land development and allocation directly, using heavy mechanization to prepare and irrigate large paddies that were worked by units of approximately twenty households. Rodenbach (1999) wrote that ancestral land rights were nonexistent; Dahou 2004 described land allocation as pure state clientelism. In 1987, the state relinquished direct allocation of land and management of the irrigated fields to elected Conseils Ruraux (CRs), of which the CR of Ross-Béthio was the best known and most important. There was no conflict between settlers and a preestablished farming group in this area; it seems that most of the displaced were pastoralists. For irrigated rice farming in the Delta, capital was the scarcest factor of production (rather than land).

Case (Abbreviation)	Country	Time Period(s)	Sources
Western Groundnut Basin	Central Senegal	1920s–1950s; 1960s+	Faye 1981; Baldé 1976; Colvin et al. 1981; Soumah 1981; Pélissier 1966; David 1980

The rise and fall of the *navétanat* in the western groundnut basin can be treated as a case study of land politics under a neocustomary (lineage-based) LTR. Here, in-migrants received parcels from local patrons or hosts but never asserted autonomous control over land. The colonial state created or upheld land systems in which Senegalese (Wolof, Serer, or Wolof-Mouride) farming populations gained or retained control over the land. Amin (1974, 14) writes that the number of in-migrants went from 60,000 per year from 1935–1940, to 40,000 per year from 1940–1958, to 11,000 per year for 1958–1961. As arable land grew scarce (due to soil erosion and demographic increase in the old groundnut basin along the Dakar-St. Louis Railway, and to population increase in the central groundnut basin), indigenous hosts gradually restricted and then stopped the current of in-migration. In-migration practically disappears over the course of the 1960s as demand for seasonal labor dropped and "rural population density became sufficient" (Amin 1974, 14). Published sources report almost no overt landlord-stranger conflict over gradual exclusion of the outsiders from land access. Suppression of the *navétanat* should not be seen as the effect of a change in state policy: the inflow of migrants to the old groundnut basin stopped in the 1940s, when the *navétanat* was in full swing, and it fell off in the western groundnut basin in the 1950s, well before the colonial administration ended the policy of subsidizing the inflow of migrants in 1961. Even with the administrative suppression of the *navétanat*, the flow of in-migrants continued in the Terres Neuves and Casamance into the 1970s. France maintained its groundnut subsidy until 1967, thus supporting high groundnut prices until that time. The classic balance of power in landlord-stranger land relationships prevailed in these settings.

Sine Saloum Region population density around 1972 was 49 persons per square kilometer (Faye 1981).

SOUTH AFRICA CASES

Case (Abbreviation)	Country	Time Period(s)	Sources
South Africa: commercial farming areas	RSA	1970–2000	Cousins 2002, 2007, Ntsebeza and Hall, 2007

Land rights allocated enforced as private property rights during the period of white minority rule were upheld by the African National Congress (ANC) government when it came to power in 1994, when it accepted a constitutional settlement and compromise that protected existing property holdings. This case appears anomalous in the context of this book's other cases of statist LTRs that have been rocked by regime change at the center of the national political system. In the South African case, even though political power was transferred to a new (rival) set of rulers in 1994, acquired land rights in the commercial farming areas were not destabilized. The Zimbabwe case shows that existence of formal private property rights per se is not sufficient to explain this outcome. However, the ANC has been under continuing and mounting pressure to overturn the old allocation (infringe upon the private property rights and forcibly acquire the land) in order to overcome the political legacy of land dispossession and redistribute land to its main constituents.

South Africa (former) homelands	RSA	1970–2000	Cousins 2002; Ntsebeza 2002, 2004; van Kessel 1997; Claassens 2005; Cotula et al. 2004; Adams and Palmer 2007; Claassens and Cousins 2008

In 2004, about 35 percent of the rural population lived in the communal areas or former "ethnic homelands" (aka bantustans). Under the *apartheid* regime, these homelands were under the administrative rule of neocustomary authorities with neocustomary-style land powers. Land rights established under the neocustomary-style LTRs were recognized by the ANC government in 1994. Since then, the legal standing and future status of these rights have been the subject of major political, policy, and legal debate. The Communal Land Rights Act of 2004 recognized the neocustomary and aligned the government with neotraditional leaders in some of South Africa's poorest rural areas. The ANC is pulled between the holders of acquired rights and the defenders of neocustomary prerogative and entitlement on the one hand, and those who see these tenure arrangements as non-liberal, not progressive, and biased against those who are often "losers" under the neocustomary rules (that is, women, youth, and newcomers) on the other. The government has favored the "traditional leaders" and those with acquired neocustomary rights. In the context of this book's other cases, it appears that the ANC government has accepted what could be considered the default position of postcolonial African governments in confirming (that is updating, not discarding) the neocustomary land regimes, even though this slights those who were expected to be among the leading beneficiaries of ANC rule.

SUDAN CASE

Case (Abbreviation)	Country	Time Period(s)	Sources
Gezira Scheme	Sudan		Abdelkarim 1986, 1991; Bernal 1997; Babikir and Babiker 2007

Irrigation and settlement schemes were created in 1925. By the time of independence in 1956, some 840,000 hectares were under irrigation in Gezira. Through this process, local inhabitants lost control of the land. Local inhabitants and in-migrants were allocated parcels of 15–40 feddans (30 feddans = 12.6 hectares) from the state; they became scheme tenants. Bernal (1997, 461) describes the scheme as governed under "direct administration." The 120,000 tenants (as of 2000) are in a contractual relationship with the Gezira Scheme authority. They are considered to be the original population. For these tenants, the strong dynamic is one of *emigration* rather than mounting demographic pressure on the land. Families cannot sell tenancies freely, however; this is regulated by Gezira scheme management. Some tenants hire laborers, including short-term laborers, who in-migrate from western Sudan and live in labor camps separate from the main/permanent settlements. Scheme tenants also establish sharecropping arrangements with migrant workers. It seems that the original scheme tenants are not facing land scarcity.

TANZANIA CASES

Kiru Valley	Northern Tanzania	1990+	Field notes

The Kiru Valley is a well-irrigated valley in the Babati District of Manyara Region. Until the 1940s, the Kiru Valley was tse-tse infested and inhabited by a small community of hunter-gatherers (the Mbugwe) in its northernmost reaches. The colonial government began tse-tse eradication and large-scale land concessions to European settlers in the 1940s, and most land in the Kiru Valley was owned by white settlers at the time of independence. In-migrants from many parts of northern and central Tanzania provided farm labor and were often allowed to farm a few acres on their own account, much like the African workers on Rift Valley farms in colonial Kenya. The Kiru Valley properties were expropriated by the state in 1967 and then leased by the government as large concessions to foreign companies. With privatization in the 1990s, the government – under the objection of the long-established, ethnically hetero-geneous communities of smallscale farmers – leased these properties to new investors. This time, many were Tanzanian citizens of Asian descent. The government's decision has been bitterly contested by the smallscale farmers who experience high levels of land scarcity. Conflict has flared between the large landowners and the smallscale farmers. The smallscale farmers have demanded that the government allocate land to them, both in the courts and by supporting parliamentary candidates who champion their demands. The LTR is deeply statist, and land competition has taken the form of politicized land-related conflict that takes place in the national arena and that pits "indigenous Tan-zanians" (a national identity restricted to black Tanzanians) against "outside investors."

Case (Abbreviation)	Country	Time Period(s)	Sources
Mamire Ward Babati District	Northern Tanzania	1980+	Field notes

This is a ward in which most people are post-1950 in-migrants. This jurisdic-tion was very sparsely inhabited until the tse-tse clearing campaigns of the late 1940s and 1950s. Land seekers from central Tanzania came to settle, either more or less spontaneously and/or via land purchases from the Gorowa Native Authority, centered at the northern end of Lake Babati. Under Ujamaa in the 1970s, settlement patterns in Mamire and the other jurisdictions in eastern Babati District were completely reorganized under the direct authority of the government. Farmers were moved from their homes and farms and relocated to administrative villages, where they received new land allocations. In 1992, the national government legally-extinguished all pre-Ujamaa land rights and claims. In-migration to Mamire Ward continued until recent years, but today, no open land remains. Those who need land either rent it or out-migrate. Land administration is completely secular and disputes are processed through a national-level system of land tribunals and courts. This is a statist LTR in an ethnically-heterogenous area of in-migration, but because no agriculturalists claim this territory on the basis of autochthony or indigeneity, there is not an indigene-stranger axis of land competition among farmers. The state does not recognize pastoralists' claims to this territory.

Case (Abbreviation)	Country	Time Period(s)	Sources
Mbulu District, Iraqw homeland	Northern Tanzania	1990s+	Börjeson 2004; Snyder 2005; Lawi 2007; Baker and Wallevik 2003; field notes

The Iraqw Da'aw, or Iraqw homeland, is located on the fertile, well-watered, western edge of the Rift Valley escarpment in Mbulu District, Manyara Region. This ethnically homogenous, densely populated microregion is one of the "islands of intensive agriculture in Eastern Africa" studied by Widgren and Sutton (2004). Pressure on the land is very high. The case is anomalous: a LTR that is largely statist in character prevails in a jurisdiction without in-migration, and in the presence of strong indigeneity-based claims to land and territory. Land is scarce; land-related tensions within families and small communities run high. Community elders and customary norms do play a role in regulating conflicts at the village level, but the statist features of the LTR mean that these conflicts can be readily channeled into the national land administration machinery, rather than bottled up at the local level. Many conflicts are "exported" out of the wards and into district-level land tribunals, where disputes are adjudicated according to secular practice and national administrative norms. Interviewees and Askew et al. (2103) stress that corruption sometimes shapes outcomes.

Giting Ward, Hanang District	Northern Tanzania	late 1980s+	Field notes; Loiske 1995; Lane 1996

This jurisdiction lies on the northern side of Mt. Hanang in the eastern part of Hanang District (Manyara Region). Barabaig pastoralists were pushed out of this area in the early- to mid-1950s when the colonial administration decided to create a yeoman class of African commercial farmers on holdings of about 500 hectares each. The statist nature of the LTR was confirmed in the Ujamaa period, when the large holdings were broken up and redistributed to smallholders and landless residents who had in-migrated to the Giting area, often to work on the large wheat farms. Since the 1980s there has not been much new in-migration. The national land administration system is the institutional arena in which the original large landholders have competed against smallholders to regain control over land they lost in the 1970s. Local land politics is structured along a class-like axis of competition (large landholders vs. smallholders).

The case differs from most of our other cases of in-migration under statist LTRs in that those who could assert claims to this territory as on the basis of indigeneity are not farmers, they are pastoralists. Their claims to the Giting area have been completely extinguished by the state, which from the 1950s onward has successfully deflected Barabaig land claims away from the Giting area and to land lying to the west and south of Mt. Hanang.

ZIMBABWE CASES

Case (Abbreviation)	Country	Time Period(s)	Sources
Zimbabwe commercial areas	Zim.	1980–2005	ICG 2004; Kriger 2007; Boone and Kriger 2010; Roe 1995; Moyo 2001; Moyo and Yeros 2005

Under colonial rule, 40 percent of the national territory (15.3 million hectares, most of the best farmland and ranchland) was assigned to white farmers and ranchers.

With independence in the 1980s, Mugabe initially affirmed the property rights granted by the ancient regime to white farmers and ranchers. Some land was acquired by the state from commercial farmers under "willing buyer, willing seller" arrangements in the 1980s and 1990s. In 2000, there were 4,500 commercial farmers in Zimbabwe. With pressure of electoral competition and societal pressure for land, the land rights of the most of these commercial farmers were expropriated under the Fast Track land reform program in 2000–2005. Approximately 35 million acres (14.1 million hectares) of land so acquired by the state was assigned to 170,000 smallholders and approximately 5,000 political elites and well-connected persons. See Chapter 10.

Zimbabwe communal areas; settlement schemes	Zim.	1980–2005	ICG 2004; Kriger 2007; Arrighi 1970; Roe, 1995, Munro 1998; Alexander 1994; Scoones et al. 2012 (for Masvingo only)

Under colonial rule, 42 percent of the national territory (16.3 million hectares) was set up as "African reserves" (Tribal Trust Lands), administered via indirect rule through officially recognized, paid chiefs. After 1980, these communal areas were administered by the state bureaucracy and the ruling party through deconcentrated Direct Councils (in association with the chiefs; see Alexander

1994). The communal areas have been zones of very high land pressure and land hunger since the 1940s, if not before. In 1980–1990, 3.5 million hectares of land acquired from commercial farmers and ranchers was used to create settlement schemes for 52,000 smallholder families under an intensively statist (directly administered) land tenure regime. Under Fast Track, the state settled 170,000 more smallholder families on the land.

References

Abdelkarim, Abba. 1986. "Wage Laborers in the Fragmented Labor Market of the Gezira, Sudan." *Africa: Journal of the International African Institute* 56/1: 54–70.

Abdelkarim, Abba. 1991. *Sudan: The Gezira Scheme and Agricultural Transition*. New York: Routledge.

Abdul-Korah, Gariba B. 2007. "'Where Is Not Home?' Dagaaba Migrants in the Brong Ahafo Region: 1980 to the Present." *African Affairs* 106 (422): 71–94.

Acemoglu, Daron and James A. Robinson. 2006. *Economic Origins of Dictatorship and Democracy*. New York: Cambridge University Press.

Acemoglu, Daron, Simon Johnson, and James A. Robinson. 2001. "The Colonial Origins of Comparative Development." *American Economic Review* 91 (5) (December): 1369–1401.

Acemoglu, Daron, Simon Johnson, and James Robinson. 2005. "Institutions as a Fundamental Cause of Long-Run Growth," in *Handbook of Economic Growth, Volume 1A*, edited by Philippe Aghion and Steve Durlauf. Amsterdam: Elsevier, 386–472.

Adams, Adrian and Jaabe So. 1996. *A Claim to Land by the River: A Household in Senegal, 1720–1994*. Oxford: Oxford University Press.

Adams, Martin and Robin Palmer, eds. 2007. "Independent Review of Land Issues, Vol. III, 2006–2007. Eastern and Southern Africa." London: Oxfam, posted at www.oxfam.org.uk/what_we_do/issues/livelihoods/landrights/index.htm (accessed 29 July 2007).

ADB. 2009. *See* African Development Bank 2009.

Addae-Mensah, J. 1986. *Population Changes and Agricultural Practices in Ghana*. Kumasi: Land Administration Research Center, University of Science and Technology. July.

Addo, N(elson) O. 1970. "Immigration into Ghana: Some Social and Economic Implications of the Aliens Compliance Order of 18 Nov. 1969." *Ghana Journal of Sociology* 6 (20): 20–42.

Adepoju, Aderanti. 1982. "Population Redistribution: A Review of Governmental Policies," in *Redistribution of Population in Africa*. John I. Clark and Leszek A. Kosinski, eds. London, and Exeter, NH: Heineman Educational: 58–84.

Adomako-Sarfoh, J. 1974. "The Effects of the Expulsion of Migrant Workers on Ghana's Economy, with Particular Reference to the Cocoa Industry," in *Modern Migrations in Western Africa*. Samir Amin, ed. London: International African Institute: 138–155.

African Development Bank (ADB). 2009. "Cameroon: Diagnostic Study for Modernization of the Lands and Surveys Sectors," ADB Country Regional Department Center (ORCE). November.

Agreement between the Zimbabwe African National Union-Patriotic Front (ZANU-PF) and the two Zimbabwe Movement for Democratic Change (MDC) formations, on resolving the challenges facing Zimbabwe, 15 September 2008, Harare, Zimbabwe, posted at www.kubatana.net/docs/demgg/mdc_zpf_agreement_080915.pdf (accessed 2 July 2010).

Akindès, F. 2004. "The Roots of the Military-Political Crises in Côte d'Ivoire." Nordic Africa Institute Research Report no. 128, Uppsala.

Akiwumi Report. 1999. *See* Republic of Kenya 1999. "Report of the Judicial Commission Appointed to Inquire into Tribal Clashes in Kenya."

Alden Wily, Liz. 2001. "Reconstructing the African Commons." *Africa Today* 48 (1): 77–99.

Alden Wily, Liz. 2003. *Governance and Land Relations: A Review of Decentralization of Land Administration and Management in Africa*. London: International Institute for Environment and Development (IIED). June.

Alden Wily, Liz and Daniel Hammond. 2001. "Land Security and the Poor in Ghana – Is There a Way Forward? A Land Sector Scoping Study." A report commissioned by DFID Ghana Rural Livelihoods Programme.

Alexander, J. 1991. "The Unsettled Land: The Politics of Land Redistribution in Matabeleland, 1980–1990." *Journal of Southern African Studies* 17 (4): 581–610.

Alexander, J. 2006. *The Unsettled Land: State-Making and the Politics of Land in Zimbabwe, 1893–2003*. Oxford: James Currey.

Alexander, J. and J. McGregor. 2001. "Elections, Land, and the Politics of Opposition in Matabeleland." *Journal of Agrarian Change* 1 (4): 510–533.

Alexander, Jocelyn. 1994. "State, Peasantry, and Resettlement in Zimbabwe." *Review of African Political Economy* 61: 325–345.

Alhassan, Osman and Takyiwaa Manuh. 2005. "Land Registration in Eastern and Western Regions, Ghana." Securing Land Rights in Africa, Research Report 5. London: IIED.

Allman, Jean Marie. 1993. *The Quills of the Porcupine: Asante Nationalism in an Emergent Ghana*. Madison: University of Wisconsin Press.

Alston, Lee J. and Bernardo Mueller. 2005. "Property Rights and the State," in *Handbook of the NIE*. Claude Menard and Mary M. Shirley, eds. Dordrecht, The Netherlands: Springer: 573–590.

Alston, Lee J., Gary D. Libecap, and Bernardo Mueller. 1999. *Titles, Conflict, and Land Use: The Development of Property Rights and Land Reform on the Brazilian Amazon Frontier*. Ann Arbor: University of Michigan Press.

Amanor, Kojo. 1999. *Global Restructuring and Land Rights in Ghana: Forest Food Chains, Timber, and Rural Livelihoods*. Livingston, NJ: Transaction Publishers. Also published under the same title in 1999, Uppsala: Nordiska Afrikainstitutet as Research Report no. 108.

Amanor, Kojo Sebastian. 1994. *The New Frontier: Farmers' Response to Land Degradation (A West African Study)*. Geneva and London: UNRISD and Zed Books Ltd.

Amanor, Kojo Sebastian. 2005. "Night Harvesters, Forest Hoods, and Saboteurs: Struggles over Land Expropriation in Ghana," in *Reclaiming the Land: The Resurgence of Rural Movements in Africa, Asia, and Latin America*. Sam Moyo and Paris Yeros, eds. London and New York: Zed Books: 102–117.

Amanor, Kojo Sebastian. 2010. "Family Values, Land Sales, and Agricultural Commodification in South-Eastern Ghana." *Africa: The Journal of the International African Institute* 80 (1): 104–125.

Amanor-Wilks, D. 2000. "Zimbabwe's Farm Workers and the New Constitution." SADC Center of Communication for Development, Harare, Zimbabwe, posted at apic.igc.org/rtable/dedooo2.htm (accessed 2 July 2010).

Amin, N. 1992. "State and Peasantry in Zimbabwe since Independence." *European Journal of Development Research* 4 (1): 112–162.

Amin, Samir. 1974. "Introduction," in *Modern Migrations in Western Africa*. S. Amin, ed. London: International African Institute: 3–126.

Amin, Samir, ed. 1974. *Modern Migrations in Western Africa*. London: International African Institute.

Amnesty International. 1997. "Cameroon: Mépris flagrant des droits de l'homme," 16 September, AFR/17/16/97.

Amnesty International. 2009. "Cameroon: Impunity Underpins Persistent Abuse." Report AFR 17/001/2009.

Amselle, Jean-Loup, ed. 1976. *Les Migrations Africaines*. Paris: Maspero.

Anderson, David. 2005. "'Yours in the Struggle for Majimbo': Nationalism and the Party Politics of Decolonisation in Kenya, 1955–1964." *Journal of Contemporary History* 39 (July): 547–564.

Anderson, David and Emma Lochery. 2008. "Violence and Exodus in Kenya's Rift Valley, 2008: Predictable and Preventable?" *Journal of Eastern African Studies* 2 (2): 328–43.

Anderson, Leslie. 2006. "Fascists or Revolutionaries? Left and Right Politics of the Rural Poor." *International Political Science Review* 27 (2) (April): 191–214.

Anderson, Perry. 1974. *Lineages of the Absolutist State*. London: New Left Books.

Anderson, Terry L. and Peter J. Hill. 1979. "An American Experiment in Anarcho-Capitalism: The Not So Wild, Wild West." *Journal of Libertarian Studies* 3 (1): 9–29.

Anderson, Terry L., and Peter J. Hill. 2004. *The Not So Wild, Wild West: Property Rights on the Frontier*. Stanford, CA: Stanford University Press.

André, Catherine and Jean-Philippe Platteau. 1998. "Land Relations under Unbearable Stress: Rwanda Caught in the Malthusian Trap." *Journal of Economic Behavior and Organization* 34 (1): 1–47.

Ansoms, An. 2009. "Re-Engineering Rural Society: The Visions and Ambitions of the Rwandan Elite." *African Affairs* 108: 289–309.

Ansoms, An. 2010. "Views from Below on the Pro-Poor Growth Challenge: The Case of Rural Rwanda." *African Studies Review* 53 (2) (September): 97–124.

Anyang'Nyong'o, P. 1987. "The Development of Agrarian Capitalist Classes in the Ivory Coast, 1945–75," in *The African Bourgeoisie*. Paul Lubeck, ed. Boulder, CO: Lynne Rienner Publishers: 185–248.

Apter, David E. 1972. *Ghana in Transition*. Princeton, NJ: Princeton University Press, second revised edition. First published in 1955 as *Gold Coast in Transition* by Princeton University Press.

ARDHO (Association Rwandaise pour la Défense des Droits de l'Homme). 1992. "Declaration sur les massacres en cours de la population de la Région de Bugesera." 10 March 1992, posted at ddata.over-blog.com/xxxyyy/0/25/58/62/bugesera-1992.pdf, accessed 13 mars 2007).

Arnold, G. 1990. "The Land Dilemma." *Africa Report* March–April: 59–61.

Arrighi, G. 1970. "Labor Supplies in Historical Perspective: A Study of the Proletarianization of the Peasantry in Rhodesia." *Journal of Development Studies* 6 (3): 197–234.

Arthur, Peter. 2009. "Ethnicity and Electoral Politics in Ghana's Fourth Republic." *Africa Today* 56 (2): 45–73.

Article 19: Global Campaign for Free Expression. 1995. "Northern Cameroon: Attacks on Freedom of Expression by Governmental and Traditional Authorities," posted at www.article19.org (accessed 1 March 2009). July.

Article 19: Global Campaign for Free Expression. 1997. "Cameroon: A Transition in Crisis," posted at www.article19.org (accessed 13 November 2009). October.

Askew, Kelly, Faustin Maganga, and Rie Odgaard. 2013. "Of Land and Legitimacy: A Tale of Two Lawsuits." *Africa: Journal of the International African Institute* 83 (1) (February): 120–141.

Association Rwandaise pour la Défense des Droits de l'Homme (ARDHO) and F. Byabarumuse. 2002. "Declaration sur les massacres en cours de la Population de la Région de Bugesera," 10 mars 1992, exhibit 6744, admitted on 14/03/2002 and registered on 14/03/2002, United Nations Tribunal Pénal International pour le Rwanda (UN-TPIR).

Austin, Dennis and Robin Luckham, eds. 1975. *Politicians and Soldiers in Ghana, 1966–1972*. London: Frank Cass.

Austin, Gareth. 1987. "The Emergence of Capitalist Relations in South Asante Cocoa-Farming, c. 1916–1933." *Journal of African History* 28 (2): 259–279.

Austin, Gareth. 1988. "Capitalists and Chiefs in the Cocoa Hold-Ups in South Asante, 1927–38." *International Journal of African Historical Studies* 21 (1): 63–96.

Austin, Gareth. 2005. *Labour, Land, and Capital in Ghana: From Slavery to Free Labour in Asante, 1807–1956*. Rochester, NY: University of Rochester Press.

Autesserre, Séverine. 2006. "Local Violence, National Peace? Postwar 'Settlement' in the Eastern D.R. Congo (2003–2006)." *African Studies Review* 49 (3) (December): 1–30.

Autesserre, Séverine. 2010. *The Trouble with the Congo: Local Violence and the Failure of International Peacebuilding*. New York and Cambridge: Cambridge University Press.

Autorité pour l'Aménagement de la Vallée du Bandama (AVB). 1971. *AVB: Opération Kossou*. Abidjan: Government of the République de la Côte d'Ivoire, AVB.

AVB. *See* Autorité pour l'Aménagement de la Vallée du Bandama 1971.

Ayee, Joseph. 2004. "Ghana: A Top-Down Initiative," in *Local Governance in Africa*. Dele Olowu and James S. Wunch, eds. Boulder, CO: Lynne Rienner Publishers: 125–154.

Azam, Jean-Paul. 2001. "The Redistributive State and Conflict in Africa." *Journal of Peace Research* 38 (4) : 429–444.

Azam, Jean-Paul and Alice Mesnard. 2003. "Civil War and the Social Contract." *Public Choice* 115 (3–4): 455–475.

Babikir, Osman Mohammed and Babikir Idris Babiker. 2007. "The Determinants of Labour Supply and Demand in Irrigated Agriculture: A Case Study of the Gezira Scheme in Sudan." *African Development Review* 19 (2): 335–349.

Babo, Alfred. 2005. "Citoyenneté et Jeu Politique en Côte d'Ivorie." *Kasa Bya Kasa* 8: 24–37.

Babo, Alfred. 2010. *Les jeunes, la terre et les changements sociaux en pays baoulé (Côte d'Ivoire).* Paris and Dakar: Editions Karthala, AfriMAP, and Le Centre de Recherches sur les Politiques Sociales (CREPOS).

Babo, A. and Droz, Y. 2008. "Conflits fonciers, de l'éthnie à la nation: Rapports interéthnique et 'ivoirité' dans le sud-ouest de la Côte d'Ivoire." *Cahiers d'Etudes Africaines* 48 (4), n. 192: 741–763.

Badiey, Naseem. 2013. "The Strategic Instrumentalization of Land Tenure in 'State Building': The Case of Juba, South Sudan." *Africa: Journal of the International African Institute* 83 (1) (February): 57–77.

Bah, T.M. 1974. "Contribution à l'étude de la résistance des peuples africains à la colonisation: Karnou et l'insurrection des Gbaya," *Afrika Zamani* 3: 105–161.

Baker, Jonathan and Hege Wallevik. 2003. "Poverty and Wealth at the Rural-Urban Interface: An Actor-Centered Perspective from Northern Tanzania." *Environment and Urbanization* 15 (2): 229–248.

Bako-Arifari, Nassirou and Pierre-Joseph Laurent, eds. 1998. "Les dimensions sociales et économiques du développement local et de la décentralisation en Afrique au Sud du Sahara." *Bulletin de l'APAD* (Association Euro-Africaine pour l'Anthropologie du Changement Social et du Développement), n. 15 (mai), special issue.

Badiey, Naseem. 2013. "The Strategic Instrumentalization of Land Tenure in 'State-Building': The case of Juba, South Sudan." *Africa: Journal of the International African Institute* 83 (1): 78–99.

Baldé, Mamadou Saliou. 1976. Un cas typique de migration interafricaine: L'immigration des Guinéens au Sénégal," in *Les Migrations Africaines*, Jean-Loup Amselle, ed.: 63–98.

Baldé, S. 2010. Centre des Etudes d'Afrique Noire (CEAN) (SciencesPo, Université de Bordeaux). "Cote d'Ivoire: Situation Institutionelle," posted at www.etat .sciencespobordeaux.fr/institutionnel/cotivoir.html (accessed 22 January 2010).

Banegas, Richard and René Otayek. 2003. "La Burkina Faso dans la crise ivoirienne: Effects d'aubaine et incentitudes politiques." *Politique Africaine* n. 89: 71–87.

Bangré, Habibo. 2004. "Côte d'Ivoire: Revision de la code de la nationalité et de la naturalisation." 21 December, Afrik.com, posted at www.afrik.com/article7981.htm (accessed 13 March 2006).

Barkan, Joel. 1995. "Elections in Agrarian Societies." *Journal of Democracy* 6 (4): 106–116.

Barkan, Joel and Michael Chege. 1989. "Decentralising the State: District Focus and the Politics of Reallocation in Kenya." *Journal of Modern African Studies* 27 (3): 431–453.

Barkey, Karen. 2008. *Empire of Difference: The Ottomans in Comparative Perspective.* Cambridge and New York: Cambridge University Press.

Baryeh, Hamidu Ibrahim (Regional Lands Officer). 1997. "Kumasi Natural Resource Management Research Project Component Study 3: Land Management and Tenure

Systems in Peri-Urban Areas of Kumasi, Ghana." Kumasi: Kumasi Lands Commission. July.

Barzel, Yoram. 1997. *Economic Analysis of Property Rights*. Cambridge: Cambridge University Press.

Bassett, T. 2003a. "'Nord Musulman et Sud Crétien': Les moules médiatiques de la crise ivoirienne." *Afrique Contemporaine* 206 (2): 13–27.

Bassett, T. 2003b. "Dangerous Pursuits: Hunter Associations (donzo ton) and national politics in Côte d'Ivoire." *Africa* 73 (1): 1–29.

Bassett, Thomas. 1993. "Introduction," in *Land in African Agrarian Systems*. Thomas J. Bassett and Donald E. Crummey, eds. Madison: University of Wisconsin Press: 13–15.

Bassett, Thomas J. 2001. *The Peasant Cotton Revolution in West Africa: Côte d'Ivoire, 1880–1995*. Cambridge: Cambridge University Press.

Bates, R. H. 2008. *When Things Fell Apart: State Failure in Late-Century Africa*. Cambridge: Cambridge University Press.

Bates, Robert H. 1981. *Markets and States in Tropical Africa*. Berkeley and Los Angeles: University of California Press.

Bates, Robert H. 2005 [1989]. *Beyond the Miracle of the Market: The Political Economy of Agrarian Development in Kenya*. Cambridge: Cambridge University Press.

Bates. Robert H. 1983. "Modernization, Ethnic Competition and the Rationality of Politics in Comtemporary Africa." in Donald Rothchild and V.A. Olorunsola, eds., *State Versus Ethnic Claims: African Policy Dilemmas*. Boulder, CO: Westview Press: 152–171.

Bayart, J.-F., S. Ellis, and B. Hibou. 1999. *The Criminalization of the State in Africa*. Bloomington and London: Indiana University Press and James Currey.

Beckman, Bjorn. 1976. *Organizing the Farmers: Cocoa Politics and National Development in Ghana*. Uppsala: Scandinavian Institute of African Studies.

Beckman, Bjorn. 1981. "Ghana: 1951–78: Agrarian Basis of the Post-Colonial State," in *Rural Development in Tropical Africa*. Judith Heyer et al., eds. New York: St. Martin's Press: 143–167.

Bekoe, Dorina, ed. 2012. *Voting in Fear: Electoral Violence in Sub-Saharan Africa*. Washington, DC: United States Institute of Peace.

Benhabib, Seyla. 2002. "Political Theory and Political Membership in a Changing World," in *Political Science: State of the Discipline*. Katznelson and Helen Milner, eds. New York: W. W. Norton: 404–432.

Benneh, George. 1988. "The Land Tenure and Agrarian System in the New Cocoa Frontier of Ghana: Wassa Akropong Case Study," in *Agricultural Expansion and Pioneer Settlements in the Humid Tropics: Selected Papers Presented at a Workshop in Kuala Lampur, 17–21 September 1985*. Walter Manchard and Wm. B. Morgan, eds. Tokyo: The United Nations University Press, posted at www.unu.edu/unupress/unupbooks/80636e/80636E09.htm (accessed 22 June 2009).

Berman, Bruce, Dickson Eyoh, and Will Kimlika, eds. 2004. *Ethnicity and Democracy in Africa*. Oxford and Athens: James Currey and Ohio University Press.

Berman, Bruce. 1998. "Ethnicity, Patronage, and the African State." *African Affairs* 97 (388): 305–341.

Berman, Bruce and John Lonsdale. 1992a. *Unhappy Valley: Conflict in Kenya and Africa. Book One: State and Class*. Athens: Ohio University Press.

Berman, Bruce and John Lonsdale. 1992b. *Unhappy Valley: Conflict in Kenya and Africa. Book Two: Violence and Ethnicity*. Athens: Ohio University Press.

Bermeo, Nancy and Philip Nord, eds. 2000. *Civil Society before Democracy: Lessons from Nineteenth-Century Europe*. London: Rowman and Littlefield Publishers, Ltd.

Bernal, Victoria. 1997. "Colonial Moral Economy and the Discipline of Development: The Gezira Scheme and 'Modern' Sudan." *Cultural Anthropology* 12 (4): 447–480.

Bernstein, Henry. 2004. "'Changing Before Our Very Eyes: Agrarian Questions and the Politics of Land in Capitalism Today." *Journal of Agrarian Change* 4 (1/2): 190–225.

Berry, Sara. 1985. *Fathers Work for Their Sons: Accumulation, Mobility, and Class Formation in an Extended Yorùbá Community*. Los Angeles and Berkeley: University of California Press.

Berry, Sara. 1988. "Concentration without Privatization? Some Consequences of Changing Patterns of Rural Land Control in Africa," in *Land and Society in Contemporary Africa*. R. E. Downs and S. P. Reyna, eds. Hanover and London: University of New Hampshire and University Press of New England: 53–75.

Berry, Sara. 1993. *No Condition Is Permanent: The Social Dynamics of Agrarian Change in Sub-Saharan Africa*. Madison: University of Wisconsin Press.

Berry, Sara. 2001. *Chiefs Know Their Boundaries: Essays on Property, Power, and the Past in Asante, 1896–1996*. Portsmouth, NH, Oxford, and Cape Town: Heinemann, James Currey, and David Philip Publishers.

Berry, Sara. 2002. "Debating the Land Question in Africa." *Comparative Studies in Society and History* 44 (4): 638–668.

Berry, Sara. 2013. "Questions of Ownership: Proprietorship and Control in a Changing Rural Terrain: A Case Study from Ghana," *Africa: Journal of the International African Institute* 83 (1): 36–57.

Beusekom. 1997. *See* von Beusekom 1997.

Bhavani, Ravi and David Backer. 2000. "Localized Ethnic Conflict and Genocide: Rwanda and Burundi." *Journal of Conflict Resolution* 44 (3): 283–306.

Bierschenk, Thomas and Jean-Pierre Olivier de Sardan. 2003. "Powers in the Village: Rural Benin between Democratisation and Decentralization." *Africa: Journal of the International African Institute* 73 (2): 145–173.

Bierschenk, T. and Olivier de Sardan, J. P. 1997. "ECRIS: Rapid Collective Inquiry for the Identification of Conflicts and Strategic Groups." *Human Organization* 56 (2): 238–244.

Bigagaza, J., C. Abong, and C. Mukarubuga. 2002. "Land Scarcity, Deficit, and Conflict in Rwanda," in *Scarcity and Surfeit: The Ecology of Africa's Conflicts*. J. Lind and K. Sturman, eds. Pretoria: Institute for Security Studies: 50–82.

van Binsbergen, Wim. 2006. "Photographic Essay: Manchester School and Background," Shikanda Portal for Wim van Binsbergen's Web sites, posted at www.shikanda.net/ethnicity/illustrations_manch/manchest.htm (accessed 10 December 2009).

Blanc, Paul. 1962. "Le problème des allogènes en Côte d'Ivoire et en Afrique de l'Ouest." *Penant: Revue de droit des pays d'Afrique*, n. 690, janvier–mars: 112–124.

Blarel, Benoit. 1994. "Tenure Security and Agricultural Production under Land Scarcity: The Case of Rwanda," in *Searching for Land Tenure Security in Africa*. John W.

Bruce and Shem E. Migot-Adholla, eds. Washington DC: The World Bank: 71–96.

Blattman, Christopher and Edward Miguel. 2010. "Civil War." *Journal of Economic Literature* 48 (1): 3–57.

Boix, Carles. 2003. *Democracy and Redistribution*. Cambridge and New York: Cambridge University Press.

Boni, Stefano. 2000. "Contents and Contexts: The Rhetoric of Oral Traditions in the *Oman* of Sefwi Wiawso, Ghana." *Africa: Journal of the International Africa Institute*, 70 (4): 568–594.

Boni, Stefano. 2005. *Clearing the Ghanaian Forest: Theories and Practices of Acquisition, Transfer, and Utilisation of Farming Titles in the Sefwi-Akan Area*. Legon, Ghana: University of Ghana Institute of African Studies.

Boone, Catherine. 2003a. *Political Topographies of the African State*. Cambridge and New York: Cambridge University Press.

Boone, Catherine. 2007. "Africa's New Territorial Politics: Regionalism and the Open Economy in Côte d'Ivoire." *African Studies Review* 50 (1): 59–81.

Boone, Catherine. 2009. "Electoral Populism Where Property Rights Are Weak: Land Politics in Contemporary Sub-Saharan Africa." *Comparative Politics* 41 (2): 183–201.

Boone, Catherine. 2012. "Land Conflict and Distributive Politics in Kenya." *African Studies Review* 55 (1) (April): 75–103.

Boone, Catherine. 2003b. "Decentralization as Political Strategy in West Africa." *Comparative Political Studies* 36 (4) (May): 355–380.

Boone, Catherine. 2007a. "Property and Constitutional Order: Land Tenure Reform and the Future of the African State." *African Affairs* 106 (October): 557–586.

Boone, Catherine. 2007b. "Winning and Losing Politically-Allocated Land Rights: Electoral Politics and Land Grievances in Kenya." Paper presented at the 2007 Annual Meetings of the African Studies Association, New York City, 19–21 October.

Boone, Catherine. 2008. "Politically-Allocated Land Rights and the Geography of Electoral Violence: The Case of Kenya in the 1990s." Paper presented at the 2008 Annual Meetings of the American Political Science Association, 30 August, Boston, MA.

Boone, Catherine. 2011. "Politically-Allocated Land Rights and the Geography of Electoral Violence in Kenya." *Comparative Political Studies* 44 (10) (October): 1311–1342.

Boone, Catherine and Dennis Duku. 2012. "Ethnic Land Rights in Western Ghana: Landlord-Stranger Relations in the Democratic Era." *Development and Change*, 43 (3) (May) 2012: 671–694.

Boone, Catherine and Norma Kriger. 2010. "Multiparty Elections and Land Patronage: Zimbabwe and Côte d'Ivoire." *Commonwealth and Comparative Politics* 48 (2) (April): 173–202.

Boone, Catherine and Lydia Nyeme. In preparation. "Land Regimes and the Political Structuring of Ethnicity: Evidence from Manyara Region, Tanzania."

Börgeson, Lowe. 2004. "The History of Iraqw Intensive Agriculture, Tanzania." *Islands of Intensive Agriculture in Eastern Africa*, Mats Widgren and John E.G. Sutton, eds. Nairobi, Dar es Salaam, Athens, and Oxford: E.A.E.P, Mkuki na Nyota, Ohio U. Press, and James Currey: 68–104.

Bosco. 2004. *See* Muchukiwa, Bosco 2004.

Boserup, Ester. 1965. *The Conditions of Agricultural Growth: The Economics of Agrarian Change under Population Pressure.* London: George Allen and Unwin.

Boserup, Esther. 1981. *Population and Technological Change: A Study of Long-Term Trends.* Chicago: University of Chicago Press.

Boutillier, J.-L. 1960. *Bongouanou, Côte d'Ivoire: Etude socio-économique d'une subdivision.* Paris: Editions Berger-Lavrault.

Boutrais, J. 1978. "Compétition foncière et développement au Nord du Cameroun: La Plaine de Mora." *Cahiers de l'ONAREST* (Office National de Recherche Scientifique et Technique du Cameroun [Yaoundé]) 1 (2): 53–90.

Bowyer-Bell, T. A. S. and C. Stoneman. 2000. "Land Reform's Constraints and Prospects: Policies, Perspectives, and Ideologies in Zimbabwe Today," in *Land Reform in Zimbabwe: Constraints and Prospects.* T. A. S. Bowyer-Bell and C. Stoneman, eds. Aldershot: Ashgate Publishing Limited: 1–23.

Brady, Henry E. and David Collier, eds. 2004. *Rethinking Social Inquiry: Diverse Tools, Shared Standards.* Lanham, MD, Boulder, CO, New York, Toronto, Plymouth, UK: Rowman and Littlefield.

Branch, Daniel and Nicholas Cheeseman. 2006. "The Politics of Control in Kenya: Understanding the Bureaucratic Executive State, 1952–78." *Review of African Political Economy* 107: 11–31.

Bratton, Michael, Robert Mattes, and E. Gyimah Boadi. 2000. *Public Opinion, Democracy, and Market Reform in Africa.* Cambridge and New York: Cambridge University Press.

Brenner, Robert. 1982. "The Agrarian Roots of European Capitalism." *Past and Present* 97 (November): 16–113.

Brett, E. A. 2005. "From Corporatism to Liberalization in Zimbabwe: Economic Poicy Regimes and Political Crisis." *International Political Science Review* 26 (1): 91–106.

Breusers, Mark, Suzanne Nederlof, and Teunis Van Rheenen. 1998. "Conflict or Symbiosis? Disentangling Farmer-Herdsman Relations: The Mossi and Fulbe of the Central Plateau, Burkina Faso." *Journal of Modern African Studies* 36 (3): 357–380.

Brown, Taylor. 2005. "Contestation, Confusion, and Corruption: Market-Based Land Reform in Zambia," in *Competing Jurisdictions: Settling Land Claims in Africa.* Sandra Evers, Marja Spierenburg, and Harry Wels, eds. Leiden and Boston: Brill Publishers: 79–102.

Brubaker, Rogers and Frederick Cooper. 2000. "Beyond 'Identity.'" *Theory and Society* 29 (1): 1–47.

Bruce, John W. 1988. "A Perspective on Indigenous Land Tenure Systems and Land Concentration," in *Land and Society in Contemporary Africa.* R. E. Downs and S. P. Reyna, eds. Hanover and London: University of New Hampshire Press and University Press of New England: 23–52.

Bruce, John W. 1993. "Do Indigenous Tenure Systems Constrain Agricultural Development?" in *Land in African Agrarian Systems.* Thomas J. Bassett and Donald E. Crummey, eds. Madison: University of Wisconsin Press: 35–56.

Bruce, John W., and Shem E. Migot-Adholla, eds. 1994. *Searching for Land Tenure Security in Africa.* Washington, DC, and Debuque, IA: The World Bank and Kendall/Hunt Publishing Company.

Bruce, John W., Shem Migot-Adholla, and Joan Atherton. 1994. "The Findings and Their Policy Implications: Institutional Adaptation or Replacement?" in *Searching for Land Tenure Security in Africa*. John W. Bruce and Shem Migot-Ahdolla, eds. Washington, DC, and Debuque, IA: The World Bank and Kendall/Hunt Publishing Company: 251–266.

Bryceson, Deborah F. 2002. "The Scramble in Africa: Re-orienting Rural Livelihoods." *World Development* 30 (5): 725–739.

Buchanan, James and Gordon Tullock. 1962. *The Calculus of Consent: Logical Foundations of Constitutional Democracy*. Ann Arbor: University of Michigan Press.

Bueno de Mesquita, Bruce and George W. Downs. 2005. "Development and Democracy." *Foreign Affairs* 84 (5) (September–October): 77–86.

Buhaug, Halvard and Jan Ketil Rod. 2006. "Local Determinants of African Civil Wars, 1970–2001." *Political Geography* 25 (3) (March): 315–335.

Buhaug, Halvard and Päivi Lujala. 2005. "Accounting for Scale: Measuring Geography in Quantitative Studies of Civil War." *Political Geography* 24 (4) (May): 399–418.

Burnet, Jennie E. n.d. "The Women and Land Studies Project: Women's Land Rights in Rwanda," the Rwanda Initiative for Sustainable Development (RISD), posted at www.law.emory.edu/WAL/WAl-studies/rwanda.htm#13 (accessed 20 December 2006).

Burnet, Jennie E. and RISD. 2003. "Culture, Practice, and Law: Women's Access to Land in Rwanda," in *Women and Land in Africa: Culture Religion, and Realizing Womens's Rights*. L. M. Wanyeki, ed. New York: Zed Books: 176–206.

Burns, Tony. 2007. "Land Administration Reform: Indicators of Success and Future Challenges." World Bank Agriculture and Rural Development Discussion Paper no. 37. Washington, DC: The World Bank.

Businge, Gerald. 2007. "Uganda's Difficult Path Towards an Agreeable Land Policy," posted at UGPulse.com, 30 March 2007 (accessed 28 July 2007).

Calas, B. 2009. "From Rigging to Violence: Mapping of Political Regression," in *The General Elections in Kenya, 2007*. J. Lafargue, ed. Nairobi: Institute Français de Recherche en Afrique (IFRA): 165–185.

Callaghy, Thomas M. 1984. *The State-Society Struggle: Zaire in Comparative Perspective*. New York: Columbia University Press.

Camara, Bakary. 2013. "The Dynamics of Land Tenure Systems in the Niger Basin, Mali." *Africa: Journal of the International African Institute*, 83 (1) (February): 78–99.

Camara, Bakary et al. 2007. "Migration et tensions sociales dans le sud-Mali." Point Sud: Centre for Research on Local Knowledge, Bamako, Mali. June.

Campbell, B. 2000. "Reinvention du politique en Côte d'Ivoire." *Politique Africaine* 78 (juin): 142–156.

Campbell, B. 2003. "Defining Development Options and the New Social Compromises in the Context of Reduced Political Space: Reflections on the Crisis in Côte d'Ivoire." *African Sociological Review* 2: 29–44.

Caramani, Daniele. 2004. *The Nationalization of Politics: The Formation of National Electorates and Party Systems in Western Europe*. Cambridge and New York: Cambridge University Press.

Carter C. B. E., Sir Morris. 1933. "Report of the Kenya Land Commission, Sept. 1933," Presented to the Secretary of State for the Colonies to Parliament by Command of His Majesty, May 1934. London: His Majesty's Stationery Office.

Carter Commission, Kenya. 1933 (aka Kenya Land Commission). *See* Carter C. B. E, Sir Morris 1993.

Centre on Housing Rights and Evictions (COHRE). 2001. *Land, Housing, and Property Rights in Zimbabwe*. COHRE Africa Programme Mission Report. Geneva: COHRE.

Chajmowiecz, Monique. 1996. "Kivu: Les Banyamulenge enfin à l'honneur!" *Politique Africaine* 64 (décembre): 115–120.

Chambers, Robert. 1969. *Settlement Schemes in Tropical Africa: A Survey of Organizations and Development*. London: Routledge and Kegan Paul Ltd.

Chambua, Samuel E. 2002. *Democratic Participation in Tanzania*. Dar es Salaam: Dar es Salaam University Press.

Chan, Stephen and Ranka Primorac. 2004. The Imagination of Land and the Reality of Seizure: Zimbabwe's Complex Reinventions. *Journal of International Affairs* 57 (2): 63–80.

Chandra, Kanchan, ed. 2012. *Constructivist Theories of Ethnic Politics*. Oxford: Oxford University Press.

Chanock, Martin. 1991. "Paradigms, Policies, and Property: A Review of the Customary Law and Land Tenure," in *Law in Colonial Africa*. Kristin Mann and Richard Roberts, eds. Portsmouth, NH, and London: Heinemann and James Currey: 61–84.

Chanock, Martin. 1998. *Law, Custom, and Social Order: The Colonial Experience in Malawi and Zambia*. Portsmouth, NH: Heinemann. First published in 1985 by Cambridge University Press.

Charlery de la Masselière, B. 1992. "Le reserrement de l'espace agraire au Rwanda." *Etudes Rurales* (janvier–juin): 99–115.

Chaumba, J., I. Scoones, and W. Wolmer. 2003a. "From *Jambanja* to *Planning*: The Teassertion of Technocracy in Land Reform in South-Eastern Zimbabwe." *Journal of Modern African Studies* 41 (4): 533–554.

Chaumba, J., I. Scoones, and W. Wolmer. 2003b. "New Politics, New Livelihoods: Agrarian Change in Zimbabwe." *Review of African Political Economy* 30 (98): 585–608.

Chauveau, Jean-Pierre. 2000. "Question foncière et construction nationale en Côte d'Ivoire." *Politique Africaine* 78: 94–125.

Chauveau, Jean-Pierre and Jean-Philippe Colin. 2010. "Customary Transfers and Land Sales in Côte d'Ivoire: Revisiting the Embdedness Issue." *Africa: The Journal of the International African Institute* 80 (1) (2010): 81–103.

Chauveau, Jean-Pierre and Paul Richards. 2008. "West African Insurgencies in Agrarian Perspective: Côte d'Ivoire and Sierra Leone Compared." *Journal of Agrarian Change* 8 (4): 515–552.

Chauveau, J.-P. 2002a. Une lecture sociologique de la loi ivoirienne de 1998 sur le domaine foncier, IRD, Réfo. Doc. de Travail n. 6, Unité de Recherche 095, sept. (46 pages).

Chauveau, J.-P. 2002b. "La loi ivoirienne de 1998 sur le domaine foncier rural et l'agriculture de plantation villageoise: Une mise en perspective historique et sociologique." *Land Reform/Réforme Agraire/Reforma Agraria*. Rome: United Nations Food and Agricultre Organization (FAO) (1): 62–79.

Chauveau, J.-P. and J-P. Dozon. 1987. "Au coeur des éthnies ivoiriennes... L'état," in *L'Etat Contemporain en Afrique*. Emmanuel Terray, ed. Paris: L'Harmattan: 221–296.

Chauveau, J.-P. and J. Richard. 1977. "Une 'périphérie recentrée: à propos d'un système local d'économie de plantation en Côte d'Ivoire." *Cahiers d'Etudes Africaines* 17: 485–523.

Chauveau, J.-P. and P. Richards. 2008. "West African Insurgencies in Agrarian Perspective: Côte d'Ivoire and Sierra Leone Compared." *Journal of Agrarian Change* 8 (4): 515–552.

Cheater, A. P. 1993. "Ambiguities and Contradictions in the Political Management of Culture," in *Socialism Ideals, Ideologies, and Local Practice*. C. M. Hahn, ed. London: Routledge: 102–116.

Chege, Michael. 2008. "Kenya: Back from the Brink?" *Journal of Democracy* 19 (4) (October): 125–139.

Chhibber, Pradeep and Ken Kollman. 2005. *The Formation of National Party Systems: Federalism and Party Competition in Canada, Great Britain, India, and the United States*. Princeton, NJ: Princeton University Press.

Chimhowu, A. O. 2002. "Extending the Grain Basket to the Margins: Spontaneous Land Resettlement and Changing Livelihoods in the Hurungwe District, Zimbabwe." *Journal of Southern African Studies* 28 (3): 551–573.

Chimhowu, A. and P. Woodhouse. 2006. "Vernacular Land Markets in Sub-Saharan Africa." *Journal of Agrarian Change* 6 (3): 346–371.

Chimhowu, A. and P. Woodhouse, 2010. "Forbidden but Not Suppressed: A 'Vernacular' Land Market in Svosve Communal Lands, Zimbabwe." *Africa: The Journal of the International African Institute* 80 (1): 14–35.

Chrétien, Jean-Pierre. 1985. "Hutu et Tutsi au Rwanda et au Burundi," in *Au Coeur de l'Ethnie: Ethnies, Tribalisme, et Etat en Afrique*. Jean-Loup Amselle and Elikia M'Bokolo, eds. Paris: Editions la Découverte: 129–166.

Chrétien, Jean-Pierre. 1991. "'Presse Libre' et propagande raciste au Rwanda." *Politique Africaine* 42 (juin): 109–120.

Chrétien, Jean-Pierre. 2000. *L'Afrique des grands lacs: Deux milles ans d'histoire*. Paris: Aubier.

Chrétien, Jean-Pierre. 2003. *The Great Lakes of Africa: Two Thousand Years of History*. Scott Straus, trans. New York: Zone Books.

Chua, Amy. 2004. *World on Fire: How Exporting Free Market Democracy Breeds Ethnic Hatred and Global Instability*. New York: Anchor Books.

Chukwuezi, Barth. 1999. "De-Agrarianisation and Rural Employment in South-eastern Nigeria." Leiden, African Studies Center, Working paper 37.

Chukwuezi, Barth. 2001. "Through Thick and Thin: Igbo Rural-Urban Circularity, Identity, and Investment." *Journal of Contemporary African Studies* 19 (1): 55–66.

Claassens, Aninka. 2005. "The Communal Land Rights Act and Women: Does the Act Remedy or Entrench Discrimination and the Distortion of the Customary?" Land Reform and Agrarian Change in Southern Africa Occasional Paper Series No. 28, Cape Town and Johannesburg: University of Western Cape School of Government, Programme for Land and Agrarian Studies (PLAAS) and Legal Resources Center (LRC). September.

Claassens, Aninka and Ben Cousins. 2008. *Land, Power, and Custom: Controversies Generated by South Africa's Communal Land Rights Act*. Cape Town and Athens: University of Cape Town Press and Ohio University Press.

Clark, John I. and Leszek A. Kosinski. 1982. *Redistribution of Population in Africa.* London and Exeter, NH: Heineman Educational.

Clay, Daniel C. 1996. "Fighting an Uphill Battle: Population Pressure and Declining Land Productivity in Rwanda." MSU International Development Working Paper no. 58. East Lansing, MI: Michigan State University Department of Agricultural Economies and Department of Economics.

Cliffe, L., J. Mpofu, and B. Munslow. 1980. "Nationalist Politics in Zimbabwe: The 1980 Elections and Beyond." *Review of African Political Economy* 18: 44–67.

Club du Sahel/OECD. 2006. *See* Ouédraogo, Hubert 2006.

COHRE. 2001. "Land, Housing, and Property Rights in Zimbabwe." COHRE Africa Programme Mission Report.

Coldham, S. 1993. "The Land Acquisition Act, 1992 of Zimbabwe." *Journal of African Law* 37 (1): 82–88.

Coldham, S. 2001. "Statute Note: Land Acquisition Amendment Act, 2000 (Zimbabwe)." *Journal of African Law* 45 (2): 227–229.

Coldham, S. F. R. 1979. "Land Tenure Reform in Kenya: The Limits of the Law." *Journal of Modern African Studies* 17 (4): 615–627.

Coldham, Simon. 1984. "The Settlement of Land Disputes in Kenya – An Historical Perspective." *Journal of Modern African Studies* 22 (1): 59–71.

Colin, J.-P., G. Kouamé, and D. Soro. 2007. "Outside the Autochthon-Migrant Configuration: Access to Land, Land Conflicts and Inter-ethnic Relationships in a Former Pioneer Area of Lower Côte d'Ivoire." *The Journal of Modern African Studies* 45: 33–59.

Colvin, L. G. et al, eds. 1981. *The Uprooted of the Western Sahel: Migrants' Quest for Cash in the Senegambia.* New York: Praeger.

Conroy-Krutz, Jeffrey. 2009. Incumbent Advantage and Urban-Rural Geography in Sub-Saharan Africa, unpub. paper, Department of Political Science, Michigan State University, 3 November 2009 (34 pages).

Constitution of Zimbabwe Amendment (No. 17) Act (2005) (Act No. 5 of 2005), 14 September.

Cooksey, Brian. 2003. "Marketing Reform? The Rise and Fall of Agricultural Liberalization in Tanzania." *Development Policy Review* 21 (1): 67–91.

Cordell, Dennis D., John W. Gegory, and Victor Piché. 1996. *Hoe and Wage: A Social History of a Circular Migration System in West Africa (Migration of Burkinabé).* Boulder, CO: Westview Press.

Cotula, Lorenzo, Camilla Toulmin, and Ced Hesse. 2004. *Land Tenure and Administration in Africa: Lessons of Experience and Emerging Issues.* London: International Institute for Economic Development (IIED). February.

Cousins, Ben. 2002. "Legislating Negotiability: Security, Equity, and Class Formation in Africa's Land Systems," in *Negotiating Property in Africa.* Kristine Juul and Christian Lund, eds. Portsmouth, NH: Heinemann: 67–106.

Cousins, Ben. 2007. "Agrarian Reform and the 'Two Economies': Transforming South Africa's Countryside," in *The Land Question in South Africa: The Challenge of Transformation and Redistribution.* Lungisile Ntsebeza and Ruth Hall, eds. Cape Town: HSRC Press: 220–245.

Crawford, Gordon. 2008. "Poverty and the Politics of (De-)Centralisation in Ghana," in *Decentralisation in Africa: A Pathway out of Poverty and Conflict?* Gordon

Crawford and Christof Hartmann, eds. Amsterdam: Amsterdam University Press: 107–144.

Crawford, Gordon and Christof Hartman, eds. 2008. *Decentralisation in Africa: A Pathway out of Poverty and Conflict?* Amsterdam: Amsterdam University Press.

Crook, R. 1997. "Winning Coalitions and Ethno-Regional Politics: The Failure of the Opposition in the 1990 and 1995 Elections in Côte d'Ivoire." *African Affairs* 96: 215–242.

Crook, Richard. 1994. "Four Years of the Ghana District Assemblies in Operation: Decentralisation, Democratisation, and Administrative Performance." *Public Administration and Development* 14 (4): 339–364.

Crook, Richard. 2008. Customary Justice Institutions and Local Alternative Dispute Resolution: What Kind of Protection Can They Offer to Customary Landholders?" in *Contesting Land and Custom in Ghana: State, Chief, and Citizen.* J. Ubink and K. Amanor, eds. Leiden: Leiden University Press: 131–154.

Crook, Richard C. 1986. "Decolonization, the Colonial State, and Chieftaincy in the Gold Coast." *African Affairs* 85 (338): 75–105.

Crook, Richard C. and James Manor. 1998. *Democracy and Decentralization in South Asia and West Africa.* Cambridge: Cambridge University Press.

Crook, Richard C. and Alan Sturla Sverrisson. 2000. "To what extent can decentralized forms of government enhance the development of pro-poor policies and improve poverty-related outcomes?" a paper presented to a workshop on political systems and development (2001 World Development Report Background Papers), Castle Donnington, UK.

Crousse, Bernard, Paul Mathieu, and Sidy M. Seck, eds. 1991. *La vallée du fleuve Sénégal: Evaluations et perspectives d'une décennie d'amenagements (1980–1990).* Paris: Karthala.

Crowder, Michael. 1968. *West Africa Under Colonial Rule.* Evanston: Northwestern University Press.

Dahou, Tarik. 2004. *Entre parenté et politique: Développement et clientelism dans le Delta du Sénégal.* Paris and Dakar: Karthala and ENDA Graf Sahel.

Dahou, Tarik, ed. 2008. *Libéralisation et politique agricole au Sénégal.* Dakar and Paris: Crepos, Enda-Graf Diapol and Editions Karthala.

Dahou, Tarik and Abdourahmane Ndiaye. 2008. "Les enjeux d'une réforme foncière," in *Libéralisation et Politique Agricole au Sénégal.* Tarik Dahou, ed. Dakar and Paris: Crepos, Enda-Graf Diapol and Karthala: 47–68.

Daley, Elizabeth. 2005. "Land and Social Change in a Tanzanian Village 2: Kinyanambo in the 1990s." *Journal of Agrarian Change* 5 (4) (October): 526–572.

Darbon, Dominique. 1992. "Un succès ambigu: L'exemple du Zimbabwe." *Société Espace Temps* 1 (1): 125–137.

Davenport, Christian. 2004. "Mass Killings and the Oases of Humanity: Understanding the Rwandan Genocide and Resistance," preliminary results of "Genodynamics: Understanding Genocide through Time and Space," an NSF-funded research project led by Christian Davenport and Allan Stam, posted at www.bsos.umd.edu/gvpt/davenport/geodynamics/data (accessed spring 2008).

David, Philippe. 1980. *Les Navétanes: Histoire des migrants saisonniers de l'arachide es Sénégambie des origines à nos jours.* Dakar and Abidjan: Nouvelles Editions Africaines.

Deininger, Klaus 2003. *Land Policies for Growth and Poverty Reduction*. Washington, DC: The World Bank.

Deininger, Klaus and Hans Binswanger. 1999. "The Evolution of the World Bank's Land Policy." *The World Bank Research Observer* 14 (2): 247–276.

Deininger, Klaus. 2003. "Causes and Consequences of Civil Strife: Micro-level Evidence from Uganda." *Oxford Economic Papers* 55: 579–606.

Deininger, Klaus. 2011. "Challenges Posed by the New Wave of Farmland Investment." *Journal of Peasant Studies* 38 (2): 217–247.

Deininger, Klaus and Rafaella Castagnini. 2006. "Incidence and Impact of Land Conflict in Uganda." *Journal of Economic Behavior and Organization* 60 (3): 321–345.

de Lame. *See* Lame 2005.

de Villiers, Gauthier with Jean Omasombo Tshonda. 1997. *See* Villiers, Gauthier de 1997.

Dembele, Ousmane. 2003. "Côte d'Ivoire: La fracture communautaire." *Politique Africaine* 89 (mars): 34–48.

Demsetz, Harold. 1967. "Towards a Theory of Property Rights." *The American Economic Review* 57 (2): 347–359.

Des Forges, Alison and Human Rights Watch. 1999. *See* HRW/Des Forges 1999.

Development Partners Group on Land in Kenya. 2005. "Joint Statement from the Development Partners Group" (a group chaired by UN-HABITAT), August, posted at www.chapterpdf.com/joint-statement-from-the-development-partners-group-for-the-kenya.pdf (accessed 25 May 2012).

Diaby, Nissoiti. 1996. "Notables et paysans dans la forêt classée, un conflit d'environnement dans l'Est de la Côte d'Ivoire," in *Democratie, Enjeux Fonciers, et Pratiques Locales en Afrique*. Paul Mathieu, P.-J. Laurent, and J.-C. Willame, eds. Bruxelles and Paris: Institut Africain-CEDAF (Centre d'Etude et de Documentation Africaines) and Editions L'Harmattan: 164–179.

Dian, Boni. 1985. *L'Economie de plantation en Côte d'Ivoire forestière*. Abidjan, Dakar, Lomé: Nouvelles Editions Africaines (NEA).

Diawara, Mamadou. 2011. "Development and Administrative Norms: The Office du Niger and Decentralization in French Sudan and Mali." *Africa: Journal of the International African Institute* 81 (3) (August): 434–454.

Diop, Mame Dagou, Chiekh Mamina Diedhiou, and Madiodio Niasse. 2009. *Sharing the Benefits of Large Dams in West Africa: The Case of Displaced People*. London and Dakar: IIED and Global Water Initiative (GWI). February.

Dorman, Sara Rich, Daniel Patrick Hammett, and Paul Nugent. 2007a. "Introduction: Citizenship and its Casualties in Africa," in *Making Nations, Creating Strangers: States and Citizenship in Africa*. Leiden, Brill, pp. 3–28.

Dorman, Sara Rich, Daniel Patrick Hammett, and Paul Nugent, eds. 2007b. *Making Nations, Creating Strangers: States and Citizenship in Africa*. Leiden: Brill.

Doujara, Hamady, Jean-François Bélières, and Demba Kébé. 2006. "Les exploitations agricoles familiales de la zone cotonnière du Mali face à la baisse des prix du coton-graine." *Cahiers Agricoles* 15 (1) (janvier–février): 64–71.

Downs, R. E. and S. P. Reyna, eds. 1988. *Land and Society in Contemporary Africa*. Hanover and London: University of New Hampshire and University Press of New England.

Dozon, J. P. 1982. "Epistémologie du 'foncier' dans le cadre des économies de planation ivoiriennes," in *Enjeux Fonciers en Afrique Noire*. E. Le Bris, E. Le Roy, and F. Leimdorfer, eds. Paris: Karthala: 56–60.

Dozon, J. P. 1985. *La société Bété*. Paris: Karthala.

Dozon, J. P. 1997. "L'étranger et l'allochtone en Côte d'Ivoire," in *Le Modèle Ivoirien en Questions: Crises, Ajustements, et Recompositions*. Bernard Contamin and Harris Memel-Fotê, eds. Paris: Karthala and Orstom: 779–798.

Dozon, J. P. 2000. "La Côte d'Ivoire entre démocratie, nationalisme, et ethnonationalisme." *Politique Africaine* 78: 45–62.

Dozon, J. P. 2008. *L'Afrique à Dieu et à Diable: Etats, Ethnies, et Religion*. Paris: Ellipses.

Duncan, Alex and John Howell. 1992. "Introduction: Assessing the Impact of Structural Adjustment," in *Structural Adjustment and the African Farmer*. A. Duncan and J. Howell, eds. London and Portsmouth, NH: Overseas Development Council in association with James Currey and Heinemann.

Dunn, John. 1975. Politics in Asunafo, in *Politicians and Soldiers in Ghana 1966–1972*. Dennis Austin and Robin Luckham, eds. London: Frank Cass and Company, Ltd.: 164–213.

Easterly, William and Ross Levine. 1997. Africa's Growth Tragedy: Policies and Ethnic Divisions." *Quarterly Journal of Economics* 112 (4) (November): 1203–1251.

Economist Intelligence Unit (EIU). 2000. *Country Profile 2000. Zimbabwe*. London: EIU.

Eisenstadt, Todd. 2011. *Politics, Identity, and Mexico's Indigenous Rights Movements*. Cambridge and New York: Cambridge University Press.

Elbow, Kent et al. 1996. *Country Profiles of Land Tenure: West Africa*. Madison, WI: Land Tenure Center.

Ellett, Rachel L. 2005. "Reemergence of the 'Other': Nationalism in Post-Nyerere Tanzania." *Canadian Review of Studies in Nationalism* 32, (1–2): 93–109.

Elliot-Teague, Ginger. 2009. "Coalition Lobbying in Tanzania: The Experience of Local NGOs." *Journal of Public Affairs* 8 (1–2): 99–114.

Ellis, Diana. 1976. "The Nandi Protest of 1923 in the Context of African Resistance to Colonial Rule in Kenya." *Journal of African History* 17 (4): 555–575.

Eltringham, Nigel. 2006. "Debating the Rwandan Genocide," in *Violence, Political Culture, and Development in Africa*. Preben Kaarsholm, ed. London and Athens: James Currey and Ohio University Press: 66–91.

Engerman, Stanley and Jacob Metzer, eds. 2004. *Land Rights, Ethno-Nationality, and Sovereignty in History*, London and New York: Routledge.

Engerman, Stanley and Kenneth L. Sokoloff. 2001. "The Evolution of Suffrage Institutions in the New World." NBER Working Paper Series, Working Paper 8512. October.

Engerman, Stanley and Kenneth L. Sokoloff. 2003. "Institutional and Non-Institutional Explanations of Economic Differences," NBER Working Paper 9989. September.

Englebert, Pierre. 2003. "Why Congo Persists: Sovereignty, Globalization, and the Violent Reproduction of a Weak State." Queen Elizabeth House Carnegie Project on Global Cultural and Economic Dimensions of Self-Determination in Developing Countries, QEH Working Paper Series no. 95, February (40 pages).

Ensminger, Jean. 1992. *Making a Market: The Institutional Transformation of an African Society.* New York and Cambridge: Cambridge University Press.

Ensminger, Jean. 1997. "Changing Property Rights: Reconciling Formal and Informal Rights to Land," in *Frontiers of the New Institutional Economics.* John N. Drobak and John V. C. Nye, eds. San Diego, London, Boston: Academic Press: 165–196.

Ermis Africa Leadership Development. See United Nations Environmental Project and Kenya Wildlife Service.

Erny, Pierre. 1995. *Rwanda 1994.* Paris: L'Harmattan.

Etherington, D. M. 1963. "Land Resettlement in Kenya: Policy and Practice." *East African Economic Review* 10 (1) (June): 22–34.

Eyoh, Dickson. 1998. "Through the Prism of a Local Tragedy: Political Liberalisation, Regionalism, and Elite Struggles for Power in Cameroun." *Africa: Journal of the International African Institute* 68 (3) (summer): 338–359.

Fairhead, James. 1989. *Food Security in North and South Kivu (Zaire), 1989.* Final Consultancy Report for Oxfam, Part I, Section 2, London: Oxfam (cited by Pottier 2002: 26).

Falola, Toyin. 2009. *Colonialism and Violence in Nigeria.* Bloomington: Indiana University Press.

Fauré, Y. 1993. "Democracy and Realism: Reflections on the Case of Côte d'Ivoire." *Africa* 63 (3): 313–329.

Faye, Aïssatou. 2006. Pouvoir local et coopération au développement à Ross-Bethio: Gestion sélective de l'offre des services fonciers et exclusion. *Bulletin de l'APAD,* 22, posted 27 mars 2006 at apad.revues.org/document92.html (accessed 7 November 2009).

Faye, Jacques. 1981. "Zonal Approach to Migration in the Senegalese Peanut Basin," in *The Uprooted of the Western Sahel: Migrants' Quest for Cash in the Senegambia.* Lucy Gallistel Colvin, Cheikh Ba, Boubacar Berry, Jacques Faye, Alice Hammer, Moussa Soumah, and Fatou Sow (New York: Praeger): 136–140.

Faye, Jacques. 2000. "Pour une nouvelle agriculture familiale et une nouvelle ruralité." *Le Quotidien* (Dakar), n. 2129, (10 mai): 8.

Fearon, James D., and Laitin, David. 1996. "Explaining Interethnic Cooperation." *American Political Science Review* 90 (4) (December): 715–735.

Fearon, James and David Laitin. 2011. "Sons of the Soil, Migrants, and Civil War." *World Development* 39 (2) (February): 199–211.

Ferguson, James. 1999. *Expectations of Modernity: Myths and Meanings of Urban Life on the Zambian Copperbelt.* Berkeley and Los Angeles: University of California Press.

Field, Alexander James. 1981. "The Problem with Neoclassical Institutional Economics: A Critique with Special Reference to the North/Thomas Model of pre-1500 Europe." *Explorations in Economic History* 18: 174–198.

Firmin-Sellers, Kathryn. 1996. *The Transformation of Property Rights in the Gold Coast: An Empirical Analysis Applying Rational Choice Theory.* Cambridge and New York: Cambridge University Press.

Fisiy, Cyprian F. 1992. "Power and Privilege in the Administration of Law: Land Law Reforms and Social Differentiation in Cameroon." Research Report no. 48. Leiden: African Studies Center.

Fisiy, Cyprian F. 1995. "Chieftaincy in the Modern State: An Institution at the Cross-roads of Democratic Change." *Paideuma* 41: 49–62.

Foot, Chris. 2008. "What is Wrong with the Proposed Constitution?" unpub. paper (21 pages). Another version appears as Kenya Landowners Federation (KLF). N.d. "An Overview of the Draft National Land Policy," posted by Mike Norton-Griffiths at www.mng5.com.

Ford, Robert E. 1993. "Marginal Coping in Extreme Land Pressures: Ruhengeri, Rwanda," in *Population Growth and Agricultural Development*. B. L. Turner II, Goran Hyden, and Robert W. Kates, eds. Gainesville: University of Florida Press: 145–186.

Ford, Robert E. 1998. "Settlement Structure and Landscape Ecology in Humid Tropical Rwanda," in *Rural Settlement Structure and Africa Development*. Marilyn Silberfein, ed. Boulder, CO: Westview Press: 167–207.

Forrest, Joshua. 2003. *Lineages of State Fragility: Rural Civil Society in Guinea-Bissau*. Oxford and Athens: James Currey Ltd. and Ohio University Press.

Forrest, Joshua. 2004. *Subnationalism in Africa: Ethnicity, Alliances, and Politics*. Boulder, CO, and London: Lynne Rienner Publishers.

Fox, Jonathan. 2004. The Difficult Transition from Clientelism to Citizenship: Lessons from Mexico." *World Politics* 46 (2) (January): 151–184.

Fred-Mensah, Ben K. 1999. "Capturing Ambiguities: Communal Conflict Management Alternatives in Ghana." *World Development* 27 (6): 951–965.

Freiku, Sebastian R. 2006. "Fulani Herdsmen, Cattle Invade Kumawu Lands." *Ghanaian Chronicle*, 5 December (electronic version, no page numbers, accessed via the Financial Times Limited, Asia Africa Intelligence Wire, via Factiva, spring 2006).

Frye, Timothy. 2004. "Credible Commitment and Property Rights, Evidence from Russia." *American Political Science Review* 98 (3) (August): 453–466.

Frye, Timothy. 2007. "Economic Transformation and Comparative Politics," in *Oxford Handbook of Comparative Politics*. Carles Boix and Susan Stokes, eds. Oxford: Oxford University Press: 940–968.

Furedi, Frank. 1989. *The Mau Mau War in Perspective*. London and Athens: James Currey and Ohio University Press.

Gadji-Dagbo, Joseph. 2002. *L'Affaire Kragbé Guabé: Un autre regard 32 ans après*. Abidjan: Nouvelles Editions Africaines.

Galvan, Dennis. 2004. *The State Must Be Our Master of Fire: How Peasants Craft Culturally Sustainable Development in Senegal*. Berkeley and Los Angeles: University of California.

Gasana, James. 1995. "La guerre, la paix, et la démocratie au Rwanda," in *Les Crises Politiques au Burundi et au Rwanda*. André Guichaoua, ed. Paris: Karthala: 211–238.

Gasana, James. 2002. "Natural Resource Scarcity and Violence in Rwanda," in *Conserving the Peace: Resources, Livelihoods, and Security*. Mark Halle, Richard Matthew, and Jason Switzer, eds. Winnipeg: International Institute for Sustainable Development (IISD): 199–246.

Gastellu, J. M. 1982. "Droit d'usage et propriété privée," in *Enjeux Fonciers en Afrique Noire*. E. Le Bris, E. Le Roy, and F. Leimdorfer, eds. Paris: Karthala: 269–280.

Gastellu, Jean-Marc. 1989. *Riches Paysans de Côte-d'Ivoire*. Paris: L'Harmattan.

Gazetted Land (Consequential Provisions) Act, 2006. Chapter 20:28 Act 8/2006. L.

Guma, 2009. "Over 29,000 Youth Militia Still Being Paid by the State." *SW Radio*

Africa Zimbabwe News, 3 April, posted at www.swradioafrica.com/News030409/ youtho30409.htm (accessed January 2010).

Gazibo, Mamoudou and Daniel C. Bach. 2012. "Introduction," in *The Neopatrimonial State in Africa and Beyond*. M. Gazibo and D. C. Bach, eds. London: Routledge: 1–6.

Gbagbo, Laurent. 1982. *Côte-d'Ivoire: Economie et société à la veille de l'indépendance, 1940–1960*. Paris: L'Harmattan.

Geertz, Clifford. 1963. *Agricultural Involution: The Processes of Ecological Change in Indonesia*. Berkeley and Los Angeles: University of California Press.

Gerring, John. 2004. "What is a Case Study and What is it Good For?" *American Political Science Review* 98 (2): 341–354.

Geschiere, Peter and Josef Gugler. 1998. "The Urban-Rural Connection: Changing Issues of Belonging and Identification." *Africa: Journal of the International African Institute* 68 (3): 309–319.

Ghana, Government of. 1999. *See* Government of Ghana. Report of the Committee on Tenant/Settler Farmers. May.

Ghana Land Administration Project. "General Information about LAP," posted at www.ghanalap.gov.gh/index1.php?linkid=48 (accessed 14 January 2008).

Gibson, Edward. 1997. "The Populist Road to Market Reform: Policy and The Electoral Coalitions in Mexico and Argentina." *World Politics* 49 (2): 339–370.

Gibson, Edward. 2004. *Federalism and Democracy in Latin America*. Baltimore, MD: Johns Hopkins University Press.

Gibson, Edward. 2005. "Boundary Control: Subnational Authoritarianism in Democratic Countries." *World Politics* 58 (1) (October): 101–132.

Gibson, Edward L. 2012. *Boundary Control: Subnational Authoritarianism in Federal Democracies*. New York and London: Cambridge University Press.

Giddens, Anthony. 1971. *Capitalism and Modern Social Theory*. Cambridge: Cambridge University Press.

Gisemba, Horace Njuguna. 2008. "The Lie of the Land: Evictions and Kenya's Crisis." Africa Policy Brief No. 2. Nairobi: Africa Policy Institute, February, with an abridged version published in 2008 in the *Sunday Nation* (Nairobi), 17 February.

Githinji, Mwangi wa. 2000. *Ten Millionaires and Ten Million Beggars: A Study of Income Distribution and Development in Kenya*. Aldershot: Ashgate.

Gizewski, Peter and Thomas Homer-Dixon. 1998. "The Case of Pakistan," in *Ecoviolence: Links among Environment, Population, and Security*. T. Homer-Dixon and Jessica Blitt, eds. Lanham, MD: Rowman and Littlefield Publishers: 147–200.

Goheen, Mitzi. 1992. "Chiefs, Sub-Chiefs, and Local Control." *Africa: Journal of the International African Institute* 62 (3): 389–411. Reproduced in part in Tom Young, ed., *Readings in African Politics*. 2003. Bloomington and Oxford: Indiana University Press and James Currey: 97–106.

Goldman, Abe. 1993. Population Growth and Agricultural Change in Imo State, Southeastern Nigeria," in *Population Growth and Agricultural Development*. B. L. Turner II, Goran Hyden, and Robert William Kates, eds. Gainesville: University of Florida Press: 250–301.

Goldstone, Jack A. 2003. "Comparative Historical Analysis and Knowledge Accumulation in the Study of Revolutions," in *Comparative Historical Analysis in the Social Sciences*. James Mahoney and Dietrich Rueschemeyer, eds. Cambridge and New York: Cambridge University Press: 41–90.

Gonné, Bernard and Christian Seignobos. 2006. "Nord Cameroun: Les tensions foncières s'exacerbent." *Revue Grain de Sel* n. 36 (septembre–novembre): 16–218.

Goody, Jack. 1980. "Rice Burning in Northern Ghana." *Journal of Development Studies* 16 (2) (January): 136–155.

Gotanegre, J.-F., C. Prioul, and P. Sirven. 1974. *Géographie du Rwanda*. Bruxelles: Editions de Boeck.

Gould, W. T. S. 1995. "Migration and Recent Economic and Environmental Change in East Africa," in *The Migration Experience in Africa*. Jonathan Baker and Tade Akin Aina, eds. Uppsala: Nordiska Afrikainstitutet: 122–148.

Gourevitch, Peter. 1986. *Politics in Hard Times: Comparative Responses to International Economic Crises*. Ithaca, NY: Cornell University Press.

Gouvernement de Transition du Zaïre, Ministère de la Communication et Press. *See* Zaire, Gouvernement de Transition du Zaïre 1993.

Gouvernement du Sénégal, Ministère de l'Agriculture. 1996. Plan d'Action Foncier (PAF) du Sénégal, October 1996 (Archives Nationales du Sénégal [ANS] poIII 4° 4016).

Government of Ghana, Committee on Tenant/Settler Farmers. 1999. "Report of the Committee on Tenant/Settler Farmers on a Study of Problems of Landlords and Tenant/Settler Farmers in Sefwi-Wiawso and Juabeso-Bia Districts, Western Region." May.

Government of Ghana. n.d. Ghana Land Administration Project, "General Information about LAP," posted at www.ghanalap.gov.gh/index1.php?linkid=48 (accessed 14 January 2008).

Government of Kenya. 2004. "Report of the Commission of Inquiry into the Illegal/ Irregular Allocation of Public Land." Nairobi: Government Printer. Released in December, chaired by Paul Ndungu.

Government of Kenya, Office of the Prime Minister. 2009. "Rehabilitation of the Mau Forest Ecosystem: A Project Concept Prepared by the Interim Coordinating Secretariat, Office of the Prime Minister for the Government of Kenya," Nairobi, September: 5, posted by the Kenya Wildlife Service at www.kws.org (accessed 26 December 2010).

Gramsci, Antonio. 1971. *Selections from the Prison Notebooks*. Q. Hoare and G. Nowell Smith trans. London: Lawrence & Wishart.

Gravel, Pierre Bettez. 1962. The Play for Power: Description of a Community in Eastern Rwanda. Ph.D. dissertation, University of Michigan, Department of Anthropology.

Gray, L. C. 1999. "Is Land Being Degraded? A Multi-scaled Investigation of Landscape in Southwestern Burkina Faso." *Land Degradation and Development* 10 (4) (July–August): 329–343.

Gray, Leslie C. and Michael Kevane. 2001. "Evolving Tenure Rights and Agricultural Intensification in Southwestern Burkina Faso." *World Development* 29 (4): 573–587.

Gready, Paul. 2010. "'You're Either with Us or against Us': Civil Society and Policy Making in Post-genocide Rwanda." *African Affairs* 109 (437): 637–657.

Great Britain, Kenya Regional Boundaries Commission. 1962. "Report of the Regional Boundaries Commission." London: Her Majesty's Stationery Office. December.

Green, Elliott. 2006. "Ethnic Politics and Land Tenure Reform in Central Uganda." A paper for the Annual Meetings of the American Political Science Association (APSA),

Philadelphia, 1 September. Revised version published in 2006 in *Commonwealth and Comparative Politics* 44 (3) (November): 370–388.

Greif, Avner. 2006. *Institutions and the Path to the Modern Economy.* Cambridge: Cambridge University Press.

Greif, Avner and David Laitin. 2004. "A Theory of Endogenous Institutional Change." *American Political Science Review* 98 (4): 633–652.

Grier, Beverly. 1987. "Contradiction, Crisis, and Class Conflict: The State and Capitalist Development in Ghana Prior to 1948," in *Studies in Class and Power in Africa.* Irving Leonard Markovitz, ed. New York and Oxford: Oxford University Press: 27–49.

Guma, L. 2009. Over 29,000 Youth Militia Still Being Paid by the State, 3 April, *SW Radio Africa Zimbabwe News*, posted at www.swradioafrica.com/News030409/youth030409.htm (accessed 22 January 2010).

Guichaoua, André. 1989. *L'Ordre paysan des hautes terres centrales du Burundi et du Rwanda.* Paris: L'Harmattan. Tome I and Tome II.

Guichaoua, André. 1992. "Le problème des réfugiés rwandais et des populations ban-yarwanda dans a région des Grands Lacs Africains: Etude présentée lors de la Réunion Conjointe OIT-HCR sur L'Aide internationale en tant que moyen de réduire la Nécessité de l'Emigration tenue à Genève les 5–8 Mai." Haut Commissariat des Nations Unies pour les Réfugiés (UNHCR), Genève. Mai.

Guichaoua, André. 1995. "Un lourd passé, un présent dramatique, un avenir des plus sombres," in *Les Crises Politiques au Burundi et au Rwanda.* A. Guichaoua, ed. Paris: Karthala: 19–51.

Guichaoua, André. 1998. "Audition de M. André Guichaoua, Professeur à l'Université Lille I." Assemblée Nationale Française, 24 mars, posted at www.voltairenet.org/article7839.html (accessed 15 February 2007).

Guichaoua, André. 1999. "Mobilité forcée dans la région des Grands Lacs," in *Déplacés et Réfugiés: La Mobilité sous Contrainte.* Véronique Lassailly-Jacob, Jean-Yves Marchal, and André Quesnel, eds. Paris: Editions du l'Institut de Recherche pour le Développement (IRD): 303–342.

Gyimah-Boadi, E. and Daddieh, C. 1999. "Economic Reform and Political Liberal-ization in Ghana and Côte d'Ivoire: A Preliminary Assessment and Implications for Nation-Building," in *State Building and Democratization in Africa.* K. Mengisteab and C. Daddieh, eds. Westport, CT: Praeger: 125–156.

Haber, Stephen, Armando Razo, and Noel Maurer. 2003. *The Politics of Prop-erty Rights: Political Instability, Credible Commitments, and Economic Growth in Mexico, 1876–1929.* Cambridge: Cambridge University Press.

Hafer, Catherine. 2003. "On the Origins of Property Rights: Conflict and Production in the State of Nature." Department of Politics, New York University, October. Published in 2006 under same title in *Review of Economic Studies* 73 (1): 119–143.

Hagberg, S. 2002. "Enough is Enough: An Ethnographic Account of the Struggle against Impunity in Burkina Faso." *Journal of Modern African Studies* 40 (2): 217–246.

Hagberg, Sten. 1998. *Between Peace and Justice: Dispute Settlement between Kara-bor Agriculturalists and Fulbe Agropastoralists in Burkina Faso* (Comoé Region [Banfora>]). Uppsala: Acta Univeisitatis Upsaliensis (268 pages).

Hagberg, Sten. 2003. "Mobilization of Rights through Organisational Structures [in Burkina]," in *Readings in African Politics.* Tom Lodge, ed. Oxford and Bloomington: James Currey and Indiana University Press: 127–138.

Hall, Peter A., and Daniel W. Gingerich. 2004. "Varieties of Capitalism and Institutional Complementarities in the Macro-Economy: An Empirical Analysis." Max Planck Institute for the Study of Societies Discussion Paper 04/5. Cologne: Max Planck Institute.

Hall, Peter A. and David Soskice. 2001. *Varieties of Capitalism: The Institutional Foundations of Comparative Advantage.* Oxford: Oxford University Press.

Haller, Tobias. 2001. "Rules That Pay Are Going to Stay: Indigenous Institutions, Sustainable Resource Use, and Land Tenure among the Ouldeme and Platha, Mandara Mountains, Northern Cameroon." *Le Bulletin de l'APAD* (en ligne), 22 (Gouvernance foncière au quotidien en Afrique), mis en ligne le 20 février 2006, apad.revues.org/148 (consulté 22 May 2012).

Hammar, A., J. McGregor, and L. Landau. 2010. "Introduction: Displacing Zimbabwe: Crisis and Construction in Southern Africa." *Journal of Southern African Studies* 36 (2): 263–283.

Hann, C. M. 1998. "Introduction: The Embeddedness of Property," in *Property Relations: Renewing the Anthropological Tradition.* C. M. Hann, ed. Cambridge: Cambridge University Press: 1–47.

Hansen, Ketil Fred. 2003. "The Politics of Personal Relations: Beyond Neopatrimonial Practices in Northern Cameroon." *Africa: Journal of the International African Institute* 73 (2): 202–246.

Harbeson, John. 1973. *Nation-Building in Kenya: The Role of Land Reform.* Evanston, IL: Northwestern University Press.

Harding, Robin. 2010. "Urban-Rural Differences in Support for Incumbents across Africa." Afrobarometer Working Paper no. 120., E. Lansing, MI, and Accra, Ghana: Michigan State University and Center for Democratic Development. June (31 pages).

Harnischfeger, Johannes. 2004. "Sharia and Control over Territory: Conflicts between 'Settlers' and 'Indigenes' in Nigeria." *African Affairs* 103 (412): 431–452.

Harold-Barry, D. 2004. "Chronology," in *The Past Is the Future.* D. Harold-Barry, ed. Harare, Zimbabwe: Weaver Press: 261–273.

Harrington, Julia. 2005. "Citizenship in Africa." *Justice Initiatives.* New York: The Open Society Institute. February.

Harris, Ron. 2003. "The Encounters of Economic History and Legal History." *Law and History Review* 21 (2) (summer): 93 parts, posted at www.historycooperative.org/cgi-bin/cite.cgi?f=lhr/21.2/harris.html (accessed 24 May 2012).

Harsch, Ernest. 2009. "Urban Protest in Burkina Faso." *African Affairs* 108 (431) (April): 268–288.

Harvey, David. 2005. *A Brief History of Neoliberalism.* Oxford: Oxford University Press.

Hatchard, J. 2001. "Some Lessons on Constitution-Making from Zimbabwe." *Journal of African Law* 45 (2): 210–216.

Hatzfeld, Jean. 2005a. *Into the Quick of Life: The Rwandan Genocide Survivors Speak.* London: Serpent's Tail. First published in 2000 as *Dans le nu de la vie*, Paris: Editions du Seuil.

Hatzfeld, Jean. 2005b. *Machete Season: The Killers in Rwanda Speak.* New York: Picador/Farrar, Straus, and Giroux. First published in 2003 as *Une saison de machettes*, Paris: Editions de Seuil.

Haugerud, Angelique. 1993. *The Culture of Politics in Modern Kenya*. Cambridge: Cambridge University Press.

Hecht, Robert M. 1982. Cocoa and the Dynamics of Socio-Economic Change in Southern Ivory Coast. Ph.D. dissertation, University of Cambridge.

Hecht, Robert M. 1985. "Immigration, Land Transfer, and Tenure Change in Divo, Ivory Coast: 1940–1980." *Africa* 55 (3): 319–336.

Hechter, Michael. 2000. *Containing Nationalism*. Oxford: Oxford University Press.

Heller, Peter. 2010. "People and Places: Can They Align to Bring Growth to Africa?" Center for Global Development Essay, posted at www.cgdev.org (acccessed 1 September 2011). September.

Henrysson, Elin and Sandra Joireman. 2009. "On the Edge of the Law: Women's Property Rights and Dispute Resolution in Kisii, Kenya." *Law & Society Review* 43 (1): 39–60.

Herbst, Jeffrey. 1990. *State Politics in Zimbabwe*. Harare: University of Zimbabwe Press.

Herbst, Jeffrey. 2000. *States and Power in Africa: Comparative Lessons in Authority and Control*. Princeton, NJ: Princeton University Press.

Herring, Ron. 2003. "The Political Impossibility Theorem of Agrarian Reform," in *Changing Paths: Institutional Development and the New Politics of Inclusion*. M. Moore and P. Houtzager, eds. Ann Arbor: University of Michigan Press: 58–87.

Hickey, Sam. 2007. "Caught at the Crossroads: Citizenship, Marginality, and the Mbororo Fulani in Northwest Cameroon," in *Making Nations, Creating Strangers: States and Citizenship in Africa*. Sara Dorman, Daniel Hammet, and Paul Nugents, eds. Leiden: Brill: 83–104.

Hien, Pierre Claver. 2003. "La dénomination de l'espace dans la construction du Burkina Faso (1919–2001)," in *Peuplement, Relations Interethniques, et Identités*. Richard Kuba, Carola Lentz, and Claude Nurukyor Somda, eds. Paris: Karthala: 23–40.

Hill, Polly. 1963. *Migrant Cocoa Farmers of Southern Ghana: A Study in Rural Capitalism*. Cambridge: Cambridge University Press.

Hintjens, Helen. 1999. "Explaining the 1994 Genocide in Rwanda." *Journal of Modern African Studies* 37 (2) (June): 241–286.

Hirschman, A.O. 1970. *Exit, Voice, and Loyalty: Responses to Decline in Firms, Organizations, and States*. Cambridge, MA: Harvard University Press.

Hochschild, Jennifer. 2009. "Searching for a Politics of Scale," in *The Future of Political Science: 100 Perspectives*. Norman H. Nie et al., eds. NY: Routledge: 248–251.

Holden, Stein T., Keijiro Otsuka, and Frank M. Place. 2009. *The Emergence of Land Markets in Africa: Assessing the Impacts on Poverty, Equity, and Efficiency*. Washington, DC: Resources for the Future.

Homer-Dixon, Thomas and Jessica Blitt, eds. 1998. *Ecoviolence: Links among Environment, Population, and Security*. Lanham, MD: Rowman and Littlefield Publishers.

Huggins, Chris. 2009. "Land in Return, Reintegration, and Recovery Processes: Some Lessons from the Great Lakes Region of Africa," in *Uncharted Territory: Land, Conflict, and Humanitarian Action*. Sara Pantuliano, ed. Bourton on Dunsmore, Rugby, Warwickshire: Practical Action Publishing: 67–94.

Huggins, Chris, Prisca Kamungi, Joan Kariuki, Herman Musahara, et al. 2006. "Land, Conflict, and Livelihoods in the Great Lakes Region: Testing Policies to the Limit." Nairobi: African Center for Technology Studies (ACTS), Ecopolicy Series no. 14.

Hugon, Philippe. 2003. "La Côte d'Ivoire: Plusieurs lectures pour une crise annoncée." *Afrique Contemporaine*, n. 2 (summer): 105–127.

Hull, C. Bryson. 2008. "Ghost of Moi Surfaces in Kenya's Violence." Reuters, 11 January, posted at www.reuters.com/article/2008/01/11/us-kenya-crisis-forest-idUSHUL08142020080111 (accessed 24 May 2012).

Human Rights Watch (HRW). 1993a. "Beyond the Rhetoric: Continuing Human Rights Abuse in Rwanda." *News from Africa Watch*, 5, (7A), Washington, DC. June.

Human Rights Watch/Africa Watch (HRW). 1993b. *Divide and Rule: State-Sponsored Ethnic Violence in Kenya*. New York and Washington: Human Rights Watch.

Human Rights Watch (HRW). 2001a. "The New Racism: The Political Manipulation of Ethnicity in Côte d'Ivoire." HRW Country Report 13 (6A), August, posted at www.hrw.org. (accessed 10 January 2003).

Human Rights Watch (HRW). 2001b. *Uprooting the Rural Poor in Rwanda*. New York: Human Rights Watch.

Human Rights Watch (HRW). 2002. "Zimbabwe: Fast Track Land Reform in Zimbabwe." Report 14 (1A).

Human Rights Watch (HRW). 2003. "Côte d'Ivoire, Trapped between Two Wars: Violence against Civilians in Western Côte d'Ivoire." Report 15 (14A).

Human Rights Watch (HRW). 2007. "'My Heart is Cut.' Sexual Violence by Rebels and Pro-Government Forces in Côte d'Ivoire," Report 19 (11A) (August).

Human Rights Watch (HRW)/Alison Des Forges. 1999. *Leave None to Tell the Story: Genocide in Rwanda*. New York: Human Rights Watch.

Humphreys, Macartan and Jeremy M. Weinstein. 2008. "Who Fights: The Determinants of Participation in Civil War." *American Journal of Political Science* 52 (2): 436–455.

Hunt, Diana. 2005. "Some Outstanding Issues in the Debate on External Promotion of Land Privatization." *(ODI) Development Policy Review* 23 (2): 199–231.

Huntington, Samuel. 1968. *Political Order in Changing Societies*. New Haven, CT: Yale University Press.

Hussein, Karim, James Sumberg, and David Seddon. 1999. "Increasingly Violent Conflict between Herders and Farmers in Africa: Claims and Evidence." *Development Policy Review* 17 (4): 397–418.

Hyden, Goran. 1980. *Beyond Ujamaa in Tanzania*. Los Angeles and Berkeley: University of California Press.

Imbs, Françoise. 1997. "Retours et reconstruction au Rwanda: Et pourtant ils vivient!" *Hérodote: Revue de Géographie et de Géopolitique* 86–87 (Special Issue: Géopolitique d'une Afrique Médiane, Yves Lacoste, ed.): 150–181.

Imbs, Françoise and A. Bart. 1994. "Le Rwanda: Les données sociogéographiques." *Hérodote* (Paris), nos. 72–73, 1ère et 2ème trimestre: 246–269.

Independent Review of Land Issues 2004. *See* Oxfam UK 2004a.

Ingelaere, Bert. 2010. "Peasants, Power, and Ethnicity: A Bottom-Up Perspective on Rwanda's Political Transition." *African Affairs* 109 (435): 273–292.

International Crisis Group (ICG). 2002. "Zimbabwe at the Crossroads: Transition or Conflict." *Africa Report* 41 (22) (March). Harare/Brussels: International Crisis Group.

International Crisis Group (ICG). 2003. "Côte d'Ivoire: The War Is Not Yet Over." *Rapport Afrique* no. 72.

International Crisis Group (ICG). 2004. "Blood and Soil: Land, Politics, and Conflict Prevention in Zimbabwe and South Africa." *Africa Report* no. 85.

International Crisis Group (ICG). 2005. "Côte d'Ivoire: Les demi-mesures ne suffiront pas." *Briefing Afrique* n. 33.

International Crisis Group (ICG). 2006. "Côte d'Ivoire: Augmenter la pression." *Africa Report* n. 40.

International Crisis Group (ICG). 2007. "Côte d'Ivoire: Can the Ouagadougou Agreement Bring Peace?" *Africa Report* n. 127.

International Monetary Fund (IMF). 2005. *International Financial Statistics Yearbook.* Washington, DC: IMF.

International Monetary Fund and International Development Association (IMF and IDA). 2002. "Côte d'Ivoire: Enhanced Initiative for Heavily Indebted Poor Countries (HIPC)." 12 March.

IRIN. 2008. "Zimbabwe: New Land Owners Face Eviction," 11 February, posted at www.irinnews.org/Report.aspx?ReportId=76682 (accessed 22 January 2010).

Isa-Odidi, Nabile. 2004. "Ethnic Conflict in Plateau State: The Need to Eliminate the Indigene/Stranger Dichotomy in Nigeria." *Human Rights Brief: A Legal Resource for the International Human Rights Community* 12 (1) (Fall): 18–23 (published by Washington, DC: American University, Washington College of Law, Center for Human Rights and Humanitarian Law).

Issacman, Allen. 1991. *Cotton Is the Mother of Poverty: Peasants, Work, and Rural Struggle in Colonial Mozambique, 1938–1961.* Portsmouth, NH: Heinemann.

Jackson, Gregory and Richard Deeg. 2006. "How Many Varieties of Capitalism? Comparing the Comparative Institutional Analyses of Capitalist Diversity." Max Planck Institute for the Study of Societies Discussion Paper 06 (2), Cologne: Max Planck Institute.

Jacob, Jean-Pierre. 2002. "La tradition du pluralisme institutionnel dans les conflits fonciers entre antochtones: Le cas du Gwendégne (Centre Ouest Burkina Faso) [Département Les Balés, around Boromo]." France, Institut de Recherche pour le Développement (IRD), Unité de Recherdre Réforme Foncière (REFO) n. 095, Doc. du travail n. 3. Avril.

Jacob, Jean-Pierre and Pierre Yves Le Meur, eds. 2010. *Politique de la terre et de l'appartenance: Droits fonciers et citoyenneté locale dans les sociétés du Sud.* Paris: Karthala.

JAG 2008. *See* Justice for Agriculture (JAG) 2008.

Jayne, T. S., David Mather, and Elliot Mghenyi. 2010. "Principal Challenges Confronting Smallholder Agriculture in Sub-Saharan Africa." *World Development* 38 (10): 1384–1398.

Jefremovas, Villia. 2002. *Brickyards to Graveyards: From Production to Genocide in Rwanda.* Albany: State University of New York (SUNY) Press.

Jenkins, Carolyn. 1997. "The Politics of Economic Policy Making in Zimbabwe." *Journal of Modern African Studies* 35 (4): 575–602.

Joireman, Sandra. 2005. "Enforcing New Property Rights in Sub-Saharan Africa: The Uganda Constitution and the 1998 Land Act." Paper prepared for the conference on Comparative Constitutionalism and Rights: Global Perspectives, Durban, South Africa, 10–13 December.

Joireman, Sandra. 2006. "The Evolution of the Common Law: Legal Development in Kenya and India." *Journal of Commonwealth and Comparative Politics* 44 (2) (July): 190–210.

Joireman, Sandra F. 2011. *Where There Is No Government: Enforcing Property Rights in Common Law Africa.* Oxford: Oxford University Press.

Jua, Nantang. 1990. *Economic Management in Neo-Colonial States: A Case Study of Cameroon, Research Reports no. 38/1990.* Leiden: African Studies Center.

Jua, Nantang. 2005. "Of Citizenship, Public Spaces, and National Imagining in Cameroun." *African Anthropologist* 12 (1) (March) 2005: 100–128.

Junisbai, Barbara. 2009. Market Reform Regimes, Elite Defections, and Political Opposition in the Post-Soviet States: Evidence from Belarus, Kazakhstan, and Kyrgyzstan. Ph.D. Dissertation, Indiana University, Department of Political Science.

Justice for Agriculture (JAG). 2008. "Destruction of Zimbabwe's Backbone Industry in Pursuit of Political Power: A Qualitative Report on Events in Zimbabwe's Commercial Farming Sector since the year 2000." JAG Trust and the General Agricultural and Plantation Workers Union of Zimbabwe (GAPWUZ), Harare, Zimbabwe, posted at www.kubatana.net/docs/agric/jag_gapwuz_destruction_agric_080508.pdf (accessed 25 May 2012) (77 pages).

Juul, Kristine and Christian Lund, eds. 2002. *Negotiating Property in Africa.* Portsmouth, NH: Heinemann.

Kaag, Mayke. 2001. *Usage foncier et usage dynamique sociale au Sénégal: L'histoire d'un bas fond et de ses defricheurs.* Amsterdam: Rosenberg Publishers.

Kabamba, Bob and Olivier Lanotte. 1999. "Guerres au Congo-Zaire (1996–1999): Acteurs et Scénarios," in *Conflits et Guerres au Kivu et dans la région des Grands Lacs.* Laurent Mathieu and J.-C. Willame, eds. Bruxelles and Paris: Institut Africain-CEDAF (Centre d'Etude et de Documentation Africaines) and Editions L'Harmattan: 99–159.

Kabera, John B. 1982. "Rural Population Redistribution in Uganda since 1900," in *Redistribution of Population in Africa.* John I. Clarke and Leszek Kosinski, eds. London, Nairobi, Ibadan: Heinemann: 192–201.

Kahl, Colin. 2006. *States, Scarcity, and Civil Strife in the Developing World.* Princeton, NJ: Princeton University Press.

Kalyvas, Stathis. 2006. *The Logic of Violence in Civil War.* Cambridge: Cambridge University Press.

Kandogo, Frederick. 2006. "Land Reform in a Regional Context: Malawian Experiences," Catholic Commission for Justice and Peace, posted at www.oxfam.org.uk (accessed 21 June 2006).

Kanongo, Tabitha. 1987. *Squatters and the Roots of Mau Mau, 1905–1963.* Athens and London: Ohio University Press and James Currey.

Kanyinga, K. 1998. "Politics and Struggles for Access to Land: 'Grants from Above' and 'Squatters' in Coastal Kenya." *European Journal of Development Research* 10 (2): 50–70.

Kanyinga, Karuti, Andrew S. Z. Kiondo, and Per Tidemand. 1994. *The New Local Politics in East Africa: Uganda, Tanzania, Kenya.* Research Report no. 95. Uppsala: Nordic African Institute.

Kapiteni, Antoine. 1998. "La première estimation du nombre des victimes du génocide des Batutsi du Rwanda de 1994, commune par commune." *Rwanda-Libération*

n. 33, avril–mai, posted at Rwanda 94, rwanda94.pagesperso-orange.fr/sitepers/dosrwand/rwframe.html (accessed 29 March 2007, 25 May 2012).

Kapur, Devesh. 1998. "The State in a Changing World: A Critique of the 1997 World Development Report." Harvard University, Weatherhead Center for International Affairs Working Paper no. 98–02.

Karlsson, Ida. 2008. "Rural-Urban Migration in Babati District, Tanzania," Arbetsrapporter, Kulturgeografiska Institutionen, Nr. 660. Uppsala: Uppsala Universitet. June.

Kasanga, Kasim and Nii Ashie Kotey. 2001. "Land Management in Ghana: Building on Traditional Authority." International Institute for Environment and Development (IIED), Land Tenure and Resource Access Series. London: IIED.

Kasara, Kimuli. 2008. "Electoral Geography and Conflict in Kenya: Examining the Local-Level Incidence of Violence in Rift Valley Province after the 2007 Election." Paper presented at the 2008 Annual Meetings of the American Political Science Association, 28–31 August, Boston, MA.

Kay, Geoffrey. 1972. *The Political Economy of Colonialism in Ghana*. London: Cambridge University Press.

Kazemi, Farhad and John Waterbury, eds. 1991. *Peasants and Politics in the Modern Middle East*. Miami: Florida International University Press.

Kelsall, Tim. 2000. "Governance, Local Politics, and Districtization in Tanzania." *African Affairs* 99: 533–551.

Kelsall, Tim. 2002. "Shop Windows and Smoke-Filled Rooms: Governance and the Re-politicization of Tanzania." *Journal of Modern African Studies* 40 (4) (December): 597–619.

Kelsall, Tim. 2004. *Contentious Politics, Local Governance, and the Self: A Tanzanian Case Study*. Research Report no. 129. Uppsala: Nordic Africa Institute. December.

Kenya. See Republic of Kenya.

Kenya Regional Boundaries Commission. 1962. See Great Britain, Kenya Regional Boundaries Commission.

Kenya Human Rights Commission (KHRC). 1996. *Ours by Right, Theirs by Might: A Study on Land Clashes*. Nairobi: KHRC, Land Rights Program.

Kenya Human Rights Commission (KHRC). 1998. *Killing the Vote: State Sponsored Violence and Flawed Elections in Kenya*. Nairobi: KHRC.

Kenya Land Alliance (KLA). 2005a. "The National Land Policy in Kenya: Addressing Customary/Communal Land Issues." KLA Issues Paper no. 4/2005. Nakuru: KLA.

Kenya Land Alliance (KLA). 2005b. "Fact Finding Mission on the Evictions in Mau Narok." Nakuru, posted at www.internal-displacement.org (accessed 26 December 2010).

Kenya Land Alliance (KLA). N.d. (2009?). "Kenya National Land Policy: Ten Myths and Misconceptions on the Draft National Land Policy." posted at http://www.kenyalandalliance.or.ke/images/Ten_Myths_and_Misconceptions.pdf. (accessed 10 May 2013).

Kepe, Thembele. 1999. "The Problem of Defining 'Community': Challenges for the Land Reform Programme in rural South Africa." *Development Southern Africa* 16 (3): 435–446.

Kigali, Secretariat d'Etat. *See* République Rwandaise 1991.

Kiggundu, Jacquie. 2008. "IDP Return Processes and Customary Land Tenure [in Burundi]." Presentation on Brookings-Bern Project on Internal Displacement hosted by Overseas Development Institute meeting, 7 February, reported in Brookings newsletter 31 July 2010.

Kiliku Report. 1992. *See* Republic of Kenya, The National Assembly 1992.

Kimble, G. T. H., ed. 1960. *Tropical Africa, Vol. 1: Land and Livelihood.* New York: Twentieth Century Fund.

Kimenyi, M. and N. S. N'Dung'u. 2005. "Sporadic Ethnic Violence: Why Has Kenya Not Experienced a Full-Blown Civil War?" in *Understanding Civil War: Evidence and Analysis.* P. Collier and N. Sambanis, eds. Washington, DC: The World Bank: 123–156.

Kinsey, B. 2010. "Who Went Where . . . and Why: Patterns and Consequences of Displacement in Rural Zimbabwe after February 2000." *Journal of Southern African Studies* 36 (2): 339–360.

Kirwin, Matthew. 2009. Communal Violence in Burkina Faso: A Multi-Level Examination. Ph.D dissertation, Michigan State University, Department of Political Science.

Kitching, Gavan. 1980. *Class and Economic Change in Kenya.* New Haven, CT: Yale University Press.

KLA. *See* Kenya Land Alliance.

Klopp, Jacqueline. 2000. "Pilfering the Public: The Problem of Land Grabbing in Contemporary Kenya." *Africa Today* 47 (1) (Winter): 7–26.

Klopp, Jacqueline. 2001. "'Ethnic Clashes' and Winning Elections: The Case of Kenya's Electoral Despotism." *Canadian Journal of African Studies* 35 (2): 473–517.

Klopp, Jacqueline. 2002. "Can Moral Ethnicity Trump Political Tribalism? The Struggle for Land and Nation in Kenya." *African Studies* (University of Witwatersrand) 61 (2): 269–294.

Klopp, Jacqueline M. 2001. Electoral Despotism in Kenya: Land, Patronage, and Resistance in the Multi-Party Context, Ph.D. dissertation, McGill University, Department of Political Science.

Knight, Jack. 1992. *Institutions and Social Conflict.* Cambridge University Press.

Kohlhagen, Dominik. 2010. "Vers un nouveau code foncier au Burundi?" *L'Afrique des Grands Lacs, 2009–2010.* Filip Reyntjens, ed. Paris: L'Harmattan: 67–98.

Koné, M[ariatou]. 1999. "Restauration de la fertilité des solds et amélioration des systèmes de culture pour le développement durable." RCI project, FAP/TPC/IVC/7821(A), August, Sous rapport n. 6, "Foncier rural et périurban."

Koné, M[ariatou]. 2006. "Quelles lois pour résoudre les problèmes liés au foncier en Côte d'Ivoire?" *Grain de Sel: Inter-réseaux développement rural*, 36 (septembre-novembre), posted at www.inter-reseaux.org (accessed 20 January 2008).

Koné, Mariatou. 2002. *Gaining Rights of Access to Land in West-Central Côte d'Ivoire.* London: International Institute for Environment and Development and IIED/GRET. March.

Korinman, Michel. 2005. "Partie du monde!" *Outre-Terre: Revue Française de Géopolitique*, n. 11: 9–18.

Kossoumna-Liba'a, Natali. 2003. "Mutations foncières au Nord-Cameroun: De la transhumance à la sédentarisation, des stratégies d'insertion et de limitation des conflits," in *Organisation spatiale et gestion des ressources et des territoires ruraux.* P. Dugué, and Ph. Jouve, eds. Actes du colloque international 25–27 février,

Montpellier, France: UMR Sagert, Centre National d'Etudes Agronomiques des Régions Chaudes (CNEARC).

Kotey, Nii A. and Marc O. Yeboah. 2003. "Report of a Study on Peri-urbanism, Land Relations, and Women in Ghana." GTZ Legal Pluralism and Gender Project (land law focal area) (as cited by Ubink 2007).

Kouamé, W. 2006. "Côte d'Ivoire: Tabou – Audiences Foraines: Un sit-in de protestation devant la justice ce matin." *Notre Voie* (18 juillet), posted at allafrica.com (accessed 15 and 19 July 2006).

Kraler, Albert. N.d. "The state and population mobility in the Great Lakes – What is different about post-colonial migrations?" University of Sussex, Sussex Centre for Migration Research, Migration Working Paper no. 24 (23 pages).

Kraxberger, Brennan. 2005. "Strangers, Indigenes, and Settlers: Contested Geographies of Citizenship in Nigeria." *Space and Polity* 9 (April): 9–27.

Krieger, Milton. 1994. "Cameroon's Democratic Crossroads, 1990–4." *Journal of Modern African Studies* 32 (4): 605–628.

Kriger, Norma 2003. *Zimbabwe's Guerrilla Veterans: Symbolic and Political Violence, 1980–1987*. Cambridge: Cambridge University Press.

Kriger, Norma 2005. "ZANU(PF) Strategies in General Elections, 1980–2000: Discourse and Coercion." *African Affairs* 104 (414): 1–34.

Kriger, Norma J. 2007. "Liberation from Constitutional Constraints: Land Reform in Zimbabwe." *SAIS Review* 27 (2): 63–76.

Kriger, Norma. 2006. "From Patriotic Memories to 'Patriotic History' in Zimbabwe, 1990–2005." *Third World Quarterly* 27 (6): 1151–1169.

Kuba, Richard and Carola Lentz. 2003. "Introduction: Historie du peuplement et relations interethniques au Burkina Faso," in *Peuplement, Relations Interethniques, et Identités*. Richard Kuba, Carola Lentz, and Claude Nurukyor Somda, eds. Paris: Editions Karthala: 5–20.

Kuba, Richard, Carola Lentz, and Claude Nurukyor Somda, eds. 2003. *Peuplement, Relations Interethniques, et Identités*. Paris: Karthala.

Kugelman, Michael and Susan L. Levenstein. 2009. *Land Grab? The Race for the World's Farmland*. Washington, DC: Woodrow Wilson Center.

Kuperman, Alan J. 2001. *The Limits of Humanitarian Intervention: Geonocide in Rwanda*. Washington, DC: The Brookings Institution.

Kydd, Jonathan, Andrew Dorward, and Jamie Morrison. 2004. "Agricultural Development and Pro-Poor Economic Growth in Sub-Saharan Africa: Potential and Policy." *Oxford Development Studies* 32 (1): 37–57.

Laasko, Liisa. 2002. "When Elections Are Just a Formality: Rural-Urban Dynamics in Zimbabwean Dominant Party Elections," in *Multiparty Elections in Africa*. Michael Cowen and L. Laasko, eds. London and New York: James Currey and Palgrave: 325–345.

Lacoste, Yves. 1997. "Geopolitique d'une Afrique Médiane." *Hérodote: Revue de Géographie et de Géopolitique* 86–87.

Lassailly-Jacob, Véronique. 1986. "Un exemple éphémère de planification du développement: l'AVB en Côte d'Ivoire centrale (1969–1980)." *Cahiers d'Etudes Africaines* 103 (26/3): 333–348.

Lassilly-Jacob, Véronique, Jean-Yves Marchal, and André Quesnal, eds. 1999. *Deplacés et Réfugiés: La Mobilité sous Contrainte*. Paris: Institut de Recherche pour le Développement (IRD) and CNHS-EHESS.

Lamb, C. 2007. *House of Stone: The True Story of a Family Divided in War-Torn Zimbabwe.* Chicago: Lawrence Hill Books.

Lame, Danielle de. 2005. *A Hill among a Thousand: Transformations and Ruptures in Rural Rwanda.* Madison: University of Wisconsin Press.

Landau, Lauren. 2008. *The Humanitarian Hangover: Displacement, Aid, and the Transformation of Western Tanzania.* Johannesburg: Wits University Press.

Lane, Charles. 1996. *Pastures Lost: Barabaig Economy, Resource Tenure, and Alienation of their Land in Tanzania.* Nairobi: Initiatives Publishers and African Centre for Technology Studies (ACTS).

Laurent, Pierre-Joseph. 1999. "Déstabilisation des Paysanneries du Nord-Kivu: Migrations, Démocratisation, et Tenures," in *Conflits et Guerres au Kivu et dans la Région des Grands Lacs: Entre Tensions Locales et Escalade Régionale.* Paul Mathieu and J.-C. Willame, eds. Tervuren and Paris: Institut Africain-CEDAF, Afrika Instituut-ASDOC, and Editions L'Harmattan: 63–84.

Lavigne-Delville, Philippe, Camilla Toulmin, Jean-Philippe Colin, and Jean-Pierre Chauveau. 2002. *Negotiating Access to Land in West Africa: A Synthesis of Findings from Research on Derived Rights to Land.* London and Paris: International Institute for Environment and Development (IIED), Groupe de récherche et d'échanges technologiques (GRET), and IRD (Institut Français de recherche pour le développement)-REFO, February.

Lawi, Yusufu Qwaray. 2007. "Tanzania's Operation *Vijiji* and Local Ecological Consciousness: The Case of Eastern Iraqwland, 1974–1976." *Journal of African History* 48: 69–93.

Lazarev, Yegor. 2011. "Land, Votes, and Violence: Political Effects of the Insecure Property Rights over Land in Dagestan," National Research University, Higher School of Economics, Basic Research Program Working Papers, Sociology WP BPR 01/SOC/2011, Moscow.

Lemarchand, René. 1970. *Rwanda and Burundi.* London: Pall Mall Press.

Lemarchand, René. 1982. "The World Bank in Rwanda: The Case of the Office the Valorisation Agricole et Pastorale du Mutara (OVAPAM)." Bloomington: African Studies Program, Indiana University.

Lemarchand, René. 1994. "Managing Transition Anarchies: Rwanda, Burundi, and South Africa in Comparative Perspective." *Journal of Modern African Studies* 32 (4): 581–604.

Lemarchand, René. 1997. "Patterns of State Collapse and Reconstruction in Central Africa: Reflections on the Crisis in the Great Lakes." *African Studies Quarterly* 1 (3), posted at web.africa.ufl.edu/asq/prev.htm (14 pages).

Lemarchand, René. 2000. "Exclusion, Marginalization, and Political Mobilization: The Road to Hell in the Great Lakes." Center for Development Studies, University of Copenhagen. March.

Lemarchand, René. 2002. "Review Article: A History of Genocide in Rwanda" (review of Mamdani 2001). *Journal of African History* 43: 307–311.

Lentz, Carola. 2000. "Ethnicity in Ghana: A Comparative Perspective," in *Ethnicity in Ghana: The Limits of Invention.* C. Lentz and Paul Nugent, eds. Houndsmills and London: Macmillan Press, and New York: St. Martin's Press: 1–28.

Lentz, Carola. 2001. "Contested Boundaries: Decentralisation and Land Conflicts in Northwestern Ghana." *Le Bulletin de l'APAD* n. 22, mis en ligne le 15 décembre 2005, apad.revues.org/50 (consulté le 25 mai 2012).

Lentz, Carola. 2003. "'Premiers arrivés et nouveau venus': Discours sur l'autochtonie dans la savane ouest-Africaine," in *Peuplement, relations interethniques, et identités*. Richard Kuba, Carola Lentz, and Claude Nurukyor Somda, eds. Paris: Kathala: 113–134.

Lentz, Carola. 2006. *Ethnicity and the Making of History in Northern Ghana*. Edinburgh: Edinburgh University Press.

Lentz, Carola and Paul Nugent, eds. 2000. *Ethnicity in Ghana: The Limits of Invention*. Houndsmills and London: Macmillan Press, and New York: St. Martin's Press.

Leslie, Winsome J. 1993. *Zaire: Continuity and Change in an Oppressive State*. Boulder, CO: Westview Press.

Leveau, Remy. 1985. *Le Fellah Marocain: Défenseur du Thrône*. Paris: Presses de la Fondation Nationale des Sciences Politiques.

Levi, Margaret. 1988. *Of Rule and Revenue*. Berkeley and Los Angeles: University of California Press.

Levine, S. 1980. "Crime or Affliction? Rape in an African Community." *Culture, Medicine and Psychiatry* 4: 151–165 (cited by Ontita 2007: 33).

Lewis, Barbara. 1980. "Ethnicity and Occupational Specialization in the Ivory Coast: The Transporters' Association," in *Values, Identities, and National Integration*. John N. Paden, ed. Evanston, IL: Northwestern University Press: 75–87.

Lewis, Barbara. 2003. "Citizens or Strangers: Ivoirian Land Law and the Succession Crisis." Paper presented at the Annual Meetings of the African Studies Association, 29 October–2 November, Boston, MA.

Lewis, Barbara. 1991. "Land, Property, and Politics: Rural Divo at the *Fin de Regime*." Paper prepared for the 1991 Annual Meetings of the African Studies Association, St. Louis, MO, 23–26 November.

Lewis, Barbara. 1992. "Political Liberalization, Economic Liberalization, and Obstacles to Rural Empowerment in Côte d'Ivoire." Paper prepared for the 1992 Annual Meetings of the African Studies Association, Seattle, WA, 20–23 November.

Ley, A. 1982. "La logique foncière de l'Etat depuis la colonisation: l'expérience ivoirienne," in *Enjeux Fonciers en Afrique Noire*. E. Le Bris, E. Le Roy, and F. Leimdorfer, eds. Paris: Karthala: 135–140.

Leys, Colin. 1975. *Underdevelopment in Kenya: The Political Economy of Neo-Colonialism*. Los Angeles and Berkeley: University of California Press.

Leys, Colin. 1996. *The Rise and Fall of Development Theory*. London and Bloomington: James Currey Ltd. and Indiana University Press.

Libecap, Gary D. 1996. "Economic Variables in the Development of the Law: The Case of Western Mineral Rights," in *Empirical Studies in Institutional Change*. Lee J. Alston, T. Eggertsson, and Douglass C. North, eds. Cambridge: Cambridge University Press: 35–58.

Lind, Jeremy and Kathryn Sturman, eds. 2002. *Scarcity and Surfeit: The Ecology of Africa's Conflicts*. Pretoria: Institute for Security Studies.

Lindbloom, Charles E. 1977. *Politics and Markets: The World's Political-Economic Systems*. New York: Basic Books.

Lipton, Michael. 1977. *Why Poor People Stay Poor: Urban Bias in World Development*. Cambridge, MA: Harvard University Press.

Liversage, H. 2004. Working Paper 3: "Rangeland Management and Land Issues [Tanzania]." New York: United Nations International Fund for Agricultural Development (IFAD).

Logan, Carolyn. 2010. The Roots of Resilience: Exploring Popular Support for African Traditional Leaders. Afrobarometer Working Paper n. 128, Michigan State University, Afrobarometer, March.

Loiske, Vesa-Matti. 1995. "Social Differentiation, Conflicts, and Rural-Urban Interaction in the Babati Area, Tanzania," in *The Migration Experience in Africa*. Jonathan Baker and Tade Akin Aina, eds. Uppsala: Nordiska Afikainstitutet: 220–233.

Lombard, Jacques. 1967. *Autorités Traditionnelles et Pouvoirs Européens en Afrique Noire: Le Déclin d'une Aristocratie sous le Régime Colonial.* Paris: Armand Colin.

Longman, Timothy. 2001. "Identity Cards, Self-Perception, and Genocide in Rwanda," in *Documenting Individual Identity: The Development of State Practices in the Modern World*. Jane Caplan and John Torpey, eds. Princeton, NJ, and Oxford: Princeton University Press: 345–358.

Longman, Timothy. 2010. *Christianity and Genocide in Rwanda*. Cambridge: Cambridge University Press.

Lonsdale, J. 1977. "When Did the Gusii (or Any Other Group) Become a 'Tribe'?" *Kenyan Historical Review* 5: 123–133.

Loveman, Mara. 2005. "The Modern State and the Primitive Accumulation of Symbolic Power." *American Journal of Sociology* 110 (6): 1651–1683.

Luebbert, Gregory. 1987. "Social Foundations of Political Order in Interwar Europe." *World Politics* 39 (4) (July): 449–478.

Lund, Christian. 1998. *Law, Power, and Politics in Niger: Land Struggles and the Rural Code*. Hamburg: LIT Verlag.

Lund, Christian. 2008. *Local Politics and the Dynamics of Property in Africa*. New York and Cambridge: Cambridge University Press.

Luong, Pauline Jones. 2002. *Institutional Change and Political Continuity in Post-Soviet Central Asia: Power, Perceptions, and Pacts*. Cambridge and New York: Cambridge University Press.

Lynch, G. 2008. "Courting the Kalenjin: The Failure of Dynastisicm and the Strength of the ODM Wave in Kenya's Rift Valley Province." *African Affairs* 107 (429): 541–568.

Lynch, Gabrielle. 2006. "Negotiating Ethnicity: Identity Politics in Contemporary Kenya." *Review of African Political Economy* 107: 49–65.

Machakos and Makueni Ranchers Association. 2007. "Memorandum to the National Land Policy Secretariat [on the DNLP]," 26 January, posted at www.mng5.com/papers/machMemo.pdf, accessed 9 May 2013.

Mackenzie, Fiona. 1998. *Land, Ecology, and Resistance in Kenya, 1880–1952*. Edinburgh: Edinburgh University Press.

MacLean, Lauren. 2010. *Informal Institutions and Citizenship in Rural Africa: Risk and Reciprocity in Ghana and Cote d'Ivoire*. New York: Cambridge University Press.

Maddox, Gregory, James Gibson, and Isaria N. Kimambo. 1996. *Custodians of the Land: Ecology and Culture in the History of Tanzania*. London, Dar es Salaam, Nairobi, and Athens: James Currey, Mkuki na Nyota, EAEP, and Ohio University Press.

Maddox, Gregory and James L. Giblin, eds. 2005. *In Search of a Nation: Histories of Authority and Dissidence in Tanzania*. Oxford, Dar es Salaam, and Athens: James Currey, Kapsel Educational Publishers, and Ohio University Press.

Mafikiri Tsongo, A. 1997. "Mouvements des populations, accès à la terre, et question de la nationalité au Kivu," in *Démocratie, enjeux fonciers, et pratiques locales en Afrique*. Paul Mathieu, Laurent, P.-J. and J.-C. Willame, eds. Paris: L'Harmattan: 180–201.

Magaloni, Beatriz. 2006. *Voting for Autocracy: Hegemonic Party Survival and Its Demise in Mexico*. Cambridge and New York: Cambridge University Press.

Maganga, Faustin. 2002. "The Interplay between Formal and Informal Systems of Managing Resource Conflicts: Some Evidence from South-Western Tanzania." *European Journal of Development Research* 14 (2): 51–71.

Magaramombe, G. and W. Chambati. 2008. "The Abandoned Question: Farm Workers," in *Contested Terrain: Land Reform and Civil Society in Contemporary Zimbabwe*. S. Moyo, K. Helliker, and T. Murisa, eds. Pietermaritzburg, South Africa: S&S Publishers: 207–238.

Mahoney, James. 2010. *Colonialism and Postcolonial Development: Spanish America in Comparative Perspective*. Cambridge University Press.

Mallya, Ernest T. 1999. "Civil Society and the Land Question in Tanzania" (first draft). Department of Political Science and Public Administration, University of Dar es Salaam, December, published by Institute of Development Studies (IDS), UK, posted at www.eldis.org/static/Doc10844.htm (accessed 1 June 2005).

Mamdani, Mahmood. 1996a. *Citizen and Subject: Contemporary Africa and the Legacy of Late Colonialism*. Princeton, NJ: Princeton University Press.

Mamdani, Mahmood. 1996b. "From Conquest to Consent as the Basis of State-Formation: Reflections on Rwanda." *New Left Review* 216: 3–36.

Mamdani, Mahmood. 2000. "Indirect Rule and the Struggle for Democracy: A Response to Bridget O'Laughlin." *African Affairs* 99 (1): 43–46.

Mamdani, Mahmood. 2001. *When Victims Become Killers: Colonialism, Nativism, and the Genocide in Rwanda*. Princeton, NJ: Princeton University Press.

Mamdani, Mahmood. 2008. "Lessons of Zimbabwe." *London Review of Books*, 30/23 (4 December): 17–21, with ensuing online discussion at *LRB*, www.lrb.co.uk/v30/n23/mahmood-mamdani/lessons-of-zimbabwe (accessed 22 December 2012).

Manby, Brownwen. 2009. *Struggles for Citizenship in Africa*. New York: Zed Books.

Mang, Henry. 2008. "Land and Labor Migrations Within Central and Southern Plateau state: Observing Latent Potentials for Conflict Due to Ideologies of Identity in Quaan Pan and Mangu Local Government Areas of Plateau State, Nigeria," a paper prepared for the 2008 annual meeting of the African Conference at the Unversity of Texas at Austin, "War and Conflicts in Africa," March 28–30.

Mang, Henry. 2009. "The Politics and Economics of 'Fadama' Irrigation and Product Sales in the Tin Mining areas of the Jos Plateau in Nigeria." A paper of the Centre for Conflict Management and Peace Studies, University of Jos, Plateau State, Nigeria, prepared for the Workshop in Political Theory and Policy Analysis, Indiana University, Bloomington, February 22–24.

Manji, Ambreena. 2001. "Land Reform in the Shadow of the State: The Implementation of New Land Laws in Sub-Saharan Africa." *Third World Quarterly* 22 (3): 327–342.

Manji, Ambreena. 2006. "Legal Paradigms in Contemporary Land Reform." *Commonwealth and Comparative Politics* 44 (1): 151–165.

Mann, Michael. 2005. *The Dark Side of Democracy: Explaining Ethnic Cleansing*. Cambridge and New York: Cambridge University Press.

Mararo, Stanislas Bucyalimwe. 1996. "Les enjeux de la guerre de Masisi." *Dialogue* (Kigale/Bruxelles), n. 192 (août-septembre): 85–95.

Mararo, Stanislas Bucyalimwe. 1997. "Land, Power, and Ethnic Conflict in Masisi (Congo-Kinshasa), 1940s–1994." *International Journal of African Historical Studies* 30 (3): 503–538.

Mararo, Stanislas Bucyalimwe. 2003. "Le Nord-Kivu au coeur de la crise congolaise," in *L'Afrique des Grands Lacs, Annuaire 2001–2*. Stefaan Marysse and Filip Reyntjens, eds. Paris: L'Harmattan: 153–185.

Maro, P. S. and W. F. I. Mlay. 1982. "Population Redistribution in Tanzania," in *Redistribution of Population in Africa*. John I. Clarke and Leszek A. Kosinski, eds. London: Heinemann: 176–181.

Marongwe, Nelson and Robin Palmer. 2004. "Struggling with Land Reform Issues in East Africa Today." *Independent Land Newsletter*, August, posted by Oxfam and Mokoro: Land Rights in Africa, accessed at http://www.mokoro.co.uk/files/13/file/lria/land_reform_highlights_eastern_africa_2004-5.pff.pdf (9 May 2013).

Marshall-Fratani, R. 2006. "The War of 'Who Is Who': Autochthony, Nationalism, and Citizenship in the Ivoirian Crisis." *African Studies Review* 49 (2): 9–43.

Martin, Susan. 1993. "From Agricultural Growth to Stagnation: The Case of Ngwa [Biafra], Nigeria, 1900–1980," in *Population Growth and Agricultural Development*. B. L. Turner II, Goran Hyden, and Robert William Kates, eds. Gainesville: University of Florida Press: 302–323.

Mascarenhas, Adolfo. 2000. "Aspects of Migration and Urbanisation in Tanzania," in *Urbanising Tanzania: Issues, Initiatives, and Priorities*. Suleiman Ngware and J. M. Lusugga Kironde, eds. Dar es Salaam: University of Dar es Salaam Press: 59–87.

Massaro, Richard J. 1998. "The Political Economy of Spatial Rationalization and Integration Policies in Tanzania," in *Rural Settlement Sturcture and African Development*, Marilyn Silberfein, ed. Boulder, CO: Westview Press: 273–310.

Mathieu, Paul. 1997. "La sécuritisation foncière entre compromis et conflict," in *Démocratie, Enjeux Fonciers, et Pratiques Locales in Afrique*. P. Mathieu, Pierre-Joseph Laurent, and Jean-Claude Willame, eds. Paris: L'Harmattan: 26–44.

Mathieu, Paul and A. Mafikiri Tsongo. 1999. "Enjeux fonciers, déplacement de populations, et escalades conflictuelles (1930–1995)," in *Conflits et Guerres au Kivu et dans la Région des Grands Lacs*. P. Mathieu and A. M. Willame, eds. Paris and Tervuren: L'Harmattan and Institut Africain/CEDAF, n. 37–38: 21–62.

Mathieu, Paul, A. Mafikiri Tsongo, and S. Mugangu Matabaro. 1999. "Insécurisation et violence: Quelques réflexions sur les causes et remèdes possibles des escalades conflictuelles," in *Conflicts et Guerres au Kivu et dans la Région des Grands Lacs*. P. Mathieu and J.-C .Willame, eds. Paris and Tervuren: L'Harmattan and Institut Africain/CEDAF, n. 37–38: 85–96.

Mathieu, Paul and J.-C. Willame, eds. 1999. *Conflicts et Guerres au Kivu et dans la Région des Grands Lacs*. Paris and Tervuren: L'Harmattan and Institut Africain/CEDAF, n. 37–38.

Mathieu, Paul, Philippe Lavigne-Delville, Lacinan Paré, Mahamadou Zongo, and Hubert Ouedraogo, with Julianne Baud, Eric Bologo, Nadine Koné, and Karine Triollet. 2003. "Sécurisé les transactions foncières dans l'ouest du Burkina Faso." Drylands Issue Paper no. 117. London: International Institute for Environment and Development (IIED).

Mathieu, Paul, P.-J. Laurent, A. Mafikiri Tsongo, S. Mugangu. 1999. "Cohabitations imposées et tensions politiques au Nord-Kivu 1939–1994: Une trajectoire conflictuelle," in *Conflicts et guerres au Kivu et dans la Région des Grands Lacs*. P. Mathieu and J.-C. Willame, eds. Paris and Tervuren: L'Harmattan and Institut Africain/CEDAF, n. 37–38: 13–20.

Mathieu, Paul, P.-J. Laurent, and J.-C. Willame, eds. 1997. *Démocratie, enjeux fonciers et pratiques locales en Afrique*. Paris: L'Harmattan.

Mathuba, B. M. 2003. "Botswana Land Policy." Paper presented at the International Workshop on Land Policies in Southern Africa, Berlin, Germany, 26–27 May 2003, posted at www.fes.de/in_afrika/studien/Land_Reform_Botswana_Botselo_Mathuba.pdf (accessed 15 June 2009).

Matter, Scott. 2010. "Clashing Claims: Neopatrimonial Governance, Land Tenure Transformation, and Violence in Enoosupukia, Kenya." *POLAR: Political and Legal Anthropology Review* 33 (1): 67–88.

Matunga, Willie. 1999. *Constitution-Making from the Middle: Civil Society and Transition Politics in Kenya, 1992–1997*. Nairobi: SAREAT.

Maupeu, Hervé. 2003. Kenya: Les élections de la Transition." *Politique Africaine* 89 (mars): 149–165.

Maxon, Robert. 1989. *Conflict and Accommodation in Western Kenya*. Rutherford, Madison, and Teaneck, NJ: Fairleigh Dickinson University Press.

Maxon, Robert. 2002a. "Colonial Conquest and Administration," in *Historical Studies and Social Change in Western Kenya: Essays in Memory of Professor Gideon S. Were*. Wm. R. Ochieng', ed. Kampala: East African Educational Publishers: 93–109.

Maxon, Robert. 2002b. "Economic and Social Change since 1963," in *Historical Studies and Social Change in Western Kenya: Essays in Memory of Professor Gideon S. Were*. Wm. R. Ochieng', ed. Kampala: East African Educational Publishers: 293–368.

Maxon, Robert M. 2003. *Going Their Separate Ways: Agrarian Transformation in Kenya, 1930–1958*. Madison, NJ: Farleigh Dickinson University Press.

May, John F. 1995. "Policies on Population, Land Use, and Environment in Rwanda." *Population and Environment* 16 (4) (March): 321–334.

Mbinji, Joseph. 2006. "Getting Agreement on Land Tenure Reform: The Case of Zambia," in *Land Rights for African Development: From Knowledge to Action*. Esther Mwangi, ed. Consultative Group on International Agricultural Research, United Nations Development Project, and International Land Coalition (CGIAR/UNDP/ILC), Collective Action and Property Rights (CAPRi) Policy Brief.

McAuslan, Patrick. 1985. *Urban Land and Shelter for the Poor*. Washington, DC: Earthscan.

McAuslan, Patrick. 1998. "Making Law Work: Restructuring Land Relations in Africa." *Development and Change* 29 (3): 525–552.

McAuslan, Patrick. 2006. "Improving Tenure Security for the Poor in Africa: Framework Paper for the Legal Empowerment Workshop – Sub-Saharan Africa." Nakuru, Kenya, October, LEP Working Paper no. 1, Food and Agriculture Organization of the United Nations, available through Oxfam at www.oxfam.org.uk/what_we_do/issues/livelihoods/landrights/index.htm (accessed 15 July 2007).

McGreal C. and E. MacAskill. 2002. Mugabe Victory Leaves West's Policy in Tatters, *The Guardian* (UK), 14 March, posted at www.guardian.co.uk/world/2002/mar/14/zimbabwe.chrismcgreal (accessed 22 January 2010).

McMann, Kelly. 2006. *Economic Autonomy and Democracy: Hybrid Regimes in Russia and Kyrgyzstan.* Cambridge and New York: Cambridge University Press.

Médard, Claire 1996. "Les conflits 'ethniques' au Kenya: Une question de votes ou de terres?" *Afrique Contemporaine*, N. Spécial 180, 4ème trimestre: 62–74.

Médard, Claire. 2009. "Elected Leaders, Militia, and Prophets: Violence in Mt. Elgon 2006–2008," in *The General Elections in Kenya, 2007.* J. Lafargue, ed. Nairobi: Institute Français de Recherche en Afrique, IFRA: 339–361.

Memo des Congolais Rwandaphones à Qui de Droit. 2004. "Processus de réunification de la RDC: Aucune change n'aboutir sans la reconnaissance du droit de tous les Congolais à l'égalité des droits," signed by Felicien Nzitatira and François Gachaha, 19 janvier, published in *Le Soft International* at lesoftonline.net, 18 février, posted by Réseau Documentaire International sur la Région des Grands Lacs Africains at www.grandslacs.net/doc/3017.pdf (accessed 20 April 2007).

"Memorandum des Communautés Hutu et Tutsi du Nord-Kivu à la Commission d'Enquête sur les Massacres de Walikale, Masisi, et Bwito (Rutshuru) en Mars et Avril 1993," 25 avril 1993. Posted by Réseau Documentaire International sur la Région des Grands Lacs Africains at www.GrandsLacs.net, at 129.194.252.80/catfiles/0656.pdf (accessed 19 avril 2007).

Meschi, Lydia. 1974. "Evolution des structures foncières au Rwanda: Le cas d'un lignage hutu." *Cahiers d'Etudes Africaines* 14 (53): 39–51.

Metzer, Jacob and Stanley Engerman. 2004. "Setting the Stage," in *Land Rights, Ethno-Nationality, and Sovereignty in History.* S. Engerman and J. Metzer, eds. London and New York: Routledge: 7–28.

Migai-Akech, J. M. 2006. "Land, the Environment and the Courts in Kenya: Background Paper for the Environment and Land Law Reports, a DFID/KLR Partnership," Nairobi: UK Department for International Development (DFID) and Kenya Law Reports (KLR), February.

Migot-Adholla, Shem E., Frank Place, and W. Oluoch-Kosura. 1994. "Security of Tenure and Land Productivity in Kenya," in *Searching for Land Tenure Security in Africa.* John W. Bruce and Shem E. Migot-Adholla, eds. Washington, DC: The World Bank: 119–140.

Migot-Adholla, Shem E., George Benneh, Frank Place, and Steven Atsu. 1994. "Land, Security of Tenure, and Productivity in Ghana," in *Searching for Land Tenure Security in Africa.* John W. Bruce and Shem E. Migot-Adholla, eds. Washington, DC: The World Bank: 97–118.

Miguel, Edward. 2004. "Tribe or Nation? Nation-Building and Public Goods in Kenya vs. Tanzania." *World Politics* 56 (3) (April): 327–362.

Mikell, G. 1989a. "Peasant Production and Economic Recuperation in Ghana." *Journal of Modern African Studies* 27 (3): 455–478.

Mikell, Gwendolyn. 1989b. *Cocoa and Chaos in Ghana.* New York: Paragon House.

Miles, William F. S. 1994. *Hausaland Divided: Colonialism and Independence in Nigeria and Niger.* Ithaca, NY: Cornell University Press.

Mitnick, Eric. 2006. *Rights, Groups, and Self-Invention.* London: Ashgate.

Moore, Jr., Barrington. 1966. *Social Origins of Dictatorship and Democracy.* Boston, MA: Beacon Press.

Moore, Mick. 1997. "Leading the Left to the Right: Populist Coalitions and Economic Reform." *World Development* 25 (7) (July): 1009–1028.

Moore, M. and P. Houtzager, eds. 2003. *Changing Paths: Institutional Development and the New Politics of Inclusion.* Ann Arbor: University of Michigan Press.

Moore, Sally Falk. 1986. *Social Facts and Fabrications: "Customary" Law on Kilimanjaro, 1880–1980.* Cambridge: Cambridge University Press.

Moore, Sally Falk. 1991. "From Giving to Lending to Selling: Property Transactions Reflecting Historical Changes on Kilimanjaro," in *Law in Colonial Africa.* Kristin Mann and Richard Roberts, eds. Portsmouth, NH, and London: Heinemann and James Currey: 108–130.

Moritz, Mark, Paul Scholte, and Saïdou Kari. 2002. "The Demise of the Nomadic Contract: Arrangements and Rangelands under Pressure in the Far North of Cameroon." *Nomadic Peoples* 6 (1): 127–146.

Moyo, S. 1986. "The Land Question," in *Zimbabwe: The Political Economy of Transition 1980–1986.* I. Mandaza, ed. Dakar, Senegal: CODESRIA: 165–202.

Moyo, S. 2000. "The Interaction of Market and Compulsory Land Acquisition Processes with Social Action in Zimbabwe's Land Reform." Paper presented at the SARIPS of the Sapes Trust Annual Colloquium on Regional Integration: Past, Present, and Future, Harare, Zimbabwe.

Moyo, S. 2001. "The Land Occupation Movement and Democratisation in Zimbabwe: Contradictions of Neoliberalism." *Millennium: Journal of International Studies* 30 (2): 311–330.

Moyo, S. and P. Yeros. 2005. "Land Occupations and Land Reform in Zimbabwe. Towards the National Democratic Revolution," in *Reclaiming the Land: The Resurgence of Rural Movements in Africa, Asia, and Latin America.* Sam Moyo and Paris Yeros, eds. London: Zed Books: 165–208.

Moyo, S. and P. Yeros. 2007. "The Radicalized State: Zimbabwe's Interrupted Revolution." *Review of Political Economy* 34 (111): 103–121.

Mozaffar, Shaheen, James R. Scarritt, and Glen Galaich. 2003. "Electoral Institutions, Ethnopolitical Cleavages, and Party Systems in Africa's Emerging Democracies." *American Political Science Review* 97 (3) (August): 379–390.

Muchukiwa, Bosco. 2004. Pouvoirs Locaux et contestations populaires dans le territoire d'Uvira au Sud-Kivu de 1961–2004. Ph.D. dissertation, Universiteit Antwerpen, Institut de Politique and de Gestion du Développement.

Mueller, Susanne D. 2008. "The Political Economy of Kenya's Crisis." *Journal of Eastern African Studies* 2 (2): 85–210.

Mueller, Susanne. 2011. "Dying to Win: Elections, Political Violence, and Institutional Decay in Kenya." *Journal of Contemporary African Studies* 29 (1) (January): 83–100.

Mueller, Susanne D. 1984. "Government and Opposition in Kenya, 1966–9." *Journal of Modern African Studies* 22 (3) (September): 399–427.

Mugangu(-Matabaro), Séverin. 1999. "La nationalité des le Kivu montagneux," in *Conflits et Guerres au Kivu et dans la Région des Grands Lacs.* Paul Mathieu and J.-C. Willame, eds. Tervuren and Paris: Institut Africain-CEDAF and L'Harmattan: 201–211.

Muhonghya Katikati, Jean-Marie. 1996. "Role et efforts de la Société Civile dans la résolution des conflits." *Dialogue* (Kigale/Bruxelles), special issue on La 'Guerre' de Masisi, n. 192 (août–septembre): 47–51.

Mumbengegwi, C. 1986. "Continuity and Change in Agricultural Policy," in *Zimbabwe: The Political Economy of Transition, 1980–1986.* I. Mandaza, ed. Dakar: CODESRIA: 203–222.

Munck, Gerardo. 2004. "Tools for Qualitative Research," in *Rethinking Social Inquiry*. H. Brady and D. Collier, eds. Lanham, MD, Boulder, CO, New York, Toronto, Plymouth, UK: Rowman and Littlefield: 105–122.

Munro, William. 2001. "The Political Consequences of Local Electoral Systems: Politics of Differential Citizenship in South Africa." *Comparative Politics* 33 (3) (April): 295–313.

Munro, William A. 1998. *The Moral Economy of the State: Conservation, Community Development, and State Making in Zimbabwe*. Athens: Ohio University Press.

Murton, J. 1999. "Population Growth and Poverty in Machakos District, Kenya." *Geographical Journal* 165 (1): 37–46.

Mutua, Makau. 2008. *Kenya's Quest for Democracy: Taming Leviathan*. Boulder, CO: Lynne Rienner Publishers.

Mutunga, Willy. 1999. *Constitution-Making from the Middle: Civil Society and Transition Politics in Kenya, 1992–1997*. Harare, Zimbabwe: MWENGO Publishers.

Naldi, G. J. 1993. "Land Reform in Zimbabwe: Some Legal Aspects." *Journal of Modern African Studies* 31(4): 585–600.

The Nation (Nairobi). 2005. "Kenyans Are 'Free to Live Anywhere,'" 1 April, posted at allafrica.com (accessed 1 April 2005).

National Civil Society Conference on Land (Kenya). 2004. "A Summary of Land Policy Principles." Kenya Ministry of Lands and Settlement, 2 April, posted at www.oxfam.org.uk/what_we_do/issues/livelihoods/landrights/downloads/kenya_land_policy_principles.rtf (accessed 27 June 2006).

National Council of Churches of Kenya (NCCK). 1992. *The Cursed Arrow*. Nairobi: NCCK.

National Council of Churches of Kenya (NCCK). *The Clashes Update: A News Bulletin of the CORDS (Christian Outreach and Rural Development Services) Department of the NCCK* (periodical, Nairobi, 1993–1996).

N'Diaye, B. 2005. "Côte d'Ivoire: The Miracle That Wasn't, Flawed Civil-Military Relations, and Missed Opportunity," in *Not Yet Democracy: West Africa's Slow Farewell to Authoritarianism*. B. N'Diaye, A. Saine, and M. Houngnikpo, eds. Durham, NC: Carolina Academic Press: 19–50.

Ndungu Commission Report. *See* Government of Kenya (GOK) 2004.

Netting, Robert McC. 1968. *Hill Farmers of Nigeria: Cultural Ecology of the Kofyar of the Jos Plateau*. Seattle: University of Washington Press.

Newbury, Catharine. 1988. *The Cohesion of Oppression: Clientship and Ethnicity in Rwanda*. New York: Columbia University Press.

Newbury, Catharine M. 1983. "Colonialism, Ethnicity, and Rural Political Protest: Rwanda and Zanzibar in Comparative Perspective." *Comparative Politics* 15 (3): 253–280.

Newbury, Catharine and David Newbury. 2000. "Bringing the Peasants Back In: Agrarian Themes in the Construction and Corrosion of Statist Historiography in Rwanda." *American Historical Review* 105 (3) (June): 832–877.

Newbury, David. 1997. "Irredentist Rwanda: Ethnic and Territorial Frontiers in Central Africa." *Africa Today* 44 (2) (April–June): 211–222.

Newbury, David. 2005. "Return Refugees: Four Historical Patterns of 'Coming Home' to Rwanda." *Comparative Studies in Society and History* 47 (2): 252–285.

Niada, Assane. 2005. "Voici les nouveau bénéficiaires de la nationalité ivoirienne." *Soir Info*, 21 juilllet, posted at www./inter-ci.com/article.php3$id_article=280 (accessed 11 July 2006).

Ninsin, Kwame A. 1989. "The Land Question since the 1950s," in *The State, Development, and Politics in Ghana*. Emmanuel Hansen and Kwame A. Ninsin, eds. London: CODESRIA Book Series: 165–183.

Nkunzumwami, Emmanuel. 1999. "La géographie du génocide au Rwanda et la justice équitable: Une clarification nécessaire par les faits." *La Nouvelle Relève* (Kigali), 26 février, posted at Michel Ognier, "Rwanda 94," rwanda94.pagesperso-orange.fr/sitepers/dosrwand/rwframe.html (accessed 25 May 2012).

Nord, Philip. 2000. "Introduction," in *Civil Society before Democracy: Lessons from Nineteenth-Century Europe*. Nancy Bermeo and Philip Nord, eds. London: Rowman and Littlefield Publishers, Ltd.: xiii–xxxiii.

Noronha, Raymond. 1985. "A Review of the Literature on Land Tenure Systems in Sub-Saharan Africa." Report no. ARU43 of the Research Unit of the World Bank Agriculture and Rural Development Department, 19 July. Washington, DC: The World Bank.

North, Douglass. 1981. *Structure and Change in Economic History*. New York: W. W. Norton.

North, Douglass. 1990. *Institutions, Institutional Change, and Economic Performance*. Cambridge and New York: Cambridge University Press.

North, Douglass and Robert Paul Thomas. 1973. *The Rise of the Western World: A New Economic History*. New York: Cambridge University Press.

Norton-Griffiths, Mike. 2008. "Some economic characterisitcs of land tenure in the agricultural areas of Kenya: A contribution to the debate on the Draft National Land Policy (May 2007)," 14 pages. Nairobi, June posted at www.mng5.com.

Norton-Griffiths, Mike, Tom Wolf, and Raul Figueroa. 2009. "Evidence Based Policy: How Does the Draft National Land Policy Measure Up?" in *Governance, Institutions, and the Human Condition*. E. W. Gachenga et al., eds. Nairobi: Law Africa Publishing: 305–329.

Norwegian Refugee Council (NRC). 2004. "Profile of International Displacement: Kenya." 30 November, posted at www.internal-displacement.org (accessed 10 January 2011).

Norwegian Refugee Council, Internal Displacement Monitoring Center (NRC). 2009a. "Whose Land Is This? Land Disputes and Forced Displacement in the Western Forest Area of Côte d'Ivoire." NRC, Geneva, and Abidjan, October, posted at www.internal-displacement.org (accessed 15 December 2009).

Norwegian Refugee Council, Internal Displacement Monitoring Center (NRC). 2009b. *Internal Displacement: Global Overview of Trends and Developments in 2008*. Geneva: NRC.

Norwegian Refugee Council, Internal Displacement Monitoring Center (NRC). 2010. *Internal Displacement: Global Overview of Trends and Developments in 2009*. Geveva: NRC.

Ntsebeza, Lungisile. 2002. "Decentralization and Natural Resource Management in Rural South Africa: Problems and Prospects." Paper presented at the Ninth Conference of the International Association for the Study of Common Property (IASCP), June 17–21, Victorial Falls, Zimbabwe, posted at dlc.dlib.indiana.edu (accessed 15 August 2007).

Ntsebeza, Lungisile. 2004. "Rural Governance in Post-1994 South Africa: Has the Question of Citizenship for Rural Inhabitants Been Settled 10 Years in South Africa's Democracy?" Paper presented at The Commons in an Age of Global Transition, the Tenth Conference of the International Association for the Study of Common Property (IASCP), 9–13 August, Oaxaca, Mexico, posted at dlc.dlib.indiana.edu (accessed 15 August 2007).

Ntsebeza, Lungisile and Ruth Hall, eds. 2007. *The Land Question in South Africa: The Challenge of Transformation and Redistribution.* Cape Town: HSRC Press.

Nugent, Paul. 1999. "Living in the Past: Urban, Rural, and Ethnic Themes in the 1992 and 1996 Elections in Ghana." *Journal of Modern African Studies* 37 (2): 287–319.

Nugent, Paul. 2010. "States and Social Contracts in Africa." *New Left Review* 63 (May–June): 35–63.

Nunn, Nathan. 2007. "Historical Legacies: A Model Linking Africa's Past to Its Current Underdevelopment." *Journal of Development Economics* 83: 157–175.

Nunn, Nathan. 2009. "Importance of History for Economic Development." *Annual Review of Economics* 1: 65–92.

Nyambara, P. S. 2001. "The Closing Frontier: Agrarian Change, Immigrants, and the 'Squatter Menace' in Gokwe, 1980–1990s." *Journal of Agrarian Change* 1 (4): 534–549.

Nyambara, P. S. 2002. "Madheruka and Shangwe: Ethnic Identities and the Culture of Modernity in Gokwe, Northwestern Zimbabwe, 1963–79." *Journal of African History* 43 (2): 287–306.

Nyamnjoh, Francis and Michael Rowlands. 1998. "Elite Associations and the Politics of Belonging in Cameroon." *Africa: Journal of the International African Institute* 68 (3): 320–337.

Nyamnjoh, Francis B. 2006. *Insiders and Outsiders: Citizenship and Xenophobia in Contemporary South Africa.* Dakar and London: CODESRIA Books and Zed Books.

Nyang'au, Issac Mbeche. 2002. The Role of the Informal Sector in Rural Development: A Case Study of Carpentry and Tailoring in Gucha District, Kenya. Master's thesis no. 20, Swedish University of Agricultural Sciences, Department of Rural Development Studiesa.

Nye, John V. C. 1997. "Thinking about the State: Property Rights, Trade, and Changing Contractural Arrangements in a World with Coercion." *Frontiers of the New Institutional Economics*, J. N. Dbovnik and J. V. C. Nye, eds. San Diego, CA: Academic Press: 121–144.

Nzabara-Masetsa, François-Xavier. 1996. "La 'Guerre' dans la Zone de Masisi." *Dialogue* (Kigale/Bruxelles) n. 192 (août–septembre): 51–67.

Nzitatira, Felicien and François Gachaha. 2004. *See* Memo des Congolais Rwandaphones.

O'Ballance, Edgar. 2000. *The Congo-Zaire Experience, 1960–98.* Houndmills, UK: Macmillan Press Ltd.

O'Brien, Kevin and Lianjiany Li. 2006. *Rightful Resistance in Rural China.* New York: Cambridge University Press.

Odegaard, Rie. 2002. "Scrambling for Land in Tanzania: Processes of Formalisation and Legitimisation of Land Rights." *European Journal of Development Research* 14 (2): 71–88.

Odegaard, Rie. 2005. "The Struggle for Land Rights in the Context of Multiple Normative Orders in Tanzania," in *Competing Jurisdictions: Settling Land Claims in Africa.* Sandra Evers, Marja Spierenburg, and Harry Wels, eds. Lieden and London: Brill: 243–264.

Odingo, R. S. 1971. *The Kenya Highlands: Land Use and Agricultural Development.* Nairobi, Kenya: East African Publishing House.

O'Donnell, Guillermo. 1993. "On the State, Development, and some Conceptual Problems: A Latin American View with Some Glances at some Post-Communist Countries." *World Development* 21: 1355–1369.

Ofei-Aboagye, Esther. 2004. "Promoting Gender Sensitivity in Local Governance in Ghana." *Development in Practice* 14 (6) (November): 753–760.

Ohlsson, Leif. 1999. "Environmental Scarcity and Conflict – A Study of Malthusian Concerns." Department of Peace and Development Research, University of Goteborg.

Ojalammi, Sanna. 2006. Contested Lands: Land Disputes in Semi-Arid Parts of Northern Tanzania: Case Studies of the Loliondo and Sale Divisions in the Ngorongoro District. Ph.D. dissertation, University of Helsinki, Department of Geography, Faculty of Science (Publications Instituti Geographici Universitatis).

Okafor, Francis C. 1993. "Agricultural Stagnation and Economic Diversification: Awka-Nnewi Region, Nigeria, 1930–1980 [SE Nigeria]," in *Population Growth and Agricultural Development.* B. L. Turner II, Goran Hyden, and Robert William Kates, eds. Gainesville, FL: University of Florida Press: 324–357.

Okoth-Ogendo, H. W. O. and John O. Oucho. 1993. "Population Growth and Agricultural Change in Kisii District, Kenya: A Sustained Symbiosis?" in *Population Growth and Agricultural Change in Africa.* Turner II, B. L, Goran Hyden, and Robert William Kates, eds. Gainesville: University of Florida Press: 187–204.

Okuro, Samuel Ong'wen. 2002. "The Land Question in Kenya: The Place of Land Tribunals in the Land Reform Process in Kombewa Division." Paper presented at the Codesria Tenth General Assembly, Kampala-Uganda, 8–12 December (cited by Henrysson and Joireman 2009).

Olivier de Sardan, Jean-Pierre. 1999. "L'espace public introuvable: Chefs et projets dans les villages nigériens." *Revue Tiers Monde* 40 (157) (janvier–mars): 139–150.

Olson, Jennifer. 1995. "Behind the Recent Tragedy: Rwanda." *GeoJournal* 35 (2): 217–222.

Olson, Jennifer Maria. 1990. The Impact of Changing Socio-Economic Factors on Migration Patterns in Rwanda. MA thesis, Michigan State University, Department of Geography.

Ominde, S. H. 1968. *Land and Population Movements in Kenya.* Evanston, IL: Northwestern University Press.

Omolo, L(eo) O(dera). 2008. "The Persecution of the Abagusii People by Their Neighboring Communities Must Come to an Immediate End." African Press International (API), 23 January 2008, posted at http://africanpress.me/2008/01/23/ (accessed 4 May 2013).

Omolo, Leo Odera. 2008. "'Sungu Sungu' Gangsters Killing Innocent People in Kisii Must Be Stopped by the Government." African Press International (API) (daily online news channel), 21 June, posted at africanpress.worldpress.com (accessed 10 May 2009).

Onoma, Ato Kwanena. 2007. "The Contradictory Potential of Institutions: The Rise and Decline of Land Documentation in Kenya." Paper presented at the Workshop on Institutional Change, 26–27 October, Northwestern University.

Onoma, Ato Kwamena. 2010. *The Politics of Property Rights Institutions in Africa.* New York and Cambridge: Cambridge University Press.

Ontita, Edward G. 2007. *Creativity in Everyday Practice: Resources and Livelihoods in Nyamira, Kenya,* Ph.D dissertation, Wageningen University (published in book form under the same imprint).

Ordeshook, P. 1993. "Some Rules of Constitutional Design." *Social Philosophy and Policy* 10 (2): 199–232.

Orvis, Stephen. 1997. *The Agrarian Question in Kenya.* Gainesville: University of Florida Press.

Ostrom, Elinor. 1990. *Governing the Commons: The Evolution of Institutions for Collective Action.* Cambridge: Cambridge University Press.

Ostrom, Elinor. 2005. *Understanding Institutional Diversity.* Princeton, NJ: Princeton University Press.

Oucho, J. O. 2002. *Undercurrents of Ethnic Conflict in Kenya.* Leiden, Boston, Köln: Brill Publishers.

Ouédraogo, Hubert. 2001. "Law and Community Based Property Rights in West Africa." *Common Property Resource Digest* 57: 1, 5.

Ouédraogo, Hubert et al. 2006. "Les réformes foncières en Afrique de l'Ouest." Report n. SAH/D(2006)560. Paris: Club du Sahel et de l'Afrique de l'Ouest (secrétariat)/OECD, août, posted at www.hubrural.org (accessed 23 June 2009).

Ouédraogo, Jean-Bernard. 1997. *Violences et communantés en Afrique Noire: La région de la Comoé entre règles de concurrence et logique de destruction (Burkina Faso).* Paris: L'Harmattan.

Ouédraogo, Sayouba. 2006. "Accès à la terre et sécurisation des nouveau acteurs autours du lac Bazège (Burkina Faso)." IIED. Dossier 138. London: International Institute for Environment and Development, Programme Zones Arides.

Ouédraogo, Souleymane. 2005. "Intensification de l'agriculture dans le plateau central du Burkina Faso: une analyse des possibilités à partir des nouvelles technologies." Doctorat en Economische Weten-Schapper, Rijksunirasiteit Groningen, Zle mani.

Outre Terre: Revue Française de Géopolitique. 2005. "Document historique I: 'Proclamation aux tribus d'Eburnie. Loi Organique de l'Etat d'Eburnie,'" *Outre Terre* n. 11: 265–268.

Oxfam UK. 2004a. *Independent Land Newsletter – Southern Africa.* June. Nelson Marongwe, editor. Later cited as "Independent Review of Land Issues (1)," posted at www.oxfam.org.uk/what_we_do/issues/livelihoods/landrights/downloads/ind_land_newsletter_sth_afr_june_2004.rtf (accessed 20 June 2007).

Oxfam UK. 2004b. *Independent Land Newsletter – Eastern Africa,* August. Nelson Marongwe, editor. Later cited as "Independent Review of Land Issues (2)," London: Oxfam UK.

Oyugi, Walter O. 2000. "Politicized Ethnic Conflict in Kenya." Addis Ababa: CAFRAD/UNPANO, 7, posted at www.dpmf.org/images/politicized-walter.htm (accessed 14 October 2008).

Pabanel, J.-P. 1991. "La question de la nationalité au Kivu." *Politique Africaine* n. 41 (mars): 32–40.

Paige, Jeffrey M. *Agrarian Revolution: Social Movements and Export Agriculture in the Underdeveloped World*. New York and London: The Free Press, 1975.

Painter, Joe and Chris Philo. 1995. "Spaces of Citizenship: An Introduction." *Political Geography*, 14 (2): 107–216.

Palmer, R. 1990. "Land Reform in Zimbabwe, 1980–1990." *African Affairs* 89 (355): 163–181.

Palmer, Robin. 1999. "The Tanzanian Land Acts, 1999: An Analysis of the Analyses." London: Oxfam UK, March, posted at www.oxfam.org.uk/what_we_do/issues/livelihoods/landrights/downloads/tananaly.rtf (accessed 20 July 2008).

Paré, Lacinan. 2001. *Negotiating Rights: Access to Land in the Cotton-Zone, Burkina Faso*. London: International Institute for Environment and Development (IIED).

Partners "Joint Statement from the Development Partners Group for the Kenya CG Meeting." August 2005. *See* Development Partners Group on Land in Kenya" 2005.

Paternostre de la Mairieu, Baudouin. 1972. *Le Rwanda, Son Effort de Développement: Antecedents Historiques et Conquètes de la Révolution Rwandaise*. Bruxelles: A. De Boeck and Kigali: Editions Rwandaises.

Peil, Margaret. 1971. "Expulsion of West African Aliens." *Journal of Modern African Studies* 9 (2) (August): 205–229.

Pélissier, Paul. 1966. *Les Paysans du Sénégal: Les Civilisations Agraries du Cayor à la Casamance*. Saint-Yieux, Haute-Vienne: Imprimerie Fabrègue.

Pélissier, Paul. 2006. "Les interactions rurales-urbaines en Afrique de l'Ouset et Centrale." *Le Bulletin de l'APAD* n. 19, mise en ligne le 12 juillet 2006, http://apad.revues.org/422 (consulté le 28 mai 2012).

Peluso, Nancy and Michael Watts, eds. 2001. *Violent Environments*. Ithaca, NY: Cornell University Press.

Percival, Valerie and Thomas Homer-Dixon. 1998. "The Case of Rwanda," in *EcoViolence: Links among Environment, Population, and Security*. T. Homer-Dixon and Jessica Blitt, eds. Lanham, MD, Boulder, CO, New York, Oxford: Rowman and Littlefield: 201–222.

Perrot, Claude-Hélène and François-Xavier Fauvelle-Aymar, eds. 2003. *Le Retour des Rois: Les Autorités Traditionnelles et l'Etat en Afrique Contemporaine*. Paris: Eds. Karthala.

Person, Yves. 1981. "Colonisation et décolonisation en Côte d'Ivoire." *Le Mois en Afrique: Revue française d'études politiques africaines* 188–189: 15–30.

Peters, Krijn and Paul Richards. 1998. "Why we fight: Voices of under-age youth combatants in Sierra Leone." *Africa: Journal of the International African Institute* 68 (2): 183–210.

Peters, Krijn. 2011. *War and the Crisis of Youth in Sierra Leone*. Cambridge and New York: Cambridge University Press.

Peters, Pauline. 2002. "Bewitching Land: The Role of Land Disputes in Converting Kin to Strangers and in Class Formation in Malawi." *Journal of Southern African Studies* 28 (1) (March): 155–178.

Peters, Pauline. 2004. "Inequality and Social Conflict over Land in Africa." *Journal of Agrarian Change* 4 (3): 269–314.

Peters, Pauline. 2013. "Conflicts over Land and Threats to Customary Tenure in Africa Today." *African Affairs* 112 (449): forthcoming in October 2013.

Phillips, Anne. 1989. *The Enigma of Colonialism: British Policy in West Africa*. London: James Currey.

Pieter van Dick, Meine. 2008. "The Impact of Decentralization on Poverty in Tanzania," in *Decentralization in Africa: A Pathway Out of Poverty and Conflict?* Crawford Gordon and Christof Hartmann, eds. Amsterdam: Amsterdam University Press: 146–166.

Pigeaud, Fanny. 2011. *Au Cameroun de Paul Biya.* Paris, Editions Karthala.

Pinkston, Amanda. 2007. Land Conflict in Ghana and Kenya. Honors thesis, University of Texas at Austin, Department of Government.

Pitcher, Anne, Mary H. Moran, and Michael Johnson. 2009. "Rethinking Patrimonialism and Neopatrimonialism in Africa." *African Studies Review* 52 (1) (April): 125–156.

Platteau, Jean-Philippe. 1995. "The Food Crisis in Africa: A Comparative Structural Analysis," in *The Political Economy of Hunger.* Jean Drèze, Amartya Sen, and Athar Hussain, eds. Oxford and New York: Clarendon and Oxford University Press: 445–553.

Platteau, Jean-Philippe. 1996. "The Evolutionary Theory of Land Rights as Applied to Sub-Saharan Africa: A Critical Assessment." *Development and Change* 27 (1): 29–85.

Platteau, Jean-Philippe. 2002. "The Gradual Erosion of the Social Security Function of Customary Land Tenure Arrangements in Lineage-Based Societies." Working Papers 2002/26, UNU-WIDER Research Paper, United Nations University, World Institute for Development Economics Research, February.

Ploch, L. 2009. *Zimbabwe.* "Congressional Research Service Report for Congress." 1 April.

Polanyi, Karl. 1957. *The Great Transformation.* Boston: Beacon. First published in 1944.

Pole Institute. 2003. "Democratic Republic of Congo: Peace Tomorrow?" Goma, March (posted at pole-institute.org, accessed 5 May 2013).

Ponte, Stefano. 2002. *Farmers and Markets in Tanzania: How Policy Reforms Affect Rural Livelihoods in Africa.* Oxford: James Currey.

Posner, D. 2004. "The Political Salience of Cultural Difference: Why Chewas and Tumbukas Are Allies in Zambia and Adversaries in Malawi." *American Political Science Review* 98 (4): 529–545.

Posner, Daniel N. 2005. *Institutions and Ethnic Politics in Africa.* Cambridge and New York: Cambridge University Press.

Poteete, Amy. 2003a. "Ideas, Interests, and Institutions: Challenging the Property Rights Paradigm in Botswana." *Governance: An International Journal of Policy, Administration, and Institutions* 16 (4) (October): 527–557.

Poteete, Amy. 2003b. "When Professionalism Clashes with Local Particularities: Ecology, Elections, and Procedural Arrangements in Botswana." *Journal of Southern African Studies* 29 (2) (June): 461–485.

Poteete, Amy. 2009. "Defining Political Community and Rights to National Resources in Botswana." *Development and Change* 40 (2): 281–305.

Pottier, Johan. 2002. *Re-Imagining Rwanda: Conflict, Survival, and Disinformation in the Late Twentieth Century.* New York: Cambridge University Press.

Pottier, Johan. 2003. "Emergency in Ituri: Political Complexity, Land, and Other Challenges to Restoring Food Security." UNFAO International Workshop on Food Security in Complex Emergencies, 23–25 September, Tivoli, posted at ftp://ftp.fao.org/docrep/fao/meeting/009/ae515e.pdf (accessed 17 April 2006).

Pottier, Johan. 2006. "Land Reform for Peace? Rwanda's 2005 Land Law in Context." *Journal of Agrarian Change* 6 (4) (October): 509–537.

Pottier, Johan and James Fairhead. 1991. "Post-Famine Recovery in Highland Bwisha, Zaire: 1984 in Its Context." *Africa: Journal of the International African Institute* 61 (4): 537–570.

Pourtier, Roland. 1997. "Congo-Zaire-Congo: Un itinéraire géopolitique au coeur de l'Afrique." *Hérodote: Revue de Géographie et de Géopolitique* 86–87 (Special Issue: Géopolitique d'une Afrique Médiane, Yves Lacoste, ed.), n. 3–4: 6–41.

Primavera, Carolien. 2005. Rural-Rural Migration in Ghana: The Effects of Out-Migration on the Sustainability of agriculture in the Upper West Region, Ghana. Master's thesis, Universiteit van Amsterdam, Faculty of Social and Behavioral Sciences, Department of Human Geography.

Pringle, Robert. 2006. *Democratization in Mali*. United States Institute of Peace (USIP) Publication, Peaceworks no. 58. October.

Prioul, Christian and Pierre Sirven. 1981. *Atlas du Rwanda*. Kigali: Imprimérie Moderne Nantasie Coueron.

Prunier, Gérard. 1995. *The Rwanda Crisis, 1959–1994: History of a Genocide*. London: Hurst.

Prunier, Gérard. 1997. "La crise du Kivu et ses conséquences dans la région des Grands Lacs." *Hérodote: Revue de Géographie et de Géopolitique* 86–87 (Special Issue: Géopolitique d'une Afrique Médiane, Yves Lacoste, ed.) n. 3–4: 42–56.

Prunier, Gérard. 2009. *Africa's World War: Congo, the Rwandan Genocide, and the Making of a Continental Catastrophe*. Oxford: Oxford University Press.

Przeworski, Adam. 1991. *Democracy and the Market*. Cambridge: Cambridge University Press.

Rabinowitz, Beth. 2013. Urban Bias and the Roots of Political Instability: The Strategic Importance of the Rural Periphery in Sub-Saharan Africa. Ph.D. dissertation, University of California, Berkeley, Department of Political Science.

Raftopoulos, B. and I. Phimister. 2004. "Zimbabwe Now: The Political Economy of Crisis and Coercion." *Historical Materialism* 12 (4): 355–382.

Ranger, T. 2004. "Nationalist Historiography, Patriotic History, and the History of the Nation: The Struggle over the Past in Zimbabwe." *Journal of Southern African Studies* 30 (2): 215–234.

Rathbone, Richard. 1993. *Murder and Politics in Colonial Ghana*. New Haven, CT, and London: Yale University Press.

Raynaut, Claude. 1977. "Circulation monétaire et évolution des structures socio-economique chez les Haoussas de Niger." *Africa* 47 (2): 160–171.

Raynaut, Claude. 1988. "Aspects of the Problem of Land Concentration in Niger," in *Land and Society in Contemporary Africa*. R. E. Downs and S. P. Reyna, eds. Hanover and London: University of New Hampshire and University Press of New England: 221–242.

Refugees International. 2004. "Analysis of the Situation of Displaced Farm Workers in Zimbabwe." Washington, DC: Refugees International.

Reno, William. 2007. "Patronage Politics and the Behavior of Armed Groups." *Civil Wars* 9 (4) (December): 324–342.

Reno, William. 1998. *Warlord Politics and African States*. Boulder, CO: Lynne Rienner Publishers.

Reno, William. 2010. "Violent Non-State Actors in Sudan," in *Violent Non-State Actors in World Politics.* Klejda Mjlaj, ed. London: Hurst and Co.: 319–341.

Reno, William. 2011. *Warfare in Independent Africa.* Cambridge and New York: Cambridge University Press.

Reyntjens, Filip. 1994. *L'Afrique des Grands Lacs en Crise – Rwanda, Burundi, 1988–1994.* Paris: Karthala.

Reyntjens, Filip. 1997. "La rébellion au Congo-Zaïre: Une affaire des voisins." *Hérodote: Revue de Géographie et de Géopolitique* 86–87 (Special Issue: Géopolitique d'une Afrique Médiane, Yves Lacoste, ed). n. 3–4: 57–77.

Reyntjens, Filip and Stefaan Marysse, eds. 1996. *Conflits au Kivu: Antécédents et Enjeux.* Antwerp: Universiteit Antwerpen, Center for the Study of the Great Lakes Region of Africa. December.

Reyntjens, Filip and Stefaan Marysse, eds. 2003. *L'Afrique des Grands Lacs, Annuaire 2001–2002.* Paris: L'Harmattan.

Republic of Kenya (ROK). 1962. Land Development and Settlement Board papers, "Settlement Schemes, 1962," Kenya Archives KNA/PC/NZA/4/14/9.

Republic of Kenya (ROK). 1964. Regional Government Agent's Office for Central Nyanza, Kisumu, "Muhoroni Settlement Scheme: Winan Division Application Forms," 13 April. Kenya Archives KNA/DC/KSM/1/5/11.

Republic of Kenya (ROK). 1966. "[Lawrance Commission] Report on the Mission on Land Consolidation and Registration in Kenya, 1965–1966", by Chairman J. C. D. Lawrance, submitted to ROK, 25 March to the Hon. T. J. Mboya, M. P., Min. of Economic Planning and Development, and Hon. J. H. Angaine, M.P., Min. for Lands and Settlement. Nairobi: ROK.

Republic of Kenya (ROK). 1978. "Land Control Board Minutes, Agendas." Taita/Taveta District. Kenya National Archives KNA/CF/5/10.

Republic of Kenya (ROK), "National Assembly [Kiliku Report]." 1992. Report of the Parlimentary Select Committee (RPSC) to Investigate Ethnic Clashes in Western and Other Parts of Kenya, Nairobi, September.

Republic of Kenya (ROK). 2002a. "Report of the Judicial Commission Appointed to Inquire into Tribal Clashes in Kenya [Akiwimi Report]." Chaired by Hon. Mr. Justice A. M. Akiwumi, presented 31 July, released October 2002.

Republic of Kenya, Ministry of Lands. 2009. Current Status of Land in the Coast [with reference to provisions of] The Draft National Land Policy of May 2007. posted at http://www.kecosce.org/downloads/land_status_coast.pdf, accessed 10 May 2013.

Republic of Kenya (ROK). 2009. Office of the Prime Minister, "Rehabilitation of the Mau Forest Ecosystem," Nairobi, September: 5, downloaded from KWS, www.kws.org (accessed 4 December 2011).

République Rwandaise. 1991. Min. de l'Agriculture, de l'Elevage, et de Forêts, Direction Générale du Génie Rural et de la Conservation de Sols, Project PNUD/FAO RWA/89/003: "Stratégie Nationale de Conservation des Sols, Evaluation des systèmes d'exploitation agricole: Rapport d'une mission de consultation," 15–10, par Innocent Ndindabahizi et Rénovat Gwabije, Kigali, avril (147 pages).

Reuters. 2000. "Zimbabwe's Mugabe Urges Blacks to 'Strike Fear in Heart of White Man,'" CNN.com, 14 December, posted at archives.cnn.com/2000/WORLD/africa/12/14/mugabe.zimbabwe/ (accessed 22 January 2010).

Reyna, S. P. and R. E. Downs. 1988. "Introduction," in *Land and Society in Contemporary Africa*. R. E. Downs and S. P. Reyna, eds. Hanover and London: University of New Hampshire and University Press of New England: 1–22.

Ribot, Jesse C. 1999. "Decentralization, Participation, and Accountability in Sahelian Forestry: Legal Instruments of Political-Administrative Control." *Africa* 69 (1): 23–43.

Ribot, Jesse C. 2004. *Waiting for Democracy: The Politics of Choice in Natural Resource Decentralization*. Washington, D.C.: World Resources Institute.

Ribot, Jesse and Nancy Peluso. 2003. "A Theory of Access." *Rural Sociology* 68 (2): 153–181.

Rice, Andrew. 2009. "Is There Such a Thing as Agro-imperialism? [Ethiopia]," *New York Times Magazine*, 22 November 2009: MM46 (New York edition).

Richards, Paul. 2006. "Forced Labor and Civil War: Agrarian Underpinnings of the Sierre Leone Conflict," in *Violence, Political Culture, and Development*. Preben Kaarsholm, ed. Oxford, Athens, and Piertermaritzburg: James Currey, Ohio University Press, and University of KwaKulu-Natal Press.

Rigby, Peter. 1977. "Local Participation in National Politics, Ugogo, Tanzania." in *Government and Rural Development in East Africa: Essays on Political Penetration*. L. Cliffe, J. S. Coleman, and M. R. Doornbos, eds. The Hague: Nijhoff: 81–98.

Riker, W. H. and D. L. Weimer. 1995. "The Political Economy of Transformation: Liberalization and Property Rights," in *Modern Political Economy*. J. S. Banks and E. A. Hanushek, eds. Cambridge: Cambridge University Press: 80–107.

Roberts, Kenneth M. Forthcoming. *Changing Course: Party Systems in Latin America's Neoliberal Era*. New York: Cambridge University Press.

Robertson, A. R. 1987. *The Dynamics of Productive Relationships*. Cambridge: Cambridge University Press.

Robinson, James and Thierry Verdier. 2002. "The Political Economy of Clientelism." Center for Economic Policy Research (Public Policy Series) Discussion Paper no. 3205. February.

Rodenbach, Etienne. 1999. La transformation des droits fonciers dans la vallée du fleuve Sénégal: Etude de trois villages. Mémoire, Ms. Economiques, Faculté des Sciences Economiques, Sociales et de Gestion, Facultés Universitaires Notre-Dame de la Paix, Namur, Belgium.

Roder, Wolf. 1964. "The Division of Land Resources in Southern Rhodesia." *Annals of the Association of American Geographers* 54 (1) (March): 41–52 (cited by Arrighi JDS, 1970, no. 43).

Roe, Emery M. 1995. "More than the Politics of Decentralization: Local Government Reform, District Development, and Public Administration in Zimbabwe." *World Development* 23 (5): 833–43.

Rogowski, Ronald. 1989. *Commerce and Coalitions: How Trade Affects Domestic Political Alignments*. Princeton, NJ: Princeton University Press.

Roitman, Janet. 2005. *Fiscal Disobedience: An Anthropology of Economic Regulation in Central Africa*. Princeton, NJ: Princeton University Press.

Rose, Laurel L. 1992. *The Politics of Harmony: Land Dispute Strategies in Swaziland*. Cambridge: Cambridge University Press.

Rossi, Georges. 1984. "Evolution des versants et mise en valeur agricole au Rwanda." *Annales de Géographie* 515 (janvier–février): 23–43.

Roth, Dik. 2003. Ambition, Regulation, and Reality: Complex Use of Land and Water Resources in Luwu, South Sulawesi, Indonesia. Ph.D. dissertation, Wageninen University.

Rowley, Charles K., ed. 1993. *Property Rights and the Limits of Democracy*. Aldershot, England: Edward Elgar.

Rugenena Mucyo, M. Balthazar. 1996. "Les massacres de 1965 et de 1991 [in Congo/Zaire]." *Dialogue* (Kigale/Bruxelles), n. 192 (août–septembre): 33–47.

Rutherford, B. 2001. "Commercial Farm Workers and the Politics of (Dis)placement in Zimbabwe: Colonialism, Liberation and Democracy." *Journal of Agrarian Change* 1 (4): 626–651.

Rutherford, B. 2007. "Shifting Grounds in Zimbabwe: Citizenship and Farm Workers in the New Politics of Land," in *Making Nations, Creating Strangers: States and Citizenship in Africa*. S. Dorman, D. Hammett, and P. Nugent, eds. Leiden: Brill: 105–122.

Sachikonye, L. M. 2003a. "From 'Growth with Equity' to 'Fast-Track' Reform: Zimbabwe's Land Question." *Review of African Political Economy* 96: 227–240.

Sachikonye, L. M. 2003b. "The Situation of Commercial Farm Workers after Land Reform in Zimbabwe." Farm Community Trust of Zimbabwe.

Sack, Robert David. 1986. *Human Territoriality: Its Theory and History*. Cambridge: Cambridge University Press.

Sadomba, W. Z. 2008. War Veterans in Zimbabwe's Land Occupations: Complexities of a Liberation Movement in an African Post-Colonial Settler Society. Ph.D. dissertation, Wageningen University.

Samuels, D. and R. Snyder. 2001. "The Value of a Vote: Malapportionment in Comparative Perspective." *British Journal of Political Science* 31 (4): 651–671.

Santiso, Carlos and Augustin Loada. 2003. "Explaining the Unexpected: Electoral Reform and Democratic Governance in Burkina Faso." *Journal of Modern African Studies* 41 (3) (September): 395–416.

Scarnecchia, T. 2006. "The 'Fascist Cycle' in Zimbabwe, 2000–2005." *Journal of Southern African Studies* 32 (2): 221–237.

Schattschneider, E. E. 1960. *The Semisovereign People: A Realist's View of Democracy in America*. New York: Holt, Reinhart, and Winston.

Scheuer, B. 2002. "La xénophobie submerge la Côte d'Ivoire." Prevention Genocides, posted at www.prevention-genocides.org/fr/campagne/textes/rapnov2000.pdf in January 2001 (accessed 15 December 2002).

Schilder, Kees. 1988. "State Formation, Religion, and Land Tenure in Cameroon: A Bibliographical Survey." Leiden, African Studies Center, Research Report no. 32/1988.

Schilder, Kees. 1994. "Quest for Self-Esteem: State, Islam, and Mundany Ethnicity in Northern Cameroon." Leiden: African Studies Center Research Series 1994/3. Aldershoot: Avebury.

Schildkrout, Enit. 1979. "The Ideology of Regionalism in Ghana," in *Strangers in African Societies*. W. A. Shack and E. P. Skinner, eds. Berkeley: University of California Press: 183–210.

Schmied, Doris. 1996. *Changing Rural Structures in Tanzania*. Rutgers, NJ: Transaction Publishers.

Schmitz, Jean. 1986. L'Etat géomètre: Les *leydi* des Peul du Fuuto Tooro (Sénégal) et du Maasina (Mali)." *Cahiers d'Etudes Africaines*, 103 (26.3): 349–394.

Schmitz, Jean. 1991. "Problèmes foncières ou territorialité politique dans la Vallée du Sénégal." Paper presented at the Centre d'Etudes d'Afrique Noire-Institut Fondamental d'Afrique Noire (CEAN-IFAN) colloquium on Etat et Société au Sénégal: Crises et Dynamiques Sociales, 22–24 October, Bordeaux.

Schwartz, Alfred. 2000. "Le conflit foncier entre Krou et Burkinabè: À la lumière de l'institution krouman." *Afrique Contemporaine* 123 (1ère trimestre): 56–66.

Scoones, Ian, Nelson Marongwe, Blasio Mavedzenge, Felix Murimbarimba, Jacob Mahenehene, and Chrispen Sukume. 2012. "Livelihoods after Land Refrom in Zimbabwe: Understanding Processes of Rural Differentiation." *Journal of Agrarian Change* 12 (4): 503–527.

Scott, James. 1976. *The Moral Economy of the Peasant: Rebellion and Subsistence in Southeast Asia*. New Haven, CT: Yale University Press.

Scott, James C. 1998. *Seeing Like a State: How Certain Schemes to Improve the Human Condition Have Failed*. New Haven, CT, and London: Yale University Press.

Seignobos, Christian. 2006. "Une négotiation foncière introuvable? L'exemple du Mayo-Rey dans le nord de Cameroun." Colloque international Les frontières de la question foncière, 2006, Montpellier, posted at www.mpl.ird.fr/colloque_foncier/communications/PDF/Seignobos.pdf (accessed 10 November 2009).

Selby, A. 2006. Commercial Farmers and the State: Interest Group Politics and Land Reform in Zimbabwe. Ph.D. dissertation in International Development, University of Oxford.

Shack, Wm. A. and Elliott P. Skinner. 1979. *Strangers in African Societies*. Berkeley: University of California Press.

Shaw, W. H. 2003. "'They Stole Our Land': Debating the Expropriation of White Farms in Zimbabwe." *Journal of Modern African Studies* 41 (1): 75–89.

Sheridan, Michael. 2004. "The Environmental Consequences of Independence and Socialism in N. Pare, Tanzania." *Journal of African History* 45 (1): 81–102.

Shenton, Robert. 1986. *The Development of Capitalism in Northern Nigeria*. Toronto: University of Toronto Press.

Shipton, Parker. 2009. *Mortgaging the Ancestors: Ideologies of Attachment in Africa*. New Haven, CT: Yale University Press.

Shipton, Parker and Mitzi Goheen. 1992. "Understanding African Landholding: Power, Wealth, and Meaning." *Africa: The Journal of the International African Institute* 62 (3): 307–325.

Shivji, Issa, ed. 1991. *State and Constitutionalism: An African Debate on Democracy*. Harare, Zimbabwe: Southern Africa Political Economic Series Trust (SAPES).

Shivji, Issa G. 1999. "Protection of Peasants and Pastoral Rights in Land: A Brief Review of the Bills for the Land Act 1998 and the Village Land Act 1998." Paper presented to the Parliamentary Committee for Finance and Economic Affairs Workshop on the Bills for the Land Act and Village Land Act, 26–28 January, Dodoma, Tanzania.

Shivji, Issa G. 2006. *Let the People Speak: Tanzania Down the Road to Neo-Liberalism*. Dakar: Council for the Development of Social Science Research in Africa (CODESRIA).

Sikor, Thomas and Christian Lund. 2009. "Access and Property: A Question of Power and Authority." *Development and Change* 40 (1): 1–22

Silberfein, Marilyn, ed. 1998a. *Rural Settlement Structure and Africa Development*. Boulder, CO: Westview Press.

Silberfein, Marilyn. 1998b. "Cyclical Change in African Settlement and Modern Resettlement Programs," in *Rural Settlement Structure and Africa Development*. Marilyn Silberfein, ed. Boulder, CO: Westview Press: 47–74.

Silberschmidt, Margrethe. 1992. "Have Men Become the Weaker Sex? Changing Life Situations in Kisii District, Kenya." *Journal of Modern African Studies* 30 (2) (June): 237–253.

Silberschmidt, M. 2001. "Disempowerment of Men in Rural and Urban East Africa: Implications for Male Identify and Sexual Behavior." *World Development* 29 (4): 656–671.

Silvestre, Victor. 1974. "Différention socio-économique dans une société à vocation égalitaire: Masaka dans le paysannat de l'Icayanya." *Cahiers d'Etudes Africaines* 14 (53): 104–169.

Simon, David. 1999. "Non Institutional Explanations for Trends in Electoral Participation in Africa's New Democracies." Presented at the Annual Meeting of the American Political Science Association, Atlanta, GA, September 2.

Skinner, E(lliott) P. 1963. "Strangers in West African Societies." *Africa: Journal of the International African Institute* 33 (4) (October): 307–320.

Skowronek, Stephen. 1982. *Building a New American State: The Expansion of National Adminstrative Capabilities, 1877–1920*. Cambridge and New York, Cambridge University Press.

Smith, Rogers. 1999. *Civic Ideals: Conflicting Visions of Citizenship in U.S. History*. New Haven, CT: Yale University Press.

Smith, Stephen. 2003. "La politique d'engagement de la France à l'épreuve de la Côte d'Ivoire." *Politique Africaine* n. 89 (mars): 112–126.

Snyder, Jack. 2000. *From Voting to Violence: Democratization and Nationalist Conflict*. New York: W. W. Norton and Company.

Snyder, Katherine. 1996. "Agrarian Change and Land-Use Strategies among the Iraqw Farmers in Northern Tanzania." *Human Ecology* 24 (3): 315–340.

Snyder, Katherine. 2005. *The Iraqw of Tanzania: Negotiating Rural Development*. Boulder, CO: Westview Press.

Solidarity Peace Trust. 2008a. "Punishing Dissent, Silencing Citizens: The Zimbabwe Elections 2008." Johannesburg, South Africa, posted at www.solidaritypeacetrust .org/?s=Punishing+Dissent (accessed 25 May 2012).

Solidarity Peace Trust. 2008b. "Desperately Seeking Sanity: What Prospects for a New Beginning in Zimbabwe?" Johannesburg, South Africa, posted at www. solidaritypeacetrust.org/download/report-files/desperately_seeking_sanity.pdf (accessed 25 May 2012).

Somé, Magloire. 2003. "Les chefferies moosé dans la vie politique du Burkina Faso depuis 1945," in *Le Retour des Rois*. Claude-Hélène Perrot and François-Zavier Fauvelle-Aymar, eds. Paris: Karthala: 219–244.

Sonin, Konstantin. 2003. "Why the Rich May Favor Poor Protection of Property Rights." *Journal of Comparative Economics* 31 (4): 715–731.

de Soto, Hernando. 2000. *The Mystery of Capital*. New York: Basic Books.

Soumah, Moussa. 1981. "Regional Migrations in Southeastern Senegal, Internal and International," in *The Uprooted of the Western Sahel: Migrants' Quest for Cash in the Senegambia*. Lucie Gallistel Colvin, Cheikh Ba, Boubacar Berry, Jacques Faye, Alice Hammer, Moussa Soumah, and Fatou Sow, eds. New York: Praeger: 161–182.

Southall, Roger. 2005. "Ndungu Report Summary." *Review of African Political Economy* 103 (March): 142–151.

Southall, Roger J. 1978. "Farmers, Traders, and Brokers in the Gold Coast Cocoa Economy." *Canadian Journal of African Studies* 12 (2): 185–211.

Spear, Thomas. 1997. *Mountain Farmers: Moral Economies of Land and Agricultural Development in Arusha and Meru*. Berkeley and Los Angeles: University of California Press.

Spierenburg, M. J. 2004. *Strangers, Spirits, and Land Reforms: Conflicts about Land in Dande, Northern Zimbabwe*. Leiden and Boston, MA: Brill Academic Publishers.

Srinivasan, Sharath. 2006. "Minority Rights, Early Warning, and Conflict Prevention: Lessons from Darfur," Minority Rights Group International (MICRO), September, accessed at minorityrights.org, 4 May 2013.

Stamm, V. 2000. "Rural Land Plan: An Innovative Approach from Côte d'Ivoire." International Institute for Environment and Development (IIED), Issue Paper no. 91.

State Failure Task Force (SFTF). 2000. "SFTF Phase III Report: Findings," by Jack A. Goldstone et al. McLean, VA: Science Applications International Corporation, 30 September, posted at www.cidcm.umd.edu/inscr/stfail (accessed 27 August 2004).

Steinfeld, Edward S. 2003. "'Painted Horses': Reform Culture and the Phenomenon of Partial Reform." MIT, October, to be published in Edward S. Steinfeld, *China's Market Visions*, forthcoming.

St. John, Patricia. 1971. *Breath of Life: The Story of the Ruanda Mission (Ruanda Mission C.M.S [Church Mission Society])*. London: The Norfolk Press.

Stone, Glen Davis. 1998. "Settlement Concentration and Dispersal among the Kofyar," in *Rural Settlement Structure and African Development*. M. Silberfein, ed. Boulder, CO: Westview Press: 75–98.

Straus, Scott. 2006. *The Order of Genocide: Race, Power, and War in Rwanda*. Ithaca, NY: Cornell University Press.

Strozeski, J. 2006. The Role of Land Ownership in Localized Conflicts between Bété and Burkinabé Households in the Central Western Forest Regions of Côte d'Ivoire. Ph.D. dissertation, Graduate School of Howard University, Department of African Studies.

Swedish International Development Cooperating Agency (SIDA). 2005. "Land Rights and Villagers: Experiences of Securing Access to Land." Land Management Programme in Tanzania (LAMP). December.

Tabutin, Dominique and Burno Shoumaker. 2004. "The Demography of Sub-Saharan Africa from the 1950s to the 2000s: A Survey of Changes and a Statistical Assessment." *Population* 59 (3–4): 455–555.

Taguem-Fah, Gilbert. 2003. "Crise d'autorité, regain d'influence et pérennité des lamidats peuls du nord-Cameroun," in *Le Retour des Rois: Les Autorités Traditionnelles et l'Etat en Afrique Contemporaine*. Claude-Hélène Perrot and François-Xavier Fauvelle-Aymar, eds. Paris: Eds. Karthala: 267–288.

Takane, Tsutomu. 2002. *The Cocoa Farmers of Southern Ghana: Incentives, Institutions, and Change in Rural West Africa*. Chiba: Institute of Developing Economies, Japan External Trade Organization.

Takougang, Joseph and Milton Krieger. 1998. *African State and Society in the 1990s: Cameroon's Political Crossroads*. Boulder, CO: Westview Press.

Tamba III, Jean-Matthew. 2004. "Senegal: Farmers Tell Government: We Will Not Be Sacrificed." *Panos* (London), 10 August, posted at allafrica.com (accessed 10 September 2004).

Tanzania National Archives (TNA). 1925. Mr. Browne, Sr. Commissioner Arusha District, Annual Report 1925, 18 January: 11 (TNA, AB.31 [1925]. File no. 1733/1/36).

Tarrow, Sidney. 1994. *Power in Movement: Social Movements and Contentious Politics.* Cambridge: Cambridge University Press.

Tarrow, Sidney and Charles Tilly. 2007. "Contentious Politics and Social Movements," in *The Oxford Handbook of Comparative Politics.* Carles Boix and Susan Stokes, eds. Oxford: Oxford University Press: 435–460.

Tassou, André. 2008. "Autorités traditionnelles et urbanisation au Nord-Cameroun: Le cas de la ville de Mokolo." Paper presented at the American Political Science Africa Initiative Workshop on Political Participation in Africa, July, Dakar, Senegal.

Tayoro, P. D. 2006. "A propos des audiences foraines: Affi N'Guessan – Il faut les empêcher." *Notre Voie* 14 juillet, posted at fr.allafrica.com/stories/200607140568.html (accessed 20 February 2008).

Teal, Francis, Andrew Zeitlin, and Haruna Maamah. 2006. "Ghana Cocoa Farmers Survey 2004: Report to Ghana Cocoa Board." Center for the Study of African Economies, Department of Economics, Oxford University, posted at www.csae.ox .ac.uk (accessed 12 May 2009).

Tegera, Aloys. 1995. "Le réconciliation communautaire: Le cas des massacres au Nord-Kivu," in *Les Crises Politiques au Burundi et au Rwanda (1993–1994): Analyses, Faits, et Documents.* André Guichaoua, ed. Paris: Karthala: 395–402.

Tettey, Wisdom J., with Boni Yao Gebe and Kumi Ansah-Koi. n.d. "The Politics of Land-Related Conflicts in Ghana: A Summary," ISSER Land Project Paper posted by isser.ug.edu.gh/index.php?option=com_content&view=article&id=162& Itemid=214 (accessed 10 June 2009). (Based on Wisdom Tettey et al. *The Politics of Land and Land-Related Conflicts in Ghana.* Issue 84 of Technical Publication, Institute of Statistical, Social and Economic Research (ISSER), University of Legon, Accra, Ghana, 2008.

Teyssier, André, Ousmane Hamadou, and Christian Seignobos. 2003. "Experiences de médiation foncière dans le Nord Cameroun." FAO Corporate Document Repository, CIRAD-TERA, TERDEL à Garoua, IRD, Observatoire du Foncier, DPGT and IRD, published in *Land Reform/Réforme Agraraire/Reforma Agraria*, n. 1: 90–103.

Thelen, Kathleen. 2005. *How Institutions Evolve: The Political Economy of Skills in Germany, Britain, the United States, and Japan.* Cambridge and New York: Cambridge University Press.

Thomas, Ian. 1982. "Villagization in Tanzania: Planning Potential and Practical Problems," in *Redistribution of Population in Africa.* John I. Clarke and Leszek A. Kosinski, eds. London: Heinemann: 182–191.

Thompson, E. P. 1963. *The Making of the English Working Class.* New York: Vintage Books.

Throup, David. 1988. *Economic and Social Origins of Mau Mau, 1945–53.* London, Nairobi, and Athens: James Currey, Heinemann Kenya, and Ohio University Press.

Throup, David and Charles Hornsby. 1998. *Multi-Party Politics in Kenya.* Athens: Ohio University Press.

Tilly, Charles. 1964. *The Vendée.* Cambridge, MA: Harvard University Press.

Toulmin, Camilla and Julian Quan. 2000a. *Evolving Land Rights, Policy, and Tenure in Africa*. London: DFID/IIED/NRI. March.

Toulmin, Camilla and Julian Quan. 2000b. "Registering Customary Rights," in *Evolving Land Rights, Policy, and Tenure in Africa*. C. Toulmin and J. Quan, eds. London: DFID/IIED/NRI: 209–212.

TPIR. *See* United Nations (Nations Unis) Tribunal Pénal International pour le Rwanda.

Tripp, Aili Mari. 1997. *Changing the Rules: The Politics of Liberalization and the Urban Informal Economy in Tanzania*. Berkeley and Los Angeles: University of California Press.

Tucker, Joshua. 2006. *Regional Economic Voting: Russia, Poland, Hungary, Slovakia, and Czech Republic, 1990–99*. New York: Cambridge University Press.

Tull, Denis M. 2003. "A Reconfiguration of Political Order? The State of the State in North Kivu (DR Congo)." *African Affairs* 102 (408) (July): 429–446.

Ubink, Janine. 2007. "Between Customs and State Law: Land Management in Peri-urban Kumasi, Ghana." Paper for the second conference of the Africa-Europe Group for Interdisciplinary Studies (AEGIS), 11–14 July, Leiden, posted at http://ecas2007.aegis-eu.org/commence/user/view_file_forall.php?fileid=815 (accessed 19 December 2008).

Ubink, Janine. 2008. "Struggles for Land in Peri-urban Kumasi and Their Effect on Popular Perceptions of Chiefs and Chieftaincy," in *Contesting Land and Custom in Ghana: State, Chief, and the Citizen*. Janine Ubink and Kojo S. Amanor, eds. Leiden: Leiden University Press: 155–182.

Ubink, Janine and Kojo S. Amanor, eds. 2008. *Contesting Land and Custom in Ghana: State, Chief, and the Citizen*. Leiden: Leiden University Press.

UNECA. *See* United Nations Economic Commission on Africa.

UNEP/KWS. See United Nations Environmental Project and Kenya Wildlife Service.

UNHCR. *See* United Nations High Commission on Refugees.

UNHCR Relief Web. 2002. Carte des Territoires du Nord Kivu, posted at reliefweb.int/node/2831 (accessed 9 January 2009 and 25 May 2012).

United Nations Development Program (UNDP). 2002. "Zimbabwe. Land Reform and Resettlement: Assessment and Suggested Framework for the Future." Interim Mission Report.

United Nations Economic Commission on Africa (UNECA). 2003. "Land Tenure Systems and Sustainable Development in Southern Africa." UNECA Southern Africa Office, Report no. ECA/SA/EGM.Land/2003/2. December.

United Nations Economic Commission on Africa (UNECA). 2004. "Land Tenure Systems and their Impacts on Food Security and Sustainable Development in Africa." ECA report no. ECA/SDD/05/09. Addis Ababa: UNCEA. December.

United Nations Environment Project and the Kenya Wildlife Service (UNEP/KWS). 2008. "Facts about Mau Forest Complex," and "Mau Complex under Siege." May. Posted by Ermis Africa Leadership Development at www.ermisafrica.org (accessed 14 January 2009).

United Nations (Nations Unis) Tribunal Pénal International pour le Rwanda (TPIR) (aka UN International Criminal Tribunal for Rwanda, or ICTR). 2002. *See* Association Rwandaise pour la Défense des Droits de l'Homme (ARDHO) and F. Byabarumuse.

Uvin, Peter. 1996. "Tragedy in Rwanda: The Political Ecology of Conflict." *Environment* 38 (3) (April): 6–16.

Uvin, Peter. 1998. "Ethnicity and Power in Burundi and Rwanda: Different Paths to Mass Violence." *Comparative Politics* 31 (3): 253–271.

Van Acker, Frank. 1999. "La 'Pembénisation' de Haut-Kivu: Opportunisme et Droits Fonciers Révisité," in *L'Afrique des Grands Lacs Annuaire, 1998–1999*. Filip Rentjens and S. Marysse, eds. Paris: L'Harmattan: 1–33.

Van Acker, Frank. 2005. "Where Did All the Land Go? Enclosure and Social Struggle in Kivu (D.R. Congo)." *Review of African Political Economy* 32 (103) (March): 79–98.

van Beusekom, Monica M. 1997. "Colonisation Indigene: French Rural Development Ideology at the Office du Niger, 1920–1940." *International Journal of African Historial Studies* 30 (2): 299–323.

Van de Walle, N. 2001. *African Economies and the Politics of Permanent Crisis, 1979–1999*. Cambridge: Cambridge University Press.

van Hoyweghen, Saskia. 1999. "The Urgency of Land and Agrarian Reform in Rwanda." *African Affairs* 98 (July): 353–372.

van Kessel, Ineke. 1997. "'One Chief, One Vote': The Revival of Traditional Authorities in Post-apartheid South Africa." *African Affairs* 96 (385) (October): 561–586.

Van Santen, José C. M. 1998. "Islam, Gender, and Urbanisation among the Mafa of North Cameroon: The Differing Commitment to 'Home' among Muslims and Non-Muslims." *Africa: Journal of the International African Institute* 68 (3): 403–426.

van Zwaneberg, R. M. A, with Anne King. 1975. *An Economic History of Kenya and Uganda, 1800–1970*. London: The Macmillan Press Ltd.

Varshney, A. 1995. *Democracy and Development in the Countryside: Urban-Rural Stuggle in India*. Cambridge and New York: Cambridge University Press.

Varshney, A. 2002. *Ethnic Conflict and Civic Life*. New Haven, CT: Yale University Press.

Vellema, Sietze, Saturnino M. Borras, Jr., and Francisco Lara, Jr. 2011. "The Agrarian Roots of Contemporary Violent Conflict in Mindanao, Southern Philippines." *Journal of Agrarian Change* 11 (3) (July): 298–320.

Vermeulen, Sonja and Lorenzo Cotula. 2010. "Over the Heads of Local People: Consultation, Consent, and Recompense in Large-Scale Land Deals for Biofuels in Africa." *Journal of Peasant Studies* 37 (4): 899–916.

Verwimp, Philip. 2003. "Testing the Double-Genocide Thesis for Central and Southern Rwanda." *Journal of Conflict Resolution* 47 (4): 423–442.

Verwimp, Philip. 2011. "The 1990–2 Massacres in Rwanda: A Case of Spatial and Social Engineering." *Journal of Agrarian Change* 11 (3): 396–419.

Villiers, Gauthier, with Jean Omasombo Tshonda. 1997. *Zaire: La Transition Manquée (1990–1997)*. Paris and Tervuren: L'Harmattan and Institut Africain-CEDAF, and Bruxelles: Cahiers Africaines, no. 27–29.

Vircoulon, Thierry and Florence Liégeois. 2010. "Violences en brousse: Le 'peacebuilding' international face aux conflits fonciers." Note de l'IFRI. Paris: Institut Français des Relations Internationales: Programme Afrique Subsaharienne, IFRI n. 13. Février.

Vlassenroot, Koen. 2004. "Land and Conflict: The Case of Masisi," in *Conflict and Social Transformation in Eastern D.R. Congo*. K. Vlassenroot and Timothy Raeymaekers, eds. Gent: Academia Press.

Vlassenroot, Koen and Chris Huggins. 2004. "Land, Migration and Conflict in Eastern D.R. Congo." *Eco-Conflicts* 3 (4) (October): 1–4. (NBI: ACTS (African Centre for Technology Studies)).

Vlassenroot, Koen and Chris Huggins. 2005. "Land, Migration, and Conflict in Eastern DRC," in *From the Ground Up: Land Rights, Conflict, and Peace in Sub-Saharan Africa*. Chris Huggins and Jane Clover, eds. Nairobi: African Centre for Technology Studies, ACTS: 115–194.

Vlassenroot, Koen and Timothy Raeymaekers, eds. 2004. *Conflict and Social Transformation in Eastern D.R. Congo*. Gent: Academia Press.

von Haugwitz, Hans-Wilhelm. 1972. *Some Experiences with Smallholder Settlement in Kenya, 1963/4 to 1966/7*. München: Weltforum Verlag.

von Hoyweghen, Saskia. 1999. "The Urgency of Land and Agrarian Reform in Rwanda." *African Affairs* 98 (July): 353–372.

Waeterloos, E. and B. Rutherford. 2004. "Land Reform in Zimbabwe: Challenges and Opportunities for Poverty Reduction among Commercial Farm Workers." *World Development* 32 (3): 537–553.

Waldner, David. 1999. *State Building and Late Development*. Ithaca, NY: Cornell University Press.

Wallerstein, Immanuel. 1967. "Class, Tribe, and Party in West African Politics," in *Party Systems and Voter Alignments: Cross-National Perspectives*. S. M. Lipset and S. Rokkan, eds. New York: Free Press: 497–518.

Wamba-dia-Wamba, Ernest. 1991. "Discourse on the National Question," in *State and Constitutionalism: An African Debate on Democracy*. Issa Shivji, ed. Harare, Zimbabwe: SAPES: 57–70.

Wanjohi, N. Gatheru. 1985. "The Politics of Land, Elections, and Democratic Performance in Kenya: A Case Study of Nakuru District." Nairobi: University of Nairobi Institute of Development Studies Working Paper no. 412. February.

Wantchekon, Leonard. 2003. "Clientelism and Voting Behavior: Evidence from a Field Experiment in Benin." *World Politics* 55 (April): 399–422.

Warner, K. 1993. "Patterns of Farmer Tree Growing in Eastern Africa." Tropical Forestry Papers 27, Oxford Forestry Institute, International Center for Research in Agroforestry, Nairobi.

Wasserman, Gary. 1973. "Continuity and Counterinsurgency: The Role of Land Reform in Decolonizing Kenya, 1962–70." *Canadian Journal of African Studies* 7 (1): 133–148.

Watts, M. 1983. "Good Try, Mr. Paul: Populism and the Politics of African Land Use." *African Studies Review* 26 (2) (June): 73–83.

Watts, Michael. 1983. *Silent Violence: Food, Famine, and Peasantry in Northern Nigeria*. Berkeley and Los Angeles: University of California Press.

Watts, Michael. 2004. "Resource Curse? Governmentality, Oil, and Power in the Niger Delta, Nigeria." *Geopolitics* 9 (1): 50–80.

WDR 2008. *See* World Bank, World Development Report 2008.

Weimer, David, ed. 1997. *The Political Economy of Property Rights: Institutional Change and Continuity in the Reform of Centrally Planned Economies*. Cambridge: Cambridge University Press.

Weingast, B. 2002. "Rational-Choice Institutionalism," in *Political Science: State of the Discipline*. I. Katznelson and H. Milner, eds. New York and London: W. W. Norton: 660–692.

Weingast, Barry R. 1995. "The Economic Role of Political Institutions: Market-Preserving Federalism and Economic Development." *Journal of Law, Economics, and Organization* 11 (1): 1–31.

Weinstein, Jeremy. 2007. *Inside Rebellion: The Politics of Insurgent Violence*. Cambridge and New York: Cambridge University Press.

Weiss, Herbert F. 1967. *Political Protest in the Congo: The Parti Solidaire Africain During the Independence Struggle*. Princeton, NJ: Princeton University Press.

Whitaker, B. E. 2005. "Citizens and Foreigners: Democratization and the Politics of Exclusion in Africa." *African Studies Review* 48 (1): 109–126.

Whiting, Susan H. 2000. *Power and Wealth in Rural China: The Political Economy of Institutional Change*. Cambridge: Cambridge University Press.

Wilkinson, Steven. 2004. *Votes and Violence: Electoral Competition and Ethnic Riots in India*. Cambridge: Cambridge University Press.

Wilks, Ivor. 1989. *Wa and the Wala: Islam and Polity in Northwestern Ghana*. Cambridge: Cambridge University Press.

Willame, Jean-Claude. 1995. "Un autre regard sur la conflictualité politique au Zaïre." *Politique Africaine* n. 60: 147–152.

Willame, Jean-Claude et al. 1997. "Zaire: Predicament and Prospects: A Report to the Minority Rights Group (USA)." Peaceworks and USIP, January, Washington, DC.

Willame, Jean-Claude. 1997a. *Banyarwanda et Banyamulenge: Violences Ethniques et Gestion de l'Identitaire au Kivu*. Bruxelles and Paris: Institut Africain-CEDAF and Editions L'Harmattan.

Willame, Jean-Claude. 1997b. "Gestion verticale et horizontale des crises identitaires: Le cas du Kivu montagneux," in *Hérodote: Revue de Géographie et de Géopolitique*, 86–87 (Special Issue: Géopolitique d'une Afrique Médiane, Yves Lacoste, ed.) n. 3–4 (1997): 78–115.

Williams, Gavan. 1981. "The World Bank and the Peasant Problem," in *Rural Development in Tropical Africa*. Judith Heyer, Gavan Williams, and Pepe Roberts, eds. New York: St. Martin's Press: 16–51.

Wing, Susanna. 2010. *Constructing Democracy in Africa: Mali in Transition*. London: Palgrave Macmillan.

Wing, Susanna. 2012. "Women's Rights and Family Law Reform in Francophone Africa," in *Governing Africa's Changing Societies: Dynamics of Reform*. Ellen M. Lust and Stephen N. Ndegwa, eds. Boulder, CO: Lynne Rienner Publishers: 145–176.

Wing, Susanna. n.d. Legal Pluralism and the Politics of Family Law Reform in Mali and Benin. Unpub. ms.

Wintrobe, Ronald. 2007. "Dictatorship: Analytical Approaches," in *Oxford Handbook of Comparative Politics*. Carles Boix and Susan C. Stokes, eds. Oxford: Oxford University Press: 363–396.

Wiseman, John. 1986. "Urban Riots in West Africa, 1977–1985." *Journal of Modern African Studies* 24 (3) (September): 509–518.

Wolf, Thomas P. 2006. "Immunity or Accountability: Daniel Toroitich arap Moi: Kenya's First Retired President," in *Legacies of Power: Leadership Change and Former Presidents in African Politics*. Roger Southall and Henning Melber, eds. Uppsala: The Nordic Africa Institute: 197–232.

Wolf, Tom. 2007. "Ethnic Mobilization versus Political Parties: A Retrospective (Kisii, 2007) Analysis, Some 2012 Scenarios, and a Current Coastal Exception That Proves the Rule?" Unpub. ms., Nairobi.

Woods, Dwayne. 2003. "The Tragedy of the Cocoa-Pod: Rent-Seeking, Land, and Ethnic Conflict in Ivory Coast." *Journal of Modern African Studies* 41 (1) (December): 641–656.

Woods, Dwayne. 2012. "Patrimonialism (Neo) and the Kingdom of Swaziland: Employing a Case Study to Rescale a Concept." *Commonwealth and Comparative Politics* 50 (3): 344–366.

World Agroforestry Center. (2006). "Improved Land Management in the Lake Victoria Basin: Final Report on the TransVic Project." Occasional Paper no. 7, Nairobi.

World Bank. 1989. *Sub-Saharan Africa: From Crisis to Sustainable Growth*. Washington, DC: The World Bank.

World Bank. 2003a. "Country Assistance Strategy: Senegal." 23 March 2003.

World Bank. 2003b. "Project Appraisal Doc. for Ghana Land Administration Project," 8 July, Report no. 25913.

World Bank. 2010. "Rising Gobal Interest in Farmland: Can It Yield Sustainable and Equitable Benefits?" Washington, DC: The World Bank. 7 September.

Xinhua News Agency. 2000. "Zimbabwean Ruling Party Unveils Election Manifesto." 23 March, posted at www.zimbabwesituation.com/march23.html (accessed 22 January 2010).

Yamano, T. and K. Deininger. 2005. "Land Conflicts in Kenya: Causes, Impacts, and Resolution." FASID Discussion Paper 2005–12–002. Foundation for Advanced Studies on International Development.

Yashar, Deborah. 2005. *Contesting Citizenship in Latin America: The Rise of Indigenous Movements and the Postliberal Challenge*. Cambridge: Cambridge University Press.

Yevou, M. 2004. "Débats sur la nationalité: Les partis se radicalisent." *Fraternité Matin*, July 15, posted at www.allafrica.com/stories, 200407150294.html (accessed 17 July 2004).

Yevou, M. 2006. "Banny aux membres de la CEI [Commission Electorale Indépendante]: Laissez les fanions de vos partis dehors." *Fraternité Matin*, March 6, posted at allafrica.com (accessed 8 March 2006).

Yoka, Lye M. 1995. "Lettres d'un Kinois à l'Oncle du Village," *Zaire Années 90*, (5) CEDAF, n. 15. Bruxelles: Institut Africain-CEDAF and Paris: L'Harmattan, 1995.

Young, Crawford. 1994. *The African Colonial State in Colonial Perspective*. New Haven, CT: Yale University Press.

Young, Crawford. 2002. "Deciphering Disorder in Africa: Is Identity the Key?" *World Politics* 54 (4): 532–557.

Young, Crawford and Thomas Turner. 1985. *The Rise and Decline of the Zairian State*. Madison: University of Wisconsin Press.

Young, Tom, ed. 2003. *Readings in African Politics*. Bloomington/Indianapolis and Oxford: Indiana University Press and James Currey.

Zaire, Gouvernement de Transition du Zaïre, Ministère de la Communication et Presse. 1993. "Livre Blanc sure la situation des Droits de l'Homme dans les Provinces du Shaba (Katanga) et du Nord-Kivu," posted by le Réseau Documentaire International sur la Région des Grands Lacs Africains at www.grandslacs.net/doc/2769.pdf (accessed 20 mars 2007).

Zeurn, Elke. 2011. *The Politics of Necessity: Community Organizing and Democracy in South Africa*. Madison: University of Wisconsin Press.

Zimbabwe Human Rights (ZHR) NGO Forum. 2002. *Human Rights and Zimbabwe's Presidential Election: March 2002.*

Zimbabwe Human Rights (ZHR) NGO Forum and the Justice for Agriculture Trust. 2007. "Adding Insult to Injury: A Preliminary Report on Human Rights Violations on Commercial Farms, 2000 to 2005."

Zindi, E. 2008. "Mutasa Warns White Farmers." 6 April in *Justice for Agriculture – PR Communique*, 7 April.

Zinyama, Lovemore. 1998. "Rural Settlement Patterns in Zimbabwe and State Manipulation of the Settlement Structure," in *Rural Settlement Structure and African Development*. Marilyn Silberfein, ed. Boulder, CO: Westview Press: 251–272.

Zolberg, Aristide. 1964. *One Party Government in Ivory Coast.* Princeton, NJ: Princeton University Press, 2nd ed. 1969.

Zougouri, Sita and Paul Mathieu. 2006. "Nouvelles transactions et formalisation des transactions foncières daus l'ouest du Burkina Faso: Le cas d'un village de la province du Houët." *Le Bulletin de l'APAD*, n. 22, Governance foncíere au quotidien en Afrique.

Index

Books in the Series (*continued from page iii*)

Orit Kedar, *Voting for Policy, Not Parties: How Voters Compensate for Power Sharing*

Robert O. Keohane and Helen B. Milner, eds., *Internationalization and Domestic Politics*

Herbert Kitschelt, *The Transformation of European Social Democracy*

Herbert Kitschelt, Kirk A. Hawkins, Juan Pablo Luna, Guillermo Rosas, and Elizabeth J. Zechmeister, *Latin American Party Systems*

Herbert Kitschelt, Peter Lange, Gary Marks, and John D. Stephens, eds., *Continuity and Change in Contemporary Capitalism*

Herbert Kitschelt, Zdenka Mansfeldova, Radek Markowski, and Gabor Toka, *Post-Communist Party Systems*

David Knoke, Franz Urban Pappi, Jeffrey Broadbent, and Yutaka Tsujinaka, eds., *Comparing Policy Networks*

Allan Kornberg and Harold D. Clarke, *Citizens and Community: Political Support in a Representative Democracy*

Amie Kreppel, *The European Parliament and the Supranational Party System*

David D. Laitin, *Language Repertoires and State Construction in Africa*

Fabrice E. Lehoucq and Ivan Molina, *Stuffing the Ballot Box: Fraud, Electoral Reform, and Democratization in Costa Rica*

Mark Irving Lichbach and Alan S. Zuckerman, eds., *Comparative Politics: Rationality, Culture, and Structure*, 2nd edition

Evan Lieberman, *Race and Regionalism in the Politics of Taxation in Brazil and South Africa*

Richard M. Locke, *Promoting Labor Standards in a Global Economy: The Promise and Limits of Private Power*

Pauline Jones Luong, *Institutional Change and Political Continuity in Post-Soviet Central Asia*

Pauline Jones Luong and Erika Weinthal, *Oil Is Not a Curse: Ownership Structure and Institutions in Soviet Successor States*

Julia Lynch, *Age in the Welfare State: The Origins of Social Spending on Pensioners, Workers, and Children*

Lauren M. MacLean, *Informal Institutions and Citizenship in Rural Africa: Risk and Reciprocity in Ghana and Côte d'Ivoire*

Beatriz Magaloni, *Voting for Autocracy: Hegemonic Party Survival and Its Demise in Mexico*

James Mahoney, *Colonialism and Postcolonial Development: Spanish America in Comparative Perspective*

James Mahoney and Dietrich Rueschemeyer, eds., *Comparative Historical Analysis in the Social Sciences*

Scott Mainwaring and Matthew Soberg Shugart, eds., *Presidentialism and Democracy in Latin America*

Isabela Mares, *The Politics of Social Risk: Business and Welfare State Development*

Isabela Mares, *Taxation, Wage Bargaining, and Unemployment*

Made in the USA
Lexington, KY
29 March 2016